OSQL Quick Reference

The osql syntax is as follows:

```
osql -U login_id [-e] [-E] [-p] [-n] [-d db_name] [-q "query"]
[-Q "query"]
[-c cmd_end] [-h headers] [-w column_width] [-s col_separator]
[-t time_out] [-m error_level] [-L] [-?] [-r {0 ¦ 1}]
[-H wksta_name] [-P password] [-R]
[-S server_name] [-i input_file] [-o output_file] [-u]
[-a packet_size]
[-b] [-0] [-l time_out]
```

Switch	Switch Definition
-U login_id	Specifies the user login ID.
-e	Specifies input to be echoed
-E	Specifies a trusted connection
-p	Specifies performance statistics to be printed.
-n	Specifies for numbering and the prompt symbol (>) to be removed from input lines.
-d db_name	Specifies a USE db_name to be issued when isql is started.
-q "query"	Specifies that a query is executed when isql is started.
-Q "query"	Specifies that a query is executed and then immediately exits isql.
-c cmd_end	Specifies a new command terminator.
-h headers	Specifies the number of rows to be displayed before showing the headers. The default is showing the headers once at the beginning for each query performed.
-w column_width	Specifies the number of characters to be displayed on each line.
-s col_separator	Specifies a character for the column separator.
-t time_out	Specifies the number of seconds before the command times out.
-m error_level	Specifies whether error messages are shown.
-L	Lists the local servers broadcasting on the network.
-?	Displays Help, summary of all switches.
-r	Specifies the redirection of error messages to the screen.
-H wksta_name	Specifies the workstation name.
-P password	Specifies the password.
-R	Specifies the SQL Server driver to use when doing a conversion for date/time and currency-to-character data.
-S server_name	Specifies the server to connect to.
-i input_file	Specifies the file that contains SQL statements.
-o output_file	Specifies the file that receives the output from isql.
-a packet_size	Specifies the packet size.
-b	Specifies that isql returns a DOS error when an error occurs.
-0	Degrades isql to an earlier version, disabling EOF batch processing, automatic console width scaling, and wide messages.
-l	Sets the number of seconds that isql will wait before the login times out.
-x max_text_size	Sets the maximum length (in bytes) of text to return.

makepipe Syntax and Switch List

```
Makepipe [/h] [/w] [/p pipe_name]
```

Switch	Switch Definition
/h	Displays help (the usage of each parameter).
/w	The wait time between read and writes, default is 0.
/p pipe_name	The pipe name; the default is abc.

`readpipe` **Syntax and Switch List**

Readpipe /sserver_name /dstring [/n] [/q] [/w] [/t]

[/ppipe_name] [/h]

Switch	Switch Definition
/sserver_name	The name of the SQL Server that just initiated the makepipe command. Do not use a space after /s. This parameter is optional if you are using the same machine for the makepipe.
/dstring	A test string to be sent to the server and back. No spaces after /d. Enclose the string in double quotes ("") if you are using spaces.
/n	The number of iterations (loops through the number of times requested).
/q	Uses query (polling) method.
/w	Specifies the wait time to pause the polling. Use with /q.
/t	Uses Transact-SQL; overrides polling. If used, /w is ignored.
/ppipe_name	Specifies the pipe to use. The default is abc.
/h	Displays help (the usage of each parameter).

BCP Switches and Syntax

Use the syntax bcp /switch or bcp -switch, such as bcp /v.

Switch	Switch Definition
-n	Native data format.
-c	Character data format.
-w	Unicode data format.
-N	Use Unicode for character data, and native format for all others.
-C	If you are loading extended characters, this switch enables you to specify the code page of the data in the data file.
-E	Use identity values in file rather than generating new ones.
-6	Use pre-7.0 data types. This option is required when loading native 6.x BCP files.
-b	The number of rows to include in each committed batch.
-m	The maximum errors to allow before stopping the transfer.
-e	The file to write error messages to.
-f	The format file used to customize the load or unload data in a specific style.
-F	The first row to start copying from in the data file when importing.
-L	The last row to end copying with in the data file when importing.
-t	The terminating characters for fields.
-r	The terminating characters for rows.
-i	A file for redirecting input into BCP.
-o	The file for receiving redirected output from BCP.
-a	The network packet size used to send to or receive from the server.
-q	This tells BCP to use quoted identifiers when dealing with table and column names.
-k	Overrides a column's default and enforces NULL values load as part of the BCP operation.
-h	The 7.0 hint options.
-U	The user account in which to log in. This account will need sufficient privileges to carry out either a read or write of the table.
-P	The password associated with the user account.
-S	The SQL server's name.
-v	The version number of BCP.
-T	Make a trusted connection to the SQL Server.

Practical

Microsoft®

SQL Server™

7.0

Brad M. McGehee

Rob Kraft

Matthew Shepker

Eric Wilson

Simon Gallagher

Tibor Karaszi

que®

A Division of Macmillan Computer Publishing, USA
201 W. 103rd Street
Indianapolis, Indiana 46290

Contents at a Glance

Practical Microsoft® SQL Server™ 7.0

This book is a revision of the previously published book "Using Microsoft SQL Server 7.0" ISBN 0-7897-1628-3

International Standard Book Number: 0-7897-2147-3

Library of Congress Catalog Card Number: 99-65507

Printed in the United States of America

First Printing: August 1999

00 99 01   4 3 2 1

Trademarks

Warning and Disclaimer

Managing Editor
Thomas F. Hayes

Project Editor
Heather Talbot

Copy Editor
Kate Givens

Indexers
Johnna VanHoose

Proofreader
Eddie Lushbaugh

Technical Editor
Trevor Dwyer

Software Development Specialist
Dan Scherf

Team Coordinator
Carol Ackerman

Interior Design
Nathan Clement
Ruth Lewis

Cover Design
Dan Armstrong
Ruth Lewis

Cover Illustrator
Nathan Clement

Layout Technician
Staci Somers

Contents

About the Authors

Brad M. McGehee is a full-time computer trainer specializing in Microsoft Windows NT Server and Microsoft BackOffice products. He is a Microsoft Certified Systems Engineer (MCSE), a Microsoft Certified Systems Developer (MCSD), a Microsoft Certified Trainer (MCT), a Microsoft Certified Systems Engineer + Internet (MCSE+I), and a Certified NetWare Engineer (CNE). He has passed more than 32 Microsoft certification tests. After receiving a bachelor's degree in Business and Economics in 1981, his first job was to teach introductory computer and BASIC programming at a community college. He is the author of four books on computers, contributing author of nine additional books on computers, and has written over 100 magazine articles. He has also worked for several computer integrators over the years, first becoming involved in networking and relational database management in the middle 1980s. He received his master's degree in Business in 1992. Throughout his career, he has been a computer consultant, developer, writer, and trainer, switching roles off and on in order not to get too bored with any one task. Currently, he lives in Overland Park, Kansas, with his wife Veronica, who is a network engineer and C++ programmer, and his daughter Anna. He can be reached at bradmcgehee@hotmail.com.

Rob Kraft has been developing applications for SQL Server since version 4.2. Having come to SQL Server as a developer, he greatly appreciates the wealth of developer tools now available in SQL Server 7.0. His developer's background also gives him a different perspective of SQL Server administration than many DBAs because he understands well what the developers are trying to accomplish. Rob is a Microsoft Certified Solutions Developer and a Microsoft Certified Trainer of SQL Server. He is also proficient with Visual Basic. Along with teaching VB classes, he presented Visual Basic 5.0 and Visual Basic 6.0 at Developer Days conferences, and he is the leader of his local Visual Basic User's group. Currently, he is at work on a project utilizing his third specialty, Project Management. Rob's hobbies include neural networks and archaeology. You can learn more about Rob or contact him through his Web site at http://ourworld.compuserve.com/homepages/robkraft.

Matthew Shepker is a SQL Server consultant and network integrator for Empower Trainers & Consultants in Overland Park, Kansas,. Matthew has been working with SQL Server for over four years in a variety of business applications, including online transaction processing, decision support systems, and other custom software. He has coauthored two other books and has written one book. Matthew is an MCSE and MCT, and is currently one test away from his MCSD. Matthew currently lives in Overland Park, Kansas, with his wife, Misty. He can be reached at mshepker@empower.com.

Eric Wilson is a Microsoft Certified Solution Developer (MCSD) and has recently started his own consulting business, WebBasix, Inc. (http://www.webbasix.com). Eric specializes in training and client/server Internet development using Visual InterDev, Visual Basic, SQL Server, and recently added Java to the list. He has recently completed all the requirements (if he ever gets around to sending in his paperwork and that darn fee) for becoming a Microsoft Certified Trainer (MCT). What's his next goal? Of course, a Microsoft Certified Systems Engineer (MCSE).

Simon Gallagher graduated in 1991 from the University of Kent at Canterbury, England, with a first-class bachelor of science with honors degree in computer science. He is currently a senior consultant, part-time instructor, and technical manager for the Indianapolis office of NewMedia, Inc. Simon is also a Microsoft Certified Professional and a Microsoft Certified Trainer in SQL Server. He also has been a Certified PowerBuilder Associate since version 3.0. Simon has been programming in PowerBuilder since Version 2.0 and has successfully fielded several different applications, ranging from a property tax reporting system to an order entry system. He has been involved with several different hardware platforms and operating systems and has a broad knowledge of databases and development languages. As part of the PowerBuilder 2.0 project team, he was working to help debug the first Informix 5.0 DBMS interface for PowerBuilder. He has also coauthored a number of books: PowerBuilder 4, 5, and 6 Unleashed, and has contributed with chapters and technical editing to other development language and database books. You can reach Simon on the Internet at raven@iquest.net. You can also explore his Web pages at http://members.iquest.net/~raven/raven.html.

Tibor Karaszi is a SQL Server trainer for Cornerstone, based in Sweden. He has been working with SQL Server for nearly 10 years as a DBA, application developer, database designer, consultant, and instructor. Tibor has also been involved in internal Microsoft education throughout Europe. In addition to certification as a Microsoft Certified Trainer, Tibor holds the Microsoft Certified Systems Engineer (MCSE) and Microsoft Certified Solution Developer (MCSD) titles and has been recognized by Microsoft as a SQL Server MVP. Tibor can be reached at tibor@cornerstone.se.

Acknowledgments

Rob Kraft would like to acknowledge the developers of SQL Server 7.0 at Microsoft for the excellent responses they provided through the private newsgroups during the three betas. Their feedback was always swift and excellent. Rob would also like to acknowledge those individuals who spend a lot of time voluntarily answering questions in the newsgroups and helping others solve their SQL Server problems. Among these volunteers are Tibor Karaszi, Kalen Delaney, Gianluca Hotz, Brian Moran, Neil Pike, Bob Pfeiff, and Steve Robinson.

To my dearest wife, Misty. Thank you for sticking by me. I love you.
—*Matthew Shepker*

Tell Us What You Think!

As the reader of this book, you are our most important critic and commentator. We value your opinion and want to know what we're doing right, what we could do better, what areas you'd like to see us publish in, and any other words of wisdom you're willing to pass our way.

As an Executive Editor for Macmillan Computer Publishing, I welcome your comments. You can fax, email, or write me directly to let me know what you did or didn't like about this book—as well as what we can do to make our books stronger.

Please note that I cannot help you with technical problems related to the topic of this book, and that due to the high volume of mail I receive, I might not be able to reply to every message.

When you write, please be sure to include this book's title and author as well as your name and phone or fax number. I will carefully review your comments and share them with the author and editors who worked on the book.

Fax: 317-581-4666

E-mail: que_proemcp.com

Mail: Executive Editor
         Macmillan Computer Publishing
         201 West 103rd Street
         Indianapolis, IN 46290 USA

introduction

Welcome to *Practical Microsoft SQL Server 7.0*. Just like
Microsoft SQL Server 7.0, this book has been a long time in
coming. The authors began this book about two years before the
release of the product. They have spent hundreds of hours
learning the ins and outs of SQL Server 7.0 through three different beta releases of the software. This book is the result of
their first-hand knowledge and experience with this important
new release.

Compared to many books that you have read on how to use
high-end applications such as SQL Server, I think you will find
this book a little different. Here's what I mean:

- The book is designed to get directly to the point with no
  wasted words. You will learn what you need to know in
  order to successfully administer SQL Server without
  wasting your time on seldom-used features.

- The book is designed around how you will use SQL Server
  on a day-to-day basis.

- You don't have to read the entire book from cover to cover
  to master administering SQL Server. You can pick the chapters you want to read, and read them in the order that
  makes the most sense to you.

- The book includes comprehensive illustrations, step by step
  instructions, side notes, cross-references, a comprehensive
  glossary, and an innovate index that makes it easy to find
  what you are looking for, even though you might not be
  sure what you are looking for.

- The book avoids, as much as possible, forcing you to learn arcane commands and syntax to use SQL Server. You will learn how to use SQL Server's graphical interface to perform most tasks.

Microsoft has put a tremendous effort into making SQL Server 7.0 a powerful but easy-to-use tool. We have also put a lot of effort into this book, making it the perfect tool to introduce you to this powerful new product. We hope you enjoy the book and find it useful.

Who Should Read This Book?

This book was written to meet the needs of IT professionals who need to learn how to install, configure, and maintain Microsoft SQL Server 7.0 on a day-to-day basis. If you fall into any of the following categories, this book is ideal for you.

NT Administrators

Many NT administrators suddenly find themselves as the database administrator of a newly purchased SQL Server. In many organizations, the budget is not large enough to justify hiring a full-time database administrator, so the NT administrator has the opportunity to take on one more responsibility, on top of all the other responsibilities he already has. If this describes your situation, you will find that this book will ease your introduction to SQL Server 7.0, making your life as an NT network administrator, and newly appointed database administrator, an easier one.

New Database Administrators

In the fast-paced world of IT, many professionals find themselves thrust into new jobs before they ever get the opportunity to learn what they are supposed to do. In many cases, that includes becoming a database administrator, even though your IT experience might be in networking, or even application development. If you are a newly appointed database administrator, you will want to master the essential database administration skills as soon as possible. This book will help you in this task, providing the essential information you need to meet the demands of your new job.

SQL Server Application Developers

In virtually every company, databases are being added to manage information. This can include traditional two-tier client/server applications, or perhaps Web browser–based applications. Whatever the application, databases such as SQL Server 7.0 are becoming more and more prevalent. This means that there is an increasing demand for SQL Server application developers who not only know how to develop applications, but who also understand how to manage SQL Server. Knowing how to administer SQL Server is a critical skill to SQL Server developers, and if you have recently found yourself developing applications for SQL Server, but don't really know much about how it is managed, this book is for you. It provides the essential basics you need to know in order to create well-designed SQL Server applications.

Web Masters and Web Developers

More and more, Web pages are being created dynamically, and the data that feeds these dynamically created pages is managed by SQL Server. If you are a Web master or Web developer who is currently thinking about using SQL Server as a back end to your Web site, or are using it already, you need to have a good foundation on how SQL Server works. You might be lucky enough to have a full-time database administrator. But if you don't, you have to become the default database administrator yourself, and you need to master the most basic SQL Server administration skills. This book will help you learn these essential skills so you can keep your Web site up and running.

Microsoft MCSE Certification Candidates

If you are like many IT professionals, you have decided to enhance your job skills by becoming professionally certified as a Microsoft Certified Systems Engineer (MCSE) or Microsoft Certified Database Administrator (MCDBA). Although this book isn't designed to prepare you to answer specific test questions, it does something even better. It teaches you how to use and manage SQL Server, providing you a better overall picture of how to use SQL Server than can a book devoted solely to preparing you for a certification test. This book makes an excellent companion study tool when preparing for the Microsoft SQL Server 7.0 Administration certification test.

IT Managers

Many IT managers find themselves spending too much time in meetings and fighting fires to spend time learning about new technology. This is unfortunate because they need to understand what specific technology can do for them. Although they might not have to understand every detail, they at least need to understand the larger picture. This book is an ideal tool for IT managers who want to learn about SQL Server 7.0, but who don't want to know every little detail. This book provides the essential information needed to use SQL Server without wasting anyone's time.

What Do I Need to Know Before I Start?

This book has been written for IT professionals who want to learn how to administer SQL Server 7.0. It assumes that you haven't had any experience with previous versions of Microsoft SQL Server, or any other high-end relational database program.

What the book does assume is that you have a basic understanding of how computers work, what a database is, and some familiarity with the NT Server operating system. You don't need to be an expert in NT Server to understand this book. But you should be familiar with how to navigate NT Server's menus and how to use some of the basic NT Server administrative tools, such as the Control Panel, User Manager for Domains, and Performance Monitor.

What This Book Contains

This book is designed to be read from beginning to end for beginners. Or if you have some previous experience with SQL Server, you can skip those chapters that you are already familiar with, and dive directly into those chapters that are new to you. After you have read the material of most interest to you, you will want to keep the book around as a handy reference when you need to look something up that you have forgotten.

The book has been organized around how you might actually use SQL Server in the real world, and is divided into these sections:

Part 1: SQL Server Basics

Part 1 is designed for those readers who are new to relational databases. It includes information on what relational databases are, how they work, and other important basic information that will provide a good foundation for understanding the rest of this book. If you are an old hand at using relational databases, you might want to skip this section.

Part 2: Installing and Configuring SQL Server

As a SQL Server database administrator, you will eventually have the opportunity to install and configure a new SQL Server 7.0 installation. This section provides lots of tips on how to not only plan a proper installation, but also on how to actually perform the installation. If SQL Server has already been installed and configured for you, you might consider skipping this section and immediately jumping into the next section on how to administer SQL Server.

Part 3: Administering SQL Server

This is one of the most important parts of this book. It teaches you the essential skills you need to manage SQL Server. This includes not only learning how to use the SQL Server administration tools, but also how to create and manage databases, schedule tasks and alerts, and maintain SQL Server on a day-to-day basis.

Part 4: SQL Server Security

SQL Server provides a comprehensive means of preventing unauthorized users from accessing SQL Server data. In this part, you will learn how to configure SQL Server security, create user accounts, and set permissions on database objects.

Part 5: Preventing Data Loss

If you have the opportunity to be a database administrator for very long at all, you will invariably get the opportunity to restore a SQL Server after it has crashed. This is never a fun task, but this Part will not only show you how to help prevent lost data, but also how to restore a SQL Server and its mission-critical data.

Part 6: Advanced SQL Server Administration

SQL Server is a powerful and comprehensive relational database program, designed to meet most enterprise business needs. Some of these needs are very sophisticated and require sophisticated tools. Part 6 teaches you how to import data into and out of SQL Server, replicate data, optimize SQL Server, and even troubleshoot SQL Server problems.

Glossary

Like every sophisticated computer application, SQL Server has its own specialized vocabulary. Although new words are introduced throughout the book, the glossary provides a comprehensive collection of terms for easy reference.

Index

Although virtually all how-to books have an index, this one is special. Unlike most indexes that simply list words chosen from the book with a page reference, this index includes concepts. In other words, even if you don't know the exact term to describe the task you want to perform, you can still easily find it in the index by looking up words that describe the concept of what you want to do. Try it, you will be surprised how powerful and useful it really is.

How This Book Makes Learning SQL Server 7.0 Easier

This book includes three important features to make learning about SQL Server 7.0 just a little easier.

Side Notes

Side notes are found throughout this book in the margins. They provide useful and important information about using SQL Server. They include tips, warnings, and other useful and interesting information.

See Also's (Cross-References)

Many times in this book you will see references to other parts of the book. This is because much of the material in the book is related, and we want you to be able to easily see this relationship, and to easily locate the material if you need to look it up.

Step-by-Step Tasks

Virtually all important SQL Server tasks have been explained to you in an easy-to-follow, step-by-step format. Whenever you need to learn how to perform a task in a chapter, look for the step-by-step task sections.

SQL Server Basics

chapter

1

Introduction to SQL Server 7.0

Learn what SQL Server is and
what it does

Useful SQL Server features

How SQL Server is integrated with
NT Server and BackOffice

What you need to know to be a
successful SQL Server DBA

SQL Server Helps You to Master Business Information

Although information is the life force of every successful business, it is also one of the most difficult business assets to manage. From many managers' perspectives, organizations produce too much information, overwhelming a manager's ability to analyze and interpret it. In other cases, managers complain that they don't have enough timely information to make important decisions. The information professional is caught in the middle. You have been charged with the responsibility of collecting critical business information and putting it in a useful form for others. If you have been managing information for some time, you already know how difficult this can be. And if you are new to information management, you will quickly learn this lesson.

Although much of the problem with information management can be placed on the managers themselves, who often don't know what information they want and how it should be presented when they get it, much of the problem has been a lack of good data management tools that easily gather and present data. Traditionally, data management tools have been very expensive, difficult to use, and inflexible. Fortunately this is changing, and at the forefront of this change is Microsoft. From an enterprise perspective, Microsoft hasn't always been on a business's short list of companies that can provide enterprise-wide data management tools. Sure, it has always been a leader when it comes to the desktop, providing top-notch office suites, but when it came to enterprise-capable tools, Microsoft offerings often fell short.

With the release of SQL Server 7.0, everything has changed. SQL Server is a full-fledged database management system that offers enterprises of any size a way to manage their data better than it has ever been managed before. SQL Server's power, flexibility, and ease of use puts SQL Server at the top of the list that once was lead by such companies as Oracle, IBM, Sybase, Informix, and others. Microsoft is now a serious database management company and SQL Server is invading enterprises at all levels, showing information managers that Microsoft has what it takes to be successful at the enterprise level.

Users, DBAs, and SQL Developers

People who use SQL Server can be divided into three major groups: Users, DBAs, and SQL Developers. *Users* are the people who add, delete, update, or query data stored on a SQL Server. They only indirectly use SQL Server because they generally access SQL Server though a custom created user-interface. The *DBA* is generally charged with the task of administering SQL Server on a daily basis. The *SQL Developer* is a programmer who designs and writes code to manipulate SQL Server data. Although all three groups are important to making SQL Server successful in an enterprise, the focus of this book is on the DBA.

This chapter introduces you to what SQL Server is and examines how its many features can come to your aid by fulfilling the information management needs of your enterprise. It also takes a look at how SQL Server is integrated with NT Server and provides a checklist of knowledge you need to master to become a successful Database Administrator (DBA).

What Is SQL Server?

Microsoft SQL Server is a client/server relational database system. What exactly is a client/server relational database system? The best way to explain it is to define it in two parts: the client/server part, and the relational database system part.

Client/server, also referred to as *distributed computing*, means that all of the data processing of a program does not occur on a single computer, as it often does on desktop, mini-, or mainframe-based computer systems. Instead, different parts of the SQL Server application run on two or more computers at the same time. For example, with SQL Server, the database engine part of the program—where the data and program code resides, and where most of the work is done—resides on a designated server computer, whereas the other part of the program, the client interface, resides on a user's desktop computer. The components of the client/server system communicate over a network as if they were one and the same program.

SQL Server is not limited to the simple example above. Multiple SQL Server databases, along with thousands of clients, can all be designed to work together, scaling to virtually any size.

A *relational database system* is a type of database architecture that has been widely adapted by software vendors (including Microsoft) for SQL Server. A relational database is divided into multiple tables of data, each of which is further divided into rows (records) and columns (fields). Think of a table as a spreadsheet, with rows for records and fields for columns. Most databases include multiple tables and other database objects.

SEE ALSO
➤ *For an illustration of a table and other database objects, see page 52-54.*

Have you used SQL Server before?

If you have used previous versions of SQL Server before, you might want to skip this chapter, focusing instead on those chapters of the book that provide the specific information you need. If you are new to SQL Server, this chapter provides an important overview, and it should not be skipped.

SQL Server supports three-tiered client/server architecture

Although SQL Server supports the traditional two-tier client/server architecture, it also supports three-tier architecture. *Three-tier client/server architecture* divides a SQL Server application into three components: 1) the user-interface tier provides user services running on a user's desktop; 2) a business rules tier running on a server that supports business services; and 3) a data tier running on another SQL Server supports data services. Although three-tier client/server architecture is hard to design, it offers many advantages over the traditional two-tier architecture, and is becoming more and more popular.

Other characteristics of relational database systems include the following:

- Virtually all modern relational database systems use the SQL language to manipulate the data in a database. SQL was developed by IBM in the 1970s and has become an industry standard. Although SQL Server is fully compliant with the latest ANSI SQL-92 standard of the SQL language, it also extends the language, adding important new features. Because of this, the version of SQL included with SQL Server is referred to as *Transact-SQL*.

- In many ways, a relational database system resembles a high-level programming language. Virtually any type of business application can be created with SQL Server to meet an organization's needs.

- A relational database system stores its data separate from the programming logic used to manipulate the data. In a two-tier client/server architecture, one SQL Server may be used to hold and manipulate data only, and another SQL Server may be used to hold the programming code and logic that is used to manipulate the data stored on the other SQL Server.

- Data integrity is critical; otherwise the data stored by SQL Server is worthless. Relational database systems include many features to help prevent bad data from being introduced.

- Business needs change almost daily, and relational databases are designed to be easily modified.

- Unlike flat-file databases, where the same data is often repeated in many different records, relational databases exclude most redundant data, reducing the need for storage space and increasing the speed upon which data can be accessed.

- Access to data can be limited by the application itself, permitting many levels of security.

SQL Server is a true client/server relational database that allows enterprises to design a distributed database system to meet their ever-changing information needs.

To learn more about Transact-SQL, see the book *Teach Yourself SQL in 24 Hours* (Sams Publishing).

A Little Background on SQL Server

SQL Server 7.0 has had a long evolution. The original release of SQL Server was in 1988, a joint product of Microsoft and Sybase that ran only under OS/2. It was a complete failure in the marketplace. Not until the release of SQL Server 4.2 for NT Server 3.1 in 1993 did SQL Server start to make some inroads into the enterprise. But even these inroads were small. In 1994, Microsoft ended its relationship with Sybase and released version 6.0 in 1995 and then version 6.5 in 1996. It wasn't until version 6.5 that SQL Server started to take off, as enterprise IT directors began to realize the power, ease of use, and low cost that SQL Server 6.5 offered.

Much of this new-found success was a result of 6.5's improved features. However, it was also due to the growing power of Intel-based servers and the move by many organizations away from file- and printer-based network operating software, such as that offered by Novell and Banyan, toward applications-based operating systems, such as NT Server. NT Server offers a low-cost platform for running server-based applications, and moving to SQL Server 6.5 was a natural extension of moving to NT Server.

With the release of SQL Server 7.0, Microsoft has finally brought SQL Server within the range of high-end databases, and more than ever, enterprises are migrating to it to handle much of their enterprise-wide information needs.

Major Features of SQL Server 7.0

SQL Server offers database administrators (DBAs) and SQL developers virtually every tool they need to create and manage a complete enterprise-wide management system. This section takes a look at some of the most important features of SQL Server 7.0. For a complete description of all the features, you will have to read the entire book.

Cost of Ownership Is Lower Than Competitors

From whatever perspective you look at it, SQL Server offers a lower total cost of ownership than any of its direct competitors. Hardware costs, server and client licenses, development costs, and on-going management costs are all lower. SQL Server leads the industry in the best price/performance and the lowest cost per transaction. Given the scrutiny IT budgets are getting these days, SQL Server's lower cost of ownership is a strong argument for organizations to check it out.

Runs Under NT Server and Windows 95/98

SQL Server runs under all versions of NT Server, including NT Server 4.0 Standard Edition, NT Server 4.0 Enterprise Edition, and it will run under Windows 2000 when it is released. It also runs under both Windows 95 and Windows 98. This ability makes SQL Server very versatile, allowing it to run on computers of any size, including laptops, desktops, and high-end servers.

Scalable to Meet Enterprise-wide Needs

Traditionally, most IT managers have considered SQL Server a lightweight when it comes to managing data. Although this may have been true in the past, this is no longer the case with SQL Server 7.0. SQL Server now supports databases over a terabyte in size, and supports up to 32 CPUs (SQL Server 7.0 Enterprise Edition). Just because SQL Server supports very large databases doesn't mean it cannot cost-effectively manage smaller databases. SQL is designed to be scalable, from small to large databases, making it a very versatile database that can fit the needs of virtually all organizations, no matter what their size.

Supports Data Replication

SQL Server includes an automatic data replication feature that allows virtually any SQL data to be replicated to another SQL Server or to any OLE DB- Compliant or ODBC-compliant database, such as IBM's DB2, Oracle, Informix, Sybase, and even Microsoft Access. Replication can be used to distribute data to remote sites, for load balancing, and to replicate data into a data mart or data warehouse. New to SQL Server 7.0 is update replication. This means that if any data replicated to remote sites is changed, these changes can automatically be propagated back to the original database.

Supports Data Marts and Data Warehouses

SQL Server's ability to manage large databases and to do replication gives it the ability to handle an enterprise's data marts or data warehouses. In addition, SQL Server includes special online analytical processing (OLAP) features and a highly tuned query optimizer to make short order of online queries.

What Are Data Marts and Data Warehouses?

Traditionally, databases have been divided into two types, based on how they are used. *Transaction-oriented* databases are ones used to insert, update, and delete records on a regular basis. An example of this would be an order-entry database for a mail order company. *Decision Support* databases are used to analyze data, which often requires sophisticated queries. An example could also be an order-entry database because managers would want to analyze who was buying what products. A problem can occur when the same database is used for both tasks, entering transactions and running queries, because both tasks occurring simultaneously can significantly affect the performance of the database. For example, an extensive query might take several hours to run, locking many records as the query is performed. This would prevent data entry staff from being able to enter or change orders as the query was running.

To prevent this type of contention, the data from transaction-oriented databases is often copied or replicated into separate databases called either data marts or data warehouses. A data mart usually contains a subset of an enterprise's total available data to be analyzed. A data warehouse usually contains virtually all the data an organization wants to query. Data marts are easier to set up and use than data warehouses, and because of this, are more popular. After data has been copied or replicated from a transaction-oriented database to a data mart or data warehouse, it can be easily queried without having any effect on the transaction-oriented database.

SEE ALSO

➤ *You'll see the Query Analyzer interface and details on this utility starting on page 232.*

Online Analytical Processing Now Built in to SQL Server

One of the biggest changes to SQL Server 7.0 is the addition of the Microsoft Decision Support Services (DSS). This powerful tool set can be used to perform online analytical processing (OLAP) without having to purchase third-party tools. It can be used for corporate reporting, data modeling, and decision support.

English Query Makes Data More Available to Casual Users

Traditionally, if a user wanted to create a custom query in SQL Server to find the answer to a question he had about the data stored in SQL Server, he either had to learn Transact-SQL, or ask someone who knows Transact-SQL to create the actual query. With the addition of English Query to SQL Server, this problem can be eliminated. English Query is a tool that enables a SQL developer to create a front end to SQL Server that enables casual users to enter SQL Server queries using English instead of using Transact-SQL. The new feature greatly expands the universe of people who are able to use SQL Server to provide the information they need to make important business decisions.

Data Transformation Services Enable Easy Exchange of Data

Moving data into and out of SQL Server has never been easy. To help reduce this burden, SQL Server 7.0 now includes the Data Transformation Services. This tool set makes it very easy to move data not only in to and out of SQL Server, but also directly between SQL Server and other databases, such as Microsoft Access or Oracle. The Data Transformation Services can save the DBA many hours over what it used to take to move data.

Supports Distributed Transactions

In many cases, enterprises need multiple SQL Servers to share the workload, which means that there must be some way for their activities to be coordinated. SQL Server is able to accomplish this task by using a tool called the Microsoft Distributed Transactions Coordinator (MSDTC). This service enables a client to make changes on multiple SQL Servers at the same time, and to ensure that either all of the transactions take place, or that none of the transactions take place. This feature ensures that transactions don't become out of sync, introducing errors in the data.

Network Independent

Although SQL Server has to run under NT Server, it is network protocol–independent. It can communicate with clients running under virtually any operating system that uses industry-standard network protocols, such as Windows NT, Windows 95/98, Windows 3.x, DOS, Novell, Banyan, and UNIX.

Built-In Fault Tolerance

Besides working with NT Server's own built-in fault tolerant features, SQL Server includes numerous features to help ensure mission critical data is not lost. SQL Server also supports Microsoft's Cluster Server software, which allows a failed SQL Server to automatically fail over to a stand-by SQL Server, with minimal disruption to clients.

Supports ANSI-92 SQL and Extensions

If you are already a SQL developer, learning to use or program with SQL Server should not be difficult because it is ANSI-92 SQL compliant. But because ANSI-92 SQL is limited, SQL

Server also includes many extensions to the language, which is called *Transact-SQL*. SQL developers will find the SQL extensions a great benefit when writing client/server applications.

Centralized Management

No matter how many SQL Servers there are in your enterprise, or where they are located, they all can be managed from one central location. This not only greatly eases the job of the DBA, but contributes to SQL Server's overall low total cost of ownership.

Visual Administration Tools and Wizards

Virtually all SQL Server management tasks can be completed through a GUI interface called the SQL Enterprise Manager. Enterprise Manager takes advantage of the new Microsoft Management Console (MMC) and includes many wizards that can make many common administrative tasks very easy to perform. SQL Server also includes a task scheduler that can automatically perform many tasks, such as backups, unattended.

SEE ALSO

➤ *MMC is shown and discussed on page 220.*

Supports Multiple Clients

SQL Server supports a wide variety of clients that enable users to insert, update, delete, and query data stored in SQL Server databases. SQL Server itself includes a variety of client tools, including SQL Server Query Analyzer and OSQL. It also works with non–SQL Server programs such as Microsoft Excel, Microsoft Access, and Crystal Reports. In many cases, organizations write their own custom clients using a development tool, such as Visual Basic. This allows organizations the greatest flexibility in creating client user-interfaces that meet their specific business needs.

Supports Many Development Tools

Creating applications in SQL Server involves creating two or more parts, depending on whether the SQL Server application uses either two-tier or three-tier client/server architecture. SQL Server development can be complex, but is made easier with a wide variety of available tools. Microsoft's Visual Studio is the most comprehensive tool set available for developing SQL Server applications, including virtually every development tool offered by Microsoft. Third-party tools are also available. If your organization does not want to develop its own SQL Server applications, it can rely on the many third-party organizations that have already written many common SQL Server applications, such as accounting or manufacturing, that can be used out of the box.

Integrates Well with Microsoft Office

If an organization had standardized on Microsoft Office as its desktop suite, it can take advantage of the tight integration between SQL Server and Microsoft Office. Data on a SQL Server can be easily downloaded into Microsoft Access or Microsoft Excel for analysis, or put into Microsoft PowerPoint for a presentation.

Internet/Intranet Connectivity

With the widespread use of the public Internet and private intranets, organizations are finding that they are an inexpensive way to share data. SQL Server can easily share data via Web sites, enabling Web browser users to access data directly from SQL Server databases. In many organizations, developers have decided to standardize on Web browsers at the standard client because they are inexpensive and easy to learn and use. In many ways, it is much easier and less expensive to create Web-related applications to access SQL Server data than it is to create conventional client/server applications. Perhaps one day Web browsers will become the standard user interface, replacing most custom-built front ends. Already you are beginning to see this as Microsoft has now adapted the Web browser metaphor for Windows 98 and Windows 2000.

Which Windows to use

Although SQL Server also runs under Windows 95/98, it is much better integrated with NT Server than Windows 95/98. Because most organizations will be running their production servers under NT Server, and not Windows 95/98, this section focuses on how SQL Server is integrated with NT Server.

How SQL Server Is Integrated with Windows NT Server and Microsoft BackOffice

SQL Server prefers NT Server to run, which is both good and bad. It is good because SQL Server has been designed to be tightly integrated with NT Server. This means that SQL Server has been optimized to run under NT Server, which contributes to SQL Server's speed and ease-of-use. It is also a bad thing because you cannot choose just any operating system to run SQL Server. But this is only a problem if you don't want to run NT Server. NT Server is a great application operating system and most people (even if they aren't NT Server fans) are willing to use it to get the many features offered by SQL Server.

NT Server Integration

NT Server offers many features that SQL Server can take advantage of. Some of these include the following:

- **SMP Support.** Out of the box, NT Server will support up to 4 or 8 CPUs (depending on which version of NT Server is used), and can support up to 32 CPUs under certain circumstances. NT Server supports true *symmetrical processing* (SMP), where the processing load is evenly distributed among each CPU for the greatest efficiency. As SQL Server is a *multithreaded* application, this mean it can take advantage of multiple CPUs, with each thread executing independently of one another. This ability is one of the reasons SQL Server scales so well.

- **Multiple Platform Support**. NT Server and SQL Server support not only Intel CPUs, but also DEC Alpha CPUs. This gives DBAs the ability to choose the CPU that best matches their needs.

- **Preemptive Multitasking**. NT Server includes a scheduling mechanism that controls the order at which program threads are run, and which ones get the highest priority. This means that any program running on NT Server, including SQL Server, is optimized to run as fast as it possibly can.

- **Reliability**. NT Server's architecture separates operating system programs from application programs. Each program running under NT Server is given its own 2GB memory space (3GB under the enterprise edition of NT Server), which is separate from all other programs, including the operating system. This means that if one program should fail, it shouldn't interfere with other running programs or the operating system. This contributes to a very stable operating system environment that can run mission-critical SQL Server applications without fear of unexpected crashes due to software-related problems.

- **Fault Tolerance**. NT Server includes it own built-in software-based fault tolerance (RAID Levels 1 and 5), and it also supports hardware RAID.

- **Central Registry Database.** All NT Server configuration information is stored in the NT Server Registry. SQL Server takes advantage of NT Server's Registry by also storing some of its configuration information in the Registry.

- **Integrated Security.** NT Server offers very good security. If implemented properly, NT Server can keep virtually all non-authorized users locked out. SQL Server can take advantage of NT Server's security, making it much easier for administrators to set up and maintain SQL Server security.

- **Background Services.** Much of the power of NT Server lies in its ability to run applications as background services. SQL Server itself takes advantage of this and runs as a series of background services.

- **Event Viewer Logging.** Important SQL Server events are automatically written to NT Server's Event Viewer. This provides a central location where administrators can look for potential problems and to troubleshoot.

- **Performance Monitoring.** When SQL Server is installed, it adds many Performance Monitor objects and counters. This allows SQL Server to be monitored using NT Server's Performance Monitor (PERFMON.EXE) tool.

You will want to master using the Performance Monitor

Although SQL Server does a lot on its own to optimize its performance, you still need to regularly monitor how well it's running. The ideal tool for this is NT Server's Performance Monitor. It enables you to view and log any of the many SQL Server statistics used to track how SQL Server is running. You will learn more about the Performance Monitor in Chapter 18, "SQL Server Optimization and Tuning Fundamentals."

- **Ease of Administration.** NT Server has always been easy to manage because of the many graphical-based administration tools provided by Microsoft. SQL Server not only has many similar graphical-based management tools, it also takes advantage of many of NT Server's tools.

Integration with Microsoft BackOffice

SQL Server is not only tightly integrated with NT Server, but also with several Microsoft BackOffice products, including Microsoft Exchange, Microsoft Internet Information Server (IIS), Microsoft Systems Management Server (SMS), SNA Server, Transaction Server, and Messaging Queue Server. Here's a brief look at how these tools integrate with SQL Server:

- **Microsoft Exchange.** Exchange is Microsoft's enterprise mail server. SQL Server can be set up to receive and send mail messages using Exchange. For example, a user could send a query request to SQL Server via a mail message, and then the query results can be emailed back to the user. Also, SQL Server can send DBAs and other users various types of alert messages, as needed.

- **Microsoft Internet Information Server.** IIS is Microsoft's enterprise Web server, and SQL Server is very tightly integrated with IIS in three important ways. First, data from a SQL Server can be automatically published as Web pages, enabling users to browse the SQL Server data with an ordinary Web browser. Second, users can query information stored in a SQL Server database by using a Web browser, and have the results quickly returned back to the Web browser. And last, dynamic Web pages can be created from information stored in a SQL Server database. These work well for both Internet and intranet Web sites.

- **Microsoft Systems Management Server.** SMS is a powerful desktop management tool that performs many tasks, including automatically taking a hardware and software inventory of all desktops and servers connected to a network. SMS requires that SQL Server be used as the database where this information is stored. Because of this, all the inventory information can be accessed like any other data stored in a SQL Server database.

- **SNA Server**. SQL Server can be integrated with IBM mainframe and AS/400 legacy applications and data using SNA Server. SNA Server acts as the physical link and translator between the legacy applications and SQL Server.

- **Transaction Server**. Transaction Server is a tool mostly for SQL Developers, not the DBA. It enables SQL Developers to more easily create multiple-tier client/server applications. Generally Transaction Server, running under NT Server, sits in the middle of a multiple-tier SQL Server architecture and is where the business rules are stored and executed.

- **Message Queue Server**. Message Queue Server is another tool mostly for SQL Developers. It is designed to make it easier for developers to create programs that can more quickly and reliably communicate with other applications by asynchronously sending and receiving messages. This is especially helpful to developers who want to integrate SQL Server with non-SQL Server applications.

SEE ALSO

➤ *To configure SQL Server to work with Microsoft Exchange, see page 297.*

What You Need to Know to Be a Successful SQL Server DBA

One single person cannot have all the necessary skills, or time, to do everything that needs to be done in order to make SQL Server work for an organization. The focus of this book is on the Database Administrator (DBA), whose job it is to install and configure SQL Server, and maintain it on a day-to-day basis. This section takes a look at who the DBA interacts with, discusses the wide variety of knowledge a good DBA must have, and takes a brief look at the day-to-day tasks of the DBA.

Before you take a look at the DBA's role in depth, let's take a short look at some of the other people who will also be involved with SQL Server. Some of those include the following:

- **SQL Developer.** If your organization is going to be developing its own SQL applications, there will be one or more people whose job it is to design and write SQL Server applications in Transact-SQL and write client front ends in some development language. Although many SQL programmers know programming, few are familiar with how networks work, how servers work, and how to administer a server. The DBA often must provide SQL programmers with the practical information they need to know about the limitations of the network hardware and SQL Server.

- **Network Administrator.** This person is responsible for setting up servers and managing network applications. Generally, this person will know everything there is to know about file and print servers, but when it comes to managing specific application servers, such as SQL Server, they may be lost. The DBA will have to work with the network administrator to determine the best way to integrate SQL Servers with the rest of the network so that network traffic is optimized. Often the DBA must rely on the network administrator to solve network-related problems that affect SQL Server.

- **Help Desk Staff.** Most larger organizations have people devoted to helping end-users over the phone or in person. The help desk staff will have to be taught how to use and support your SQL Server applications so they can help others. As the DBA, you may be responsible for ensuring that they are trained not only on how to use the client software, but have a basic understanding of the SQL Server application in order to properly troubleshoot problems. Often it will be someone here who first alerts you to a potential SQL Server problem.

- **End-Users.** Although end-users spend the most time with computer applications, they are often the most neglected when it comes to training. They are also often ignored when it comes to seeking their input on how to make a SQL Server application better. Although the DBA probably won't be responsible for training users, the DBA may be involved in ensuring that proper end-user training is done, and for soliciting feedback on current SQL Server applications.

As the DBA, it may be your job to coordinate the efforts of all the people listed here. If you are from a small organization, you may find yourself playing multiple roles, if not all these roles. Nobody said this job was easy.

Skills Needed to Be a DBA

The responsibilities of the DBA are diverse, and the skills necessary to be a good DBA are varied as well. Some of the skills a DBA should possess include the following:

- **A Solid Understanding of NT Server**. Because SQL Server is so intimately tied to NT Server, the DBA must have a good understanding of how NT Server works and how to manage it. For example, the DBA should know how to manage users and groups, change local and share permissions, change the security policy, modify the Registry, manage shares, stop and start services, use the Event Viewer, set up fault tolerance, run the Performance and Network Monitors, understand domain design, and be familiar with basic NT Server troubleshooting.

- **An Intimate Knowledge of SQL Server**. It goes without saying that the DBA should have a good understanding of SQL Server.

- **Familiarity with Data Backup and Restore**. As most SQL Server databases are mission critical, the DBA's biggest challenge is to ensure that the data is available when needed. No matter how the SQL Server databases are backed up, the DBA must be very familiar with the backup tools (SQL Server, NT Server, or third-party) and how to use them to quickly restore a crashed database.

Project management skills are a plus

If you want to become an effective DBA, it is very useful to have some project management skills and experience. In some cases, a DBA might be put in charge of deploying SQL Server throughout an entire enterprise, or be responsible for upgrading all current SQL Server 6.5 servers to 7.0. The more you know about project management, the more successful you will be at managing larger projects.

T-SQL and the DBA

Although learning Transact-SQL is an important skill for the DBA, this book focuses on how to administer SQL Server though the many GUI administrative tools provided. Where appropriate, this book also includes some Transact-SQL examples.

- **An Understanding of Business Processes**. This may be the hardest part for the DBA to master. Every SQL Server database, in one way or another, models (imitates) one or more business processes. The better the DBA understands these processes, the more the DBA can contribute to SQL Server's success at achieving them. It is sometimes easy to forget that the reason SQL Server has been implemented in the first place is to cost-effectively fulfill some critical business need, and that it is not there just to provide some of us with high-paying jobs.

- **A Basic Understanding of Relational Database Design**. SQL Server databases can be very complex, and the DBA has to understand how they are designed in order to be able to optimize and tune them.

- **A Basic Understanding of Transact-SQL**. Although the DBA does not have to be a Transact-SQL programmer, it is still useful to know the basics, such as how to create a simple query using the SELECT statement. The more Transact-SQL the DBA knows, the more valuable the DBA becomes.

- **A Meticulous Approach to Work**. Although this statement can be made for almost any job, it is especially important for the DBA. Most SQL Databases contain mission critical data that if lost, could significantly affect the success of a business. The DBA must very careful when performing all tasks to ensure data is never lost, or that the database isn't down any longer than it has to be for routine maintenance.

What Exactly Does a DBA Do?

Up to now, the duties of the DBA have been described in general terms. Now let's take a specific look at some of the many varied tasks the DBA does on a regular basis:

- **Install and Upgrade SQL Server**. When a new SQL Server computer needs to be installed, or upgraded from an old to a new version, it is the DBA who will do the work. Installing a new SQL Server computer probably won't be a common event, unless you work for a very large organization. Fortunately, most new installations are routine. SQL

Server upgrades are another story. Although they may not occur often, they can be very time consuming and troublesome. Problems range from finding the time to make the upgrade so that business operations are not affected, to unexpected bugs that can devastate a database. Upgrades involve much planning and need to be approached very methodically.

- **Create and Manage Databases**. It is usually the job of the DBA to create and manage the databases used for storing data.

- **Manage Database Users and Security**. Managing user security is one of the biggest jobs of the DBA. As people's responsibilities change, or as people leave or join an organization, user accounts have to be created and the correct database permissions set. It is the job of the DBA to balance the need for security with the ability of people to easily access the data they need to do their jobs.

- **Perform Database Maintenance**. SQL Server databases are very complex, and to help prevent the loss of data, the DBA is responsible for performing regular database maintenance tasks to help catch and fix any errors before they become major problems.

- **Back Up and Restore Databases**. Of all the jobs the DBA has, this is probably the most important, and boring. Even the most fault-tolerant server can fail, destroying all the data stored on it. Regular backups help to ensure that data will not be permanently lost. The DBA is responsible for developing a disaster recovery plan to deal with potential data loss, no matter how it happens. Although most of us think of server crashes as the main cause of data loss, there are may others. Some of them include user error, accidents, theft or vandalism, fire, and acts of nature. The DBA must be prepared for every eventuality.

- **Transfer Data Between SQL Server and Other Applications**. Although our ultimate goal is to store all of an organization's data in one location in a single format, this is currently impossible. Enterprise data is often scattered throughout an organization, and stored in many formats.

The job of the DBA can be stressful

Being in charge of mission-critical data can take its toll in stress for many DBAs. In many cases, the data you manage and guard is the life force of the company, and should the data ever be lost, the life of the company could be in jeopardy. The best way to deal with this kind of stress is to take every precaution you can to prevent potential problems. This way, you can get a good night's sleep every night.

Some data may be on mainframes, some on UNIX servers, and some in SQL Server. As a DBA, you often must move data from various applications to SQL Server, and from SQL Server to other applications. How often you have to transfer data depends on your organization. Some DBAs transfer data daily between SQL Server and other applications, and other DBAs transfer data only occasionally.

- **Manage Data Replication**. If your organization takes advantage of SQL Server's replication ability, it is the duty of the DBA to both set up and manage replication. Depending on the needs of the business, this can range from simple to very complex.

- **Regularly Monitor and Tune SQL Server**. As a DBA there will be one type of complaint you hear more often than any other, and that is complaints about database response time. Everybody wants instant response time, and when they don't get it, they complain. As the DBA, you will be blamed for it, even though it is often out of your control. SQL databases are very complex and have many limitations when it comes to speed. Although some tasks are fast, some are inherently slower. Often when you make a change to speed up one task, this in turn slows down another task. On a regular basis, the DBA must monitor SQL Server database performance and take active steps to tune it for optimum performance. This is a never-ending job because most databases change over time, which means that they have to be tuned differently as they change.

- **Schedule Events**. Many of the routine tasks of the DBA, such as database backups, can be automated using SQL Server's task scheduler. The DBA is responsible for identifying common tasks that can be automated, implementing them, and then following up to be sure the tasks are occurring as scheduled. Also, the DBA can set up SQL Server to provide alerts when critical events occur, which can be emailed to the DBA, providing constant feedback on the status of all the SQL Servers under the DBA's supervision.

- **Troubleshoot Problems**. Troubleshooting problems is a constant challenge for the DBA. Problems never seem to go away for long. As soon as you solve one, a new one you have never seen before appears. Although a thorough understanding of SQL Server is the best tool you have to begin troubleshooting, there is no substitute for experience. The longer you are a DBA, the better you will become at troubleshooting.

- **Work with Others to Keep SQL Server Running**. As was mentioned earlier, the DBA does not work alone. A SQL Server is just one small part of a large network that makes up just a small part of any organization. The DBA works with many other people throughout the organization to ensure that the SQL Servers the DBA is responsible for are meeting the business needs they were designed to meet.

SEE ALSO

➤ *To install SQL Server, see page 111.*

➤ *To create and manage databases, see page 256.*

➤ *To perform database maintenance, see page 308.*

➤ *To back up and restore a database, see page 476.*

➤ *To transfer data from SQL Server using DTS, see page 510 or using BCP, see page 520.*

➤ *To replicate SQL Server data, see page 542.*

Become a Microsoft Certified Professional to Enhance Your Skills

For now and the foreseeable future, the demand for DBAs will outstrip the supply, providing many new and high-paying jobs. Experts on Microsoft SQL Server will have no problem finding jobs as a DBA at Microsoft Solution Providers, system integrators, consulting firms, corporations, and government agencies alike in the United States and worldwide. Although it is not a prerequisite to finding a job as a SQL Server DBA, you should consider becoming Microsoft-certified in SQL Server by participating in Microsoft's Certified Professional (MCP) program. This section takes a brief look at what an MCP is, the benefits of becoming certified, and how to become certified.

What Is a Microsoft Certified Professional?

When you begin your job search to find a SQL Server DBA position, it is very difficult to prove to potential organizations that you really know a particular product as well as you claim. It is all too easy for applicants to "fudge" their resume to claim that they are experts on the product. Microsoft realized that this was an on-going problem in the computer industry, so it established its MCP program. The purpose of the program is to enable computer professionals to prove their knowledge and mastery of Microsoft products by taking and passing one or more rigorous certification tests.

What Certification Programs Does Microsoft Offer?

Microsoft currently offers seven certification programs. They include:

- **Microsoft Certified Product Specialist (MCPS)**. This is the easiest certification to attain because you only have to pass one test. You can choose from a wide variety of tests, but if you are interested in proving your skill on SQL Server, you will want to take the System Administration for Microsoft SQL Server 7.0 test. After you pass a particular test, such as the one for SQL Server, you become an MCPS for the particular product you pass the test on. These same tests also count toward other Microsoft certifications.

- **Microsoft Certified Database Administrator (MCDBA)**. If your desire to specialize as a DBA, then this is the cerification you will want to attain. It is designed for professionals who implement and administer SQL Server databases. To recieve this certification, you must pass five Microsoft Certification exams. The first four tests you must pass are referred to as core exams, which include tests on Administering Microsoft SQL Server 7.0, Designing and Implementing Database with Microsoft SQL Server 7.0, Implementing and Supporting NT Server 4.0, and Implementing and Supporting NT Server in the Enterprise.

The last of the five tests can be selected from a group of optional tests, including tests on Designing and Implementing Data Warehouses using Microsoft Sql Server 7.0, Microsoft Internet Information Server, Visual Basic 6, and several others.

- **Microsoft Certified Systems Engineer (MCSE).** This is one of the hottest, if not *the* hottest, industry certification you can earn. It is designed for networking professionals and requires that you pass a total of six tests. Four of the tests must be from Microsoft's Operating System group of tests, which includes tests on the topic of Networking Essentials, Windows 95, NT 4.0 Workstation, and NT 4.0 Server, among others. Then you have to take two elective tests, which are generally available on each Microsoft BackOffice product, such as SQL Server. If your goal is to become a DBA, and you want to maximize your earning power and job opportunities, this is the certification to get.

- **Microsoft Certified Solution Developer (MCSD).** This certification program is designed for developers. It consists of four tests. The first three must be taken from a pro-scribed list of tests. The last test is an elective of your choos-ing. One of the electives is a test called Implementing a Database Design on Microsoft SQL Server 7.0. This test is designed for developers who will be writing applications in Transact-SQL for SQL Server. This same test may also be taken as an elective for the MCSE program. If you want to be a DBA, but are more interested in programming than network support, this is the ideal certification for you.

- **Microsoft Certified Professional + Internet (MCP+I).** Attaining this certification requires three tests. The tests are on NT Server, TCP/IP, and the Internet Information Server. As a DBA, you might want to consider this certifica-tion if the SQL Servers you want to administer serve as back ends to a Web server.

- **Microsoft Certified Systems Engineer + Internet (MCSE+I).** This is the most difficult of all Microsoft certifications to attain. It requires a total of nine tests: seven required and two optional. It is designed for those who want to specialize in the Internet. Like the MCP+I, you might want to consider this certification if you are the DBA of a SQL Server that is used to support Internet and intranet applications.

- **Microsoft Certified Trainer (MCT).** This is a special certification for people who want to train at Microsoft certified Training Centers (CTEC). People who teach Microsoft Certified Classes at CTECs must become an MCT before they can teach, and must be certified separately on each class they teach.

To learn more about Microsoft Certification, see Microsoft's Web site at www.microsoft.com/train_cert.

chapter

2

SQL Server and Database Fundamentals

Learn the nature and structure of
SQL Server 7.0

Explore essential aspects of
administration

Learn what you need to know about
databases, including objects and
architecture

What is Transact-SQL and how much
does a DBA need to know?

Do I need to read this chapter?

This chapter is designed for people new to SQL Server. If you have used previous versions of SQL Server, you may want to skip this chapter and go immediately to a chapter that covers a topic that interests you. If this is the first time you have ever used any version SQL Server, you will definitely want to read this chapter. It provides important foundational material you need to understand before reading further in this book.

Server-to-server ratio

Each physical server running NT Server can only run a single copy of SQL Server. An organization may have as many SQL Servers and it needs.

SQL Server Fundamentals

When people think of SQL Server, they often have different pictures in their heads of what SQL Server really is. Some people think of it as a database. Others think if it as a physical server. And others think of the BackOffice product sold by Microsoft.

In Chapter 1, "Introduction to SQL Server 7.0," I defined SQL Server as a client/server relational database system. In this section, you learn exactly what SQL Server really is.

What Exactly Is SQL Server?

SQL Server can be best understood by taking a look at how it works.

- First, SQL Server is a computer program that resides on a single computer running NT Server. SQL Server isn't a physical server itself, but a computer program that runs on a physical server. Only one copy of SQL Server can run on a single physical server at a time, although an organization can have as many physical servers running SQL Server at it needs. Generally, each SQL Server is managed as a separate entity, although multiple SQL Servers can be managed from a central location.

- Second, each separate copy of SQL Server has the ability to manage one or more separate databases. In addition, each database is distinct from one another, and managed separately. The number of databases each copy of SQL Server can manage is dependent on the server hardware, the size of the database, and how the database is used.

- Third, it is a good idea to separate in your mind SQL Server from the databases it manages. SQL Server is software written specifically to manage databases, whereas a database is a special data structure designed to hold data. Although they are both intertwined, they are very much distinct from one another (see Figure 2.1).

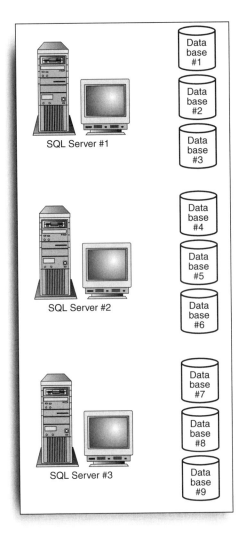

FIGURE 2.1

SQL Server should be thought of as separate from the databases it manages. Each separate SQL Server can manage one or more separate and distinct databases. The number of databases managed by SQL Server depends on the capability of the physical server running SQL Server.

- Fourth, although SQL Server is used to create and manage databases, it takes more than this to make SQL Server useful to an organization. A database isn't too useful if people cannot easily search, insert, update, or delete records from it. This generally requires that a SQL Server developer write custom-written Transact-SQL code to produce the desired results. This is referred to as a *SQL Server application*.

What is an NT service?

An NT service is a program that runs in the background of NT Server without any user interface. To administer a service, it must be accessed by a separate program that has a user interface.

■ Fifth, from an administrative point-of-view, SQL Server can be divided into two major parts: the core SQL Server services and the SQL Server management tools. The core SQL Server services consist of the *SQL Server Engine* and the *SQL Server Agent*. They are referred to as services and will be discussed in more detail in the section called "SQL Server Architecture Fundamentals" later in this chapter. The core services are always running in the background of NT Server and in a sense are the "real" SQL Server. You are not able to see this critical part of SQL Server, but you can interact with it using the second part of SQL Server, which includes the SQL Server management tools. SQL Server includes a variety of management tools that enable you to interact with SQL Server.

As you can see, SQL Server has many different aspects. Generally, when you refer to "SQL Server," you are referring to the core SQL services, which make up the real heart of SQL Server.

What Makes SQL Server a Client/Server Database System?

SQL Server is the "server" part of a client/server relational database system. SQL Server is used to manage the databases that are used by the people who do the "real" work in most organizations. The databases managed by SQL Server act as repositories of data, storing data such as sales information, inventory, or any kind of data used by an organization.

In order for people to get data both in and out of SQL Server databases, a "client" is required. Both parts—server and client—are required to produce the desired results of a well-managed information system. These parts are then tied together by a custom-written Transact-SQL application.

When you purchase SQL Server, you only purchase the "server" part of a client/server relational database system, not the "client" part. Although SQL Server does include some software that acts as an administrative client, in that it enables the DBA to access and manage SQL Server over a network, it doesn't provide the client software necessary for the typical user. This software must be purchased or custom created.

Figure 2.2 shows how SQL Server and client software work together.

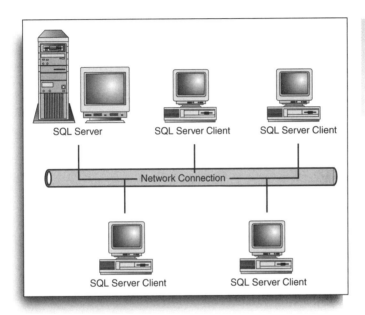

SQL Server

SQL Server Client

SQL Server Client

Network Connection

SQL Server Client

SQL Server Client

FIGURE 2.2

SQL Server requires client-side software in order to be useful.

This illustration is an example of a simple SQL Server client/server design. It has a single SQL Server managing a single database running on a single physical server. The illustration also shows four separate user workstations, each running a copy of the client software necessary to access the SQL Server database over a network. In order for anyone to access the database on the server running SQL Server, such as to search, insert, update, or delete a record, she performs the task at a workstation. Each workstation must be running client software that has been designed to access the database on the SQL Server over a network connection. Whenever a user needs to access the database, the client software sends a command to the SQL Server over the network using a language the SQL Server is able to understand. After SQL Server has acted on the request from the client software, it can respond to the client software as appropriate. For example, if a user wants a listing of all the sales made on a certain date for a particular store, the user can type in the request at the client, where the message is sent to the SQL Server. After the SQL Server receives the request, it will process it, and then send the results of the request back to the client who requested it.

In most cases, the client software running on the workstation must be custom-written to work properly with the database managed by SQL Server. Although it is possible to use such programs as Microsoft Excel or Microsoft Access to act as a client to SQL Server without any special programming, it requires that the user know a great deal about both SQL Server and their client software to do any productive work. Because most users will be untrained in SQL Server and in database techniques in general, custom-written client software is usually required. This enables a developer to write a client that is easy to use by untrained individuals.

As you may have already guessed, this book focuses on how to administer SQL Server, not how to write client software or SQL Server client/server applications. What you learn in this book is only part of the overall picture, albeit an important one. As a SQL Server DBA, you will be part of a larger team that works together to apply SQL Server to meeting your organization's information management needs.

How do you create client software?

Writing client software to access data from a database managed by SQL Server is a complex task requiring programmers with client/server application knowledge and experience. Virtually any programming language can be used to write client software. One of the most popular is Microsoft's Visual Basic. Generally, client software is written as part of a larger development project that includes designing and writing a SQL Server client/server application in Transact-SQL.

SQL Server Administration Fundamentals

As I mentioned in the previous section, the program code that represents SQL Server runs as two major services under NT Server. Because they are NT services, they cannot be directly controlled by the DBA. This means that using one or more of a wide variety of techniques must indirectly control them. This section takes a brief look at some of the tools available to the DBA to manage the two core SQL Server services.

Managing SQL Server Using GUI-Based Tools

SQL Server includes a variety of GUI-based tools that enable the DBA to manage its two core services. The major tools include:

- **SQL Server Enterprise Manager**: Usually referred to just as "Enterprise Manager," this tool is the most important of all the SQL Server administration tools. This is the tool most used by the DBA as she administers SQL Server. You will learn how to use this powerful administration tool as you read throughout this book. Enterprise Manager is also a Microsoft Management Console (MMC) snap-in. In other words, Enterprise Manager isn't a standalone program, it is part of Microsoft's new MMC strategy. MMC is a new user-interface environment that can be used to manage any of the newer breed of Microsoft BackOffice programs. Eventually, MMC will become the standard user interface for NT Server and all Microsoft BackOffice products.

- **Enterprise Manager Wizards**: To make the life of the DBA a little easier, Enterprise Manager includes a wide variety of wizards that step you through many typical DBA-related administrative tasks. A *wizard* is a tool that steps you through configuring a specific aspect of SQL Server. The wizards are available from the Enterprise Manager.

- **SQL Server Query Analyzer**: Usually referred to as the "Query Analyzer," this tool enables the DBA or SQL developer to directly administer SQL Server using Transact-SQL statements. Transact-SQL can be entered interactively, or it can be run from stored procedures or scripts from the Query Analyzer.

- **SQL Server Service Manager**: Usually referred to as the "Service Manager," this tool enables you to stop and start the SQL Server services.

- **SQL Server Profiler**: Usually referred to as the "Profiler," this tool enables you to directly monitor communication between SQL Server and client software.

- **SQL Server Client Network Utility**: Usually referred to as the "Client Network Utility," this tool is used to configure the Network Libraries and DB Library options for SQL Server administrative client software.

- **Other Tools**: SQL Server includes many other tools besides the ones listed here. They will be introduced throughout the book as appropriate.

Although these tools, and more, are automatically loaded when SQL Server is installed onto a physical server, they also can be loaded onto any Windows 95/98, Windows NT Workstation, or Windows NT Server computers. This means that you don't have to be physically present at a SQL Server to administer it. By loading these tools on remote computers, you are able to remotely manage SQL Server.

It is important to keep in mind that each of these tools is used to indirectly administer SQL Server. When these tools are used, they communicate with the appropriate SQL Server service, either configuring it to your needs, or enabling you to perform any necessary functions, such as creating a new database or backing up and restoring a database. The next section on the SQL Server architecture provides a detailed explanation of how this works.

SEE ALSO

➤ *For more information on using the SQL Server Setup program, see page 143.*

➤ *For more information on using the SQL Server Client Configuration Manager, see page 184.*

➤ *For more information on using the SQL Server Profiler, see page 572.*

SQL Server Architecture Fundamentals

To be a good DBA, and to be able to troubleshoot SQL Server problems, you need a basic understanding of how SQL Server works. This section takes a high-level look at SQL Server's architecture. In this section, you will learn about:

- Client/server architecture
- Client architecture
- The network connection
- SQL Server architecture

If after reading this section you want to learn more about how SQL Server works, read the section in the SQL Server Books Online called "SQL Server Architecture."

Client/Server Architecture

The best way to understand how SQL Server works is to take a look at all the parts of the SQL Server client/server architecture. Figure 2.3 presents a high-level overview of this architecture.

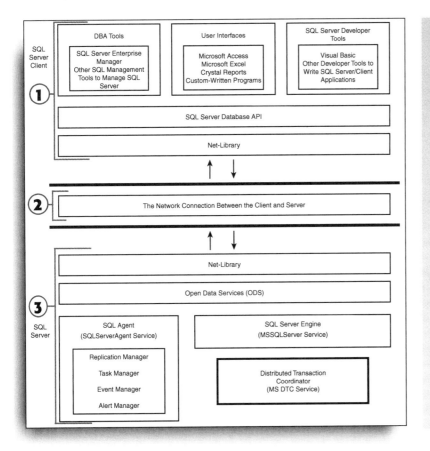

FIGURE 2.3
The SQL Server client/server architecture.

(1) The SQL Server client is made up of many parts. Each part works together to communicate with SQL Server over a network connection.

(2) The SQL Server client and SQL Server must be connected by a common transport protocol over a network connection. Virtually any type of physical network architecture is supported.

(3) SQL Server isn't just a single program, it is a combination of many components that all work together in order to communicate with a wide variety of client software.

What about multiple-tier client/server architecture?

This section focuses solely on the more common two-tier client/server architecture, although SQL Server supports multiple-tier architecture.

The overall SQL Server client/server architecture includes three important components:

- **SQL Server client software:** The client component is used to access SQL Server and the databases managed by SQL Server. Client software includes software to both administer and use SQL Server remotely over a network connection.

- **Network connection:** This is the network connection that physically connects the client software to SQL Server. It is what enables the client software to speak directly to the SQL Server core services. If the client and SQL Server software are on the same physical server, this component is skipped.

- **SQL Server:** This is the SQL Server program, which includes a variety of components, including the core SQL Server services: the SQL Agent and the SQL Server Engine.

All three components work together to provide the necessary functionality that makes SQL Server a great tool for organizations to manage many of their informational management needs. Now that you have looked at the big picture, let's look at each individual component in depth.

SQL Server Client Architecture

SQL Server's client architecture can be divided into three major components:

- The client application software
- The SQL Server Database API
- The Net-Library

The Client Application Software

Client application software refers to the program used to access SQL Server. This may be a custom-written program, or it may be a program purchased from a third-party vendor. Client application software can be divided into three categories: DBA Tools, SQL Server Developer Tools, and User Interfaces.

DBA Tools include any of the SQL Server administration tools that come with SQL Server, and any custom-written tools you may want to create to manage SQL Server. The SQL Server Enterprise Manager is considered the key DBA Tool, and like all other SQL Server client software, it can be used to remotely attach to SQL Server to perform necessary administration tasks.

SQL Server Developer Tools include any programming tool, such as Visual Basic or Visual Studio, that can be used to create custom-written client/server applications, including user interfaces. These tools generally run on development workstations and only connect with SQL Server as necessary during the development process.

User Interfaces include any tool designed to enable a typical database user to access and manipulate the data stored in SQL Server databases. These can include off-the-shelf tools such as Microsoft Access, Microsoft Excel, Crystal Reports, or any third-party program designed to access SQL Server data. It also includes any custom-written software designed to enable typical users to access SQL Server data.

The SQL Server Database API

Client application software cannot communicate directly with SQL Server; it must first go through a database *applications programming interface* (API). This acts as an intermediary between the application software and SQL Server.

SQL Server supports a variety of database APIs, including *OLE DB*, *ODBC*, *DB-Library*, and *Embedded SQL*. Whenever a programmer decides to write a client application for SQL Server, he or she has to pick an appropriate database API. As a SQL Server DBA, you generally don't care which database API is used as it doesn't generally affect how you perform your work.

The Net-Library

Both the SQL Server client software, and SQL Server, run as processes on a computer. A *process* refers to all the resources allocated on a computer necessary to run a program. Because of this, the term *process* is often used to refer to either client software or SQL Server as it is running.

Anyone can write his own SQL Server administrative program

SQL Server has been designed so that anyone with enough ambition can write his own administrative tools. Microsoft has included something called SQL Distributed Management Objects (SQL-DMO) with SQL Server. This is a COM-based object model that enables a programmer to use virtually any programming language to write custom SQL Server administrative programs.

SQL Server supports Universal Data Access

One of the banes of corporate application designers has been the problem of dealing with many different data storage formats. Some corporate data is stored in spreadsheets, some in file-based databases, some in relational databases, and on and on. Traditionally, it has been difficult to gather all this data into a single, easily available source. To help resolve this problem, SQL Server supports what Microsoft refers to as Universal Data Access (UDA). This technology allows SQL Server to easily connect widely diverse data into one central location where it can be easily queried.

Want to know more about database APIs?

To find out more about SQL Server database APIs, search for the phrase "Client Components" in the SQL Server Books Online.

For the SQL Server client process to speak to the SQL Server process, an Interprocess Communication (IPC) must occur. This can be a local IPC or a network (remote) IPC. If it is a local IPC, both the client and SQL Server processes must be running on the same computer. If it is a network IPC, the client process and the SQL Server process communicate over a network connection.

There isn't a single IPC mechanism. If fact, SQL Server supports many different types of IPC mechanisms, including *named pipes, shared memory, multiprotocol, Windows sockets, Novell SPX/IPX, DECNet, AppleTalk,* and *Banyan VINES.* Each of these are just names of different types of IPC mechanisms supported by SQL Server to enable a client and SQL Server process to communicate with each other.

To support each different IPC mechanism, SQL Server implements the mechanisms as Net-Libraries. A *Net-Library* is the programming code, generally as a Dynamic Link Library (DLL), that is loaded by both a client and SQL Server, in order to have a common way to communicate.

When you install client software on a workstation, you will have to load an appropriate Net-Library, or it will be unable to communicate with SQL Server.

Keep in mind that the client application, database API, and the Net-Library are all required parts of any SQL Server client.

SEE ALSO

➤ *For more information on the various IPC mechanisms supported by SQL Server, see page 126.*

➤ *For more information on how to install a Net-Library for a client, see page 185.*

The Network Connection

In most cases, the SQL Server client will communicate with SQL Server over a network. The type of network chosen makes little difference to the two components as long as the computer running the client and the computer running SQL Server use the same transport protocol and have a common Net-Library.

SQL Server

Similar to the SQL Server client, SQL Server has several components that you should be familiar with. They include the following:

- Net-Library
- Open Data Services (ODS)
- SQL Agent Service
- SQL Server Service
- Distributed Transaction Coordinator Service

Net-Library

This is the SQL Server version of the Net-Library described previously. Both the client and the server need a common Net-Library to communicate. Unlike the client, who can run only a single Net-Library at one time, SQL Server can run multiple Net-Libraries simultaneously. This allows a SQL Server to communicate simultaneously with multiple clients at the same time, no matter which Net-Library each client is using.

Open Data Services (ODS)

Open Data Services (ODS) is a server-side programming applications programming interface (API) used for creating client/server integration with external application systems and data sources. It acts as an interface between the server Net-Libraries and server-based applications.

Developers can use ODS to write applications to distribute SQL Server data to the outside computing environment. Developers can access ODS through such client-side programming APIs as DB-Library and Open Database Connectivity (ODBC). This is of more interest to developers than DBAs.

SQL Server Service

The SQL Server service (MSSQLServer) is the SQL Server engine. It enables users to query, insert, update, and delete data stored in databases. In many ways, the SQL Server service is the heart and soul of SQL Server.

DBA duties and "Open Data"

Although the use of Open Database Connectivity and other open database technologies, such as OLE DB, and standards, such as COM, are of more interest to developers, they do have implications important for DBAs. The capability of nonunique systems to communicate means that you might end up with data in a variety of storage types. One of Microsoft's goals with SQL Server is to incorporate heterogeneous data storage sources as seamlessly as possible. You might never have to write the programs that access data in Word, a Mac graphics program, or a DB2 mainframe, but eventually you might be asked to manage those data sources as well.

The SQL Server service is responsible for managing all SQL Server database files, executing all Transact-SQL statements and stored procedures, and allocating its own resources among concurrent users.

Under NT Server, the SQL Server service runs as a standard NT Server service. Optionally, it can be run as an *executable*. Under Windows 95/98, the SQL Server service runs as an executable only because Windows 95/98 doesn't support background services like NT Server does.

SQL Executive Service

The SQL Executive Service (SQLExecutive) is used for scheduling and automating a variety of DBA management tasks, for creating alerts that can be sent to a DBA about potential SQL Server problems, and is used for event auditing. Within the SQL Executive Service is a group of four "managers" that have specific tasks. They include the Task Manager, Event Manager, Alert Manager, and the Replication Manager. These four managers are coordinated by another component of this service called the Scheduler. Here's what the four managers do:

- **Task Manager:** This manager causes one or more designated tasks to be carried out when a specified event occurs. For example, when it reaches 1:00 AM, a database backup can be automatically made. The designated tasks can be implemented as Transact-SQL statements, scripts, or NT command shell scripts.

- **Event Manager:** This manager writes SQL Server events to the NT Server Event Viewer log.

- **Alert Manager:** This manager sends one or more designated individuals a message, via email or pager, when a specified event on SQL Server has occurred.

- **Replication Manager:** This manager is used during the replication process to schedule when replication will occur.

Under NT Server, the SQL Agent runs as a standard NT Server service. Under Windows 95/98, the SQL Agents runs as an executable only because Windows 95/98 doesn't support background services like NT Server does.

The power of alerts

Sending alerts is an example of Microsoft's tight integration between two of its products: SQL Server and Exchange. SQLMail, a built-in feature of SQL Server that manages mail messages, is a powerful tool for communicating messages both from and to SQL Server.

SEE ALSO
➤ *For more information on creating scheduling tasks, see page 284.*

Distributed Transaction Manager Service

The *Distributed Transaction Manager (MS DTC)*, which runs as a service, isn't a required SQL Server service. It acts as a *transaction manager* and is used when a SQL Server application has been written that modifies data on two or more SQL Servers as part of a single transaction. It guarantees that each data modification on each server will either be 100% complete on all the servers, or in the event of an aborted transaction, any partial modification is rolled back on all the affected servers so the data doesn't become corrupted.

Normally, this service is only started and run when its specific features are needed. Most common SQL Server applications don't use this service. Unless your specific SQL Server client/server application requires this service, you won't use it.

As you can see, SQL Server's architecture is complicated. Actually, it is much more complicated that described in this section. There is much more hidden detail. Fortunately, you don't need to know every detail as you learn how to use SQL Server. The material presented in this section is more than enough to understand the procedures described in this book.

> **Other SQL Server architecture sources**
>
> For additional information on SQL Server's architecture, check out the book, *Microsoft SQL Server 7.0 Unleashed*, from Sams Publishing.

Database Fundamentals

A database is where SQL Server stores its data. Although this may at first seem like a straightforward statement, it has many implications for the DBA. This section takes a look at exactly what is meant by a SQL Server database, and covers these topics:

- The physical and logical database
- System and user databases

The Physical and Logical Database

Every SQL Server database is composed of two parts: the physical database and the logical database. The *physical database* consists of the physical files that make up a database. The *logical database* is that part of the database that is visible to a user.

A SQL Server physical database is made up of two or more physical operating system files. At a minimum, one of these two files will contain the database information and the other will contain the database's transaction log. *Transaction log* files contain the information used to recover a database. Both types of files are themselves made up of smaller units, including *pages* (8K chunks of data) and *extents* (made up of 8 contiguous pages). You will learn more about pages and extents later in the chapter in the section titled "Database Architecture Fundamentals."

A physical database isn't of much direct use to the casual database user. Instead, users are presented with a logical view of the data, which is stored as *database objects* such as tables, views, and so on. You will learn more about database objects later in this chapter in the section "Database Object Fundamentals."

As a DBA, you need to concern yourself more with the physical side of databases than the logical side because, as a DBA, you are responsible for creating and managing the physical database. Although you might become involved in the logical side, this is generally delegated to the database designer and SQL developer.

System and User Databases

SQL Server uses special databases, called *system databases*, to keep track of itself and the databases it manages. These databases are created when SQL Server is first installed and are constantly used by SQL Server as it carries out its various tasks. You will learn more about system databases later in this chapter in the section titled "Database Architecture Fundamentals."

Databases that you create for the needs of your organization are called *user databases*. You can create these whenever you need them. A single copy of SQL Server can maintain a single user database, or hundreds of separate databases, depending on your organization's needs. SQL Server manages each database separately from one another.

What happened to database devices?

If you have ever used a previous version of SQL Server, you may be asking yourself why a discussion of database devices is missing from this book. Database devices, which were preallocated physical files where databases and transaction logs were created and stored, are no longer necessary in SQL Server. This means that SQL Server 7.0 is in many ways much easier to use than previous versions of SQL Server.

SEE ALSO

➤ *For more information on how to create user databases, see page 256.*

Database Object Fundamentals

As I mentioned earlier, a database has both a physical and logical side. This section takes a look at that logical side by describing the kinds of logical database objects that make up a physical database. As a DBA, it is important to understand the type of objects a SQL Server database can contain, even though you probably won't be actively involved in creating them. This is generally left to the database designer or SQL developer.

The phrase *database object* refers to a logical component of a database that contains either data or is used to interact with data. The objects introduced in this section include

- Tables
- Views
- Roles
- Indexes
- Datatypes
- Defaults
- Stored procedures
- Triggers
- Constraints

> **A logical database starts out as an empty shell**
>
> Later in the book when you learn how to create a SQL Server database, what you are actually creating is an empty shell, or container, that will eventually be populated by SQL Server database objects. Creating a new database is just the first of many steps when developing a database for production use.

Tables

Tables are the most important objects within a database because this is where data is stored. Each database can store up to two billion tables. Tables are made up of *rows* (records) and *columns* (fields) (see Figure 2.4). Each table can have up to 1,024 columns and an unlimited number of rows (only limited by disk space and performance issues).

FIGURE 2.4
Tables are made up of rows and columns.

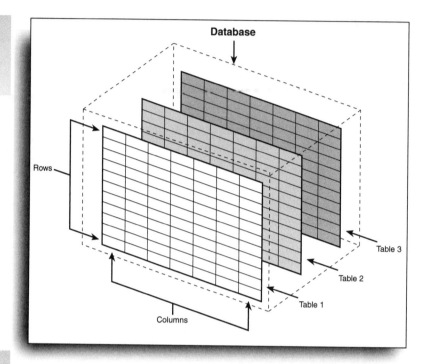

Views

Views, or virtual tables, are created to provide alternate ways to view data stored in tables. Views can be created to display a subset of data from a table, or two or more tables can be linked and combined to create a view (see Figure 2.5). Views themselves don't contain data; they only point to selected data and present it visually.

Roles

The *role* object is new to SQL Server. A role enables you to group one or more users into a single unit that can be used to apply a given set of permissions. Any user who is assigned to that role takes on the permissions assigned to that role. One or more roles can be defined per database, each one enabling you to grant a different set of permissions to each role, depending on the needs of the organization. Every SQL Server database comes with some default role objects.

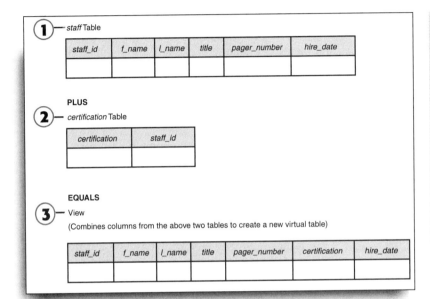

FIGURE 2.5
Views don't store data; they only present it visually.

1 The *staff table* is an independent database table.

2 The *certification table* is an independent database table.

3 A view can be used to combine two separate tables into a virtual table.

Indexes

Indexes are database objects used to speed up data access and to ensure entity integrity of a table. Indexes contain ordered pointers that point to data stored in tables, allowing SQL Server to quickly locate data. Without indexes, SQL Server would have to search every row in a table to find a particular piece of data. Indexes, like indexes in a book, allow SQL Server to quickly locate data in a table.

SQL Server uses two different types of indexes: clustered and nonclustered (see Figure 2.6).

- A *clustered index* forces the rows in a table to be physically stored in sorted order, using one or more columns (indexes can include one or more columns) from the table to sort the rows by. A table may only have one clustered index.

- A *nonclustered index* is a physical data structure separate from the table that points to the data in a table. The pointers are themselves sorted, making it easy to quickly locate data within a table. A table may include an index for every column in a table, although this would be uncommon. Generally, only columns that benefit from sorting have indexes.

FIGURE 2.6

SQL Server supports clustered and nonclustered indexes.

1 In a clustered index, all the data in the table is physically sorted. Note that the `staff_id` column is used to physically sort the table.

2 This is an unsorted table. Note that the last column is not a table column. It is used as an identifier for the physical location of each row in the table.

3 A nonclustered index is an object separate from the table. The table remains in the same physical order in which it was created. The nonclustered index here is sorted by `staff_id`. The pointer column points to the physical location in the table where the row is stored, so it can be located quickly.

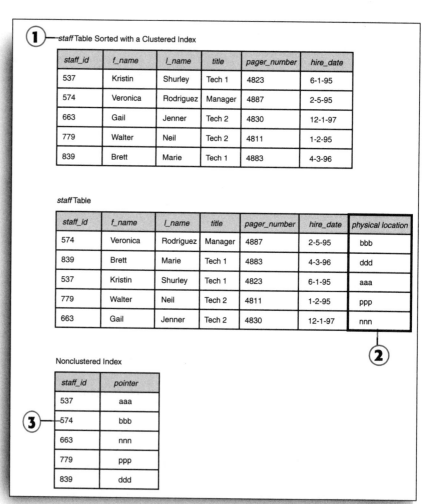

1 *staff* Table Sorted with a Clustered Index

staff_id	f_name	l_name	title	pager_number	hire_date
537	Kristin	Shurley	Tech 1	4823	6-1-95
574	Veronica	Rodriguez	Manager	4887	2-5-95
663	Gail	Jenner	Tech 2	4830	12-1-97
779	Walter	Neil	Tech 2	4811	1-2-95
839	Brett	Marie	Tech 1	4883	4-3-96

staff Table

staff_id	f_name	l_name	title	pager_number	hire_date	physical location
574	Veronica	Rodriguez	Manager	4887	2-5-95	bbb
839	Brett	Marie	Tech 1	4883	4-3-96	ddd
537	Kristin	Shurley	Tech 1	4823	6-1-95	aaa
779	Walter	Neil	Tech 2	4811	1-2-95	ppp
663	Gail	Jenner	Tech 2	4830	12-1-97	nnn

2

Nonclustered Index

staff_id	pointer
537	aaa
574	bbb
663	nnn
779	ppp
839	ddd

3

SEE ALSO

➤ *For more information on how to use indexes to speed up the performance of SQL Server, see page 580.*

Datatypes

Datatypes define or describe the type of data that can be entered into a column and how SQL Server stores it. Whenever a SQL developer creates a new table, the developer must assign each column in the table a datatype. For example, a column with the numeric datatype is designated to store numbers, not letters. Datatypes are often used by database designers to prevent data-entry people from entering the wrong type of data into a particular column of a row. SQL Server offers both built-in and user-defined datatypes.

Defaults

Defaults are values that are automatically entered into columns when a user enters no values into them during data entry. When a SQL developer creates a table, the developer has the option of creating a default entry for any column in the table. For example, if most business addresses stored in a table are from Kansas, a default of "KS" could be created for the State column that would be automatically entered into every newly created row, saving the data entry person a little bit of typing. Of course, the data entry person could override the default if necessary.

Stored Procedures

Stored Procedures are very powerful and flexible database objects that enable you to automate many tasks. They are made up of precompiled Transact-SQL statements that carry out a predetermined task, or series of tasks. Transact-SQL developers write their own stored procedures to automate many data processing tasks. SQL Server includes many predefined stored procedures, referred to as *system-stored procedures*. One example of a system-stored procedure is sp_help. When run, this stored procedure provides information about a particular database object that you specify. All built-in stored procedures begin with the characters sp_. Various useful stored procedures are described throughout this book.

55

What happened to rules?

If you are familiar with previous versions of SQL Server, you may wonder what happened to the rule database object. Rules still exist, but only for backward compatibility reasons. Constraints serve the same purpose as rules, and should always be used in new SQL database design and application development

How can I learn more about database objects?

If you would like to learn more about database objects, do a search in the SQL Server Books Online on "Logical Database Components."

Triggers

Triggers are a special type of stored procedure that executes when specific events occur to a table. For example, when data in a table is inserted, updated, or deleted, a trigger can be made to automatically fire, executing a series of Transact-SQL statements. SQL developers often use triggers to help ensure data integrity and perform other tasks.

Constraints

Constraints are used to enforce data integrity. They define specific rules regarding what can and cannot be allowed in a column. Constraints are generally added to a table by the SQL developer when the table is first created. There are five types of constraints: Primary Key, Foreign Key, Unique, Check, and Not Null.

Database Architecture Fundamentals

In this section you take a closer look at the physical side of SQL Server databases. You will take a look at what makes up a physical database, along with looking at the system databases that SQL Server uses to manage itself and other databases. You will learn about

- Database architecture
- Database transaction log
- System databases
- System tables
- Master databases
- MSDB databases
- Model databases
- Tempdb databases

Database Architecture

Every SQL Server database is made up of two or more physical operating system files. SQL Server databases can consist of three different types of physical files:

- **Primary data file:** Every database includes at least one primary data file. This file is designed to hold database objects, such as tables and indexes. This file is also used to point to the rest of the files that constitute the database. Although not required, primary data files have a file extension of .mdf.

- **Secondary data file:** A database will only have a secondary data file if the primary data file isn't large enough to hold all the data. A database might have none, one, or many secondary data files. The accepted file extension for a secondary data file is .ndf.

- **Log file:** Every database has a log file, which is used to log all information before it is written to a primary or secondary data file. This data is used to help recover a database should it be damaged. A single database may have a single log file, or multiple log files if the original one runs out of room. The accepted file extension for a log file is .ldf.

Each database file type is itself made up of two components, which include the following:

- **Page**: The smallest data unit used in SQL Server is called a page. A page holds 8K (8192 bytes) of data, and is used to hold database objects. There are seven different kinds of pages used in SQL Server, including: data, index, log, text/image, global allocation map, page free space, and index allocation map. Each serves a specific purpose in SQL Server. For example, data pages hold database objects, index pages hold indexes, log pages hold log data, and so on.

- **Extent**: By combining eight contiguous pages (64K) together, you have an extent. An extent is the basic unit used to create tables and indexes. There are two types of extents: uniform and mixed. A uniform extent's space is dedicated to a single object, such as a single table or index. A mixed extent can be shared by up to eight different objects.

As a DBA, you generally don't need to be concerned about the details of how SQL Server allocates space in a database. SQL Server automatically performs this process as needed.

The Database Transaction Log

Whenever a database is created, a transaction log is created at the same time. A transaction log is used to automatically record all changes made to a database, before the changes are actually written to the database. This is an important *fault tolerant* feature of SQL Server that helps prevent a database from becoming corrupted.

SQL Server considers a *transaction* a set of operations (Transact-SQL statements that change a database) that are to be completed at one time, as if they were a single operation. To maintain data integrity, transactions must either be completed fully, or not performed at all. If for some reason, such as a server failure, a transaction is only partially applied to a database, the database has become corrupted.

SQL Server uses a database's transaction log to prevent incomplete transactions from corrupting a database. Here is how SQL Server uses the transaction log to prevent data corruption:

- A user performs some task at the client that modifies the database.

- When a transaction begins, a begin transaction marker is recorded in the transaction log. Following this marker is a before and after image of the database object being changed. This is followed by a commit transaction marker in the transaction log. Every transaction made is recorded like this in the transaction log.

- Periodically, a *checkpoint* process occurs, and all completed transactions recorded in the transaction log are applied to the database. This process also creates a checkpoint marker in the transaction log, which is used during the recovery process to determine which transactions have and have not been applied to the database.

- A transaction log will continue to grow, retaining all the transactions, until it is backed up. At that point the transactions are removed, making room for more transactions.

Should a server fail between the time when a transaction is entered and stored in the transaction log, and before it is applied to the database, or if the server should fail during the exact moment when the transaction log is being applied to the database, the database doesn't become corrupted.

When a server is restarted, SQL Server begins a recovery process. It examines the database and transaction log, looking for transactions that were not applied, and for transactions that were partially applied but not completed. If transactions in the transaction log are found that were not applied, they are applied at this time (*rolled forward*). If partial transactions are found to have been made, they are removed from the database (*rolled back*). The recovery process is automatic, and all the information necessary to maintain a database's integrity is maintained in the transaction log. This ability substantially increases SQL Server's fault tolerance.

> **Learning more about SQL Server fault tolerance**
>
> As a DBA, one of your most important jobs is to prevent data loss. You will learn how to prevent data loss in Part V of this book, "Preventing Data Loss."

System Databases

When SQL Server is installed for the first time, the setup program creates a number of system databases that are used internally by SQL Server to not only track itself, but to track the user databases it manages. These include the following:

- **Master**: The *Master* database is used to track all SQL Server system level information. It is also used to track all other databases and to store SQL Server configuration information.

- **Msdb**: The *Msdb* database is used by the SQL Server Agent service to track job, alert, and operator information.

- **Model**: The *Model* database is used as a template to create all new user databases. It includes the 17 standard database catalog tables.

- **Tempdb**: The *Tempdb* database is used to hold all temporary tables or other objects created as SQL Server performs its work.

In addition to these system tables, the SQL Server setup program also installs two user databases: Pubs and Northwind. These are sample databases that you can experiment with. If you don't want to use either the Pubs or Northwind databases, they can be deleted.

Every database has both a logical and a physical name. The logical name is the name given to the database by SQL Server and is used internally by SQL Server. The names listed previously are the logical names of the databases included with SQL Server. The physical name is the name of the operating system file that holds the logical database.

When each system database is created, its accompanying transaction logs are also created. Each system database is also assigned a default size when it is first created, but these databases can grow as needed.

Figure 2.7 illustrates the four system databases, along with their vital statistics. It is a good idea to become familiar with each of the system databases so that you can easily recognize them when using SQL Server.

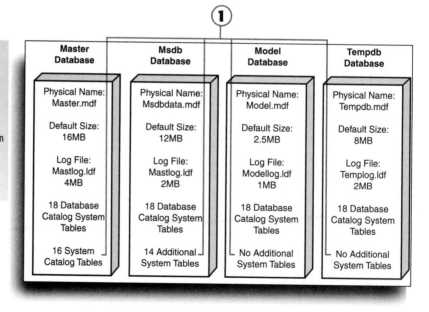

FIGURE 2.7

You should become familiar with the SQL Server system databases.

① This shows default system tables only and doesn't include special tables required for replication.

Master Database	Msdb Database	Model Database	Tempdb Database
Physical Name: Master.mdf	Physical Name: Msdbdata.mdf	Physical Name: Model.mdf	Physical Name: Tempdb.mdf
Default Size: 16MB	Default Size: 12MB	Default Size: 2.5MB	Default Size: 8MB
Log File: Mastlog.ldf 4MB	Log File: Mastlog.ldf 2MB	Log File: Modellog.ldf 1MB	Log File: Templog.ldf 2MB
18 Database Catalog System Tables	18 Database Catalog System Tables	18 Database Catalog System Tables	18 Database Catalog System Tables
16 System Catalog Tables	14 Additional System Tables	No Additional System Tables	No Additional System Tables

Both system and user databases contain special table objects called system tables. These are automatically created whenever a database is first created. *System tables* are used to store data that tracks information on all SQL Server and database activities. Every database, whether system or user, includes 17 identical system tables, commonly referred to as *database catalog tables*. In addition to these common system tables, the Master and Msdb databases each include special system tables that are unique to themselves.

The following section first takes a look at the 17 database catalog tables common to both system and user databases, and then it takes an individual look at each of the SQL Server System databases, along with their unique system tables.

The Model Database and the Database Catalog System Tables

When a new database is created, it always includes the standard 17 system catalog tables. These tables are actually copied from the Model database whenever a new database is created. The sole purpose of the Model database is to act as a template for new databases. The Model database includes only the 17 system catalog tables, no others.

Some DBAs and database designers like to modify the Model database so that whenever a new database is created, it also includes the modifications. Some examples of common modifications to the Model database include adding user-defined datatypes, constraints, defaults, stored procedures, and others. Any change made to the Model database is automatically reflected in any new databases when they are created.

How to View System Tables

System tables are just any other tables found in SQL Server, which means that you can easily view their contents. In some cases the contents of systems tables will be obvious, but in other cases, their contents look like gibberish. The easiest way to view a system table is to use Query Analyzer.

To view system tables

1. From Query Analyzer, select the database whose systems tables you want to view.

2. In the Query Analyzer's query window, type in the following:

```
select * from tablename
```

where *tablename* is the name of the system table you want to view.

3. Now execute the query. The contents of the system table will be displayed.

Database Catalog Tables

The 18 database catalog tables are used by each database to track information on how the database is designed and used. They include the following:

- **sysallocation:** Includes a row for each allocation unit managed by SQL Server.

- **syscolumns:** Includes one row for every column of a table, for every column of a view, and for every parameter used in a stored procedure in the database.

- **syscomments:** Includes one or more rows containing the SQL definition statements (creation text) for every view, rule, check constraint, default, trigger, and stored procedure object in the database.

- **sysconstraints:** Includes information on all the constraints used in the database.

- **sysdepends:** Includes one row for every table, view, or stored procedure that is referenced by another view, trigger, or stored procedure in the database.

- **sysfilegroups:** Includes one row for each filegroup stored in a database.

- **sysfiles:** Includes one row for each file in a database.

- **sysforeignkeys:** Includes one row for every foreign key constraint found in all the tables of a database.

- **sysfulltextcatalogs**: Lists all the full-text catalogs for this database.

- **sysindexes:** Includes one row for every clustered index, non-clustered index, tables without an index, plus additional rows for each table that stores text or image data in the database.

- **sysindexkeys**: Includes one row for each table and index in a database.

- **sysmembers**: Includes one row for each member of a role.

- **sysobjects:** Includes one row for every table, view, log, rule, default, trigger, and stored procedure in the database.

- **syspermissions**: Includes rows designating specific object permissions assigned to users, groups, and roles for a database.

- **sysprotects**: Includes information on permissions that have been applied to security accounts.

- **sysreferences:** Includes one row for every referential integrity constraint used on a column or table in the database.

- **systypes**: Includes one row for every default and user-defined datatype used in the database.

- **sysusers**: Includes one row for each NT Server user, NT Server group, SQL Server user, or SQL Server role in the database.

Master Database

The Master database is SQL Server's most important database, storing such information as the available databases, the amount of space allocated to each database, ongoing processes, user accounts, active locks, system error messages, and system stored procedures.

Besides the 18 database catalog tables common to all SQL Server databases, the Master database includes an additional 16 specialized system tables commonly referred to as the *system catalog* (or data dictionary). These tables include the following:

Do I need to learn the system tables?

Although it might seem over-whelming at first, it is a good idea to learn the purpose of each sys-tem table. As a DBA, you will need to know them in order to manage and troubleshoot data-base problems.

Don't manually change a system table

A system table is virtually like any table found in a SQL Server data-base. Its records can be viewed, inserted, updated, or deleted. Although it is possible to make changes, don't. All changes to any system table must be made through Enterprise Manager, Transact-SQL statements, or stored procedures. If you make a change manually, you could not only damage the table's contents, but you could cause SQL Server to crash. As a matter of fact, SQL Server prevents you from making changes directly to a system table unless you first make a configura-tion change.

- **sysaltfiles:** Includes a row for each file managed by SQL Server.

- **syscacheobjects:** Includes information on how SQL Server's cache memory is being used.

- **syscharsets:** Includes information on the installed character sets and sort orders.

- **sysconfigures:** Includes system configuration values to be used at the next startup of SQL Server.

- **syscurconfigs:** Includes current SQL Server configuration values.

- **sysdatabases:** Includes information on the databases being managed by SQL Server, including database name, owner, and status.

- **sysdevices:** Includes information on devices, such as the disk dump or tape dump device.

- **syslanguages:** Includes the installed language sets.

- **syslockinfo:** Includes information on active locks in all the databases managed by SQL Server.

- **syslogins:** Includes all the user account information, including name, password and configuration information.

- **sysmessages:** Includes all the system error messages available to SQL Server.

- **sysoledbusers:** Includes a row for each user and password mapping for a specified linked server.

- **sysperfinfo:** Includes a representation of all the SQL Server performance monitor counters.

- **sysprocesses:** Includes information on all current processes, including process IDs, logon information, and the current status of each logged on user.

- **sysremotelogins:** Includes information on all users logging in from remote SQL Servers.

- **sysservers:** Includes one row for each remote server that this SQL Server can access.

Msdb Database

The Msdb database is used by the SQL Executive Service to schedule alerts, tasks, and replication. It also stores a history of every backup and restore made to every database managed by SQL Server.

The Msdb database includes the standard 18 system catalog tables, plus 14 specialized tables that are used by SQL Server agent. These specialized tables include

- **sysalerts:** Includes information on user-defined alerts.

- **syscatagories**: Includes information on all the categories SQL Server uses to organize jobs, alerts, and operators.

- **sysdownloadlist**: Includes a queue of download instructions for all target servers.

- **sysjobhistory:** Includes a complete history of the success or failure of every scheduled task or alert.

- **sysjobs**: Includes information on scheduled jobs.

- **sysjobschedules**: Includes information on jobs scheduled for execution.

- **sysjobservers**: Includes information on the associations or relationships of a specific job with one or more target servers.

- **sysjobsteps**: Includes information on each step that a particular job needs to execute.

- **sysnotifications:** Includes a list of which operators are associated with which alerts, and how the operators are to be alerted.

- **sysoperators:** Includes a list of all the operators who are to receive alerts from SQL Server, along with contact information.

- **systargetservergroupmembers**: Includes information on which target servers are currently participating in a multiserver group.

- **systargetservergroups**: Includes information on which target server groups are currently participating in a multiserver environment.

- **systargetservers**: Includes information on which target servers are currently participating in a multiserver operation domain.

- **systaskids**: Includes task-related information for backward compatibility with previous versions of SQL Server.

There are additional System tables used to store backup and restore information that are not included here.

Tempdb Database

The Tempdb database is a shared database that is used by all SQL Server databases and all database users. It is used to store temporary information, such as sorting information when a temporary index is created during a query on a non-indexed table. Like all databases, it includes the 18 default database catalog system tables.

Any temporary tables created as the result of user actions are automatically deleted when that user disconnects from SQL Server. Also, all temporary tables created in Tempdb are deleted every time SQL Server is stopped.

What Is Transact-SQL?

When you communicate with SQL Server, ultimately, you are speaking to it using Transact-SQL. Transact-SQL is the language that SQL Server understands. Whenever you use SQL Enterprise Manager to create or manage a database, SQL Enterprise Manager translates your request into Transact-SQL, which is submitted to SQL Server for execution.

If you like, you can directly communicate with SQL Server using Transact-SQL. As a DBA, you will usually find it more convenient to manage SQL Server using SQL Enterprise Manager, or other SQL Server tools, rather than typing in Transact-SQL statements. But there are some SQL Server tasks that can only be done using Transact-SQL. In other instances, it is more efficient to use Transact-SQL to perform some tasks instead of using a GUI interface.

Transact-SQL is a superset of the industry-standard ANSI-92 SQL relational database manipulation language. It was developed by Microsoft to communicate to SQL Server and includes many enhancements not included in the ANSI-92 version.

Isn't Transact-SQL more a subject for database developers rather than DBAs? No. Although DBAs don't need to become expert Transact-SQL programmers, they do need to know the basics. As a DBA, you need to know how to use Transact-SQL to create, manage, and query data in SQL Server databases. You also want to be able to talk intelligently with SQL developers, and that requires a basic understanding of the programming language they use to create SQL Server client/server applications.

Unlike most programming languages, Transact-SQL isn't designed to perform general tasks. For example, you cannot use it to write a spreadsheet program or use it to control an automated assembly line. It is a specialized language designed specifically for creating, managing, and extracting information from relational databases.

Most common programming languages are procedural in nature. This means that the programmer specifies in the code itself how the program should execute. For example, if a programmer wants to search through a group of records, looking for a specific piece of data, the code is written in such a way as to evaluate one record at a time—field by field—until all the records are examined. If a match is found, the results are displayed onscreen or printed in a report. The programmer is responsible for specifying exactly how the search should be conducted.

Transact-SQL isn't a procedural language. Instead, the Transact-SQL programmer specifies what results are desired, and then submits the request to SQL Server. It is up to SQL Server to decide how to go about searching for the data. After it has been decided how to best search for the data, it conducts the search, and then produces the results, often called a results set, or results output. In addition, SQL Server doesn't search for data in a database, record by record. Instead, SQL Server searches entire data sets (a table, for example) instead. This means that SQL Server can find data quickly, even if the database is large.

> **The advantages to knowing Transact-SQL**
>
> Some DBAs would assert that knowing Transact-SQL is just as important to DBAs as to developers. Why? In a word, the answer is performance. Keep in mind that many applications are written by a group of developers who each create a portion of the code for an application. If you have poor performance, you can use the Query Analyzer to find some of the problems, but you'll need to understand why the code is creating such a problem in order to try and resolve it.

Transact-SQL statements can be divided into three major categories: data definition, data manipulation, and data control. *Data definition* statements are designed for defining a database, modifying its structure after it is created, and dropping it when you are done with it (CREATE, DROP). *Data manipulation* statements are used for entering, changing, and extracting data (INSERT, UPDATE, DELETE, SELECT). *Data control* statements provide a way to protect a database from corruption (GRANT, REVOKE).

ANSI-92 SQL is very limited in that it doesn't include the standard control-of-flow statements that are commonly found in most programming languages. For example, it doesn't include any IF-THEN or WHILE statements that are used to control how a program executes. Because of this limitation, ANSI-92 SQL must be used along with another programming language in order to create programs that access SQL Server data.

One of the major enhancements Microsoft has made to ANSI-92 SQL is the addition of many features that make Transact-SQL more like a standard programming language, reducing the need for using another programming language to perform many tasks. Transact-SQL includes many control-of-flow statements, along with local variable, stored procedures, and triggers, all of which aren't available in ANSI-92 SQL. Transact-SQL can be used standalone for many applications, or it can be combined with other languages, such as Visual Basic or C++, to create powerful client/server applications.

Transact-SQL is ANSI-92 compliant, which means that any SQL scripts written for other ANSI-92–compliant SQL database programs will run unmodified in SQL Server. Keep in mind that if a developer creates a program using any of the Transact-SQL enhancements not included in ANSI-92, these scripts won't run under non-Microsoft SQL databases. The only way to ensure portability among SQL database programs is to not use any of the neat Transact-SQL features and stick only with ANSI-92, but this reduces the power of SQL Server, which is no fun at all.

Batches and performance

The use of batches is an example of how knowing something about Transact-SQL can help you optimize your system's performance. When writing a SQL application, a developer often can choose to submit one transaction per batch, or multiple transactions per batch. In some cases, but not all, submitting multiple transaction per batch is much faster. This is because a batch with multiple transactions only needs to be parsed once, and it only travels over the network one time. Multiple transactions in multiple batches must be parsed and sent over the network multiple times. The more you know about Transact-SQL, the better you will perform your job.

There are two ways to submit Transact-SQL statements to SQL Server for execution. The first is to use an interactive tool, such as the SQL Server Query Analyzer, to enter Transact-SQL statements, one or more at a time. This enables the DBA to directly interact with SQL Server.

The other common way to use Transact-SQL to communicate with SQL Server is to use Transact-SQL scripts. A script is a collection of one or more batches of Transact-SQL statements designed to perform some specific action. A script is similar to a standard computer program.

When a script is submitted to SQL Server, the following occurs:

- The script is parsed.
- The code is then optimized.
- The code is then compiled.
- Finally, the code is executed, statement by statement.

All this happens automatically and very quickly, and the results, if any, are returned.

Transact-SQL is a powerful language, one that you should take the time to learn if you intend to be a full-time DBA. Although you will learn some Transact-SQL in this book, it isn't enough to become competent with it. You need to purchase a book or take a class on Transact-SQL programming. Although it is not the easiest language to learn, learning it will pay for itself many times over as a SQL Server DBA.

Where to read up on Transact-SQL

Two books that introduce Transact-SQL include
Teach Yourself Transact-SQL in 21 Days, by Bennett Wm. McEwan & David Solomon (Sams Publishing).
Microsoft SQL Server 7.0 Unleashed (Sams Publishing).

part

II

Installing and Configuring SQL Server

chapter

3

Planning a SQL Server Installation

Learn how SQL Server will be used •

Learn how SQL Server will fit into •
your current network

Protect SQL Server data •

Learn SQL Server software •
requirements

Learn SQL Server hardware •
requirements

Learn Installation •

What if I already have SQL Server 7.0 running?

If you already have SQL Server 7.0 up and running, and you don't intend to add any more copies soon, you may want to skip this chapter. On the other hand, reading this chapter may offer some suggestions on how to better fine-tune your current installation.

Planning Is an Important First Step

Planning a new SQL Server installation isn't an easy undertaking. Whether you are installing a single SQL Server to be used by a dozen people, or a large distributed SQL Server installation with 10 servers and 500 users, you need to go through the same planning process, carefully examining how SQL Server and your SQL Server application will fit into your organization.

This chapter takes a look at many of the planning issues you should consider even before you purchase your first copy of SQL Server. You have heard this time and time again, but it bears repeating. If you carefully plan your SQL Server installation, you will make fewer mistakes, the overall costs will be lower, you will come closer to meeting your schedule, and you will be able to sleep at night, not having to worry about how you are going to explain problems, mistakes, and cost overruns to your boss.

The first time you read this chapter, you will want to read through it quickly for an overview of what you must do to plan a new SQL Server installation. Later, when it is closer to the time you will begin formally creating your SQL Server installation plan, you will want to reread the chapter more closely, with pen and paper nearby, taking notes about the planning issues that specifically affect your situation.

Although this chapter focuses on planning issues, the next chapter, "Installing SQL Server," covers how to actually install SQL Server. It includes such information as how to choose the correct net-libraries, character set, dictionary order, and so on, along with explicit step-by-step instructions on how to install and configure SQL Server.

Although I wish I were able to tell you exactly how you should plan your installation, there is no way to do this in a book. Every situation is different, and only general guidelines and suggestions are offered here. Also keep in mind that there is no single right way to plan an installation. There are many right ways, each with their own combination of strengths and weaknesses. It is your job to create the best possible SQL Server installation plan given your unique circumstances and available resources.

How Will SQL Server Be Used in Your Organization?

How SQL Server is used to meet your organization's business needs significantly affects the implementation planning process. SQL Server is a very flexible tool and can perform many tasks, but many tasks are mutually exclusive. For example, although a single SQL Server can easily handle a busy transaction-based sales database where hundreds of entries are made every hour, the same SQL Server is unable to perform adequately if multiple marketing managers want to perform extensive queries at the same time. This is because transaction processing functions and decision support functions conflict and require SQL Server to be configured differently.

How SQL Server will be used in your organization is very important to know, and you must plan every task you want SQL Server to perform. This section takes a look at some of the most important questions that need to be answered early in the planning process. You must evaluate each question and answer it according to your organization's unique needs.

This section takes a look at the following questions:

- Will SQL Server be used mostly to manage transactions?
- Will SQL Server be used mostly to perform decision support?
- Will SQL Server be a back end to an Internet/intranet server?
- Will SQL Server be used for graphics or multimedia?
- How will SQL Server applications be developed?
- How many users will access SQL Server simultaneously?
- Where will users be located in relation to SQL Server?
- How mission critical will SQL Server applications be?

The answers to each of these questions can significantly affect how you plan a SQL Server installation. Each question will be examined one at a time.

What are OLTP and OLAP?

OLTP, or online transaction processing, and OLAP, or online analytical processing, are the latest buzzwords to describe transaction-oriented processing and decision support, respectively.

Will SQL Server Be Used Mostly to Manage Transactions?

It is probably fair to say that most organization's database needs fall into the area of managing transactions. Managers want to track every sale, every purchase, every inventory item, every staff member, every client, every prospect, and on and on. Some organizations may only have a few dozen transactions a day, whereas others may have hundreds of thousands. Although most transactions are still input by hand, many more are being input via scanners or other non-traditional methods.

Planning a SQL Server installation to handle large numbers of transactions is significantly different than planning one to be used mostly for decision support. This is because in a *transaction-oriented environment*, generally a single record, or set or related records, is affected by each transaction. As long as each transaction is distinct, hundreds or even thousands of records can be open simultaneously by hundreds of users. A *decision support environment* is much different. Generally, one or more managers will be issuing complex queries that affect thousands of records, if not all the database's records, more or less simultaneously. Large queries cause many records to become *locked*, which prevents them from being changed.

If a database is used both ways simultaneously, the different types of database access will clash, significantly slowing down the overall access speed of the database, if not disrupting its use completely. Ideally, a single database should be used for one type of database access or the other, not both.

If SQL Server will be used mostly for transactions, consider these questions:

- What percentage of your SQL Server application will be transaction-oriented? The more heavily transaction-oriented it is, the less suitable it will be able to support decision support needs. If decision support is also needed, perhaps SQL Server *replication* is called for.

- How many transactions an hour, day, week, or month will there be? This will directly affect how much processing power the computer hardware needs, along with needed disk space.

- Will transactions be entered 24 hours a day, or limited to a particular time period? Will these transactions be evenly spaced throughout the year, or will there be significant seasonal fluctuations? This can affect how you will maintain and back up your data.

- Will transactions be entered by hand? by scanner? other? This will affect how your SQL Server application will be designed.

- Where will transactions be entered? In close proximity to SQL Server? same city? same state? same country? This can affect your WAN connectivity needs, along with the potential need for coordinating transactions between physically separated SQL Servers.

As you will find out throughout the book, configuring SQL Server for transaction processing is much different than configuring it for decision support.

SEE ALSO

➤ *For more information on replication, see page 541.*

➤ *For more information on optimizing SQL Server, see page 563.*

Will SQL Server Be Used Mostly to Perform Decision Support?

Although transaction management has been the traditional use of relational database applications, decision support has become more and more important as organizations are becoming more intensely competitive. *Data warehouses* (used to store virtually all an organization's data) and *data marts* (used to store departmental or divisional data) have become popular. By storing large quantities of detailed and summarized data, and by using new analytical techniques, organizations are learning more about their customers and business than they never knew before.

Using SQL Server to perform decision support requires a much different configuration than does one for managing transactions. If an organization wants both functions to be performed by SQL

Server, they will need to have at least two separate, but connected SQL Servers, each performing the tasks they are designed to perform. Some of the questions that must be answered when planning for a decision support application include:

- How much data will need to be stored? And for how long? This affects your plan for purchasing disk space and how you intend to perform backups of large quantities of data.

- How many people will be accessing the data simultaneously? This can affect SQL Server hardware requirements.

- How fast do you want results to be returned from queries? Decision support generally requires greater processing power, and the faster you need results, the more powerful your hardware will need to be.

- How real-time must the data be? There are different ways data can be moved from a transaction-oriented database into a decision support database. How fast you need the data for analysis affects these choices.

One of the more common ways that organizations distribute the transaction processing and decision support aspects of a database is to use replication. Replication is used to copy data from the transaction-based SQL Server to a decision support-based SQL Server. This way, the two distinct tasks can be distributed over two separately configured SQL Servers.

SEE ALSO

➤ *For more information on SQL Server replication, see page 541.*

Will SQL Server Be a Back End to an Internet/Intranet Server?

The Internet revolution has found an entirely new use for SQL Server—as a back end for an Internet or intranet server. SQL Server is being used as a database that supplies information to Web servers and browsers, to perform transaction processing for online sales, and even to store Web pages that are created dynamically based on the needs of the user at a Web browser.

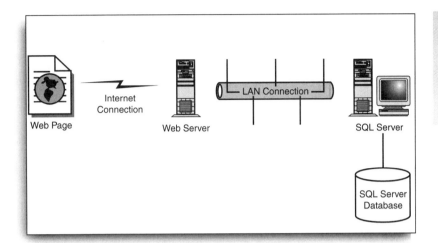

FIGURE 3.1
SQL Server is becoming a popular back end to Internet and intranet servers.

The technology used to integrate SQL Server and Web servers is changing and improving rapidly. Before long, Web applications may become the most popular reason to use SQL Server. When planning to integrate SQL Server with a Web server, consider the following:

- Will SQL Server be a back end for the Internet, or an intranet? This can affect your hardware and software requirements.

- What kind of security will be required to protect the data stored in SQL Server? The type of data stored in SQL Server, and who has access to it, can affect your plans on how to secure the data.

- Will SQL Server mostly be used to provide data based on Web-based queries? To manage transactions? To create Web pages? This can affect your plans on how to interconnect SQL Server and your Web server.

- How many page hits can be expected an hour, day, week, month, and year? Will the hits be consistent, or vary over time? This can affect your hardware decisions.

- What development tools will be used to integrate SQL Server with Web servers? This can affect who will be chosen to develop your SQL Server applications and how they will be maintained.

SQL Server works with virtually any Web server

SQL Server can be used as a back end database to virtually any Web server; you don't have to use Microsoft's Internet Information Server.

Visual InterDev works with SQL Server

Microsoft's Visual InterDev software development tool makes it easy to incorporate SQL Server with an Internet or intranet Web site. It includes special features that enable you to create a Web site using SQL Server and doesn't require custom programming.

Will SQL Server Be Used for Graphics or Multimedia?

Although using SQL Server to store graphics and other multimedia has yet to catch on, it is becoming more and more of a consideration for many organizations. Traditionally, graphics and multimedia have been stored in a format (*BLOB*) that could not be directly manipulated by the database. This is changing. SQL Server 7.0 has new features that make it easier to store and manipulate this data.

Like the other uses of SQL Server listed previously, using SQL Server for storing graphics and multimedia data requires a much different planning process. When planning to use SQL Server to store graphics or multimedia data, find answers to these questions:

- What kind of data will SQL Server store, and how much of it will there be? Graphics and multimedia come in many forms, and you need to consider what they will be. Also, the amount of graphics and multimedia directly affects storage requirements.

- How will the data need to be accessed and manipulated? Will SQL Server be used just to store the data, or to manipulate it? What kind of software will be using the data, and how? This will affect your software choices and the hardware used by the users.

- Will the graphics and multimedia data need to be used in combination with other types of data, such as transactions? This can affect your application development and other software needs.

How Will SQL Server Applications Be Developed?

Although SQL Server is a very powerful tool in its own right, it cannot perform any business tasks until one or more SQL Server applications have been developed to perform these tasks. SQL Server itself cannot work alone; it must always be partnered with an application.

Although this book, and specifically this chapter, focuses on planning how to install SQL Server, the topic of application development isn't covered, as it is beyond the scope of this book. Nevertheless, it is still an important planning issue. In most cases, the application development process is the key to the success of any SQL Server installation, much more so than selecting the right hardware to run SQL Server on. Ultimately, the success of any SQL Server installation is dependent on the application(s) created for it.

You will want to find answers to these questions:

- Who will be developing your SQL Server applications? Will they be written by staffers or contractors? Will application development be outsourced? Will you purchase an off-the-shelf application?

- How soon will you need the application?

- Who will be responsible for coordinating the planning of the integration of the SQL Server and application installation process?

- Who will support the application after it is installed? Who will create the documentation? Who will train the users?

- What development tools will be used to create the application?

How Many Users Will Access SQL Server Simultaneously?

The answer to this question depends in large part on the answers to some of the previous questions. For example, most transaction-oriented SQL Server applications have more users than those that support decision support. The number of users who access SQL Server simultaneously significantly affects not only how the application is designed, but how SQL Server is installed, configured, and maintained.

Be sure you get answers to the following questions before beginning the planning process:

SQL Server applications are easier than ever to write

SQL Server 7.0 includes many new features to make writing applications much easier than previous versions of SQL Server. If you want to write applications for SQL Server, you will want to seriously consider purchasing Microsoft's Visual Studio, which includes many development tools to make Transact-SQL programming much easier and more efficient.

- How many users will be simultaneously accessing data? This basic question affects both hardware needs and how the SQL application will be developed.

- What will be the nature of their access? Will they be entering transactions or performing extensive queries? As discussed earlier, these two types of functions are usually mutually exclusive.

- Will users need to access SQL Server 24 hours a day, 7 days a week? Or just during a standard 40-hour week? This will affect when SQL Server can be maintained and backed up.

- Will the number of users increase over time? This will affect what will need to be purchased now, and in the future.

- What kind of client will be used to access SQL Server? SQL Server supports many applications, some of which are better than others when it comes to handling large numbers of users.

- What is an acceptable response time for users? Everyone wants users who are productive and happy. What is the maximum amount of latency you can get away with, while still keeping your users productive and happy? *Latency* refers to the amount of time your users have to wait from when they query SQL Server, and when they get their first results from SQL Server based on the query.

Where Will Users Be Located in Relation to SQL Server?

An important logistical consideration when planning a SQL Server installation is the location of the users in regard to SQL Server. It is becoming the norm for more and more users to access SQL Server data using methods other than a fast LAN connection. Staffers from remote offices, and even from their homes, need access to an organization's data.

How SQL Server is implemented, such as a single server, or as many distributed servers, or replicated servers, is significantly affected by how people need to access its data. It also affects the hardware and communications links required to keep everyone connected. You need answers to these questions:

- How will users access SQL Server data—via a fast LAN link? a fast WAN link? a slow WAN link? dial-up remote access? the Internet? This can affect application development and the necessary hardware to make the client/server connection.

- Will there be any international users? This can affect application development and how long SQL Server has to be available during the day to users.

- How many users will access the SQL Server via the various links? This affects hardware speed and capacity needs.

- What are the acceptable response times for users when they access SQL Server data? This affects both client and server speed and capacity needs.

- How will remote connections to SQL Server be used? For transactions? Decision support?

How Mission Critical Will the SQL Server Applications Be?

Although some SQL Server applications aren't critical to the operation of a business, others are its lifeblood. It's not unheard of for an organization to go out of business because it lost its computing infrastructure.

The more critical a SQL Server application is to a business, the more that has to be spent on ensuring SQL Server will not go down. This can mean the use of highly reliable hardware, even redundant hardware using fail-over servers, which can significantly add to the total cost of a SQL Server installation.

Because this issue is so important, it will be covered more thoroughly in several sections of this book, including more information later in this chapter. Ask yourself these questions when creating your SQL Server plan:

Get your network administrators involved

Planning for a SQL Server installation cannot be done in isolation. It is important that you involve the people responsible for your network's design and management. In many cases, they may know the users of the network much better than you do.

For related information…

For more information on preventing data loss, see Part V of this book, "Preventing Data Loss."

- If the SQL Server is down, will it cost your organization money? If so, how much for every hour SQL Server is down? If it only costs your business $100 an hour for down time, this isn't enough to justify spending tens of thousands of dollars on redundant hardware and software. But if being down costs your organization thousands of dollars an hour, this extra cost is easily justified.

- Does your installation plan include how to deal with short down times? disasters? You will need a disaster recovery plan ready to go before your SQL Server goes into production.

- Does your organization's management have an appreciation for the importance of devoting sufficient resources to keeping a mission-critical SQL Server up and running all the time? You may have to battle for the necessary funds.

Hopefully, these questions have sparked many more questions that need to be answered during the SQL Server installation planning process. How your organization uses SQL Server significantly influences the planning process and must be your first step when creating a plan. But this is just a start. There are many other things to consider, and they are described in the following sections.

Always test SQL Server before adding it to your network

Before adding a SQL Server to your current network, you should seriously consider testing it thoroughly in regards to how it will affect network traffic. Although your current network may be working fine, the addition of a SQL Server, and the additional network traffic generated by it, could disrupt your current network traffic in unexpected ways.

How Will SQL Server Fit into Your Current Network?

Although the previous section dealt with how SQL Server will be used in your organization, this section deals with how SQL Server will fit into your current network. If your network is like most networks, it includes a combination of many different technologies and vendors, each with their own strengths and weaknesses. In addition, it may be also overloaded with traffic and perhaps it is even an administrative nightmare to manage.

Just your luck—you now have to make your current network even more complex by adding one more application, and not a simple one at that. Perhaps SQL Server is being introduced to solve some old problems and will make your overall network and management information tasks that much easier, but then again, adding SQL Server may do just the opposite. In any event, it is your job to add SQL Server to your network to accomplish the goals described in the previous section.

The goal of this section is to help you plan how to fit SQL Server into your existing network, and it will cover these important topics:

- Which network and desktop operating systems are you currently using?
- How well will your current network infrastructure work with SQL Server?
- What is the NT Server Domain Model?
- What is your NT Server Naming Scheme?

Which Network and Desktop Operating Systems Are You Currently Using?

The single most important impact of deploying SQL Server in a network is that it only runs under Windows NT Server. No other network operating systems need apply. This statement makes the assumption that SQL Server running under Windows 95/98 will not be used for networked-based applications.

If you already have NT deployed, at least you already have a basic understanding of how NT works. But if you will be bringing NT into your network for the first time to support SQL Server, or perhaps as part of a network operating system change over, you are facing much more work that just planning a SQL Server installation.

Adding to the complexity are the desktop operating systems currently in use. Fortunately, SQL Server works with most desktop operating systems, even with some not available from Microsoft.

Network Operating Systems

SQL Server, along with NT, can co-exist in virtually any network operating system environment, including the following:

How will Windows 2000 Affect SQL Server 7.0?

As this book was being prepared, Windows 2000 was still in beta. The information about 2000 that is provided in this book is based on the beta version, not on the final release version.

- Windows NT Workstation 4.0 (SP4 or greater), Windows 95, Windows 98
- Windows NT Server 4.0 (SP4 or greater), Windows 2000
- Novell NetWare (3.x, 4.x, IntraNetWare)
- AppleTalk
- Banyan VINES
- UNIX
- DEC PATHWORKS
- OS/2, LAN Server

The only requirement is that your network support at least one of the following *transport protocols*:

- TCP/IP
- IPX/SPX (NWLink)
- NetBEUI

Given that TCP/IP is the most heterogeneous and versatile of all the transport protocols, it is probably the one you will select to use with SQL Server.

Desktop Operating Systems

Choosing a desktop operating system is somewhat more problematic than selecting a network operating system. Not only do you have to use desktop operating systems compatible with SQL Server, but you must also have one that is compatible with the client software you will use to connect with SQL Server.

Even at this time, many corporate desktops are still running 16-bit desktop operating systems. The move to 32-bit operating systems, such as Windows 95, Windows 98, and NT Workstation, has been slow in the corporate world. This may affect client development because you may not be able to take advantage of the most current 32-bit development tools if not all of your workstations are using 32-bit software.

It is possible that you may have to consider upgrading most, if not all, of your desktops to a 32-bit operating system before you implement SQL Server into your organization. And in many cases, this means upgrading hardware at the same time.

SQL Server supports clients running on most desktop operating systems, including

- DOS
- Windows 3.x
- Windows for Workgroups 3.x
- Windows 95 and Windows 98
- NT Workstation
- Novell NetWare Networking Client Software
- Macintosh
- UNIX

Of course, the application client software must also run on one or more of the above desktop operating systems. In many cases, the choice of the application client will be more of a limiting factor than which clients SQL can communicate with.

One of the most important reasons for establishing what desktop operating systems will be used to access SQL Server has to do with being able to establish an Inter-Process Communication (IPC) link between the desktop clients and SQL Server. This is accomplished by loading the correct Net-Libraries at both the client and server, which enables the two to communicate over a network. SQL Server includes many Net-Libraries, which are discussed more in Chapters 4, "Installing SQL Server" and Chapter 5, "Installing SQL Client Utilities." If a particular desktop operating system will not run any of the Net-Libraries included with SQL Server, the operating system is incompatible with SQL Server. If the desktop client is a Web browser, Net-Libraries aren't required.

How Well Will Your Current Network Infrastructure Work with SQL Server?

Installing one or more SQL Servers can dramatically affect LAN performance on a preexisting network. As a part of your planning process, you will need to determine your current bandwidth use, estimate the bandwidth that will be used by your

---

NT Workstation is an ideal administrative client

If you will be managing a SQL Server remotely from a desktop, the ideal operating system to run the Microsoft Management Console and the SQL Enterprise Manager is NT Workstation. It not only offers superior security, 32-bit performance, and robustness, but also it is the only desktop operating system that is 100% compatible with NT Server.

NT Server's Performance Monitor and the Network Monitor Agent

NT Server's Performance Monitor tool can be used to measure network activity if you have also loaded the Network Monitor Agent. The Network Monitor Agent can be loaded from the Control Panel Network Services dialog box in NT Server.

SQL Server applications, and determine where you need to make the necessary changes and improvements in order to accommodate the additional network traffic.

None of these tasks are easy, but they are necessary if you don't want any unexpected surprises. Many organizations that have installed SQL Server-based client/server applications and didn't take this step have quickly discovered how overloaded their network actually was once the application was put into production, resulting in horrible network performance. Don't let that happen to you.

Many tools exist in the market to determine current bandwidth utilization, including the *Network Monitor* tool that began shipping with NT Server 4.0 (and is also included with Microsoft's Systems Management Software). If your network is large, including many switches and routers, you will have your job cut out for you determining current bandwidth. No matter how you go about collecting bandwidth utilization, you need to collect this information over a period of time in order to accurately determine your current utilization.

Much harder than determining your current utilization is predicting how much additional traffic your SQL Server–based client/server applications will take up. This is affected by many factors, including the number of SQL Servers, number of clients, the nature of the tasks being performed, and so on. There are client/server traffic simulation products available, but the only really true test is to conduct a realistic pilot test, measure the traffic, and then extrapolate it to your network.

Only after you have done this, and then compared it to your network's current utilization, will you know if your current network is up to the challenge of running the new application, or if you will need to make some changes to deal with the new traffic. The more accurately you plan this step, the happier everyone will be with the final results when the application is up and running.

When evaluating your current network infrastructure to see how well it will work once the client/server application is running, consider the following issues:

- Is your network designed around a distributed or collapsed backbone? Generally, a collapsed backbone design can support more traffic.

- What media are you using—Ethernet? Fast Ethernet? Token-Ring? FDDI? ATM? some combination of these? Will you have to upgrade to faster media? Fast Ethernet seems to have caught on as the least expensive way to get lots of bandwidth.

- Are your servers and clients using shared or switched media? Using switched media is an inexpensive way to increase available bandwidth.

- How are you segmenting your network—with routers? switches? The new Layer 3 switches seem best for internal networks, and routers seem best to connect with WANs.

- What protocol or protocols are being used? The fewer protocols used, the more bandwidth available. SQL Server works with all the major transport protocols, with TCP/IP being the best all-around choice because of its robustness and popularity.

- How do you connect your LANs together over geographic areas? Which WAN transport are you using? What is its bandwidth utilization? SQL Server client/server applications can potentially cause havoc with slow WAN connections.

- Will some of your clients use remote access to access SQL Server? Are these connections fast enough, or do you need to move to a faster connection, such as moving from dial-up modems to ISDN?

As part of the process of planning your SQL Server installation, you will want to reconsider your entire network infrastructure, ensuring that it will meet the needs of your SQL Server applications now and in the future. Don't skip this step; it is very critical to the success of your SQL Server installation.

What is an NT Server domain?
A domain is a logical grouping of users and computers in a single administrative unit. An organization may have a single NT Server domain, or it may have multiple domains. If multiple domains are used, they must be arranged in a proper domain model.

What Is the NT Server Domain Model?

Whether you will be using NT Server 4.0 or Windows 2000, you will have to consider how your current NT Server domain model will affect SQL Server's installation. Under NT 4.0, you can choose from the Single Domain, Master Domain, Multiple Master Domain, and the Complete Trust models. Under Windows 2000, you have the additional flexibility offered by the Active Directory.

SQL Server will work under virtually any domain model. So whether you are adding NT Server to your network for the first time and can choose any model, or you already have an established domain model that meets your needs, adding SQL Server into the mix is generally not a problem.

There are two issues that affect how SQL Server integrates with NT Server: the SQL Server Service Account and security.

SQL Server uses two main services to perform its work: the SQLServerAgent service (used to perform administrative tasks, such as scheduling jobs) and the MSSQLServer service (the SQL Server engine). Both services must be assigned an NT user account to log on. Both services can use the same service account, or they can use separate accounts. What is important is that this account or accounts must exist in the designated accounts domain of a multiple domain NT network (single domain networks aren't a problem). These same accounts must also be used by all SQL Servers in the organization if they are to communicate with each other. This also means that all SQL Servers within an NT network must all have the ability to access the accounts domain where the service accounts exist.

The second issue is security. SQL Server offers two security choices: *Windows NT Authentication* (which only allows Windows NT logins) and *SQL Server Authentication* (which allows both SQL Server and Windows NT logins).

If your entire network uses only NT Server, you can choose Windows NT Authentication, which offers superior SQL Server Security. But if you are using a mixed operating system network, and some of the clients who will be accessing SQL Server aren't using NT networking, you will have to use SQL Server Authentication instead.

If you are adding NT Server to your current network, you have the ability to design your domain model to fit the needs of SQL Server. If you have a current NT network, and if it follows all of Microsoft's recommendations for proper design, you probably won't have any problems installing SQL Server. The only problem that can arise is if your current NT domain model isn't properly designed. If this is the case, you may have to redesign it properly before installing SQL Server.

> **How can I learn more about NT Server domains?**
>
> If you are new to NT Server domains, check out this book for information: *Windows NT Server 4 Professional Reference* by Karanjit S. Siyan, Ph.D (New Riders).

SEE ALSO

➤ *For more information on the MSSQLServer service and the SQLServerAgent service, see page* 47.

➤ *For more information on how to create the SQL Server service account, see page* 135.

➤ *For more information on SQL Server security, see page* 358.

What Is Your Windows NT Server Naming Scheme?

The naming scheme used by SQL Server and NT Server are different and can cause a multitude of problems if not carefully examined before SQL Server is installed. This is because SQL Server uses the NetBIOS names of NT Servers as its own name, and because it also can use NT accounts as SQL Server login IDs. The problem that occurs is that NT's naming scheme follows different rules than SQL Server's naming scheme. If any of the NT names automatically used by SQL Server don't follow SQL Server's naming scheme, SQL Server won't work as expected.

To prevent any problems, the best solution to this dilemma is to use the least common denominator between the two naming schemes for all NT computer names and user accounts. Use it at all times when creating names for NT Server. If you currently have an NT network that breaks any of these rules, you will have to change any names that violate these SQL Server naming rules (also referred to as *identifier* rules) before installing SQL Server. They include the following:

- Names must not exceed 128 characters. NT Server NetBIOS names must not exceed 15 characters.

Quoted identifiers are an exception

The naming scheme described in the body of the text isn't your only option, although it is the recommended naming scheme. SQL Server supports quoted identifiers. Basically, this means you can use any name you want, and even include spaces in names, if you enclose the name in quotations or square brackets.

- Names must not include any spaces. NT Server NetBIOS names should also not include spaces.

- Names must begin with an uppercase or lowercase letter, or the symbol _. Names can also begin with @ or #, but these have special meaning and should not be used in most cases. NT Server NetBIOS names can begin with any letter, number, and most symbols.

- Characters in names after the first letter may be any letter, number, or the symbols @, _, #, or $. NT Server NetBIOS names can include all letters, numbers, and most symbols.

Plan How to Protect SQL Server Data

In a previous section you were asked to assess how mission critical your SQL Server application would be. More than likely, any data you store in SQL Server is important to your organization, or why would you even bother collecting and storing it in the first place? The question you must ask is how would it affect your organization if the data were lost. The more valuable the data, the more time you need to spend ensuring that it is well protected.

This section takes a look at some of the data protection issues associated with planning a SQL Server installation. It takes a look at these issues:

- How will you secure your data?
- What type of fault tolerance will you use?
- How will you back up your data?
- Do you have a formal disaster recovery plan?

Part IV, "SQL Server Security," and Part V, "Preventing Data Loss," cover how to protect your data using SQL Server.

How Will You Secure Your Data?

SQL Server needs to be protected from non-authorized access from both inside and outside your organization. The most common method is to use either NT Server's or SQL Server's security options, but will they be adequate to protect your data? Data security is an issue many DBAs don't think much about, relying on the software to take care of it. But as many organizations have learned, it is almost impossible to protect data from a determined foe, and basic software security is often not enough. Read the following questions to evaluate and plan how you need to deal with security issues in your SQL Server installation plan:

- How will you prevent internal users from accessing non-authorized SQL Server data? Will you rely on SQL Server's Windows NT Authentication or SQL Server's Authentication Mode? Will you require other third-party security protection methods?

- Will you need to develop some type of internal security policy, such as minimum password lengths, forced password changes, and so on? How will you enforce this?

- If your internal network is connected to the Internet, how will you protect it from external threats? Will you need a firewall or proxy server?

- If SQL data is available via the Internet or an intranet, how will it be protected? How will you authenticate users? Will you need to encrypt your data?

- How will you audit your security plan to ensure that data isn't being compromised?

When planning for your SQL Server security, it is a good idea to bring in an organization's management to participate. It is ultimately up to management to determine how valuable SQL Server data is, and to allocate the necessary resources to protect it.

What Type of Fault Tolerance Will You Use?

Fault tolerance describes what steps the DBA takes to help ensure that the physical hardware running SQL Server stays up and running without downtime. The degree of fault tolerance that is used depends greatly on how mission critical the data is to an organization. Some organizations can operate successfully for days if their SQL Server is down, whereas others can potentially lose ten of thousands of dollars every hour their SQL Server is down.

Fault tolerant techniques can range from the very simple, which any DBA can set up, to the very complex, requiring networking specialists to set up. Choosing the best method to prevent hardware downtime isn't easy, and the first step to planning this aspect of a SQL Server installation is to get answers to these questions:

- Exactly how mission critical is your SQL Server application? How much are you willing to spend to ensure that you have virtually 100% up time?

- Is NT Server-based fault tolerance adequate for your SQL Server?

- Is hardware-based RAID, and other hardware-based fault tolerance, adequate for your SQL Server?

- Does your SQL Server need to be clustered in order to have server fail-over capability?

- Is the location of the SQL Server hardware secure? Many kinds of software attacks can only be executed at a physical server, and keeping them physically secure is considered the best barrier for protection.

- How will you regularly evaluate how effective your fault tolerant plan is working and what will you do to proactively prevent unexpected downtime?

Like SQL Server security issues, it is important to involve an organization's management when evaluating risks associated with server downtime, and getting them to provide adequate resources to ensure SQL Server data is available whenever needed.

How Will You Back Up Your Data?

Even the best and most expensive fault tolerant SQL Server hardware will not always protect your valuable data. Because of this, you will need to back up your SQL Server data on a regular basis. Backing up SQL Server data isn't always an easy task.

Although a SQL Server database can be backed up at any time, even when it is being used, it can create a substantial performance penalty. Deciding when to back up is a critical decision. Also, transaction logs need to be backed up regularly throughout the day, not only to ensure up-to-date backups, but also to truncate the transaction log so it will not fill up.

And then there are the issues of what software to use to back up your data, and what hardware to use. There are many choices that have to be made, and your decisions will significantly affect the success of your backup plan. Consider the following when planning your SQL Server backup strategy:

- What backup software will you use to back up SQL Server data? Will you use SQL Server's software? third-party software?

- Will you back up to disk or to tape? Will you be backing up over the network or from the physical SQL Server?

- How will you ensure the integrity of your SQL Server data before and after you make backups? When will this be done?

- Will users need to access the data 24 hours a day, 7 days a week? Or will there be dead times when backups can be made?

- How often will you back up your SQL Server database? How often will you back up your SQL Server transaction logs?

- How long will it take to perform the necessary backups? How will this affect when you can backup?

- Who will back up SQL data?

- Where will backups be stored? How long will backups be kept?

- What procedures will you have in place to ensure that backups are good?

- What procedures will you have to ensure that the appropriate people know how to properly and quickly restore data from backups?

> **Warning about third-party backup software**
>
> If you choose to use third-party backup software to back up SQL Server data, be sure that the software includes a backup agent specifically designed to back up SQL Server 7.0 databases and transactions logs. Not all third-party backup software has this capability.

Of all the important tasks the DBA is responsible for, maintaining good backups is probably the most important.

SEE ALSO

➤ *For more information on how to back up a database, see page 453.*

Do You Have a Formal Disaster Recovery Plan?

Your disaster recovery plan should be comprehensive

Hopefully, your organization has a formal, written disaster recovery plan. As a DBA, you will need to augment that plan for SQL Server. If your organization doesn't have a formal disaster recovery plan, now is the time to create one.

You might think that having expensive fault-tolerant hardware and a comprehensive backup strategy in place would be all the protection you need. But what if your expensive server was stolen or sabotaged, or the building caught fire or was flooded? Although we don't like to think about disasters, they do happen, and could happen to your organization.

Although it is impossible to consider every possibility, it is important to evaluate all the most common risks, what would happen if they were to occur, and how they would affect your organization's ability to survive. At the very least, you will want to consider the following:

- What are all the possible risks your SQL Server and its data face?

- If you lose all your hardware and data, do you have offsite backups you can use to restore the data on new hardware? How long would it take to start from scratch to get access to your data?

- Is your data so mission critical that your organization should invest in a hot site that duplicates your data, so it can immediately take over in the case of a disaster?

- Who will be responsible for creating and maintaining your disaster recovery plan? Who will implement the plan should it have to be used?

- How will you determine if your disaster recovery plan works?

When planning a new SQL Server installation, disaster planning often seems to be one of the last things considered. Don't let this happen. This needs to be considered early in the planning stage because it can directly affect many of your implementation decisions.

Protecting your data is a full-time job, and must be planned from the start. As the DBA, make it your responsibility to ensure your organization's data is well protected.

Plan Your SQL Server Software Requirements

This section will be short because many software-related issues have already been discussed in earlier sections. SQL Server, like all database programs, run in the context of desktop and network operating systems. This section covers these areas:

- What clients will be used to access SQL Server?
- What operating system will you use to deploy SQL Server?
- What licensing method will you use?

Although you have many options when selecting software to work with SQL Server, you will find that if you stick with Microsoft products, you will save yourself a lot of integration-related headaches. Although SQL Server can work with many non-Microsoft products, the implementation isn't always great. Obviously, Microsoft encourages you to stick with their products. Personally, I feel their products range from good to great (although not perfect). By sticking to an all-Microsoft software solution, you will have much fewer problems.

What Clients Will Be Used to Access SQL Server?

Although SQL Server supports a wide variety of clients, you will have a lower total cost of ownership if you exclusively use NT Workstation, either 4.0 or Windows 2000, as your desktop operating system. NT Workstation is easier to maintain and more robust than any other desktop operating system and should be your choice if your client hardware will support it.

If your hardware isn't quite up to running NT Workstation, the next best choice is Windows 98. Its hardware requirements are fewer, and its total cost of ownership is a close second to NT Workstation.

Of course, you may be faced with constraints not under your control and be forced to use other client operating systems. If you do, be sure to thoroughly test these clients with your SQL Server application to see that they perform as you expect them to.

Besides using a conventional desktop operating system to run your client software, you may consider using Web browsers, network PCs, or Microsoft's Terminal Server. Each of these methods has its strengths and weaknesses, and the methods may or may not meet your needs. At the very least, you want to consider them during your planning process.

What Operating System Will You Use to Deploy SQL Server?

I have already discussed how SQL Server will generally run only under Windows NT Server. The only decision you have here is whether you want to run SQL Server under NT 4.0 (using the latest Service Pack) or under Windows 2000. If choosing NT 4.0, you also have the choice to run under the regular version or the Enterprise Edition.

If you are purchasing new copies of NT Server to run SQL Server, you should probably choose Windows 2000 (when it becomes available), unless you already have many NT 4.0 servers that you don't plan to upgrade for a while, and you want all your servers to have the same version of NT Server.

Whether you choose the regular or Enterprise edition of NT Server 4.0 depends on whether you need the extra features provided by the Enterprise edition, such as more capacity and fault tolerance features.

When making your decision, don't make it based on how much you can save in the initial purchase price. The largest cost of any software is the installation and support costs, and you should purchase the version of NT that best meets your overall needs.

What Licensing Method Will You Use?

Although the cost of licensing software isn't your biggest cost when planning a SQL Server installation, it can be significant. You will have to purchase server licenses for both NT Server and SQL Server for every SQL Server you want to deploy. And for each desktop accessing SQL Server, you will have to purchase client desktop operating system licenses, NT Server client licenses, and SQL Server client licenses. If you will have people access SQL via a Web server, you will have to purchase an addition license for this.

The biggest licensing cost will be for your clients to access SQL Server. Microsoft offers two different ways to purchase client licenses: per server and per client.

When you purchase client software licenses by server, the licenses are associated with that single server and cannot be used for other servers. If you have 100 people who need to access a single SQL Server, you have to purchase 100 client licenses. If those same 100 people need to access a second SQL Server, an additional 100 client licenses have to be purchased. This adds up to 200 client licenses for 100 people and two SQL Servers. Additional client licenses would have to be purchased for each additional SQL server purchased.

When you purchase client software by client, the client license is associated with a specific desktop, and not a server. Like the first example above, if 100 people need to access a single SQL Server, 100 client licenses have to be purchased. But if a second, third, or any additional SQL Servers are purchased, no additional client licenses have to be purchased because a client license associated with a client can be used to access an unlimited number of SQL Servers. Obviously, this is the least expensive way to purchase client licenses.

Why would anyone ever choose to license client software by server? There is one instance where it is less expensive. Consider

Before you buy

Microsoft's licensing requirements change from time to time, and you will want to check with your Microsoft Solution Provider to find out the latest licensing requirements as part of your planning process.

a situation where there is a single SQL Server and 100 people who need to access it, but at any one time only 50 out of the 100 need to access it simultaneously. If this is the case, licensing by server is less expensive than licensing by client. Under licensing by server, only 50 client licenses have to be purchased. Under licensing by client, 100 client licenses have to be purchased.

Microsoft permits organizations to make a one-time change from per server licensing to per client licensing, should you decide this is the best way for you to save money. Microsoft doesn't allow a change in the other direction.

Plan Your SQL Server Hardware Requirements

Selecting the right server hardware to run SQL Server will be one of the hardest things to do because there are so many variations to choose from. And many of the decisions that affect your server hardware needs depend on how you answered many of the questions asked earlier in this chapter.

The goal of this section is to get you to think about all the various possibilities, with a look at some of the pros and cons of each. This section covers these topics:

- Choosing hardware from the NT Server Hardware Compatibility List
- Selecting the hardware platform
- Selecting the CPU
- Do you need multiple CPUs?
- How much RAM do you need?
- Selecting a fast I/O controller
- Selecting hard disk capacity
- Do you need hardware RAID?
- Do you need clustered servers?
- Selecting a CD-ROM
- Selecting a backup device

- Selecting the Network Interface Card
- Selecting an NT Server Role for SQL Server
- Selecting an NT Server file system for SQL Server

Ultimately, you will want to choose server hardware that adequately performs the tasks you want to accomplish with your SQL Server application. Generally, this translates into purchasing the fastest hardware you can afford with the necessary capacity to grow with your organization for the next year or two.

Choosing Hardware from the NT Server Hardware Compatibility List

When it comes time to choose hardware to run NT Server and SQL Server, there is one cardinal rule: The hardware selected must be on Microsoft's NT Server Hardware Compatibility List (HCL). NT can be a finicky operating system, and the only way to ensure that NT Server and SQL Server will run without hardware-related problems is for all your hardware to be on the HCL. This isn't to say that hardware not on the HCL will not work, but you cannot be sure, and with the mission-critical nature of most SQL Server installations, why take an unnecessary risk to save a few dollars?

NT Server's HCL is updated periodically and is available at their Web site, which is the best place to find it. The copy of the HCL that comes on the NT Server CD is always out of date, and may not include the latest and greatest hardware. The HCL can be found at the following URL:

```
http://www.microsoft.com/hwtest/hcl
```

Check the HCL carefully

When checking out potential hardware to see if it is on the HCL, be sure to check for exact model numbers. Just because a similar item is on the HCL doesn't mean that it will work under NT. I know this from personal experience. Check the model numbers!

Selecting the Hardware Platform

SQL Server 7.0 only runs on Intel or Alpha microprocessors, and you have to decide which platform best meets your needs.

Intel microprocessors are popular because they are relatively inexpensive, widely available, widely supported, and offer many options to meet virtually any business need. On the other hand, Intel microprocessors aren't the fastest available.

Alpha microprocessors are known for their blazing speed and have the ability to scale well. But they are more expensive than Intel microprocessors, aren't as widely available or supported, and their servers have less options.

The decision isn't easy. Generally speaking, pick the hardware platform that best meets your needs for speed.

Selecting the CPU

After you have selected the hardware platform, it is safe to say that you will always want to purchase the fastest microprocessor available from the vendor. The cost difference between the fasted microprocessor and slower ones in a family of micro-processors is insignificant when compared to the entire cost of installing SQL Server.

You will also want to purchase a microprocessor with the largest amount of L1 and L2 cache you can get. This is especially important with the L2 cache. You will want an L2 cache of at least 512KB, and the greater the size of your databases, the faster your server will perform.

Do You Need Multiple CPUs?

The answer to this question depends on many of the answers to the questions asked previously in this chapter, and that is why it is so important to explore all the planning questions in this chapter before making any buying decisions. Larger databases with many users who access it require a server with greater power.

SQL Server 7.0 under NT 4.0 Enterprise Edition and Windows 2000 scale up to 8 CPUs, providing a tremendous amount of processing power that can meet almost any organization's data-base needs. SQL Server knows how to take advantage of multi-ple CPUs, and adding them can significantly boost SQL Server's performance.

Except for small SQL Server databases that you know won't grow much in the future, I would always recommend purchasing a server that can support more CPUs than you currently need so that you can add them if circumstances change. If you purchase a server with exactly the number of CPUs you think are needed (and no spare slots), and are wrong, you will have to purchase a new server, which is much more expensive than purchasing a server with CPU room to spare in the first place.

How Much RAM Do You Need?

The amount of RAM needed, like the number of CPUs, depends on how SQL Server will be used. SQL 7.0 will automatically take advantage of all the RAM you throw at it, so it is impossible to have too much RAM.

Of all the options you have to speed up SQL Server's performance, adding more RAM makes the greatest difference. Ideally, you should have enough RAM to hold the entire database and its application in RAM so that SQL Server will never have to read from the hard disk during normal operations. This may or may not be practical depending on the size of your database and your budget. But with the price of RAM constantly coming down, you need to consider purchasing as much RAM as you can afford.

After your SQL Server application is up and running, you can use NT Server's Performance Monitor tool to evaluate whether additional RAM is needed, and how much.

Determining the appropriate amount of RAM for a new SQL Server application is difficult, and can only be estimated. Only after running an application for a while do you have the necessary information to accurately determine your application's RAM requirements.

SEE ALSO
➤ *For more information on how to use NT Server's Performance Monitor to determine the RAM needs of SQL Server, see page 577.*

Selecting a Fast I/O Controller

After RAM, disk I/O is probably the most significant bottleneck when it comes to running SQL Server. When selecting the hardware to run SQL Server, you will want to specify the fastest SCSI, PCI-based disk I/O subsystem available, and you will probably want to purchase a system with at least two or more I/O controllers, depending on the number of physical disk drives that are to be used. The more I/O controllers you have, the faster your server can move data from disk drives to RAM, and the faster your system will be.

More than likely, any I/O controller you purchase will have onboard RAM cache to help speed up data access. Keep in mind that SQL Server and NT Server don't work properly with write-back caches, only read-ahead caches. If your I/O controller supports write-back cache, be sure that there is a way to disable this feature.

Selecting Hard Disk Capacity

The amount of hard disk space you need depends entirely on how much data you intend to store and manage with SQL Server. This can be as little as a gigabyte, or as much as a terabyte. The amount of space is also dependent on whether you will be using RAID for fault tolerance, as RAID requires additional space to store parity information.

When specifying hard disk capacity, start with a figure that will meet current needs and the estimated needs for the next year. There is no point purchasing more hard disk space than you need, especially with the constantly falling prices of hard disks. But be sure your server has room to grow, either internally or externally, should your plans change and your disk capacity needs increase significantly.

Do You Need Hardware RAID?

Although NT Server includes built-in software-based RAID, it is slow and should only be used in the smallest SQL Server installations. Ideally, when you specify an I/O subsystem, you will want to specify one that is capable of RAID level 5 and also offers hot-swappable disks. This will add very little to the overall cost of your SQL Server installation and provide some of the biggest return on your investment in terms of the fault tolerance it provides.

Do You Need Clustered Servers?

With the introduction of Microsoft's clustering solution, and similar products from other vendors, it is now possible for organizations to rely on PC-based servers for 24-hour, 7-day a week performance. Adding clustering to your SQL Server installation can be expensive, often more than doubling the cost of the hardware to run SQL Server, but if your SQL Server application is mission critical, this can be a small price to pay for peace of mind. Clustering solutions aren't easy to plan or install, and you will want to take extra time to research all the various clustering options before making a decision.

Selecting a CD-ROM

Without a doubt, you will want to add a CD-ROM to your SQL Server hardware. Be sure to specify a SCSI device (to match your controller), but don't worry about the speed. Most CD-ROMs will be used to load software, where speed in unimportant.

Selecting a Backup Device

You will want to spend a lot of time carefully considering how you will back up your SQL Server data because of the obvious importance of this necessary task. The size of your SQL data bases, how often they are backed up, how many people will be accessing the data simultaneously when backups are performed, and how fast you need to back your data up all factor in your determination of what type of backup device you need. You will also want to consider how you intend to restore data in case of problems and how much time it will take.

Ideally, you will want to purchase a backup device that not only can automatically back up all your data without manual intervention, but that can also be extremely fast and offer its own built-in fault tolerance.

SQL Server 7.0 Enterprise Edition required for Microsoft clustering

If you want to take advantage of Microsoft's clustering solution provided with NT Server 4.0's Enterprise Edition, you will have to purchase the Enterprise Edition of SQL Server 7.0.

Selecting the Network Interface Card

Although network I/O usually doesn't present a bottleneck for smaller SQL Server installations, it can play a factor in larger installations. You will need to determine how much bandwidth all your clients will require when they simultaneously access a single SQL Server, and ensure that you have adequate capacity to meet peak loads.

At the very least, you will want to purchase a single PCI-based, 10/100 Ethernet NIC (or comparable Token-Ring card). If a single card won't meet the required bandwidth capability, you may have to use multiple NICs, or even split the load among two or more SQL Servers in order to balance the load.

Selecting an NT Server Role for SQL Server

NT Server 4.0 can be installed to run under any one of three server roles: *Primary Domain Controller* (PDC), *Backup Domain Controller* (PDC), and *Member Server* (MS). Although SQL Server will run under any of these roles, the server role you should select is the MS. Both PDCs and BDCs are used in login authentication and Directory Services replication, which can put an extra load on the server. An MS, on the other hand, doesn't participate in these tasks, and can devote more of its resources to serving SQL Server.

Selecting an NT Server File System for SQL Server

NT Server supports both the FAT and NTFS file systems, and either can be used to run SQL Server. There is no question that you should select the NTFS file system. Some of the benefits of NTFS include the following:

- Handles very large partitions and file sizes
- Includes built-in fault tolerance features
- Offers superior file security

FAT cannot offer any of the above, and should not even be considered for any SQL Server installation.

At this point we end our discussion of the types of questions you should be asking yourself when planning a new SQL Server installation. The next step is to begin creating, and eventually carrying out, the plan. The next section takes a brief look at how to do this.

Formalizing and Carrying Out the Plan

As suggested earlier in this chapter, after you have reviewed this chapter, you need to read it again more carefully, and take careful notes of any question you must get answers to. As you can imagine, not every possible question is discussed here, and you will want to add your own questions that you need to get answers for. This chapter is simply a starting point.

This section takes a brief look at some of the major steps you might perform when carrying out a SQL Server installation, from the initial plan to the final installation.

Evaluate Your Needs

The purpose of this chapter is to help you begin evaluating your needs, which always raises lots of questions. Because of the difficulty of this task, it is often skipped when people begin the process of planning a new SQL Server installation. But this is the most important step because it is the basis for performing all the remaining steps.

Although we all have time constraints, you must take the time to carefully evaluate all your needs, ask lots of questions, and get satisfactory answers to them all. This will take time, but time spent here will pay off later with a smoother and more successful installation.

Training

One issue that has not yet been discussed, which should be addressed early in the planning process, is the need for training. The best SQL Server installation in the world cannot be

> **Purchase a disk defragmentation program**
>
> NTFS is subject to file fragmentation, which can contribute to slow disk I/O performance. To keep you SQL Server running at peak performance, you will want to defrag your SQL Server regularly. NT 4.0 doesn't include any built-in file defragmentation utilities, and you will want to purchase a third-party tool to perform regular, automatic disk defragmentation. Windows 2000 includes a basic defrag tool that enables you to manually defrag a server, but you will probably still want to purchase a third party tool that can automatically perform disk defragmentation.

successful unless everyone involved knows how to carry out his or her part successfully. Some of the training issues you need to consider include:

CTECs offer Microsoft training

Certified Technical Education Centers (CTECs) offer a wide variety of classes on SQL Server, including training for the DBA, Transact-SQL developer, and special classes on SQL Server optimization, client/server design, and decision support.

- Training developers on the necessary tools to create the SQL Server application.
- Training the DBAs to install and manage SQL Server.
- Training the end users who will be using the SQL Server application.
- Training managers so that they are aware of the limitations and possibilities of SQL Server and related hardware and software.

Training is often forgotten until the end of the project. This is a mistake. Training issues need to be defined early in the process so everyone can take advantage of the necessary training to carry out their parts satisfactorily.

Write Down the Plan

Be sure that your entire SQL Server installation plan is written down in detail. Not only will you want to put it in report form for people to read, you may want to use project management software, such as Microsoft's Project, to help you manage all the details. Project management isn't an easy task, and project management tools can make your task a little easier.

Your plan should include such details as how you intend to test your SQL Server application and installation before it is put into production. In many cases, you may want to conduct a pilot before final rollout to catch any unforeseen problems.

Cost Out the Plan

As you obtain answers to all your questions, you will need to begin attaching costs to your plan. This is also a difficult part of creating the installing plan, and because of this, guesses are often used instead of reasoned estimates or hard costs. As much as possible, don't guess costs; find out what they are by asking lots of questions of the right people. The cost of many projects such as these are poorly appraised, and because of this, cost overruns occur, which not only hurt your reputation, but also detract from the ultimate success of the project. When you have to guess, guess on the conservative side, which means guess on the high side rather than the low side. Your goal is to present a realistic picture of the total costs of a project.

Get the Plan Approved

After you have everything planned well, including accurate cost estimates, you are ready to get the plan approved. If you have done a good job, getting approval for the project should not be difficult. But if your planning job is sloppy or incomplete, can you blame a manager for not immediately approving your plan?

Implement the Plan

After the project is approved, now the fun (or stressful) part comes into play—you get to see how well your plan works. This will include many tasks, probably over a long period of time, depending on the nature of the project. As you implement your plan, you will find out things you didn't plan for, and you will have to change your plan accordingly. But this is part of any project implementation. The best thing to keep in mind is that the more carefully you have planned your SQL Server implementation, the smoother the implementation will occur.

chapter

4

Installing SQL Server

What You Need to Know Before Installing SQL Server 7.0

This chapter covers new installs only

This chapter focuses on new SQL Server installations. For information on how to upgrade previous versions of SQL Server to version 7.0, see Chapter 6, "Upgrading SQL Server from 6.5 to 7.0."

Whereas the previous chapter, "Planning a SQL Server Installation," provided a high-level overview of how to plan a SQL Server installation, this chapter focuses on the details of how to install SQL Server.

Compared to previous versions of SQL Server, version 7.0 is much easier to install. It's so easy, it might lull you into thinking that you don't really need to do much planning to install it. But don't be fooled into believing this. SQL Server is still a very complex product and its installation takes careful consideration.

Caution: Know where you're going before you start

Please read this chapter over in its entirety before attempting to install SQL Server for the first time. You will find that reading the entire chapter and following its suggestions can be a great time saver in the long run. At some point when you are ready to install SQL Server for the first time, you can use the step-by-step part of this chapter as your personal guide to installing SQL Server.

The first part of this chapter takes a high-level look at the setup process, describing all the decisions you must make during the installation process. Next is a step-by-step look at performing an actual installation. The last part of this chapter describes how to perform some preliminary steps to get SQL Server up and running after it is installed, such as how to register your server and create server groups using SQL Enterprise Manager.

Minimum Hardware and Software Requirements

How do I install SQL Server on Windows 95/98?

Although this chapter focuses on how to install SQL Server on NT Server, most of the material also applies to installing SQL Server on Windows 95/98. Areas where there are significant differences between how they are installed will be highlighted in notes like this one.

Before you begin thinking about installing SQL Server, you must have the correct hardware and software prepared and up and running. This means all the hardware has to be on Microsoft's NT Hardware Compatibility List (HCL) and properly installed and configured. It also means that NT Server must be installed and configured properly. You will want to verify and test all the hardware and the NT installation thoroughly. Many of the problems that occur during SQL Server installation are because these preliminary steps have not been done properly.

This section describes the minimum hardware and software requirements to run SQL Server. As was discussed in Chapter 3, you will want to outfit your SQL Server with the appropriate hardware to meet the needs of your SQL Server application, which is generally much greater than the minimum requirements listed here. The minimum hardware requirements are just enough to get SQL Server to run, but not enough for a production system. The following minimum hardware requirements apply to both the NT Server and Windows 95/98 SQL Server installations.

The minimum hardware requirements include

- CPU. One Intel 32-bit 80x86-based CPU (such as the Pentium, Pentium Pro, or Pentium II running at 133MHz or higher) or one DEC Alpha AXP CPU.

- RAM. 32MB.

- Disk Space. A minimum install requires about 80MB (doesn't include management tools or Books Online), a typical install requires about 185MB (includes management tools but doesn't include Books Online), and a full install takes about 210MB (includes management tools and Books Online).

- CD-ROM. Only required if installing SQL Server from CD. SQL Server can be installed from a network share point.

- I/O Subsystem, Display, Keyboard, Mouse. Any NT Server supported hardware will work.

- Network Card. Required if running SQL Server on a network. Optional if running standalone.

The minimum software requirements include the following:

- Operating System. SQL Server must be installed on Windows NT Server Version 4.0, Service Pack 4 or later; Windows NT Workstation 4.0, Service Pack 4 or later; Windows 95; or Windows 98.

Server Hardware Preparation and Settings

There are two important things you need to do with your hardware before installing SQL Server, and both of them only apply to you if you are using a RAID-based disk array. First, if the I/O

Use a current version of the HCL

All hardware must be on the NT Server hardware compatibility list (HCL) if you are installing SQL Server on NT Server. If you are installing SQL Server on Windows 95/98, you must use the Windows 95/98 HCL. To get the most recent version, visit Microsoft's WWW site at www.microsoft.com.

Books Online can run from CD

If you don't want to install Books Online because of hard disk space limitations, it can run from the SQL Server CD instead.

How do I install SQL Server on clustered NT Servers?

Installing SQL Server on to clustered NT servers isn't covered in this book. If you want to learn more about how to perform this type of installation, search for "Cluster Server" in the SQL Server Books Online.

controller for your disk array supports write-back caching, be sure to turn it off. Most, but not all, write-back caching schemes currently implemented by manufacturers don't work with SQL Server. Using this feature will corrupt your data, so don't even think about using it. Second, be sure the disk volumes on your RAID disk array have already been created before loading SQL Server. These will need to be in place in order to be ready to store the built-in SQL Databases (such as Master), and any new databases you create.

NT Server Software Settings

When configuring NT Server before SQL Server is loaded, there are a variety of options you need to consider and appropriately configure. They include choosing the proper NT Server role, sizing and locating the swap file, setting background and foreground tasking, and setting the file cache size. Each of these are described below.

NT Server Role

When installing NT Server 4.0, you must specify a role, either Primary Domain Controller (PDC), Backup Domain Controller (BDC), or Member Server (MS), that the server will take on. Although SQL Server will run on NT Server, no matter what role it is playing, the optimum role is MS. As an MS, NT Server will devote as much of its resources to SQL Server as possible, which makes for a faster SQL Server. Both PDCs and BDCs have a certain amount of overhead due to their participation in client authentication and Directory Service synchronization, which take away server resources from SQL Server.

Sizing and Locating the Pagefile

By default, NT Server creates a *pagefile* (pagefile.sys) automatically. The pagefile is used to provide NT Server with additional virtual memory, allowing NT Server to run programs that require more RAM than the server actually has. *Virtual memory* is a combination of RAM and the space allocated in the pagefile.

Although a pagefile provides many benefits, it also produces one major problem. Data stored in the pagefile (instead of RAM),

---

How do I know which role NT Server has been configured for?

If you intend to install SQL Server on a preexisting NT Server, you can determine it's role by running the Server Manager tool, from the Administrative Tools (Common) program group on your Start menu. To determine the role of the current NT Server, note the phrase in the Type column on the screen next to the server in question. If the last word is Primary, the server is a PDC; if the last word is Backup, it's a BDC; Server means it's an MS. If the NT Server is a PDC or a BDC, and you want to change the role to an MS, you have no choice but to reload NT Server because a PDC or BDC cannot be reconfigured to an MS.

significantly reduces the overall speed of the server, sometimes dramatically affecting performance. Although there isn't much you can do to speed up the use of a pagefile, there are a couple of things you can do.

First, the default size of a pagefile depends on the amount of RAM you have in the server when NT Server is first installed. The minimum and maximum size chosen by NT Server might or might not be appropriate for your situation. The only way to know for sure is to use NT Server's Performance Monitor to keep a watch on it after the server goes into production. By using the Paging File|%Usage counter of Performance Monitor, you will be able to tell exactly how much of the pagefile is being used, and you can change it appropriately—either increasing or decreasing it—based on your application. Until you have the opportunity to put your SQL Server into production, go ahead and use the pagefile size that is automatically created by NT Server.

NT Server automatically places the pagefile on the same drive as the NT system files. If you want optimum SQL Server performance, place the pagefile on a drive separate from the drive that holds the NT System files, but *not* in a RAID volume with your data. By placing the pagefile, NT system files, and SQL Server data on separate physical drives, there is less contention for data access, which helps to speed up overall hard disk access, boosting SQL Server's performance.

Pagefile size and Windows 95/98

You don't need to manually assign Windows 95/98 a fixed pagefile size. If fact, if you do, you might end up slowing down SQL Server. Let Windows 95/98 automatically determine the appropriate pagefile size, which is the default setting.

Changing NT Server's pagefile settings

1. Log on to NT Server as a user with administrative rights.
2. Click the Start button.
3. Click Settings.
4. Click Control Panel. This displays the Control Panel screen.
5. Double-click the System icon. This displays the System Properties dialog box.
6. Click the Performance tab.
7. Click the Change button under the Virtual Memory heading. This displays the Virtual Memory dialog box (see Figure 4.1). This screen can be used to change the size of a pagefile, and to move it from one disk drive to another.

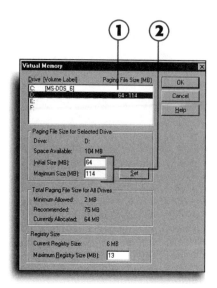

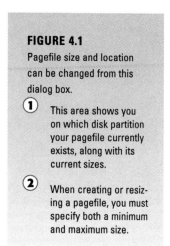

FIGURE 4.1

Pagefile size and location can be changed from this dialog box.

① This area shows you on which disk partition your pagefile currently exists, along with its current sizes.

② When creating or resizing a pagefile, you must specify both a minimum and maximum size.

8. To change the size of the pagefile, first click the drive where the pagefile is located. This is done in the Drive window at the top of the screen.

9. Next, enter the Initial Size (MB) and the Maximum Size (MB) for the pagefile in the appropriate boxes, and then click the Set button. This saves the new pagefile setting.

10. To move the location of the current pagefile, first click the drive where you want the pagefile to be located. This is done in the Drive window at the top of the screen.

11. Next, enter the Initial Size (MB) and the Maximum Size (MB) for the pagefile in the appropriate boxes, and then click the Set button. This saves the new pagefile setting. The Drive window at the top of the screen will now show two pagefiles, the old one and the new one.

12. To remove the old pagefile, click the drive where the old pagefile is located. Next, in both the Initial Size (MB) and the Maximum Size (MB) boxes, enter a zero. Then, click the Set button. This will remove the old pagefile.

13. When you are finished, click OK. You will then be prompted to reboot your computer. Go ahead and reboot the computer now. After the computer is rebooted, the new settings will go into effect.

SEE ALSO

➤ *For more information on how to use the NT Server Performance Monitor to monitor SQL Server, see page 565.*

Setting Foreground and Background Tasking

By default, after installing NT Server, NT sets the application performance of any foreground application to None. This means that the foreground application you are running doesn't get a priority boost over the applications currently running in the background. By default, all user applications running under NT Server are assigned a CPU priority of 7 (priorities range from 0–31, with 0 the lowest and 31 the highest). When SQL Server is in production, this is the setting you will want to maintain, as you want SQL Server to get all the CPU cycles it can. But while you are setting up the server and using many foreground applications, you might want to temporally boost the foreground application priority to make your life a little more productive.

Changing the priority of foreground applications in NT Server

  1. Log on to NT Server as a user with administrative rights.

  2. Click the Start button.

  3. Click Settings.

  4. Click Control Panel. This displays the Control Panel screen.

  5. Double-click the System icon. This displays the System Properties dialog box.

  6. Click the Performance tab. This tab is used to change the performance of foreground applications (see Figure 4.2).

  7. To change the priority of foreground applications, move the slider between None and Maximum. There are three settings. None means that the foreground application receives no priority boost from the default priority of 7. A setting between None and Maximum boosts foreground applications to a priority of 8. A setting of Maximum boosts a foreground application to a priority of 9.

  8. After you are finished setting the foreground application performance, you can exit by clicking OK.

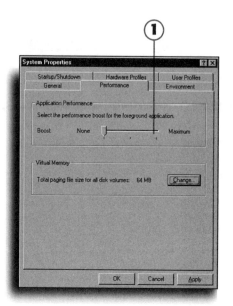

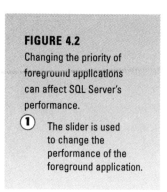

FIGURE 4.2

Changing the priority of foreground applications can affect SQL Server's performance.

① The slider is used to change the performance of the foreground application.

If you do make this change, don't forget to return it to a setting of None when SQL Server is put into production.

Setting NT File Caching

After loading NT Server, but before loading SQL Server, the NT Server File Caching setting is set to Maximize Throughput for File Sharing. But after you load SQL Server, the installation process automatically changes this setting to Maximize Throughput for Network Applications. Assuming that SQL Server is the only application running on this physical server, leave the setting at Maximize Throughput for Network Applications. This influences how much RAM is devoted to file caching by NT. A setting of Maximize Throughput for Network Applications reduces the amount of RAM dedicated to file caching and gives it to the application for use. This allows SQL Server to take advantage of the additional RAM for its own use, speeding up its overall performance.

Verifying the current NT File Caching setting

1. Log on to NT Server as a user with administrative rights.
2. Click the Start button.

3. Click Settings.

4. Click Control Panel. This displays the Control Panel screen.

5. Double-click the Network icon. This displays the Network dialog box.

6. Click the Services tab, which displays the screen in Figure 4.3.

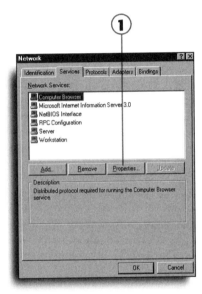

FIGURE 4.3

You must select the Service from this dialog box.

① The properties dialog box of the Server service is where you change NT Server file caching.

7. Double-click Server in the Network Services box. This displays the Server dialog box (see Figure 4.4).

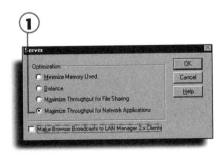

FIGURE 4.4

To optimize SQL Server, set the NT Server File Caching setting to Maximize for Network Applications.

① The best setting for SQL Server is Maximize Throughput for Network Applications.

8. If the Maximize Throughput for Network Applications option isn't chosen, choose it by clicking the appropriate radio button.

9. When you are finished, click OK.

If you made a change to the optimization setting, you will be prompted to reboot NT Server for the changed setting to take effect.

SEE ALSO

➤ *For more information on how to tune SQL Server for optimum performance, see page 581.*

Two versions of SQL Server come on CD
The SQL Server distribution CD contains two versions of SQL Server: one for Intel CPUs, and one for Alpha CPUs. Their respective folder names on the CD are: \I386 and \Alpha.

Different Ways to Install SQL Server

When it's time to load SQL Server on to a server, you have several installation options, which include:

- Installing from cd
- Installing from a network share point
- Installing withSystems Management Software (SMS)

Let's take a look at each option, and discuss its pros and cons.

Installing from CD

Windows 95/98 doesn't support all SQL Server features
Although SQL Server can be installed on Windows 95/98, not all SQL Server features are supported. Some of the major exceptions include the following: replication is limited to acting as a subscriber, database size is limited to 4GB, and text searching capabilities are limited.

The most common way to install SQL Server is from the CD provided by Microsoft. All that is required to install SQL Server from a CD is a CD-ROM.

There are no real disadvantages of installing SQL Server from CD, although you might want to consider the following points:

- You might want to install many copies of SQL Server with the least amount of effort possible.
- You might only have one CD that contains SQL Server.
- Some or all of the physical servers don't have their own CD-ROM.

If any of the above statements are true, you might want to consider one or more of the following alternative ways to install SQL Server.

Installing from a Network Share Point

If you need to install multiple copies of SQL Server, and especially if you only have a single CD with SQL Server, you might want to copy the appropriate SQL Server setup files from the CD to a network share point that can be accessed by everyone authorized to install SQL Server.

If you want to create a network share point for installing SQL Server, all you have to do is create a new folder on a file server and give it an appropriate name, such as SQL Setup Files, and then copy into it the appropriate folders from the SQL Server CD. After the appropriate files are copied, share the folder and assign the necessary security. At this point, any authorized user can connect to the shared folder and install SQL Server.

Besides the convenience of using a network share point to install SQL Server, it is often faster to install SQL Server from a network share point than a CD.

You might want to consider the network bandwidth available to you when installing SQL Server over a network sharepoint. As you might imagine, during the setup process itself, over 100MB of data will be sent over the network. If the network isn't busy, this shouldn't be a problem, but if the network is very busy, you might want to time your installs when the network is less busy, so as not to interfere with regular network traffic. This also implies that your network share point is accessible via a fast LAN link, not a slow WAN link.

As service packs become available for SQL Server 7.0, you will also want to add them to your SQL Server share point to make them easy to access.

Finding out more about network shares

If you have never created a network share using NT Server, do a search for "network share" in the NT Server Books Online.

Installing SQL Server With Systems Management Software

Is SMS a good choice for installing SQL Server?

Unless you have a very large number (more than 10) of new SQL Servers you want to install, using SMS for unattended installation is probably not worth the effort. SQL Server installations can be tricky, and an SMS unattended installation of SQL Server assumes that the installation isn't tricky and will be uneventful.

If you still think you want to use SMS to install SQL Server, be sure you conduct a small pilot test first to work out any unforeseen problems.

If your organization currently is using Microsoft's Systems Management Software (SMS) BackOffice product (version 1.2 or later), and if you need to install many copies of SQL Server throughout your organization, you might want to consider using SMS to perform the installation for you automatically and unattended. Although SMS can be used to push a new installation, it cannot be used to upgrade older SQL Servers.

To make your job of automatically pushing and installing SQL Server using SMS easier, the following files are included on the SQL Server CD:

- Smssql70.pdf. This is the Package Definition Format (PDF) file that is used by SMS to create an SMS package, and a job, that will perform the push installation to remote servers.

- Sql70ins.cmd. This is a batch file that is used to detect the computer platform (Intel or Alpha), and then run the correct version of setup.exe. It also is used to install SQL Server, along with the SQL Server Books Online.

- Sql70ins.ini. This is a script file that is used for unattended installations. This file has to be manually edited so that setup.exe knows exactly how you want SQL Server installed. If you need to install SQL Server more than one way on different servers, you will have to create a separate copy of this file for every different type of installation you need.

- Sqlrem.cmd. This is a batch file that is used to detect the computer platform when running an unattended removal of SQL Server using SMS.

- Sql70rem.ini. This is a script file used for an unattended removal of SQL Server using SMS.

If you aren't an SMS guru, these files will be meaningless to you. But if you want to use SMS for performing unattended installations of SQL Server throughout your organization, you will need to let your SMS guru know about the above files, along with the additional information on unattended installations in the SQL Server Books Online.

SQL Server Installation and Configuration Options

Whether you install SQL Server from a CD, from a network share point, or by using SMS, you will need to carefully think through the following SQL Server installation issues.

This is a very important, and lengthy, look at all the options you have when installing SQL Server. Each option is examined closely, providing the information you need to properly install and configure SQL Server. After this section is a step-by-step look at the actual installation process, which requires that you have already evaluated all the following options and made the appropriate decisions to meet your specific needs. These sections cover:

- SQL Server naming rules
- Entering registration information
- Choosing an installation type
- Choosing network support
- Choosing a character set
- Choosing a sort order
- Choosing a Unicode collation
- Choosing Management Tools
- Choosing where to install SQL Server
- Choosing where to store SQL Server data
- Entering a service account
- How to create a service account
- Choosing to auto-start SQL Services

SQL Server Naming Rules

Before installing SQL Server, it is important to understand SQL Server's naming rules; they are different from the naming rules used by NT Server. For example, NT Server permits names that are not legal for SQL Server. This can cause a problem because SQL Server uses the name of the NT Server as its own name. If the name of the NT Server where SQL Server is to be installed doesn't follow the SQL Server naming rules, the SQL Server installation will fail. In addition, SQL Server can use NT usernames as login IDs, which means that NT usernames must also follow SQL Server naming rules. Because of this, it is important that any NT naming scheme you select must correspond with SQL Server's naming scheme. To ensure a successful SQL Server installation, be sure that your NT naming scheme follows these SQL Server naming rules:

- Names must not exceed 128 characters.
- Names must not include any spaces.
- Names must begin with an uppercase or lowercase letter, or the underscore symbol _. Names can also begin with @ or #, but these have special meaning and should not be used in most cases.
- Characters in names after the first letter may be any letter, number, or the symbols @, _, #, or $.

If all your NT names follow these rules, SQL Server can successfully co-exist with NT Server.

Entering Registration Information

As is typical for Microsoft products, you will be asked to enter a name, company, and product registration number. The number is on the CD case, and probably should be written down in some central location for easy referral in case the CD case is ever misplaced.

Choosing an Installation Type

SQL Server offers three different installation types: Typical, Minimum, and Custom.

Typical Installation

This option automatically installs SQL Server and the client utilities using all default installation options. This means that minimal decisions will have to be made by the installer. This option automatically installs SQL Server and Books Online. This option takes about 163MB of disk space. It doesn't automatically load the Full Text Search software, development tools, or sample files.

Compact Installation

This option loads the absolute minimum number of files to operate SQL Server, and uses all default installation options. A Compact Installation is like a Typical Installation, except the Management Tools and Online Books are not loaded. This option takes about 74MB of disk space.

Custom Installation

This option enables you to not only choose exactly which SQL Server components you want to load, but it also gives you the option to choose many different SQL Server options, instead of just automatically accepting default options. The custom installation options include the following choices:

- Network protocols
- Character set
- Sort order
- Utilities to install
- Which online documentation to install
- Where to place program files
- Where to Place Data Files
- Which Service Accounts to Use for SQL Server Services
- Whether to Start SQL Services Automatically
- Which Program Group to Place SQL Server Icons

Choosing Custom Installation gives you the greatest flexibility of choice, and is the one you should probably choose. This chapter assumes you will be selecting Custom Setup and explains each of the various options you can choose from.

Windows 95/98 defaults to TCP/IP Sockets

If you install SQL Server on Windows 95/98, the default Network Library is TCP/IP Sockets.

Choosing Network Protocols

For clients to communicate with SQL Server over a network connection, they must share a common Interprocess Communication (IPC) mechanism in order to send network packets back and forth between the client and SQL Server. SQL Server supports several different IPC mechanisms, which are implemented as Network Libraries in the form of Dynamic Link Libraries (DLL). If both the client and SQL Server don't share a common Network Library, they cannot communicate.

By default, SQL Server uses the Named Pipes, TCP/IP, and Multi-Protocol Network Libraries, but you can add additional Network Libraries to SQL Server if needed to support a wider variety of client types. Although SQL Server itself has the capability to support multiple Network Libraries simultaneously, SQL clients don't have this capability. This means that it is generally easier to load multiple Network Libraries on SQL Server than it is to change all the clients to support a single Network Library on SQL Server.

In a Typical or Minimal SQL Server installation, Named Pipes, TCP/IP Sockets, and Multi-Protocol are the only Network Libraries automatically installed. A Custom installation lets you choose additional Network Libraries during setup, or they can be changed later through SQL Setup.

Before you decide to add additional Network Libraries, read about each available Network Library, so you can learn whether or not it is required. Loading unnecessary Network Libraries take away valuable RAM from SQL Server that could be used by the SQL Server to speed up its performance.

SEE ALSO

➤ *For more information on IPC mechanisms and SQL Server architecture, see page 45.*

Named Pipes Network Library

Traditionally, NT Server and BackOffice products have used the Named Pipes IPC mechanism to communicate with each other, and SQL Server is no exception. When using Named Pipes, SQL Server listens for communications from clients using the `\\sql_server_name\pipe\sql\query` hidden share, where `sql_server_name` is the name of the computer where SQL Server is installed.

Most Microsoft-based client operating systems have the capability to communicate with SQL Server using Named Pipes, and if all your SQL Server clients use Named Pipes, this single Network Library will be the only Network Library you need to load.

If desired, the Named Pipes Network Library can be removed, but only after SQL Server has been installed. Named Pipes is required during the installation process; otherwise the installation process will fail.

Multi-Protocol Network Library

The Multi-Protocol Network Library supports *remote procedure calls* (RPC). This means that SQL Server can use most of the IPC mechanisms supported by NT, including TCP/IP Sockets, NWLink, and Named Pipes. It also supports Multi-Protocol encryption to protect passwords and data as they move between clients and SQL Server.

The Multi-Protocol Network Library is more flexible than Named Pipes, and because of this, you might want to make it your only Network Library, assuming all the clients support it. If you do, remember not to remove the Named Pipes Network Protocol until SQL Server has been fully installed.

As a compromise, many DBAs leave both Names Pipes and Multi-Protocol Network Libraries for the greatest flexibility for servicing the needs of SQL clients.

TCP/IP Sockets Network Library

If your network is 100% TCP/IP-based, you might want to consider using the TCP/IP Sockets Network Library. It uses the standard TCP/IP Sockets Network API as the IPC mechanism.

If you choose this option, you can change the TCP/IP port number that SQL Server uses to listen for client communication. The default port is 1433, which is the official port number assigned to SQL Server by the Internet Assigned Number Authority.

If your clients will access SQL Server via a proxy server, you can enter its IP address when you complete the setup screen.

NWLink (IPX/SPX) Network Library

If your network is mostly made up of Novell servers and uses the IPX/SPX transport protocol, and if some or all of the clients who will be accessing SQL Server use the Novell SPX protocol exclusively to communicate, you will have to load the NWLink Network Library. This network library provides the capability for Novell SPX clients to communicate with SQL Server.

If you choose this network library, you will be prompted to enter the Novell Bindery Service Name, which is used to register SQL Server on the Novell Network. This name is generally the computer name of the SQL Server.

If your Novell network uses TCP/IP instead of IPX/SPX, this network library isn't required.

AppleTalk ADSP Network Library

If your network has Apple Macintosh–based clients who will be communicating with SQL Server using AppleTalk, you will have to install this network library.

If you select this option, you will be prompted for an AppleTalk Service Object Name, which is usually the computer name of the computer running SQL Server.

If your Apple Macintosh–based clients use TCP/IP instead of AppleTalk, this network library isn't required.

Banyan VINES Network Library

If your network has any clients running the Banyan VINES Sequenced Packet Protocol (SPP) that communicates with SQL Server, you will have to install this network library. Currently, this network library is available for Intel platforms only, not Alpha platforms.

If you select this option, you will be prompted for a StreetTalk Service Name, which has a format of *servicename@group@org*, where *servicename* is the StreetTalk service name used by SQL Server, *group* is the group, and *org* is the organization.

The Banyan VINES software for NT must first be installed on NT Server before SQL Server and the Banyan VINES Network Library is installed.

Choosing a Character Set

A character set is a collection of uppercase letters, lowercase letters, numbers, and symbols that are recognized by SQL Server. Traditionally, character sets have had 256 characters, but this can vary depending on the language supported by the character set. The first 128 characters of each of the character sets supported by SQL server are identical. It is the remaining characters that can vary significantly from one character set to another.

SQL Server includes 14 character sets, but only one can be selected at a time. Whatever character set is selected, it is critical that the same one is used both for SQL Server and for its clients; otherwise, many characters might not be recognized when information is sent back and forth between the client and server. It is also important that all your SQL Servers that need to intercommunicate also have the same character set; otherwise, you might receive unexpected results.

It is important that the correct character set be chosen during the installation process. Although a character set can be changed at a later time, it requires that the rebuild your databases and reload your data (a major task!).

By default, SQL Server chooses the ISO Character Set (Code Page 1252). This character set is also known as the ISO-8859-1, Latin 1, or ANSI character set. This character set is compatible with the Windows 95/98 and Windows NT operating systems, and it provides the greatest compatibility with most other world languages. Unless you have a good reason, you should leave this as the default character set.

Other characters sets include

- Multilingual. Use this character set when your SQL Server clients are MS-DOS–based and use extended characters.

- U.S. English. Although this character set sounds like it might be an appropriate one, and although it has been traditionally popular in the United States, this character set includes many block graphical characters that aren't used in databases. Only choose this option if you need to maintain backward compatibility with legacy applications.

- Arabic

- Baltic

- Central European

- Chinese, simplified

- Chinese, traditional

- Cyrillic

- Greek

- Hebrew

- Korean

- Japanese

- Turkish

Choosing a Sort Order

Another decision you must make is which sort order to select. A sort order determines how SQL Server resolves queries and sorts data. Different sort orders can produce different output. For example, take a look at the following lists of last names, and notice how they are sorted differently when using different sort orders:

Dictionary Sort Order, Not Case Sensitive

Mcgehee
McGovern
McGovney

Dictionary Sort Order, Case Sensitive

McGovern
McGovney
Mcgehee

Binary Sort Order

MCGOVNEY
McGovern
mcgehee

As you can see, the sort order you choose can produce unexpected results. There are three important reasons why you need to choose the right sort order at installation time. First, if you later decide to change the sort order, you will have to rebuild your database and reload your data. Second, your client software must use the same sort order as your SQL Server. If it doesn't, unpredictable results will occur. And last, all the SQL Servers you have in your organization that need to intercommunicate must have the same sort order, or unexpected results can occur.

The default sort order for the ISO character set is Dictionary Order, Case-Insensitive. This produces the kind or results you are used to. Unless you have a very good reason, leave this sort order as the default.

The available sort orders depend on which character set you choose. If you chose the default ISO Character Set, you can choose from these sort orders:

- Dictionary Order, Case-Insensitive. The default choice, and also the most common choice; it presents data in the order you have learned to expect.

- Binary Order. Provides the fastest sorting, but strings aren't sorted in standard dictionary order. Data is instead sorted based on the ASCII values of the strings. For example, using a binary sort, "Zen" comes before "apple."

- Dictionary Order, Case-Sensitive.

- Dictionary Order, Case-Insensitive, Uppercase Preference.

- Dictionary Order, Case-Insensitive, Accent-Insensitive.

- Danish/Norwegian Dictionary Order, Case-Insensitive, Uppercase Preference.

A warning about changing sort orders

Changing sort orders after creating one or more databases can affect login ID passwords. For example, if you move from a non–case sensitive to a case sensitive sort order, users will have to type passwords in uppercase to be authenticated. Moving from case sensitive to non–case sensitive sort order means users can't log in at all unless a previous password was all uppercase.

If you have to change sort orders, besides rebuilding all your databases, plan on changing all your user passwords. You might change the passwords before you rebuild your databases, making them compliant with whatever your new sort order requires.

- Icelandic Dictionary Order, Case-Insensitive, Uppercase Preference.

- Swedish/Finnish (standard) Dictionary Order, Case-Insensitive, Uppercase Preference.

- Swedish/Finnish (phonetic) Dictionary Order, Case-Insensitive, Uppercase Preference.

If you choose a character set other than the ISO character set, you will have slightly different sort orders to choose from. See the SQL Books Online for details on the available sort orders for the various characters sets included with SQL Server.

Choosing a Unicode Collation

SQL Server has the capability to store standard ASCII characters (as described previously) and Unicode characters. Unicode characters can represent over 64,000 different characters, while ASCII characters can only support 256 different characters. After choosing a Character Set and Sort Order when installing SQL Server, you are also asked to choose a Unicode Collation type, which acts as a sort order for Unicode data stored in SQL Server. The SQL Server installation program will provide a default Unicode Collation based on the Character Set and Sort Order you have previously chosen. Unless you have a good reason not to, you should always leave the Unicode Collation to the default value suggested to you by the installation program. If you change the default value, your data might not sort as you would expect.

Choosing Management Tools

Another choice you must make is which SQL Server Management Tools you want to load. You will probably not want to load them all, especially on a production server where disk space is at a premium. The tools you may load include the following:

- SQL Server Enterprise Manager. This key tool is a must-load on all SQL Servers as it provides direct access to managing SQL Server.

- SQL Server Profiler. This tool is used to monitor traffic between SQL Server and clients. Only load this on servers you think you will be running it from.

- SQL Server Query Analyzer. This tool is used to communicate to SQL Server via Transact-SQL. You will probably want to load this on most, if not all, servers for convenience.

- Version Upgrade Wizard. This tool makes it easier to migrate from 6.x SQL Servers to SQL Server 7.0. Only load it if you need to migrate. This tool isn't available when SQL Server is loaded on to Windows 95/98.

- Client Configuration. This is used to verify which DB-Library is installed on a client, and to configure the client to communicate with SQL Server. It also installs the makepipe and readpipe programs that are used to test whether the Named Pipes IPC is working properly between SQL Server and a client. Generally, you won't need to load this on a SQL Server.

- Development Files. These are files needed by OLEDB developers to create programs using ODBC, DB-Library, ODS, DMP, ESQL, and MS DTC. If this doesn't apply to you, don't load them.

- Sample Files. These are sample files designed for developers to view and learn from. If this doesn't apply to you, don't load them.

No matter which of these options you decide to load, the following utilities and files are automatically loaded. They include BCP, ISQL, OSQL, ODBC, and DB-Library.

Choosing Where to Install SQL Server

You can choose where SQL Server is to be installed, or you can go with the SQL Server defaults. The default drive and folder is c:\Mssql7, and the following subfolders are created under \Mssql7:

- Binn. 32-bit client and server executable files and DLLs, along with help files.
- Books. SQL Server Books Online.
- DevTools. This folder, and its subfolders, are only created if you choose to load the optional development tools and samples.
- Ftdata. Only loaded if you install the optional Full-Text Search components. Used to hold full-text catalog files.
- HTML. Holds HTML and related files.
- Install. Installation scripts and output files.
- Jobs. Stores information on SQL Server jobs.
- Upgrade. Version Upgrade Wizard files. Not created if you don't install the Upgrade Wizard.

Choosing Where to Store SQL Server Data

Along with being able to choose the location of the SQL Server program files, you can also specify the location of where SQL data is to be stored. By default, the SQL Server setup process creates these folders underneath the c:\Mssql7 directory:

- Backup. This is where SQL Server puts all backup devices by default.
- Data. This is where SQL Server stores database and transaction log files by default.
- Log. This is where SQL Server stores error log files.
- Repldata. If replication is used, SQL Server uses this directory for replication tasks.

Although the Log and Repldata directories are good places to keep their respective information, you will probably want to choose different drives and directories to store your database, transaction logs, and backup devices. Which ones you choose will depend on your physical server configuration and the nature of your data. Quite often, SQL database and transaction log files are stored on a RAID 5 disk array for maximum fault tolerance, but your exact needs, as defined in the previous chapter on planning, will determine where you will store your data.

Creating a Service Account

SQL Server is made up of two major services: the SQLServerAgent and the MSSQLServer services. SQLServerAgent is responsible for routine maintenance tasks such as handling alerts, tasks, events, and replication, whereas MSSQLServer is the SQL Server engine that directly manages databases.

> **Don't forget the MSDTC service**
>
> Although the MSSQLServer and SQLServerAgent services are the two key services used by SQL Server, there is also one more service, the MSDTC service. Because it is optional and not commonly used, it isn't discussed in this section. But if you do decide to use it, it will have to have a service account just like the other two SQL Server services.

As NT Services, the two key SQL Server services run continuously in the background, whether or not a user is logged in to NT Server. And like most NT Services, the two key SQL Server services are generally automatically started whenever NT Server is rebooted. As NT initializes, it starts all necessary services. Part of the initialization process is that every service must "log on to" NT Server, similar to how a user must log on to NT Server in order to access network resources.

An NT service can log on in two different ways. First, it can log on using NT's built-in LocalSystem account. This is a special security account reserved for the use of NT services. When a service logs on to NT using the LocalSystem account, the service runs under the security context of the physical server where the service is running. This means that the service has permission to operate on the local server, but that it may not interact with the rest of the network. For most NT services, this limitation isn't a problem.

Although both SQLServerAgent and MSSQLService can run under the local security context of a single server, this limit restricts their capability to communicate with other SQL Servers. This might be adequate for small, single-server SQL Server installations, but when multiple SQL Servers are installed that need to interact, using the LocalSystem account will not work.

Windows 95/98 doesn't need service accounts

If you install SQL Server on to a Windows 95/98 computer, you don't need to create a service account. Windows 95/98 is unable to run services. Instead, they run in the background as any other background program does.

This leads us to the other way a service can run under NT Server, and that is by logging on under an NT user account specially created for use by a service. By logging on under a standard NT user account, a service then runs under the security context of the domain where the account is located. Normally, this would be an organization's accounts domain.

To allow SQLServerAgent and MSSQLServer the greatest flexibility, you will probably want to create a special NT Server service account using the User Manager for Domains (only a user with administrative privileges can create this account). Although you might create separate service accounts for each service, this is unnecessary. You need only create one service account, and both services can share the same account to log in. In fact, if you have multiple SQL Servers spread throughout your enterprise, you will want to use the same NT service account for all your SQL Servers. This simplifies administration and helps to ensure that all the SQL Servers can communicate.

The NT service account should be created in your NT Accounts Domain. This is the domain where all your NT user accounts reside. This assumes that SQL Server is located in either an accounts domain, or a resource domain that has access to an accounts domain through a trust relationship.

The NT service account should be created before SQL Server is installed, but it isn't required. This is because you are prompted for the name of the service account during the SQL Server installation process. If you forget to create the account before installing SQL Server, the LocalSystem account will be used instead. After SQL Server is installed, the service account can be changed by changing the startup values of the service using the Services icon in NT's Control Panel.

When you create an NT service account to run SQLServerAgent and MSSQLServer, you will need to configure the account this way:

- The account must belong to the NT Server's Domain Admins global group.
- The Change Password at Next Logon option *must not* be selected.

- The Password Never Expires option *must* be selected.
- A password should be assigned to prevent someone from logging on to NT using this account. Also, this account should not be used to log on to NT. It is to be used by the SQL Server services only.
- The account *must* be given these advanced user rights. Act as Part of the Operating System, Increase Quotas, Log On as a Service, and Replace a Process Level Token. If you create the account before installing SQL Server, the setup process will automatically assign these rights for you.

Don't make any other changes to the account, such as restricting hours, adding a login script, or restricting the account to specific machines. Any of these options can prevent the service account from logging on properly.

The following section guides you through all the necessary steps to create an NT service account to be used by SQLServerAgent and MSSQLService.

SEE ALSO

➤ *For more information on SQL Server service accounts, see page 47.*

How to Create a Service Account

This section is designed for those DBAs who are not familiar with how to use NT Server's User Manager for Domains program to create a new account. If you are familiar with this procedure, you might want to skip this section. This section steps you through the entire process.

Creating a new service account to be used by the SQLServerAgent and MSSQLServer services

1. Log on to NT Server using an account with administrative rights.

2. Load NT Server's User Manager for Domains program (see Figure 4.5).

Create the service account in the Accounts Domain

When you create a service account with User Manager for Domains on an NT Server, be sure this account is created in the Accounts Domain. An Accounts Domain is the domain in an NT network where all user accounts are created. By default, the domain selected by User Manager for Domains might not be the Accounts Domain. If it isn't, you will need to select the Accounts Domain by selecting Select Domain from the User drop-down menu before creating the service account.

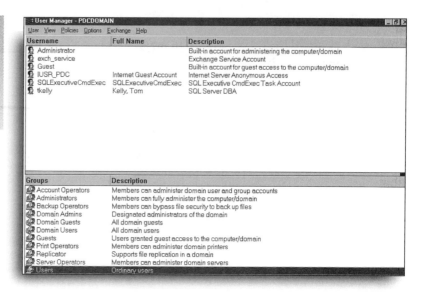

FIGURE 4.5

The SQL Server service account is created with NT Server's User Manager for Domains.

3. To create a new user account that will be used as SQL Server's service account, click the User drop-down menu, and select New User.

The New User dialog box appears (see Figure 4.6).

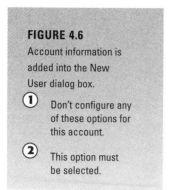

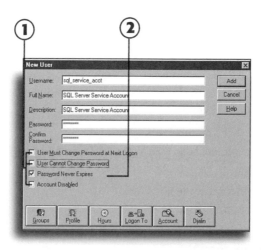

FIGURE 4.6

Account information is added into the New User dialog box.

① Don't configure any of these options for this account.

② This option must be selected.

4. The first step is to enter a Username for the service account. Although any legal NT account name can be used, keep in mind that you will also want to follow SQL Server's naming

rules, which are more restrictive than NT Server's naming rules. You will also want to select a name, such as `sql_service_acct`, that is self-documenting.

5. Next, enter a descriptive full name for the account. The Full Name field is optional, but useful to help document the purpose of this NT account.

6. Next, you can enter an optional description in the Description field to further document the purpose of this account.

7. Next, enter a password in the Password and Confirm Password fields. It is important to enter a password to prevent users from using this account to log on to NT Server. Like any password, select one that is hard to guess.

8. Be sure to deselect the check next to User Must Change Password at Next Logon. If you don't deselect it (it is selected by default), the SQL services will fail when they try to start up because NT Server will be asking the service to enter a new password, and of course the service has no idea about how to enter a new password.

9. The User Cannot Change Password check box is irrelevant to this account, so you can check it, or not, as you please.

10. Be sure to select the Password Never Expires check box. Most organizations force users to change their password periodically. If you don't select this option, and if the account expires, the SQL Services will fail when they are restarted.

11. Don't select the Account Disabled check box, unless you want to temporally prevent anyone, or the services, from using this account.

12. After the initial dialog box is completed, there is one more step before the account can be created. Click the Groups button at the bottom of the dialog box, and the Group Memberships dialog box appears (see Figure 4.7).

FIGURE 4.7

The service account must be added to the Domain Admins global group.

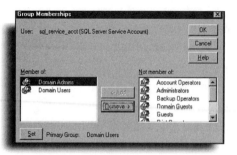

FIGURE 4.7

The service account must be added to the Domain Admins global group.

13. You must make this service account a member of the Domain Admins global group. To do this, click once on Domain Admins from the Not Member Of box, and then click the Add button. This will move the Domain Admins group to the Member Of box. Leave the Domain Users global group where it is. Click OK when you have completed this step.

    You are returned to the New User dialog box.

14. If you are happy with this account, click Add, and then Close to exit the New User dialog box.

15. If you have not yet installed SQL Server, this is the last step you need to perform to create the service account. You may remember from the previous section that the service account must also be assigned certain User Rights before it can be used. If you create this account now, and load SQL Server later, when you tell SQL Server the name of this service account, the SQL Server setup program will automatically assign the necessary User Rights to the account.

    On the other hand, if you are creating this account after having already loaded SQL Server, you will have to manually add the necessary User Rights to this service account. To do this, perform these additional steps. Remember, you don't need to do these steps if SQL Server has yet to be loaded.

16. To add the necessary User Rights to the SQL Server service account, select User Rights from the Policies drop-down menu.

    The User Rights Policy dialog box appears (see Figure 4.8).

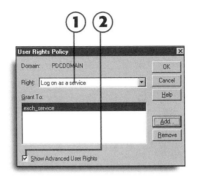

FIGURE 4.8

Some advanced user rights have to be added to the service account.

(1) The rights are chosen from this list box.

(2) The Show Advanced User Rights check box must be selected.

17. From the User Rights Policy dialog box, click the check box next to Show Advanced User Rights. This is required because advanced user rights are not automatically displayed in this dialog box unless this option is selected.

18. You must add the following advanced user rights to the SQL Server service account:

- Log on as a service.

- Act as part of the operating system.

- Increase quotas.

- Replace a process level token.

To add each of these advanced user rights, click the Right list box menu. From the list box, select one advanced user rights from the list above, such as Logon as a Service. This displays the advanced user right in the Right list box.

19. After the advanced user right is selected and is displayed in the Right list box, next click the Add button, and the Add Users and Groups dialog box appears (see Figure 4.9).

20. After the Add Users and Groups dialog box is displayed, click the Show Users button. This displays all user accounts in the Names window.

21. Use the scroll bar in the Names windows to find the service account you created, and then click once on the account name so that it is highlighted.

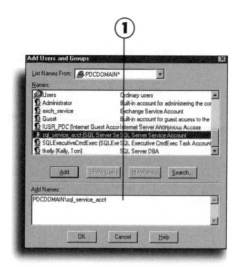

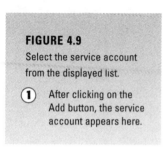

FIGURE 4.9

Select the service account from the displayed list.

① After clicking on the Add button, the service account appears here.

22. Next, click the Add button, and the account name is added to the Add Names window. And last, click the OK button. This will return you to the User Rights Policy dialog box, and the service account will now be displayed in the Grant To window.

23. Repeat steps 18 through 22 for each of the advanced user rights listed previously. After you are done, click the OK button from the User Rights Policy dialog box, and you will be returned to the User Manager for Domains main window.

At this point, the service account has been properly set up. You can exit User Manager for Domains, and you are ready to install SQL Server.

Installing SQL Server

Now that you have thoroughly considered all the possible SQL Server installation options, and you have created your SQL Server service account, you are ready to do an actual installation. So let's begin.

Installing SQL Server

1. Log in to NT Server with an account that has administrative rights.

2. Be sure there are no other programs running in the foreground, such as the NT Event Viewer, Registry Editor, or any other NT administrative tools. These instructions also assume that no version of SQL Server is currently running on the server.

3. If you are installing SQL Server from a CD, follow these steps to start the SQL Server Setup program:

   Insert the SQL Server CD into the CD drive. In a few seconds, the SQL Server Setup program will auto-start and display this screen (see Figure 4.10).

All examples are from NT Server

This example shows screens from installing SQL Server on NT Server only. Installing SQL Server on Windows 95/98 is very similar.

Microsoft Internet Explorer must be loaded

Before you can load SQL Server, you must have already loaded Microsoft Internet Explorer Version 4.10 or later.

A copy of Internet Explorer is provided on the SQL Server installation CD in case you don't already have a copy of it installed.

FIGURE 4.10
The SQL Server auto-start screen.

From this screen you have several options. To start SQL Server Setup, select Install SQL Server 7.0 Components. The next screen allows you to select which components you want to load (see Figure 4.11).

FIGURE 4.11
This screen allows you to choose which components you want to install at this time.

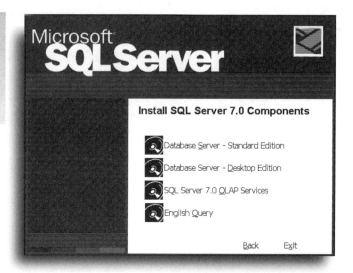

If you have NT Server's CD auto-start feature turned off, you can manually start the SQL Server Setup program. To do this, change to the root directory of the SQL Server installation CD and run the setup.bat program. This will open the first SQL Server setup screen.

4. If you are installing SQL Server from a network share point, change to the folder at the share point that contains SQL Server and run setup.bat.

5. From the Install SQL Server 7.0 Components screen, select Database Server—Standard Edition if you want to load SQL Server on NT, or choose Database Server—Desktop Edition if you want to load SQL Server on Windows 95/98.

6. Next is the Select Install Method screen (see Figure 4.12).

Normally, you will want to install SQL Server on the computer where you are currently located. If so, the default option of Local Install—Install to the Local Machine will

work for you. If you want to install SQL Server to a remote
computer, you can by choosing Remote Install—Install
to a Remote Machine. Once you have made your decision,
click Next.

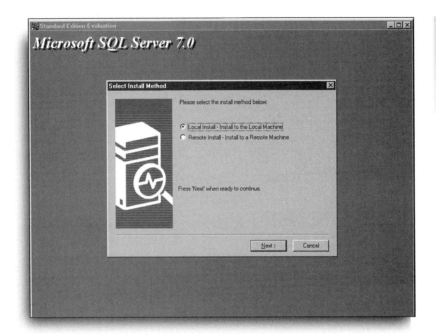

FIGURE 4.12
You must choose where
you want to install SQL
Server.

7. Next is the Welcome screen (see Figure 4.13). The SQL
   Server Setup program is a wizard that steps you through the
   entire setup process. To continue with the setup, click Next.

8. Next is the Software License Agreement screen. If you
   accept the agreement, click Yes to continue. You must select
   Yes if you want to install SQL Server.

9. Next is the User Information Screen. Here, enter your
   name and company nameAfter you have entered this information, click Next to continue.

10. Next is SQL Server Setup screen. Here, enter the 10 digit
    CD Key. This number is found on the yellow stick attached
    to your CD case. After you have entered the key, click Next
    to continue.

FIGURE 4.13
The Setup program
begins with this Welcome
screen.

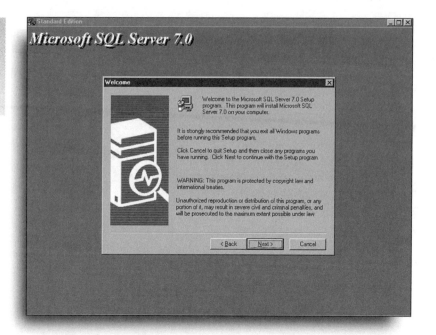

11. Next is the Setup Type Screen (see Figure 4.14). First, you
    must select whether you want to perform a Typical,
    Minimum, or Custom installation. You learned about these
    setup options earlier in the chapter. In this tutorial, you will
    take a look at the Custom installation as it provides the most
    flexibility when installing SQL Server. Click the radio but-
    ton next to Custom. Next on this screen you must decide
    where you want to place the SQL Server program and data
    files. You may install them in the same location, or separate
    locations. Use the Browse buttons to select a location other
    than the default locations suggested. Use the available space
    guidelines at the bottom of the screen to help select the
    most appropriate location. After you have completed this
    screen, click Next to continue.

12. Next is the Select Components Screen (see Figure 4.15).
    Here, you must choose those SQL Server components you
    want to load. Notice on the left side of the screen are the
    Components, and on the right side of the screen are the
    Sub-Components. First, you choose a component by

clicking inside the check box, and if applicable, you choose a subcomponent by clicking in a check box. As you choose the appropriate components for your installation, note that you can gauge the size of the installation by watching the available disk space at the bottom of the screen. After you have completed this screen, click Next to continue.

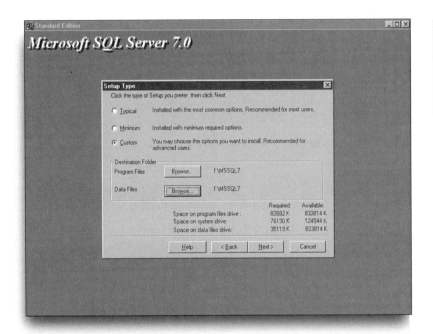

FIGURE 4.14
You must choose how you want to install SQL Server.

13. Next, the Character Set/Sort Order/Unicode Collation Screen appears (see Figure 4.16). You choose both the Character Set and Sort Order from the appropriate list box at the top of the screen. You choose the Unicode Collation from the list box at the bottom of the screen. You can also select the Unicode character sensitivity from the check boxes at the bottom of the screen. After you have completed this screen, click Next to continue.

14. Next, the Network Libraries screen appears (see Figure 4.17). For every Network Library you install, you must also enter some corresponding information. See the earlier section on Network Libraries for an explanation of how to complete this screen. Generally, the defaults will work fine. After completing this screen, click Next to continue.

FIGURE 4.15
You must select which SQL Server components and subcomponents you want to load.

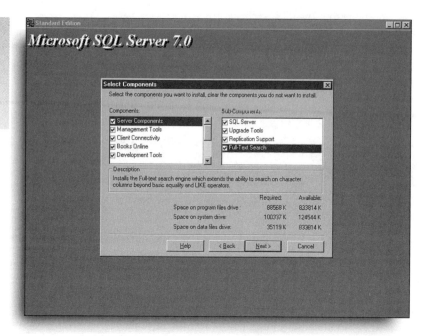

FIGURE 4.16
You must select the proper Character Set, Sort Order, and Unicode Collation

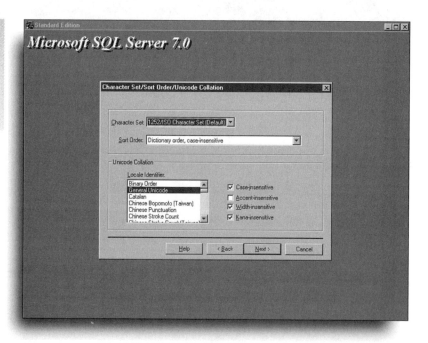

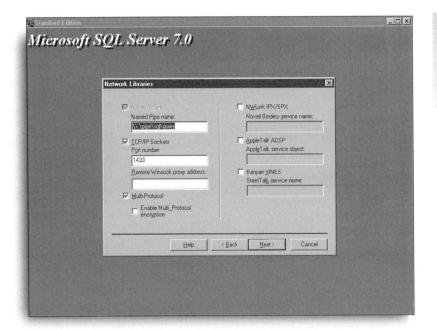

FIGURE 4.17
You must select one or more appropriate network libraries.

15. Next, the Services Accounts screen appears (see Figure 4.18). Here, you can specify that the same Service Account be used for all three SQL Server services, or you can enter a different Service Account for each of the three services. If you want to use the same Service Account for all the services, be sure to select Use the Same Account For All Services. Auto-start SQL Server Service. Then, you will want to select Use a Domain User account and then type in the name of the appropriate service account in the Username text box, enter the corresponding password in the Password text box, and the name of the NT Server domain where the account exists in the Domain text box.

If you want to use the Local System account instead of a domain user account for the service account, you can by selecting the Use the Local System account radio button. But if you choose this option, your SQL Server won't be able to communicate with any other SQL Servers.

If you want to use a different service account for each of the SQL Server services, you must select the Customize the

Settings For Each Service radio button, and then fill out the Service Settings for each separate service.

After you are finished entering your choices, click Next to continue.

FIGURE 4.18
You must decide on the service account you want to use for the SQL Server services.

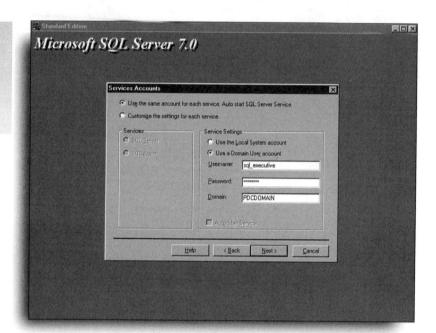

16. Next, the Choose Licensing Mode screen appears. You can choose from the Per Server or Per Set Modes, as was described earlier in this chapter. Select the appropriate mode, then click on Next to continue.

17. The Start Copying files screen now appears. Assuming you don't want to make any changes to the responses you have already made, click Next to begin copying the files to SQL Server. After about 10–15 minutes, depending on the speed of your computer, the installation will be complete.

18. The very last screen you will receive will be to prompt you to reboot your server, or to wait until later. Assuming you can reboot your server now without interruption to users, reboot your server now. After the computer reboots, SQL Server will have been installed and is now ready to run.

Congratulations, SQL Server is now installed. Unfortunately, your work isn't done yet. Although SQL Server is installed, you still need to perform some initial configuration before SQL Server is ready to perform any work. The next section describes the most basic steps that need to be performed before using SQL Server.

Post-Installation Issues

After SQL Server has been installed, there are several steps you need to complete before you can say that SQL Server is ready to run. Some of these steps are one-time steps you perform to ensure SQL Server was installed properly and to prepare SQL Server to run properly in the future. These steps are covered in this section. Other steps include configuring, tuning and optimizing, establishing login IDs and database user IDs, and of course creating new databases. These topics are covered later in this book.

This section focuses on these preliminary steps:

- Verifying SQL Server was installed correctly
- How to register SQL Server with SQL Enterprise Manager
- How to create Server Groups
- How to add a password to the SA account

You will want to perform these steps almost immediately after installing SQL Server.

Verifying That SQL Server Was Installed Correctly

After SQL Server is installed, you should take a few minutes to verify that SQL Server was installed and running properly. Use the steps described in the following sections to verify the installation.

Verify That the Program and Data Folders Were Created

Use NT's Explorer to verify that SQL Server's program files and data files were installed into the folders you specified when running the SQL Server Setup program.

Each folder should contain additional folders that match those listed earlier in this chapter. Check to see that all the subfolders in both the program and data folders are there.

You will also want to verify the contents of the /data subfolder that is under the data folder you specified. This is where SQL Server creates and stores a variety of default databases and transaction logs. The /data subfolder should include these files (see Figure 4.19):

- Distmdl.mdf and Distmdl.ldf (only found if optional replication objects were loaded)

- Northwnd.mdf and Northwnd.ldf

- Master.mdf and Mastlog.ldf

- Model.mdf and Modellog.ldf

- Msdbdata.mdf and Msdblog.ldf

- Pubs.mdf and Pubs_log.ldf

- Tempdb.mdb and Templog.ldf

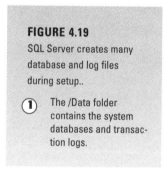

FIGURE 4.19

SQL Server creates many database and log files during setup..

① The /Data folder contains the system databases and transaction logs.

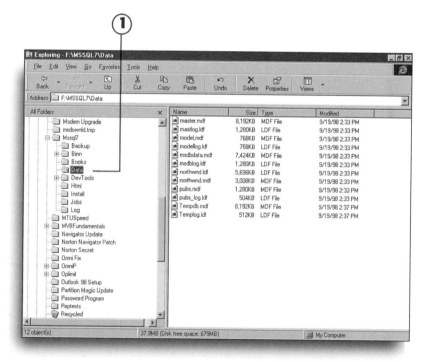

Verify That All the SQL Server Management Tools Are Loaded

Verify that all the SQL Server Management Tools you specified during setup were installed. The easiest way to verify this is to click Start, Programs, Microsoft SQL Server (Common). This will display a menu listing all the programs, utilities, and online documentation that you specified during setup.

Verify That the SQL Server Services Are Loaded and Running

When you installed SQL Server, its two main services—SQLServerAgent and MSSQLServer—were installed and set to automatically start (assuming you specified them to auto-start). When SQL Server is first installed, the two services aren't automatically started the first time until NT Server is rebooted.

Verifying that these two services were installed, and manually starting them for the first time

1. Start the NT Control Panel, and then double-click the Services icon. This displays the Services dialog box (see Figure 4.20).

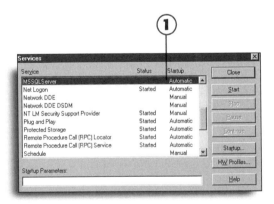

FIGURE 4.20

The SQL Servers can be verified by examining them through the Control Panel Services dialog box.

① Note that the MSSQLServer service is currently not started. The area below the Status is blank. The SQLServerAgent service cannot be seen from this figure. You must scroll down to see it.

2. Scroll down the list of services until you first see the MSSQLServer service (see Figure 4.20). If you have not rebooted since loading SQL Server, it should have a blank Status. And under Startup, it should have a setting of Automatic.

3. To manually start the service, click it once so that it is high-lighted, and then click the Start button. After about half a minute, the status will change to Started, and the service is now running.

4. Scroll down a little further and you should then see SQLServerAgent, and it should also have a blank Status and a Startup setting of Automatic.

5. To manually start the service, click it once so that it is high-lighted, and then click the Start button. After about 10–15 seconds, the status will change to Started, and the service is now running.

6. If everything is correct, you can exit the Services dialog box and the Control Panel.

What if the services aren't there? If the services aren't listed, your SQL Server installation failed miserably and you will have to start over, but this would be rare.

You might have noticed that under the Startup column was the word Manual instead of Automatic. If you are facing this situation, you probably forgot to choose the auto-start option when you installed SQL Server. This is easy to fix.

Choosing auto-start

1. One at a time, select each of the SQL Server services from the Services dialog box and click the Startup button. This displays the Service dialog box (see Figure 4.21).

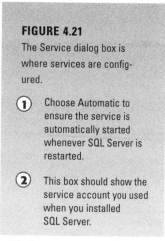
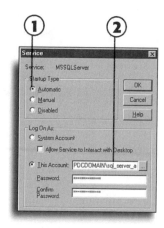

FIGURE 4.21
The Service dialog box is where services are configured.

① Choose Automatic to ensure the service is automatically started whenever SQL Server is restarted.

② This box should show the service account you used when you installed SQL Server.

2. In this box, select Automatic as the Startup type.

3. Click OK, and you'll be returned to the Services dialog box (refer to Figure 4.21).

4. Repeat steps 1–3 for the other SQL Server service.

5. The last step is to manually start the services as described earlier. If the services don't start as described, and if you get an error message, go to the troubleshooting section of this chapter for more guidance on how to resolve this problem.

Verify That You Can Log In to SQL Server

The last way you can verify that SQL Server has been installed properly is to try to log in and run a small query. If you can perform both of these steps successfully, you know SQL Server has been installed without any problems.

This section will demonstrate how to log in using the ISQL tool, which is the command-line–based program provided with SQL server used to run Transact-SQL commands. Although there are other SQL Server programs or utilities that you could use instead, this one is being recommended for this test because there is less that could go wrong when performing the test.

Load and log in to ISQL, and run a small query to verify that SQL Server is installed correctly

1. Go to NT's command prompt.

2. At the command prompt, type the following and press Enter:
   ```
   isql /Usa /P
   ```

3. If everything is working as it should be, the ISQL prompt should appear instead of the command prompt. It looks like this:
   ```
   1>
   ```

4. Type the following query to test whether SQL Server will respond. Press Enter after each line.
   ```
   select @@servername
   go
   ```

5. Assuming everything is working, the name of your server should be displayed at the ISQL prompt. The response should look *similar* (the server name and numbers will vary) to this:

```
-- -- -- -- -- -- -- -- -- --
PDC
 (1 row affected)
Network packet size (bytes): 4096
1 xact:
Clock Time (ms.): total = 321 avg = 321 (3.12 xact per
sec.)
1>
```

6. To exit the ISQL program, type exit at the ISQL prompt and press Enter, and you will be returned to NT's command prompt.

If everything worked as described, you know SQL Server has been installed properly and is working correctly. If you run into any problems or error messages, see the troubleshooting section later in this chapter.

Registering SQL Server

When you are confident that SQL Server is installed and working properly, the next step is to register it with SQL Enterprise Manager. SQL Enterprise Manager is the main program used to manage SQL Server. It has the capability to not only manage a local SQL Server, but also multiple SQL Servers connected anywhere to the same physical network. But before SQL Enterprise Manager is able to so this, you must tell SQL Enterprise Manager about the various SQL Servers you may have, and that is done through a process called registration. When a SQL Server is registered with a copy of SQL Enterprise Manager, that copy of SQL Enterprise Manager has the capability to manage that SQL Server, no matter where it is on the network.

Registration is a one-time process, although you can unregister and re-register any SQL Server from any copy of SQL Enterprise Manager as desired.

There are two ways to register a SQL Server using SQL Enterprise Manager, either manually, or through the

---

SQL Server might have to be registered multiple times

Copies of SQL Enterprise Manager might exist on the same physical server as SQL Server, or it can be loaded on to any NT-based computer. If you have a copy of SQL Enterprise Manager on your workstation, you will have to register all the SQL Servers you want to manage from your desktop. If you also want to manage your SQL Servers from a copy of SQL Enterprise Manager on another computer, you can, but you will also have to register all the servers with that copy of SQL Enterprise Manager as well, and so in, for every copy of SQL Enterprise Manager you have installed throughout your organization.

Registration Wizard. This section will take a look at both methods, starting with the Registration Wizard.

Registering a SQL Server Using the Registration Wizard

Before you try to register a SQL Server with SQL Enterprise Manager, be sure that SQL Server is installed and running properly. If it isn't, you will be unable to register it with SQL Enterprise Manager.

Registering a SQL Server with SQL Enterprise Manager for the first time

1. From the Microsoft SQL Server Program Group, start the SQL Server Enterprise Manager. This loads the Microsoft Management Console (MMC) (see Figure 4.22).

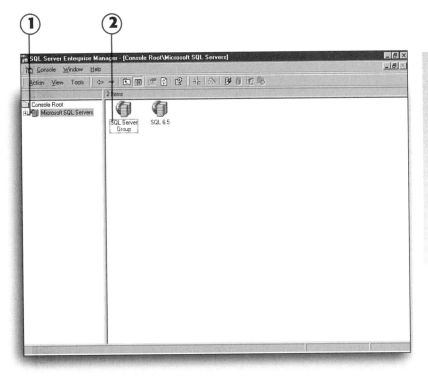

FIGURE 4.22

This shows SQL Enterprise Manager loaded into the MMC.

① The Console Root displays a tree of SQL Server groups and servers in the containers window.

② Currently, the default SQL Server Group is displayed in the contents window.

2. You are ready to start the Registration Wizard. To start the Wizard, right-click Microsoft SQL Servers, which is listed under the Console Root (see Figure 4.22). This displays several selections (see Figure 4.23), and you want to select Register SQL Server.

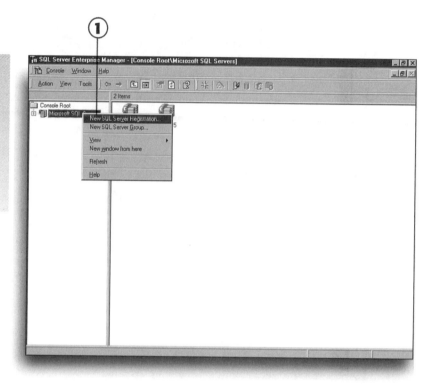

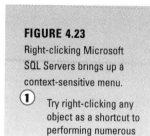

FIGURE 4.23

Right-clicking Microsoft SQL Servers brings up a context-sensitive menu.

① Try right-clicking any object as a shortcut to performing numerous tasks.

3. After selecting New SQL Server Registration, the first screen of the Registration Wizard appears (see Figure 4.24). Click Next to continue.

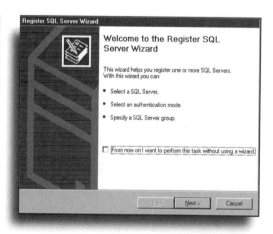

FIGURE 4.24

The Registration Wizard steps you through the process of registering a SQL Server with SQL Enterprise Manager.

4. Next, the wizard asks you to select which SQL Server you want to register (see Figure 4.25). The available SQL Servers appear on the left side of the screen. If your server isn't displayed, it might not be installed properly, or the two SQL Server services might not have been started. Assuming your server is displayed, click the server you want to register so that it is displayed in the Available servers box, and then click Add. This moves the SQL Server to the right side of the window under Added Servers. You can register more than one SQL Server at a time if you like.

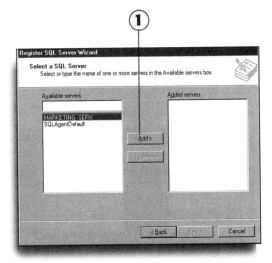

FIGURE 4.25

Select from the available servers those you want to register.

① To register the server, you must click Add. This moves the server from the Available servers box to the Added Servers box..

5. After you have added one or more SQL Servers to the Added Servers window, click Next, and you are asked which connection option you want to use to connect SQL Enterprise Manager to SQL Server (see Figure 4.26). You have two choices: Windows NT Authentication or SQL Server Authentication. If this is the first SQL Server installation in your organization, choose SQL Server Authentication for now; this can be changed later if you change your security mode. But if this isn't the first SQL Server to be installed, choose the security mode that your other SQL Servers are currently using. The following examples assume you have chosen SQL Server Security. After you have made your selection, click Next.

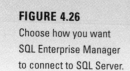

FIGURE 4.26

Choose how you want SQL Enterprise Manager to connect to SQL Server.

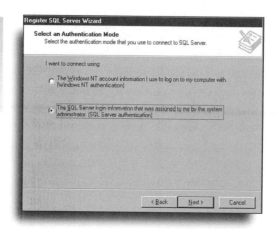

6. Next, the wizard wants you to choose whether SQL Enterprise Manager will remember your login name and password. The first option, Login Automatically Using My SQL Server Account Information, can be chosen if you want SQL Enterprise Manager to remember your login name and password. This way, every time you start SQL Enterprise Manager, you won't have to re-enter this same information over and over.

If you don't want SQL Enterprise Manager to remember your login name and password, choose the option Prompt for the SQL Server account information when connecting.

If you choose the first option, enter **SA** as the Login name, and use a blank for the Password. You must use this login name and password when you first register a new SQL Server because you have not yet assigned the SA account a password, nor have you created any other login names. Click Next to continue.

7. The next screen of the Registration Wizard (see Figure 4.28) lets you add a SQL Server to a server group. From the screen, you can add the SQL Server to the default SQL Server Group, you can create a new server group and add the SQL Server to it, or you can add the server to a pre-existing group (other than the default group). *Server groups* are used to group similarly used SQL Servers for

management purposes, and are completely optional. For
example, if you have many SQL Servers, you might put
some of them into the Marketing group, some in the
Production group, and others in the Accounting group. All
server groups do is enable you to group similar SQL Servers
for display in SQL Enterprise Manager, nothing more.
Select whichever option best meets your needs, and then
click Next to continue.

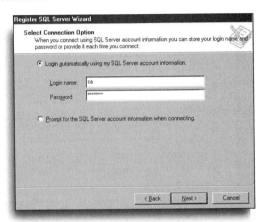

FIGURE 4.27
Enter your login ID
and password.

FIGURE 4.28
The Registration Wizard
enables you to add the
SQL Server to a server
group.

8. The Registration Wizard displays its final screen (see Figure
4.29). If you need to make any changes, you can by clicking
the Back button. Otherwise, if you are happy with your
choices, click Finish. The Register SQL Server dialog box

appears, and you should get a message where you are told that the registration was successful. If you get an error message, see the troubleshooting guidelines later in this chapter.

FIGURE 4.29

The final Registration Wizard screen.

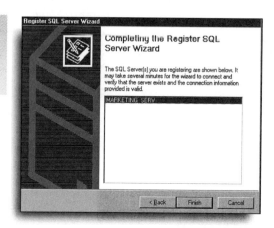

9. Click Close, and you are returned to the SQL Enterprise Manager. Under the Console Root, you will see the heading Microsoft SQL Servers. Click the plus sign next to this heading, and one or more SQL Server groups will be displayed under the heading. If you have not created any new server groups, the only one listed will be the default SQL Server Group. To view the newly registered SQL Server, click the plus sign next to the appropriate server group, and all the servers in this group will be displayed. If a SQL Server doesn't show up under one of the server groups, it has not been properly registered with SQL Enterprise Manager.

SEE ALSO

➤ *Windows NT Authentication or SQL Server Authentication are covered in detail in Chapter 11; see page 358.*

Registering SQL Server Manually

If you don't want to use the Registration Wizard to register a SQL Server, you don't have to.

Manually registering a SQL Server with SQL Enterprise Manager

1. The first step is to turn off the Registration Wizard. After it is turned off, then from this time on, you will be able to manually register any SQL Server with SQL Enterprise Manager. To turn the Registration Wizard off, you must first start it by right-clicking either the Microsoft SQL Server's heading, on any server group, or on any registered SQL Server, and then selecting the Register SQL Server option. This displays the first screen of the Registration Wizard.

2. To turn off the Registration Wizard, select the option on the wizard screen that says From Now on I Want to Perform This Task Without Using a Wizard, and then click Cancel. This will close the Registration Wizard and also prevent the Registration Wizard from running each time you register a SQL Server.

3. Now, to register a SQL Server with SQL Enterprise Manager manually, right-click either the Microsoft SQL Server's heading on any server group, or on any registered SQL Server, and then select the Register SQL Server option. This displays the Registered SQL Servers Property dialog box (see Figure 4.30).

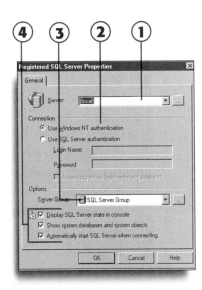

FIGURE 4.30
This property sheet is used to register a new SQL Server manually.

① Enter the SQL Server name here, or browse for it by clicking on the ... button.

② Select the appropriate type of authentication here.

③ Select which server group the SQL Server should join.

④ Normally, you will want to select all these options.

4. Complete this dialog box using the same type of information described earlier when the Registration Wizard was described. One difference between this dialog box and the information requested by the Registration Wizard is at the bottom of the box are these three options:

- Display SQL Server State in Console. If you choose this option, SQL Enterprise Manager regularly polls the MSSQLServer service to see if it is running, and displays a green light at the server icon in the console when it is running, and a red light if the service isn't running.

- Show System Databases and System Objects. If you choose this option, all system database and objects are displayed in the console. Otherwise they are not.

- Automatically Start SQL Server When Connecting. Assuming that the MSSQLServer isn't set to auto-start, this option can be used to automatically start this service when you first connect to this server.

By default, all three options are chosen now, and are automatically chosen when using the Registration Wizard. You can make any choice you deem appropriate. When you have completed the screen, you can register the server by clicking OK.

How to Edit a SQL Server's Registration Information

Sometimes you might need to edit a SQL Server's registration settings, such as when you change the login ID or password you originally used to register a SQL Server.

Make any changes to a registered server

1. From SQL Enterprise Manager, display the SQL Server whose registration you want to change.

2. Right-click the server's name and then select Edit SQL Server Registration from the menu. This displays the Registered SQL Server's Property box, which was shown in Figure 4.30.

3. Make any necessary changes. When finished, click OK to save the settings and return to SQL Enterprise Manager.

How to Unregister a SQL Server from SQL Enterprise Manager

From time to time you might need to unregister a SQL Server from SQL Enterprise Manager.

Unregistering a SQL Server from SQL Enterprise Manager

1. From SQL Enterprise Manager, display the SQL Server whose registration you want to remove.

2. Right-click the server's name that you want to unregister, and then select Delete SQL Server Registration from the menu.

3. A confirmation box appears, asking you to click Yes if you want to remove the SQL Server, or to click No to cancel this operation. Click Yes to unregister the SQL Server.

Managing SQL Server Groups

Although you can create new server groups from the Registration Wizard, or from the Registered SQL Server's dialog box, you can also create, rename, and delete server groups manually. You can also change a SQL Server from one group to another if you like.

Managing SQL Server groups

1. From SQL Enterprise Manager, click the plus sign next to the Microsoft SQL Servers heading. This displays all current server groups below it. Right-click the Microsoft SQL Server Heading, or any of the current server groups, and then select New SQL Server Group from the menu. This displays the Server Groups dialog box (see Figure 4.31).

FIGURE 4.31
Server groups can be added, renamed, and removed from this dialog box..

2. To create a new server group, enter the name of the new group in the Name box and click OK. This will automatically make this group a first-level server group. If you want, you can choose to create second-level groups by selecting the Sub-Group Of option. This enables you to make a new group a subgroup of any pre-existing group. In most cases, first-level server groups are more than adequate.

3. If you want to remove a server group, right-click the name of the server group you want to remove, and then select Delete from the menu. The group is removed immediately without warning.

Assigning a System Administrator Password

One of the first things you will want to do is add a password to the SA account. The SA has the capability to perform any function on SQL Server, and you want to prevent unauthorized users from logging on to the SQL Server.

Adding a password to the SA account

1. From SQL Enterprise Manager, open the folder that represents the SQL Server which needs its SA password changed, then open the security folder.

2. Click once on the Logins folder, and then on the right side of the console window, the currently available login IDs are displayed.

3. Right-click the SA login ID, and select Properties from the menu; the SA Properties dialog box appears (see Figure 4.32).

4. To add a password to the SA account, enter one in the box labeled Password. You will note that the password box is filled with asterisks. This means nothing, as there is currently no password for the SA login ID. Be sure you pick a password that isn't easy to guess.

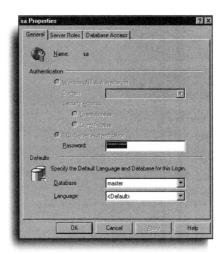

FIGURE 4.32
Login ID properties are changed here.

5. After you have added a password, click OK. This will save the password and close the dialog box. At this time you will need to go back to the registration for this SQL Server and edit it to indicate the new password for the SA account, assuming you used the SA account to register the server.

The rest of this Properties screen will be described later in the book.

At this point, SQL Server is working and is ready to be configured for whatever application you are using it for.

Troubleshooting a SQL Server Installation

If you carefully followed all the advice and instructions in this chapter, you should not experience any problems installing SQL Server. Almost any problems that you run into are because you left out a step, or made a mistake during the installation process. This section will look at some common installation problems and how to correct them.

How to Identify SQL Server Installation Problems

There are many different ways that you can learn that your SQL Server installation has gone awry. These include

- Error Messages. The most common feedback SQL Server will provide you with are error messages. Although the messages you receive might not always be accurate, the first assumption you should make when receiving an error message is that it is accurate and you need to get to the cause of it. Some messages are obvious, whereas others are very obscure. If you cannot determine from the message itself what the problem is, write the message down in its entirety and first look it up in SQL Server's Books Online. If you don't find the message there, try looking it up in Microsoft's TechNet (you have to be a subscriber to receive it) or on Microsoft's web site.

  If you can't find the error message, you will want to check out NT Server's Events Viewer (application log) for possible related messages, and you can check the SQL Server error logs, if there are any, for clues. The SQL Server error logs are located in the \log folder of the folder where SQL Server is installed. Find the file called Errorlog and open it with Notepad or WordPad. All the error logs are ASCII files and can be easily viewed with any text editor. SQL Server error logs are hard to interpret, but they might give you a clue to what has happened.

- Installation Not Verified. If you tried to verify the installation as described earlier in the chapter, and the problem appears to be something missing from the installation that should be there, you have two choices. Either you can run setup again over the current installation, or you can first delete the current bad installation, and then reinstall all over again.

Common Installation Problems and Their Solutions

The following sections describe some of the most common problems people run across when installing SQL Server.

Using the Wrong Version of NT Server

Using the incorrect version of NT Server, or are using an older Service Pack, can cause a wide variety of problems, many of them hard to diagnose. If the installation produces obscure error messages with any apparent reason, be sure to check that the version of NT Server you are using is appropriate. If you discover you have the wrong version, uninstall SQL Server, upgrade NT Server to an acceptable version, and then reload SQL Server.

File Open During Installation

During the installation process, SQL Server replaces some NT Server files. If any of these files happen to be open during installation, they can cause a critical error message to be displayed onscreen. This is why it is important for no other programs to be running when SQL Server is installed. If you do discover that you have one or more NT utilities open that might be causing the problem, close them, and then click the Retry button displayed by the message. If this doesn't work, you might have to abort the SQL Server install and try again, this time without any programs running.

MSSQLServer or SQLServerAgent Will Not Start

This is probably the most common problem faced when installing SQL Server. Follow these steps to help you narrow down the possible cause of this problem:

- Have you created a service account as described earlier in this chapter?
- Was the service account properly created, with administrative rights and the other advanced user rights that are required?
- Was the service account created in the proper NT accounts domain?
- Was the service account entered properly when requested during the installation process? Did you accidentally use your NT logon account as the service account?
- Have you made any typos?

If you cannot figure out the problem, delete the service account you created and create a new one, carefully following the advice provided in this chapter. Then go to the Control Panel, where the services are, and be sure you have selected the service account for both services, along with specifying the correct passwords. More often than not, the mistake is a simple one that is easily corrected.

SEE ALSO

➤ *For more information on troubleshooting SQL Server, see page 599.*

How to Remove SQL Server

Removing SQL Server from a physical server

1. Be sure you have either transferred or backed up any data stored in any databases on the SQL Server you are about to remove.

2. Run the SQL Server Setup program. It will detect that SQL Server is currently loaded on the server, and will give you the opportunity to remove SQL Server. The first screen that appears is the SQL Server welcome screen. Click Next to continue.

3. The next screen wants to know which computer has the copy of SQL Server you want to remove. By default, the current SQL Server is selected. Click Next to continue.

4. The next screen wants to know what you want to do. Select the option Work With Existing SQL Server. Click Next to continue.

5. The next screen offers a variety of options. To remove SQL Server, choose the Remove SQL Server option, and select Next. You will receive a confirmation message. Select Yes to remove SQL Server. SQL Server will then remove itself from your server.

chapter

5

Installing SQL Client Utilities

Management tools require proper permissions

Only a user who has been assigned appropriate permissions is allowed to use any of the Management Tools. Because of this, you will only want to load this software on workstations where the users will have the proper permissions.

What Are the SQL Server Management Tools?

Once SQL Server has been installed, it is time to think about loading the SQL Server Management Tools on workstations that will be used to remotely administer SQL Server. You may also want to load the Management Tools on SQL Server developer workstations as well.

The SQL Server Management Tools are the same Management Tools you were given a chance to load when you installed SQL Server. The advantage of loading the Management Tools on other workstations is that you have the ability to remotely manage any SQL Server from virtually any computer, not just from the physical server SQL Server is running on.

The SQL Server Management Tools can be loaded onto NT Server, NT Workstation, and Windows 95/98 desktops. Unlike some of the Management Tools included with SQL Server 6.5, SQL Server 7.0 Management Tools cannot be run under Windows 3.x or DOS.

This chapter describes the Management Tools, shows you how to install them, and provides detailed information on how to use the SQL Server Client Configuration Utility, which is used to configure SQL Server Management Tools after they have been installed onto a workstation.

SQL Server Management Tools

SQL Server includes a wide variety of client-based administrative tools that can be used to manage SQL Server. During the installation process, you can load as few or as many of the Management Tools as you think you need. SQL Server provides you with these options:

- **SQL Server Enterprise Manager:** If you want to remotely manage SQL Server, then installing the SQL Server Enterprise Manager onto your workstation is necessary. This program allows the DBA to perform virtually any SQL Server administrative task.

- **SQL Server Profiler:** This tool is used to monitor and record SQL Server database activity between SQL Server and clients. Only load this tool on workstations that perform this task.

- **SQL Server Query Analyzer:** This tool is used to manually send Transact-SQL statements and stored procedures to the SQL Server database engine. You will probably want to load this on most, if not all remote management workstations. This is a tool you may want to load onto SQL Server developer's desktops, as it gives developers direct access to SQL Server so they can run interactive Transact-SQL statements and SQL scripts.

- **Client Diagnostic Utilities:** This tool is used to verify which DB-Library is installed on a client, and to configure the Management Tools to communicate with SQL Server over a network. It also installs the *makepipe* and *readpipe* programs which are used to test whether or not if the Named Pipes IPC is working properly between SQL Server and a client. Generally, you will want to load this onto any client that uses any of the SQL Server Management Tools. This tool is described in depth later in this chapter, in the section titled, "How to Use the Client Diagnostic Utilities."

SEE ALSO

➤ *For more information on makepipe and readpipe, see page 241.*

- **MS DTC Client Support:** The Microsoft Distributed Transaction Coordinator (DTC) tool provides DTC client support. It only needs to be loaded onto clients that run a SQL Server application that requires it.

- **Development Files:** These are files needed by OLE DB developers to create programs using ODBC, DB-Library, ODS, SQL-DMO, Embedded SQL for C, and MS DTC. Generally, only SQL Server developers will want these files.

- **Sample Files:** These are sample files designed for developers to view and learn from. As with the development files, only SQL Server developers will want these files.

Enterprise Manager is part of the Microsoft Management Console

As part of Microsoft's effort to make administrative tasks as easy as possible, Enterprise Manager is now a part of Microsoft's Management Console (MMC). The MMC is a shell program that contains plug-in programs, such as Enterprise Manager. The MMC defines a new standard user interface and can run multiple plug-in programs simultaneously. For example, you can manage both SQL Server 7.0, SNA Server 4.0, and Internet Information Server 4.0 all from the same MMC. These means you don't have to switch between programs to manage your network software.

173

- **Replication Conflict Resolution Tool**: Used to help resolve replication conflicts between two SQL Servers. You will only need this tool if you are implementing replication on your SQL Servers.

No matter which of the above options you decide to load, the following utilities and files are automatically loaded. They include bcp, isql, osql, ODBC, and DB-Library.

SEE ALSO

➤ *For more information on bcp, see page 520.*
➤ *For more information on isql and osql, see page 236.*

Choosing Online Documentation to Install on Clients

During the client install process, you will also be asked if you want to install the online documentation onto the client. You can choose to load any of these online documentation options:

- **Books Online:** This is the massive and comprehensive documentation of SQL Server, and is a must for virtually every client, whether the client is a SQL Server management or a developer's workstation. It will take about 11MB of disk space, but it is worth it. If you don't want to take up this much space on the client, you can always install the Books Online onto a network share point and then connect to it whenever necessary. You also have the option to run it from a locally installed CD player.

Management Tool Hardware and Software Requirements

Just as you need the right hardware and software to install SQL Server, you also need the right hardware and software to install the SQL Server Management Tools. This section takes a look at the minimum *and* recommended hardware and software.

Hardware Requirements

If your client is running NT Server or NT Workstation, make sure that all of the hardware is on Microsoft's NT Hardware Compatibility (HCL) list. If your client is running under Windows 95/98, make sure that all the hardware is on the appropriate Windows' HCL. Hardware requirements include:

- **CPU:** Minimum requirements include an Alpha AXP or an Intel 32-bit (80486) processor. Recommended is an Intel Pentium-based system running at 200MHz or higher.

- **RAM:** Minimum requirement is 32MB. Recommended is 32MB or more for Windows 95/98, or 64MB or more under NT Server or Workstation.

- **Display and Graphics Adapter:** Any display and graphics adapter on the HCLs will work. Recommended is at least a 15" display with at least 1,024 × 768 resolution.

- **Disk Space:** The minimum requirement for installing all of the Management Tools is about 73MB. Since you will probably not be loading all of the options, you should be able to get by with less.

- **CD-ROM Drive:** Only required if installing the Management Tools from CD.

- **Network Interface Card:** Any operating system compatible card will work. Recommended is a dedicated switched 10Mbit or 100Mbit card if you are accessing one or more SQL Servers heavily from the remote workstation.

Software Requirements

Will SQL Server run on NT 5.0?

Of course. Whenever Windows 2000 is released, SQL Server 7.0 will run on it with no problems.

The software requirements for the SQL Server Management Tools include two components: the desktop operating system and the network software.

- **Desktop Operating System:** The minimum requirement is either NT Server 4.0 or NT Workstation 4.0 (Service Pack 4), or Windows 95 or Windows 98. It is recommended to always use the latest *service pack* for all of these operating systems.

- **Network Operating System:** SQL Server Management Tools run under the same network operating systems as SQL Server, which include NT Server, Novell, Banyan, and Apple.

How do I create a network share point?

1. Select an NT Server where you want to create the share point.

2. Create a folder on the NT Server using Explorer.

3. Copy the Management Tools from the SQL Server distribution CD to the newly created folder.

4. Share the folder using Explorer.

5. Set the permissions on the shared folder to "Read" for all SQL Server administrators, and "No Access" for all other users.

Where to Install the Management Tools From

SQL Server Management Tools can be installed from three locations:

- **SQL Server Distribution CD:** The Management Tools can be loaded directly from the distribution CD by running the SQL Server Setup program. This is the same program used to install SQL Server.

- **Network Share Point:** The most flexible way to install the Management Tools is to install them from a SQL Server share point on your network. Starting the Management Tool installation process is done by running setup.bat, the same program used to install SQL Server. If you intend to load many copies of the Management Tools onto desktops, this is the most efficient way.

- **Remotely From Most Desktops:** The SQL Server Management Tools can be loaded from virtually any desktop that has access to the SQL Server source files (either from CD or a network share point). Once the setup process is started on the workstation, you are given the option to remotely install the Management Tools from the current workstation, whether or not it already has a copy of the Management Tools on it. This option will be discussed in more detail later in this chapter.

Microsoft currently does not formally support the installation of the Client Tools using Systems Management Server (SMS). But this does not preclude you from installing them using SMS. All it means is that you will have to create your own installation scripts to perform the installation. This, of course, is best left up to an SMS expert, not the average DBA.

How to Install the SQL Server Management Tools

Installing the SQL Server Management Tools is a simple process. In fact, the steps required to load the Management Tools are a subset of the steps required to load SQL Server. This means you are already familiar with the process. Here are the steps required to load the SQL Server Management Tools onto a workstation:

How to Install the SQL Server Management Tools

1. If you are installing the Management Tools onto NT Server or Workstation, logon with an account that has NT Server administrative rights. If you are installing the Management Tools onto a Windows 95/98 desktop, you can logon using any legal user account.

2. Be sure there are no other programs running before you begin the installation process. If there are, exit them before continuing. Also, check to see if there are any old versions of any SQL Server Management Tools on the workstation. If there are, you will want to remove them before loading the new version.

3. If you are installing SQL Server from a CD, follow these steps to start the SQL Server Setup program:

Installation under NT Server demonstrated here

The screens used in this tutorial were taken from an installation onto NT Server. Installing the Management Tools under NT Workstation and Windows 95/98 is almost identical. You should have no problem loading it using these same instructions, although some of the screens may look slightly different.

Insert the SQL Server CD into the CD drive. In a few seconds, the SQL Server Setup program will auto-start and display this screen (see Figure 5.1).

From this screen you have several options. Click on "Install SQL Server 7.0 Components" option.

4. In the next screen (see Figure 5.2) you must select which SQL Server 7.0 components you want to load. Click on "Standard Edition" or "Desktop Edition"

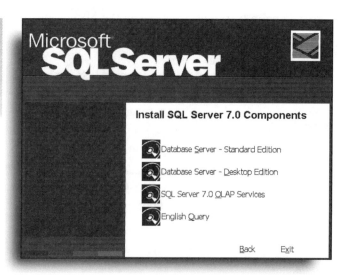

5. In the next screen (see Figure 5.3) you must select where you want to install the tools

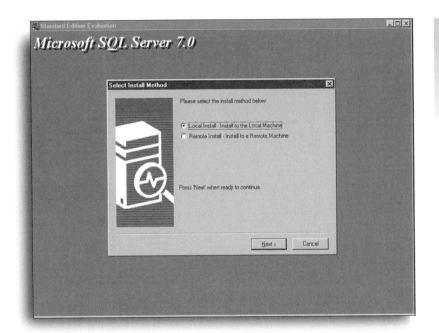

6. After finally going through all of the introductory screens, the first actual SQL Server setup screen is displayed (see Figure 5.4).

If you have NT Server's CD auto-start feature turned off, you can manually start the SQL Server Setup program. To do this, change to the root folder on the SQL Server, then run setup.bat.

If you are installing SQL Server from a network share point, change to the folder at the network share point that contains SQL Server, then run setup.bat.

7. The SQL Server Setup program is a wizard that steps you through the entire SQL Server setup process. Although this is the same procedure you used to load SQL Server, you will not repeat all the same steps. In this case, you will only be loading the SQL Server Management Tools.

FIGURE 5.4

This is the beginning SQL Server Setup screen

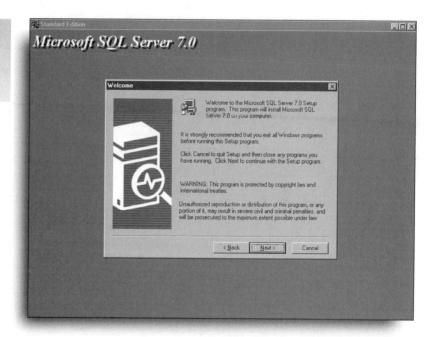

At the bottom of the first screen you have the option of canceling the setup process at any time, and you have the ability to go back and forth, from step to step, by clicking on the Next and Back buttons (The Back button will not appear until a later screen). To continue with the setup, click on the Next button.

8. The next screen (see Figure 5.5) is the Microsoft License Agreement. Click on Yes to proceed.

9. In the next screens (see Figure 5.6 and Figure 5.7) you must enter your name, company name, and serial number. Click Next
to proceed.

10. The next screen we must deal with is the Setup Type screen (see Figure 5.8). In order to install the administrative tools, you must click the radio button next to "Custom." Before you proceed, check that the destination folders are correct. If not, you can change them by clicking on the appropriate Browse button. Also check to ensure you have plenty of space available on your computer's hard disk to install the management tools. When you are ready, click the Next button.

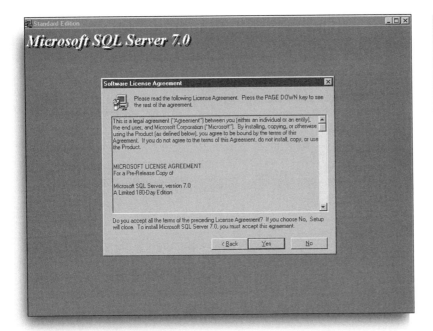

FIGURE 5.5
You must accept the
Microsoft License before
you can proceed.

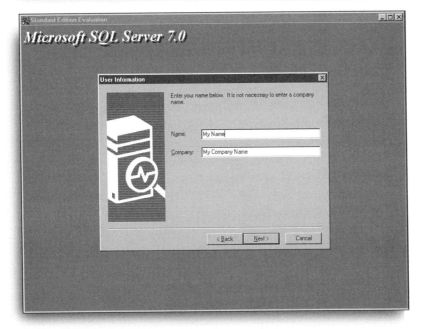

FIGURE 5.6
You must enter your
user information.

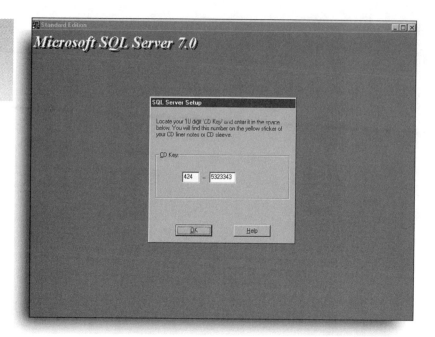

FIGURE 5.7
You must enter the CD-Key.

11. In the Select Components screen (see Figure 5.9), you must select which components you want to load and deselect the components you don't want to load. Generally, you will want to place a checkmark next to Management Tools, Client Connectivity (required), and Books Online (optional). If you highlight the Management Tools option, the sub-components are displayed in the Sub-Components window. Here, you can select which of the many management tools you want to load. Select only those you need. After you have selected all the components you need, once again verify that you have enough disk space to load them. When you are done with your selections, click Next.

12. Finally, you are done answering questions and have arrived at the last screen. Assuming you are satisfied with your selections, click the Next button to begin installing the management tools.

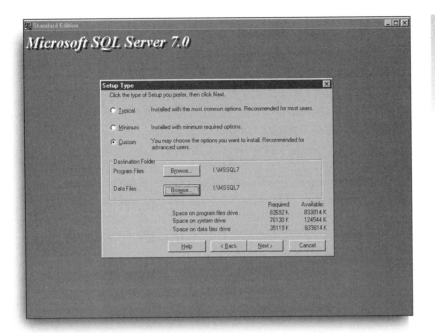

FIGURE 5.8
You select which components you want to load from this screen.

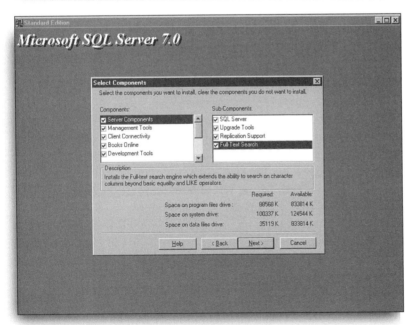

FIGURE 5.9
You choose which administrative tools you want to load from this screen.

ODBC drivers are automatically updated

Whenever the SQL Server setup program is used to install the Management Tools onto an NT or Windows 95/98 client, the current SQL ODBC drivers will be updated if there is not already a newer version installed. This allows clients that use ODBC to access SQL Server 7.0 to function correctly.

After clicking the <u>N</u>ext button, the files you specified are copied to your computer. When the installation process is done, you will be returned to one of the original setup screens (refer to Figure 5.2). To exit this screen, click Exit.

Once the Management Tools have been loaded, you can verify that they work by going to the workstation's Start Menu and then selecting <u>P</u>rograms. There, you should see the Microsoft SQL Server menu option, where most of the Management Tools can be started. To verify that the tools work properly, chose one and run it, seeing if you can connect to a remote SQL Server. Of course, you will have to have a legal account and the necessary permissions on SQL Server for this test to work. If you can make a connection to a SQL Server, then you know the tools have been installed successfully.

In most cases, once you have installed the Management Tools, you should be able to use them immediately without any additional configuration. But if your network is not a pure Microsoft Windows network, then you may have to change some configuration options using the SQL Server Client Configuration Utility, which is discussed in the next section.

How to Use the Client Configuration Utility

The SQL Server Client Configuration Utility is used to configure Management Tools so they can successfully communicate with a SQL Server. In most cases, you should not have to run this program because the defaults that were used when the Management Tools were loaded will work for most workstation configurations. But if you find out that your client software will not communicate with SQL Server, then you can use this utility to properly configure the client software so it can communicate with SQL Server.

This section is divided into four parts. The first part describes how to load the Client Configuration Utility. The last three parts describe the various options available on each of the three screens that make up the configuration utility.

How to Start the Client Configuration Utility

In most cases, you will have installed the Client Configuration Utility when you installed the other Management Tools onto a workstation. If you did not load this utility, you must load it following the steps described above. Once the Client Configuration Utility has been installed, you can start it by following these steps:

Starting the Client Configuration Utility

1. Log onto the workstation using an account with the appropriate permissions.

2. To load the Client Configuration Utility, click on the Start button, then click on <u>P</u>rograms, then click on Microsoft SQL Server 7.0, then click on Client Network Utility.

3. Next, the Microsoft SQL Server Client Configuration dialog box appears (see Figure 5.10). This utility includes three tabs that separate each of the three main options. They include the General, Network Libraries, and DB Library Options tabs. Each of the three tabs are described in the following sections.

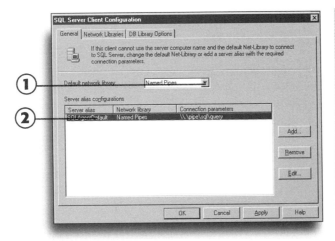

FIGURE 5.10

The Client Configuration dialog box.

(1) Use this list box to select which default Net-Library you want this client to use.

(2) The Network protocol configurations box is reserved for handling special exceptions and is rarely used.

General

The General tab (see Figure 5.10) has two sections. At the top portion of the screen you are able to specify which Net-Library you want to use as the default network protocol for this workstation. The second part of the screen is used to specify optional network protocol configurations.

As you may remember when you installed SQL Server, you had to specify one or more Net-Libraries to load. This is the software used to make a network connection between SQL Server and client software. While you can load and run more than one Net-Library at a SQL Server, only one Net-Library can be loaded and active in a client at a time. In order for a client to communicate over a network with SQL Server, both must be running the same Net-Library, otherwise they cannot communicate.

SEE ALSO

➤ *For more information on Net-Libraries, see page 126.*

By default, the Net-Library installed for the Management Tools when it is installed onto Windows NT is Named Pipes. If you are installing the Management Tools onto a Windows 95/98 workstation, the default Net-Library is TCP/IP.

Assuming that default Net-Library installed on the Workstation matches one of the Net-Libraries on the SQL Server you want to communicate with, then the Management Tools will be able to communicate with SQL Server without any changes. But if there is no match, then you will have to select a Net-Library at the client that matches one of the Net-Libraries running at SQL Server. Or you must add the appropriate Net-Library on the SQL Server so the Management Tools can communicate with SQL Server. Either way works fine, but it is generally easier to add them to the SQL Server than to the workstations.

If you need to change the default network protocol for a workstation, you can by selecting the appropriate protocol from the Default network library list box.

Security mode is affected by the Net-Library choice

If you intend to use the NT Authentication mode of security in SQL Server, then the client must run either the Named Pipes, Multi-Protocol Net-Libraries, or TCP/IP.

The Server Alias Configurations part of the General tab screen is only used for special cases. It is only used if you run into any of these situations:

- The Management Tools are on a workstation running Windows NT connecting to a SQL Server running under Windows 95.
- You need to add a unique network protocol configuration for communications between a specific SQL Server and a workstation running the Management Tools.
- The SQL Server that you want to communicate with from a workstation running the Management Tools listens on a non-standard port.

Generally, you will not need this option.

Network Libraries

The Network Libraries tab is used solely to display which Network Libraries that are currently installed on the workstation and to let you know their version number. See Figure 5.11.

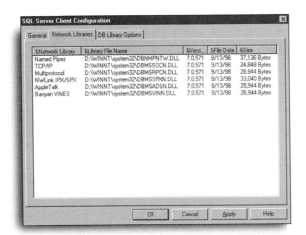

Configuring a custom network protocol

If you ever need to learn how to configure a custom network protocol for a workstation, search for "Setting Up Network Protocol Configurations" in the SQL Server Books Online.

FIGURE 5.11

This tab only shows which Network Libraries are currently installed.

This tab is often helpful during troubleshooting to see if the Network Library being used by the Management Tools is the most recent version or not.

DB-Library Options

The main purpose of the DB-Library tab (see Figure 5.12) is for you to determine whether or not you have the most current version of the DB-Library files installed on the client.

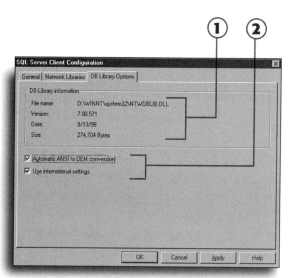

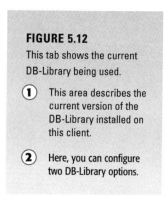

FIGURE 5.12

This tab shows the current DB-Library being used.

(1) This area describes the current version of the DB-Library installed on this client.

(2) Here, you can configure two DB-Library options.

Another part of the DB Library Options tab is the two check boxes that can be used to configure how the DB-Library communicates with SQL Server. Here is what they do:

- **Automatic ANSI to OEM:** When this option is selected, it tells DB-Library to convert characters from the OEM (original equipment manufacturer) to ANSI format when communicating from the client to SQL Server, and to convert characters from ANSI to OEM when communicating from SQL Server to the client. This option is often required because the character set used by SQL Server is different from the one used by the client operating system. This option automatically makes the proper translation of character sets.

This setting should be selected if the client is running Windows NT or Windows 95/98. If a Windows 3.x client is being used, this option should not be selected.

- **Use International Settings:** When this option is selected, it allows DB-Library to get the date, time, and currency format settings from the local operating system rather use hard-coded setting. This option should be selected if the client is running Windows NT or Windows 95/98.

Troubleshooting a Management Tools Installation

As long as you follow the instructions, you should rarely have any difficulty installing the SQL Server Management Tools. If you do, follow these guidelines to help resolve the problem.

How to Diagnose the Problem?

After the Management Tools have been installed, try them out. If you can make a successful connection to a SQL Server, then everything is working as it should. If you cannot make a connection, you will probably be presented with an error message. Use this error message as your guide to what you should do next. At the same time, if you are running Windows NT, check the Event Viewer for any related messages.

If the error message is obvious, then take the necessary steps to correct the problem. If the message is not obvious, look it up in the SQL Server Books Online on one of the SQL Server's already installed in your organization. If the message is not listed there, then look it up in Microsoft's TechNet (available by subscription from Microsoft) or on Microsoft's WWW site.

How to Resolve the Problem

If you cannot determine what the problem is from the error message, or you did not receive an error message, then try the following steps to resolve the problem:

Un-installing Management tools in troubleshooting

1. Remove the Management Tools from the client by using the Control Panel Add/Remove Program icon.

2. Be sure that any older versions of the Management Tools have been removed from the client.

3. Reboot the computer.

4. Reinstall the Management Tools following the instructions exactly as described above.

5. Check to see if you can now access a SQL Server using one of the Management Tools.

If you are still having a problem, first determine if the Management Tools are acting any differently than they did the first time you loaded them. If they are, then note the differences (such as new error messages) and take appropriate action. If the same problem repeats itself after reloading the Management Tools, and you have exhausted all error messages and their causes, it's time to get outside help.

SEE ALSO

➤ *For more information on troubleshooting SQL Server, see page 599.*

6

Upgrading SQL Server From 6.5 to 7.0

Plan a strategy for your upgrade

Anticipate problems and learn how to avoid them

Follow the step-by-step guide to upgrading

Many users of Microsoft SQL Server 6.5 have looked forward to the long-awaited (and often delayed) release of the SQL Server 7.0 product. However, if you're like many DBAs, you're dreading the possible problems that can stem from an upgrade at least as much as you're looking forward to finding out what you can do once you get the product installed. This chapter walks you through both the planning stage of an upgrade and the actual upgrade using SQL Server's innovative and time-saving wizard. But, to help minimize problems and data loss, you'll also find some advice on how to resolve upgrade issues before you dive in.

Developing an Upgrade Strategy and Plan

Upgrading SQL Server

As you begin to examine upgrade plans for SQL Server 6.x to 7.0, it should be pointed out that although the two systems cannot run simultaneously on the same machine, they can exist on the same machine. You can switch between the two during the upgrade process (assuming you have enough disk space to keep a live copy of your 6.5 databases).

The plan and strategy for an upgrade is different from the plan and strategy for a new installation. In an upgrade, you have already decided on a platform and are currently running SQL Server. You may have many large production databases and hundreds of users that depend on the databases, or you may have small development databases with a few users. In many ways, upgrading an existing SQL Server is more critical than installing a new SQL Server. The existing SQL Server contains data being used and depended on by your organization.

With your organization depending on these databases, it is easy to see why it is important to develop a plan that enables you to upgrade to the new release with the least amount of risk. If the upgrade is not successful, your plan should allow you to return the system to its pre-upgrade state.

First Rule of Upgrading

Never underestimate the difficulty of an upgrade. Remember the first rule of upgrading: *Expect something to go wrong*; when it does, make sure that you can get the system back and running to its previous state. Creating an upgrade plan is essential. I was once involved with what was to be a simple upgrade for a banking organization that gave me a six-hour window to get their high-powered SQL Server multiprocessor upgraded from SQL Server

4.21 to SQL Server 4.21a. No problem, right? After all, the upgrade was not even a major revision number—just a revision letter. Nothing could go wrong...NOT! Five hours later, when the SQL Server was still not working correctly and tech support was trying to resolve the problem, we opted to restore the system to the pre-upgrade state. After the SQL Server was restored, it did not work either! It appears that the problem had to do with the SQL Server registry entries. This was not a problem because our upgrade plan called for backing up the system registry. After the registry was restored, the SQL Server was up and running with no problems, and the upgrade was pushed off to another day, awaiting information from tech support.

The moral of this story is never underestimate the potential problems that might be encountered during an upgrade, and be overly cautious. It's better to have too many files backed up and ready to restore than not enough.

The Word Is Out—SQL Server 7.0 Version Upgrade Wizard

The database upgrade process for SQL Server 7.0 is unique compared to previous versions and upgrades. In previous versions, SQL Server applied whatever changes were necessary to the existing databases as well as upgraded the code and registry settings. As stated earlier, SQL Server 7.0 made many fundamental changes to the SQL Server storage engine including increasing the size of a data page from 2KB to 8KB. The net result of all the changes (improvements) to SQL Server 7.0 prevents the previous 6.x databases from being upgraded. Instead, the upgrade process involves installing SQL Server 7.0, and then using the Version Upgrade Wizard to import the existing 6.x databases into SQL Server 7.0. Also, unlike previous releases of SQL Server, Microsoft leaked information to the public during the development cycle and held several seminars openly talking about SQL Server 7.0 and the upgrade process. The SQL Server 7.0 upgrade process via the Version Upgrade Wizard has not been very popular with some of the press (early reviews). The complaints do not stem from the difficulty of the task or from problems encountered during upgrades. The real fear seems to be that existing databases cannot be upgraded in place, but must be exported into new 7.0 databases, increasing the amounts of disk space required to keep live copies of SQL Server 6.5 databases around. However, Microsoft knew that an upgrade process that did not upgrade the existing databases would immediately cause a lot of anxiety to the existing customer base. So, Microsoft needed the upgrade to be bullet proof and simple. One sure way to bullet proof the process is to test as many databases as possible with the Version Upgrade Wizard. Microsoft did just that. Microsoft set out to upgrade several hundred databases to find and correct any problems. They also encouraged many of their partners to upgrade databases in what amounted to an impressive programming and testing effort. So after all this testing, the one draw back the Version Upgrade Wizard has is the disk space requirements if you want to keep copies of the 6.5 databases around and don't have a new box or enough disk space on your current machine. In all fairness, Microsoft has tried to do all they can to ease the pain by enabling you to use drives located on your machine, network drives, direct pipeline, or tape.

The Version Upgrade Wizard was designed for ease of use, performance, and fault tolerance. The Version Upgrade Wizard is not a souped-up version of the 6.x Transfer Manager or BCP. As a matter of fact, the data transfer is not performed with BCP but OLE DB. Upgraded databases are defaulted to 6.x compatibility mode, which is good news for those of you concerned about key words or changes in ANSI SQL. Following are some highlights of the Version Upgrade Wizard:

- Easy to use wizard
- Performs fast data transfer mechanism (NOT BCP or Transfer Manager)
- Maintains 6.x compatibility (can be changed to 7.0 after the upgrade)
- Gets customers quickly to SQL Server 7.0
- Stop and Go capabilities

- Ensures data integrity
- Converts all databases or select individual databases for upgrading

Even if the wizard works great though, still execute a well-planned backup plan with a fall back strategy.

When upgrading an existing SQL Server 6.x to SQL Server 7.0, you have two options available:

- Upgrade the existing SQL Server (single computer)
- Install a new SQL Server and use the Version Upgrade Wizard to migrate the databases to the new server (two computers)

SEE ALSO

➤ *For more information on developing a back-up strategy, see page 455.*

Upgrade the Existing SQL Server (Single Computer)

If you are upgrading an existing SQL Server 6.x installation to SQL Server 7.0 on the same machine, SQL Server 7.0 will be installed on the machine along with SQL Server 6.5. The two versions cannot run simultaneously; however you can easily toggle between the two systems. You use the SQL Server 7.0 Version Upgrade Wizard to export your 6.5 databases to disk, tape, or network drives and then import them into SQL Server 7.0.

Installing a New SQL Server 7.0 Computer to Migrate Existing 6.x Databases (Two Computers)

In this upgrade process, you are dealing with two machines. Because you are not installing SQL Server 7.0 on the same machine as SQL Server 6.5, you are in a good upgrade position. You can migrate all your databases at once or a few at a time. You and your users will have access to the 7.0 server and the 6.x server after the upgrade process because the 7.0 and 6.5 servers are on different computers.

SEE ALSO

➤ *For more information on hardware requirements, see page 112.*

Advantages of using the Upgrade Wizard

I think the Version Upgrade Wizard opens up upgrade possibilities that were not available in previous versions. For instance, if you are in an organization that is thrifty, you may not have an available NT test server to load the latest release of SQL Server, upgrade your databases, and test your applications. Instead you are required to upgrade the production server and hope and pray the existing applications work without a hitch. With SQL Server 7.0, if you don't have a test server, find yourself a hefty client workstation running Windows NT Workstation or NT Server and install SQL Server 7.0 on the desktop. Use the Version Upgrade Wizard to bring over your production databases and test them locally. When everything checks out, you can confidently upgrade the production server. If you find a problem, you can correct it prior to upgrading the production server.

Unsupported upgrades

Upgrades from SQL Server version 4.2x systems are not supported in SQL Server 7.0. These 4.2x systems must first be upgraded to SQL Server 6.5.

General Version Upgrade Wizard Information

If you have two computers, you can access both databases after the upgrade process has ended. When upgrading on a single machine, the state of your SQL Server 6.5, after the SQL Server 7.0 Version Upgrade Wizard completes, depends on the method selected to transfer the databases. If you have enough disk space on your server to install SQL Server 7.0 without removing SQL Server 6.x's data devices, you can use a direct pipeline to transfer the data. The direct pipeline approach is the best approach to take when performing an upgrade. The direct pipeline approach transfers the data and objects in memory from SQL Server 6.x to SQL Server 7.0, leaving the SQL Server 6.x intact. The direct pipeline approach also offers the best upgrade performance. If you do not have enough disk space to upgrade without removing your SQL Server 6.x databases first, you will have to export the SQL Server 6.x data and objects to tape or a network share. The taped drive option is the faster of the two options; however, if you don't have a tape drive use the network drive option.

Version Upgrade Wizard Steps with Tape Drive and Network Drive Options

The following is a list of the steps taken by the Version Upgrade Wizard when using a tape drive or network:

1. Exports 6.x. objects.
2. Shuts down SQL Server 6.x.
3. Exports 6.x data.
4. Backs up and deletes 6.x devices.
5. Starts SQL Server 7.0.
6. Imports SQL Server 6.5 objects into SQL Server 7.0.
7. Imports SQL Server 6.5 data into SQL Server 7.0.

Version Upgrade Wizard Steps Using the Direct Pipeline Options

The following is a list of the steps taken by the Version Upgrade wizard when using a direct pipeline:

1. Exports SQL Server 6.x objects.

2. Shuts down SQL Server 6.x.

3. Starts SQL Server 7.0.

4. Imports SQL Server 6.x objects.

5. Exports and imports data from SQL Server 6.x to SQL Server 7.0.

Behind the Scenes with the Version Upgrade Wizard

Take a close look at what the Version Upgrade Wizard is doing after you have answered all of the required questions to transfer SQL Server 6.x databases to SQL Server 7.0.

Installing SQL Server 7.0

The first thing to happen in the upgrade process is the installation of SQL Server 7.0. At this time, you will set up the server with required information such as SQL Server Agent account information and the proper sort order and character set.

Step 1—Validate the 6.x Databases

The Version Upgrade Wizard examines the SQL Server 6.x database to try and detect any possible problems that may occur in the upgrade process.

Step 2—Export Server Settings

After the Version Upgrade Wizard has validated the 6.x databases, the Server configuration information is exported (scripted out).

Step 3—Export MSDB Database and Replication Information

The msdb database in SQL Server 7.0 is quite different from the msdb found in SQL Server 6.5. Several 6.5 system tables no longer exist and new 7.0 tables have been added. In this step the Version Upgrade Wizard exports the msdb database objects and SQL Executive objects. If the server is being used in replication, replication information is also exported out.

Step 4—Export Logins

The Version Upgrade Wizard then exports the login information. The login information is exported based on default users located in databases being exported. The security model is also exported.

Step 5—Export the Database Objects

The next step in the process is to export the 6.x objects. Objects are scripted per database. The Version Upgrade Wizard generates the required script to create the file/filegroups and the databases. Files are a one-to-one mapping with the 6.x devices. (You can change them during the upgrade process.) The database objects are then exported in the following order:

- User-defined datatypes
- Tables and clustered indexes
- Rules and defaults
- Stored procedures, triggers, and views

Step 6—Import 6.x Server Settings into 7.0

After all database objects are exported, the 6.5 SQL Server is shut down, and the SQL Server 7.0 server is started. The 6.x Server settings exported earlier are loaded into SQL Server 7.0.

Step 7—Create SQL 7.0 Databases

The SQL Server 7.0 filegroups and files are created.

Step 8—Converts the SQL 7.0 *MSDB* Database

The msdb database in SQL Server 7.0 is quite different from the 6.x msdb. Therefore, the 6.x objects are converted to the 7.0 format.

Step 9—Import Logins

The user logins are imported into SQL Server 7.0.

Import 6.x Objects into 7.0 Databases

The scripts created for the various database objects are loaded into the 7.0 server.

Export/Import 6.x Data into 7.0 Database

The data is exported from 6.x and imported into the 7.0 database using OLE DB.

Import 6.x SQL Executive Settings into 7.0

The converted SQL Server 6.x Executive settings are imported into SQL Server 7.0.

Update Statistics and Verify Object and Data Transfer

Update statistics is performed and the objects and data transferred are verified. At a bare minimum, the transfer of all objects is verified along with the number of rows for each table. The wizard can be configured to do a more extensive CRC check.

Estimating the Amount of Disk Space Required to Upgrade

Use the Version Upgrade Wizard to estimate the disk space requirements. The disk space requirements estimates show the amount of space required to perform a direct pipeline (leaving SQL Server 6.x intact) or if you remove SQL Server 6.x.

The Upgrade Plan

Before you begin to upgrade an existing SQL Server installation, it is important to create an upgrade plan. The Upgrade Wizard provides different mechanisms for recovery from data loss. However, you should have the capabilities to recover the databases without relying on the Version Upgrade Wizard, in case yours is the one database in a million where the wizard does not perform correctly.

The following sections provide an example of an upgrade plan to upgrade an existing SQL Server installation to SQL Server 7.0.

1. Determine whether you have the required disk space. Make sure that you have the required amounts of disk space to upgrade your existing SQL Server. Because SQL Server 7.0 does a complete installation, you need between 74MB to 190MB depending on the type of SQL Server installation

> **Use the direct pipeline transfer mechanism**
>
> When performing an upgrade, use the direct pipeline transfer mechanism of the Version Upgrade Wizard, if possible. The direct pipeline offers the best performance and leaves your 6.x databases intact.

you select. As a rough estimate, you need 1.5 times your current databases' size in disk space to perform a direct pipeline. If you are upgrading a SQL Server 4.2x installation, you need to upgrade to 6.5 first.

2. Determine proper amount of tempdb space. Make sure that the 6.x database Server being upgraded has tempdb set to at least 25MB.

3. Make sure NT and SQL Server have the proper service pack installed. SQL Server 7.0 requires NT Services Pack 4 or later, for Windows NT and the miniservice pack. The SQL Server 6.5 server must be on Service Pack 3 or later.

4. Estimate downtime and schedule the upgrade with users. Estimate the amount of time you expect the upgrade to take. Remember that the larger the database, the longer the upgrade takes. Don't forget to give yourself time to perform any necessary backups before the upgrade begins, time to test the upgraded server, and time to handle any possible problems—including going back to the original installation, if necessary. After you have determined the amount of time required to perform the upgrade, schedule a date with your users to perform the upgrade. If you have a Microsoft Technical Support contract, notify tech support of your upgrade plans and check for any last minute instructions or known problems.

On the day of the upgrade, follow these steps:

Performing the actual upgrade

1. Perform database maintenance. Before backing up the databases, perform the following DBCC commands on each database: CHECKDB, NEWALLOC, and CHECKCATALOG.

2. Check the SQL Server's open databases' configuration parameter. Make sure that the SQL Server's open databases' configuration parameter is equal to or greater than the number of databases on your server (including master, pubs, model, and tempdb). If the parameter is less than the total number of databases on your system, use the SQL

Enterprise Manager or the system stored procedure `sp_configure` to increase the value.

3. Back up all databases. Perform SQL Server backups on the databases, including the `master` database. If possible, shut down SQL Server and use the Windows NT backup facilities to back up the SQL Server directories, including all the SQL Server devices for possible restoration.

4. Back up the NT Registry. Back up the NT System Registry again, in case you need to restore the system to the original SQL Server installation.

5. Turn off read-only on databases. For any databases that have the `read only` option set to `TRUE`, use `sp_dboption` to set the `read only` option to `FALSE`. The `CHKUPG` utility reports any databases in read-only mode.

6. Make sure that no SQL Server applications are executing. Before upgrading the SQL Server, ensure that no one is using SQL Server.

7. Upgrade the server. Run the setup program and select the Upgrade SQL Server option.

The Fall Back Plan

An SQL Server upgrade is a straightforward process, but because you are usually dealing with valuable data and systems that can be down only for a limited time, upgrades should be treated with extreme caution and care. Just as important as a good upgrade plan is a good fall back plan in case the upgrade does not go as smoothly as you hoped. Here are some suggestions on how to protect yourself. Above all, make sure that you have the backups (tapes, and so on) to return your SQL Server to its earlier state if necessary.

Suggestion 1: Complete System Backup Recovery Plan

If possible, shut down the SQL Server before the upgrade and perform a backup of the SQL Server directories and all the data devices. You must shut down SQL Server to back up files that the SQL Server is using, such as devices. If the upgrade fails for some reason, you can restore the SQL Server directories,

Keep a copy of the Registry

Always make sure that you have a valid backup of the Windows NT System Registry before starting any upgrade.

devices, and the NT Registry, returning your system to its earlier setup.

Suggestion 2: Complete Database Backups—Reinstall Previous Version

Perform SQL Server database backups on the databases, including the master. Make sure that you have all the valid SQL Server configuration information such as the server name, character set, sort order, network configuration, and device and database layouts. If you cannot get the SQL Server 6.5 upgrade to work correctly, having the database dumps and the required SQL Server information enables you to reinstall your previous SQL Server system and reload your databases if necessary.

Suggestion 3: Complete System Backup and Database Backups

Perform suggestions 1 and 2. You never can be too careful!

The bottom line is that the information and data completely recover your system if the upgrade fails. Play it safe. Have a backup plan to use if the backup plan fails!

Upgrading SQL Server

As stated in Chapter 5, the upgrade process is done via the Version Upgrade Wizard. All the databases can be migrated at one time or you can selectively upgrade them one at a time. Before starting the upgrade, make sure that you have performed all the items on the upgrade checklist described in Chapter 5. If you did not read the upgrade section, it is highly recommended that you go back and read the Version Wizard Upgrade section in Chapter 5. The Version Upgrade Wizard provides a very easy user interface to migrate your SQL Server 6.x databases to SQL Server 7.0. The Version Upgrade Wizard is extremely smart. At any step in the process you can pause or halt the wizard. You can then later pick up where you left off or you can restart the process all over again. If you pick up from where you left off, the wizard does not redo things that have already been completed successfully. For example, each table is treated as an individual transaction. If the wizard successfully completes the export and import of Table A, but fails on Table B, halt the process, correct the problem, and then restart the process. The wizard does not redo Table A because it was exported and imported successfully, instead it begins with Table B (where you left off).

As a reminder, although the Version Upgrade Wizard offers some fallback protection (when using the direct pipeline), make sure that you have done the following:

- Performed database backups
- Backed up SQL Server files, devices, and directories
- Backed up the NT Registry
- Have adequate disk space to perform the upgrade
- Set TempDB tempdb to 25MB or greater

Switching Between SQL Server 6.5 and SQL Server 7.0

SQL Server 7.0 and SQL Server 6.5 can't run simultaneously on the same machine. However, you can easily toggle back and forth between SQL Server 6.5 and SQL Server 7.0 using the switch SQL Server option. When you install SQL Server 7.0 on the same machine, as an existing SQL Server 6.5, the Windows Start Menu contains a new item called Microsoft SQL Server Switch (Common), shown in Figure 6.1.

Select the menu item and a message box appears, stating that SQL Server is restoring SQL Server 6.5 (or 7.0) information. Using the Window Start Menu option, you can switch from SQL Server 6.5 to SQL Server 7.0. This enables you to toggle back and forth between 6.5 and 7.0 during or after the upgrade process (see the following Last Minute Suggestion). As stated earlier, you should be prepared to fallback to SQL Server 6.5 without relying on the switch over option (that is, you have full recovery capability).

Last-minute suggestion

If possible, during the upgrade process, find enough disk space so you don't have to remove your SQL Server 6.5 devices. I know that on very, very large databases or organizations with very little cash, you will have to remove the 6.5 devices to make room for the 7.0 databases. If you can upgrade SQL Server 6.5 to 7.0 without removing the SQL Server 6.5 databases, you will be able to easily fall back to SQL Server 6.5. Using the switch option, you can switch back to 6.5 if you find your applications are having trouble with SQL Server 7.0 or you encounter problems during the upgrade.

FIGURE 6.1

Windows Start Menu—
Microsoft SQL Server
Switch.

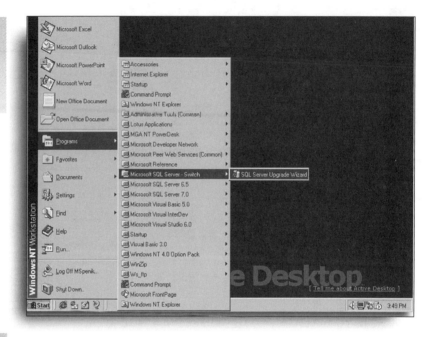

Assumption for installation options

The following walkthrough of the upgrade assumes that you did not select upgrade databases during the installation process. The example also uses the direct pipeline for the object and data transfer.

Step 1: Run the Version Upgrade Wizard

From the Windows Start menu, select the Microsoft SQL Server Switch and then select the Version Upgrade Wizard Option (refer to Figure 6.1). The SQL Server Version Upgrade dialog box appears, as shown in Figure 6.2.

The first screen is merely a welcome screen. Review the text and click the Next button.

FIGURE 6.2

SQL Server Version Upgrade Wizard dialog box.

Step 2: Select Object Transfer Options

The Object Transfer Selection dialog box, shown in Figure 6.3 appears. Using this selection dialog box, you can determine what you want to export and import into SQL Server 7.0. The default values are to export and import both objects and data, use Named pipes for data transfer (that is, data pipeline). You can change any of the defaults; for example, you can transfer the data via tape or select data validation to occur after an exhaustive data integrity check that performs checksums (CRC) to ensure the integrity of the data transferred. After you have selected your options, click the Next button.

FIGURE 6.3
Object Transfer Selection dialog box.

Step 3: Servers Logon

The Servers Logon dialog box appears, shown in Figure 6.4. Select the 6.x server you want to export data from the combo drop-down box. Enter in the sa password and any special command line options required to start the server. Select the 7.0 server you want to import the data into using the combo drop-down box. Enter the sa password and any special command line options required to start the 7.0 server. Click the Next button. A dialog box appears that tells you that the computer is stopping SQL Server (7.0) and restarting SQL Server (6.5) and that all users need to be off the servers. After the SQL Server has restarted, the Code Page Selection dialog box, shown in Figure 6.5, appears.

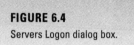

FIGURE 6.4
Servers Logon dialog box.

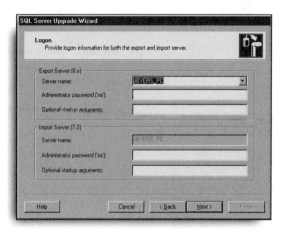

Step 4: Code Page Selection

The Code Page Selection dialog box enables you to select the code page used to generate the script files used to upgrade (see Figure 6.5). It is recommended that you take the default selection. To continue, click the Next button.

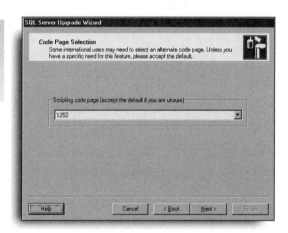

FIGURE 6.5
Code Page Selection dialog box.

Step 5: Select Databases to Upgrade

The Database Selection dialog box appears, shown in Figure 6.6.

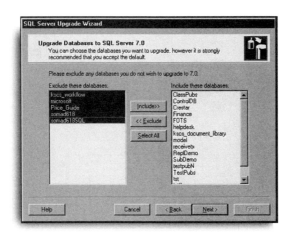

FIGURE 6.6
Database Selection dialog box.

Select the databases you want to upgrade and click the Next button.

Step 6: 7.0 Database Creation

The Database creation dialog box, shown in Figure 6.7, appears. To have your 7.0 databases created with the default options, data files located in the SQL Server 7 data directory, and a one-to-one mapping of SQL Server 6.5 devices to SQL Server 7.0 files, use the default setting. To change to the files or locations, click the Edit button. To use existing databases already created in 7.0, select the Existing Database option. To run a customized script to create the databases, select the Script option and give the path and filename of the script to execute. After you have made your selection, click the Next button.

Estimating Disk Space Requirements

If you want to determine whether you have the necessary disk space to perform a direct pipeline upgrade or an upgrade without SQL Server databases, you can use the Database Creation dialog box. To estimate disk space, perform the following:

1. Click the Edit button; the SQL Server Upgrade Wizard dialog box, shown in Figure 6.8, opens.

207

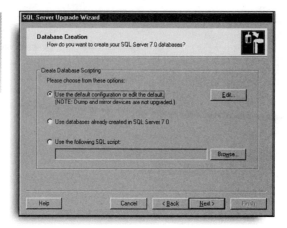

FIGURE 6.7
Database Creation dialog box.

FIGURE 6.8
SQL Server Upgrade Wizard dialog box.

2. Click the Advanced button; the Proposed Database Layout dialog box, shown in Figure 6.9, appears.

3. Click a database in the Proposed Database Layout window. The Drive Summary window displays the estimated space required by SQL Server 7.0 and the amount of free space available on the selected drive. To view the space requirements with the SQL Server 6.x files removed, click Options on the menu and select Free Space Includes 6.x files.

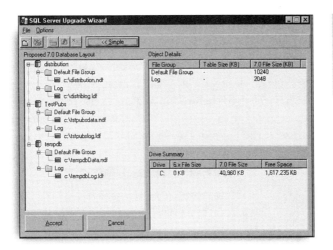

FIGURE 6.9
Proposed Database
Layout dialog box.

Step 7: System Configuration Options

The System Configuration Options dialog box, shown in Figure 6.10, appears. The default values are to transfer existing server settings and SQL Executive settings as well as turn ANSI Nulls off and mixed mode of quoted identifiers. After you have made your selection, click the Next button.

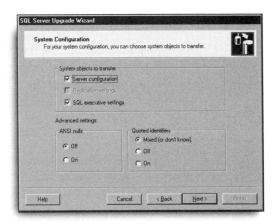

FIGURE 6.10
System Configuration
Options dialog box.

Step 8: Review Upgrade Selections

The Review Upgrade Selections dialog box, shown in Figure 6.11, appears. This dialog box gives you the opportunity to review all of your upgrade option selections and make any necessary changes before moving on to the upgrade. When you are satisfied with your upgrade selections, click the Finish button to start the upgrade.

FIGURE 6.11
Review Upgrade
Selections dialog box.

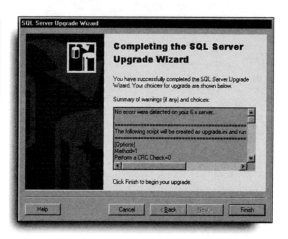

Step 9: SQL Server 7.0 Upgrade in Progress

The Version Upgrade Status dialog box, shown in Figure 6.12, appears. This dialog box provides you with information about the current progress of the upgrade such as the tasks being executed, task status, start time, and end time. You can pause the current task by clicking the Pause button, pause between steps, close out the upgrade process, or resume a paused task.

When the upgrade has completed successfully, an Upgrade Complete dialog box appears.

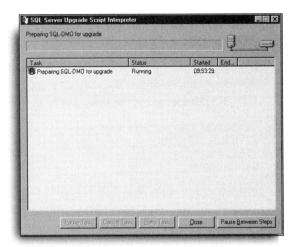

FIGURE 6.12
Version Upgrade Status
dialog box.

Upgrade Troubleshooting

The Version Upgrade Wizard provides useful and easy-to-access information regarding errors that occur during the upgrade process. If an error does occur during the upgrade process, you will get an Informational Files Found dialog box, shown in Figure 6.13.

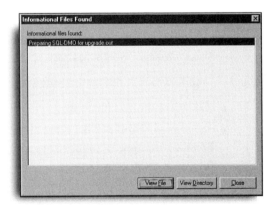

FIGURE 6.13
Informational Files Found
dialog box.

You can then select to view the information files to see what problem occurred with the particular object. You can then try to correct the problem and resume or redo the upgrade process.

Upgrade Subdirectories and Contents

To troubleshoot the upgrade process, it helps to know how the upgrade subdirectories are created and what the contents of each directory are. The main upgrade directory is the subdirectory UPGRADE located off of the main SQL Server directory.

Whenever you perform an upgrade, a subdirectory is created off of the upgrade directory that has the following format:

```
Machine name_date_time
```

For example, on the KSCSINC server, the full path is:

```
C:\MSSQL7\UPGRADE\KSCSINC_041898_125255
```

This directory contains the following:

- .OUT files—For each stage of the upgrade process
- .OK files—For all scripts run on 6.x and 7.0
- .ERR files—Errors encountered during a stage in the upgrade process

The upgrade subdirectory created whenever you run the upgrade process also has a subdirectory for each database upgraded with the following naming convention:

```
Number Database Name
```

For example, the full path of the database Finance is as follows:

```
C:\MSSQL7\UPGRADE\KSCSINC_041898_125255\001Finance
```

This subdirectory contains the following:

- .OK files—For each successful object transfer
- Script files—For each database object with file extensions based on the type of object (for example, Table = .tab, stored procedure = .prc, and so on)

7.0 Compatibility with 6.x Applications

SQL Server 7.0 leaves upgraded databases in a 6.x compatibility mode. Therefore, your applications should run without a hitch. You might run into problems where applications or tools that used SQL Server system tables might no longer work due to system table changes in 7.0. To upgrade a database to SQL Server 7.0 compatibility, use the stored procedure `sp_dbcmptlevel`.

Removing SQL Server

If you want to remove an SQL Server installation, do not delete the SQL Server directories. Run Add/Remove Programs located in the Control Panel or select the Uninstall SQL Server 7.0 option from the SQL Server 7.0 program group, shown in Figure 6.14.

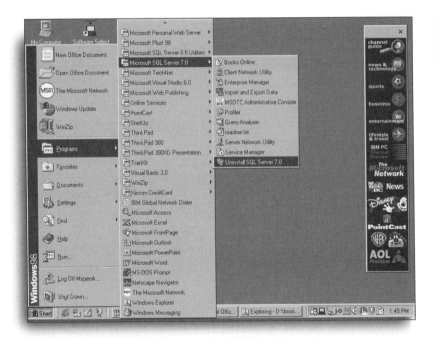

FIGURE 6.14
The Uninstall SQL Server 7.0 menu option.

An Are You Sure dialog box, shown in Figure 6.15, appears. To continue deleting SQL Server 7.0, select Yes.

FIGURE 6.15
The Are You Sure You Want to Remove SQL Server dialog box.

An Uninstall dialog box appears and begins the uninstall process. A progress indicator is displayed to show you the progress of the uninstall. After SQL Server is uninstalled, you must manually delete a few files like backup devices or unattached files/file-groups. Remove the leftover files by removing the SQL Server home directory, MSSQL7, which is left over after a file removal.

Upgrade Planning FAQ

The following are some frequently asked questions about upgrade planning:

Q I read somewhere that if I planned not to migrate some databases or to migrate a few databases at a time, I should beware of cross database dependencies. What exactly is that?

A The Version Upgrade process creates user logins based on the default logins located in databases being migrated. If a login is not created because a database is not migrated, future objects owned by the login fail when other databases are migrated; this is called cross database dependency. For example, suppose you have a user login called Test1 that defaults to the pubs database, but the user owns objects in a database called Finance. If you do not migrate pubs (before Finance), when the Version Upgrade Wizard creates the objects owned by Test1, the object creation fails because Test1 does not exist.

Q If I have 6.5 replication setup, do I need to do anything special when upgrading?

A Make sure you upgrade the distribution server first to SQL Server 7.0, which supports both 7.0 and 6.5 publishers and subscribers.

Q **Can I install SQL Server on an NT Server that is also a Primary or Backup Domain Controller?**

A Yes, you can install SQL Server on a PDC or BDC; it is not recommended and you are much better off if you can dedicate a machine to SQL Server. If you must use your PDC or BDC, add more memory and, if possible, additional processors.

SEE ALSO
➤ *For more information on developing a back-up strategy, see page 455.*
➤ *For more information on hardware requirements, see page 112.*

part

III

Administering SQL Server

SQL Server Tools

Explore the graphic interface of the
Enterprise Manager and the MMC

Learn how to graphically display
queries and tables

Find the shortcuts you need with
administration wizards

This chapter introduces the tools that will help you in the navigation and administration of SQL Server 7.0. Like many other new product releases from Microsoft, SQL Server 7.0 uses the Microsoft Management Console (MMC) as an all-in-one interface.

But still, the MMC is not the only tool that can be used. Your old buddies bcp and isql are still around, however isql has an upgrade as well, called the osql. At the end of the chapter, you'll find a description of each of the wizards. The wizards themselves are pretty straightforward. A step by step lesson on using the wizard would be unnecessary because that's what a wizard is—a set of steps. Instead, I've included a quick reference to what each wizard does and how it can make your life a little easier.

This chapter will hopefully be used as a reference guide to the SQL Server Tools and Wizards. I'll try not to be too wordy during this chapter; after all, it is a lot of material, and I do want you to actually get through this book. So let's cut to the chase...

Using the Microsoft Management Console (MMC)

Third-party snap-ins

Third-party vendors are also able to produce *snap-in* components that you can use to administer other applications.

The Microsoft Management Console is the new user interface (UI) for SQL Server 7.0. MMC is used for all the latest additions to the Windows NT and BackOffice family. This makes it a more common tool for doing administration throughout your enterprise.

Adding a new component is easy. First, you'll launch the Enterprise Manager and then add a new component (snap-in) to it.

The MMC is part of the installation of SQL Server 7.0. Even if you have installed it with prior utilities, the installation will make sure you have the latest edition. After SQL Server is installed, MMC is ready to be used. Unless the MMC is already running, you need to launch the MMC. There is no MMC application sitting by itself. Start SQL Server 7.0 by selecting from Start,

Programs, SQL Server 7.0, Enterprise Manager. This launches the Enterprise Manager within the MMC.

Adding a snap-in tool

1. From MMC Select Console, select the Add/Remove snap-in (Ctrl+M).

2. At the bottom of the Dialog box, select Add.

3. Select from the available Snap-ins (see Figure 7.1) for the an example of the snap-in dialog box.

FIGURE 7.1

The Add Standalone Snap-In dialog box. This lists the available components that can be snapped into the MMC.

One really nice thing you can do with the MMC is to add HTML pages. For instance, you can add a snap-in for a Web page. This Href could be the link to Microsoft's FAQ sheets or Bug lists, or even personal notes or SOPs (standard operating procedures) that you might develop to make life a little easier for you DBAs.

To add a Web page, follow steps 1–3. When you're at step 4:

4. Select Link to Web Address.

5. Add the information for the link.

That's it! The link will produce a page in the MMC from the appropriate source. Figure 7.2 shows the MMC with a Web page added.

FIGURE 7.2
This page could be any site you want internal to your organization or an external such as Microsoft's Help site.

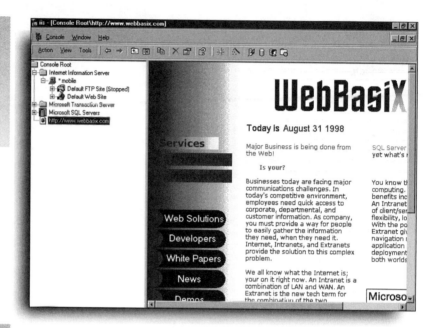

Migrating from 6.5 to 7.0 utilities

If you are crossing over from SQL Server 6.5, you will notice that some of your utilities are no longer around. They have most likely been merged with another utility, or have been abandoned altogether. Another thing worth mentioning is that the shortcut buttons for the actively used programs are no longer around.

Working with the Tree and Details Pane

The MMC produces a Tree and Detail pane, much like that of Windows Explorer. This should make the learning curve a bit easier. The navigation for the most part is user friendly. The left pane resembles the Tree view structure while the right pane is a detail view. The right view can also display HTML pages as you might have experienced if you followed the previous example.

So, how do you find the tools that you so desperately need? That's what this book is for. I've spent quite a few frustrating hours trying to find the common tools from the previous SQL Server versions, only to find the tool right in front of me with a different name. You will be rediscovering all your favorite utilities throughout this chapter, and possibly adding a few new favorites to the list.

SQL Enterprise Manager Overview

SQL Server Enterprise Manager is your gateway into the UI for SQL Server. Anything you could do with the previous versions of Enterprise Manager you can do with the MMC version. The key is finding out how. This chapter will discuss the ins and outs of navigating around the MMC SQL Enterprise Manager.

The SQL Enterprise Manager Screen

As you might notice from Figure 7.3, the Enterprise Manager has changed in appearance quite a bit. Even though the appearance has changed, the functionality has not. The top menu bar has three items: Console, Window, and Help:

- The Console menu enables you to open other consoles, create a new console, add or remove snap-ins, save the current settings, and exit the MMC.

- The Window menu functions just like Window menus of other Microsoft MDI (Multiple Document Interface) applications (such as Word and Excel), enabling you to tile the open frames Horizontally, Cascade, and so on.

- Help provides information about the MMC and not the current snap-in component. For help on SQL Server 7.0, see the section in this chapter titled "SQL Server Books Online."

Below the main menus are the menu items, which gain access to SQL Server. Starting from the left you'll find Action, View, and Tools:

- Action enables you to do things such as register a new server or server group. The Action item also has the Views and Tools menus listed for redundancy.

- Views provide a listing of the different types of views available to you. You can select large, small, list, or detail views of the icons and their associated properties. If you are used to the Explorer view menu, this should be second nature to you.

- The Tools menu lists all the SQL Servers tools and wizards. You can back up a database; start, stop, and configure replication; and launch tools such as the Query Analyzer, Profiler, and so on.

- To the immediate right of the menus are other toolbar items. The toolbar items are basically shortcuts to the most often used items from the menu bar. Some of the common buttons displayed here are Back, Forward, Refresh, Register Database, New Database, New Login, and so on.

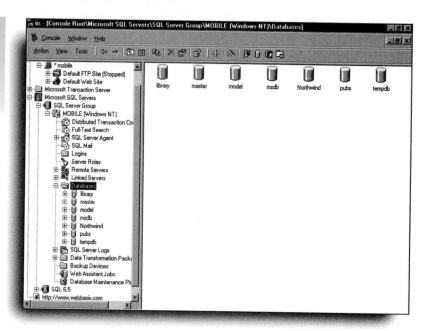

FIGURE 7.3
The extended view of a SQL Server database as viewed from the MMC.

The Enterprise Manager might have a new look, but underneath it is really the same old utility you've always used. Give it a week and you'll soon forget the differences between the new MMC look and the old Enterprise Manager shell.

Query Designer

SQL Server 7.0 also has what resembles the Query By Example (QBE) found in Microsoft Access, which can be a replacement for MS Query. The actual name for this application is the Query Designer and is part of the Visual Database Tools. The Query Designer is a great tool; however, it isn't listed as a SQL Server tool. In fact, it's a little hard to find unless you know where to look for it.

View the expanded table information (Query Designer)

1. From the Enterprise Manager, expand the Northwind database and then expand the tables.

2. Right-click the Categories table.

3. Select Open Table, and then Return All Rows

After you have opened the table, the entire screen is enveloped with the Query Designer. The Query Designer enables you to view the properties, perform select queries, action queries (insert, updates, deletes and create table queries), SQL syntax validation, sorting, filtering, and group by's.

Most likely you will only be looking at the Results pane, which shows the current results from the query; however, you have three more views to choose from or add to the current view. These three optional views are Show Diagram, Show Grid, and Show SQL Pane.

The Show Diagram Pane

This pane enables you to graphically display the database table or tables. By default, only the current table you have opened will be shown in this view. To add another table, simply right-click anywhere in that pane (except for, of course, on a graphical representation of a table). A pop-up box will appear with some options; you are only concerned with the Add table. This will actually show all tables and views that are available in your database. Add the products table. Notice that the relationship is graphically represented as well with a line and key on one end and an infinity icon on the other. This shows a one-to-many relationship with the CategoryID on the Categories table as the primary key. You can select individual columns or select them all by selecting the appropriate check boxes next to each column name.

The Show Grid Pane

This pane enables you to add more detailed information to the query being created. For example, you can select the sort order for a particular column, alias, or criterion. This is all done in a visual fashion.

SQL refresh

The Results pane doesn't automatically refresh its results. To refresh the results, click the red exclamation point.

Advantages of the Query Designer

Because the Query Designer isn't considered an admin tool I just provided a quick introduction here. Feel free to experiment with this "implementation tool." It will help you create complex queries much quicker than using the Query Analyzer (discussed later in this chapter); after the queries are designed, they can be placed in the Query Analyzer and tested for performance.

Alternate removal

You can also use the Add/Remove Programs from the Control Panel to add or remove SQL Server.

The Show SQL Pane

This pane shows you the actual SQL statement generated by the selections made with the previous views. You can now copy and paste code from this window into the Query Analyzer, a VB, or VI project, and so forth.

SQL Server Setup

SQL Server Setup is used to install, reinstall, reconfigure, or uninstall your SQL Server. The Setup program can be used to rebuild the Master database; change the network support options; add a language; change the character set, or sort order; set the server options; and change security options.

To access the install for the first time or after the installation has already taken place, you need to insert the CD-ROM and run the set-up program, or wait for the auto-start. To uninstall SQL Server 7.0, you can select the Uninstall option from the SQL Server program group. Choose Start, Programs, Microsoft SQL Server 7.0, Uninstall SQL Server 7.0.

SEE ALSO

➤ *For more information on installing SQL Server, see page 122.*

SQL Server Service Manager

SQL Server Service Manager is used for starting, stopping, and pausing SQL Server (MSSQLServer), SQL Server Agent, and the Microsoft Distributed Transaction Coordinator (MSDTC).

The SQL Service Manager can be launched from the SQL Server Program Group. Choose Start, Programs, Microsoft SQL Server 7.0, Service Manager. The SQL Server Service Manager is now a taskbar application. When launched, it is located in the task area next to the clock. SQL Server Manager can also be used to start and stop the Microsoft Search (MSSearch) service. The MSSearch Service provides full-text indexing and querying capability to SQL Server.

For shortcut access to SQL Server Service Manager tasks, right-click the SQL Server Service Manager icon in the taskbar (see Figure 7.4), and click one of the available commands. The icon resembles a tower box (PC/Server tower box) with a white circle in the lower-right corner. Depending on the server's state (condition), a different figure and color will be inside of the circle. The three states for the server are

Stopped   White circle with a red square

Paused   White circle with two black bars

Started   White circle with a green triangle

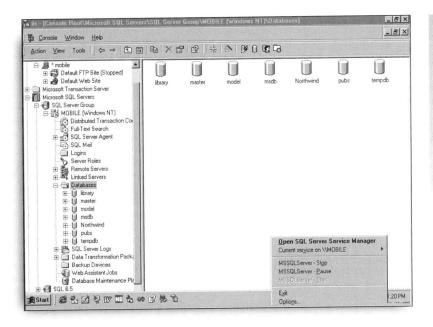

FIGURE 7.4
The SQL Server Service Manager as a taskbar icon, with the available options. To show these options, right-click the icon. To launch the Service Manager, double-click the icon.

SQL Server Service Manager also enables you to

- Open the SQL Server Service Manager dialog box.
- Select a service.
- Start, continue, pause, or stop the selected service.
- Set options for the selected service.
- Get information about the SQL Server Service Manager application.
- Exit the application.

SQL Server Client Configuration Utility

SQL Server Client Configuration is used for managing the client configuration for DB-Library, Net-Libraries, and any custom defined network connections.

The SQL Server Client Configuration Utility is located in the program group for SQL Server. From the Start menu, choose Programs, Microsoft SQL Server 7.0, Client Network Utility. As you might have noticed, it is referred to as the Client Network Utility in the program group; however, after it is launched, the title bar indicates the Client Configuration Utility. I'll bet you're glad I told you this. By the way, it's referred to as the *Client Configuration Utility* and the *Network Configuration* program in Books Online.

When to configure a client

You should configure the client only when you

- Set the default client Net-Library to a selection other than Named Pipes.

- Add a different configuration entry for communicating with a specific server.

- Set DB-Library options.

Configuring a client Net-Library to communicate with a server is optional. Named Pipes is the default client Net-Library, installed during SQL Server Setup for computers running Microsoft Windows NT or Microsoft Windows 95/98. This should be fine in most cases. If, however, this protocol doesn't connect with your server, you will need to reconfigure the clients with the correct configuration.

For the Server process, SQL Server listens to Named Pipes, TCP/IP Sockets, and Multiprotocol Net-Libraries protocols on computers running Windows NT. However, Named Pipes is not supported on the Windows 95/98 platform. SQL Server installed on computers running Windows 95/98 listens to the server TCP/IP Sockets and Multiprotocol Net-Libraries. If the connection is local to the Server (such as a client and server on the same computer), SQL Server will then listen to the server Shared Memory Net-Library.

The default client Net-Library for SQL Server clients making remote connections is Named Pipes, which isn't supported on servers running Windows 95/98. Clients connecting to servers running Windows 95/98 should use the SQL Server Client Configuration to perform one of the following options:

- Change the default client Net-Library.
- Define a configuration entry for a client Net-Library on which the server running Windows 95/98 is listening.

SQL Server Performance Monitor

The SQL Server Performance Monitor integrates with Windows NT Performance Monitor (see Figure 7.5). This provides up-to-the-minute activity and any performance problems, as well as a way to diagnose system problems that might occur. Using the SQL Server Performance Monitor can indicate ways to increase or improve performance.

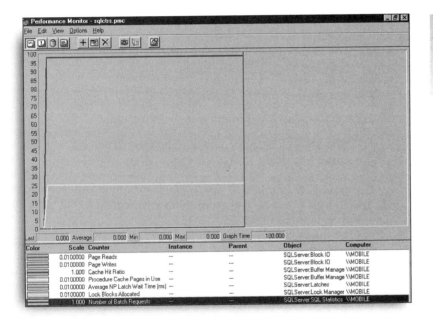

FIGURE 7.5

The SQL Server Performance Monitor.

SQL Server Profiler

The SQL Server Profiler is a great utility to see a continuous record of server activity in real time. SQL Server Profiler monitors events produced through SQL Server, filters these events based on user-specified criteria, and displays the trace output to the screen, a file, or a table. You can even replay previously captured traces.

Monitoring with SQL Server Profiler

SQL Server Profiler is a graphical tool that enables system administrators to monitor engine events in Microsoft SQL Server. Events are the new way of communicating to and from SQL Server. With engine events, a COM object can intercept these events and act accordingly. Examples of engine events include the following:

- Transact-SQL SELECT, INSERT, UPDATE, and DELETE statements.
- Login connects, fails, or disconnects.
- RPC (remote procedure call) batch status.
- The start or the end of a stored procedure.
- The start or the end of an SQL batch.
- An error written to the SQL Server error log.
- A lock acquired or released on a database object.
- A cursor that is opened.

The data generated about each event can be captured and saved to a file or back to a SQL Server table for later analysis. To collect the engine event data you set up traces. Examples of the event data captured within a trace include

- The type (class) of event, such as Object:Created, which indicates a database object was created.
- The name of the computer the client is running.
- The ID of the object affected by the event, such as a table name.
- The SQL Server name of the user issuing the statement.
- The text of the Transact-SQL statement or stored procedure being executed.
- The time the event started and ended.

You can filter event data so that only a subset of the event data is collected. This enables you to collect only the event data you are interested in. For example, if you are only interested in a particular user or the effects of a certain database, you can filter on those specifics and ignore all others. You could also set filters on items taking longer than expected, such as a query that takes longer than the 40 seconds.

SQL Server Profiler also allows (captured) event data to be replayed against SQL Server. This will effectively re-execute the saved events as they originally occurred.

SQL Server Profiler can be used to

- Monitor the performance of SQL Server.
- Debug Transact-SQL statements and stored procedures.
- Identify slow-executing queries.
- Troubleshoot problems in SQL Server. For example, you can capture the events that might be leading to a potential problem and then replicate the process on a test system to isolate and fix the problem.
- You can actually test SQL statements or stored procedures by walking-through them. You can single-step through statements, one line at a time, to confirm that the code works as expected.

Figure 7.6 shows the initial tabbed dialog for creating a trace.

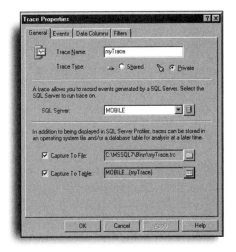

FIGURE 7.6
Running a trace is one of the valuable functions you can perform using the SQL Server Profiler.

SEE ALSO
➤ *For details on creating traces, see page 572.*

SQL Server Query Analyzer

SQL Server Query Analyzer provides a graphical interface to analyze the execution plan of a query or multiple queries, view the data results, and recommend indexes.

The SQL Server Query Analyzer resembles the Query window found within Enterprise Manager of SQL Server Version 6.5. If you are familiar with Version 6.5, this tool should be a snap; however, if SQL Server is completely new to you, don't fuss. This is an extremely easy tool to use. Let's start with the execution of a simple query.

If you haven't already done so, launch The Query Analyzer. This can be accomplished from within the MMC or from the Start menu.

Using Query Analyzer

1. From the MMC, select Tools and SQL Server Query Analyzer. You can also select Programs, SQL Server 7.0, Query Analyzer from the Start menu.

2. Connect to your local SQL Server. Use trusted connection if you have admin privileges on your machine. This will log you in as the sa (System Administrator). If you are not the admin to your machine, log in with the sa user and password (if any) that you specified during the install.

3. Select pubs from the combo box in the query window. This will be the database you will run the query from. Alternatively, you could specify the Use statement before your query.

4. Type the following in the top window pane if more than one is showing:
   ```
   SELECT * FROM authors
   ```

5. Select the method of execution. Four different execution options are available:

   • Standard Execution (Ctrl+E) displays the results in the text file fashion. Figure 7.7 shows this query with Standard Execution.

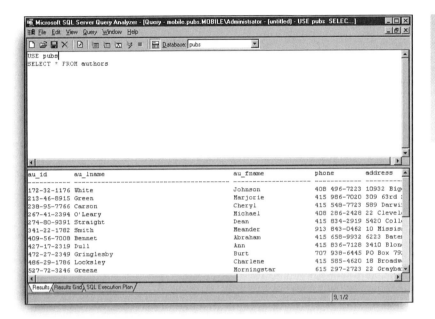

FIGURE 7.7
The Query Analyzer showing the resultset in a standard file display using Standard Execution (Ctrl+E).

- Execute to Grid (Ctrl+D) provides a more viewing friendly format (see Figure 7.8), providing a spreadsheet or table–like structure (a column, row layout).

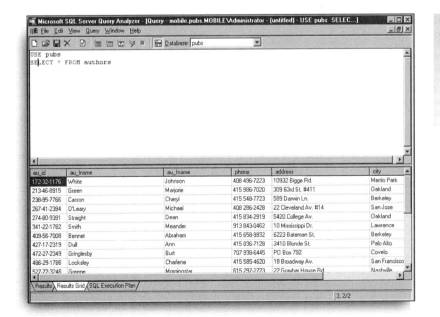

FIGURE 7.8
The Query Analyzer showing the resultset in a grid style display using Execute to Grid (Ctrl+D).

- Execution Plan (Ctrl+L), shown in Figure 7.9, shows the actual execution process that took place. This query didn't show anything exciting because you only had one table involved, but if you run a more complex query with inner or outer joins, you will find the graphical representation.

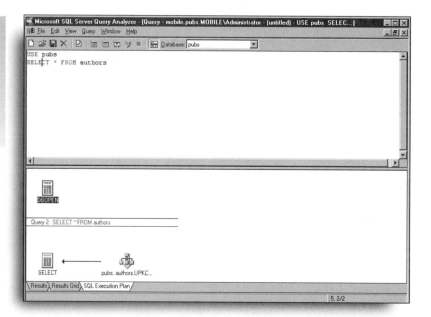

FIGURE 7.9
The Query Analyzer showing the execution plan that took place when executing this query.

Access to execution methods

Each of these can run from the Query tab on the menu bar, and each has a corresponding button on the Query Window.

- Index Analysis (no shortcut) should most likely tell you that it was unable to recommend any indexes. However, if you start writing complex queries that are used often, you should paste your queries in this utility and test them for index suggestions.

SQL Server Books Online

SQL Server Books Online is a great resource to have on hand. The MS books online help guide is becoming the standard way to access help with Microsoft Applications, Services, and Programming languages. The books online is a one stop shop for all your questions relating to a particular product, and in some cases they merge related products.

Books Online has a simple navigation piece, as shown in Figure 7.10. Books online will resemble the MMC or windows explorer. The left-hand side has a tree view structure while the right hand side has an IE (Internet Explorer Web viewer). The pages rendered in the right hand pane are simple HTML pages (you can even view the source if you want to touch up on you HTML).

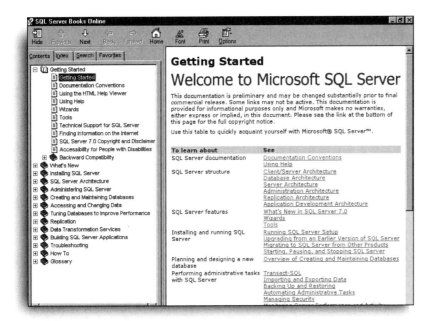

FIGURE 7.10

An example of Books Online.

Searching by Contents

A content search is like searching a book based on the outline of the chapters. The chapter outline is viewable as a tree structure. Clicking a book in the left-hand pane will open the book revealing pages, or chapters. Click a page and the page will be displayed in the right-hand pane. Clicking a chapter (resembling another book) will open more chapters, and more pages in the left page.

Searching by Index

Searching by index will search all words that were indexed when creating the help materials. Occasionally, you might not find the item you are looking for and will need a more general search. Use the Search tab for more general searches.

Using the Search Tab

The Search tab enables you to enter a word and search every document for that word. The left-hand pane will fill with matching documents that contain your requested word(s).

Favorites Tab

Synchronizing the left and right window panes.

When you are using the Index search or the generic Search tab, by selecting the Contents tab you can sync-up your current location to the location of the contents in a book. This will show you exactly what book, chapter, and page you are currently reading from.

The Favorites tab is an easy-to-use bookmark. If you like the information you've found and want to make it easier to find later, simply select the Favorites tab. The bottom of the tab will show your current topic. Click Add to save the item in your Favorites list. If you need to delete an item, simply select it and press the delete button.

If you are unsure how some of the utilities work, or have just forgotten, remember the wizards are great learning tools. They do an excellent job of pointing out the necessary tasks that are being completed. After running through the wizards a few times, you should have a good understanding of the whole process. Even if you don't, there's always this book, or the Books Online.

BCP

To bulk copy data from one SQL Server database to another, data needs to be bulk copied into a data file and then to a database. The bcp utility performs this bulk copy operation.

SEE ALSO
➤ For more information on BCP's use and parameters, see page 520.

ISQL Utility

The isql is a command-line utility that enables you to enter Transact SQL statements, system-stored procedures, and script files saved on your hard drive. The isql utility uses the DB-Library to communicate with Microsoft SQL Server. SQL Server 7.0 added functionality that isn't available with the DB-Library and is therefore not functional with isql. For example,

Unicode ntext data cannot be retrieved. To make up for this, the osql utility was created to support the range of the new SQL Server 7.0. osql will discussed shortly; for now let discuss the isql and its functionality.

The syntax for isql is as follows:

```
isql -U login_id [-e] [-E] [-p] [-n] [-d db_name]
➥[-q "query"] [-Q "query"]
[-c cmd_end] [-h headers] [-w column_width]
➥[-s col_separator]
[-t time_out] [-m error_level] [-L] [-?] [-r {0 ¦ 1}]
[-H wksta_name] [-P password]
[-S server_name] [-i input_file] [-o output_file]
➥[-a packet_size]
[-b] [-O] [-l time_out] [-x max_text_size]
```

Table 7.1 shows the definitions of the switches used in isql.

isql/w versus Query Analyzer

SQL Server 6.5 had a window interface, which ran MS Query if you ran isql/w from a command line prompt. This tool no longer exists. You should use the SQL Server Query Analyzer instead.

TABLE 7.1 Switches for isql

Switch	Switch Definition
-U login_id	Specifies the user login ID.
-e	Specifies input to be echoed.
-E	Specifies a trusted connection.
-p	Specifies performance statistics to be printed.
-n	Specifies for numbering and the prompt symbol (>) to be removed from input lines.
-d db_name	Specifies a USE db_name to be issued when isql is started
-q "query"	Specifies that a query is executed when isql is started.
-Q "query"	Specifies that a query is executed and then immediately exits isql.
-c cmd_end	Specifies a new command terminator.
-h headers	Specifies the number of rows to be displayed before showing the headers. The default is showing the headers once at the beginning of each query performed.
-w column_width	Specifies the number of characters to be displayed on each line.

continues...

TABLE 7.1 Continued

Switch	Switch Definition
-s col_separator	Specifies a character for the column separator.
-t time_out	Specifies the number of seconds before the command times out.
-m error_level	Specifies whether error messages are shown or not.
-L	List the local servers broadcasting on the network.
-?	Displays Help, summary of all switches.
-r	Specifies the redirection of error messages to the screen.
-H wksta_name	Specifies the workstation name.
-P password	Specifies the password.
-S server_name	Specifies the server to connect to.
-i input_file	Specifies the file that contains SQL statements
-o output_file	Specifies the file that receives the output from isql.
-a packet_size	Specifies the packet size.
-b	Specifies that isql returns a DOS error when an error occurs
-0	Degrades isql to an earlier version, disabling EOF Batch Processing, Automatic console width scaling, and Wide messages.
-l	Sets the number of seconds that isql will wait before the login times out.
-x max_text_size	Sets the maximum length (in bytes) of text to return.

osql

The osql utility is a new command-prompt utility for ad hoc, allowing interactive execution of Transact-SQL statements and scripts. If you are familiar with the isql utility, osql will be a breeze.

The osql utility was created to replace isql; however, isql remains for backward compatibility. New features supported by osql include

- Access to columns defined with the ntext data type (a Unicode data type with a maximum length of 1,073,741,823 character)
- Access to columns with data longer than 255 characters defined by char, varchar, nchar, and nvarchar. The osql utility uses the ODBC API (application programming interface) instead of the DB-Library (used by isql).

Except for these new features, osql and isql support the same functionality.

The osql syntax is as follows:

```
osql -U login_id [-e] [-E] [-p] [-n] [-d db_name]
➥[-q "query"] [-Q "query"]
[-c cmd_end] [-h headers] [-w column_width]
➥[-s col_separator]
[-t time_out] [-m error_level] [-L] [-?] [-r {0 ¦ 1}]
[-H wksta_name] [-P password] [-R]
[-S server_name] [-i input_file] [-o output_file] [-u]
➥[-a packet_size]
[-b] [-O] [-l time_out]
```

Table 7.2 shows the definitions of the switches used in osql.

TABLE 7.2 Switches for osql

Switch	Switch Definition
-U login_id	Specifies the user login id.
-e	Specifies input to be echoed.
-E	Specifies a trusted connection.
-p	Specifies performance statistics to be printed.
-n	Specifies for numbering and the prompt symbol (>) to be removed from input lines.
-d db_name	Specifies a USE db_name to be issued when isql is started

continues...

TABLE 7.2 Continued

Switch	Switch Definition
-q *"query"*	Specifies that a query is executed when isql is started.
-Q *"query"*	Specifies that a query is executed and then immediately exits isql.
-c *cmd_end*	Specifies a new command terminator.
-h *headers*	Specifies the number of rows to be displayed before showing the headers. The default is showing the headers once at the beginning for each query performed.
-w *column_width*	Specifies the number of characters to be displayed on each line.
-s *col_separator*	Specifies a character for the column separator.
-t *time_out*	Specified the number of seconds before the command times out.
-m *error_level*	Specifics whether error messages are shown.
-L	Lists the local servers broadcasting on the network.
-?	Displays Help, summary of all switches.
-r	Specifies the redirection of error messages to the screen.
-H *wksta_name*	Specifies the workstation name.
-P *password*	Specifies the password.
-R	Specifies the SQL Server driver to use when doing a conversion for date/time, and currency-to-character data.
-S *server_name*	Specifies the server to connect to.
-i *input_file*	Specifies the file that contains SQL statements.
-o *output_file*	Specifies the file that receives the output from isql.
-a *packet_size*	Specifies the packet size.
-b	Specifies that isql returns a DOS error when an error occurs.
-0	Degrades isql to an earlier version, disabling EOF Batch Processing, Automatic console width scaling, and Wide messages.
-l	Sets the number of seconds that isql will wait before the login times out.
-x *max_text_size*	Sets the maximum length (in bytes) of text to return.

makepipe and readpipe

makepipe and readpipe are diagnostic utilities that can be used if you are unable to connect to Microsoft SQL Server. To use these tools, a makepipe is issued on the server. The server then listens for a readpipe.

Using diagnostics

1. From the Start menu select Run.

2. Type in `cmd`.

3. Click OK.

4. Repeat steps 1–3 once more. You should now have two command windows open.

5. Select one of the windows.

6. Type in `makepipe`.

7. Press Enter. It should say `waiting for client to connect...`, as shown in Figure 7.11

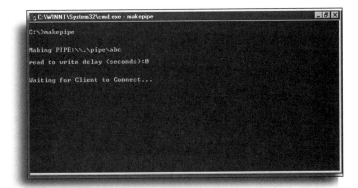

FIGURE 7.11
Starting the makepipe procedure.

8. Select the other open command window.

9. Type `readpipe /s[machine_name] /d"Test One"`, (see Figure 7.12). Don't type spaces after the `/s` or `/d`; replace `machine_name` with your computer name. Use quotes after `/d` if you want to send more that one word.

10. Press Enter.

FIGURE 7.12

This screen shows the outcome of using makepipe and readpipe.

When the `machine_name` **parameter is optional**

You can actually leave off the *machine_name* parameter when testing on the same computer.

Watch each screen to see the messages being displayed. They will appear simultaneously because they are on the same machine. The operation could be a bit slower on a busy network if you were actually talking between two machines.

11. When you are finished, type **exit** followed by **[return]** in the readpipe command window. Use Ctrl+C to cancel the operation in the makepipe window. Use the Exit command to close the window.

makepipe and readpipe have a fairly straightforward switch list. Hey, at least it's short.

Makepipe switch list

```
Makepipe [/h] [/w] [/p pipe_name]
```

/h	Displays help (the usage of each parameter).
/w	The wait time between read and writes, default is 0.
/p	The pipe name; the default is abc.

Readpipe switch list

```
Readpipe /sserver_name /dstring [/n] [/q] [/w] [/t]
➥[/ppipe_name] [/h]
```

/sserver_name	The name of the SQL Server that just initiated the makepipe command. Do not use a space after /s. This parameter is optional if you are using the same machine for the makepipe.
/dstring	A test string to be sent to the server and back. No spaces after /d. Enclose the string in double quotes (""), if you are using spaces.
/n	The number of iterations (loops through the number of times requested).
/q	Uses query(polling) method.
/w	Specifies the wait time to pause the polling. Use with /q.
/t	Uses Transact-SQL; overrides polling; if used /w is ignored.
/ppipe_name	Specifies the pipe to use; default is abc.
/h	Displays help (the usage of each parameter).

SQL Server Wizards

SQL Server wizards help you create your database objects and services without the fear of always looking for your notes on how to do something correctly. Having a wizard walk you through each task is a great way to learn what needs to be done. Just about everything has a wizard. You might have previously avoided a certain task simply because you didn't have the time to research how to do it. As you all know, or will learn at some point, unless you understand a procedure completely, you're going to make mistakes. Your time is precious enough without having to recover from mistakes. If you aren't certain what you're doing, or whether you're doing it right, let the wizard be

243

your guide. Some of these wizards are simple, whereas others are more complex. If you are teaching yourself SQL Server, you will be glad that wizards exist. Otherwise, you might never actually know where to begin. All these wizards are available from the Tools menu, by selecting the Wizards option (see Figure 7.13).

FIGURE 7.13
The available wizards.

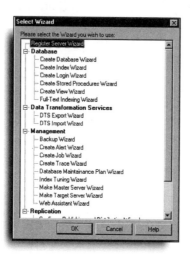

Each section will cover a new wizard and the main steps to the wizard, giving as much detail as possible without overdoing it. Wizards are, well, wizards—they are supposed to make the hard or perplexing tasks easier. So with that in mind, let's being our Wizard tour.

Register Server Wizard

The Register Server Wizard, obviously, registers you server. Registering your server is the process of telling SQL Server the Server Name that you want to register, the type of security your are using, your login and password (if not using trusted), and the server group you want to be part of.

You can create a new server group when creating a database. A database can only be part of one group.

Security Wizard

The Security Wizard automates the task of creating logins for a SQL Server. The wizard enables you to specify either an NT User account or create a SQL Server Authentication.

SEE ALSO
➤ *For more information on implementing security, see page 357.*

Create Database Wizard

The Create Database Wizard automates the task of creating a database. The wizard walks through the primary steps for creating a database. These steps include the database name, the database files, the log files, the initial size of the files, and how these files will grow. Tables aren't created at this point. They are created by Transact-SQL statements or by right-clicking a database and selecting New Table.

SEE ALSO
➤ *This topic is covered in more detail on page 261.*

Create Alert Wizard

When an error occurs or when SQL Server fires an event, they are entered into the SQL Server Application Event log. The SQL Server Agent reads the Application Event log and does a comparison of the events to an alert (which you define). If a match is found, an alert is fired.

SEE ALSO
➤ *For more information about creating alerts, see page 291.*

Create Job Wizard

A Job is something that is executed on a regular basis. The Job can be a Transact-SQL statement, and executable, or even a script (VBScript). For example, you might want to clean out all the hits your database tracks for a certain Web page. This can be done each day, week, month, or even year. The job can be simple or very complex.

SEE ALSO
➤ *Chapter 9 shows you how to schedule jobs; see page 284.*

Database Maintenance Plan Wizard

The Database Maintenance Plan Wizard actually creates a series of jobs that help your database perform its best. For instance, it can schedule backups on a regular basis and check for any inconsistencies.

SEE ALSO

➤ *Creating a maintenance plan is discussed on page 311.*

Create Index Wizard

Indexes are created automatically when you create PRIMARY and UNIQUE constraints; however, you might also want to create indexes on other fields that will be queried often. The create Index wizard enables you to select a table and then create indexes on a given field. If indexes already exist, the wizard will notify you of this. You can specify the index as a clustered index (if one does not already exist), a non-clustered index, unique index, the fill factors can also be selected. If an item cannot be indexed, such as a picture data type field which stores the information in a binary format (not good for indexing), SQL Server will block out that field for indexing.

Create Stored Procedures Wizard

Stored procedures are compiled queries. Why would you want to have compiled queries and what are they? Every time you run a query, the SQL Engine must examine the query and make sure that all the fields and tables are valid. Then, it must decide to execute the query.

When you create a stored procedure, all of this is done once. Not having the overhead of finding the best path to take when running a query can save on performance.

SEE ALSO

➤ *Chapter 15 shows a helpful use for a stored procedure; see page 500.*

Create View Wizard

A view is a virtual table that represents a different way of viewing a current table. This could be used for a variety of factors,

including but not limited to displaying all the pertinent information for a very large table, and displaying a subset of non-
sensitive data. Security permissions can be administered to
allow only HR to see the whole table that shows salary,
whereas ordinary users see basic information from the view.

DTS Import/Export Wizard

The DTS (Data Transformation Services) Wizard enables you to
easily use DTS to import or export heterogeneous information
using OLE DB and ODBC; you can also copy database schemas
and data between relational databases.

Heterogeneous data is data that is stored in different file formats.
Using DTS with OLE DB and ODBC enables you to retrieve
data from one file format and use it with another.

SEE ALSO

➤ *For information on using views for more secure data, see page 431.*

Web Assistant Wizard

The Web Assistant Wizard generates HTML pages based on
SQL Server data, queries, stored procedures, and so on. The
HTML files can be published so that they are viewable by the
company's intranet or over the Internet for the world to view.
The pages themselves don't query the database and are therefore
not dynamic. However, Jobs can be created that regularly recreate the pages, or a trigger could launch a task to re-create the
page whenever an item is inserted, updated, or deleted.

Configuring Publishing and Distribution Wizard

The Configure Publishing as Distribution Wizard can be used
for

- Configuring a server for publication.
- Selecting the databases for publication.
- Selecting servers to subscribe to publications.
- Configuring a server as a distributor.
- Specifying the location of the database.

- Specifying the location of the log file.
- Enabling other publishers to use the current server as a distributor.
- Choosing a remote server as the remote distributor for a publisher.
- Registering subscribers to the publishers.

Create Publication Wizard

The Create Publication Wizard is used to enable a database to be used for publication. Part of preparing a database for publication is selecting tables or stored procedures to be published as articles.

Pull Subscription Wizard

> **You must set up publication and distribution before Push or Pull**
>
> If you have not set up publication and distribution, the wizard will initiate the Publication and Distribution Wizard first. After this has been completed, you will be allowed to run the Pull Subscription Wizard.

The Pull Subscription Wizard will help you create subscriptions to publication.

You can use the Pull Wizard to

- Specify which publication you to subscribe to.
- Specify the name of the destination server used for the subscription.
- Change Subscriber properties.
- Synchronize the schedule with the publisher.
- Manage the visibility of the subscription to other subscribers.
- Specify if the subscription is updateable.
- Specify the priority for each subscriber during conflicts

Push Subscription Wizard

The Push Subscription Wizard will help you in creating subscriptions to publications.

You can use the Push Wizard to

- Specify which server of server groups will receive the publication as a subscriber.

- Install the Destination Database.
- Specify scheduling.

Uninstalling Publishing and Distribution Wizard

If you uninstall the Publishing and Distribution Wizard you are effectively disabling Publishing and Distribution on your server. All publications on the server are dropped. All subscriptions to these publications are dropped. The distribution database is also deleted.

Disabling (uninstalling) publishing and distribution doesn't affect subscriptions received from other publishers.

Manual deletion required

Although the subscriptions are dropped at the publisher, subscription information at the subscribers must be deleted as well. This information doesn't perform a cascade deletion of subscribers.

chapter

8

Managing Databases

This chapter covers database creation and management. Creating or implementing a design for a SQL Server database means planning, creating and maintaining the database.

As we delve into creating a database, you might be asking the question "Why aren't we talking about creating devices first?" "Where are the devices?" "Why can't I find a way to create devices?"

If SQL Server is new to you, this won't matter or make any sense, but for those SQL Server old timers...I have some news for you. Devices are finally gone. Let's all take a moment and bow our head to the SQL Server gurus who finally took this headache out of our lives forever.

In previous releases of SQL Server, a device was a storage area for your database file and log files. You first allocated disk space by creating a device with a certain amount of storage space, for example, 10MB for the data device, and maybe 2MB for a log device. You actually didn't need to create separate devices for a log and data file. However, if you didn't create separate devices, you couldn't do separate backups.

After you created the device, you could then create a database. When creating the database, you specified where the database would reside as well as where the log would reside. One database could spread across multiple devices and a single device could hold multiple databases. To me this was not a very organized data structure. To make it worse, if the database was filled to capacity (and so was the device), you first had to increase the size of the device, and then you could increase the size of the database.

Expanding a device is no longer necessary (it's no longer there). In fact the SQL Server team did us a favor. By creating everything on a file basis, the log and data files are automatically separated. Creating a data device and a log device is no longer part of the process of creating a database.

If this seems foreign and a bit scary, just take a deep breath and relax. The rest of this chapter is devoted to starting you from the ground up. Just follow through the examples and take this chapter one step at a time. By the end, everything will become very clear to you. And to those of you who are new to SQL Server, you should be thanking the SQL Server team because they took the overhead of device understanding and maintenance out of the learning curve.

Planning SQL Server Databases

The complexity of a database application can vary greatly. Having a robust design means allowing the database to grow as your users and data grows. You need to consider the number of users who will be logged on to the system at any one time and the number of transactions each user is performing.

Keep in mind, when planning your database you should be thinking not only about the effect it will have on your hardware, but also about the logic behind the database.

Estimating Database Size

Understanding how data is stored is important for deciding how much space needs to be allocated for the database itself. Data is stored in pages and extents. The sizing has changed from previous releases of SQL Server.

- Pages. A *page* is the fundamental unit of data storage for SQL Server. In Version 7.0 the page size is 8KB. This is increased from 2KB for earlier versions. SQL Server 7.0 can have 128 pages per megabyte of disk space (1 MB = 1024 KB, 1024 / 8 = 128)

  The start of each page has a header that takes up 96 bytes to store information about the page. Data is stored in data rows. Rows are placed in order after the header. A row cannot span two pages, so the maximum amount of space a single row can use is 8060 bytes.

- Extents. An *extent* is eight contiguous pages, or 64KB. Two types of extents exist: mixed and uniform. A mixed extent shares its space with up to eight objects. A single object owns uniform extents, and only that object can use all eight pages. When a table or index is created, it allocates pages from a mixed extent. When a table has grown to eight pages, it is switched to a uniform extent.

Estimating the Size of Your Database

We now know the maximum amount of data that can be stored in each row. We can now also figure out how many pages and extents will be needed when we build our database. Then we can figure out, based on some complex theory of ours, how much the database will grow, right? That was the way we used to do it, or at least that was the suggested way of doing it. Most of us just created the database, guessed on the size needed, and then added space when needed. Thankfully, SQL Server 7.0 decided to do some fine-tuning in this arena.

Estimating the size of a database just got a whole lot easier with SQL Server 7.0. Before, if you wanted to accurately estimate the size of you database, you needed to figure out how much data would be stored in each row of each table, and then guess/estimate the amount of data that would be entered into the database.

Believe me when I say that this was hardly ever accurate. Now I'm sure that there are plenty of people out there that have done a terrific job with this; however, this is one of my least favorite things to do. We should be spending more of our time creating a great design rather than trying to figure out how many megabytes of a 20GB hard drive will need to be reserved.

With SQL Server 7.0, you don't even need to do an estimation if you don't want to. You can tell the SQL Server to allow the database to grow automatically. If you don't want your database to be able to take over the whole hard drive, well, that's okay too. SQL Server 7.0 enables you to specify the maximum amount of space you want to allow the database to occupy. Be aware that if you don't specify the maximum size, you are telling SQL Server that it is okay to use the whole hard drive if necessary.

You'll revisit this in a little while when you create your database. First, you need to understand a few more things.

Planning the SQL Server Database Transaction Log

Transaction logs are not as complicated as data files. Transaction logs simply contain a series of log records. These records contain all the necessary information needed for the recovery of the database in the unfortunate event of system crash or hardware failure.

By default, when creating a log for SQL Server 7.0 the size of the transaction log is 25 percent. This is used primarily as a rough estimate, and you can change the size according to your needs.

How Does a Transaction Log Work?

A transaction log records all the data modifications done to your database. This includes INSERTS, UPDATES, and DELETE statements, or stored procedures. They are recorded in real time (as they execute). It records the start of each transaction, and it stores all the information necessary to undo the modifications if needed. The log file continues to grow, and gets truncated only when a full database backup is completed or if the Truncate Log on Checkpoint option has been set. A check point is issued whenever SQL Server is sure that the data has been successfully written to disk.

The process of recording a transaction to a data file

1. An application or other means sends a modification statement to the database.

2. The data being modified is read into memory.

3. Modifications are then recorded in the transaction log on the disk.

4. If all goes well, a checkpoint is issued in the transaction log, and the data is written to the database. However, if something bad happens, a rollback can be issued that returns the data to its normal state.

How to Create a SQL Server Database and Transaction Log

The database and transaction log goes hand and hand with SQL Server 7.0. Because it is tied together, we will cover the creation of both objects at the same time.

You can create a database and transaction log by three different methods:

- The old-fashioned Transact-SQL command CREATE DATABASE
- Enterprise Manager
- SQL Server's new wizards

When creating a database, you are defining the name, size, and the location of the database. All other parameters are optional.

Creating a database actually creates a duplicate of the model database. If you find you are repeating several tasks in each database after you create it, you can actually modify the model database with the new tables, stored procedures, and so on. The next time you create a database, those changes will be in your new database as well.

Creating a Database and Transaction Log with Transact-SQL

CREATE DATABASE has changed significantly from previous versions of Microsoft SQL Server.

The syntax is as follows:

```
CREATE DATABASE database_name
[ON {
[PRIMARY](NAME = locgical_file_name,
    FILENAME = 'path_and_file_name'
    [, SIZE = size]
    [, MAXSIZE = max_size]
    [, FILEGROWTH = growth_increment]
    }[,...n]
]
[LOG ON
    {
```

```
    (NAME = logical_file_name,
    FILENAME = 'path_and_file_name'
    [, SIZE = size])
    }[,...n]
]
[FOR RESTORE]
```

PRIMARY

This option specifies the primary filegroup. The primary file-group must contain all the system tables for the database. A database can have only one PRIMARY filegroup. If one is not specified, the first one listed will become the PRIMARY. (We will be discussing file grouping later in this chapter).

FILENAME

This is the path and filename of the file you are creating. The file must be located on the same server as SQL Server. It can be on a different hard drive as long as it is on the same physical machine.

SIZE

Specifies the size in megabytes you want to allocate to your database. The minimum value is 1MB, and the default is 3MB for data files, and 1MB for log files.

MAXSIZE

This option enables you to specify the maximum size to size to which your file can grow. The default allows your file to grow until the disk is full.

FILEGROWTH

This option enables you to specify the growth increment of the file itself. This setting cannot exceed the MAXSIZE setting. A value of 0 will indicate no growth is allowed. The default is 10 percent, meaning that each time it grows it will allocate an additional 10 percent to itself.

Clearer results in the Query Analyzer

If you run this in the SQL Server Query Analyzer the response you get is better than the old version. In previous versions, the Results pane displayed something like `This command did not return any data,` (which meant that everything went just fine).

In Version 7.0 your Results pane should display something more specific as shown in Figure 8.1.

For example, to perform this operation, enter the following into a SQL Server code editor, such as Query Analyzer.

```
CREATE DATABASE myDatabase
ON
        PRIMARY (NAME=myDatabase_data,
        FILENAME = 'C:\mssql7\data\myDatabase.mdf',
        SIZE=10MB,
        MAXSIZE=15MB,
        FILEGROWTH=25%)
LOG ON
        (NAME=myDatabase_log,
        FILENAME='C:\mssql7\data\myDatabase.ldf',
        SIZE=4MB,
        MAXSIZE=6MB,
        FILEGROWTH=2MB)
```

Figure 8.1 shows the CREATE DATABASE Transact SQL statement in action.

FIGURE 8.1
The results of the space allocation in the SQL Server Query Analyzer.

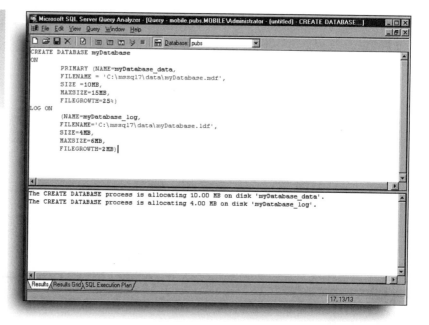

SEE ALSO

➤ *Appendix A contains several examples and more information on creating objects with Transact-SQL on page 641.*

➤ *For more information on using the Query Analyzer, see page 232.*

➤ *If you prefer to use the osql utility, see page 238.*

Create a SQL Server Database with Enterprise Manager

Creating a Database and Transaction log from within Enterprise manager is relatively simple.

Creating a database in Enterprise Manager

1. Open Enterprise manager. Choose Start, Programs, SQL Server 7.0, Enterprise Manager.

2. On the left pane, open Microsoft SQL Servers.

3. Open SQL Server Group.

4. Scroll down to Databases and right-click, as shown in Figure 8.2.

5. Select New Database.

6. Fill in the name for your database.

7. Select the options you want. For now take all the defaults.

8. Click OK.

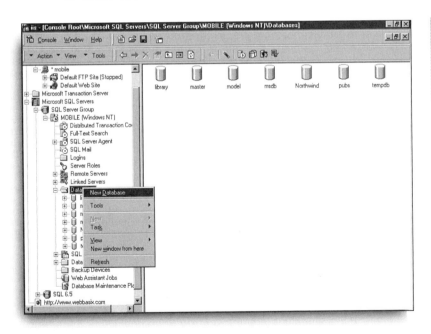

FIGURE 8.2
Creating a database with a right-click!

That's it! You just created a database and log file with the Enterprise Manager. All the defaults were used so you may want to make some changes, but for now this was sufficient.

Optional Settings

When creating your database with the Enterprise Manager, you have the option of changing the defaults as you did with the Transact-SQL Statement. A few additional items were done for you when using the Enterprise Manager. For instance, the following list shows some of the options available to you in the dialog box (they are in no particular order, and can be set in order you may choose):

General and Transaction Log tabs are shown in Figures 8.3 and 8.4.

- Filename:

  Created based on the Database Name.

  Extensions of _Data are added for the Data file and _Log for the Log file.

FIGURE 8.3
Naming the database with Enterprise Manager.

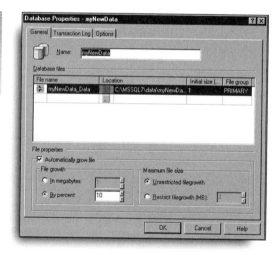

- Location:

  The file was placed in the Default location (the installation directory of SQL Server).

  Extensions were also attached to the Data and Log location names.

FIGURE 8.4

Viewing the corresponding Transaction log file information.

- Initial Size:

  1MB was allocated for the Data file.

  1MB was allocated for the Log file.

- File Properties:

  Both are set to:

  Automatically grow

  Grow by 10 percent

  Have unrestricted growth

The Options tab appears as shown in Figure 8.5:

- No items were selected for the available options on the Options tab. We will be discussing what each option can do later in this chapter.

How to Create a SQL Server Database Using the Create Database Wizard

Now let's close the loop by creating a Database and Transaction Log with the wizard. The wizard will walk you through the creation of a Database and Log step by step. You can leave the defaults or change them if you wish to experiment.

FIGURE 8.5

Database options you can set using Enterprise Manager.

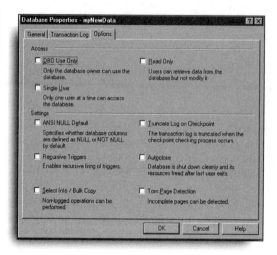

Creating a Database and Transaction Log with the wizard

1. From inside the MMC choose Tools, Wizards. All the objects that have wizards are listed in alphabetical order.

2. After you select Databases the tree should expand to show you a list of the available wizards for Databases.

3. Click the Create Database Wizard and then click OK.

4. By now, all this should look familiar to you. After the Splash screen, you are prompted for the database name and where it will reside on the hard drive.

5. Edit the data filename and initial size. You can also add more data files(using more data files will be discussed later in this chapter). The following lists some of the options you can alter:

   Data file options:

   Autogrow the file (y/n) (default is yes)

   How fast should it grow? (default is by 10%)

   How big should it grow? (default is unrestricted)

6. Edit the log filename and initial size. Additional log files can be added as well. The following shows you some of the options and defaults, but the defaults are usually acceptable:

Log file options:

Autogrow the file (y/n) (default is yes)

How fast should it grow? (default is by 10%)

How big should it grow? (default is unrestricted)

7. The next screen indicates that everything is ready and you can click Back to review what you have done, Cancel to cancel the operation, or Finish to complete the operation.

8. After the operation has finished, you will be prompted for the Set Up a Maintenance Plan. Select No.

How to Delete (Drop) a SQL Server Database

The action of deleting a database is referred to as *dropping a database*. You can drop a database whenever you are finished with it. You will probably be adding and dropping databases frequently during the design phase. During production, you want to be extremely careful about dropping databases; after all, during development the only people using the database should be developers and beta testers. If something goes wrong, you can say that's just part of development. If something goes wrong when your system is fully online, you can bet that head will roll.

You can drop a database by executing the DROP DATABASE statement shown in Listing 8.1 or by using SQL Server Enterprise Manage.

LISTING 8.1 Dropping a Database with Transact-SQL

```
1 DROP DATABASE database_name [,…n]
2
3 Example: dropping a single database
4 DROP DATABASE library
5
6     Example: dropping multiple databases
7     DROP DATABASE library, pubs, and northwind
```

Dropping a database in previous versions

In previous versions of SQL Server, if you dropped the database and the device from Enterprise Manager, you still needed to delete the file from the hard drive. This is not the case with Version 7.0. Using the Enterprise Manager or the DROP DATABASE statement will also delete the corresponding file.

Dropping a Database with SQL Server Enterprise Manager

1. Open MMC.
2. Open the Database folder.
3. Right-click the database you want to drop.
4. Select Delete (drop is not available as an option).
5. You a prompted with a confirmation box. Select Yes.

Things to Consider When Dropping a Database

When dropping a database you should consider the following:

- With the Transact-SQL command DROP DATABASE, you can delete several databases at once.
- The Enterprise Manager will only allow you to drop one database at a time.
- After you drop a database, any Login ID that used the dropped database as its default will now use the master database.
- You should always back up that master database after any database is added or deleted.

Restrictions of Dropping Databases

Warning: Dropping the msdb system database

SQL Server enables you to drop the msdb system database; however, it is unwise to do so. The msdb database is used for the following important services: SQL Server Agent, Replication, SQL Server Web Wizard, Data Transformation Services (DTS).

Even if you are not currently using these services, it is wise to not delete the msdb.

There are a few restrictions to keep in mind when you drop a database.

You cannot drop databases that are

- Currently opened for reading or writing by another user.
- Currently being restored.
- Publishing any of its tables (part of SQL replication).

In addition, you cannot drop the following system databases:

- Master
- Model
- Tempdb

SEE ALSO

➤ *You might want to generate a message to avoid having tables deleted accidently; see page 687 for more information.*

Setting SQL Server Database Options

A number of database options can be set for each individual database. Only the System Administrator or the Database owner can change these options. Changing these options will only modify the current database; it will not effect other databases.

Database options can be modified with the sp_dboption system stored procedure, or by using SQL Server Enterprise Manager. Using SQL Server Enterprise Manager only gives you a subset of the available options. Sp_dboption will only affect the current database, but to modify serverwide settings, use the sp_configure system stored procedure.

After you make a change, a checkpoint is automatically issued, making the change immediate.

SQL Server Database Options

Following is a listing of the more common database options. For a detail on each option, see your Books Online.

An asterisk (*) indicates Enterprise Manager can perform this operation; otherwise, it is a stored procedure option only.

*ANSI null default

Controls whether the default value for all data types is NULL. Microsoft defaults to Not Null. If this setting is checked, the default reverses for that database.

When issuing a CREATE TABLE unless the creator explicitly states NOT NULL, the rule will apply to the table creation as well.

ANSI Nulls

When set to TRUE comparisons of any value to a NULL will evaluate to a NULL. When set to FALSE only comparison of non-Unicode values will evaluate to TRUE if and only if both values are NULL.

ANSI Warnings

When set to TRUE, error warnings are displayed.

*autoclose

When set to TRUE, the database automatically closes when the last user breaks a connection. This is very useful for desktop environments, but should be avoided in cases where connections are contiguously being made and dropped. The amount of overhead generated for opening and closing a database can have a negative effect on a production environment.

*autoshrink

When set to TRUE, SQL Server will periodically shrink the database files if necessary.

*dbo use only

When set to TRUE, only the dbo has access to the database. Use this option when performing database fixes.

published

Used for replication, when published is set to TRUE publication is enabled. Setting this to false disables publication.

*read only

TRUE indicates the database is read-only. FALSE allows read/write access.

*recursive triggers

When set to TRUE, this allows recursive triggers to fire. When set to FALSE (the default), triggers cannot fire recursively. A recursive trigger is one that fires on the originating table, causing an update on another table, which then causes an update on the originating table.

Disconnecting users with dbo use only?

This will not disconnect any active users; however, users who aren't logged on won't be able to do so until the option has be set back to FALSE.

*select into/bulk copy

This allows the database to accept non-logged actions such as SELECT INTO and the bcp utility.

*single user

This allows only a single user to access the database.

subscribed

When subscribed is set to TRUE, the database can be subscribed to for publication.

*torn page detection

When *torn page detection is set to TRUE SQL Server will detect incomplete disk reads to be flagged. Power failures or other system malfunctions can cause torn pages.

*Truncate Log on Checkpoint (*trunc. Log on chkpt.)

When this is set to TRUE, SQL Server truncates the transaction log whenever it encounters a checkpoint. This is mainly used for development so that the transaction log doesn't become full too often. You should not use this option in a production system.

*Auto create statistics

When set to TRUE, statisics are generated for a query optimization if the statistics are missing.

*Auto update statistics

When set to TRUE, statisics are generated for a query optimization if the statistics are out of date.

Set Database Options Using the *sp_dboption*

Follow these steps for changing database options using the sp_dboption.

Syntax:

```
sp_dboption ['database'] [,'option'] [,'value']
```

Example:

```
sp_dboption 'pubs', 'read only', 'true'
```

To view the current status of the pubs data base, issue the following command:

```
sp_dboption 'pubs'
```

All the settings that have been activated are listed.

Getting all available options for sp_dboption

Executing the `sp_dboption` without any parameter will return all the options available.

Database Options Using SQL Enterprise Manager

When using the SQL Enterprise Manager to change database options, you are only presented with a subset (about half) of the actual list.

Changing the database options through Enterprise Manager

1. Open the Server Group.
2. Open the Server.
3. Open the Databases.
4. Right-click the database you want to change, and then click Properties.
5. Select the Options tab.
6. Select the option(s) to change.
7. Click OK when finished.

Files and Filegroups

Files and filegroups are the new storage structure for SQL Server. A database is stored in a file structure, and then a default filegroup is created when you create your database. Other files can be added to your design. These files can then be grouped together based on user-defined filegroups. In most cases, you will only use the default filegroup and have only one file for your database structure. As we will see, however, once you feel comfortable with the file and filegroup concept, performance can be increased and administration can be made easier.

We will start off by looking at the file and the three different types of files. Then, we will add filegroups and assign files to filegroups.

Files

As mentioned earlier, SQL Server creates databases and logs based on a file structure instead of the Disk Device specification from previous releases. This allows the databases and log files to scale with greater ease. Each file can only by used by one database. It cannot be shared between multiple databases. When a database is dropped from DROP DATABASE or Enterprise Manager, the associated file is deleted as well.

Microsoft SQL Server has three types of files:

- Primary. The primary file is the default file for a database. Every database must have at least on primary data file. The default and recommended file extension is .mdf.

- Secondary. Secondary data files are other (non-primary) data files in the database. It is not necessary to have secondary data files, but as we will see they have a definite purpose in providing scalability and performance enhancements. The default and recommended extensions is .ndf.

- Log. A log file is the storage area for all the changes to the databases. Every database must have at least one log file. The default and recommended extension is .ldf.

Forcing default file extensions?

SQL Server will not enforce the recommended file extension. They are simply there to help you manage your database files.

Filegroups

When a database is created, the primary filegroup contains the primary file. Other filegroups (user defined filegroups) can be created and grouped for allocation and administration purposes. You create a filegroup as a named collection of files. No file can be a member of more that one filegroup.

Three types of filegroups exist:

- Primary. The primary filegroup contains the primary data file and any other data files not assigned to another filegroup.

- User-defined. User-defined filegroups are created using the FILEGROUP keyword when using CREATE DATABASE or ALTER DATABASE statements.

Transaction logs versus filegroups

Transaction logs are not part of filegroups. Transaction logs are managed by themselves as separate entities.

■ Default. The default filegroup is the group that is created when no filegroup is specified during a table creation. Only one filegroup can be the default in each database.

The following uses the CREATE DATABASE statement to create a primary data file, a user-defined filegroup, and a log file. You then issue an ALTER DATABASE statement to change the default filegroup to the user-defined filegroup.

```
USE MASTER
GO
    Two dashes are comment markers
    Create the database

CREATE DATABASE myNewData
ON
PRIMARY (NAME=myNewData_data,
FILENAME = 'c:\mssql7\data\myNewData.mdf',
SIZE=10MB,
MAXSIZE=15MB,
FILEGROWTH=10%)
    FILEGROUP myNewData_FG1
        (NAME = 'myNewData_FG1_DAT1',
        FILENAME = 'c:\mssql7\data\myNewData_FG1_DAT1.ndf',
        SIZE=3MB,
        MAXSIZE=10MB,
        FILEGROWTH=10%),
        (NAME = 'myNewData_FG1_DAT2',
        FILENAME = 'c:\mssql7\data\myNewData_FG1_DAT2.ndf',
        SIZE=3MB,
        MAXSIZE=10MB,
        FILEGROWTH=10%)
    LOG ON
        (NAME = myNewData_log,
        FILENAME = 'c:\mssql\data\myNewData.ldf',
        SIZE=5MB,
        MAXSIZE=15MB,
        FILEGROWTH=10%)
    GO
    --Use Alter to change the default filegroup
    ALTER DATABASE myNewDB
    MODIFY FILEGROUP myNewData_FG1 DEFAULT
    GO
```

Additionally, you can create files in specific filegroups. Then, if you create a heavily used file in a filegroup on the D drive and another heavily used file on the E drive, when a memory intensive query is being performed you can have the query performed in parallel.

Documenting SQL Server Database Creation Steps

Documenting SQL Server Database Creation Steps or the structure of the database can be useful for a number of reasons, but of course the main and most compelling is a back up of the work you have done. This will not necessarily save you from data loss, but it will save your schema, and a database schema is a horrible thing to lose.

Microsoft SQL Server has a script generator that makes it easy for you to document, and if necessary rebuild, your database. The script generator can build the database and the objects created in the database. You have a choice of selecting anywhere from all of the objects to just a single one. You can take the script from one database and run it in another to create exact duplicates of stored procedures, rules, triggers, etc. You can generate scripts for the following objects:

- Tables
- Stored Procedures
- Triggers
- Indexes
- Views
- Users and Groups
- User-defined data types
- Logins
- Rules
- Defaults
- Table Keys/DRI

The schema can be saved into a single file or you may want to break them up on a per object basis. Regardless of your method, you no longer have a good excuse for an undocumented database.

Generate a script from SQL Server Enterprise Manager

1. Expand the server group.

2. Expand the server.

3. Expand the databases.

4. Right-click on the appropriate database, as shown in Figure 8.6.

5. Click on Tasks.

6. Select Generate SQL Scripts.

7. Select the options you want to generate in the dialog, as shown in Figure 8.7.

You can preview the file first or simply click OK to save it to a file.

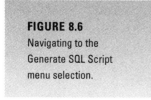

FIGURE 8.6
Navigating to the Generate SQL Script menu selection.

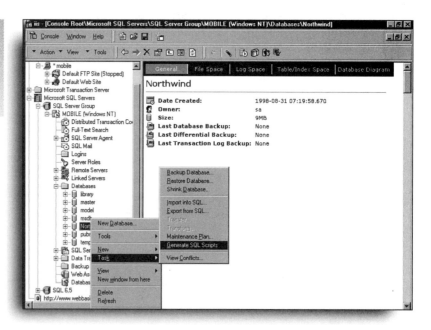

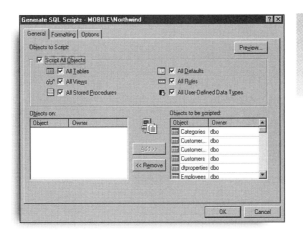

FIGURE 8.7

Available options during Script Generation.

SEE ALSO

➤ *For more information on establishing a backup strategy to prevent all data loss, see page 455.*

➤ *Appendix A contains several examples and more information on creating objects with Transact-SQL on page 641.*

➤ *For more information on using the Query Analyzer, see page 232.*

➤ *If you prefer to use the osql utility, see page 238.*

➤ *You might want to generate a message to avoid having tables deleted accidently; see page 687 for more information.*

chapter
9

Scheduling Tasks and Alerts

Understand what SQL Server Agent is

Understand how to configure
SQL Server Agent options

Create jobs to perform routine tasks

Create alerts to monitor SQL Server

Install SQL Mail and use it with
alerts and jobs

One of the primary goals of SQL Server 7.0 is to make life easy for the database administrator (DBA). SQL Server 7.0 manages its own memory requirements and database file sizes, and has numerous wizards to assist you in performing a variety of tasks. However, perhaps one of the most useful tools is the SQL Server Agent. SQL Server Agent essentially acts like an assistant that spares you from the tedium of performing tasks that occur on a regular basis. It also monitors the server for you and notifies you if a problem occurs. In addition, it is the workhorse behind the replication process. Specifically, SQL Server Agent is a tool used to do the following:

- Immediately alert you, or someone else, if a problem occurs.
- Solve problems and prevent potential problems automatically.
- Perform routine maintenance without DBA assistance.
- Delay low priority processing until the server is less busy.
- Easily and regularly share data with other data stores.

As you probably already know, many things have to be done to keep a Database Management System (DBMS) functioning efficiently. SQL Server Agent acts as an administrative assistant for you by automatically performing most of the maintenance and support that SQL Server requires. This chapter covers how you can configure the SQL Server Agent to manage the following:

- Jobs. Jobs are actions, such as backing up a database, that can be scheduled to execute on a recurring basis.
- Alerts. Alerts are events, like maximum allowed logons has been reached, that you can define and have SQL Server Agent watch for. SQL Server Agent then notifies you when a defined event occurs.
- SQL Mail. SQL Mail is a feature of SQL Server that allows it to send and receive email.

Replication

SQL Server Agent also administers SQL Server replication.

The chapter is separated into four sections. The first section provides an overview of the SQL Server Agent and gives you step-by-step instructions for its configuration. The following three sections cover jobs, alerts, and SQL Mail, providing step-by-step instructions for use along with examples and explanations of the features. The sections don't need to be read in sequence, but you should read the section on SQL Server Agent first.

SEE ALSO

➤ *For more information on how SQL Server 7.0 has automated replication, see page 553.*

SQL Server Agent Overview

SQL Server Agent is a program designed to run in the background on a Windows NT Server, just like the SQL Server engine itself. In Windows NT terms, SQL Server Agent is a *service*. To understand the capabilities and functionality of SQL Server Agent, it is important to remember that the SQL Server Agent service isn't part of the SQL Server service. Both SQL Server Agent and SQL Server represent distinct processes to the operating system and therefore both can run independently of the other. However, SQL Server Agent relies on SQL Server to store the information it needs to carry out its instructions. Specifically, SQL Server Agent stores data in the MSDB database in SQL Server. If the SQL Server service isn't running, the SQL Server Agent service can't access data about jobs to execute and alerts to monitor.

By designing SQL Server Agent as a separate process, Microsoft saves the SQL Server service from the burden of job, alert, and replication management. The SQL Server service is free to focus on just the tasks of data management.

The SQL Server Agent, as mentioned previously, acts like an assistant to the DBA. It can automate regular DBA functions such as database backups. It can monitor SQL Server for errors and upon finding one, either execute a job to correct the problem or send an email notification to a DBA. It also coordinates the synchronization and replication of data with other DBMSs. Without the SQL Server Agent, most DBAs would spend hours every night of the week backing up databases and transaction logs, as well as performing other operations that prepare SQL

Formerly known as

In previous versions of SQL Server, SQL Server Agent was known as SQL Executive.

Server to run more efficiently the next day. Additionally, DBAs would probably not be aware of problems with SQL Server until someone using the SQL Server contacted the DBA about the problems. If you don't desire these self-administration features (as is often the case on test systems), you don't have to run the SQL Server Agent service.

SEE ALSO

➤ *For more information on general DBA tasks, see page 27.*

➤ *For more information on automating back-ups with SQL Server Agent, see page 453.*

The SQL Server Agent Functions

The primary role of the SQL Server Agent service is to monitor, maintain, and support the operations of the SQL Server service. It does this by controlling the following functions:

- Job Management. Running routine maintenance tasks such as database backups and index re-creations on defined schedules.

- Alert Management. Sending notifications through email when problems occur. Corrective action can also be taken by running jobs.

- Event Management. Monitoring the Windows NT Application Log for the conditions that are defined by alerts.

- Replication Management. Distributing data from SQL Server to other database management systems through a process called replication. Replication is discussed in detail in Chapter 17.

SQL Server Agent Configuration

SQL Server Agent usually requires customization for each server. All of SQL Server Agent's properties are maintained through the Properties dialog shown in Figure 9.1. These properties include the following:

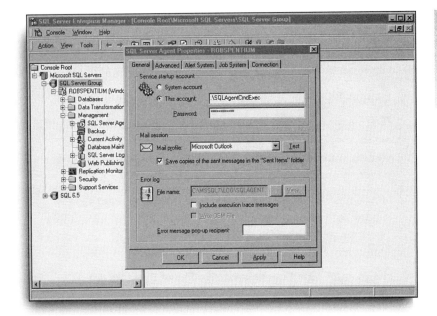

FIGURE 9.1

This dialog is used to set up and configure SQL Server Agent..

- The account SQL Server Agent uses to log on to NT.
- The account SQL Server Agent uses to log on to SQL Server.
- The account SQL Server uses to log on to an email server.
- The location of the SQL Server Agent Error Log..
- The default operator to notify if an error occurs.
- The limits placed on the size of the job history log.

Other SQL Server Agent properties related to alerts and jobs are covered in their respective sections later in this chapter.

How to Configure the SQL Server Agent to Log On to NT

The Service Startup Account is the account that the SQL Server Agent service uses to log on to NT Server. When SQL Server Agent logs on, it can do so with the System Account, or with an NT User Account. The System Account is an account built into NT Server for services running on NT Server that won't be interacting with other computers. The permissions on the System Account are restricted to accessing objects, such as directories and printers, controlled by that NT server.

If SQL Server is going to be replicating data to other servers, sending or receiving email, or running tasks that need to access files on other servers, SQL Server Agent should be configured to log on to NT Server using an NT User Account.

Assign an NT User Account to the SQL Server Agent service

1. Create the NT User Account using the NT program User Manager for Domains. The NT User Account should be configured as shown in Figure 9.2 and as follows:

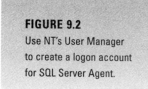

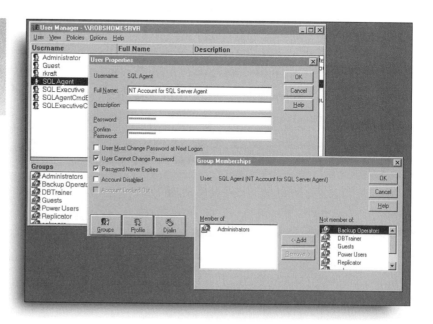

- Disable User Must Change Password at Next Logon.

- Enable User Cannot Change Password.

- Enable Password Never Expires.

- Make the account a member of the Administrators Group.

- Grant the account the advanced right of Log On as a Service Right from the Policies, User Rights menu .

2. Click Add to save the new NT Account and exit User Manager.

3. In Enterprise Manager, right-click SQL Server Agent and select Properties to open the Properties dialog.

4. Choose the General tab (selected by default) and click the This Account option in the Service Startup Account frame as shown in Figure 9.3. Type the name of the NT User Account just added to the This Account box, and then type the NT User Account password in the Password box and click OK.

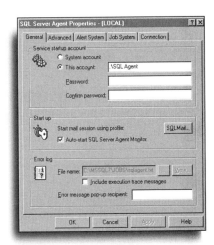

FIGURE 9.3

Select the account SQL Server Agent uses to log on to NT Server from the General tab in SQL Server Agent Properties.

5. A dialog prompts you to restart the SQL Server Agent service. This causes SQL Server Agent to log off of NT server and then log on again using the newly assigned NT User Account.

How to Configure SQL Server Agent to Log On to SQL Server

The information on the Connection tab controls how SQL Server Agent logs on to SQL Server. This information is unrelated to the information on the General tab, which controls how SQL Server Agent logs on to NT Server. SQL Server operates under one of two possible security modes; see Chapter 11, "Introduction to SQL Security," for an explanation of these modes.

Select Use Windows NT Authentication to have SQL Server Agent log on to SQL Server with the same account it uses to log on to NT Server. Windows NT Authentication is recommended. If you want SQL Server Agent to log on to SQL Server with a different account than the one used to log on to NT Server, select Use SQL Server Authentication and select the desired administrative account from the SysAdmin logon ID drop-down list. You also need to provide the Password for this account as shown in Figure 9.4.

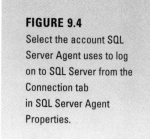

FIGURE 9.4
Select the account SQL Server Agent uses to log on to SQL Server from the Connection tab in SQL Server Agent Properties.

SEE ALSO

➤ *For more information on NT security, see page 371.*

How to Set the Location of the SQL Server Agent Error Log

SQL Server Agent keeps a detailed log of the actions it initiates. The log tracks alerts fired, replication, jobs executed, and the complete output messages from the jobs. You can configure SQL Server Agent to log Errors, Warnings, Informational Messages, or any combination of those three. You can also specify the name and location of the error log files. Just like the error log for the SQL Server service, the SQL Server Agent service creates a new log file each time SQL Server Agent is restarted. The last ten log files are kept automatically.

You can specify the location of the SQL Server Agent Error Log from the General tab of SQL Server Agent's properties. To view the contents of the SQL Server Agent Error Log, right-click the SQL Server Agent in Enterprise Manager and choose Display Error Log.

SEE ALSO

➤ *For more information on using the error log to troubleshoot problems in SQL Server, see page 602.*

How to Configure SQL Server Agent to Automatically Restart SQL Server

Both SQL Server and SQL Server Agent can be configured to restart automatically if they are unexpectedly stopped. Check the boxes in Restart Services on the Advanced tab of SQL Server Agent's properties for this to take effect, as shown in Figure 9.5.

Selecting this option causes SQL Server Service Manager to regularly check whether SQL Server and SQL Server Agent are executing.

Using Notepad with the Error Log

The contents of the SQL Server Agent Error Log may be browsed with any text editor.

Configuring Service Polling Interval

The frequency with which SQL Server Service Manager checks on the status of SQL Server and SQL Server Agent can be configured by setting the Polling Interval (Seconds) option of SQL Server Service Manager. Right-click the SQL Server Service Manager (running on your taskbar) to reach this option.

283

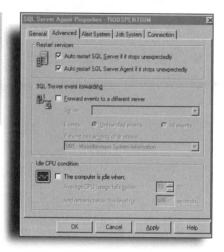

FIGURE 9.5

You can configure SQL Server and SQL Server Agent to automatically restart if either one fails.

How to Manage Jobs

The most frequently used capability of SQL Server Agent is job management. Jobs can be created to automate administrative duties like backing up databases, dropping and re-creating indexes, replicating data to other servers, checking data integrity, and performing long running operations such as creating databases during off hours. Jobs can also be used for non-administrative purposes like sending an application report through email.

Jobs in SQL Server 7.0 provide a powerful replacement for the task capabilities of previous releases. Jobs are comprised of steps. Steps are similar to tasks in SQL Server 6.x. A job represents a sequence of steps to execute. In the past, DBAs often scheduled tasks to execute based on a best guess of when preceding tasks would complete. With the new job architecture of SQL Server 7.0, all related steps (formerly tasks) execute upon completion of their dependent steps.

Job management involves six general steps

1. Creating a job. Defining the job owner and the SQL Server it executes on.

2. Creating steps. Defining what each step does when it runs.

3. Sequencing steps. Defining the order in which the steps execute.

4. Setting job options. Specifying operators to be notified when the job succeeds or fails.

5. Scheduling jobs. Determining the date and times when a job will execute. A job can be scheduled to run once or on a recurring basis.

6. Monitoring jobs. Verifying that jobs are running successfully and on the desired schedules.

Creating Jobs

Some of the wizards provided with SQL Server automatically create jobs for you. You can modify these jobs, or you can create your own jobs for the tasks that have no associated wizard. Every job requires at least one job step. A step is a specific action taken by a job. Each job may have multiple steps. For example, a weekly maintenance job may perform a database consistency check in the first step, optimize the indexes in the second step, and finally back up the database in the third step.

You can create, modify, or delete a job by selecting the desired job with a right-click of your mouse. The following sections explain the various steps involved in creating a new job.

General Job Information

When you create a new job you will see the dialog shown in Figure 9.6. Here you need to provide the following information:

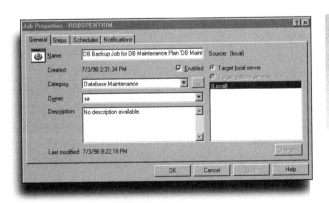

FIGURE 9.6

The name and owner of a job are entered in the General tab of the Job Properties dialog..

- Name—a unique and meaningful name for your job.

- Category—although not necessary, this enables you to group your jobs together for more useful viewing.

- Owner—a user with SysAdmin privileges will own most jobs, but you can allow other users to create their own jobs. Non-SysAdmin users generally don't have the same privileges as SysAdmin users, so their jobs may fail if they attempt to perform restricted activities (like delete a database).

- Description—provide a longer explanation of what the job does when necessary.

- By default, the new job will be enabled and targeted to run on this SQL Server.

Job Steps

Job steps are the specific actions that a job takes. The Steps tab of the Job Properties dialog lists all the steps currently assigned to the job. Editing or creating a new step presents the dialog shown in Figure 9.7.

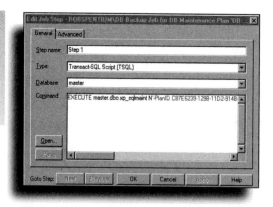

FIGURE 9.7
Job steps represent the specific actions carried out during the execution of a job.

You can create seven different types of steps, but four of these (Replication Distributor, Replication Transaction-Log Reader, Replication Merge, and Replication Snapshot) are used only for replication. The other three, which you are most likely to use, are

- Operating System Command (CmdExec). This type of step enables you to run a command (.cmd), batch (.bat) file, or any executable (.exe) program that doesn't have a graphical interface.

- Transact-SQL Script (TSQL). This type of step enables you to run an SQL query on SQL Server.

- Active Script. This type of step allows various scripting languages such as VBScript, JavaScript, and even Perl to programmatically manipulate the SQL Server and other objects.

For more information about the four replication tasks, see Chapter 17.

Transact-SQL Script steps run an SQL command when executed. The following example shows a Transact-SQL Script step to back up the pubs database:

```
BACKUP DATABASE pubs TO pubsdump WITH INIT
```

Transact-SQL Script steps must specify the database they run in. Choosing the database from the drop-down list in the Database box does this.

Active Script steps are a very powerful new feature of SQL Server 7.0. Using various scripting languages, you can create a step to manipulate almost any aspect of SQL Server. The languages enable you to manipulate the code objects that make up SQL Server. Manipulating SQL Server with code is generally easier than using SQL Server's stored procedures, and it also is less likely that you would have to change your code with subsequent releases of SQL Server. Here is an example of Visual Basic Script code that executes another job. If you have a job that performs some database operations, and you would like for it to execute the database backup when it completes, you could add an Active Script step with the following Visual Basic Script code:

```
Dim oSQL
Set oSQL = CreateObject("SQLDMO.SQLServer")
oSQL.Connect "NTServer1", "sa", ""
oSQL.JobServer.Jobs("Northwind Full DB Backup").Start(1)
set osql = nothing
```

> **Jobs owned by non-SysAdmin users**
>
> Users other than SysAdmin can create and administer their own job. SQL Server restricts user jobs to Operating System Command steps only and the user can only administer the jobs they create. User jobs run within the permissions assigned to the SQL AgentCmdExec account.

With Active Scripts you can create jobs that would modify the SQL Server in almost any way conceivable. Please see the Books Online for a description of the SQL Server object model (DMO).

Operating System Command steps are useful because they can run other programs, most often batch (.bat) or command (.cmd) files. A batch file might contain statements to import data into SQL Server from another database using the bulk copy program. A batch file could also run the OSQL program. The OSQL program provided with SQL Server allows a group of SQL statements, commonly called a script, to be run on the SQL Server. A batch file could run the OSQL program to create a table in SQL Server, and then run the bulk copy program (BCP) to import data into the newly created table, and then run the OSQL program again to create indexes on the table. This is but one example of what can be done with jobs and the OSQL program.

What happened to ISQL

The OSQL program replaces the ISQL program in previous releases. The ISQL program is still available, but does not provide as many features as the new OSQL program.

Sequencing Steps

The Steps tab of the Job Properties dialog enables you to easily change the order of execution of your steps. Simply choose the up or down arrows in the lower-left corner of the dialog to change the order of the selected step. You can also specify that the job begins execution from a step other than the first step by selecting the step to start in from the Start Step drop-down list. This feature enables you to restart a job that failed while skipping the steps that ran successfully.

How to Schedule Jobs

Jobs can be scheduled to run any one of the four ways shown in Figure 9.8.

FIGURE 9.8

Jobs can run at startup, when the CPU isn't busy, on a recurring basis, or one time.

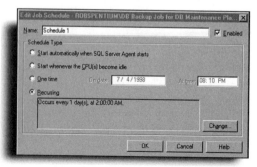

- Start Automatically when SQL Server Agent Starts. The job will begin running when SQL Server Agent is started.

- Start whenever the CPU(s) become idle. This setting is designed to allow SQL Server Agent to execute a job during periods of low activity. SQL Server Agent's definition of CPU Idle can be modified on the Advanced tab of the SQL Server Agent's Properties dialog.

- One Time. A job can be scheduled to run One Time on the date and time entered. One Time jobs are used for operations that you may want to perform when no one else is on the server, like creating new databases.

- Recurring. Most jobs are scheduled to run multiple times based on the schedule defined for the job in the Job Schedule dialog box shown in Figure 9.9.

Run any job immediately

Any job can be run immediately by right-clicking the job and selecting Start.

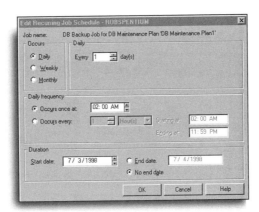

FIGURE 9.9
SQL Server provides a dialog that allows a lot of flexibility for scheduling jobs.

SQL Server also enables you to create multiple schedules for any job. This is useful in situations where it isn't easy to create a single schedule that covers when the job should run. For example, you may desire to run a backup job at 11:00 PM on week nights, and at 6:00 PM on the weekend. You can create two separate schedules for the same job to accomplish your desired schedule.

How to Modify Job Notifications

It is often important that you know if a job doesn't run successfully. You can learn about jobs that fail immediately by assigning an operator for the job to notify in the event of a failure. To do

Lack of notification may not mean success!

I recommend that you initially be notified on both failure and success of a job (Whenever the job completes). If you are only notified when the job fails, and the job doesn't even run, you will probably assume that it ran successfully.

so, select the Notifications tab of the job, and select the desired method of notification.

How to View Jobs

Figure 9.10 shows a list of SQL Server jobs.

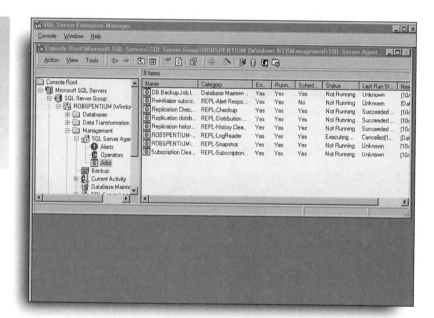

View the list of jobs defined to SQL Server

1. Expand the server group that contains the SQL Server to be administered.

2. Expand the SQL Server that has the list of jobs you want to view.

3. Expand the Management folder.

4. Expand the SQL Server Agent.

5. Click the Jobs group.

From this screen you can see at a glance if any jobs are currently executing and the status of the last execution of each job. You can click any column name above the jobs to sort the window in ascending or descending order (by clicking a second time).

To view a history of all the previous executions of a particular job, right-click the desired job from the view, and then select View Job History. The job history gives you detailed information about the success or failure of each job. This information can be invaluable to help you solve problems that occur during job execution.

By default, SQL Server keeps a record of the last 1000 jobs ran, up to a maximum of 100 per job. The 100 per job maximum prevents the history table from being filled with records from a single job.

It is possible to change the number of history records kept by changing the SQL Server Agent properties on the Job System tab as shown in Figure 9.11.

If you have fixed size databases

If you have not elected to let your databases dynamically resize themselves, increasing or not limiting the number of history rows kept may require an increase in the size of the MSDB database to provide enough space for all the data.

FIGURE 9.11

You can increase the length of time SQL Server maintains historical data about job execution by configuring SQL Server Agent.

The number of rows kept *per job* can also be configured. This prevents jobs that run frequently, like replication jobs, from dominating the contents of the entire history log.

Alerts and Operators

SQL Server Agent has the ability to notify you when various events occur on SQL Server. SQL Server Agent monitors the messages written to the Windows NT Event log, and if it finds a message that you told it to look for, it can notify you that the event has occurred. For example, if more users attempt to connect to SQL Server than you have licenses for, SQL Server writes a message to the Windows NT Application Log. SQL Server Agent considers this message an event, and you can configure SQL Server Agent to email you when this event occurs.

SQL Server Agent reads the Windows NT Application Log continuously for events that were written by SQL Server. When an event written by SQL Server is found, SQL Server Agent looks to see if you have defined an alert for the event and if you have, SQL Server Agent initiates the alert response. The alert response can be one or both of the following:

- Notification. The alert sends a message to an operator to notify the operator of the condition of SQL Server.

- Job Execution. The alert executes a previously defined job that has been created to resolve the problem.

Alerts provide you with quick notification when a problem occurs and can be used to relieve some of your administrative chores.

SQL Server Agent uses an object called an operator when sending email messages. An operator is usually associated with an email account, but it can also be associated with pager software or a network ID.

Managing Operators

You must define an operator before you can configure an alert or job to send an email message to an individual. Creating an operator associates the operator name with one or more of the following:

- An email account name in a MAPI-compliant email system.

- A pager account name in a MAPI-compliant email system.

- A net send name for machines running the NT Messenger service.

You can create operators for a variety of purposes including the following:

- Providing you notification when excessive failed logon attempts occur.

- Providing notification to a tape librarian when a backup completes and a new tape is required.

- Providing notification to a user when an application job completes.

- Providing notification to a developer when an error related to a database is encountered in an application.

How to View Operator Information

You can view a list of existing operators in SQL Enterprise Manager by expanding the SQL Server Agents folder and clicking the Operators icon (see Figure 9.12).

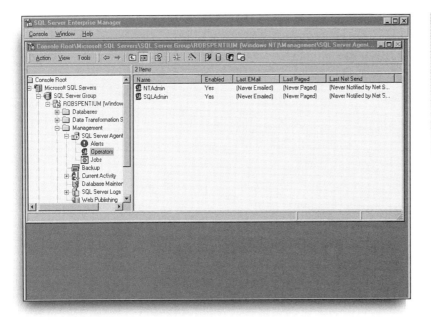

FIGURE 9.12
Operators are the people SQL Server knows about. SQL Server can send email messages to operators from Alerts and Jobs..

How to Create Operators

You can create, modify, and delete operators by right-clicking the operators group or a specific operator. When creating a new operator or modifying an existing operator, you will see the dialog shown in Figure 9.13.

FIGURE 9.13

This dialog enables you to define operators who you will notify when alerts are fired or tasks fail.

Many mechanisms of notification

SQL Server Agent can send notifications to operators through one or more of the following: email, pager, and net send. You should integrate SQL Server Agent with SQL Mail before defining email or pager operators. SQL Mail configuration is covered in the next section of this chapter.

Create an operator

1. Choose the Operators tab and right-click New Operator.

2. Enter an operator name. Only SQL Server uses the operator name; it isn't part of the email system. The operator name is associated with the E-mail Name entered below it.

3. Type the operator's email name from your email system in the E-mail Name field. Click the Test button next to the email name to send a test message to the email account to verify that it is set up correctly.

4. If the email server supports pager notifications, a name can also be entered as the Pager E-Mail Name in the Operator dialog box.

5. Select the Notifications tab in the Operator dialog box to display all alerts currently defined to SQL Server, and the alerts assigned to this operator. From this tab you can select which events this particular operator should be notified about.

Managing Alerts

Alerts provide a proactive mechanism for monitoring the performance of SQL Server. DBAs who work on servers without an alert mechanism usually don't know about problems until users report application problems. Alerts can even notify you before a problem occurs by integrating with NT Performance Monitor or monitoring warning messages in the NT Event Log.

How to Create Alerts

Creating an alert associates an event, usually an error in SQL Server, with an action to take when the event occurs.

Use the Alerts dialog shown in Figure 9.14 to configure alerts. Right-clicking the Alerts group in SQL Server Agent and selecting New Alert opens the dialog. You need to provide the following information:

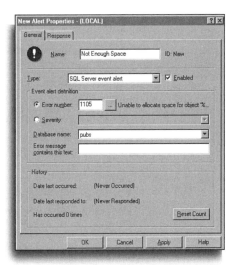

FIGURE 9.14

Use this dialog to create an Alert. Alerts notify you immediately when a problem occurs in SQL Server.

Use the following steps to define a new alert

1. Assign the alert a Name.

2. Define the event that causes the alert. You can choose to have SQL Server Agent look for either a specific error number or all errors in the selected Severity level.

   - Error Number. In most cases you should create alerts to look for specific error numbers. To find the error number associated with a specific error, click the button containing the ellipses. A dialog is displayed as shown in Figure 9.15. Using this dialog, you can search for the error number associated with the text you enter.

Errors must be in the NT Eventlog

Alerts will only work for error numbers that are logged. By default, SQL Server doesn't log all messages, particularly informational messages. However, you can enable logging for any messages by editing the message and selecting Always Write to Windows NT Eventlog..

FIGURE 9.15

If you don't know the error number for a particular message, you can search for it. Enter a keyword in the error message and click Find.

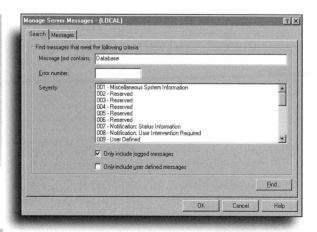

Why execute a job when an alert fires?

You may wonder what sort of job you would execute when an error occurs. That usually depends on the specific error. For example, if you define an alert to fire when a database is out of space, you could have the alert execute a job that increases the size of the database.

- Severity. An alert defined on a severity level will be executed when any error assigned that severity level occurs. Severity level alerts are designed to let you know about all the errors that you didn't anticipate. If you anticipate certain errors, like exceeding the number of allowable users, you should define an alert on that particular error number. But in either case, you should use the severity level alerts to provide you with notification of problems that were not anticipated. A number of severity level alerts are already defined as examples. I recommend that you use these predefined severity level alerts.

3. After defining what condition SQL Server Agent will look for, you need to define the action to take when that condition occurs. Select the Response tab to define the action to take if the event occurs. The alert can send an email message to one or more operators, it can execute a job, or it can do both.

4. For alerts that send email, the alert can send the error message contained in the Windows NT Application Log by enabling Include Error Message Text In. If the alert sends email, choose the intended recipients in the Operators to Notify frame.

5. For alerts that execute jobs, select the Execute job check box and then select the job name from the drop-down list.

How to View Alert Information

To view the alerts defined to SQL Server (see Figure 9.16),
select the Alerts icon in the SQL Server Agent group.

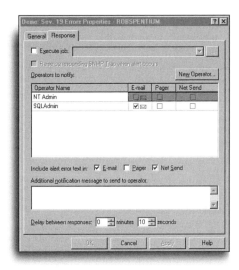

FIGURE 9.16
You can see at a glance
the error number each
alert is defined for, the
last time the alert was
fired, the total number of
times the alert has fired,
as well as other informa-
tion. More details can be
found in the SQL Server
Agent Error Log.

From this screen, you can see when an alert was last fired and
how many times it has fired. Additional information about a particular firing of an alert can be found in the SQL Server Agent
Error Log.

How to Set Up SQL Server to Send Email

As you are by now aware, SQL Server is designed to take care of
itself after you have configured it. However, no matter how well
SQL Server is configured, and no matter how well all of its tasks
are automated, there will still be times when SQL Server is faced
with a situation it can't resolve or a situation that needs your
immediate attention. When such times occur, SQL Server needs
to be able to contact you as swiftly as possible so that you can
deal with the situation before it gets worse, and SQL Mail is the
best method for this.

SQL Mail is the component of SQL Server that enables SQL
Server to send messages through email. SQL Mail can
communicate with any Mail Application Programming Interface

**Understand email before setting
up SQL Mail**

Getting SQL Mail working the first
time isn't easy. I think this is primarily due to the number of
accounts involved: the account you
use to log on to NT Server, the
account you use to log on to SQL
Server, the account SQL Server
uses to log on to NT Server, the
email profile name SQL Mail uses
to log on to email, the recipient
email name of the SQL Server
email account, and the display
name of the SQL Server email
account. Read on for clarification
of how these accounts interact.

Which email client do you have?

Are you confused by the variety of email products from Microsoft? You are not alone. Microsoft has the following products:

On Windows for Work groups 3.11, a client called Microsoft Mail;

On Windows 95, a client called Microsoft Exchange Outlook and Outlook Express

For Windows NT, an email server called MS Mail Postoffice; an email server called Microsoft Exchange; an email client called Exchange Client; and an email client called Windows Messaging.

Separate NT Account for SQL Server and SQL Agent?

If SQL Server Agent logs on to NT with an NT Account different from SQL Server, you also need to create an email account for SQL Server Agent, or associate both the email profile for the SQL Server Agent NT Account and the email profile for the SQL Server NT Account to the same email account. If this sounds confusing, that is because it is. I highly recommend that SQL Server and SQL Server Agent use the same NT Account to simplify configuring email, as well as other security permissions, on SQL Server.

(MAPI)–compliant email systems such as Microsoft Exchange, Lotus Notes, and Groupwise. SQL Server can send email messages under the following conditions:

- When a SQL Server alert occurs.
- When an NT Performance Monitor threshold is exceeded.
- Upon completion or failure of a scheduled job.
- From within stored procedures written by your programmers.

Understanding how SQL Server interacts with email and getting SQL Mail running on SQL Server can challenge any SQL DBA. Five fundamental steps must be completed to make SQL Mail function. The details of the five steps listed here vary depending upon the version of NT Server, SQL Server, email server, and email client that you are using:

Enabling SQL Mail

1. Create an email account for SQL Server on the email post office.
2. Reconfigure SQL Server to log on to NT Server with an NT user account so that it can access the email post office.
3. Install a mail client on the NT Server running SQL Server.
4. Configure SQL Mail with a logon account.
5. Start the SQL Mail client for SQL Server.

SEE ALSO
➤ *For more information on Transact-SQL, see page 639.*

Creating a Mail Account for SQL Server

The first step is to create an email account that SQL Server can use to log on to the email system. Like any other user of email, SQL Server must log on to the email system so that it can send and receive messages. In most companies, the email administrator is responsible for creating the email logon account. Companies using email usually devote a server to processing email.

Verifying How SQL Server Logs On to NT Server

By default, the SQL Server Service (MSSQLServer) logs on to NT Server using the System Account. If the email server is running on a different server than the SQL Server, SQL Server must be changed to log on to NT Server using an NT User account to access the email server.

Configure SQL Server to log on to NT Server with an NT User account

1. Open Enterprise Manager and right-click the SQL Server to be configured.

2. Select Properties.

3. Select the Security tab to see the dialog shown in Figure 9.17.

4. Select the This Account option.

5. Enter the name of the NT User account that SQL Server will use to log on.

6. Enter the NT User account's password in the space provided.

SQL Server runs best alone!

This isn't a recommendation to install SQL Server and your email server, especially Exchange, on the same NT Server. Both SQL Server and email servers use a lot of resources and processing power and should be placed on separate machines whenever possible.

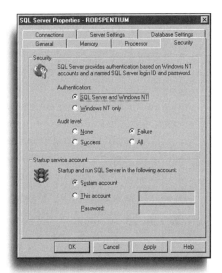

FIGURE 9.17

You can configure SQL Server to log on to NT with a user account so that SQL Server can access resources like email on other servers.

Security in Windows 95/98

If you are running the Windows 95/98 version of SQL Server, you won't be able to change this option. Don't worry because you don't need to. SQL Server is basically running under the same account as the user that logged into Windows 95/98 and will use the email account associated with the user currently logged on to send email.

Separate NT Account for SQL Server and SQL Agent?

Once again, if you created separate NT Accounts for SQL Server and SQL Server Agent, you will have to perform this step twice, once for each account. I recommend not using the default Exchange profile name MS Exchange Settings so that you can distinguish between the profiles in SQL Server.

Profile name

The profile name only has meaning on this machine. The profile name (the default is MS Exchange Settings or Microsoft Outlook) is associated with the NT User account that is **currently logged on to the NT Server** (which is why it is important that you are currently logged on with the same account SQL Server uses to log on to NT). This profile is used by default when a user or service such as SQL Server executes the email client to access an email server. In summary, the NT User account is associated with a profile name, which is then associated with an email account on a particular email server.

This NT User account should have administrator privileges on the NT Server that SQL Server is running on, and it should be configured as shown in Figure 9.2 earlier in this chapter.

After changing the NT User account assigned to the SQL Server service, stop and restart SQL Server. This causes SQL Server to log on to NT server using the assigned NT User account and gives SQL Server the permissions that are assigned to the NT User account.

If the email server is a non-Microsoft server, additional software may be required. For example, if the post office is on a NetWare server, Gateway Services for NetWare needs to be installed so that permissions to the NetWare directory containing the post office can be granted.

Installing a Mail Client on NT Server

Before you set up the Mail Client on the NT Server running SQL Server, log on to NT Server using the same NT User account that you now have the SQL Server service using to log on to NT. This assures that any profile or Registry entries you create while setting up the interface to mail will be accessible to the SQL Server service when it attempts to connect to email.

A variety of email client packages are available that can be used to connect to SQL Server. The main goal of this step is to ensure that you can use your email client and the email account created for SQL Server to send email from this NT Server. Space doesn't permit me to describe how to set up every possible email client, but most of them are conceptually the same. The following steps show you how to set up Microsoft's most popular clients, Outlook, Exchange, and Windows Messaging.

Configure Microsoft Outlook or Microsoft Exchange Client

1. Create an email profile.
   1. Open Control Panel and execute the Mail program.
   2. Choose Show Profiles.
   3. Choose Add.
   4. Select Microsoft Exchange Server and choose Next.

5. Type a Profile name and choose Next. If this is the first profile you have created for this NT account on this machine, the default name of MS Exchange Settings will be used. To change the default name, create a second profile, and then delete the default profile.

6. Choose the name of your email server and the name SQL Server uses to log on to the email server.

2. Run the Microsoft Exchange or Outlook client program.

3. If the program is configured to prompt for a profile, choose the profile just created from the drop-down list. Otherwise, the client is connecting with a default account, which should be the profile just created.

4. If a connection can be made to the email system, send a message to the SQL Server email account to verify that it can send and receive messages.

Configure Microsoft Windows Messaging

1. Install Windows Messaging from the Windows NT Setup tab of the Add/Remove programs group in the Control Panel.

2. Start Windows Messaging from the Main group on the Program menu to connect to the SQL Server email account.

3. Supply the mailbox name and password that were created for the email account by your email administrator.

Configure SQL Mail with a Logon Account

You now need to tell SQL Server what email profile (if you are using Exchange or Outlook), or what mailbox name and password (if you are using Windows Messaging) to use to log on to email. This should be done twice, once for SQL Server and once for SQL Agent. You can set the email profile for SQL Server Agent on the General tab of the SQL Server Agent Properties dialog; and you can set the email profile for SQL Server from either the General tab of SQL Mail properties, or from the Settings tab of the SQL Server Properties dialog as shown in Figure 9.18.

Display name versus log on name

The name used to log on to an email server can be different from the Display name. Display names are seen in address books and are usually first name and last name (Bill Gates). Email logon names are usually the same as the account name that is used to log on to NT (bgates).

Send email to the Display name

When sending email, send it to the Display name.

Changing passwords

If the email password of the email account is changed in the email system, the password also has to be changed for SQL Mail. This can be done through SQL Enterprise Manager. This isn't necessary with the Microsoft Exchange client when connecting to a Microsoft Exchange server because the email password is synchronized with the NT user account password. However, if the NT user account password changes, it also needs to be changed in SQL Server properties.

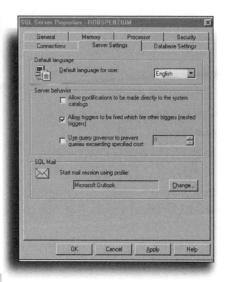

FIGURE 9.18
This dialog lets you enter the email profile name that SQL Server will use to connect to your email server.

Separate NT Account for SQL Server and SQL Agent?

If your SQL Server and SQL Server Agent log on to NT with different accounts, be careful in assigning profiles in SQL Server. The email profile created for SQL Server Agent is assigned in the SQL Server Agent properties. The email profile created for SQL Server is assigned in either the SQL Mail properties or the SQL Server properties.

Starting SQL Mail

You can configure SQL Mail to start automatically each time SQL Server is started or you can start it manually. To configure SQL Mail to start automatically, check the box on the Settings tab of the SQL Server Properties dialog as shown in Figure 9.18.

To start SQL Mail manually, expand the SQL Server, right-click SQL Mail, and select Start.

Troubleshooting

SQL Server offers many tools to assist in determining why jobs, alerts, and SQL Mail are not functioning as expected. The general tools for resolving any problem related to SQL Server are

- The SQL Server Error Log
- The SQL Server Agent Error Log
- The Applications Log on the NT Event Viewer

For jobs, each job history can be examined by right-clicking the specific job and selecting Job History. For alerts, you can examine the last time the alert was fired and how many times it has been fired by clicking the Alerts icon in SQL Server Agent.

The steps to troubleshooting jobs, alerts, and SQL Mail are outlined in the next three sections.

Troubleshooting SQL Server Agent

If SQL Server Agent doesn't start and cannot be started
manually, examine the following:

- The NT User Account SQL Server Agent uses to log on
  to NT Server. You may need to re-enter the password if it
  has changed.

- The SQL Server account SQL Server Agent uses to log on
  to SQL Server. You may need to re-enter the password if it
  has changed.

- The error logs for SQL Server Agent, SQL Server, and NT.

Troubleshooting Jobs

In the past I ran across two general types of errors related
to jobs:

- The job doesn't execute on the schedule set up for it.

- The job appears to execute but the desired action
  doesn't occur.

To resolve errors of the second case, examine the job history for
the particular job that isn't executing correctly. Some steps, such
as steps that run .bat files, will return a successful completion
message if SQL Server Agent is able to successfully *start* the .bat
file running. SQL Server Agent doesn't know if the actions performed from the .bat file are successful or not.

In resolving any trouble related to job execution, examine
the following:

- Is the SQL Server Agent Service running?

- Is there an error in the Windows NT Application Log?

- Are there error messages in the SQL Server Agent
  Error Log?

- Is the job enabled?

- Is the schedule type correct?
- Are the schedule date and times correct (is it past the end date)?
- Is the schedule enabled?
- Are the job steps sequenced so that all steps will execute?

Troubleshooting Alerts

If an alert did not fire when expected, examine the following:

- Is the SQL Server Agent Service running?
- Is there an error in the Windows NT Application Log?
- Are there error messages in the SQL Server Agent Error Log?
- Is the alert enabled?
- Are the alert's Last Occurred and Count values changing? If they are not changing, there may be a problem with the response being fired. Compare the date and time of the error to the dates and times the alert is enabled and providing notification. Also test the email address or Pager address.

Troubleshooting SQL Mail

If you are unable to start SQL Mail, examine the following:

- Does SQL Server log on to NT using an NT User Account?
- Is SQL Server assigned an email profile to use to log on to the email server?
- Can you log on to NT Server with the NT User Account SQL Server uses? Can you open the email client (Outlook) using the email profile SQL Server uses to log on to the email server?
- Can you send and receive email from the email client (Outlook)?
- Is there an error in the Windows NT Application Log?
- Are there error messages in the SQL Server Agent Error Log?

If SQL Mail is started but email isn't being sent from Alerts and jobs, examine the following:

- Are there error messages in the SQL Server Agent Error Log?
- Is SQL Server Agent assigned an email profile to log on to the email server?
- Does SQL Server Agent log on to NT using an NT User Account?
- Can you log on to NT Server with the NT User Account SQL Server Agent uses? Can you open the email client (Outlook) using the email profile SQL Server Agent uses to log on to the email server?
- Can you send and receive email from the email client (Outlook)?
- Is there an error in the Windows NT Application Log?

SEE ALSO

➤ *Chapter 19 lists several methods for general troubleshooting; see pages 603 and 635 for more details and resources.*

chapter

10

Maintaining SQL Server

Document your SQL Servers   •

Create a formal SQL Server
maintenance plan   •

Monitor log files, security, user
activity, and performance   •

Manage current databases and
create new ones   •

Maintain SQL Server software
and indexes   •

Manage User Accounts   •

Backup databases and logs   •

Maintaining SQL Server Over the Long Haul

After you have SQL Server and your databases up and running, you might think you have time to take it easy. After all, isn't most of the hard work over after your SQL Server databases are up and running? If you think this is true, you're in for a big surprise. Many of the tasks you have performed up to now are designed to get SQL Server up and running. Now its time to dig in for the long haul. As the DBA, it is your job to ensure that your SQL Server databases stay in production, no matter what. To accomplish this, you must carefully look after and pamper your SQL Servers.

Checklist makes your job easier

To help make your life a little easier as a DBA, at the end of this chapter is a SQL Server Maintenance Checklist you can use as an outline to create your own SQL Server maintenance plan.

Unfortunately, SQL Server doesn't have the ability to automatically tell you what needs to be done to it to keep it in tip-top shape. As the DBA, you must learn the necessary maintenance tasks you need to perform on a regular basis in order to keep SQL Server humming.

The purpose of this chapter is to help you along, describing the kinds of tasks you must perform on a regular basis to ensure SQL Server stays in production. Rest assured, your work is cut out for you.

Document Your SQL Servers

One of the most important, but ignored, tasks of the DBA is to thoroughly document how each of your SQL Servers and their databases are configured. When any SQL Server is first installed and configured, and when any changes are made to SQL Server settings, every step and configuration option needs to be documented. This includes the creation of any new databases and any configuration changes that are made to the databases.

Documentation is important for many reasons, including the following:

- To help restore a server after it crashes.

- To help troubleshoot a server when it begins to exhibit problems.

- To help optimize SQL Server over time.

- To help others, assuming the DBA isn't available, understand how and why SQL Server is configured the way it is.

Documentation can take many forms, including written documentation on paper (as in a diary), text files created as a result of a Transact-SQL query, word processing documents, databases, or as Transact-SQL scripts. Whatever way is chosen to document a SQL Server and its databases, all the information must always be kept up-to-date and be readily available. Please don't store your documentation on the same SQL Server or on servers you are documenting.

Things that should be documented include

- All SQL Server configuration settings should be documented. This can be easily done by running the sp_configure stored procedure and saving the output as a text file (see Figure 10.1).

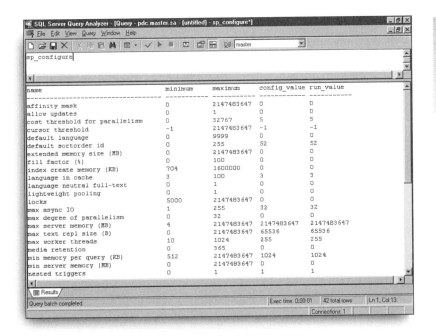

> **Use Transact-SQL scripts to document SQL Server**
>
> When possible, use Transact-SQL scripts to document your SQL Servers and databases. This way, you can use them to quickly re-create the configuration should they be lost. While scripts are a great documentation tool, they are of little value if they aren't kept up-to-date. Whenever you make a SQL Server or database change that affects a script, that script must be updated immediately for it to be of value. How to create a Transact-SQL script is beyond the scope of this book.

FIGURE 10.1
Documenting each SQL Server's configuration is important.

How to run sp_configure

1. Load the SQL Server Query Analyzer.

2. In the Query Pane, type

   sp_configure

3. Select Query from the menu bar, and then select Execute.

4. The results are immediately displayed in the Results Pane.

- A Transact-SQL script should document every database managed by SQL Server so that it (along with all of its database objects) can be re-created if necessary. You will have to learn more about Transact-SQL before you will be able to perform this task.

- All tasks and alerts need to be documented so they can be easily re-created.

- All special procedures, such as BCPing data on a daily basis from a non-SQL Server database to SQL Server, should be documented.

- All login IDs, database user IDs, groups, and their related permissions need to be documented so they can be re-created easily. Transact-SQL scripts can be used to document these items.

- The results of any performance monitoring, along with what steps you took to tune SQL Server's performance, and why you implemented them, should be documented. Ideally, the results of your tuning should also be included.

- Any problems, and their solutions, should be documented so that if they occur again, you don't have to reinvent the wheel to resolve them.

- The disaster recovery plan for your SQL Servers should be included as part of the documentation. This includes such important information as a step-by-step procedure on how to restore a crashed SQL Server or individual databases.

It is all too easy to skip this important step, especially if you are already overworked. If you have to, budget time in your schedule for the specific task of creating and maintaining your documentation. Maintaining documentation should be considered as important as making daily backups.

SEE ALSO

➤ *For more information on using the SQL Server Query Analyzer, see page 232.*

➤ *For more information on creating a disaster recovery plan to prevent data loss, see page 454.*

Create a Formal SQL Server Maintenance Plan

The focus of this chapter is on how to maintain SQL Server and its databases in order to keep them up and running all the time. This is no small effort, but the job is made easier by creating a formal SQL Server maintenance plan that outlines every step that needs to be taken on a periodic basis. Although each situation is different, the suggestions in this chapter should provide you with most of the information you need to create such a plan.

Most parts of a SQL Server maintenance plan have to be repeated on a regular basis. Because of this, creating a formal plan might best be done using some type of software that helps to remind you of the tasks that need to be performed. Some of the software you might want to consider to use to create a formal maintenance plan include the following:

- Word Processor or Spreadsheet. Word processors and spreadsheets offer great flexibility when it comes to enabling you to create a formal maintenance plan. They also enable you to create nice looking output, especially handy if you have to present your plan to a supervisor. On the other hand, word processors and spreadsheets don't include any easy way to automatically notify you of tasks to perform. If your SQL Server management tasks are light, all you might need is to print a check list on paper and post it above your desk. But if your management tasks cover multiple SQL Servers, a word processor or spreadsheet may not adequately meet your needs.

- Project Management. Project management software, such as Microsoft Project, are great tools for managing large and complex projects. They not only enable you to list every possible step that needs to be done, but also enable you to delegate tasks, track costs, track job completion, and print out nifty charts showing overall progress. On the other hand, project management software is difficult to learn and set up. Unless you're managing a huge number of SQL Servers, you may want to find a simpler tool to use.

311

- Scheduling. Scheduling software, such as Microsoft Outlook, makes it easy to enter recurring tasks and to be provided reminders to complete them (see Figure 10.2). It can even record each task you performed in a history log. The software is also easy to learn and use. This tool is especially useful for the typical DBA who manages a range of SQL Servers by him or herself, and doesn't need the power of project management software.

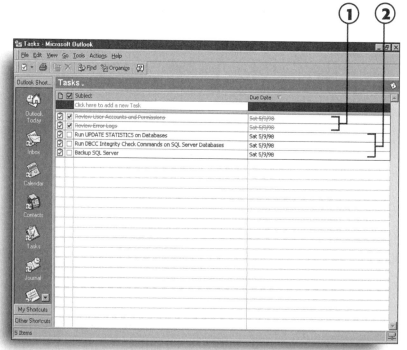

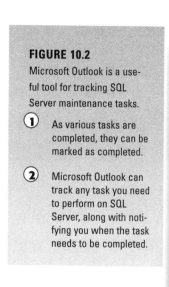

FIGURE 10.2

Microsoft Outlook is a useful tool for tracking SQL Server maintenance tasks.

1. As various tasks are completed, they can be marked as completed.

2. Microsoft Outlook can track any task you need to perform on SQL Server, along with notifying you when the task needs to be completed.

- Database. As a DBA, you may want to create your own custom tool to manage your SQL Server administrative tasks, and what better tool to select than a database. If you like to program, you can even use SQL Server itself to create your own custom application. Or if you prefer not to program, select a database like Microsoft Access, which doesn't require programming. If you choose this route, be sure that others besides yourself are able to use your application in case you aren't available when needed.

Whichever tool or tools you choose to track your maintenance plan, use this chapter (and the summary at the end of the chapter) as a guide to what tasks you need to perform, and when. Revise the plan as needed. Virtually every organization using SQL Server is constantly changing, which means that how you maintain SQL Server and its databases must also change. Keep the plan up-to-date and be sure you follow it. Otherwise, you have wasted a lot of your time.

Monitor Log Files

Although some SQL Server–related errors produce error messages onscreen as they happen, many don't. It is the DBA's responsibility to monitor SQL Server log files to find the not-so-obvious errors that can occur.

The SQL Server error logs are the most comprehensive place to find SQL Server errors, and should be reviewed daily in order to locate any potential problems. Many of the messages found in the error logs are only informational in nature and can be ignored.

SQL Server produces comprehensive log files for both the MSSQLServer and SQLServerAgent services. Both types of log files are stored in the \Mssql7\Log\ folder. MSSQLServer log files are assigned the first name of Errorlog, and SQLServerAgent log files are assigned the first name of Sqlagent. SQL Server maintains not only a current error log for each service, but it also maintains the previous six versions of each. The name of the current MSSQLServer log is Errorlog, with each subsequent log having a number appended to it (Errorlog.1, Errorlog.2, and so on). The name of the current SQLServerAgent log is Sqlagent.out, with each subsequent log having a number appended to the first name (Sqlagent.1, Sqlagent.2, and so on).

All log files are stored in the ASCII format and can be viewed with any text editor. Besides using a text editor, you can display both service's log files using SQL Enterprise Manager.

How to View the MSSQLServer Log Using SQL Enterprise Manager

The following steps show you how to view the MSSQLServer log file using SQL Enterprise Manager.

Viewing the MSSQLServer log file

1. Load SQL Enterprise Manager.

2. Select the SQL Server whose log file you want to display by clicking the plus sign next to the server's name. This displays all the server's objects.

3. Click on the plus sign next to the Management object.

4. Display the logs by clicking the plus sign next to the SQL Server Logs object.

5. To view any of the error logs, click the log you want to view. This displays the error log in the Details pane (see Figure 10.3).

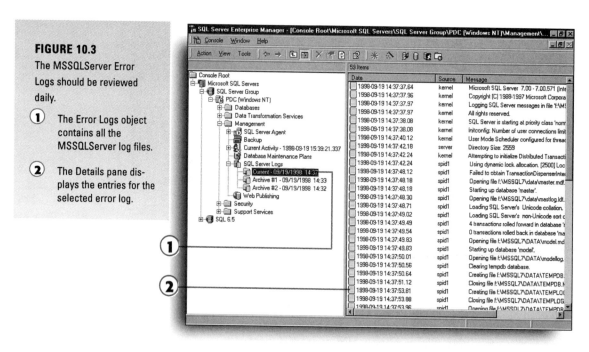

FIGURE 10.3

The MSSQLServer Error Logs should be reviewed daily.

① The Error Logs object contains all the MSSQLServer log files.

② The Details pane displays the entries for the selected error log.

How to View the SQLServerAgent Log Using SQL Enterprise Manager

The following steps show you how to view the SQLServerAgent log files from SQL Enterprise Manager.

Viewing the SQLServerAgent log file

1. Load SQL Enterprise Manager.

2. Select the SQL Server whose log file you want to display by clicking the plus sign next to the server's name. This displays all the server's objects.

3. Display the SQLServerAgent logs by right-clicking the SQL Server Agent object, and then select Display Error Log. This displays the SQL Server Agent Error Log (see Figure 10.4).

4. To view differnt types of error messages, click the list box and select the type of errors to display.

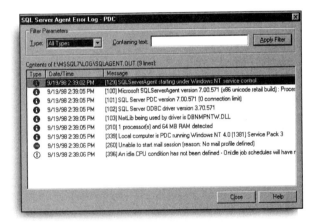

FIGURE 10.4
The SQLServerAgent error logs should be reviewed daily..

Examining the NT Server Event Viewer Logs

Although the SQL Server error logs are a good place to start looking for potential problems, the NT Event Viewer provides two additional logs to track: the System and Application logs. The System log is used to track NT-related messages, and should be viewed to find any potential NT problems that could affect SQL Server. The Application log stores messages from application programs running on NT, including many messages from SQL Server. The SQL Server messages you see here are also duplicated in the SQL Server error log, but not all error messages found in the SQL Server Error Logs are found here. The advantage of viewing SQL Server messages here, rather than from the SQL Server Error Logs, is that you can see them in context with other non–SQL Server error messages that could affect SQL Server, which might provide clues to some problems.

Make it one of your daily tasks to review these logs. Some small SQL Server problems can turn into bigger problems, and unless you look for them every day, you won't be able to discover them before they come back to haunt you.

How to View NT Server Event Viewer Messages

The following steps show you how to view SQL Server messages using NT Server's Event Viewer.

Viewing the NT Server Event Viewer messages

1. Load NT Server's Event Viewer.

2. To view the Application log, select Log from the main menu and select Application. This displays the NT Server Application log (see Figure 10.5).

3. To view the System log, select Log from the main menu and select System. This displays the NT Server Application log.

SEE ALSO

➤ *For more information on how to troubleshoot SQL Server using error logs, see page 602.*

Use the Event Viewer's Filter option

When viewing messages using the NT Event Viewer, use the Filter option to selectively view error messages. For example, you can choose to view only SQL Server error messages, or only Warnings. You can decide exactly what you see.

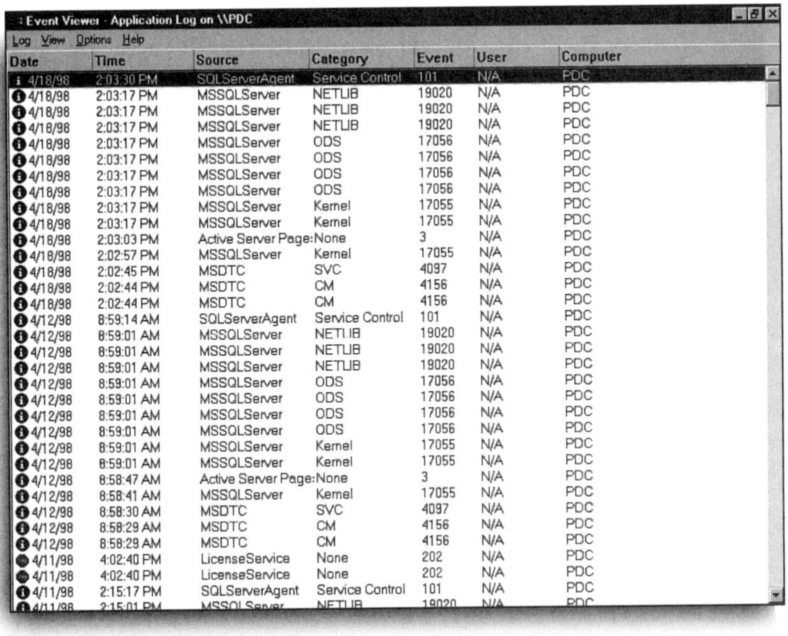

FIGURE 10.5

The NT Event Viewer Application Log should be reviewed daily.

Monitor Security

As the DBA, you are responsible for ensuring that only authorized individuals have access to only those SQL Server database objects they need to access. Users should not be able to access any database object unless they have a need to access it.

Audit Current Accounts and Permissions

Part IV, "SQL Server Security," discusses SQL Security basics, and as the DBA, you need to be very familiar with them. Besides the basics of creating new login Ids and database user Ids, and assigning permissions, the DBA is responsible for ongoing security, which means you need to regularly review who is accessing your SQL Server databases, and what they are doing with the data. On a regular basis (at least once a month), you should perform the following:

- Review all the login IDs to verify that all of them are still needed. People leave the organization and often change jobs

How to verify NTFS and share permissions

1. Log on to NT Server with administrative permissions.

2. Start NT Server's Explorer.

3. To verify share level permissions on a folder, right-click the shared folder and choose Sharing. This displays the Properties dialog box. Next, click the Permissions button. This displays the Access Through Share Permission dialog box, which displays the current share level permissions for this share.

4. To verify NTFS permissions on a folder, right-click on the folder and choose Sharing. This displays the Properties dialog box. Next, click the Security tab. Then click the Permissions button. This displays the Directory Permissions dialog box, which displays the current NTFS permissions for this folder.

within an organization, and as soon as anyone no longer needs their login ID, it should be deleted. Hopefully your organization has an internal procedure to notify you of such changes. But even then, you need to take the responsibility to regularly review all login IDs and verify their need to exist.

- Review database user Ids for necessity as well. Although an individual may still need a login ID to access SQL Server, she may not still need access to databases she has had access to in the past. After you have determined which login IDs are legitimate, verify which databases they need access to.

- Next, you will want to verify the permissions each individual needs in each database. This sounds like a lot of work, and it is. But without performing such an audit on a regular basis, you cannot ensure that your data is properly protected.

- Don't forget to regularly verify the NTFS and Share permissions used on the physical servers running SQL Server. This includes both the SQL Server program folders and the data folders. Although the normal way to access SQL Server database data is through SQL Server, you want to prevent unauthorized users from accessing the data through the folder structure. An unauthorized person may not be able to do much with the data if he accesses through the file system, but he might be able to damage or erase it. Regularly check folder access permissions using NT Server's Explorer tool to insure they are adequate to protect your SQL Server data.

Use NT Server's Audit Capability to Monitor Use

Limit use of NT Security Logging

Don't leave NT Security Logging on all the time; it can use valuable CPU time that can be better devoted to running your SQL Server applications. Audit sparingly, only when you think there may be problems with unauthorized access.

If you want to track successful or unsuccessful access to SQL Server files or data on NTFS partitions, you can take advantage of NT Server's built-in auditing capability. These audit results are written to NT Server's Event Viewer Security Log where they can be reviewed for potential problems. NT Server's auditing capability is made available through two separate NT Server tools: the User Manager for Domains and the Explorer. Both tools work together to permit comprehensive auditing of any SQL Server.

Turn on NT Server's auditing capability to track successful folder and file access on NTFS partitions

1. Log on to NT Server as a user with administrative rights.

2. Load NT Server's User Manager for Domains program (see Figure 10.6).

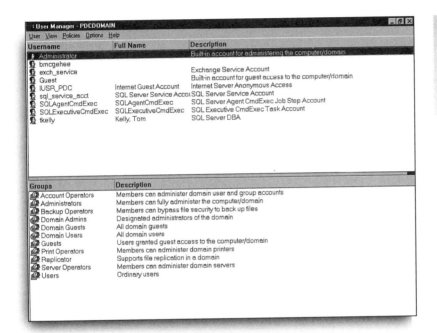

FIGURE 10.6

NT Server's User Manager for Domains is used to turn on auditing.

3. From the Policies drop-down menu, select Audit, and the Audit Policy dialog box appears (see Figure 10.7).

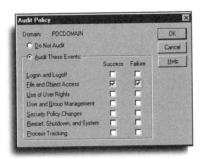

FIGURE 10.7

Select the File and Object Access audit event from this dialog box.

NT Server enables comprehensive auditing

Virtually every activity that occurs on an NT Server can be audited. If you want to learn more about how NT Server auditing works, check out the book *Inside Windows NT Server 4*, by Drew Heywood, published by New Riders.

4. In the Audit Policy dialog box, click Audit These Events. This causes all the audit events to become ungrayed (see Figure 10.7).

5. Depending on whether you want to audit successful or failed events, select one or both of the options next to the File and Object Access audit events.

6. Click the OK button after you are finished to save the settings and exit the dialog box. The User Manager for Domains can now be exited by selecting Exit from the User menu.

7. Now that you have told NT Server you want to audit File and Object access, you have to tell it which folders or files you specifically want to audit. This is done using NT Server's Explorer. Load Explorer and then select the folder where your SQL Server data is stored on your server (see Figure 10.8).

FIGURE 10.8

Select the folder that contains the SQL Server databases you want to audit.

① You may choose to select an entire folder by clicking the folder.

② If you like, you can audit specific files by highlighting the

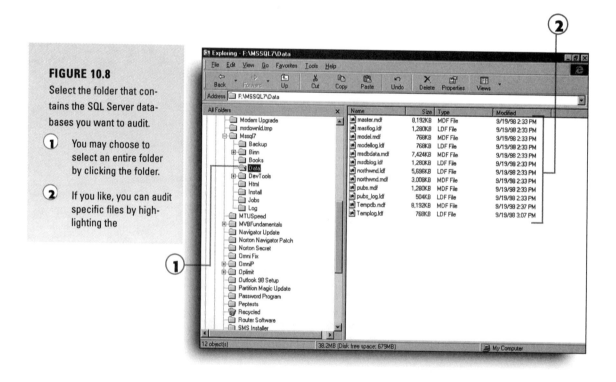

320

8. You now have to decide whether you want to audit one or more individual files, or one or more folders that contain various SQL Server data files. If you want to audit an entire folder, you must select one at a time and turn auditing on for it. If you want to audit one or more files in a single folder, you can select one or more at the same time by holding down the Control key and clicking the files you want to audit.

9. After you have selected a folder or files to audit, right-click the selected object, and then select Properties from the pop-up menu. This displays the Data Properties dialog box. Then click the Security tab (see Figure 10.9).

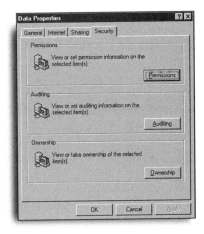

FIGURE 10.9
Select the Auditing button to choose what features you want to audit.

10. Click the Auditing button to display the Directory or File Auditing dialog box shown in Figure 10.10 (the actual box depends on whether you are auditing a folder or files; both are very similar).

11. The Directory or File Auditing dialog box requires you to first specify who you want to audit. You can choose from individuals or groups. If you want to audit every potential access, select the Everyone group, which includes all NT users in the accounts domain. To select users or groups to audit, click the Add button, and the Add Users and Groups dialog box appears (see Figure 10.11).

321

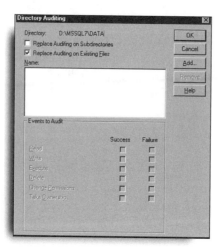

FIGURE 10.10

The Auditing dialog box is where you specify the events you want to audit.

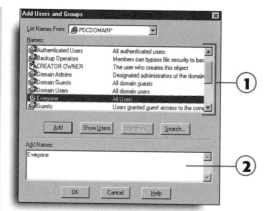

FIGURE 10.11

This dialog box is used to select which user(s) or group(s) you want to audit.

① You can select one or more users or groups from this box.

② This box shows you which users or groups you selected from the above box.

12. From the Add Users and Groups dialog box, select a user or group and click the Add button, which adds the user or group to the box at the bottom of the dialog box. Repeat this process until you are finished, and then click OK. This returns you to the Auditing dialog box, which now contains the names or groups you added in the previous step (see Figure 10.12).

13. The last step before you are done is to select which types of events you want to audit. You can choose either the success

or failure of six different events. Most likely, the Read, Write, and Delete events will be the ones you choose, especially if you are auditing SQL Server database file access. Of course, you can choose to audit any events you want. After you have selected which events you want to audit, click OK, and you will be returned to the Explorer. If desired, you can repeat these steps on additional files or folders.

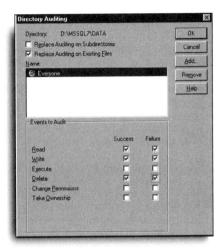

FIGURE 10.12
Now you can specify which events you want to audit.

14. Now that auditing has been turned on, anytime someone you selected in steps 11 and 12 tries to take an action you are auditing on the files or folders you have specified, an alert will be written to NT Server's Event Viewer Security log. To view this log at any time, start the Event Viewer and select Security from the Log main menu. This displays the Security log (see Figure 10.13).

15. Every audited event is displayed in the Security log. To find additional information about a specific event, you can double-click any event and the Event Detail dialog box appears (see Figure 10.14), which displays additional information.

Learning about NTFS permissions

It is important to understand NTFS permissions before you begin to audit files and folders with NT Server. To learn more about NTFS permissions, check out the book *Inside Windows NT Server 4*, by Drew Heywood, published by New Riders.

FIGURE 10.13

Audit events are displayed in the Security log of the Event Viewer.

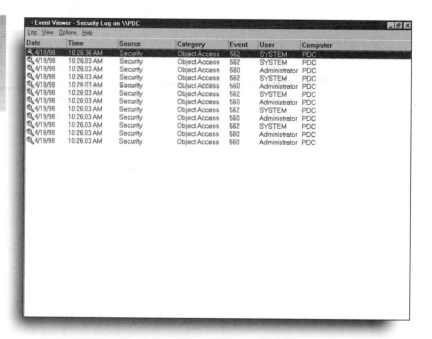

FIGURE 10.14

Audited event details are shown here..

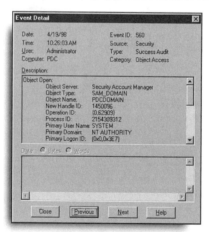

16. After you are done reviewing the audited events, you may exit the Event Viewer by selecting Exit from the Log drop-down menu.

17. When you are done auditing after a period of time, remember to turn off auditing.

Monitor User Activity

While auditing security is important, monitoring normal user activity within SQL Server databases is also important. The more you know how SQL Server databases are being used, the better information you have to help tune and optimize your SQL Servers.

Three main tools you can use to monitor user activity within SQL Server databases are

- Current Activity Window
- SQL Server Profiler
- NT Server Performance Monitor

Each tool provides a variety of different ways to monitor SQL Server user activity.

Current Activity Window

This tool, which is described in detail in Chapter 19, "Troubleshooting SQL Server," enables the DBA to view a current graphical snapshot of user activity (see Figure 10.15). It enables you to view all the users who are currently logged into SQL Server, along with the processes they are running and a listing of which locks they have open. It also includes information about blocked processes. Not only does the Current Activity Window provide this information, it enables the DBA to select and kill any process at will. This can be useful when a user starts a process that significantly affects the performance of SQL Server and needs to be stopped before it would end on its own.

The DBA should consider reviewing the information in the Current Activity Window one or more times a day, especially when diagnosing potential problems.

SQL Server Profiler

The most powerful tool available to monitor user activity is the SQL Server Profiler, which is discussed in detail in Chapter 19, "Troubleshooting SQL Server." It enables the DBA in either real time or in log files to monitor user activity over a period of

325

time. Time series data such as this is useful to find potential performance bottlenecks and to troubleshoot problems (see Figure 10.16).

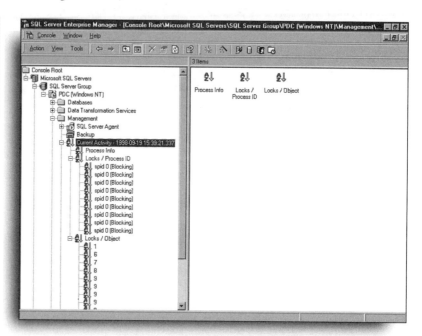

FIGURE 10.15
The Current Activity window provides a current snapshot of user activity.

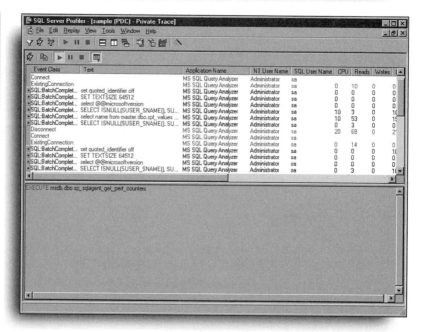

FIGURE 10.16
The SQL Server Profiler is a powerful way to monitor user activity.

Some of the activities that the SQL Server Profiler can monitor include the following:

- User access methods
- User activity metrics
- Number of times an object is accessed
- Lock contention and deadlocks
- Which processes may be blocking others
- Which users or applications are heavily used
- Performance bottlenecks

Ideally, the DBA should regularly monitor user activity with the SQL Server Profiler. Although the DBA will always want to use this tool when attempting to resolve a current problem, she should use it on a weekly or monthly basis to gauge typical user activity in order to monitor exactly what is happening.

NT Server Performance Monitor

Besides the normal performance counters that the NT Server Performance Monitor uses to track system resource usage, it can also be used to monitor user activity, tracking such items as an individual's CPU and disk usage within SQL Server.

The DBA should consider using these user activity counters to monitor usage in a Performance Monitor log over daily or weekly periods in order to track usage trends.

SEE ALSO
➤ *For more information on using the NT Server Performance Monitor, see page 577.*

Monitor SQL Server Performance

Although SQL Server is to a limited degree self-tuning, there is much room for improvement. SQL Server needs regular monitoring to determine whether there are any bottlenecks preventing it from running as fast and efficiently as possible. Only by regularly monitoring your SQL Server's performance will you be able to identify bottlenecks and resolve them. The main tool used to monitor SQL Server's performance is NT Server's

What is a bottleneck?

A server bottleneck refers to a part of the server that is being overused so much that it is maxed out in capacity. In turn, this bottleneck acts as a limiting factor in the server, slowing down its overall performance. For example, a server's CPU can become a bottleneck, running at virtually 100% capacity. This prevents the server from performing any faster, even if other server resources are being underused.

Performance Monitor. In addition, SQL Server has the ability to send performance information to an SNMP management console.

NT Server's Performance Monitor

The most commonly used tool to monitor SQL Server performance is NT Server's Performance Monitor. When SQL Server is loaded on to NT, it adds a number of Performance Monitor objects. Each object includes many individual counters. A *counter* is used to measure one specific aspect of SQL Server's performance. For example, by monitoring the counter that tracks the number of transactions per second SQL Server is performing, the DBA can get a good idea of how busy SQL Server really is (see Figure 10.17).

What is a Performance Monitor Object?

An *object* is just a grouping of related counters. A *counter* is a measured statistic, such as the percent usage of a CPU or a disk drive. When you load SQL Server, it adds many new objects and counters that can display much information about how SQL Server is performing.

FIGURE 10.17
NT Server's Performance Monitor is used to monitor SQL Server's performance.

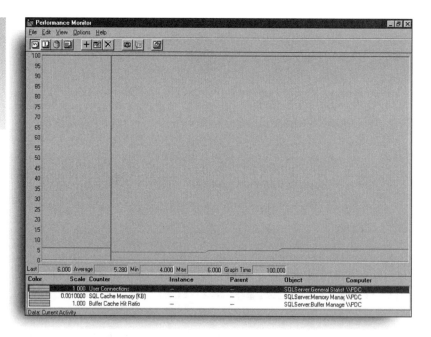

There are more than 100 SQL Server–specific counters, plus more than 350 other counters that are specific to NT Server. Although you would never need to use all these counters to monitor SQL Server, there are perhaps 15–20 that you may want to monitor on a regular basis in order to gauge SQL Server's performance.

SEE ALSO

➤ *For more information on optimizing SQL Server, see page 563.*

SNMP Monitoring

Although most SQL Server monitoring is performed through tools provided by either SQL Server or NT Server, the DBA has the option of monitoring much of SQL Server's activity through the use of a third-party SNMP Management console, such as Hewlett-Packard's OpenView.

SNMP, or Single Network Management Protocol, is part of the TCP/IP protocol suite. It was designed as a standard way to allow SNMP Management console software to communicate with network hardware and software from other vendors. SNMP uses client/server technology. The SNMP Management console acts as the client, and the device or software being monitoring acts as the server. Running on the server component is a program referred to as an SNMP Agent, and a *MIB* (Management Information Base). The *SNMP Agent* is the program code that makes the SNMP Agent work, and the MIB describes the kind of information the SNMP Agent can provide an SNMP Management console upon request.

Whenever an SNMP Management Workstation wants information about any SNMP device, it sends it a request. The SNMP Agent receives the requests and responds with an answer to the SNMP Management console. In addition, the SNMP Agent has the ability to send messages, called traps, to the Management console to notify the console of predefined events, such as a security breach.

When SQL Server is installed, both SNMP Agent software and a MIB are also loaded. Together, these two pieces communicate with an SNMP Management console, allowing a SNMP Management Workstation to query SQL Server for performance data, and allowing SQL Server to send the SNMP Management console traps as defined by the DBA. In order to work, the server running SQL Server must be running TCP/IP and the NT SNMP service.

> **What is an SNMP Management Console?**
>
> The term *SNMP Management Console* generally refers to any third-party program written to communicate with SNMP agents, and to display the resulting information onscreen. For example, an SNMP Management Console can be used to display SQL Server performance data, instead of using the Performance Monitor tool. Currently, Microsoft doesn't sell an SNMP Management Console. It must be purchased from other vendors.

> **How do I set up SNMP Monitoring?**
>
> If you want to learn how to set up SNMP Monitoring, do a search for *SNMP (SQL Setup)* in the SQL Server Books Online.

Manage Current and Create New Databases

As the DBA, another important area you are responsible for is to create and maintain databases. Most of this is covered in detail in Part III, "Administering SQL Server," although this section acts to bring all the information together to help remind you of the tasks you need to perform on a regular basis. Some of the following tasks need to be performed on a consistent schedule, whereas others will only need to be carried out as necessary.

Size and Create New Databases

From time to time, you will need to create new databases for new projects. This means you will also need to learn how to estimate their sizes so you can create them large enough to meet your needs. Although SQL Server dynamically increases database sizes, it is more efficient overall to try to create a database at the optimum size. Whenever a database is automatically resized, it temporarily takes away processing resources from SQL Server that could be used to meet the needs of clients instead.

Monitor Database and Transaction Size

After a database is in production, it is important to monitor its size and the size of its transaction log. You don't want to find out that your hard disk is running out of space due to the increasing size of your databases and their transaction logs.

The NT Performance Monitor provides one of the easiest ways to regularly monitor available disk space and the size of your databases and transaction logs.

SEE ALSO
> *For more information on using the Performance Monitor, see page 577.*

Scheduled Data Imports or Exports

Many organizations regularly export or import data to and from SQL Server on a scheduled basis. For example, you might need to import raw data from a mainframe into SQL Server daily for decision analysis or other uses. Or you might export data from a SQL Server into another database for additional data processing.

SEE ALSO
➤ *For more information on importing and exporting data in SQL Server, see page 510.*

Managing Replication

If you use SQL Server's database replication feature, you will need to monitor it regularly to ensure there are no problems. You may also need to change various replication features or reconfigure published or subscribed articles.

SEE ALSO
➤ *For more information on how to set up replication in SQL Server, see page 542.*

Scheduling Events and Alerts

Many of the routine tasks needed to maintain SQL Server databases can be automated by creating scheduled events and alerts. As the DBA, it is your responsibility to determine what events and alerts need to be set up, and to set them up.

SEE ALSO
➤ *For more information on scheduling events and alerts, see page 284.*

Maintaining SQL Server Software

Generally, after SQL Server is installed, the SQL Server software itself should not require much attention. But as Microsoft strives to improve its products, it comes out with Service Packs and new versions of the software that require you to update the SQL Server software.

Updating SQL Server with Service Packs

Service Packs are how Microsoft provides interim bug fixes and small improvements to SQL Server. To find out whether a new Service Pack has become available, you will have to watch Microsoft's Web site at www.microsoft.com, as it doesn't automatically notify SQL Server owners that they have become available.

Usually, Service Packs are cumulative, which means that all new Service Packs includes all the older Service Packs.

Installing a Service Pack is generally an easy task, but nevertheless, you will want to plan its installation. First, don't install the Service Pack immediately after it becomes available. Microsoft has had a bad habit of releasing Service Packs that sometimes cause more problems that they solve, although this problem has become better. Ideally, wait a month or two after the release of the Service Pack, and watch the SQL Server news groups and other SQL Server–related news to find out if there are any known problems with the Service Pack.

If you find out that a Service Pack has no major problems, schedule a time when you can take your SQL Server down, as you will have to take it out of production during the Service Pack's installation. Be sure to plan for plenty of time. Try not only to have enough time to install the Service Pack, but also enough time available in case you need to reload your server from scratch should the worst happen.

Before loading the Service Pack, make a complete backup of all your SQL Server databases, as well as the entire server where the Service Pack is to be installed. Also plan on upgrading all your SQL Servers at the same time, as there is the possibility that if you upgrade one but not another, and the servers need to interact, the interaction may not work because of the differences in the software.

After the Service Pack has been installed, bring the server back up and test it thoroughly to ensure that it is functioning properly. Please don't let this section scare you away from installing Service Packs. Rarely are there problems, but you need to be prepared for the worst.

Upgrading Your Software

About every one and a half to two years, Microsoft releases a new version of SQL Server. Just keep in mind that this event will occur, and that you need to plan for it. You may not want to upgrade immediately, but at some point you must, if you want to take advantage of all the new features that are offered.

Manage User Accounts and Permissions

One of the least interesting routine tasks the DBA is responsible for is to maintain user accounts and permissions. New users always need to be added, former users need to be removed, and permissions need to be changed. This is an ongoing DBA task that is performed on a regular basis.

Database user account management can be divided into these major categories:

- Adding new login and database user IDs
- Modifying current login and database user IDs
- Managing object permissions

If you want to streamline these tasks, develop a system so that any required changes to accounts and permissions are forwarded to you automatically. Either create a paper form that can be filled out and sent to you, or perhaps an e-form that can be emailed to you over your network. Whatever system you choose, the more efficient the system, the less work you will have to do (you will make fewer corrections) and the happier your users will be (they will have the necessary data access when they need it).

SEE ALSO

➤ *For more information on managing user accounts, see page 376.*

➤ *For more information on managing user permissions, see page 420.*

Verify the Integrity of SQL Server Databases

Although SQL Server does its best to ensure that all the databases it is managing are functioning properly, sometimes problems can arise. These include both logical and physical inconsistency problems internal to a database. Before these problems can rear their ugly heads and cause major problems, it is a good idea to regularly run some of the built-in SQL Server DBCC commands that are used to verify the integrity of databases.

DBCC (Database Consistency Checker) commands are built into SQL Server to perform a wide variety of maintenance tasks. Two of the most commonly used DBCC commands to verify database integrity include

- DBCC CHECKCATALOG. Used to verify the consistency between system tables.
- DBCC CHECKDB. Used to validate the allocation and structural integrity of data and indexes of tables in a database.

Ideally, both DBCC commands should be run before and after each database is backed up. They should be run before a backup to ensure the data is okay and is able to be restored. There is no point in backing up databases that cannot be restored because of some integrity problem. They should be run after a backup because additional transactions probably will have occurred between the time of the initial runs of these commands and the actual backup. If you are backing up data during a period of no database activity, the second run of the commands is unnecessary.

You should always run these DBCC commands before you back up, but sometimes this isn't possible. These commands can take many hours to run on very large databases, and it isn't recommended that you run them when users are accessing a database heavily. This presents a problem for large databases and databases that are used 24 hours a day. In these cases, you may have to schedule specific down times to run these.

SEE ALSO

➤ *For more information on using these DBCC commands, see page 611.*

Maintain Database Indexes

SQL Server is very smart, making use of the information available to it in order to optimize its own performance. One of the best examples of this is when SQL Server runs a query. Through SQL Server's built-in query optimizer, SQL Server is able to select from a table's one or more indexes and choose one or two of them that will help it execute a query the fastest. But for this to work, information about the indexes, referred to as the index statistics, must be current. The query optimizer uses the statistics kept for each index to determine which index to use. If the index statistics are out of date, the query optimizer may not make the best decision when selecting an index, and the resulting query may run much slower than it could if more current index statistic information were available.

Whenever an index is created, the index statistics are automatically updated. But as rows in tables are changed, and the various table indexes change, the index statistics for each index are not updated. This means that over time, the index statistics become out of date, becoming less useful over time. Depending on how much data is changed in a table, index statistics could become out of date in as little as a single day, or it might take weeks or months before the statistics became out of date. It all depends on how many rows are changed in a table.

Because an index's statistics are not automatically updated, it is up to the DBA to determine which indexes in which tables need to have their statistics updated using the UPDATE STATISTICS command, which is designed specifically for updating an index's statistics.

After the analysis of how much data is changed in each table, the DBA needs to develop a plan to run the UPDATE STATISTICS command on the appropriate tables at the appropriate times. Some tables may need to be updated every day, some every week, some every month, and some less often. Fortunately, this task can be assigned to SQL Server's scheduling function so that they are performed automatically.

Besides scheduling necessary UPDATE STATISTICS on tables, the DBA must constantly evaluate whether the current implementation plan is appropriate, and to make any necessary changes regarding the use of any tables change over time.

Besides ensuring that index statistics are up to date, another responsibility of the DBA is to regularly review the various databases and determine whether any new indexes need to be added (to optimize speed) or deleted (because they are not being used). This is an ongoing task that the DBA needs to add to his or her schedule.

Run UPDATE STATISTICS before backing up data

When you schedule running the UPDATE STATISTICS command on a table, ideally it should be run before a scheduled backup. That way, if the data should ever need to be restored, it will be restored with the most current index statistics.

Backup Databases and Transaction Logs

Because this topic is covered in-depth in Part V, "Preventing Data Loss," this section will be kept short. It goes without saying that as the DBA, one of the most important and critical jobs you have is to make regular backups of your databases and transaction logs. But there are other related jobs that fall into this category that many DBAs often forget:

- Backing up system databases whenever they change.
- Verifying backups to ensure that they are good.
- Keeping a copy of the backups off premises for extra protection.
- Developing a formal disaster recovery procedure, and testing it.
- Training others on how to restore data if the DBA is unavailable.
- Documenting database design, including maintaining up-to-date Transact-SQL scripts that can be used to re-create databases.
- Developing a procedure to identify old data that can be removed from production databases and archived.

Although most DBAs know they need to perform regular backups of their user databases, many forget some of these steps, which all play an important part of an organization's total backup strategy. Key to this strategy is writing a plan, and then following the plan.

NT Server-Related Maintenance Tasks

As a DBA, you may or may not be the network administrator for the NT Servers that are running SQL Server. Whether you are the network administrator or not, you must ensure that these regular network administrator–related tasks are performed that directly affect SQL Server's performance. Here are some of the regular network-administrative tasks that need to be done to insure SQL Server runs properly:

- Back up NT Server's Registry and system files. If you ever need to restore an NT Server running SQL Server, you will need to be able restore it to the state it was in before the failure. Otherwise, you will have to start building the NT Server from scratch, which can be time-consuming.

- Monitor all of NT Server's Event Viewer logs. They may contain reports of problems that don't directly affect SQL Server now, but could in the future if they aren't corrected.

- Regularly run a defragmentation utility to ensure that data files are contiguous. This can substantially increase the speed of file access, boosting SQL Server's overall speed. Schedule the defrag process to occur when your SQL databases aren't in heavy production.

- Monitor available hard disk space on the server. Because SQL Server's database and transaction log files can increase dynamically, it is possible to run out of hard disk space. Use NT Server's Performance Monitor tool to send you an alert if hard disk space gets beyond a specified amount of free disk space.

- Monitor NT Server's paging file (pagefile.sys) to see if it's large enough. By default, pagefile.sys is created to expand between a minimum and maximum size. If the pagefile.sys should ever fill up, it can lock NT Server, along with SQL Server. Use NT's Performance Monitor to track its size.

- Monitor the performance of the server hardware using NT's Performance Monitor, isolating bottlenecks and resolving them as necessary.

- As Service Packs are released for NT Server, be sure that they are installed as necessary, but only after first verifying that there are no problems with the Service Pack.

- As required, be sure the physical server's hardware is running properly and is updated as necessary to keep up with the needs of the users accessing the SQL Server data stored on it.

If there is a separate NT Server network administrator, you must work with him or her to ensure that all these tasks are performed

Finding information on NT Server

The details on how to perform these tasks are beyond the scope of this book. For a good reference on using NT Server, check out the book *Inside Windows NT Server 4: Administrator's Resource Edition* by Drew Heywood (New Rider's Press).

as needed. Ideally, as the DBA, you will also want to have NT Server Administrator rights and permissions to any SQL Server to administrator.

Working with Developers

Often, as a DBA, you will have the opportunity to work with SQL Server developers who are maintaining or creating new SQL Server applications. If so, you may find yourself performing many of the following tasks because of this relationship:

- Create new databases and objects at the request of developers.
- Back up and restore development databases.
- Create login IDs.
- Offer suggestions to the developers based on your knowledge and experience of the hardware that SQL Server is running on, and share your knowledge of SQL Server and how your users use data managed by SQL Server.

Often, there is some friction between the DBA and developers. For example, a developer may want a certain permission to perform some task. But as the DBA, you may not want to assign the permission because the developer could misuse it. These kinds of problems arise all the time, and the more the DBA knows about SQL Server development, the less this should be a problem.

How to Use the Database Maintenance Plan Wizard

SQL Server includes many wizards that can make your life as a DBA just a little easier. Or so it seems. One of the wizards included with SQL Server is the Database Maintenance Plan

Wizard. Its purpose is to automatically create a database maintenance plan on a per database basis. It has the ability to schedule the following jobs for you:

- Rebuild database indexes.
- Run the UPDATE STATISTICS command on the database.
- Specify page checking against extent structures in the database.
- Check the allocation of text and image columns in the database.
- Schedule database backups.
- Schedule transaction log backups.
- Generate a report showing what the plan successfully and unsuccessfully accomplished.

The Database Maintenance Plan Wizard steps you through a series of questions, asking you if and when you want to schedule any of the steps. After you are done creating the plan, the plan is automatically created for you, and it automatically runs as scheduled. At first glance, it may seem that this wizard may be a great time saver. And for the beginning DBA, this may be true. The problem with the wizard is that it is too limiting, just as many wizards are. In many cases, you may want to perform maintenance tasks that are not permitted by the wizard, or you may want to choose configuration options that are also not permitted by the wizard. In this case, the only option is to set up these same maintenance tasks manually using the SQL Server Agent.

Only you can decide whether the Database Maintenance Plan Wizard meets your needs as a DBA. I suggest you try it and decide for yourself. The following section describes how to use the Database Maintenance Plan Wizard, and the section after this one describes how to modify a currently existing plan created with the wizard.

SEE ALSO
➤ *For more information on setting up maintenance tasks, see page 276.*

How to Use the Database Maintenance Plan Wizard

The following steps show you how to use the Database Maintenance Plan Wizard to create a maintenance plan for a single database on a SQL Server.

Create a maintenance plan with the Database Maintenance Plan Wizard

1. Start the SQL Enterprise Manager, and select the SQL Server you want to currently work with.

2. From the Tools menu, select Database Maintenance Planner. This displays the Database Maintenance Plan Wizard Welcome screen (see Figure 10.18).

FIGURE 10.18

The welcoming screen of the Database Maintenance Plan Wizard..

3. Read the screen, and when you are done, click Next. This displays the Select Databases screen (see Figure 10.19).

4. Here, you must select which database or databases you want to create a maintenance plan for. You can select: all databases, all system databases, all user databases, or you can select any combination of databases. Click on the radio button of your choice, then click Next.

5. This displays the Update Data Optimization Information screen (see Figure 10.20).

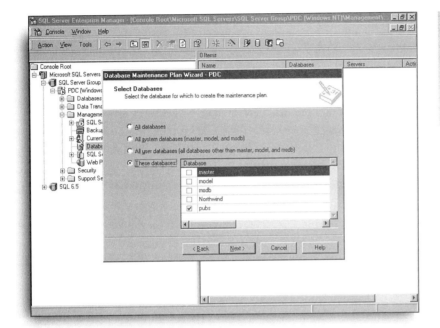

FIGURE 10.19
Use this screen to select the database or databases you want to create a maintenance plan for.

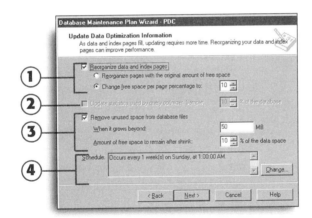

FIGURE 10.20
Here, you can decide how you want the database optimized.

(**1**) Used to drop and rebuild all the index pages of the tables in a database.

(**2**) Used to update the optimization statistics of a database.

(**3**) Used to reclaim empty space in a database.

(**4**) Used to schedule when you want the tasks on this page to be automatically carried out by SQL Server.

In section 1, Reorganize Data and Index Pages is used to determine whether you want to rebuild all the indexes in a database. The option Reorganize Pages with the Original Amount of Free Space refers to rebuilding the indexes using the same FILLFACTOR as was originally used when the indexes were created. FILLFACTOR refers to the amount of empty space in a newly created index. This empty space is used to store index information when new records are added to a table. The greater the FILLFACTOR, the less often an index

341

needs to be rebuilt. At the same time, the greater the FILLFACTOR, the more space that is taken up by a table's index. If you are not familiar with the FILLFACTOR option, and you want to rebuild the indexes in this database, you should choose this option.

If you are familiar with how the FILLFACTOR option works, you may want to select the Change Free Space per page percentage to option. Whatever number you enter in the box, the resulting FILLFACTOR will be the inverse. For example, if you enter **10** in the box, the FILLFACTOR will be 90.

In section 2 of the screen, you decide whether you want to run the UPDATE STATISTICS command on the tables in the database. As was mentioned earlier in this chapter, running this command can help speed up queries when they are run against this database. If you rebuild a database's indexes, you don't need to run this command because the act of rebuilding a database automatically accomplishes the same thing as the UPDATE STATISTICS command. If you decide to choose the Update the Statistics Used by the Query Optimizer option, you also have the option to choose the Sample % of the database. This option determines what percentage of a table is evaluated when running the UDPDATE STATISTICS command. The higher the value, the more accurate the results of the command, but the longer it takes to run.

In section 3 of the screen, you can determine whether or not you want unused space in a database to be reclaimed. For example, the textbox for the When It Grows Beyond option is checked, it determines at what point SQL Server should reclaim space. The default value of 50MB means that whenever the unused space in a database exceeds 50MB, that SQL Server should reclaim space. When the amount of unused space is lower than 50MB, no space is reclaimed. You get to choose this value. Also, you get to choose one more option. While it may be a good idea to reclaim wasted database space, you don't want to leave none. Some empty space is required to re-create indexes. This means you have to determine how much free space to leave. You get to enter this amount as a percentage of the total data space available in the database. For example, if your database is 100MB, and you leave the default value of 10% in the Amount of Free Space to Remain After Shrink at 10%, then 10MB will be kept for free space. Don't make this amount so small that you cannot rebuild your indexes, or the next time you try to rebuild your database's indexes, the operation will fail.

In section 4, you must tell the wizard how often you want to perform the tasks listed on this page of the wizard. By default, they are performed once a week on Sunday at 1:00AM, which may not be what you want. You can easily change when these tasks are performed by clicking on the Change button and completing the necessary information on the screen that appears. In it, you can specify any day or any time to run these tasks.

After you have completed this screen, click Next.

6. The next screen of the wizard is the Database Integrity Check (see Figure 10.21).

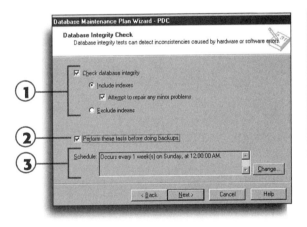

FIGURE 10.21

You can decide which integrity tests you want to run on the database.

① Determines which integrity checks, if any, are performed.

② Determines, in relation to when backups are performed, when these integrity checks are performed.

③ Determines when the tasks on this page are run.

In section 1 of this screen, you determine whether or not any integrity checks are run on a database. By running this option, you can find out if there are any problems with a database, and maybe even fix minor problems. Sometimes, running a complete integrity check on your database can take a long time, especially if your database is large. Ideally, you should run the integrity check on all the indexes and attempt to repair any problems. But if you find that the check takes too much time, you can decide to exclude the indexes in the check, which will help to reduce the amount of time it takes to run the check.

In section 2 of this screen, you determine when these checks are run, in relation to when backups are performed. Almost always, you will want to choose to perform these tests before doing a backup. This way, if the tests fail, the backup will not be performed. There is not much point in backing up a database if the database is damaged.

In section 3 of this screen, you determine when the tasks on this screen will run just as you did on the previous screen of this wizard.

When you are finished with this screen, click Next.

7. The Specify the Database Backup Plan screen is displayed (see Figure 10.22).

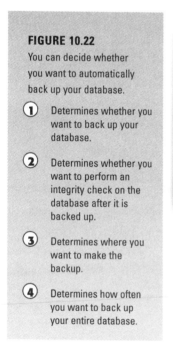

FIGURE 10.22

You can decide whether you want to automatically back up your database.

(1) Determines whether you want to back up your database.

(2) Determines whether you want to perform an integrity check on the database after it is backed up.

(3) Determines where you want to make the backup.

(4) Determines how often you want to back up your entire database.

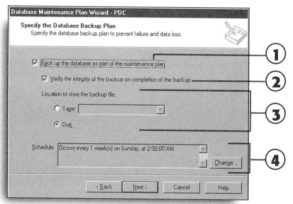

Section 1 is used to determine whether or not you want to perform a complete backup of your database. In most cases, you will want to perform a complete backup of each database daily.

Section 2 is used to determine whether or not you want the integrity of the database to be checked after the backup is complete. This is recommended, assuming you have time to run the tests, to ensure that you have a good backup of the database.

Section 3 determines where the backup will be made. Select the Tape option if you will be backing up to tape, or select the Disk option if you will be backing up to disk.

Section 4 allows you to schedule when you want to back up the database, and works like the previous screens of the wizard.

When you are finished with this screen, click Next.

8. The Specify Backup Disk Directory screen appears (assuming you chose to back up to disk on the previous screen of the wizard). See Figure 10.23.

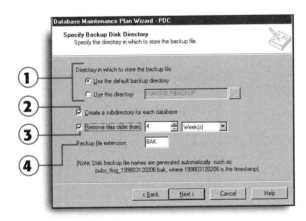

FIGURE 10.23

You must tell the wizard where you want your disk backups to be stored.

(1) Determines where you want to store your disk backup.

(2) Determines whether you want each database disk backup to be stored in a different folder.

(3) Determines how long you want to store your disk backups.

(4) Determines what file extension will be used for disk backup files.

Section 1 is used to determine where you want your disk backups to be stored. If you want them to be stored in SQL Server's default backup folder, you can choose this option, but it is not a good idea. This is usually on the same hard disk where your original files are stored, and if the hard disk fails, you will lose both your original and backup of your databases. Instead, you should use the Use This Directory option and specify a folder located on a hard disk separate from where the original database is being stored.

Section 2 is used to determine whether you want all your database disk backups to be included together in one folder, or if you want every database to be in a separate subfolder. Choose whichever works best for you.

Section 3 is used to determine how long your disk backups will be kept. The default is four weeks. Remember that disk backups take up a lot of space, so you don't want to store too many backups.

Section 4 is used to indicate what file extension you want to use for your disk backups. The default is BAK. There is no good reason to change this, unless you like to confuse yourself and others.

When you have completed this screen, click Next.

9. The Specify the Transaction Log Backup Plan screen is displayed (see Figure 10.24).

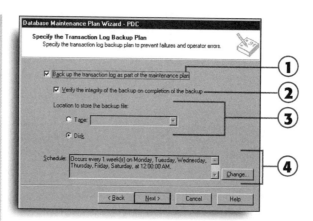

FIGURE 10.24

This screen is used to determine whether you want to back up your transaction log on a regular basis.

(1) Determines whether you want to back up a database's transaction log.

(2) Determines whether you want to check the integrity of the backup after the transaction log is backed up.

(3) Determines where you what to store your transaction log backups.

(4) Determines when and how often you want to back up a database's transaction log.

This screen is almost identical to the previous screen (see Figure 10.22) used to determine whether you want to back up your entire database. All the options are the same and will not be repeated here.

After you have completed this screen, click Next.

10. The Specify Transaction Log Backup Disk Directory screen appears (see Figure 10.25).

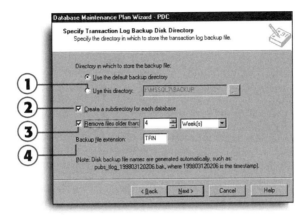

FIGURE 10.25
This screen is used to determine where you want to store your disk backups of transaction logs.

(1) Determines where you want to store your transaction log disk backup.

(2) Determines whether you want each transaction log disk backup to be stored in a different folder.

(3) Determines how long you want to store your backups.

(4) Determines what file extension will be used for backup files.

This screen is almost identical to the previous screen (see Figure 10.23) used to determine the location of your databases. All the options are similar and will not be repeated here.

After you have completed this screen, click Next.

11. The Reports to Generate screen appears (see Figure 10.26).

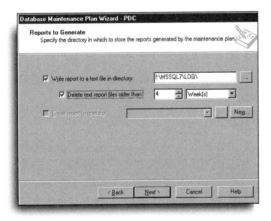

FIGURE 10.26
You can decide whether you want a report generated of the results of maintenance plan after it is run.

After a maintenance plan has run, you can have a report automatically generated letting you know whether each step in the plan was completed successfully or unsuccessfully. You can choose to have the report written to a text file, and even emailed to you. If you choose the email option, SQL Server must already be configured for email. Because text reports are not automatically deleted after they are written, you will probably want to have them automatically overwritten by selecting the Delete Text Report Files Older Than option and setting the amount of time you want the files to be kept.

After you choose how you want a report created, click Next.

12. Next is the Maintenance History screen (see Figure 12.27).

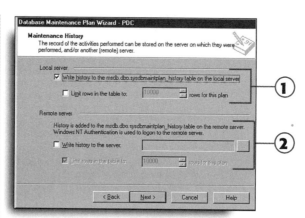

Section 1 is used to choose whether you want to maintain a permanent record of every time a maintenance plan runs in the MSDB database of the local server. By default, every plan will be stored forever, unless you limit the number of rows by selecting the Limit Rows in the Table To option.

Section 2 is similar, except for storing the data in the local MSDB database, you can store in a table on another SQL Server. Why would you want to do this? If you have more than one server, you can use this option to force all the SQL Servers to write all their history information to the same SQL Server, which makes it easier for you to view and analyze all the history of your plans for all your servers at one time.

13. And finally, at last, is the final screen of the wizard (see Figure 10.28).

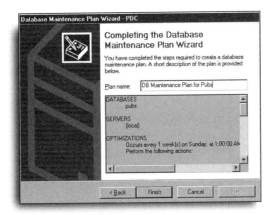

FIGURE 10.28
The last screen of the wizard enables you to go back and make changes.

Here, you have the ability to review your choices, and to make changes if desired. To review your choices, click the scroll bar. If you want to make changes, click the Back button. When you are happy with all your choices, click Finish. After a few seconds, a message appears letting you know that the plan has been created. Click OK to remove the screen.

SEE ALSO

➤ *For more information on how to configure SQL Server for email, see page 297.*

How to Change a Database Maintenance Plan

When you create a Database Maintenance Plan, the plan itself shows up in two different locations of the SQL Enterprise Manager. The first place is under the Database Maintenance Plans object under the SQL Server where it was created (see Figure 10.29).

Every database maintenance plan you create for each database managed by SQL Server is displayed in the details pane of SQL Enterprise Manager. Each plan can be individually viewed and changed from this pane.

Besides showing up under the Database Maintenance Plans object, the actual jobs that are created by SQL Server to run the plan are displayed in the details pane when the Jobs object is selected (see Figure 10.30).

FIGURE 10.29
Each plan for every database you create is listed in the details pane..

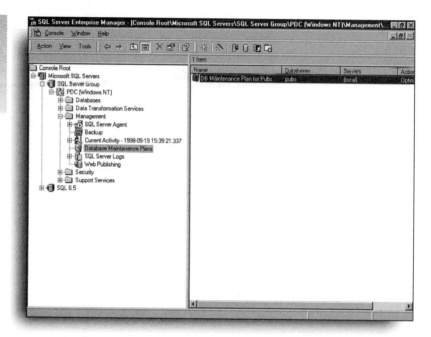

FIGURE 10.30
Each job that is created by the Database Maintenance Plan Wizard appears in the details pane.

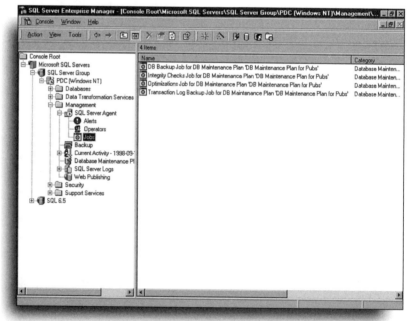

In Figure 10.30, you can see that the Database Maintenance Plan Wizard created four separate SQL Agent Jobs to perform the plan. Each job can be manually viewed and changed like any other job.

After one or more jobs have been created by the Database Maintenance Plan Wizard, they can be viewed and changed at any time.

1. Load the SQL Enterprise Manager, and then select the SQL Server you want to work with.

2. Click the Database Maintenance Plans object so that all the available maintenance plans appear in the details pane (see Figure 10.30).

3. To view or change a maintenance plan, right-click the plan you want to work with, and select Properties from the pop-up menu. This displays the Maintenance Plan dialog box (see Figure 10.31).

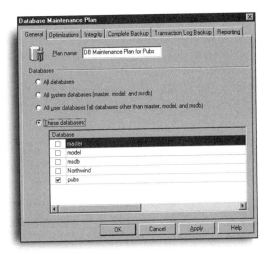

FIGURE 10.31
You can edit a maintenance plan from this dialog box.

4. From here, you can select the appropriate tab and then view or change any of the settings you originally selected when you first created the plan.

5. When you are finished, click OK. This will save any changes you made to the plan. You will see a message telling you that the changes were made, and you will have to click OK to remove the message.

SEE ALSO

➤ *For more information on how to view and edit jobs, see page 284.*

SQL Server Maintenance Checklist

After reading this chapter, you may wonder how you are going to keep track of all the tasks you need to perform to maintain SQL Server. To make this task easier, the following section summarizes the many tasks into various time frames. What you need to do now is to create your own checklist. Use this as your guide, but customize it to meet your unique circumstances.

As mentioned earlier in this chapter, you should automate this checklist by entering it into a software tool, such as Microsoft Outlook or Project, where you can not only be reminded of your regular tasks, but also where you can track what you have and have not done.

Daily Tasks

- Review the SQL Server error log for potential problems.
- Review the NT Event Viewer error logs, which include the System and Application logs, for potential problems.
- Periodically throughout each day, the DBA should review the Current Activity Window, looking for potential problems that need immediate resolution.
- Verify that replication is working as expected.
- Monitor database and transaction log sizes.
- Add new login and database user IDs as needed.
- Modify current login and database user IDs as needed.
- Manage object permissions as needed.

- Run DBCC commands on your databases to ensure their integrity.
- Run UPDATE STATISTICS as needed.
- Rebuild indexes as needed.
- Back up system and user databases and transaction logs, and keep copies off-site.
- Back up the NT Registry and system files.
- Monitor server hard disk and pagefile.sys space.

Weekly Tasks

- Run UPDATE STATISTICS as needed.
- Rebuild indexes as needed.
- If you are only backing up transaction logs daily, be sure to do a full database backup at least once a week.
- Monitor overall NT Server performance with Performance Monitor.

Monthly Tasks

- Audit current login IDs, database user IDs, and permissions to ensure that they are current and don't permit anyone more access than they need.
- Audit NT Server NTFS and share permissions to ensure that unauthorized users cannot improperly access SQL Server programs or data.
- Use NT Server's auditing capability to track successful and unsuccessful folder and file access.
- Use the SQL Server Profiler to monitor user activity within all production databases to determine usage trends.
- Use NT Server's Performance Monitor to track and analyze SQL Server user activity and overall performance.
- Verify that backups are good by actually restoring selected databases onto test servers.

Other Scheduled Tasks

- Whenever a SQL Server or a new database is put into production, it must be thoroughly documented. And whenever any change is made to any SQL Server or database, these changes also must be documented.
- Update your formal SQL Server maintenance plan as your SQL Server environment changes.
- Create and size new databases as needed.
- Create events and alerts as needed.
- Set up replication as needed.
- Import and export data from and to SQL Server as needed.
- Regularly review and update the disaster recovery plan.
- Apply SQL Server Service Packs as required.
- Apply NT Server Service Packs as required.
- Work with developers as required.

part

IV

SQL Server Security

chapter

11

Introduction to SQL Security

SQL Server Security Basics

Before anyone can access SQL Server, or the data stored in databases by SQL Server, he must first be authenticated by SQL Server. In other words, SQL Server must determine whether the user trying to access SQL Server is an authorized user or not. If SQL Server considers the user an authorized user, the user is let in. If the user isn't considered an authorized user, access is denied.

SQL Server supports two different types of user authentication: Windows NT Authentication and SQL Server Authentication. If Windows NT Authentication is used, this means that NT Server's built-in security is used to authenticate the user. If SQL Server Authentication is used, SQL Server's own built-in security is used, and Windows NT Security isn't used.

So when a user logs in to SQL Server, which authentication method will be used? This depends on you, the DBA. It is your responsibility to configure which security mode SQL Server will use when authenticating users. By selecting a security mode, you determine which authentication method SQL Server will use to authenticate users.

A *security mode* refers to how SQL Server authenticates a user when she attempts to access SQL Server. SQL Server offers two security modes: the Windows NT Server Authentication Security Mode and the SQL Server Mixed Authentication Security Mode. Don't confuse these with Windows NT Authentication and SQL Server Authentication, which are authentication methods, not modes.

The *Windows NT Server Authentication Security Mode* uses the NT Windows Authentication method only to authenticate users. This means that whenever a user attempts to access SQL server, Windows NT Security is used to authenticate the user. If the user cannot be authenticated by Windows NT Server, the user is denied access.

The *SQL Server Mixed Authentication Security Mode* enables a user to be authenticated by either Windows NT Authentication or SQL Server Authentication. This means that if a user attempts to access SQL Server, Windows NT Authentication is tried first to authenticate the user. If that fails, SQL Server Authentication is tried next. If the user cannot be authenticated by either authentication methods, the user is denied access.

As you might guess, the SQL Server Mixed Authentication Security mode is much more flexible than the Windows NT Server Authentication Security Mode. Because of this, the SQL Server Mixed Authentication Security Mode is the default security mode of SQL Server.

This chapter is the first of three chapters on SQL Server Security. This chapter provides an overview of how SQL Server security works, explaining in detail the two security modes. Chapter 12, "Managing Users," describes how to create SQL Server accounts. Chapter 13, "Assigning User Permissions," describes how to assign users the necessary permissions to access database information. All three chapters are closely related and should be read together as a single unit, as all three chapters are closely intertwined.

Planning SQL Server Security

As with every aspect of configuring and using SQL Server, you should carefully plan how you want to implement SQL Server security. SQL Server offers a variety of security-related choices, with each one offering different sets of advantages and disadvantages. As you read this chapter, and the next two, you will need to find answers to these questions before setting up the security features of SQL Server:

- Which security mode is the most appropriate for your organization? Should you select the more flexible SQL Server Mixed Authentication Security Mode, or the more restrictive Windows NT Server Authentication Security Mode?

- How tight should your security be? Some organizations have little need for security, whereas others need very tight security. The tighter the security requirements, the more work that is involved in setting it up.

An authentication method is different from a Security mode

An *authentication method* is a built-in SQL Server process that you cannot directly configure. A *security mode* is a configurable option that enables you to choose which authentication method SQL Server uses to authenticate users.

Doesn't SQL Server have three security modes?

If you used any previous version of SQL Server, you may have noticed something missing from this chapter. In the past, SQL Server offered three security modes: Standard Security, Integrated Security, and Mixed Security. Under SQL Server 7.0, there are only two security modes. The new Windows NT Server Authentication Security Mode is most like the older Integrated Security Mode, and the new SQL Server Mixed Authentication Security Mode is most like the older Mixed Security mode. The older Standard Security mode no longer exits, as its functionality is built in to the new SQL Server Mixed Authentication Mode. All older SQL Server programs should be able to take advantage of one of these two new security modes.

- What tasks need to be performed in your databases (such as inserting, updating, deleting, or querying data), and who will perform these tasks? The answers to these questions determine what login IDs, database user IDs, roles, and groups will be required, along with what permissions are to be assigned to each.

- After SQL Server security has been set up, it is important that your security plan include a way to monitor the effectiveness of the overall plan. The needs of users constantly change, which means that your security needs will change. You must have a standard way to deal with change, while still ensuring the level of security your organization needs.

As you read this section on SQL Server security, you may want to have paper and pen at hand to take notes, roughing out your security needs and the tasks you will need to perform to put them into place.

The SQL Server Security Architecture

SQL Server's security is multifaceted, involving both the network operating system and SQL Server itself. In this section, we introduce you to some basic SQL Server security terminology, take a look at the various barriers put up between users and SQL Server's data to prevent unauthorized access, and how SQL Server authenticates users. This high-level look at SQL Server's security architecture will help you understand what is happening in the background to help protect your valuable data.

SQL Server Security Building Blocks

SQL Server uses a variety of security-related terms that you must understand before reading the rest of this chapter. The following terms are key to understanding SQL Server security.

- Login ID. Whenever a user wants to access SQL Server, the user must provide a login ID in one form or another. The *login ID* acts as a key that unlocks the door to SQL Server and enables the user to enter and gain access to specific databases managed by SQL Server. If a user's account uses Windows NT Authentication, the user's SQL Server login ID is the same as his NT Server logon ID. In addition, the user doesn't have to manually re-enter his login ID when he attempts to access SQL Server. If a user's account uses SQL Server authentication, he will have to manually enter his login ID and password before he can gain access to SQL Server.

- Database user ID. Before a user can access a database managed by SQL Server, she must have a database user ID for that specific database. Each separate database includes a system table that holds all the database user IDs that have been granted access to the database. If a user doesn't have a database user ID in the database they want to access, she cannot access it. Generally, the database user ID for a user is the same name as her login ID. Here's how it works. After SQL Server has authenticated a user, the user must choose which database managed by SQL Server she wants to access. When the user attempts to access a database, the user's login ID is checked against the list of database user IDs stored in the database's system table. If there is a match, the user is allowed into the database. If there is no match, access is denied. A user will have a database user ID for each database she has been given access to.

- Roles. Previous versions of SQL Server contained database groups in each database. Database groups are no longer used in SQL Server 7.0. Instead, roles are used. A role is very similar to a group in that SQL Server login IDs, NT Server logins, groups, and other roles can be assigned to the same role, and then permissions can be assigned to the role. Anyone who is a member of a role will have the permissions that are assigned to the role. SQL Server comes with many predefined roles, and you can create your own. A user may belong to more than one role at the same time.

- Application Roles. This is a special type of role that is assigned to a specific application that has been designed to access SQL Server data. For example, if a user needs to access a specific type of data, instead of explicitly assigning permission to the user to access the data, the user is given access to the data by using the application that has been assigned an application role. This means that a user can only gain access to the data by using this specific application. Application roles are assigned to applications, not users.

- Groups. The word *group* in SQL Server security terminology refers to NT Server global groups. These groups are created and managed with NT Server's User Manager for Domains administrative tool. SQL Server understands global groups and even enables you to assign SQL Server permissions to them if you are using Windows NT Authentication.

SEE ALSO

➤ *For more information on login IDs, see page 378.*

➤ *For more information on database user IDs, see page 382.*

➤ *For more information on roles, see page 383.*

Barriers to Accessing SQL Server Data

Before any user can access data in a SQL Server database, he must pass four major barriers, all in the proper order (see Figure 11.1). To pass each barrier, users need a "key" to unlock the various barriers. By providing four ways to prevent unauthorized users from accessing SQL Server data, you can be assured that your data won't easily be compromised.

The first major barrier a user must transverse is the user's network operating system. Although this is generally NT Server, it can be any network operating system that can co-exist with NT Server and SQL Server. Generally speaking, a user must provide a valid network account name and password to be authenticated and logged on to the network. All this does is get the user onto the network. It doesn't automatically allow her access to SQL Server.

What is an NT Server global group?

NT Server uses global groups to group users with similar data access needs. For example, if everyone in the development department of an organization needs access to a specific database, they all could be grouped together in a global group named `gg_development`. SQL Server recognizes global groups and enables the DBA to assign specific database permissions to a global group.

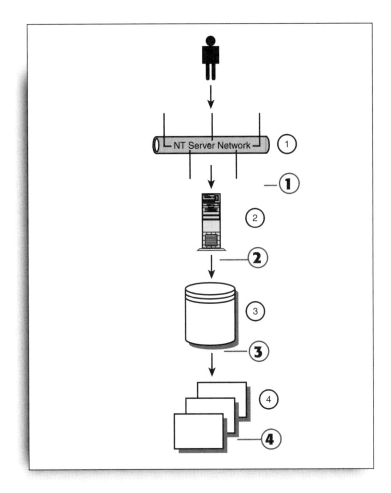

FIGURE 11.1

Users must past four barriers before they can access SQL Server data.

(1) The network operating system; the user must log on to the network.

(2) SQL Server authentication; the user must have a SQL Server user account.

(3) Database authentication; the user's ID must be in a system table of the database.

(4) Object authentication; the user must be assigned permissions.

After a user has access to the network, the next step is for the user to be authenticated by SQL Server using Windows NT Authentication or SQL Server Authentication. To be authenticated by SQL Server, the user must provide SQL Server with a valid login ID and password. If the user is being authenticated by Windows NT Authentication, the user's NT Server network account name is used as the SQL Server login ID. In fact, the user doesn't even have to enter the login ID. SQL Server can automatically determine the login ID itself. If SQL Server Authentication is authenticating the user, the user must manually enter a valid SQL Server login ID and password.

Just because a user has access to SQL Server doesn't mean that he has access to any of the databases managed by SQL Server. The next step is for the user to be authenticated by the database he wants to access. Unless a user has a database user ID in a system table of the database he wants to access, he cannot access it. This is done on a database by database basis. A user may be given permission to access all the databases managed by SQL Server, or the user may just be given permission to access one or two databases.

Last of all, even though a user may have permission to access a database, this doesn't automatically grant the user permission to access the data stored in the objects of the database, such as tables. A user must be given specific permission to access database objects, on an object-by-object basis. Just because a user has been given permission to one table doesn't mean she automatically has permission to access other tables.

As you can see, users have many barriers to cross before accessing SQL Server data. Although the four barriers make it very difficult for unauthorized users to access your data, at the same time it makes it harder for you to set up SQL Server security. Depending on your security requirements, setting up security can be complex and time consuming. Microsoft realizes that setting up and maintaining SQL Server security can be difficult. Because of this, it has included many features that make your job as the DBA much easier. You will learn more about these features as you read this section of the book.

User Authentication

When a user attempts to gain access to SQL Server, he can be authenticated in one of two ways: either by Windows NT Authentication or SQL Server Authentication. Don't confuse these with security modes, which are a distinct, but related topic. Security modes are discussed in more detail in the next section of this chapter.

Windows NT Authentication takes advantage of NT Server's built-in security, which includes such features as encrypted authentication, passwords that expire, minimum length

---

What exactly is a permission?

A *permission* is the right assigned to a user enabling him to access a specific object in a SQL Server database. By default, users don't have any permission to access any object in a SQL Server database. The DBA or other authorized user must assign permissions to a user.

passwords, account lockout, and restricted access based on computer names. Windows NT Authentication comes into play when a user attempts to connect to a SQL Server and must be authenticated before proceeding to later barriers.

When SQL Server is asked to authenticate a user, instead of asking the user to enter a login name and password, SQL Server uses the login name used by the user when he logged on to NT Server. SQL Server asks NT Server for the account name used by the user when he logged on to NT Server. Then SQL Server compares that name to a list of authorized login IDs in a SQL Server system table. If it finds a match, SQL Server authenticates the user, enabling the user to pass this barrier. Note that the password isn't checked. This is because SQL Server is trusting that NT Server has already done the proper security checking to verify who the user is. All this occurs in the background, unbeknownst to the user.

Windows NT Authentication works with either the Windows NT Server Authentication Security Mode or the SQL Server Mixed Authentication Security Mode.

SQL Server Authentication doesn't use any of NT Server's built-in security features. Instead, SQL Server itself is totally responsible for authenticating users who want to access SQL Server. For example, after a user has logged on to NT Server and been authenticated by NT Server, the user is past the first barrier to gaining access to SQL Server data. The next step is to pass the second barrier, or SQL Server itself. Under SQL Server Authentication, a user will be required to enter both a login ID and password. This information is then compared to a system table managed by SQL Server that includes a list of all authorized login IDs and passwords. If there is a match, SQL Server will authenticate the user and let in. If the user's login ID or password aren't found in the SQL Server system table, the user is denied access.

SQL Server Authentication is commonly used in three instances. First, many older SQL Server applications were designed to use this authentication method. If you want to run such an application under SQL Server 7.0, you have no choice but to use

More on NT Server security

Most NT Server security features are configured using NT Server's User Manager for Domains program. If you aren't familiar with this tool, you need to learn more about it. Check out the book *Inside Windows NT Server 4.0* by Drew Heywood, published by New Riders (ISBN: 1-56205-860-6).

Windows 95/98 doesn't support NT Server authentication

If you run SQL Server under Windows 95/98, it won't support Windows NT Authentication. Windows 95/98 only supports SQL Server Authentication, which means you have no choice but to set up SQL Server to use the SQL Server Mixed Authentication Security Mode.

SQL Server Authentication, unless you want to rewrite the application. The second reason to use this authentication method is if you run SQL Server under Windows 95/98. Windows 95/98 only supports SQL Server Authentication, not Windows NT Authentication. The last reason this method is used is if the client operating system used is non–Windows-based, and you have no choice but to use SQL Server Authentication. Examples of this include clients running Novell client software or users accessing SQL Server via a Web browser. This is because only Windows-based client operating systems support NT Server authentication.

SQL Server Authentication is only supported under the SQL Server Mixed Authentication Security Mode. The NT Server Authentication Security Mode doesn't support it.

What Is a Security Mode?

In the previous section we took a look at the two ways SQL Server can authenticate users: Windows NT Authentication and SQL Server Authentication. Each of these describes how a user can be authenticated by SQL Server.

Closely related to these two authentication methods is what is referred to as a security mode. A *security mode* refers to how you as the DBA configure SQL Server to authenticate users. SQL Server supports two different security modes:

- Windows NT Server Authentication Security Mode. If you set up SQL Server to use this security mode, SQL Server can only use Windows NT Authentication to authenticate users.

- SQL Server Mixed Authentication Security Mode. If you set up SQL Server to use this security mode, SQL Server can use Windows NT Authentication or SQL Server Authentication to authenticate users into SQL Server.

As a DBA, you must decide which security mode is most appropriate for your organization, and then configure SQL Server appropriately. The following two sections describe these two security modes in detail, and also show you how to configure SQL Server to use them.

SQL Server Mixed Authentication Security Mode

After installing SQL Server for the first time, SQL Server is automatically set to the SQL Server Mixed Authentication Security Mode. This means that a user is able to connect to SQL Server using either Windows NT Authentication or SQL Server Authentication. This option provides the most flexibility for the DBA, because users of virtually any type can be authenticated by SQL Server.

How a User Is Authenticated Using the SQL Server Mixed Authentication Security Mode

Because the SQL Server Mixed Authentication Security Mode permits either Windows NT Authentication or SQL Server Authentication, SQL Server must perform several steps whenever a user first tries to access SQL Server. Although the following steps are hidden from the user, here is what SQL Server does underneath the surface to authenticate a user under the SQL Server Mixed Authentication Security Mode:

1. When a user attempts to connect to SQL Server and become authenticated by SQL Server, the first thing SQL Server does is evaluate whether the user is connecting from either a trusted or non-trusted network connection.

2. If the user is connecting using a non-trusted connection, SQL Server automatically assumes that SQL Server Authentication will be used to authenticate the user. This is because Windows NT Authentication doesn't work over a non-trusted connection. This will most commonly occur when the client being used by the user is a non-Windows product, or if the user is connecting over the Internet using a Web browser. The user will be prompted to enter his SQL

Should I choose the SQL Server Mixed Authentication Security Mode?

Unless you have a specific reason not to enable any users into SQL Server using SQL Server Authentication, choosing this mode gives you the most flexibility when defining a security scheme for SQL Server. Even if virtually all database users will be using Windows NT Authentication to access SQL Server, using this mode is still a good choice.

What is a trusted connection?

A *trusted connection* is any connection that takes advantage of NT Server's built-in security. In order for a trusted connection to take place, either the Named Pipes TCP/IP, or the Multi-Protocol network libraries must be used for both the client and SQL Server. If the network library being used is any network library other than Named Pipes TCP/IP, or Multi-Protocol, the network connections is non-trusted, and Windows NT Authentication cannot be used.

367

Server login ID and password before he can be authenticated by SQL Server.

3. If the user is connecting using a trusted connection, the next thing SQL Server does is attempt to authenticate the user with Windows NT Authentication. This means that SQL Server will verify that the logon information provided by the user when she logged on to NT Server will be used to also log in to SQL Server. If there is a match between the SQL Server login ID and the SQL Server login ID stored in a system table of SQL Server, the user is authenticated and allowed into SQL Server. Should the user's application unnecessarily prompt the user to enter a login ID and password, the user can just bypass this prompt and directly access SQL Server (see Figure 11.2).

FIGURE 11.2
If Windows NT Authentication is being used, you can bypass login screens such as this one.

4. If SQL Server cannot automatically authenticate the user using Windows NT Authentication, SQL Server will attempt to authenticate the user with SQL Server Authentication. The user must then enter a valid SQL Server login ID and password to be authenticated.

5. Under any situation where an unauthorized user attempts to access SQL Server, his access will be automatically denied and an error message will appear.

How to Implement the SQL Server Mixed Authentication Security Mode

Because the SQL Server Mixed Authentication Security Mode is the default security mode of SQL Server, you don't have to do anything to configure it for use. The following steps show you how to verify that your server is currently using the SQL Server Mixed Authentication Security Mode, and shows you how to change it to this mode in case someone else has already changed SQL Server to the Windows NT Authentication Security Mode.

Configure SQL Server to use the SQL Server Mixed Authentication Security Mode

1. Start the SQL Enterprise Manager using a login ID with an appropriate SQL Server role.

2. From the scope pane, display the available SQL Servers.

3. Right-click the SQL Server you want to modify and then select Properties from the pop-up menu. This displays the SQL Server Properties dialog box (see Figure 11.3).

FIGURE 11.3
The SQL Server Properties dialog box is used to configure SQL Server security, among other tasks.

4. From the SQL Server Properties dialog box, select the Security tab. This displays the Security window (see Figure 11.4).

5. If the radio button next to SQL Server and Windows NT is selected, your SQL Server is already configured to use SQL Server Mixed Authentication Security. If this radio button isn't selected, select it now.

FIGURE 11.4
You configure the SQL
Server Authentication
Security Mode from this
screen.

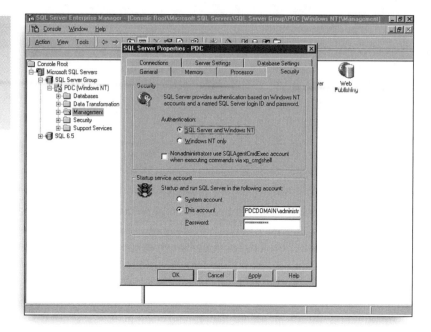

6. After you have selected the appropriate option, click OK. This will return you to the SQL Enterprise Manager's main screen.

7. Assuming you changed the Authentication Security Mode in step 5 above, you must restart the MSSQLServer service before it will go into effect. You may use any of the many methods available to stop and start this service. In this example, we will use the SQL Enterprise Manager to restart the service.

8. First, you must stop the MSSQLServer service. To do this, right-click the appropriate SQL Server and select Stop from the pop-up menu. After a few seconds, the icon next to the server will change from a green arrow to a red dot, indicating that the service has stopped.

9. Now you must restart the service. To do this, right-click the appropriate SQL Server and select Start from the pop-up menu. After a few seconds, the icon next to the server will change from a red dot to a green arrow, indicating that the service has been restarted.

The SQL Server is now using the newly chosen security mode, and will continue to use it until it is changed again.

Using the Windows NT Authentication Security Mode

If you decide to choose the Windows NT Authentication Security Mode, only the Windows NT Authentication mechanism is used to authenticate users for SQL Server. If you choose this option, you must ensure that all the client software used by the users who want to access SQL Server are running a Windows-based client and can connect to the SQL Server using a trusted connection. This option is much more restrictive than the SQL Server Mixed Authentication Security Mode because it doesn't permit SQL Server Authentication. You should only choose this option if you know that you will never run into a situation where your users will ever want to connect to SQL Server with a non-Microsoft client.

How a User Is Authenticated Under the Windows NT Authentication Security Mode

Authentication under the Windows NT Authentication Security Mode is much simpler than under the SQL Server Mixed Authentication Security Mode.

Whenever a user attempts to access SQL Server, SQL Server automatically attempts to authenticate the user by using the NT Server login used by the user when she logged into NT Server. The user doesn't have to enter a login ID or password to access SQL Server. This is true even if the application she is using prompts the user to log in. If the application prompts the user to log in, the user can ignore the prompt.

Assuming that the user's NT Server login ID has been added to SQL Server, the user is automatically authenticated. If a user tries to log in to SQL Server using SQL Server security, and he isn't authorized to access SQL Server using NT Windows authentication, his attempt will fail.

How to Configure the Windows NT Authentication Security Mode

If you want to select the Windows NT Authentication Security Mode, you will have to configure SQL Server to use it. This section shows you how to configure SQL Server to use the Windows NT Authentication Security Mode.

Configure SQL Server to use the Windows NT Authentication Security Mode

1. Start the SQL Enterprise Manager using a login ID with an appropriate SQL Server role.

2. From the scope pane, display the available SQL Servers.

3. Right-click the SQL Server you want to modify and then select Properties from the pop-up menu. This displays the SQL Server Properties dialog box.

4. From the SQL Server Properties dialog box, select the Security tab. This displays the Security window (see Figure 11.5).

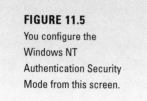

FIGURE 11.5
You configure the Windows NT Authentication Security Mode from this screen.

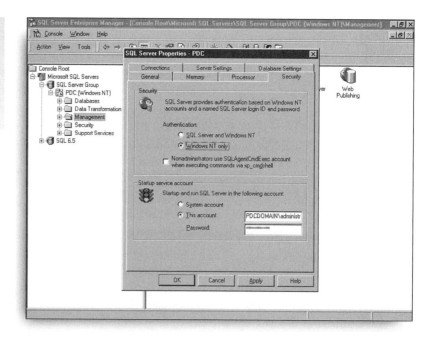

5. To select the Windows NT Authentication Server Mode, select the radio button next to Windows NT only.

6. After you have selected the appropriate option, click OK. This will return you to the SQL Enterprise Manager's main screen.

7. You must restart the MSSQLServer service before the new security mode will go into effect. You may use any of the many methods available to stop and start this service. In this example, we will use the SQL Enterprise Manager to restart the service.

8. First, you must stop the MSSQLServer service. To do this, right-click the appropriate SQL Server and select Stop from the pop-up menu. After a few seconds, the icon next to the server will change from a green arrow to a red dot, indicating that the service has stopped.

9. Now you must restart the service. To do this, right-click the appropriate SQL Server and select Start from the pop-up menu. After a few seconds, the icon next to the server will change from a red dot to a green arrow, indicating that the service has been restarted.

SQL Server is now using the newly chosen security mode, and will continue to use it until it is changed again.

Selecting an Authentication Security Mode is just the first step you must take when setting up security for a SQL Server. In the next two chapters you learn how to create user accounts and set permissions.

SEE ALSO
➤ *For more information on login IDs, see page 378.*
➤ *For more information on database user IDs, see page 382.*
➤ *For more information on roles, see page 383.*

chapter

12

Managing Users

How Do Users Gain Access to SQL Server?

More often than not, access to SQL Server data needs to be limited to selected groups and people. As you learned in the previous chapter, "Introduction to SQL Security," SQL Server provides a comprehensive security system that can work alone (SQL Server Authentication), or be integrated with NT Server's security system (Windows NT Authentication).

The authentication method that is used to log users in to SQL Server depends on whether SQL Server has been set up for the Windows NT Server Authentication Security Mode or the SQL Server Mixed Authentication Security Mode.

In this chapter, you will learn how to create and manage the necessary login IDs, database user IDs, NT Server global groups, and SQL Server roles necessary to enable users to access SQL Server and the databases managed by it. How you create and manage this will be directly affected by which SQL Server Security Authentication Mode you have selected and configured for SQL Server, as described in the last chapter.

In the next chapter, you will learn about permissions, which are the last barriers users must pass before they can gain access to SQL Server data. After you finish this chapter, you will have a well-rounded view of how to implement user security in SQL Server.

SEE ALSO

➤ *For more information on the two SQL Server supported security modes, see page 357.*

Introduction to SQL Server Accounts

System tables are important to SQL Server security

Login IDs are stored in the syslogins table of the Master database. Database User IDs are stored in the sysusers table of each separate database.

One of the main jobs of the DBA is to manage SQL Server accounts. This includes creating new accounts, changing current accounts, and dropping accounts as needed.

SQL Server uses two types of user accounts:

- Login ID. This is the user account name used by SQL Server to identify users who want to access SQL Server. For example, if users want to access SQL Server, they must first log in to SQL Server by providing an appropriate login ID and password (see Figure 12.1). After users have logged into SQL Server, this doesn't mean they can automatically access data in a database managed by SQL Server. Before they can do this, users must also have an appropriate database user ID to access a database. Login IDs are stored in the syslogins table in the Master database.

- Database User ID. After users have logged in successfully to SQL Server using a login ID, they must have an appropriate database user ID in every database they want to access (see Figure 12.1); otherwise, they are denied access. Every separate database has a special system table, called the sysusers table, that tracks who may access it. In this table are the database user IDs that have permission to access the database. So if users have a login ID, they may only access a database if they also have a database user ID in the sysusers table of the database. If they do not have a database user ID in the sysusers table, they may not access the database. Note that users don't have to separately log in to a database. Whenever users attempts to access a database, SQL Server automatically checks the database's sysusers table to see whether it contains a database user ID for the user. If it does, the user is allowed in; otherwise, the user is denied access. In most cases, a user's database user ID is the same as the user's login ID, although this isn't required.

Users can be assigned a SQL Server login ID in two different ways. One way is to use the user's NT Server user account as the user's SQL Server login ID, or you can ignore the user's network account and make up your own SQL Server login ID.

If SQL Server is set up to use the SQL Server Mixed Authentication Security Mode, this means that either Windows NT Authentication or SQL Server Authentication can be used to authenticate the users and enable them into SQL Server. You can choose either method for a SQL Server user account as best meets your needs.

The four user barriers to accessing SQL Server data

Before users can access any SQL Server data, they must first pass four barriers. First, they must have a network login ID and password to access the network that SQL Server is running on. Second, they must have a login ID to gain access to SQL Server. Third, they must have a database user ID to access a database. And fourth, they must have the proper permission to access data stored in SQL Server objects, such as tables or views. By default, no user has access to any SQL Server data.

How to refer to the login ID and database user ID

The term *login ID* is sometimes referred to as *login name* or *login account* in other references. Also, the term, *database user ID* is often referred to as *user*, *username*, or *user account* in other references.

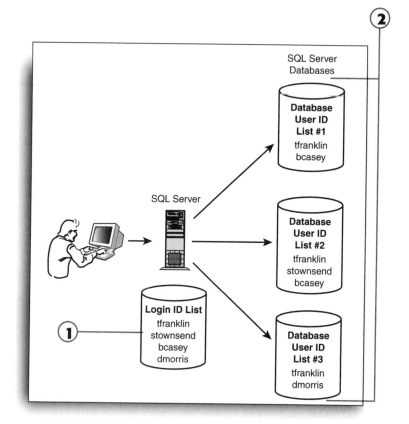

FIGURE 12.1

Both a login ID and database user ID are required before users can access any SQL Server database.

(1) In this example, there are four different login IDs that have permission to access this SQL Server.

(2) Although there are four login IDs that have potential access to SQL Server databases, in database number one, only two users have their login ID in the database's system table. In database number two, only three users have access to this database, and in database number three, only two users have access to this database.

If SQL Server is set up to use the Windows NT Server Authentication Security Mode, only Windows NT Authentication can be used to authenticate users and enable them into SQL Server.

You will learn how to perform all these tasks later in this chapter.

How to Create and Manage Login IDs

Before any user can access SQL Server, she must first have a SQL Server login ID. As the DBA, it is your job to determine which users need access to SQL Server, and then create the necessary login IDs.

This section is divided into two parts. First, you learn how to create login IDs for users who will be using Windows NT Authentication to gain access to SQL Server. Second, you will learn how to create login IDs for users who use SQL Server Authentication to access SQL Server. Keep in mind that you don't have to use both authentication methods if you don't want to. You can use one or the other, or any combination of both, depending on your user's needs.

This section focuses on giving you the big picture of how to create login IDs. The specific steps on how to create login IDs using SQL Enterprise Manager will be covered later in this chapter.

Creating Login IDs Under Windows NT Authentication

If you are running SQL Server under either the Windows NT Server Authentication Security Mode or the SQL Server Mixed Authentication Security Mode, you have the ability to create SQL Server login IDs using Windows NT Authentication.

If you remember from the previous chapter, Windows NT Authentication means that NT Server, not SQL Server, is used to authenticate users who want to access SQL Server. For example, whenever users log on to NT Server, they must enter an NT user account name, a password, and the name of the domain where their user account resides. This information is then authenticated by an NT Server domain controller in the NT Server domain. When users are authenticated by NT Server, they are given what is called an access token. An access token is much like a custom-made key that enables users to access the various network resources that they have permission to access. After users have the access token, and assuming that Windows NT Authentication is being used, the user can now attempt to access SQL Server, which is of course is just another resource available on a network. When users attempt to connect to SQL Server, SQL Server then compares their NT Server account name (which is a part of the access token) to the list of login IDs in its syslogins table in its Master database. If there is a match, the user is automatically logged in to SQL Server without any

Do I have to always log in when requested?

Some programs used to remotely access SQL Server always display a login screen when they are first started. If Windows NT Authentication is being used, the user can skip this screen by clicking the Cancel button. The user will be automatically logged in to SQL Server.

further authentication needing to be done. This process is invisible and automatic for the user.

Now that you know how SQL Server uses the NT Server user account name as the SQL Server login ID, let's take a look at how to tell SQL Server to do this. By default, no NT Server user account has the capability to access SQL Server until you have told SQL Server that the NT Server user account may access SQL Server.

There are two different ways you can tell SQL Server to use an NT Server user account name as a SQL Server login ID. The first way is to assign the specific NT Server user account name to SQL Server. In other words, you configure SQL Server so that it knows to enable a specific NT Server user account name as a login ID and to use Windows NT Authentication to login this user to SQL Server.

The second way to permit users to access SQL Server using Windows NT Authentication is to assign an NT Server global group to SQL Server. Here, you configure SQL Server using an NT Server global group instead of a user account name. This means that anyone who belongs to the global group is automatically able to access SQL Server. In this particular case, users who are members of a global group assigned to SQL Server are not given specific login IDs. Instead, these users are managed as a group, not separately.

As a DBA, your goal should be to use NT Server global groups instead of using individual NT Server user account names when configuring SQL Server security. This is because it is much easier, and less work, to manage a collection of global groups than it is to manage many individual users.

There is a potential problem you must be aware of when using global groups with SQL Server. What if you want to use a particular global group to enable users to access SQL Server, but you don't want everybody in the global group to access SQL Server. One way to resolve the problem is to modify the global group so that it doesn't contain the users you want to exclude. But this isn't always possible because global groups are also used within NT Server to manage permissions. If you cannot modify

What are NT Server global groups?

Global groups in NT Server are used to group users together who have a common need to access a particular resource, such as SQL Server. Users can belong to one or more global groups. Global groups are created and managed using the User Manager for Domains, an NT Server-based administrative utility. Before you can use the User Manager for Domains, you must have the proper administrative rights.

DBAs need to create their own Sysadmin account

Everyone who is to be the DBA of a SQL Server needs to have a login ID created, along with being assigned the Sysadmins role. This is a special role that enables the user to perform any SQL Server administrative function. Of course, don't assign the Sysadmins role to users who don't need full administrative rights.

the global group, SQL Server provides the ability to exclude selected users who are a member of a global group from accessing SQL Server. This will be demonstrated later in this chapter.

Whenever you install SQL Server, it automatically configures SQL Server to allow the NT Server Administrator's local group to have access to SQL Server. This means that any NT Server user account name that is a member of the Administrator's local group can automatically access SQL Server in the role of a Sysadmin. When the Administrator's local group is displayed in SQL Administrator, it is shown to be a member of the "builtin" domain. This isn't a real SQL Server domain. It is just SQL Server's way of dealing with this special case. Also note that this group isn't a global group, but a local group. Normally, only global groups are added to SQL Server. This is the only exception. As a DBA, you cannot add local groups to SQL Server.

This automatic capability of SQL Server to make all NT administrators Sysadmins of SQL Server isn't necessarily a good thing. Normally, you will want to separate the functions of managing NT and SQL Server by having different people perform different functions. If you like, you can remove this entry so that NT administrators cannot by default be Sysadmins.

Later in this chapter you will learn how to assign both NT Server user account names and global groups to access SQL Server.

Creating Login IDs Under SQL Server Authentication

If you are running SQL Server under the SQL Server Mixed Authentication Security Mode, you have the ability to create SQL Server login IDs using SQL Server Authentication.

If you remember from the previous chapter, SQL Server Authentication is handled entirely from SQL Server. NT Server doesn't become involved. For example, users must first log on to their network operating system, such as NT Server. After they have been authenticated by the operating system and logged on to the network, they now have the ability to attempt to access

SQL Server. When they attempt to access SQL Server, they are required to manually log in to SQL Server by entering their SQL Server ID and a password. After SQL Server receives this information, it checks its syslogins system table to see if the user's login ID and password match. If so, the user is logged in. If not, the user is denied access.

Creating a login ID for use with SQL Server Authentication is an easy process, generally performed using the SQL Enterprise Manager. You will learn how to manually add a SQL Server login later in this chapter.

How to Create and Manage Database User IDs

When users have been assigned a login ID, no matter which authentication mode is being used to authenticate the user, every user must also have a database user ID in every database they want to access.

For example, if a user has been assigned the login ID tfranklin, and he wants to access a database managed by SQL Server, he must have a database user ID in the database he wants to access. Generally, the login ID used by the user is added to the sysusers table of the database. This, in effect, is how the database user ID is created. Normally, the login ID and database user ID are identical, which makes managing user accounts much easier for the DBA. Unfortunately, the login ID and database user ID don't have to be identical. It is possible to assign a particular login ID a different database user ID in a database. Although this is possible, it isn't recommended as it can make your job as the DBA much more complex than it has to be.

Fortunately, adding a database user ID is a very simple step that is normally done when a user's login ID is first created. Creating both the login ID and the database user ID can be created in the same step, which is described later in this chapter.

How to Manage SQL Server Roles

So far there has been little mentioned about what a SQL Server role is. In essence, a role is a grouping of users who have similar SQL Server access needs. But roles are just a little more complex than this. For example, there are a variety of different types of SQL Server roles, including the following:

- Predefined server roles
- Predefined database roles
- The public role
- Custom database roles

In this section you take a look at the various types of SQL Server roles there are, and how you can use them to make your job as the DBA just a little easier.

Predefined Server Roles

In previous versions of SQL Server it was hard to delegate administrative tasks to others. For example, you might want to designate yourself as the senior DBA with the ability to perform any SQL Server task that needs to be performed. In addition, you might want to delegate some of the administrative tasks to others, while at the same time restricting exactly what they can do. Although this was possible in previous versions of SQL Server, it was difficult to implement. SQL Server 7.0 has solved this problem by including what are called predefined server roles (also known as fixed server roles).

SQL Server 7.0 includes a total of seven different predefined server roles, each with different sets of administrative permissions. This enables you to assign a variety of administrative helpers with different levels of ability to help you administer SQL Server. All you have to do is add their login ID to the role. All server roles are predefined by SQL Server. You don't have the ability to create your own server roles.

What happened to SQL Server groups?

If you have used any previous version of SQL Server, you may have noticed that SQL Server groups are no longer used. Instead, they have been replaced by SQL Server roles, which are much more flexible and powerful tools to manage users within a database.

383

Predefined server roles are defined at the SQL Server level, not at the database level. This means that anyone who belongs to one of these predefined server roles has specific permissions to manage SQL Server and all the databases managed by SQL Server. The administrative tasks they can perform depend solely on which predefined server role they have been assigned. Predefined server roles include

- System Administrators (sysadmin). This is the most powerful of all the roles. Anyone who belongs to this role can perform any task with SQL Server, including overrule any of the other predefined server roles. This role is equivalent to the SA account in previous versions of SQL Server.

- Database Creators (dbcreator). They have the ability to create and alter individual databases.

- Disk Administrators (diskadmin). They have the ability to manage disk files.

- Process Administrators (processadmin). They have the ability to manage the various processes running in SQL Server.

- Security Administrators (securityadmin). They have the ability to manage logins for a server.

- Server Administrators (serveradmin). They have the ability to configure serverwide settings.

- Setup Administrators (setupadmin). They have the ability install SQL Server replication and to manage extended procedures.

Generally, you won't need all these roles when delegating SQL Server administrative tasks to assistants. In many cases, you will probably assign your assistants to one or two roles, giving them the specific permissions they need to perform the tasks you have delegated to them.

You will learn how to assign users to predefined server roles later in this chapter.

Predefined Database Roles

In many ways, predefined database roles are similar to predefined server roles. Predefined database roles assign specific types of permissions to each of the nine predefined roles. The major difference between predefined server roles and predefined database roles is that predefined database roles are specific to a database and don't cross databases. Like predefined server roles, predefined database roles can be used by you to help distribute the SQL Server administrative burden to others. Predefined database roles include

- Database Owner (`db_owner`). They have ownership permission of a database and can perform any configuration or maintenance tasks within a given database. They can also perform all the activities of all the other database roles, and can override any of the other roles. In previous versions of SQL Server, this role is most similar to the DBO database user ID.

- Database Access Administrator (`db_accessadmin`). They have the ability to manage database user IDs for a database.

- Database Data Reader (`db_datareader`). They have the ability to view any data from all the table objects in a database.

- Database Data Writer (`db_datawriter`). They have the ability to insert, modify, or delete any data from all the table objects in a database.

- Database Data Definition Language Administrator (`db_ddladmin`). They have the ability to create, modify, or delete any objects in a database.

- Database Security Administrator (`db_securityadmin`). They have the ability to manage database user IDs and roles in a database, along with managing statement and object permissions within a database.

- Database Backup Operator (`db_dumpoperator`). They have the ability to back up a database.

- Database Deny Data Reader (`db_denydatareader`). A special role that enables members to change database schema, but not see the data in a database.

- Database Deny Data Writer (`db_denydatawriter`). A special role that prevents members from changing any data in a database.

What happened to the SQL Server alias?

In previous versions of SQL Server, you could create an alias. An alias was a way to enable users with a login ID to enter a database using a database ID that belonged to someone else. The main purpose of an alias was to enable developers into a database under the database user ID of DBO instead of their own database user ID. This was done to ensure that all the objects that were created by the developers were owned by the DBO, not the developers themselves. Whoever creates an object in SQL Server is the owner of the object. Now that SQL Server 7 has a **db_owner** role, which enables a developer to access a database as the database's owner, alias's are no longer needed or used.

As a DBA, you will probably not use most of these predefined database roles. You will probably just need a few in order to delegate some of your administrative tasks to your assistants. And as with predefined server roles, users can belong to more than one predefined database role at the same time.

The Public Role

The public role is similar to the public group that was used in previous versions of SQL Server. When created, every database has the public role by default, similar to how each database has predefined database roles. What is unique about this role is that every database user ID in a database automatically belongs to this role. In many ways, it is similar to the NT Server's Everyone group. You cannot add or remove users from the public role, or modify it in any way. All you can do with it is assign permissions to it. Any permissions assigned to the public role automatically are assigned to all database user IDs in the database. The public role is especially handy if you want to assign the same permissions to all database users in a database at the same time.

Custom Database Roles

As a general rule of thumb, you will want to take advantage of as many of the built-in roles as you can. Why reinvent the wheel? On the other hand, you may run into situations where none of the built-in roles meet your needs. If this is the case, SQL Server gives you the capability to create your own custom database roles.

If you are using Windows NT Authentication and use NT Server global groups to manage users, you may find that you don't really need to create custom database roles as you can gain the same effect by using global groups instead grouping like users. But if you aren't an NT Server administrator and don't have permission to create the global groups you need, or if you are using SQL Server Authentication, you may have no choice but to create custom database roles to help better manage your users.

Use global groups instead of custom database roles when posible

Assuming you have the ability to create NT Server global groups and use Windows NT Authentication, you should always use global groups instead of custom database roles to manage users. Using global groups instead of custom roles generally reduces the amount of time you have to spend managing both NT Server and SQL Server user accounts because global groups can work with both NT Server and SQL Server. Custom database roles only work with SQL Server. In addition, global groups can span multiple SQL databases, whereas roles are specific to a database, which makes them slightly less flexible than global groups.

When you create custom database roles, keep the following in mind:

- Custom database roles, as is true for any SQL Server role, are used to group like users that need the same set of permissions to access SQL Server objects.

- Custom database roles are created within a single database and cannot span multiple databases.

- Users can belong to more than one custom database or built-in role at a time.

- Custom roles can include NT Server users, NT Server global groups, SQL Server database user IDs, and other SQL Server roles.

You will learn how to create and manage custom database roles later in this chapter.

How to Manage Users Using SQL Enterprise Manager

You may have wondered why the actual techniques used to manage users has been saved until now, instead of being introduced when they were first discussed. The reason is because most SQL Server user account management tasks are performed at the same time, not in separate, distinct steps. Now that you have read all about the various aspects of managing SQL Server accounts, it's time you learned how to manage them using SQL Enterprise Manager.

In the following sections, you will learn how to:

- Use the SQL Server Create Login Wizard to manage SQL Server accounts

- Manually use SQL Enterprise Manager to manage SQL Server accounts.

After you become more and more familiar with managing SQL Server security, you will soon find out that it is often much easier to manually maintain user accounts than it is to use the SQL Server Create Login Wizard. Although the wizard is easy to use, it isn't very flexible.

> **Advanced users can use Transact-SQL to manage users**
>
> Virtually everything that is described in this chapter on how to use SQL Enterprise Manager to manage user accounts can be performed by using Transact-SQL statements. If you want to learn more about how to use Transact-SQL to manage user accounts, see SQL Server's Books Online.

How to Use the SQL Server Create Login Wizard to Manage SQL Server Accounts

In this section, you will learn how to create login IDs and database user IDs using the SQL Server Create Login Wizard. Although not as powerful or flexible as performing these same tasks manually with SQL Enterprise Manager, the SQL Server Create Login Wizard is a good tool for DBAs new to SQL Server.

Using the SQL Server Create Login Wizard

1. Start the SQL Enterprise Manager using a SQL Server login ID that belongs to the Sysadmin's role. This displays the SQL Enterprise Manager's main screen.

2. Click the SQL Server Tools drop-down menu and select Wizards. This displays the Select Wizard dialog box (see Figure 12.2).

FIGURE 12.2

The Select Wizard screen is where you select from all the available SQL Server wizards.

3. Click on the plus sign next to Database to display all of the wizards that are applicable to databases, including the Create Login Wizard. To start the Create Login Wizard, click on it, then click OK. This displays the first screen of the Create Login Wizard (see Figure 12.3).

FIGURE 12.3
This is the introduction screen to the Create Login Wizard.

4. After you have read the screen, click Next to continue. This displays the Select Authentication Mode screen (see Figure 12.4).

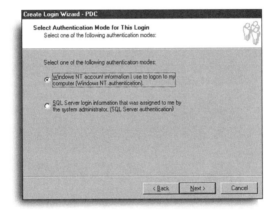

FIGURE 12.4
This screen enables you to choose which authentication method you want to use for the new login ID you are currently creating.

5. As you learned earlier in the chapter, a login ID can be created using either Windows NT Authentication or SQL Server Authentication if you are in the SQL Server Mixed Authentication Security Mode, or only using Windows NT Authentication if you are in the Windows NT Server Authentication Security Mode. In this example, SQL Server is set up for the SQL Server Mixed Authentication Security Mode, and both authentication options are available.

389

Can I mix authentication modes?

As long as SQL Server is set up to use SQL Server Mixed Authentication Security Mode, you can mix authentication modes for your SQL Server login IDs.

Normally, you will want to select the Windows NT Account Information I Use to Logon to my Computer (Windows NT Authentication) option. This is because most of your users will already have NT Server user accounts and you will want to use them as your SQL Server login IDs. If any of your users will not have NT Server user accounts, you can choose the second option, SQL Server Login Information That was Assigned to Me by the System Administrator (SQL Server Authentication).

Note at the bottom of the dialog box that you have the option to move back if you want to make any changes to your previous choices. All you have to do is click the Back button. For now, click the Next button to continue. The dialog box that appears next depends on which authentication security mode you selected in the previous screen. If you selected Windows NT Authentication, the screen in Figure 12.5 appears. If you selected SQL Server Authentication, the screen in Figure 12.6 appears.

FIGURE 12.5

This screen appears when you are setting up a login ID using Windows NT Authentication.

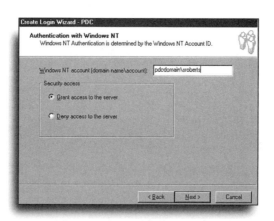

6. If you selected Windows NT Authentication for this login ID and are using the screen displayed in Figure 12.5, you must enter two pieces of information. First, you must enter the domain name and NT Server user account name that you want to use as the login ID for SQL Server. You must enter both the domain name and username, separated by a backslash. Notice that you cannot browse for the name.

Under Security Access, you must select from either Grant Access to the Server or Deny Access to the Server. In almost all cases, you will choose the first option. The second option is only used if you have previously added an NT Server global group to SQL Server and this account belongs to the group, but you don't want that user to be able to access SQL Server.

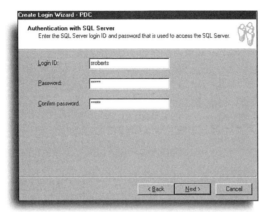

FIGURE 12.6
This screen appears when you are setting up a login ID using SQL Server Authentication.

If you selected SQL Server Authentication for this login ID and you are using the screen displayed in Figure 12.6, you must enter a login ID and a password (the password is entered twice). This will be the login ID and password the user must use every time she logs into SQL Server.

After you have completed one or the other of these screens, click Next to continue. This displays the Grant Access to Security Roles dialog box (see Figure 12.7).

Login IDs must follow SQL Server naming rules

Whenever you create a new login ID, using either Windows or SQL Server Authentication, the login ID used must follow the standard SQL Server naming rules as described in Chapter 4, "Installing SQL Server."

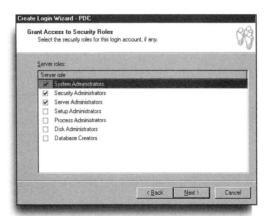

FIGURE 12.7
You can delegate SQL Server administrative tasks by assigning a login ID to one or more prede-fined server roles.

7. This screen appears no matter which authentication mode you selected earlier. This screen enables you to assign this login ID to one or more predefined server roles. In most cases, you won't assign any of these to users because most users don't need the administrative permissions these roles confer. After you are finished with this screen, click Next to continue. This displays the Grant Access to Databases dialog box (see Figure 12.8).

FIGURE 12.8
This screen is used to add database user IDs to each database the user needs to access.

8. This screen enables you to designate which databases will be accessible to this login ID. What it does is automatically enter the user's login ID as the database user ID for each database you select in this screen. After you are through selecting one or more databases for this login ID to access, click Next to continue. This displays the final screen of the Create Login Wizard (see Figure 12.9).

FIGURE 12.9
This final screen summarizes all your choices for this login ID.

9. This last wizard screen summarizes all the choices you made as you completed this wizard. If you want to make any changes, you can click the Back button and make any necessary corrections. If you are happy with your choices, you can click Finish to end the wizard and create the login ID.

The Create Login Wizard can only be used to create one login ID at a time. Also, you may have noticed that you were not given many choices about how the login ID was created. This can be corrected by using the SQL Enterprise Manager as described later in this chapter. By creating a login ID manually, you have much more flexibility and many more choices.

How to Create, Modify, and Delete SQL Server Login IDs

Although the Create Login Wizard enables you to create new login and database user IDs, you may find the Create Login Wizard too restrictive to perform many tasks. This section shows you how to manually manage login and database user IDs. You should become familiar with each of the following procedures if you want to master all aspects of SQL Server account management:

- How to display SQL Server account information
- How to create and configure login IDs
- How to delete a login ID
- How to create and configure database user IDs
- How to create and configure database roles
- How to delete a database user ID or database role
- How to configure a server role

You won't necessarily perform these manual steps in this order. You can perform them in any order that best meets your needs.

How to Display SQL Server Account Information

Before you take a look at how to create and configure SQL Server login IDs, database user IDs, and roles, let's take a look at how you can view information about them. Very often, as a DBA, you will need to just check user information to see how a particular user is configured. Also, by beginning here, you will have a better feel for using SQL Enterprise Manager in later sections when you begin to actually create or configure user accounts.

How to View Login ID Information

SQL Enterprise Manager makes it easy to view all of a SQL Server's login IDs. As a DBA, you will probably spend a lot of time viewing login information in your day-to-day management of SQL Server.

Viewing SQL Server login ID information using SQL Enterprise Manager

1. Start SQL Enterprise Manager using an account with Sysadmins privileges.

2. Using your mouse in the Scope pane, select the SQL Server you want to work with and open its folder to display all of SQL Server's options.

3. Click the Security folder, then the Logins folder. All the SQL Server's login IDs are displayed in the Details pane (see Figure 12.10).

   Take some time now to view the login ID information presented:

   - The Name column lists each login ID. Notice in this example that many of the accounts are proceeded with an NT Server domain name, such as PDCDOMAIN. Any login ID that is proceeded with a domain name is using Windows NT Authentication. Names that are not proceeded with a domain name use SQL Server Authentication. Here, this includes the SA and sroberts login IDs.

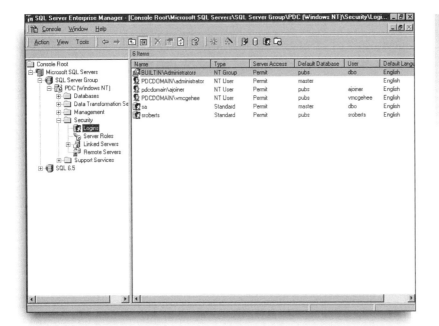

FIGURE 12.10
SQL Enterprise Manager
enables you to view all
the login IDs from the
same window.

- The Type column provides additional information
  about the login ID. If the type is NT User, this login
  ID was created in NT Server and has been added as a
  SQL Server login ID. If the type is NT Group, this
  means that any NT user who belongs to this NT
  Server global group has the ability to access SQL
  Server using the global group as the login ID. In this
  case, individual NT users aren't assigned their own
  SQL Server login ID. Instead, they use the global
  group as their login ID. If the type is Standard, this
  login ID was created using SQL Enterprise Manager
  and not NT Server.

- The Default Database column shows which database
  each login ID uses as its default database. All login IDs
  must be assigned a default database. This is the database they are automatically logged in to whenever they
  first access SQL Server.

- The User column is the database user ID this user has been assigned for the default database he is automatically logged in to when he first accesses SQL Server. In most cases, this will be the same database user ID that is assigned for the login ID for every database he has been given access to.

- The Default Language column isn't normally used if the <Default> language option is used when creating a new login ID. If you choose a specific language for a login ID, it will be displayed in this column.

4. To view specific information about any of the login IDs, right-click the login ID you want to find more information about and select Properties from the pop-up menu. This displays the login ID's Properties dialog box (see Figure 12.11).

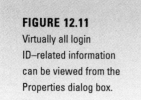

FIGURE 12.11
Virtually all login ID–related information can be viewed from the Properties dialog box.

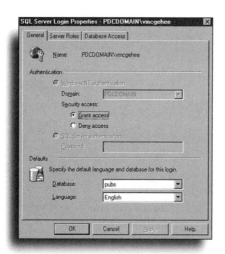

The Properties dialog box is divided into three tabbed screens: General, Server Roles, and Database Access. The General tab (see Figure 12.11) displays authentication and default information. The Server Roles tab (see Figure 12.12) shows which Server Roles the login ID belongs to. The Database Access tab (see Figure 12.13) shows which databases the login ID has database user IDs in, along with showing which Database Roles in each database the user belongs to. Each of these tabs will be explained in more detail later in this chapter.

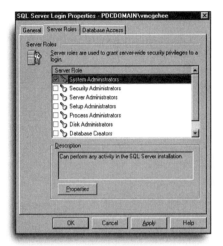

FIGURE 12.12
Every Server Role the login ID belongs to is displayed on this screen.

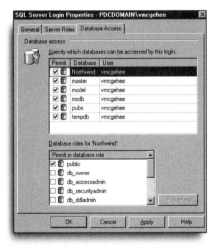

FIGURE 12.13
Every database a login ID can access, along with database roles for each database, are listed on this screen..

Notice that virtually every login ID setting can be viewed from these three tabs. In most cases, you will use this Properties dialog box for viewing most login ID information. In addition to this view of the login ID information, there are several other views you need to become familiar with, which are discussed in the next couple of sections of this chapter.

5. After you are finished viewing login ID information, click Cancel to exit the Properties dialog box.

You will find that this technique for viewing login ID information is the most useful of all the different ways available to view SQL Server account information.

How to View Database User ID Information

Although you can use the method mentioned previously to view some database user ID information, there is another way to view it. As you know, database user IDs are associated with specific databases. One way of viewing database user ID information is to go to a specific database managed by SQL Server to view database user ID information.

Viewing database user ID information from the perspective of a database

1. Start SQL Enterprise Manager using an account with Sysadmins privileges.

2. Using your mouse in the Scope pane, select the SQL Server you want to work with and open its folder to display all of SQL Server's options.

3. Click the plus sign next to the Databases folder in the Scope pane so that all the databases managed by SQL Server are displayed.

4. Now click the plus sign next to the database folder whose database user IDs you want to view.

5. Click the Database User folder. This displays all the database user IDs for this database in the Details pane (see Figure 12.14).

The Name column displays the database user IDs that have been added to this database, indicating who has the ability to access this database. The Login Name column lets you know which login ID is associated with the various database user IDs who have access to the database.

6. To view additional information about the database user IDs listed for a database, right-click a database user ID in the Details pane and select Properties from the pop-up menu. This displays the database user ID's Properties dialog box (see Figure 12.15).

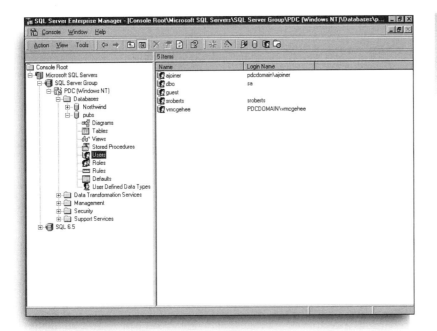

FIGURE 12.14
You can view database
user IDs by database.

FIGURE 12.15
This screen shows you
which database roles this
particular database user
ID belongs to.

The Properties dialog box displays all the defined database
roles for this database, and also shows you which ones this
particular database user ID belongs to. The rest of the features of this screen will be discussed in a later section of
this chapter.

7. To exit this dialog box, click Cancel.

Although you might find this option to view database user IDs handy when you want to quickly determine who is able to access a particular database, you will probably find it easier to view the same information from viewing the login ID information as described in the previous section.

How to View Database Role Information

Although database role information can be viewed using the technique just described, it can also be viewed from the perspective of the database role instead of the database user ID.

Viewing database role information from the perspective of the role itself

1. Start SQL Enterprise Manager using an account with Sysadmins privileges.

2. Using your mouse in the Scope pane, select the SQL Server you want to work with and open its folder to display all the SQL Server's options.

3. Click the plus sign next to the Databases folder in the Scope pane so that all the databases managed by SQL Server are displayed.

4. Now click the plus sign next to the database folder whose database user IDs you want to view.

5. Click the Roles folder. This displays all the database roles for this database in the Details pane (see Figure 12.16).

In the Name column is a listing of all the database roles for this particular database. In the Role Type column is either the word Standard or Application. Standard means that it is a normal database role, whereas Application means that this is an application database role. You will learn more about database roles later in this chapter.

6. If you want to find out more information about any of the database roles listed, right-click the database role in the Details pane and select Properties from the pop-up menu. This displays the database role Properties dialog box (see Figure 12.17).

FIGURE 12.16
This screen lists all the database roles for this particular database.

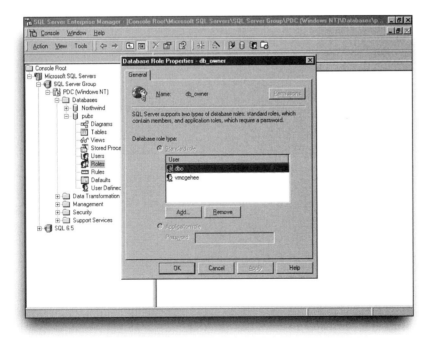

FIGURE 12.17
This screen shows you which database user IDs belong to a particular database role.

The Properties dialog box is used to show you which database user IDs from this database belong to this particular database role.

7. To exit this dialog box, click the Cancel button.

You will probably find it easier to use the login ID folder, as described earlier, to view this same information.

How to View Server Role Information

Many times you will want to view the various server roles for your SQL Server and determine which login IDs belong to them.

Viewing which login IDs have been assigned to which server roles

1. Start SQL Enterprise Manager using an account with Sysadmins privileges.

2. Using your mouse in the Scope pane, select the SQL Server you want to work with and open its folder to display all the SQL Server's options.

3. Click the Sercurity folder, then click the Server Roles folder in the Scope pane so that all the server roles are displayed in the Details pane (see Figure 12.18).

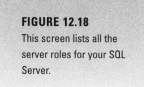

FIGURE 12.18
This screen lists all the server roles for your SQL Server.

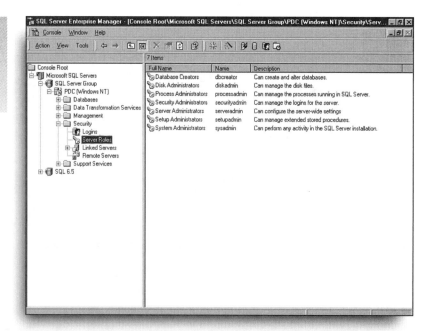

The complete name of the server role is displayed in the Full Name column, and the short name of the server role is displayed in the Name column. The Description column describes what this server role can do.

4. To find out which login IDs have been assigned to each server role, right-click a server role and choose Properties from the pop-up menu. This displays the server role's Properties dialog box (see Figure 12.19).

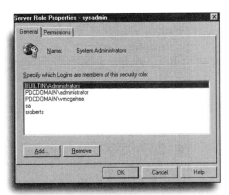

FIGURE 12.19
This screen lists all the server roles for your SQL Server.

The Properties dialog box has two tabs: General and Permissions. The General tab (see Figure 12.19) tells you which login IDs have been assigned this particular server role. The Permissions tab (see Figure 12.20) shows you all the various permissions the role has been assigned.

5. Click Cancel to exit the dialog box.

This is the only place you can view server role information, so you need to become familiar with this viewing option.

FIGURE 12.20
This screen lists all the
permissions that have
been assigned to the
server role.

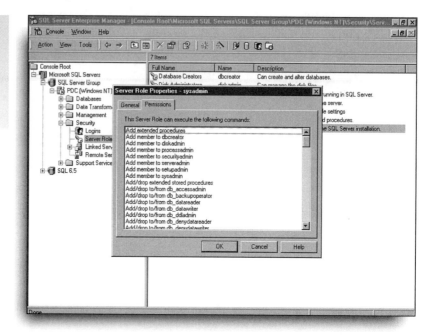

How to Create and Configure Login IDs

Now that you are familiar with how to view login ID information, it is time to learn how to create and configure a new login
ID. What you will learn in this section is how to create most
new login IDs. You will also follow similar steps to reconfigure a
current login ID.

Creating and configuring a new login ID manually

1. Start SQL Enterprise Manager using an account with
   Sysadmins privileges.

2. Using your mouse in the Scope pane, select the SQL Server
   you want to work with and open its folder to display all the
   SQL Server's options.

3. Click on the security folder, then click on the Logins folder.
   All the SQL Server's login IDs are displayed in the Details
   pane.

4. To create a new login ID and configure it for use, right-click
   the Logins folder and select New Login from the pop-up
   menu. This displays the New Login dialog box
   (see Figure 12.21).

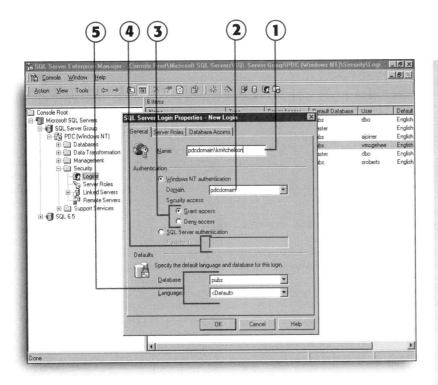

FIGURE 12.21

Use this dialog box to create new login IDs.

(1) Enter the new login ID here.

(2) If you want to use Windows NT Authentication for this login ID, select the appropriate NT Server domain from this list box.

(3) Select whether you want to grant or deny access to this login ID.

(4) If you want to use SQL Server Authentication, enter a password here.

(5) You must select a default database for this user to access when she logs in to SQL Server. You don't have to enter a language if you want to use the default us_english language.

5. Before you begin to complete this dialog box, you must first determine whether you want to use Windows NT Authentication or SQL Server Authentication for this particular login ID. This is important because it determines how you will enter the Name. If you will be using Windows NT Authentication, you must enter a preexisting NT Server username in the Name box, or an NT Server global group. Unfortunately, you cannot browse for potential NT Server usernames or global groups; you must type it in from memory, spelled exactly like the NT Server user account name or global group name. If you will being using SQL Server Authentication, you can enter any name you want in the Name box for the new login ID, as long as it follows standard SQL Server naming standards.

6. If you are using Windows NT Authentication for this login ID, you must select the Windows NT Authentication option button and then select the NT Server domain name from the list box to which the NT Server user account belongs. When you do this, the Name box will change, adding the

405

Why don't I enter a password for Windows NT Authentication?

You don't need to enter a password for Windows NT Authentication because NT Server, not SQL Server, is used for authentication. When users log on to NT Server, entering their user account name and password, they are authenticated by NT Server, and SQL Server doesn't have to repeat the authentication.

name of the NT Server domain before the NT Server account name, separated with a backslash. This is required; otherwise, SQL Server cannot create the login ID. Under Security Access, the option button next to Grant Access is automatically selected. This means that this login ID has been granted access to SQL Server, which is generally your goal when you create a new login ID. The reason the Deny Access option is available is to deny an NT Server user account from SQL Server access that happens to belong to an NT Server global group that has been granted access to SQL Server. If you design your NT Server global groups correctly, you should never have to deal with exceptions such as this.

7. If you are using SQL Server Authentication for this login ID, you must select the SQL Server Authentication option button, and then enter a password for this login ID.

8. In the Database list box you must select which database you want to be this login ID's default database. This is the database the login ID is automatically logged in to when it accesses SQL Server. By default, users are assigned the Master database as their default database. This isn't a good idea because you don't want just anyone to be able to log into the Master database. You should always select the database that this login ID will most often use. You can leave the Language list box as is, set to <Default>. This means that the default language will be us_english.

9. Technically speaking, you now have entered all the information you have to enter to create the new login ID. If you wanted to, you could click OK now and the login ID would be created. But in most cases, you will want to consider completing both the Server Roles and Database Access tabs on the New Login dialog box. Why? Because it is generally easier to assign login IDs to server roles, and to add database user IDs now rather than later. This is your choice and you can do whatever is easiest for you. I am going to assume you want to complete all three tabs now.

10. Click the Server Roles tab. This displays the Server Roles screen (see Figure 12.22).

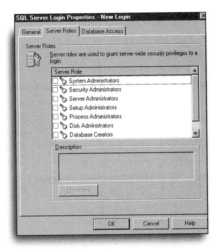

This screen enables you to assign this login ID to one or more separate server roles. Only assign a login ID to a server role if that user needs to have SQL Server administra-tive privileges. In most cases, you won't assign the login IDs you create to a server role. If you do need to assign a login ID to a server role, just click in the box next to the role or roles you want the login ID to have.

11. Click the Database Access tab. This displays the Database Access screen (see Figure 12.23).

Database user IDs are added to a login ID from this screen. Notice that the top scroll box has a Database column. This column lists every database that is available for access on this SQL Server. To permit users to access a database, and to add a database user ID to the database, all you have to do is click the box in the Permit column that matches the database you want them to access. When you do this, the login ID will appear in the User column, and this becomes their database user ID for that database. Note that the login ID and data-base user ID are identical. This is normal and preferred. Although it is possible to change the database user ID in the

User column, it is unwise because there will no longer be an obvious link between the login ID and database user ID. You can permit a login ID to access as many databases as you like.

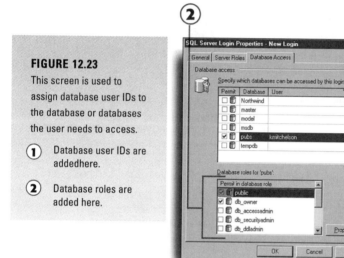

FIGURE 12.23

This screen is used to assign database user IDs to the database or databases the user needs to access.

(1) Database user IDs are added here.

(2) Database roles are added here.

12. The Database Roles scroll box is used to assign the user to one or more database roles. These can be predefined database roles, or custom roles you create. Note that the public database role has already been selected for you. This is normal and cannot be undone. Remember, all database user IDs in a database always belong to the public role. If you like, you can add the database user ID to as many database roles as needed. Note that you must do this for each separate database that you allow them to access. In this example (Figure 12.23), the database roles you see marked are for the Pubs database. Each database has its own set of database roles.

13. Notice the Properties button on this screen. This button enables you to view and modify which database user IDs belong to a specific database role. Click the Properties button, and the Database Role Properties dialog box appears (see Figure 12.24).

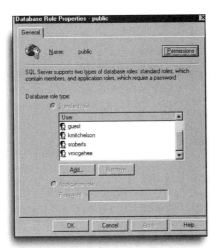

FIGURE 12.24
This screen is used to view, add, and remove database user IDs from a database role.

You can use this dialog box to view, add, or remove database user IDs from the database role that was selected when you clicked the Properties button. You will learn more about this screen later in this chapter.

14. Click the Cancel button to exit this dialog box.

15. After you have completed all the options for this login ID, you can create the login ID by clicking OK. The New Login dialog box closes, and the login ID is created and is displayed in the Details pane of the Logins folder.

After you gain experience with SQL Server, you will find that this technique is the easiest and fastest way to create a new login ID.

How to Delete a Login ID

There are many reasons for deleting a login ID from SQL Server. One reason might be because the user no longer needs access to SQL Server to complete his job. Or, the user may leave the company. In either case, you will want to remove his login ID from SQL Server to ensure the best security.

Whenever you delete a login ID, you also automatically delete any database user IDs that may be in the databases managed by SQL Server. This is done automatically.

Delete the login ID from SQL Server before deleting the NT Server user account

If users are leaving your organization, be sure to delete the login ID from SQL Server before deleting the NT Server user account using the User Manager for domains. If you delete the NT Server user account first, you won't be able to delete the login ID from SQL Server. If this happens to you, you will have to re-create the NT Server user account using the User Manager for domains. This will enable you to delete the login ID from SQL Server. Then you will again have to delete the NT Server user account.

Before you can delete a login ID, you must ensure that the user doesn't own any database objects in any of the databases. If she does, her login ID cannot be deleted. Before you can delete the login ID, you will have to either delete the objects the user owns, or transfer the ownership of the objects to another user. After a user no longer owns any database objects, you can delete the login ID.

Deleting a login ID from SQL Server

1. Start SQL Enterprise Manager using an account with Sysadmins privileges.

2. Using your mouse in the Scope pane, select the SQL Server you want to work with and open its folder to display all the SQL Server's options.

3. Click on the security folder, then click on the Logins folder. All the SQL Server's login IDs are displayed in the Details pane.

4. Right-click the login ID you want to delete, and then select Delete from the pop-up menu.

5. A dialog box appears asking you if you really want to delete this login ID. Click OK to delete the login ID.

SEE ALSO

➤ *For more information on database object ownership, see page 423.*

How to Create and Configure Database User IDs

More often than not, you will use the login ID properties screen to add login IDs to databases, as described earlier in this chapter. But that isn't your only choice. If you like, you can create and configure database user IDs from the perspective of the database instead of the login ID. This section shows you how to create and configure database user IDs for preexisting login IDs. If you want to create a database user ID for a new user using this method, you will have to first create a new login ID for that user.

Creating and configuring a database user ID

1. Start SQL Enterprise Manager using an account with Sysadmins privileges.

2. Using your mouse in the Scope pane, select the SQL Server you want to work with and open its folder to display all the SQL Server's options.

3. Click the plus sign next to the Databases folder in the Scope pane so that all the databases managed by SQL Server are displayed.

4. Now click the plus sign next to the database folder where you want to create the new database user ID.

5. Right-click the Database User folder and select New Database User from the pop-up menu. This displays the New User dialog box (see Figure 12.25).

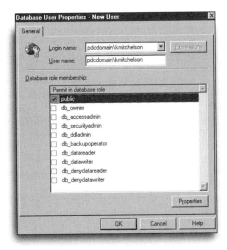

FIGURE 12.25
This screen is used to add a new database user ID.

6. From the Login Name list box, select the preexisting login ID you want to grant access to this database. This list box will only include login names that have yet to be granted access to this database. After you select the login name, the User Name box is automatically filled in for you. This means that the login ID you selected is used as the database user ID for this database, which is what you want.

7. The Database Role Membership scroll box contains a list of all the database roles for this database. If needed, you can assign the newly created database user ID to one or more

database roles by clicking the appropriate box. Notice that the public database role is already selected. This is because every database user ID must belong to the public database role of a database. The Properties button at the bottom of the screen displays the same Database Role Properties screen (see Figure 12.24) you saw when you create the database user ID when you learned how to create login IDs earlier in this chapter. You will learn more about this later in this chapter.

8. Click OK to create the database user ID. The New User dialog box disappears and the newly created database user ID appears in the Details pane.

After you gain some experience with SQL Server, you will probably find that you rarely use this method of creating a database user ID.

How to Create and Configure Database Roles

This section shows you how to create standard and application database roles within a given database. Although each database has many predefined roles, you may find that you need to create your own. This section shows you how.

Creating and configuring a new database role

1. Start SQL Enterprise Manager using an account with Sysadmins privileges.

2. Using your mouse in the Scope pane, select the SQL Server you want to work with and open its folder to display all the SQL Server's options.

3. Click the plus sign next to the Databases folder in the Scope pane so that all the databases managed by SQL Server are displayed.

4. Now click the plus sign next to the database folder where you want to create the new database user ID.

5. Right-click the Database Role folder and select New Database Role from the pop-up menu. This displays the New Role dialog box (see Figure 12.26).

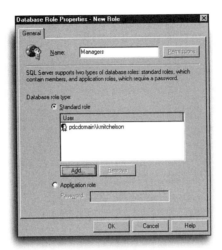

6. In the Name box, enter a new name for the database role you want to create following standard SQL Server naming conventions.

7. Next, you must select whether you want to create a standard or application database role. If you select Standard Role, you have the option of adding one or more database user IDs to the role at this time. Or, you can skip this step now and add database user IDs later using the previous techniques already described in this chapter. If you select Application Role, you must also enter a password.

8. After you have finished this screen, click OK to create the new database role. This will close the New Role dialog box and then display the new role in the Details pane.

Remember that database roles are created on a database-by-database basis. Database roles are not shared between databases.

How to Delete a Database User ID or Database Role

As part of your day-to-day responsibility of maintaining SQL Server, you will often find it necessary to remove current database user IDs from databases, and somewhat less often, remove database roles that are no longer needed.

When you remove a database user ID from a database, what you are doing is preventing that login ID from accessing that particular database. Removing a database user ID only removes the database user ID from a single database at a time, and it doesn't affect the user's login ID. If you want to remove users permanently from SQL Server, you will have to remove their login ID, as described earlier in this section. You cannot remove a database user ID from a database that is the owner of one or more database objects. You either have to delete the database object first, or transfer the ownership of the object to another database user ID.

The only database roles you can remove from SQL Server are those that have been created by you or another DBA. You cannot remove built-in database roles. If a database role has one or more database IDs associated with it, you must remove them before removing the database role itself. If you try to delete the database role without removing any database user IDs first, you will get an error message.

The following sets of steps will show you how to delete both database user IDs and database roles.

Deleting a database user ID from a database

1. Start SQL Enterprise Manager using an account with Sysadmins privileges.

2. Using your mouse in the Scope pane, select the SQL Server you want to work with and open its folder to display all the SQL Server's options.

3. Click the plus sign next to the Databases folder in the Scope pane so that all the databases managed by SQL Server are displayed below the folder.

4. Click the plus sign next to the name of the database where you want to delete the database user ID. This displays a number of folders below the database name.

5. Click the Database Users folder. This displays all the current database user IDs for this database in the Details pane.

6. In the Details pane, right-click the database user ID you want to delete and select Delete from the pop-up menu.

7. A message box appears asking you to confirm the deletion. Click Yes to delete the database user ID.

Deleting a database role

1. Start SQL Enterprise Manager using an account with Sysadmins privileges.

2. Using your mouse in the Scope pane, select the SQL Server you want to work with and open its folder to display all the SQL Server's options.

3. Click the plus sign next to the Databases folder in the Scope pane so that all the databases managed by SQL Server are displayed below the folder.

4. Click the plus sign next to the name of the database where you want to delete the database user ID. This displays a number of folders below the database name.

5. Click the Database Roles folder. This displays all the database roles for this database in the Details pane.

6. In the Details pane, right-click the database role you want to delete and select Delete from the pop-up menu.

7. A message box appears asking you to confirm the deletion. Click Yes to delete the database role.

How to Configure a Server Role

As was discussed earlier in this chapter, server roles are used to give login IDs various levels of SQL Server administrative privileges. You can assign a login ID to a server role when you create a login ID, as described earlier in this chapter, or you can assign a login ID to a server role as described in this section. Most likely, you will use the login ID technique described earlier because it is generally more convenient that this option.

Server roles are built into SQL Server. New server roles cannot be created nor can they be deleted. Your only option when configuring a server role is to add or remove login IDs from them. Here's how.

Adding or removing a login ID from a server role

1. Start SQL Enterprise Manager using an account with Sysadmins privileges.

2. Using your mouse in the Scope pane, select the SQL Server you want to work with and open its folder to display all the SQL Server's options.

3. Click the security folder, then click the Server Roles folder. This displays all the server roles in the Details pane.

4. To add a login ID to a server role, right-click the server role where you want to add the login ID and select Properties from the pop-up menu. This displays the Properties dialog box (see Figure 12.27).

FIGURE 12.27

Login IDs can be added and removed from server roles using this screen.

5. To add a login ID to this server role, click the Add button. This displays the Add Members dialog box (see Figure 12.28).

FIGURE 12.28

You can select one or more login IDs from this dialog box to add to the current server role.

6. To select one or more login IDs to add to this server role, click each login ID you want to add to the server role. Every time you click a login ID, it will be highlighted, and remain highlighted unless you click it again. After you have selected the login IDs you want to add to the server role, click OK. This returns you to the Properties dialog box with the newly added login IDs displayed in it.

7. When you are finished, click OK. This will close the Properties box and add the login IDs you selected to this server role.

You can add login IDs to server roles whenever you need to. But keep in mind that delegating administrative privileges to users is sometimes a risky proposition and you don't want to overdo it. Only give login IDs the absolute minimum privileges they need to accomplish the tasks you have assigned them.

SEE ALSO

➤ *For more information on the two SQL Server security modes, see page 358.*

➤ *For more information on database object ownership, see page 427.*

chapter

13

Assigning User Permissions

Permissions Determine Who Can Access Data

In the last chapter, you learned how to create and manage login IDs that are used to control access into SQL Server. You also learned how to create and manage database user IDs, which are used to control access into individual SQL Server databases. Although you have come a long way to permitting users to access data stored in SQL Server databases, there is still one more barrier. Even though a user may have a valid login ID and database user ID, a user cannot access any data in a database unless he has been given explicit permissions to access the objects stored in the database (see Figure 13.1).

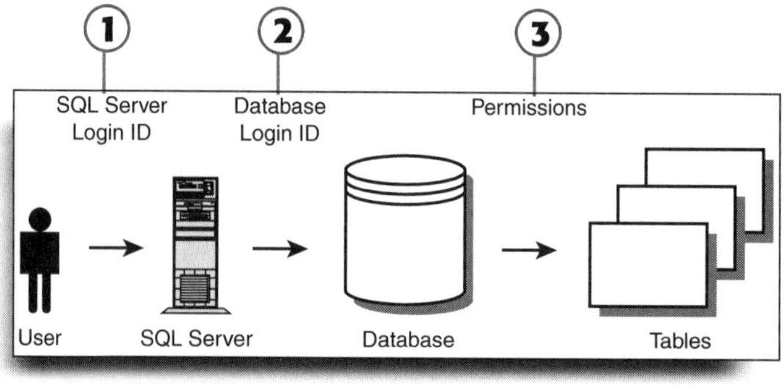

FIGURE 13.1
Database users must go through several barriers before they can access data.

(1) A login ID is used to enable a user access to SQL Server, but nothing else.

(2) A database user ID is used to enable a user access to a specific database managed by SQL Server, but nothing else.

(3) Permissions are assigned to users to enable them to access objects within a database, such as the tables that contain data.

Permissions are used in SQL Server to specify which users are permitted to access which database objects, and what they are allowed to do to with those objects. For example, a user named jknox (which user) may be given access to the sales table (which object), in order to make changes to it (what they are allowed to do to the object). If a user isn't given explicit permission to access an object, she cannot access it.

Permissions can be assigned to *users* (including NT Server accounts and SQL Server accounts), *groups* (NT Server global groups), and *roles* (including predefined server roles, predefined database roles, and custom database roles). For ease of administration, it is generally easier to assign permissions to groups and roles instead of individual users. It is much easier to assign a permission once to a group of 50 users than it is to assign this same permission 50 different times to 50 individual users.

SQL Server has three different types of permissions that can be assigned: statement, object, and implied. *Statement permissions* enable users to execute specific Transact-SQL statements that are used to create database objects, or to back up databases and transaction logs. For example, before a user can create a new table in a database, he would have to be granted the necessary statement permission. *Object permissions* determine what a user may do to a preexisting database object. For example, before a user could view data in a specific table, she would have to be granted the necessary object permission. *Implied permissions* are permissions that can only be performed by members of predefined server and database groups, or owners of database objects. For example, anyone who belongs to the Sysadmins role has the ability to do anything he wants within SQL Server. Or the owner of any database object has the ability to perform any activity of an object he owns, but not to objects others own.

Permissions are assigned to users based on what they need to do with the data stored by SQL Server. Some users may only need to view data, others may need to query data and produce reports, others may need to change data, and so on. One of the major responsibilities of the DBA is to determine which users need access to which objects, and what permissions they need.

Before granting permissions to users, it is important for the DBA to carefully plan the permissions needs of the users. The more careful the planning, the easier it will be for the DBA to implement and manage permissions.

Permissions assigned to one database are independent of permissions assigned to another database. If a user needs access to tables in two different databases, that user must have database user IDs in both databases, and the necessary permissions granted in each database for each object they need to access.

SEE ALSO

➤ *For more information on NT security see page 371.*

Implied permissions are new to SQL Server 7.0

If you have used previous versions of SQL Server, you may be surprised to learn about implied permissions. This is a new category of permissions that has been added to SQL Server 7.0. But don't let this confuse you; although the term is new, the concept behind it is not. *Implied permissions* are just another way of referring to the default permissions that have been traditionally assigned to the SA and DBO. In SQL Server 7.0, these permissions have been given a name, and they have also been expanded in scope, as you will learn later in this chapter.

Statement versus object permissions

When you compare statement permissions to object permissions, note that statement permissions affect actions that affect tasks that can be performed to a database, whereas object permissions affect actions that affect individual objects within a database. Statement permissions are associated with specific users and object permissions are associated with objects.

Statement Permissions

Statement permissions are given to users who either need the ability to create a database or database objects, or who need to back up databases and their transaction logs. If you think about this for a moment, this means that very few people other than SQL Server developers or backup assistants ever need to be assigned statement permissions.

Whenever you assign a user a statement permission, you are in essence giving that user the ability to execute specific Transact-SQL statements. They include the following:

- CREATE DATABASE: Includes the ability to create a new database on a specific SQL Server.

- CREATE DEFAULT: Includes the ability to create a default value that is automatically entered into a table column whenever the column is left blank when a new row is added to a table.

- CREATE PROCEDURE: Includes the ability to create a stored procedure.

- CREATE RULE: Includes the ability to create a rule that is used to validate data entered into a column whenever a new row is added to a table.

- CREATE TABLE: Includes the ability to create a new table inside a database.

- CREATE VIEW: Includes the ability to create virtual tables, which are used to display a subset of a table, or to join two or more tables into a single virtual table.

- DUMP DATABASE: Includes the ability to back up a database.

- DUMP TRANSACTION: Includes the ability to back up a database's transaction log.

The above database tasks can be performed using Transact-SQL statements as shown, or by using SQL Enterprise Manager. In either case, a user must be granted explicit permissions to perform them, one statement permission at a time. You can assign a user a single statement permission, all of them, or any subset of the available statement permissions.

Learning Transact-SQL makes your job easier

Although this book has avoided as much Transact-SQL as it can, it cannot be completely ignored. If you want to excel at your job as a DBA, you will need to eventually master Transact-SQL.

Although statement permissions can be assigned to users, groups, and roles, they are rarely ever assigned to them. How come? First of all, I have already mentioned that very few users ever need statement permissions in the first place. But more importantly, the main reason you seldom will ever assign statement permissions to users, groups, or roles is because SQL Server already includes predefined server and database roles that serve the same purpose. For example, the predefined server role—Sysadmin—or the predefined database role—db_owner— are used to perform virtually any task that can be accomplished by a user who has been assigned statement permissions. In effect, this means that you will rarely, if ever, assign a statement permission to a user. Instead, if a user needs the capability to perform one or more statement permissions, what you will do is assign that user to a predefined server or database role that can perform the actions required instead.

In many ways, assigning statement permissions is an archaic way of assigning these types of tasks to users. The preferred method is to use the built-in server and database roles that are new to SQL Server 7.0.

SEE ALSO

➤ *For more code examples using T-SQL, see Appendix A of this book beginning on page 639.*

> **Built-in server and database roles**
>
> Server and database roles were discussed in the previous chapter. In case you have forgotten what they are, here is a brief review. Server roles enable the DBA to delegate portions of the SQL Server administrative tasks to users without giving them too much power. Anyone assigned to one of the available server roles is automatically granted specific administrative rights. Database roles are assigned at the database level, and like server roles, delegate certain permissions to the members of the role to perform specific tasks within the database, such as to create database objects.

Object Permissions

The most common type of permissions assigned to users, groups, and roles are object permissions. Object permissions determine who may access a preexisting database object, and how they access the object.

Whenever you assign a user an object permission, you are in essence giving that user the ability to execute specific Transact-SQL statements on objects within a database, including the following:

- DELETE: Includes the ability to delete a table or view in a database.
- EXECUTE: Includes the ability to execute a stored procedure.

- INSERT: Includes the ability to add a new row into a table, or into a table through a view.

- REFERENCES: [Declarative referential integrity (DRI)]: Includes the ability to link two tables together using a common column. It is rare that a user would need this object permission.

- SELECT: Includes the ability to search for and view data from a view, table, or column.

- UPDATE: Includes the ability to change data in a table, column of a table, or in a table through a view.

The above object-related tasks can be performed using Transact-SQL statements (as shown above), SQL Enterprise Manager, or indirectly through the use of any client front-end application that uses Transact-SQL statements to access SQL Server data on a SQL Server. No matter how a user accesses objects in a database, each user must be given explicit permissions to perform them, one object permission at a time.

SEE ALSO

➤ *For a discussion and listing of database objects, see page 51.*

Implied Permissions

An implied permission is a permission that a user gets just from the fact that she belongs to a predefined server or database group, or because she is the owner of a database object. Implied permissions cannot be assigned to users. Instead, a user who needs an implied permission must be added to a predefined group that already has the permission. Implied permissions can be assigned to users, groups, or custom roles by adding them to a predefined server or database role. They can also be assigned to users, groups, or custom roles by assigning any of these as the owner of a specific database object (which would be very rare).

Server Roles

Server roles were introduced in the last chapter, "Managing Users." Now let's take another look at them and how you might use them to assign implied permissions to users.

The only reason you would want to assign any user to any of the predefined server roles is if you want to delegate some of your SQL Server administrative duties to others, such as assistants. There are a wide variety of server roles included with SQL Server. Some of them are very useful, such as the Sysadmin, who has the ability to perform any function in SQL Server. Others, though, such as Processadmin, are very specialized and rarely need to be used.

The available server roles include the following:

- System Administrators (sysadmin): This is the most powerful of all the roles. Anyone who belongs to this role can perform any task with SQL Server, including overrule any of the other predefined server roles. This role is equivalent to the SA account in previous versions of SQL Server.

- Database Creators (dbcreator): They have the ability to create and alter individual databases.

- Disk Administrators (diskadmin): They have the ability to manage disk files.

- Process Administrators (processadmin): They have the ability to manage the various processes running in SQL Server.

- Security Administrators (securityadmin): They have the ability to manage logins for a server.

- Server Administrators (serveradmin): They have the ability to configure serverwide settings.

- Setup Administrators (setupadmin): They have the ability to install SQL Server replication and to manage extended procedures.

Exactly what implied permissions does each role have?

The list of implied permissions each server role has is extensive. The best way to see them is to view them through the SQL Enterprise Manager. To view the implied permissions for any server role, right-click the server role and select Properties. When the Properties dialog box appears, click the Permissions tab. This screen displays all the implied permissions for each server role.

Be careful about assigning server roles

Whenever you assign any user to a server role, you are giving them the potential ability to damage your SQL Server and its data. So be wary about who you give this power to.

Predefined server roles are defined at the SQL Server level, not at the database level. This means that anyone who belongs to one of these predefined server roles has specific permissions to manage SQL Server and all the databases managed by SQL Server. The administrative tasks they can perform depends solely on which predefined server role they have been assigned.

Database Roles

SQL Server offers nine predefined database roles, all of which have been assigned a variety of implied permissions. Like server roles, you can use database roles to help distribute the SQL Server administrative burden to others. The available database roles include

- Database Owner (db_owner): They have ownership permission of a database and can perform any configuration or maintenance tasks within a given database. They can also perform all the activities of all the other database roles, and can override any of the other roles. In previous versions of SQL Server, this role is most similar to the DBO database user ID.

- Database Access Administrator (db_accessadmin): They have the ability to manage database user IDs for a database.

- Database Data Reader (db_datareader): They have the ability to view any of the data from all the table objects in a database.

- Database Data Writer (db_datawriter): They have the ability to insert, modify, or delete any data from all of the table objects in a database.

- Database Data Definition Language Administrator (db_ddladmin): They have the ability to create, modify, or delete any objects in a database.

- Database Security Administrator (db_securityadmin): They have the ability to manage database user IDs and roles in a database, along with managing statement and object permissions within a database.

- Database Backup Operator (db_dumpoperator): They have the ability to back up a database.

- Database Deny Data Reader (db_denydatareader): A special role that enables members to change database schema, but not see the data in a database.

- Database Deny Data Writer (db_denydatawriter): A special role that prevents members from changing any of the data in a database.

Database roles are assigned at the database level, not at the SQL Server level. This means that anyone who you assign to a database role in one database has the implied permissions of that role in that database, not in any other database. As with server roles, you will probably not assign too many users to database roles. In most cases, only SQL Server developers should be assigned any of the available database roles.

Database Object Owners

Whenever a user with the proper statement permission creates a new object in a database, such as a table, he becomes the database object owner (DBOO) of that object. Database object owners have implied permissions on all the objects they own, which gives them the ability to perform any activity on that object, such as SELECT, INSERT, UPDATE, DELETE, and so on. They have complete control of the objects they create.

As you can imagine, allowing just anyone to be a database object owner isn't a good idea. Normally, the only people who should ever create new database objects are SQL developers or the DBA, not ordinary users.

Understanding Permission Precedence

As you have already learned, permissions can be assigned to users, groups, and roles for any given database object. Because of this, a user may be subject to many different sets of permissions. For example, the user tfranklin (see Figure 13.2) may have been assigned some specific permissions to a table named INVENTORY. At the same time, tfranklin might be a member of one or more groups, and a member of one or more roles.

FIGURE 13.2

Users can be subject to a wide variety of permissions.

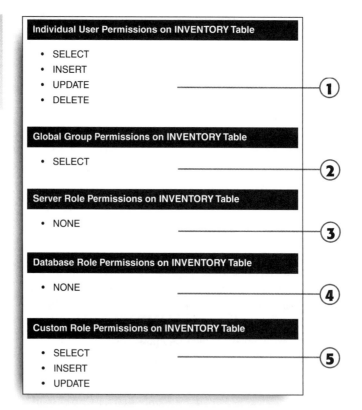

So what permissions does a user really have if they have been granted various permissions, especially if the permissions conflict with one another? The following "rules" apply to the setup shown in Figure 13.2:

- Any SQL Server user can be assigned one or more statement or object permissions for a specific database object.

In this case (1), tfranklin has been assigned four different object permissions.

- Assuming a user is being authenticated into SQL Server using Windows NT Authentication, they may be a member of one or more NT Server global groups. Each global group they are a member of can have its own set of permissions. In this case (2), tfranklin is a member of a single global group that has been assigned a single object permission.

- Any SQL Server user can be assigned to one or more server roles, conveying on them a variety of administrative-related implied permissions. In this case (3), tfranklin has not been assigned to any server roles.

- Any SQL Server user can be assigned to one or more database roles, conveying on them a variety of administrative-related implied permissions for this particular database. In this case (4), tfranklin has not been assigned to any database roles.

- Any SQL Server user can be assigned to one or more custom roles, and each role can be assigned its own set of permissions. In this case (5), tfranklin is a member of a single custom role that has been assigned three object permissions in the INVENTORY table.

In essence, a user's "net" permissions are the sum total of all the permissions they have been assigned. In our example, tfranklin is subject to five different sets of permissions. In this case, the "net" sum of all these permissions is that tfranklin has SELECT, INSERT, UPDATE, and DELETE permission on the INVENTORY table.

What happens if a user belongs to a group that has been assigned specific permission to view a table, but you don't want one of the members of the group to view it? One option is, of course, to remove the user from the group. But this may not always be possible. Groups aren't only used by SQL Server, they are also used by NT Server, and the user may need to belong to the group in order to access resources on an NT network.

The way to do this is to specifically deny access to the user. This is generally done on a case-by-case basis. For example, let's say that user `estraight` is a member of an NT global group named MARKETING that has been given `SELECT` permission to view the `INVENTORY` table (see Figure 13.3). You want everybody in the MARKETING group to have `SELECT` permission except `estraight`.

FIGURE 13.3

Access denied always wins out over other permissions.

(1) As an individual user, `estraight` has been denied access to the `INVENTORY` table.

(2) As a member of a global group, `estraight` has been granted SELECT permission on the `INVENTORY` table.

(3) Normally, permissions are additive, which means they get all the permissions. But access denied is an exception. Because `estraight` has been denied access as an individual user, she cannot gain access to it even though she is a member of a group that does have access.

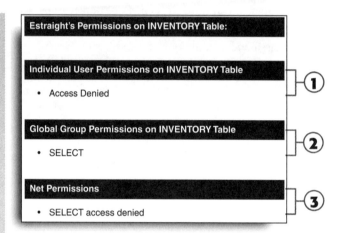

To prevent `estraight` from having `SELECT` permission on the `INVENTORY` table, all you have to do is deny access to `estraight`. This can be done at the individual level (as in the example), or by membership of another group or custom role. Whenever a user has been denied access to an object, this overrules any permission they may have otherwise obtained from belonging to a group or role that offers them that permission. You will learn how to deny access to users later in the "Understanding Permission Precedence" section.

From this discussion, you may have concluded that assigning permissions to users can be a complex task. Keep in mind that each user is subject to five different levels of permissions, and that permissions can be statement, object, and implied. And you must set these for each object in a database for each user. If hundreds of users need to access hundreds of objects in a database, how will you ever manage permissions? Although permissions can be complex, they can also be very simply managed by following some techniques listed in the "Best Practices for Managing Permissions" section later in this chapter.

Using Views and Stored Procedures to Enforce Security

As you know, a database can be made up of many different objects, even hundreds of objects. In many cases, users will have to have access to most, if not all, of these objects to perform their work. As mentioned in the previous section, assigning permissions to each and every object can be a complex undertaking.

One way to minimize the amount of time you spend assigning permissions to database objects is to make frequent use of views and stored procedures in your databases. Of course, this means that whoever develops the database has to cooperate and make good use of them. The more you make use of views and stored procedures, the fewer permissions you will have to assign. Here's why.

Remember, a view is a virtual table. It either enables you to display a subset of a single table or to combine two or more tables into a single view. If used correctly, a database application can be designed in such a way as views are always used to enable users to access data. This means that permissions only need to be assigned to views, not to individual tables. This really can be a time savings when a view is actually a peek into two or more tables. If a view isn't used, you have to assign permissions to every table a user wants to see. But with a view, the permissions only need to be added one time.

A more significant time savings can be gained by using stored procedures. Remember that a stored procedure is actually a string of Transact-SQL statements precompiled as a single object. Stored procedures have the ability to access any database object and perform any activity on it. A single stored procedure could conceivably access dozens, if not hundreds, of database objects. For example, say that you wanted your users to enter orders into a database. Such an activity might touch many different database objects. Normally, to give permission to each user, each object would have to be given the necessary permissions. That's a lot of work. But if a stored procedure were used to access all the objects, only the stored procedure would need the permission, not each individual object accessed by the stored procedure.

By now, you should see how the proper use of views and stored procedures can significantly reduce the amount of permissions you must assign to individual objects.

For permissions to behave as just described, every object affected by a view or stored procedure must be owned by the same user. This is referred to as an unbroken ownership chain.

Understanding Ownership Chains

An *ownership chain* refers to the dependencies that one object in a database has with other objects in the same database. For example, a table might be created in a database. Next, based on the newly created table, a view might be created. And then this view might be used as part of a stored procedure (see Figure 13.4). The view is dependent on the table, and the stored procedure is dependent on both the view and the table.

FIGURE 13.4

A non-broken ownership chain.

① This stored procedure, which is dependent on the view and table objects below it, is owned by user jknox.

② This view object is owned by the user jknox.

③ This table object is owned by the user jknox.

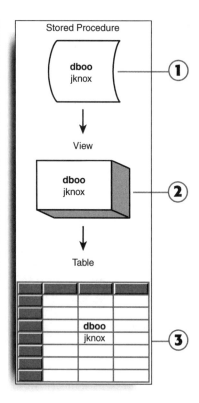

As you have already learned, whoever creates an object in a database becomes the database object owner (dboo) of that object. In the previous example, each of the three objects could all be owned by the same dboo, or each of three objects could have different dboos. If the same dboo owns all the objects in the ownership chain, this is referred to as a *non-broken ownership chain*. But if more than one dboo owns the three objects, this is referred to as a *broken ownership chain*.

Non-Broken Ownership Chains

So how does the ownership chain affect permissions? If the ownership chain is non-broken (all the objects in the chain have the same dboo), and if the dboo wants to grant permission to the highest object in the chain (the stored procedure in our example) to a user, the dboo only needs to grant the permission based on the highest object in the ownership chain, not to all the objects in the chain (see Figure 13.4). Separate permissions don't have to be granted to each object in the chain, even though a user has access to all of them because of the chain of ownership. This feature makes the DBA's job much easier because ownership chains are a common occurrence in all SQL Server databases.

A Broken Ownership Chain

What happens to permissions in a broken ownership chain? Let's assume that the dboo of a stored procedure wants to grant permission to it, but the dboo isn't the owner of the other objects in the ownership chain (see Figure 13.5). If this is the case, the dboo of the stored procedure will have to obtain the permission from the dboos of the other objects in the ownership chain first. Although this is possible, it is a lot of administrative work. After the dboo of the stored procedure has all the necessary permissions from the other dboos, the dboo of the stored procedure can grant permission of it to others.

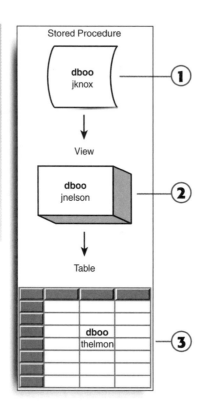

FIGURE 13.5

A broken ownership chain.

① This stored procedure, which is dependent on the view and table below it, is owned by jknox.

② This view is owned by jnelson.

③ This table is owned by thelmon.

How to Prevent Broken Ownership Chains

To prevent broken ownership chains, the same owner must own all the objects in a database. This means that as a DBA, you must not assign statement permissions to individual users, where each user would become the owner of any database object he or she created. So how do you allow database developers into a database to create objects, and at the same time retain a non-broken ownership chain? The only way to ensure a non-broken ownership chain is to educate developers to specify the dbo as the owner of an object whenever they create an object. By default, whenever a user, such as a developer, creates a new database object, they become the object of that object if they do not specifically assign the dbo as the object owner. This means that if there are many developers creating objects in a database, and they don't specifically specify the dbo as the object owner then the object is created, they the ownership chain within the database will be broken.

In previous versions of SQL Server this was a major problem because object ownership cou7ld not be changed. In SQL Server 7.0, object ownership can be changed using the sp_changeobjectowner system stored procedure. So if one or more of your developers don't specifically assign the DBO as the object owner of every object they create, you have the ability to correct this problem after the fact. In a large database with many objects, this can be very time concumming. Ideally, you need to educate your database developers how to properly assign object ownership when they create thier objects.

Maintaining a non-broken ownership chain can save the DBA much administrative time.

Best Practices for Managing Permissions

As you can see, there are many facets to managing permissions on a SQL Server. Some people may think that there are too many options, making permission management more difficult than it should be. SQL Server offers so many options to allow the DBA the greatest flexibility. Every SQL Server installation is different and they all have special needs. The wide variety of permission options makes it possible to meet all these special needs.

For those of you who want to minimize the job of managing permissions, this section is devoted to listing some of the best practices for managing permissions. If you follow them, you will find that managing permissions isn't all that difficult. But when you run into a situation where these best practices don't meet all your needs, then you can take advantage of some of the more complex features of SQL Server.

These best practices include the following:

- Always start assigning permissions from the largest group or role (largest by membership) first, and then narrow down as needed. For example, start by assigning permissions to the Public role first. If that doesn't meet all your needs, assign permissions to NT Server global groups next (assuming you are using Windows NT Authentication) or custom roles (if you are using SQL Server Authentication). If this still doesn't meet all your needs, assign permissions to specific users.

- Try to avoid assigning individual users permissions unless there is no other choice, such as when required to prevent access.

- Ideally, place group users in NT Server global groups for assigning permissions (assuming the users use Windows NT Authentication), or custom roles (assuming SQL Server authentication.

- Only assign users to built-in server roles who need administrative access to SQL Server.

- Don't give users more permissions than they need to perform their specific job.

- Avoid having users belong to more than one NT Server global group, custom role, or built-in role.

- Avoid adding groups to roles, and roles to roles.

- Don't assign statement permissions unless you absolutely have to.

- Use view and stored procedures often when creating a database application in order to reduce the number of objects that need to be assigned permissions.

- Maintain an unbroken chain of ownership.

If you follow these best practices, you will find that managing permissions on SQL Server isn't as difficult as you might have first thought.

How to Display Information on Permissions

Before you learn how to grant or revoke permissions for users, groups, and roles, you will take a quick look at how to view both statement and object permissions. This will not only help to orient you to how to work with permissions, but will also show you how to perform a task you will be performing on a regular basis as a DBA. First, you will learn how to view the current object permissions for all users, groups, and roles for a single database using

SQL Enterprise Manager. Then you will learn how to view object permissions for all users, groups, and roles using SQL Enterprise Manager. Keep in mind that permissions are managed on a database-by-database basis, and that you must perform these steps on every database you want to view the permissions on.

How to View Statement Permissions

Viewing statement permissions is an easy task using SQL Enterprise Manager.

Viewing statement permissions

1. Start SQL Enterprise Manager using an account with Sysadmins privileges.

2. In the Scope Pane, select the SQL Server you want to work with and open its folder to display all the SQL Server's options.

3. Click the plus sign next to the Databases folder in order to display all the databases being managed by this SQL Server.

4. Right-click the database you want to work with, and then select Properties from the pop-up menu. This displays the database's Properties dialog box (see Figure 13.6).

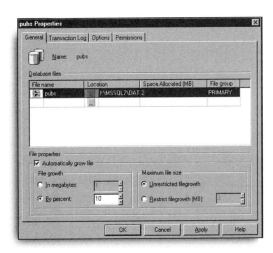

FIGURE 13.6
The database Properties dialog box.

5. Next, click the Permissions tab of the Properties dialog box. This displays the statement permissions screen, although this name isn't displayed on the screen (see Figure 13.7).

FIGURE 13.7

Statement permissions for a single database can be viewed from this screen.

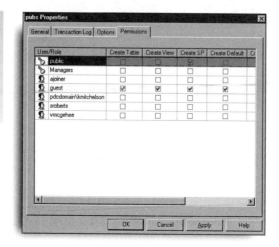

In the first column of this screen, under the heading User/Role, is a listing of all the database user IDs for this database. Keep in mind that this column can include any user, group, or role. In the other columns are the various statement permissions that can be potentially assigned. Also note that this screen doesn't show all the available statement permissions; you must scroll across the screen to see them all.

6. After you have seen the various statement permissions that have been assigned, you can exit this screen by clicking Cancel. This returns you to SQL Enterprise Manager's main screen.

You can view statement permissions anytime you need to for every database managed by SQL Server.

How to View Object Permissions

Viewing object permissions is just a little more difficult than viewing statement permission. You can either view them from the perspective of users, groups, or roles, or from the perspective of the objects themselves. This section shows you how to view statement permissions both ways.

Viewing object permissions from the perspective of the user, group, or role

1. Start SQL Enterprise Manager using an account with Sysadmins privileges.

2. In the Scope pane, select the SQL Server you want to work with and open its folder to display all of SQL Server's options.

3. Click the plus sign next to the Databases folder to display all the databases being managed by this SQL Server.

4. Next, click the plus sign next to the database where you want to view the statement permissions. This displays all the database's folders.

5. The next step depends on whether you want to view object permissions for users and groups, or for custom roles. If you want to view object permissions for users and groups, click the Users folder so that all of the users and groups are displayed in the Details Pane. If you want to view object permission for custom roles, click the Roles folder so that all the roles, predefined and custom, are displayed in the Details pane.

6. This step assumes that you have decided to view object permissions on users and groups, or custom roles. In either case, this step works the same. From the Details pane, right-click a user, group, or custom role whose object permissions you want to view, and then select Properties from the pop-up menu. This either displays a user and group Properties dialog box (see Figure 13.8), or a role Properties box.

7. Next, click the Permissions button. This displays the permissions screen for the user, group, or custom role you previously selected from the Details pane (see Figure 13.9).

First note that there are two radio buttons at the top of this screen. By default, the List All Objects button is selected. When this button is selected, all objects belonging to the database are displayed onscreen. If List Only Objects with Permissions for this User is selected, only those database objects for which the user has any permission are listed.

FIGURE 13.8
This is the a user's
Properties dialog box..

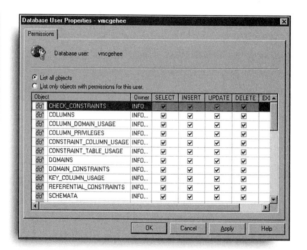

FIGURE 13.9
Object permissions for a
user, group, or role can
be viewed from this
screen.

In the first column is an icon that represents the type of
database object. The second column, Object, gives the name
of the object. The Owner column shows who owns the
object. The remaining columns list all the available object
permissions. A check in any of the boxes under any of the
object permission columns indicates that this user has that
permission on the object in question. As you scroll up and

down, looking at all the objects in a database, you may notice that not all objects have all object permissions. For example, stored procedures only have the Execute object permission.

8. After you are finished viewing the object permissions, you can exit the screen by clicking Cancel. You then must click the Cancel button again to return to SQL Enterprise Manager's main screen.

Viewing object permissions from the perspective of individual database objects

1. Start SQL Enterprise Manager using an account with Sysadmins privileges.

2. In the Scope Pane, select the SQL Server you want to work with and open its folder to display all of SQL Server's options.

3. Click the plus sign next to the Databases folder to display all the databases being managed by this SQL Server.

4. Next, click the plus sign next to the database where you want to view the object permissions. This displays all the database's folders.

5. Now you have to decide which object's permissions you want to view. You can choose from these folders: Tables, SQL Server Views, Stored Procedures, Rules, Defaults, and User Defined Datatypes. Click the folder that contains the database object you are looking for. Clicking the folder displays all the related objects in the Details pane.

6. Right-click one of the objects in the Details pane, and then select Properties from the pop-up menu. This displays the Properties dialog box of the object you selected (see Figure 13.10).

7. To display the permissions for this object, now click the Permission button. This displays the object permissions screen, although this name isn't displayed on the screen (see Figure 13.11).

FIGURE 13.10
The Properties dialog box contains the Permissions button.

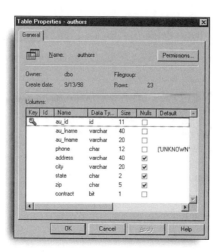

FIGURE 13.11
An object's object permissions can be viewed from this screen.

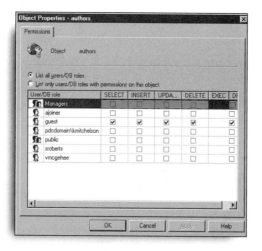

First note that there are two radio button at the top of this screen. By default, the List All Users/DB Roles button is selected. When this button is selected, all users, groups, and roles for this database are displayed on the screen. If the List Only Users/DB Roles with Permissions on this Object option is selected, only those users, groups, and roles that have any permissions at all for this object are listed.

The first column shows an icon. A single head indicates either a user or group. Two heads indicate a role. All the users, groups, and roles for this database are under

User/DB Role. The remaining columns indicate the object permissions available for this object. A check mark indicates that a user, group, or role has been granted the associated object permission. Note that not all the object permissions are available. This is because not all objects have all object permissions.

8. After you are finished viewing the object permissions, you can exit by clicking Cancel twice, first for the permissions screen, and a second time for the Properties dialog box. This returns you to the SQL Enterprise Manager main screen.

How to Grant and Revoke Permission

In the previous section, you learned how to view statement and object permissions. In this section, you will build on what you just learned and learn how to grant and revoke statement and object permissions. The actual mechanics of setting permissions is easy to learn. What is difficult, as has already been described in this chapter, is how to best apply them. As a beginner to assigning permissions, you will want to adhere to the best practices discussed earlier. If you do, you will find your job as a DBA much easier.

Permissions take effect immediately

Whenever a statement or object permission is granted or revoked, it happens immediately. A user doesn't have to log out and log in again in to be affected by a change in permissions.

How to Grant and Revoke Statement Permissions Using SQL Enterprise Manager

The granting and revoking of statement permissions uses the same screens you saw in the last section. But this time, you will learn how to either grant or revoke statement permissions for users, groups, and roles.

Remember that no user has any permission to access any database object until it has been assigned to them. When you grant a statement permission to a user, you are giving that user permission to perform a specific task, such as create database objects or back up a database or transaction log. That user retains the statement permission you gave him until it has been specifically revoked. After a permission has been revoked, the user no longer can perform the same task until he has been granted that same statement permission again.

Granting or revoking statement permissions for a user, group, or role

1. Start SQL Enterprise Manager using an account with Sysadmins privileges.

2. In the Scope pane, select the SQL Server you want to work with and open its folder to display all of SQL Server's options.

3. Click the plus sign next to the Databases folder to display all the databases being managed by this SQL Server.

4. Right-click the database you want to work with, and then select Properties from the pop-up menu. This displays the database's Properties dialog box.

5. Next, click the Permissions tab of the Properties dialog box. This displays the statement permissions screen, although this name isn't displayed onscreen (see Figure 13.12).

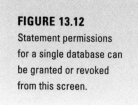

FIGURE 13.12
Statement permissions for a single database can be granted or revoked from this screen.

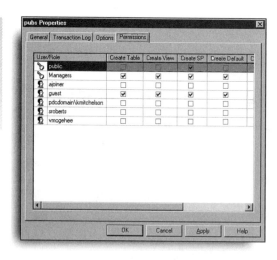

This is the same screen you saw earlier in this chapter. In the first column of this screen, under the heading User/Role, is a listing of all the database user IDs for this database. Keep in mind that this column can include any user, group, or role. In the other columns are the various statement permissions that can be potentially assigned. Also note that this screen doesn't show all the available statement permissions; you must scroll across the screen to see them all.

6. To grant any of the seven statement permissions to any of the users, groups, or roles displayed in the first column, click the appropriate box under the appropriate column. A check mark will appear in the box (see Figure 13.2). The actual statement permission isn't granted until you have clicked Apply or OK.

7. To revoke a statement permission that has been previously assigned, click the check in the box that represents the statement permission you want to revoke from a user, group, or role. When you click the check box, it changes to a red *X*, indicating that the statement permission is to be revoked (see Figure 13.13). The actual statement permission isn't revoked until you have clicked Apply or OK.

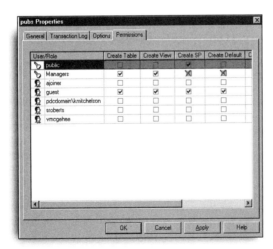

FIGURE 13.13
A red X indicates that the statement permission is to be revoked.

8. After you have granted or revoked any statement permissions, you can exit this screen by clicking OK. This returns you to SQL Enterprise Manager's main screen.

You may grant or revoke statement permissions any time you want. Just keep in mind that it is actually very rare to assign anyone statement permissions. More typically, predefined database roles are used to accomplish the same effect.

How to Grant and Revoke Object Permissions Using SQL Enterprise Manager

When you learned how to view object permissions for users, groups, and roles, you discovered that there were two ways to view them. You could either view the object permissions from the perspective of the user, group, or role, or from the perspective of the database object itself. The same is true for granting or revoking object permissions. In most cases, you will probably be granting or revoking object permissions from the perspective of the user, group, or role because this is much more intuitive than from the perspective of a database object. Because of this, this section will only demonstrate how to grant or revoke object permissions from the perspective of the user, group, or role.

If you want to grant or revoke permissions from the perspective of the database object, you can, using virtually the same steps described in the next set of steps.

Remember that no user has any permission to access any database object until it has been assigned to her. When you grant an object permission to a user, you are giving that user permission to perform some task on a pre-existing object, such as to SELECT, INSERT, UPDATE, or DELETE the object. That user retains the object permission you gave her until it has been specifically revoked. After a permission has been revoked, the user no longer can perform the same task until she has been granted that same object permission again.

Granting or revoking object permissions from the perspective of the user, group, or role

1. Start SQL Enterprise Manager using an account with Sysadmins privileges.

2. Using your mouse in the Scope pane, select the SQL Server you want to work with and open its folder to display all of SQL Server's options.

3. Click the plus sign next to the Databases folder to display all the databases being managed by this SQL Server.

4. Next, click the plus sign next to the database where you want to view the object permissions. This displays all of the database's folders.

5. The next step depends on whether you want to grant or revoke object permissions for users and groups, or for custom roles. If you want to grant or revoke object permissions for users and groups, click the Users folder so that all the users and groups are displayed in the Details pane. If you want to grant or view object permission for custom roles, click the Roles folder so that all the roles, predefined and custom, are displayed in the Details pane.

6. This step assumes that you have decided to grant or revoke object permissions on either users and groups, or custom roles. In either case, this step works the same. From the Details pane, right-click a user, group, or custom role whose object permissions you want to grant or revoke, and then select Properties from the pop-up menu. This either displays a user and group Properties dialog box, or a role Properties box.

7. Next, click the Permissions button. This displays the permissions screen for the user, group, or custom role you previously selected from the Details pane (see Figure 13.14).

   The first column contains an icon that represents the type of database object. The second column, Object, gives the name of the object. The Owner column shows who owns the object. The remaining columns list all the available object permissions. A check in any of the boxes under any of the object permission columns indicates that this user has that permission on the object in question. As you scroll up and down, looking at all the objects in a database, you may notice that not all objects have all object permissions. This is because not all objects have all object permissions.

447

8. To grant any of the six object permissions to any of the users or groups displayed in the first column, click the appropriate box under the appropriate column. A check mark will appear in the box (see Figure 13.14). The actual object permission isn't granted until you have clicked Apply or OK.

FIGURE 13.14

Object permissions for a user, group, or role can be granted or revoked from this screen.

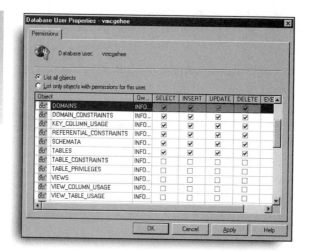

9. To revoke an object permission that has been previously assigned, click the check in the box that represents the object permission you want to revoke from a user or group. When you click the check box, it changes to a red *X*, indicating that the object permission is to be revoked (see Figure 13.15). The actual object permission isn't revoked until you have clicked Apply OK.

10. After you are finished viewing the object permissions, you can exit the screen by clicking OK. You them must click OK again to return to SQL Enterprise Manager's main screen.

Like statement permissions, you can grant or revoke object permissions anytime you need. But unlike statement permissions, you will be spending a lot of time managing object permissions for your database users. By following the best practices described earlier in this chapter, you will find that managing user permissions isn't as bad as you might have originally thought.

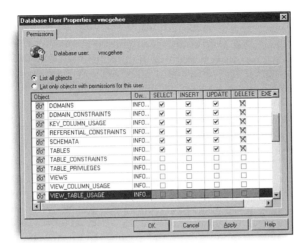

FIGURE 13.15
A red *X* indicates that an
object permission is
being revoked.

chapter

14

Backing Up Databases

Identify the potential causes of data loss •

Learn the benefits of, and options for, redundant data •

Plan a viable backup strategy •

Use SQL Server's tools to implement your backup plan •

Preventing data loss may be the most important function that you perform as a Data Base Administrator (DBA). Every day the information you keep in databases is used to support business decisions, track customer activity, record financial position, provide customer support, and much more. If all this data suddenly vanished, what impact would that have on your organization? Would your employees be able to continue to work as usual without noticing, or would many employees be unable to do their job at all? Would your organization suffer any financial loss from losing the database? Could they re-create the data that was lost? These are the questions that you hope you will not have to learn the answer to, and the information provided in this chapter will help prevent these situations from occurring.

This chapter describes the tools available in SQL Server to help you prevent data loss. The most important of these tools is the SQL Server Backup. Therefore, multiple examples of backups are provided along with step-by-step instructions for backing up your databases. Additional options for preventing data loss, such as mirroring hard drives, are also covered in this chapter. Finally, a list of issues to consider when deciding which backup strategy best suits a particular SQL Server is included, along with recommended solutions.

Features that prevent data loss

NT Server also provides features that help prevent data loss, such as marking bad sectors, mirroring, and better security. These techniques are not available in the Windows 9x version of SQL Server and are usually sufficient reasons for running SQL Server on NT Server rather than Windows 9x.

Possible Causes of Data Loss

Before you look at the various tools you have to prevent data loss, you should identify the possible causes of data loss so that you can select a way of preventing data loss that best fits your environment. Some of the possible causes of data loss include

- Hard disk crashes.
- Accidental data corruption. For example, someone may delete or modify data unintentionally.
- Malicious data corruption. For example, a disgruntled employee may intentionally delete or modify data.
- Natural disasters, such as fires, floods, and earthquakes.
- Theft.
- Viruses.

Several of the possible causes of data loss, such as fires and floods, can affect your entire data center. Therefore, it is a good idea to keep a backup copy of your critical data at a location that will probably not be affected by the same disaster.

The best way to recover from one of these disasters is to have a plan ready for dealing with the situation should it occur. Creating a plan to prevent data loss can be time-consuming, tedious, and intimidating, but if you ever have to go through recovery, you will be glad that you prepared for it. The amount of effort invested in a backup strategy is usually proportional to how important your data is. The more important your data is, the more time you will spend ensuring that procedures are in place to prevent the loss of that data. It is very important to put a backup plan in place to protect the system from the many types of failures that may occur. Though the odds of your data center being struck by a tornado may be small, it is worth an extra day of effort to create a plan that protects the data from that possibility.

The steps you take to prevent data loss also depend on the type of disaster that you are trying to protect against. The tools for protecting your data are listed in the next section, but the majority of this chapter focuses on the most flexible and productive tool for preventing data loss, the SQL Server Backup.

> **Is your business required to take backups offsite?**
>
> Many government agencies and regulated businesses are required by law to send a copy of critical data to another site nightly. This can be achieved by carrying a backup tape offsite, or transmitting a backup across a network to a remote site.

Ways to Prevent Data Loss

You can do a number of things to prevent the loss of data, and most DBAs usually implement multiple procedures to protect their data. Some of the alternatives for preventing data loss include the following:

- **Maintaining Redundant Data.** Redundant data stores the databases in more than one location and updates both locations at the same time. Tools for maintaining redundant data include
  - Disk Mirroring and Duplexing (RAID 1)
  - Disk Striping with Parity (RAID 5)

- Clustering
- Replication
- **Performing a Periodic Data Backup.** On a regular basis, usually daily, make a copy of the database and keep it in another location, often on a magnetic tape. Tools to perform backups include
    - SQL Server Backups
    - Third-Party Backup Products
    - Operating System Level File Copies (NT Explorer)

Maintaining Redundant Data

Of the four ways to store duplicate copies of databases presented here, mirroring is the easiest and least expensive to implement. Clustering is a promising new technology that will become commonplace in large shops within a few years, but it is currently an immature technology in the Windows NT environment and is best reserved for companies that are willing to take the risk of working with new technologies.

Disk Mirroring

Disk mirroring protects your databases by using a duplicate copy of a hard disk partition on a different physical hard disk. This not only protects the data in the event that one hard disk fails; it also means that SQL Server can continue to operate even after the hard disk fails. If a failure occurs, SQL Server automatically begins using the data on the mirrored hard disk. Disk Mirroring is a feature of the Windows NT operating system and is therefore transparent to SQL Server.

Disk Duplexing

Disk duplexing, shown in Figure 14.1, works just like disk mirroring, but in addition, it also uses a separate hard disk *controller* to read and write from the mirrored disk. This provides additional protection against the possibility of a hard disk *controller* failure. Both disk mirroring and disk duplexing are often referred to as Redundant Array of Inexpensive Disks (RAID) Level 1.

Standby SQL Servers

A standby server is another alternative that combines database backups with data redundancy. After a backup is performed, it is immediately restored onto a different SQL Server. This second SQL Server exists just in case the primary server fails, in which case, the backup SQL Server would be started as the primary server and take over processing. SQL Server offers some features that help ease the implementation of standby servers. See the online documentation for the details.

Redundant data is only available for Windows NT Server

The techniques for maintaining redundant data described in this section are not available in the Windows 9x version of SQL Server.

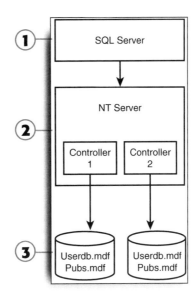

FIGURE 14.1
Disk duplexing uses separate controllers to make simultaneous updates to duplicate files on separate hard disks.

1 SQL Server requests NT Server to save data to a hard drive.

2 NT Server, implementing disk duplexing, sends the write commands to two different Disk Controllers.

3 Each Disk Controller writes the same data changes to a different hard drive.

Disk Striping with Parity

Disk striping with parity (RAID 5) is another hard disk protection feature offered with Windows NT. The process, which is also transparent to SQL Server, writes files across multiple physical hard disks, but provides a logical view of just a single hard disk (see Figure 14.2). The *with parity* part of disk striping with parity indicates that the operating system generates a piece of information called a parity strip for each file. It writes the parity strip to a hard disk that does not contain another piece of the file. If a single hard disk on the system fails, the operating system uses the information in the parity strip to rebuild the piece of the file that was contained on the lost disk. The operating system and SQL Server can continue to run without the failed hard disk because the missing information is rebuilt in memory until a new hard disk is installed.

Although RAID 1 and RAID 5 are available with Windows NT, it is also possible to implement them by purchasing more sophisticated hardware and third-party software. Implementing RAID with sophisticated hardware costs more than using RAID with Windows NT, but hardware RAID usually offers better performance than Windows NT RAID.

Mirroring within SQL Server is no longer available

Previous versions of SQL Server offered an option for mirroring database files through SQL Server. This option has been removed in SQL Server 7.0 because Windows NT can perform mirroring more efficiently.

How do I implement RAID 1 or RAID 5?

For steps to implement RAID 1 or RAID 5, see Help for Disk Administration in your NT Server manuals.

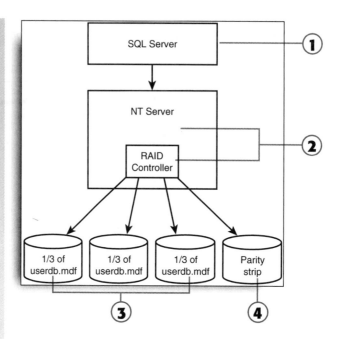

FIGURE 14.2

Disk striping with parity splits a file over multiple disks.

(1) SQL Server requests NT Server to save data to a hard drive.

(2) NT Server, implementing disk striping with parity, creates the parity strip by analyzing the data it intends to write to three hard drives.

(3) NT Server writes one-third of the data on drive 1, a second third on drive 2, and the final third on drive 3.

(4) NT Server finishes by writing the parity strip on drive 4.

Clustering

Clustering is a new technology for Windows NT. The goal of clustering is to prevent processing down time by having multiple servers capable of taking over the processes of any server that fails. A typical cluster may consist of two NT Servers, both running cluster software, and both running a copy of SQL Server. The cluster software, however, makes the two NT Servers and SQL Servers look like a single server on the network as shown in Figure 14.3.

The cluster can be configured to do all the processing on one physical server, or it can split the processing. For example, for SQL Server, two application databases could be running on the first SQL Server in the cluster, and three more could be running on the second SQL Server. If the operating system of one NT Server fails, the other NT Server in the cluster will recognize this and take over the hard drives and processing of the first NT Server.

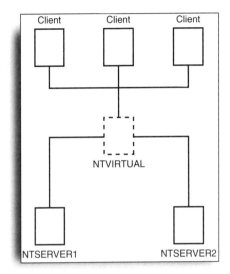

FIGURE 14.3
Client PCs connect to
NTVIRTUAL, unaware
that it is a virtual, rather
than a physical, NT
Server.

Details about implementing clustering on NT Server and SQL Server are beyond the scope of this book, but here are some things to consider:

- Microsoft's Clustering Server (MSCS) requires the Enterprise Edition of NT Server.

- SQL Server clusters are only supported on the Enterprise Edition of SQL Server.

- You must have a separate license for each NT Server and SQL Server in the cluster.

- Although the cluster is transparent to the client, and no client software or additional licenses are required, the only protocols currently supported are TCP/IP and Named Pipes.

- Clustering only offers protection from an operating system failure! If a hard drive crashes, or the power is lost to one of the machines, the other machine will not be able to take over the processes of the first machine. Clusters do not eliminate the need for RAID systems and backups!

SQL Server Clustering is designed for the Enterprise Version

You might be able to get a SQL Server clustered with the standard edition, but Microsoft does not support it..

Third-party NT clustering

Microsoft is not the only game in town when it comes to clustering on NT Server. Several companies, for example Veritas, have been offering clustering solutions on NT Server for a number of years and currently may offer a product that is better suited to your needs.

Microsoft is rapidly improving the capabilities of its clustering technologies. To get more information about MSCS, go to Microsoft on the Web at www.microsoft.com. Instructions for configuring MSCS can be found in the online MSCS Administrator's Guide, available with Windows NT Server, Enterprise Edition.

Replication

Replication is really not designed as a mechanism for preventing data loss, but it can, in desperate situations, be taken advantage of to perform that function. Replication copies data changes as they occur on one SQL Server to another SQL Server. The reason replication does not work well as a data redundancy tool is that all the connecting client computers usually have to be reconfigured to begin using the replication server, and the replication processes on SQL Server need to be altered as well.

SEE ALSO

➤ *To learn more about replication see page 542.*

Periodic Data Backup

In addition to maintaining redundant copies of the database files to protect SQL Server from a hard disk failure, it is important that you periodically back up the databases and send them to an offsite location. This protects your databases from disasters that might destroy an entire data center. Database backups also give you a recovery point to return to if significant information in the database is corrupted or deleted. Disk mirroring, for example, does not provide any benefits against accidental deletion of data because the data is deleted from both the primary and the mirrored copy. Three methods of performing periodic backups are described in the following sections.

Operating System File Backups

Perhaps the easiest method for backing up data is to use an operating system level copy command. For example, Windows NT Explorer can be used to copy the database files to a directory on another server. However, to do this safely SQL Server must not be running. If SQL Server is running and users modify data during the file backup, the backup copy may capture only some of the rows affected by the data modification as described in this example:

1. Using Windows NT Explorer, a backup of a database file is started.

2. During the backup, a new customer and a new order are added to the database as a single transaction.

3. The Windows NT Explorer backup has already backed up the customer table so it does not contain the new customer; however, it does capture the new order in the backup.

The result of this scenario is a backup that contains an order for a customer, but the backup does not contain the information about the customer. If this backup is restored into SQL Server, the referential integrity between customers and orders is lost.

Third-Party Product Backups

Another way to back up the database files periodically is to use a third-party product or Windows NT's backup tool. Because SQL Server has built-in backup functionality, you may wonder why you would consider a third-party product. Many people turn to other backup products because they need to back up non–SQL Server data in addition to the SQL Server data and they don't want to have to learn and maintain multiple backup products. Third-party products simplify Windows NT Server maintenance by performing the backups for both SQL Server and the other applications on the NT Server.

Before you use a third-party backup product, make certain that the product is capable of backing up SQL Server 7.0 database files by reading the product documentation or talking to the vendor. Also, learn how the backup software handles user modifications that occur during the backup like the one described in the preceding section.

Thoroughly test third-party backup software before using it

I recommend testing the backup product on a non-production server first. Also, before you use it on a production server, stop the SQL Server and use Windows NT Explorer to copy the database files to another disk or tape device. The reason for my extreme caution is that I have seen a third-party backup program corrupt the database it was attempting to back up and the database was lost.

SQL Server Backups

The SQL Server backup is the most versatile and reliable method you have to back up data. In addition to backing up entire databases, SQL Server can do the following:

- Back up specific database files.
- Back up the transaction log.
- Perform a differential backup.

SQL Server backups are more reliable than other methods of backing up database files because they never back up partial transactions, and therefore they maintain the integrity of the data. SQL Server backups also are dynamic, which means you can back up the database while it is in use. To maintain data integrity, a DBMS needs to be able to restore the database to the way it looked at a single point in time. In SQL Server's case, that single point in time image is the way the database looked when the backup process began. But what happens if a user attempts to modify the database during the backup? Here is an example: The following steps in Figure 14.4 illustrate how a SQL Server backup maintains data integrity when a user attempts to modify the database it is backing up.

SQL Server also offers a variety of options for backing up less than the entire database. Partial backups are useful when backups need to execute frequently on SQL Servers used for a lot of data entry or data modification.

Full Database Backups

Obviously, SQL Server can back up an entire database. Full database backups are recommended at least weekly for every site. It takes less time to restore a database if the full database backup is recent because fewer additional differential or transaction log backups need to be applied. A full database backup *must be* performed before a differential or transaction log backup. Database backups copy every allocated extent in the database to the backup file without examining the data on the extent. Therefore, the backup contains user tables, system tables, indexes, and all other objects in the database.

Unused space is not backed up

Space that was allocated but contains no data will not be copied to the backup. This results in backup files that are smaller than the database, and it speeds up the backup and restore processes.

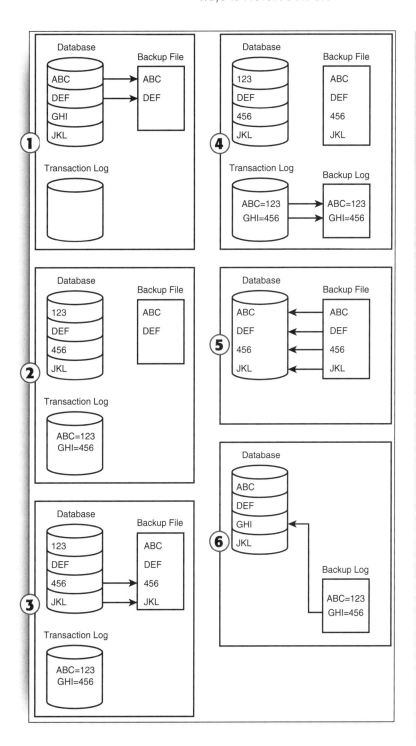

FIGURE 14.4

A SQL Server backup creates a single point in time image of the database.

(1) SQL Server begins copying data to the backup file.

(2) In one statement, a user modifies some data that SQL Server has not yet backed up, and some that it has backed up.

(3) When SQL Server reaches this now modified data, it copies the data to the backup file with the modifications.

(4) When SQL Server finishes backing up the database, it then backs up the portion of the transaction log that was written during the database backup.

(5) If a restore is necessary, SQL Server will restore the database to the image on the backup.

(6) Then, SQL Server will rollback the transactions contained in the back up of the transaction log that were executed during the database backup and that were on pages that had not been backed up. This reverses the changes made to the database during the backup, and leaves the database in the same state that it was at the beginning of the backup.

Frequency of backups

Frequent transaction log backups are required to implement a robust Standby SQL Server. Transaction logs are usually backed up hourly or even more frequently in such environments.

Transaction Log Backups

Because a full database backup can take a long time, you may prefer to back up a smaller portion of the database during the week and perform full database backups only on the weekend. One way to back up a smaller portion of a database is to back up just the data in the transaction log. The transaction log is a separate file that just records the changes that are made to the database. A transaction log backup copies the changes recorded in the transaction log that have been made to the database since the last transaction log backup (the entire transaction log is backed up if there are no prior log backups). Some DBAs back up transaction logs as frequently as every hour. This reduces the potential amount of data loss if a failure occurs because you usually lose all the changes that were made after the last database backup when restoring.

A transaction log backup contains only the modifications that occurred to the database since the previous transaction log backup. A common backup strategy is to back up the Full Database in the early morning, possibly at 3:00 AM, and then perform transaction log backups during the day, possibly at 10:00 AM, 1:00 PM, and 4:00 PM. If a failure occurs at 5:00 PM, modifications made between 4:00 PM and 5:00 PM may be lost. To restore the database to the image it contained at 4:00 PM, you must restore the Full Database, and then the 10:00 AM backup, and then the 1:00 PM backup, and finally the 4:00 PM backup. If any of the transaction log backups are missing or unusable, the restoration can proceed no further. For example, if the 1:00 PM transaction log backup was lost, the database can only be recovered to 10:00 AM; the 4:00 PM backup cannot be restored without first restoring the 1:00 PM backup.

SEE ALSO
➤ *For steps to recover a database from backup see page 485.*

➤ *For information on how to set up automated backups, see page 479 and subsequent sections later in this chapter.*

Differential Backups

Differential backups offer another alternative for backing up just part of a database. Differential backups do not use the transaction log; instead, they take a new image of the entire database.

This new image is smaller than the original full backup because it only contains the data that changed since the last full backup. Differential backups may or may not be smaller than transaction log backups, it depends on the nature of the data modifications. However, the advantage that differential backups have over transaction log backups is restoration speed. For example, if a single row in a table is modified twenty times after the full database backup and is then restored from a transaction log, it is modified twenty times during restoration as well. However, if it is restored from a differential backup it is only modified once with the last (twentieth) value. Figure 14.5 illustrates various SQL Server backups.

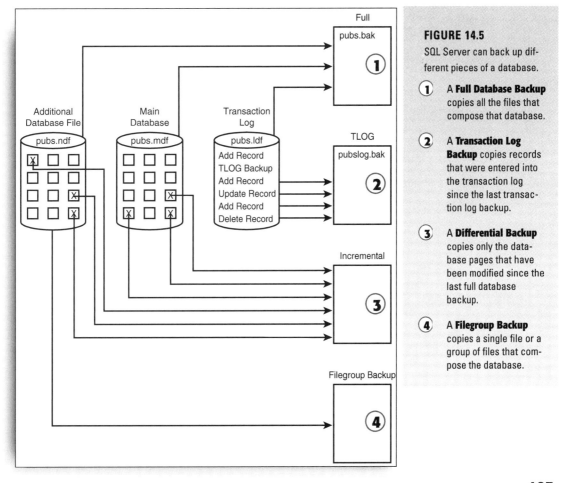

FIGURE 14.5

SQL Server can back up different pieces of a database.

1. A **Full Database Backup** copies all the files that compose that database.

2. A **Transaction Log Backup** copies records that were entered into the transaction log since the last transaction log backup.

3. A **Differential Backup** copies only the database pages that have been modified since the last full database backup.

4. A **Filegroup Backup** copies a single file or a group of files that compose the database.

Database File Backups

A database can be comprised of many files on the hard disk. If the database is large and cannot be backed up in a single night, database file backups can be used to back up a piece of the database each night.

For example, a database is split between dbfile1, dbfile2, and dbfile3, and the transaction log is on file dblog1. A full database backup is made on Sunday at 1:00 AM. Dbfile1 is backed up on Monday at 10:00 PM. Dbfile2 is backed up on Tuesday at 10:00 PM. On Wednesday, dbfile2 is lost and needs to be restored. The steps to restore the database are:

General steps for restoration

1. Back up the transaction log.
2. Restore *dbfile2* from the Tuesday 10:00 PM backup.
3. Apply the transaction log beginning on Tuesday at 10:00 PM.

Establishing a Backup Strategy

As an administrator, you need to create a plan or strategy to ensure that all data is backed up appropriately. This plan should answer the following questions:

- What data should be backed up?
- Which type of backups (differential, transaction log, or file-group) should you implement?
- What special considerations are there for Web servers, OLTP servers, DSS servers, or servers active 24 hours a day?
- How frequently will each database be backed up?
- What medium will the backups be created on?
- What data protection should the Operating System and Hardware provide?
- Who is responsible for the backups?

- Where will backups be stored?

- How long will backups be retained?

- How will successful backups be verified?

- How long will it take to restore from a backup if a failure occurs?

- How will the backup and restore strategy be tested?

- Who will document and maintain the backup and restore strategy?

Guidelines for answering these questions are provided in the following section.

Considerations for a Backup Strategy

The following list of questions and answers should help give you some tips or hints on creating your own back-up strategy or resolving issues that might arise. Although there is no way to predict every problem or outcome, I've tried to offer some recommendations you might find useful, too.

What data should be backed up?

Answer: At a minimum, the system databases master and msdb should be backed up. If the server is a Replication Distributor, the *distribution* database should be backed up. Finally, the user databases containing application data should be backed up.

The *master* database contains information vital to the operation of the entire SQL Server. If any changes to this database are lost, the SQL Server may be unable to restart successfully.

The *msdb* database contains information about all the jobs, alerts, and notifications on the SQL Server. This includes information about all the replication schedules. It can be very time-consuming or even impossible to reconstruct all this information if it is lost.

The *distribution* database is created when a SQL Server is configured as a Replication Distributor. The database contains information about the most recently published data and the

> **Backing up read-only databases speeds recovery**
>
> Some companies with read-only databases may decide not to back up those databases because they can always reload them from the original source data if necessary. I recommend backing up these databases anyway because it takes less time to restore them from backup than it does to re-import the data.

concurrency of the data maintained at the subscribers. Losing this database requires all the publishers to re-synchronize with all the subscribers before replication can begin again.

Obviously, the user databases containing the data used by your applications should be backed up regularly.

Recommendation: Back up *all* databases except tempdb.

SEE ALSO

➤ *For a detailed explanation of the players and roles involved with replication, see page 543.*

Which type of backups (differential, transaction log, or filegroup) should you implement?

Answer: The answer primarily depends on how frequently data is backed up, and the size of the databases. Generally you should not use filegroup backups unless your database is so large that you cannot backup the entirety of it with a full backup. You should use transaction log backups when you want to keep changes that have occurred, but don't want to impact performance by performing a full database backup. Transaction log backups are usually performed at regular intervals between full backups. Finally, you should use differential backups when you want to minimize the time it will take to restore a database. For example, it will be quicker to restore from a full database backup and one differential backup, than a full database backup, and fifteen transaction log backups. A good guideline might be to perform a differential backup in place of every sixth transaction log backup.

Recommendation: Perform Full backups daily, transaction log backups hourly, and differential backups every 6th hour (if the database is large and restoration time is critical).

What special considerations are there for Web servers, OLTP servers, DSS servers, or servers active 24 hours a day?

Answer: Decision Support Servers (DSS) usually have very few data modifications that cannot be recreated easily. Some companies do not even bother to back these databases up. I believe they should be backed up because recovery will be easier, but a daily Full backup is usually sufficient. Extremely large DSS servers (Data Warehouses) may require filegroup backups to be most efficient. Online Transaction Processing (OLTP) servers are very active and require frequent transaction log backups to frequently capture the data being entered with minimal impact to the users. Web servers and other servers that are active 24 hours a day present the toughest challenge. You can probably agree that they should be backed up, but the time to back them up is unclear. You need to discover at least one time each week when the server is at low activity to perform a full database backup. Transaction log backups should probably be hourly with differential backups every six hours.

Recommendation: Perform Full backups on DSS servers daily. Perform Full backups on OLTP servers daily, and transaction log backups hourly. Perform Full backups at least weekly on 7X24 servers and a mix of transaction log and differential backups between the full backups.

How frequently will each database be backed up?

Answer: The answer to this question is based on two factors: the number of data modifications that occurs on SQL Server and the amount of data that your company is willing to risk losing if a failure should occur. Nightly backups may be sufficient for servers with low transaction volumes, but for servers with a lot of daily activity, hourly or semi-hourly backups may be more beneficial to reduce the impact of a system failure. Servers with data redundancy through RAID 1 or RAID 5 may feel comfortable backing up less frequently but should remember that data redundancy does not protect the data from some threats, like fires.

Recommendation: Back up master whenever it changes, msdb and distribution daily, and all user databases daily if time and space permit. If time does not permit, back up user databases weekly.

> **How can you determine when your database is least active?**
>
> NT Performance Monitor is the tool to use to determine periods of low or high activity on SQL Server. With Performance Monitor, you can log selected statistics for a period of a few weeks, and then use Performance Monitor to view the contents of the log and compare activity levels. Two key counters to monitor to determine peak activity are SQLServer:General Statistics—User Connections and SQLServer:Buffer Manager—Page Requests/sec.

Alternative offsite backup strategy

To get a copy of your data offsite, one alternative to backing up to tape is to copy the backups across the network to a server residing at a remote location. Another alternative, usually for small databases, is to back up to a removable hard drive.

What medium will the backups be created on?

Answer: You can back up your databases to either disk or tape. Backing up to disk includes local hard disks or any hard disk that the server can access through the network. Backing up to tape makes use of Windows NT tape software to copy a database onto a magnetic tape.

Recommendation: Back up to disk if space allows. Include the SQL Server backup files in a scheduled Windows NT or third-party tape backup of the entire operating system after the SQL Server backups complete. Although you can back up directly from SQL Server to tape, SQL Server can write to disk much faster than it can write to tape with less performance impact.

What data protection should the operating system and hardware provide?

Answer: The type of data redundancy enabled by the operating system and hardware can affect your decision about frequency and type of backups.

Recommendation: This is entirely restricted by your budget. Hardware RAID 5 systems are becoming practical and inexpensive. At a minimum, mirror the partition containing the *master* database files if possible. For better security, SQL Server databases should be placed on a separate NTFS partition with extremely restricted access.

Who is responsible for the backups?

Answer: At the majority of sites the DBA is delegated this responsibility and schedules the backups to run automatically. At some sites, users who have the permission to back up the database perform backups when they are ready to. In any case, a DBA should be involved to ensure that a backup plan exists and to review it.

Recommendation: The DBA should be responsible.

How long will backups be retained?

Answer: Companies often retain backups for an extended time rather than overwrite the same backup file every night. This enables them to load the backup to a test system to research current problems and to recover to that point if bad data has been accumulating for days. The traditional retention period for a database backup is one week because most backups are written to tape and that tape is reused every seventh day.

Recommendation: Retain database backups for one week.

Where will backups be stored?

Answer: Backups can be stored on the same hard disk as the database, but this is pointless because the most common failure is a hard disk failure and this would destroy the backups as well. Backups can be stored on a separate hard disk on the same machine or on another server on the network if the space is available. Backups can also be placed on tape and the tape can be sent offsite.

Recommendation: Back up to tape (better yet, back up to hard disk, and then copy the backup to tape). Make sure that the tape is taken offsite (not left in the tape drive). If space permits, back up to another server as well.

How will successful backups be verified?

Answer Someone should know if the backup jobs run successfully. You can accomplish this by having the backup job send email indicating its success or failure.

Recommendation: Have the backup job send you email on both success and failure of backups. If you do not have the backup job send you notification on success as well as failure, you may mistakenly assume the backup succeeded when it did not run at all.

How long will it take to restore from a backup if a failure occurs?

Answer: You should have a good idea of how long it takes to recover from a backup if a failure occurs. Because users must wait while the databases are restored, restoration should be as quick as possible and the need for a quick restoration may affect your backup strategy. For sites that cannot afford long downtimes, a backup SQL Server should be considered.

How long should you keep a backup?

Depending on where you live and what your line of business is, you might encounter government requirements that you keep backups for three to seven years. In such cases, you should consider putting a backup copy on CD-ROM or DVD. These storage mediums are less likely to deteriorate or be subjected to magnetic corruption than hard disk and tape backups.

Recommendation: Test your restore strategy to determine whether the restoration time is acceptable.

How will the backup and restore strategy be tested?

Answer: It is not enough to assume that the backup is successful just because the job terminated with a success message. You should also restore the database from the backup copy and test the applications against it to ensure that the backup copy is valid. SQL Server can examine the data on a tape to see if it is valid for recovery, but the only way to be sure that it can actually *be* recovered is to recover it.

Recommendation: Back up your databases to tape using SQL Server. Stop SQL Server and back up all database files using Windows NT Explorer. Destroy the original database files, restart SQL Server, and attempt to recover the databases from the backup tape. Repeat these steps whenever the environment changes in any way that affects part of the backup and restore process. Environment changes include operating system changes (from NT 4.0 to 5.0 or when adding a service pack), new backup software or new versions and fixes to existing backup software, and hardware changes (hard disks, machine, tape drives, or brand of tape).

Who will document and maintain the backup and restore strategy?

Answer: Documenting the steps to take to recover databases greatly simplifies the process if the need ever arises. With good documentation, the recovery can be performed without the help of the DBA.

Recommendation: Create a Disaster Recovery Plan that details the actions to take in response to various types of failures (hard disk failures, machine failures, network failures).

Considerations for Immediate Backups

Most of your database backups will be performed by jobs executed by SQL Server Agent. However, there are times when you may need to perform an immediate backup of a database, outside of the normal backup schedule.

You should perform an immediate backup of the master database any time it is modified. Although this may sound as if the master needs to be updated many times a day, in most environments the master is not modified very frequently. It is important to keep the master database current because if the server configuration changed since the last backup and a restoration is attempted, SQL Server may be unable to restart! Actions that update the master database include

- Creating, altering, or deleting a database or database file.
- Altering a transaction log.
- Adding or removing remote servers.
- Adding or removing login IDs.
- Changing server configurations.

There are also times when you should perform an immediate backup of other databases. You might want to back up a database after creating indexes, because index creation can take a long time and it is often faster to restore a database from backup than to re-create the indexes. You should also immediately back up a database after performing any operations that are not recorded in the transaction log. Examples of such nonlogged operations include

- Backing up the Transaction log with `No_log` or `Truncate_Only`
- Importing data with `Select Into/Bulk Copy` enabled
- Creating a permanent table using the `Select Into` statement

The problem with nonlogged operations is that, by definition, the modifications they make to the database are not recorded in the transaction log. This makes it impossible to perform transaction log or differential backups after this point. Therefore, if your backup strategy is anything but a full database backup each time, you should immediately perform a full or differential database backup after the nonlogged operation.

SEE ALSO

➤ *Turn to page 520 for examples and a demonstration on how to use the BCP utility.*

Examples of Backup Strategies

This section describes backup strategies that can be implemented in various scenarios.

Scenario 1. SQL Server has less than five hundred megabytes of data and is primarily a decision support server (few data modifications).

Recommended backup strategy

1. Back up master and msdb nightly to files on the hard disk.
2. Back up user databases nightly to files on the hard disk.
3. After the SQL Server backups complete, have Windows NT copy NT files and the SQL Server back up files to tape.
4. Take the tape offsite when the backup is complete.

Scenario 2. SQL Server has two gigabytes of data. The database is used for accumulating data entry and is heavily modified during the day.

Recommended backup strategy

1. Back up master and msdb nightly to files on the hard disk.
2. Back up user databases nightly to files on the hard disk.
3. Back up user databases every hour during the day with a transaction log backup. Transaction log backups take less time than full backups and thus affect system performance for a shorter amount of time.
4. After the SQL Server backups are complete, have Windows NT copy NT files and the SQL Server back up files to tape.
5. Take the tape offsite when the backup is complete.

Scenario 3. SQL Server has two gigabytes of data. The database is split across several database files with the most frequently modified tables on one database file on a separate hard disk. The tables on the other database files are modified infrequently. Server downtime needs to be kept to a minimum.

Recommended backup strategy

1. Back up master and msdb nightly to files on the hard disk.

> **When to consider a differential backup**
>
> This is where you may consider a differential backup or two. You could run one at 12:00 and another at 6:00 in place of the transaction log backups. The benefit of doing this would be to decrease restoration time.

2. Back up user databases nightly to files on the hard disk.

3. Back up the highly active database file every hour during the day with a database file backup.

4. After the SQL Server backups are complete, have Windows NT copy NT files and the SQL Server back up files to tape.

5. Take the tape offsite when the backup is complete.

Scenario 4. SQL Server has one hundred gigabytes of data. It is comprised of multiple databases; some are large, some are small, some are frequently modified, and others are not. The largest database, split across multiple files, takes 26 hours to back up. Server downtime needs to be kept to a minimum. The SQL Server supports a 7X24(7 days a week, 24 hours a day) operation.

Recommended backup strategy

1. Back up master and msdb nightly to files on the hard disk.

2. Back up small databases nightly to files on the hard disk.

3. Perform a filegroup backup on the largest database. Back up a different filegroup each night to spread the total 26 hours of backing it up across seven nights. Perform a full database backup for large databases weekly at a period of low activity.

4. Perform differential backups on the large active databases every hour (differential backups take less time to recover from than transaction log backups).

5. Perform transaction log backups on the large low activity databases once per day (their transaction logs are small).

6. After nightly SQL Server backups complete, have Windows NT copy NT files and SQL Server backup files created that night to tape.

7. Take the tape offsite when the backup is complete.

Although a SQL Server backup can execute while users are on the system, the performance of the applications may be degraded. Because of this, most full database backups are usually performed at low activity times. However, the degradation of performance is not the only factor that constrains when a SQL Server backup runs. The other factor to consider is the amount

Measuring for least active times

Most DBAs know which databases are most active and when they are most active if the databases are used internally by the company. However, databases supporting Web servers may be active steadily around the clock. To get a good measure of the period during the week of least activity, use the NT Performance Monitor and create an hourly log of the average number of User Connections during a three or four week period.

Backing up large databases

Unfortunately, for databases this large you will probably have to backup directly to tape, unless you are fortunate enough to have hundreds of gigabytes of free disk space available.

Backing up to other servers

One alternative to keep in mind when backing up databases is that you can back them up to other servers. Any hard drive that your NT Server can access, including NetWare servers, can be used as a destination for your backup files. Backing up to a server connected with low bandwidth is discouraged because it can negatively affect the performance of other traffic on your network, as well as the amount of time the backup process runs.

of time it takes the backup to execute. A database backup may last from a few minutes to several hours, depending on the size of the database and the speed of the backup media.

Implementing SQL Server Backups

In this section, you will be shown the step-by-step instructions for backing up databases and transaction logs for any of the backup methods provided by SQL Server. The section begins with an introduction to SQL Server Backup Devices and explains the role of backup devices in performing your SQL Server backups. After you are shown how to create backup devices you will be shown how they are used through the instructions for backing up a database. Because there are many types of database backups (full, transaction log, filegroup, and differential), a separate section is provided for each to guide you through the type of backup you have chosen to perform.

Microsoft now provides three different ways to execute SQL Server backups in Enterprise Manager:

- Immediate backups can be performed from the menu for a specific database.
- Scheduled backups run a job that executes the sqlmaint.exe program and can perform full database or transaction log backups.
- Scheduled backups can also use Transact-SQL to perform any type of database backup.

Although there may be multiple methods for performing a specific type of backup, this chapter focuses on the method that is easiest to implement for the given scenario.

How to Create a Backup Device

A *backup device* is nothing more than a pointer to a location where the backup of your database will be placed. You can create a backup device at any time from a Backup folder in SQL Enterprise Manager, or you can wait to create a backup device until the time you actually back up your database. The backup device is used when you perform an immediate backup of your database, and you can also use it in scheduled database backups. A backup device can specify the name of a file on a hard drive that will be written to when the backup runs, or it could specify the name of a tape drive.

Creating a backup device does *not* create an actual file until the SQL Server backup executes.

Creating a backup device

1. Open the SQL Server Enterprise Manager and expand your SQL Server.

2. Expand the **Management** folder and right-click on the **Backup** folder.

3. Select **N**ew **Backup Device.** Each backup device has just two pieces of information as shown in Figure 14.6.

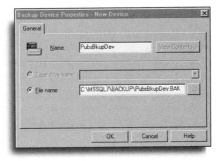

FIGURE 14.6

Create a Backup Device by providing a logical name and a physical location for the backup to be written to.

- The Name is an alias used by the backup command when it creates an actual backup copy of a database.

- The Tape drive name or Disk filename is the actual physical file location the backup device will write to.

4. For tapes, enter the Tape drive name, which is usually something like `\\.\TAPE0`. For disk files, enter the Disk filename, which is usually something like `\\NTServer\backups\Monday\master.bak`.

5. Click OK to finish. You should see this backup device name in the Backup folder.

How to Perform an Immediate Backup

You can immediately back up a database by either running an existing backup job, or by selecting Backup Database from the specific database's pop-up Task menu. When backing up a database through the database's pop-up Task menu, you will see the dialog shown in Figure 14.7.

FIGURE 14.7
The Backup Database dialog box enables you to immediately back up any database.

Advantage to differential backups

Differential backups usually take longer to execute than transaction log backups, but they also usually take less time to restore from. The differential backup should be retained until the next full database backup, or the next differential backup, is performed.

Performing an immediate database backup

1. In Enterprise Manager, right-click the database name. Select **All Tasks, Backup Database...** from the pop-up menu.

2. The dialog in Figure 14.7 appears. Enter a Name for the backup (or use the default name provided). Include a Description for tracking information.

3. Click the type of backup you want to perform:

   ▪ **Database - Complete**   The default option selected.

   ▪ **Database - Differential**   A differential backup makes a copy of all the changes that have occurred in the database since the last full database backup.

   ▪ **Transaction Log**   The most common reason for immediately backing up the transaction log is to prevent the transaction log from becoming full. If you have configured the transaction log file to automatically grow larger when necessary, this is not a concern unless the hard drive containing the transaction log is almost out of space. This option is disabled if Truncate Log on Checkpoint is true for this database.

- **File and Filegroup**   This option is also disabled if Truncate Log On Checkpoint is true for this database. A filegroup backup copies just a few of the actual operating system files that make up a database. Filegroup backups are used when you don't have enough time to back up the entire database.

4. Click the Add button to select either a Tape or Disk destination for the database backup.

5. Enter the name of a file to back up to, or select an existing backup device to backup to.

6. Select one of the following Action options:

   Click Append to Media if you want to add this database backup to other backups that already exist on the tape.

   Click Overwrite Existing Media if you want to replace the contents of the tape or file you are backing up to.

7. Choose OK tobegin the immediate backup.

How to Schedule Automatic Backups

Database backups should be performed frequently and regularly. The best way to accomplish this is to create a SQL Server job for the SQL Server Agent to execute on a scheduled basis. Because backing up a database affects the performance of the SQL Server, it is generally best to perform backups during periods of low activity, often in the early hours of the morning.

You have three mechanisms for creating a backup job:

- Use the Database Maintenance Plan Wizard. This is recommended because it also schedules other database maintenance activities that should be performed on a regular basis.

- Create a schedule for a backup through the immediate backup interface. This is the easiest option. It is just like an

Backups and the transaction log

When you perform an immediate transaction log backup it becomes part of your transaction log chain; therefore, you should retain this backup in case you need to restore the database before you get the chance to do another full or differential database backup.

Where are your system databases?

Are you looking for your system databases (master, model, msdb, tempdb) but don't see them in the databases group? If so, you can view them by right-clicking your SQL Server name, selecting Edit SQL Server Registration, and selecting the check box labeled Show System Databases.

Backup performance impact really isn't all that bad

Despite my many warnings about the impact of performing a backup while users are on SQL Server, the performance impact of backups in SQL Server 7.0 really is not extremely significant. This is a vast improvement over previous versions. However, because you have to pick a time during which to do your backups, why not pick low activity times? The really good news is that you should not be extremely concerned if you need to perform a full database backup while users are active. There is a very good chance they won't even notice.

immediate backup, except that you click the Schedule button and select your schedule before clicking OK.

- Write the Transact-SQL yourself and create a job to execute it. This option takes the longest to set up, but offers you the most flexibility and features.

How to Schedule a Full Database or Transaction Log Backup Using a Wizard

The easiest way to schedule a full database backup is to use the Database Maintenance Wizard.

Scheduling a database backup

1. Click the database in SQL Enterprise Manager that you want to create the scheduled backup for.

2. Execute the **Database Maintenance Plan Wizard** from the **Management** group of wizards.

3. Choose the Next button until you reach the step named **Specify the Database Backup Plan**, shown in Figure 14.8.

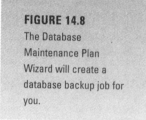

FIGURE 14.8
The Database Maintenance Plan Wizard will create a database backup job for you.

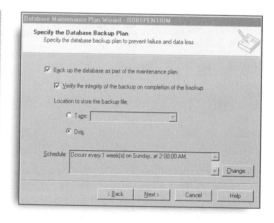

4. Click the change button to create a schedule for running the backup.

5. Enter either a Tape Drive or a Disk Directory that the backup will be written to. The backup process will generate a backup filename.

6. If you want the backup job to delete old files from the same directory to free space on the hard drive, click the Remove Files Older Than option and enter a number of weeks.

7. Click Next. You will be presented with a screen showing all the same options for backing up the transaction log that you just saw for the database.

After you have verified your selections, the wizard will generate one job for the database backup and another job for the transaction log backup. You can make modifications to these jobs and their execution schedules as you would any other job.

SEE ALSO

➤ *For information about the other steps in the Database Maintenance Plan Wizard, see page 338.*

➤ *For information on modifying and maintaining jobs, see page 284.*

How to Schedule a Differential or Filegroup Backup

Differential and filegroup backups are probably easiest to schedule through the Backup Database dialog on the database's All Tasks menu. Use the same procedure you would use to perform an immediate backup, but click the Schedule button and select the schedule you want the backup to run on before selecting the OK button.

How to Create a Job to Schedule a Backup

I highly recommend using the wizards to create backup jobs when you are getting started, but eventually you will want to modify those jobs, or perhaps add a backup step to an existing job. Therefore I am providing this simple example of creating a backup job from scratch, and showing you an example of the SQL.

Using Transact-SQL to schedule a differential or filegroup backup

1. In Enterprise Manager, expand the **Management** group and then expand SQL Server Agent and right-click the Jobs group. Select New Job.

2. Provide a Name for the job and then select the Steps tab.

3. Choose the New command button on the Steps tab of the Job Scheduling dialog and you will see the dialog shown in Figure 14.9.

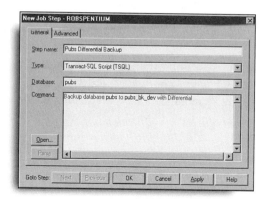

4. In the General tab, enter a name for the step, perhaps `Pubs Differential Backup`.

5. Select Transact-SQL Script from the Type drop-down list for the step type.

6. Select the name of the database you want to back up from the Database drop-down list.

7. The last step is to enter in the Command text box the Transact-SQL that the job will execute to back up the database.

The syntax for performing a full database backup of the pubs database to a backup device named `pubs_bk_dev` is

```
BACKUP DATABASE pubs TO pubs_bk_dev
```

To perform a differential backup to pubs

```
BACKUP DATABASE pubs TO pubs_bk_dev WITH DIFFERENTIAL
```

To perform a filegroup backup to pubs of the `authors` file in the `titles` filegroup

```
BACKUP DATABASE pubs FILE = 'authors', FILEGROUP =
'titles',
TO pubs_bk_dev
```

SEE ALSO

➤ *Detailed information about jobs can be found beginning on page 284.*

chapter
15

Restoring SQL Data

Understand how to restore from
different types of back-ups ●

Restore a database from a full
database backup ●

Restore from a differential or
transaction log backup ●

Restore the master database with or
without a backup ●

Restore to a specific point in time ●

Database Administrators seldom look forward to the task of restoring a database. This isn't because a restoration is difficult, but rather because the stakes can be very high. Restoring a database means that the current database on the SQL Server is over-written with a copy of the database from a previous backup. If all goes well, you begin working with the restored version of the database, but if the restoration fails, the database may be lost forever.

Hopefully, you will never need to restore a database and will rarely need to review this chapter. However, it is a good idea to read it at least once so that you are familiar with the restore operations, know what you will need to restore a database, and know how to prepare to make a restore as simple and accurate as possible.

After reading this chapter, you will be able to

- Restore a database from a full database backup
- Restore from a differential or transaction log backup
- Restore the master database with or without a backup
- Restore to a specific point in time

The chapter presents step-by-step instructions for performing each of these tasks.

Restore Overview

> **SQL Server will create the database during restore**
>
> In previous versions of SQL Server, you had to create the database before you could restore it. The process has changed in SQL Server 7.0. SQL Server can create the database for you if it doesn't already exist.

The SQL Server restore command is used for two reasons. The primary reason is to restore a database that has become corrupt. The causes of database corruption include hard disk failure and the accidental deletion of data. The other use of SQL Server's restore command is to copy data from one SQL Server to another. This is a good way to populate other SQL Servers with data for software development, testing, consistency checks, and remote processing.

You must have a backup of a database before the database can be restored. If you have not already done so, please read Chapter 14, "Backing Up Databases," for information about creating database backups.

The restore process always begins by restoring from a full data-base backup, unless you are restoring a database filegroup.

After the restore from the full database backup, you should sequentially restore either differential, database file, or transac-tion log backups if you have them, depending on the strategy you used when you backed up the database.

Microsoft improved the restore process considerably in SQL Server 7.0. You no longer need to know all the steps by which a database was originally created to restore the database from a backup. In fact, the database doesn't even need to exist when you restore it; the restore process can create it for you. SQL Server 7.0 offers a variety of ways to restore databases. The various options for backing up and restoring data provide you with the tools to back up your databases effectively in any environment. This section describes the restoration options available and the considerations for implementing database restores.

> **SQL Server 7.0 can only restore databases backed up with 7.0**
>
> You cannot restore SQL Server 6.5 database backups into SQL Server 7.0. Likewise, SQL Server 7.0 backups cannot be restored into previous versions of SQL Server. To bring a SQL Server 6.5 database into a SQL Server 7.0 server, use the Upgrade Wizard described in Chapter 6, "Upgrading SQL Server from 6.5 to 7.0."

Ways to Restore Databases

When you are ready to begin restoring a database, you will have one or more of the following types of files to restore from:

- **Full database backup**. A file containing an image of the entire database taken at a specific point in time.

- **Transaction log backup.** A file containing before and after images of each modification made to a database in the order that they occurred.

- **Differential database backup.** A single point in time image of all the changes made to the database since the last full database backup.

- **File or filegroup backup.** An exact copy of one or more of the operating system files that make up the logical database.

The steps you take to restore a database depend on the type of backup files you have to restore from, as well as the type of fail-ure you are trying to recover from. In most cases, you will want to restore the most current data possible, so you will need to start by determining exactly what data is lost.

Scenario 1

Perhaps the best way to learn about SQL Server's restore options is with an example. Let's assume that you have a server with three hard drives and no data redundancy (no mirroring or striping of the hard drives). One of the hard drives crashes and you discover that you can no longer access the pubs database on SQL Server. For this example you will assume that all the database files are on the D: drive, and all the transaction log files are on the E: drive as shown in Figure 15.1.

FIGURE 15.1

Example of database file placement on multiple drives.

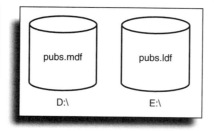

pubs.mdf   pubs.ldf

D:\   E:\

Restoring files for this sample

1. Determine which hard drive crashed, and which database files were on that hard drive.

   If the database is lost. If you discover that the D: drive containing the pubs database crashed, the transaction log for the pubs database on the E: drive may still be intact. By backing up what is still in the transaction log, you will be able to restore all the transactions that occurred up to the moment of the crash. To back up the transaction log when the database is lost, open a query analyzer window and enter the following command:

   `Backup Transaction Pubs with No_Truncate`

   The `No_Truncate` option tells SQL Server to make a backup copy of the contents of the transaction log, but SQL Server should not attempt to connect to the pubs database (because it isn't there) while doing so.

If the transaction log is lost. If you discover that the E:
drive containing the pubs transaction log crashed, the pubs
database itself is still intact. However, you cannot make
modifications to the database because the transaction log
doesn't exist and therefore there is no place to record your
modifications. You can re-create the transaction log by stopping and restarting SQL Server. During startup, when SQL
Server is unable to locate the log file, it will create a new log
file for the database automatically.

2. You are now ready to begin restoring the pubs database from
   its backup image. The first backup file you restore should
   contain the most recent full database backup of pubs. The
   full database backup contains an image of the database as it
   looked at the specific point in time the backup was made.
   When the restoration from the full database backup is complete, you are ready to move to the third and final step.

3. If you have performed any backups since the last full database backup, you will probably want to restore those backups as well. The number of additional files you restore will
   depend on your backup methodology:

   · If you have performed only transaction log backups since
     the last full database backup, you will restore each log
     backup beginning with the oldest and continuing through
     the most recent.

   · If you have performed differential backups since the last
     full database backup, you will want to restore the most
     recent differential backup.

   · If you have performed both transaction log and differential
     backups, you will want to restore using the method that
     will give you the most current image in the shortest
     amount of time.

For example, assume that you performed a full database backup
last night at 3:00 AM, transaction log backups at 10:00 AM, 1:00
PM, and 4:00 PM, and a differential backup at 2:30 PM, as
shown in Figure 15.2.

FIGURE 15.2
A backup scenario with both transaction logs and differential backups.

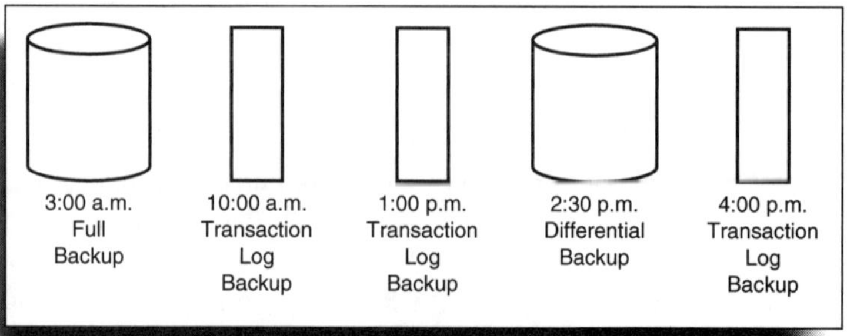

| 3:00 a.m. Full Backup | 10:00 a.m. Transaction Log Backup | 1:00 p.m. Transaction Log Backup | 2:30 p.m. Differential Backup | 4:00 p.m. Transaction Log Backup |

A crash occurs at 4:01 PM. To restore the database to what it looked like at 4:00 PM, you can perform either one of the following two sets up steps.

Options for restoring after a scheduled backup

1. Restore from the full database backup taken last night at 3:00 AM.

2. Restore the transaction log backup taken at 10:00 AM.

3. Restore the transaction log backup taken at 1:00 PM.

4. Finally, restore the transaction log backup taken at 4:00 PM.

Or...

1. Restore from the full database backup taken last night at 3:00 AM.

2. Restore the differential backup taken at 2:30 PM.

3. Finally, restore the transaction log backup taken at 4:00 PM.

The recommended approach is the second list because it requires fewer steps and because differential restores are usually faster than transaction log restores.

The steps for restoring files after the most recent full backup depend on your backup and restore strategy. Each possible strategy is explained in the following sections with examples.

Applying Transaction Logs

After the restore from the full database backup is complete, each transaction log backup can be restored. When a transaction log backup is restored, the transactions contained within it are

---

Change Recovery Completion State on all but your last file

Any time you plan to restore more than one file you will need to change the Recovery Completion State for all but the last file restored. The Recovery Completion State is a flag that indicates to SQL Server whether the recovery process is complete and users can begin using the database. Make sure you select an option that leaves the database able to restore additional transaction logs, unless you are on the final backup file to be restored.

Illustrations show logical file contents

This illustration doesn't represent the physical contents of the backup files. The physical contents are stored in a format that only the SQL Server database understands, not in SQL.

re-applied to the database. The original UPDATE, INSERT, and DELETE transactions entered by the users are re-executed and database pages are re-modified. Due to the nature of transaction log restores they *must* be restored in sequence. An illustration of the logical contents of the transaction log backup is shown in Figure 15.3.

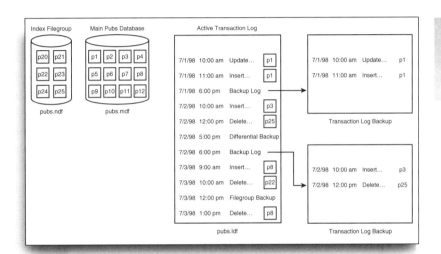

FIGURE 15.3
Transaction Logs *must* be restored in sequence.

Here is an example of restoring from transaction log backups.

Restoring from transaction log backups

1. On Sunday, you backed up the full database.

2. On Monday evening, you backed up the transaction log.

3. Again on Tuesday evening, you backed up the transaction log.

4. A hard disk failure occurs on Wednesday morning.

5. To restore as much of the database as possible, you immediately back up the transaction log. This saves all the transactions that were entered Wednesday morning prior to the failure.

6. Next, restore the database from the full database backup taken on Sunday.

7. Then, restore the transaction log backup from Monday evening.

Assumptions of this example

These examples assume the failure did not affect the hard drive containing the transaction log. If the active transaction log is lost along with the database, recovery of transactions entered since the last backup isn't possible.

**When a transaction log
is unusable**

If any log in the chain of transaction logs is unusable, transaction
logs that were created after the
unusable transaction log also cannot be restored. In this example, if
the Monday log is unavailable or
damaged, you will not be able to
restore the Tuesday evening or
Wednesday morning transaction
log backups.

8. Restore the transaction log backup from Tuesday evening.

9. Finally, restore the transaction log backup made on Wednesday morning immediately after the failure.

When restoring transaction logs, all files except the very last log restored need to be restored in a way that leaves the database non-operational so that subsequent log files can be applied.

Applying Differential Backups

After the restore from the full database backup is complete, the differential backup can be applied. Unlike transaction logs, only one differential backup image is applied. Differential backups taken after the full database backup, but before the most recent differential backup, can be discarded. Restoring a differential backup replaces only pages in the database that changed since the full database backup. The logical contents of a differential backup file are shown in Figure 15.4.

FIGURE 15.4
Differential restores
replace only pages that
have changed in the
database since the full
database backup.

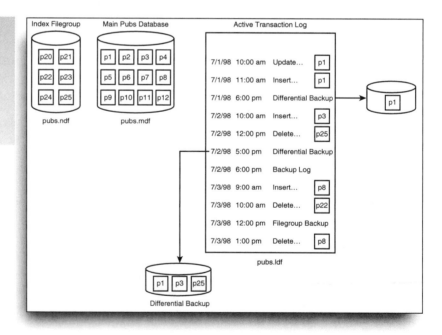

Restoring a differential backup

1. On Sunday, you backed up the full database.

2. On Monday evening, you performed a differential backup.

3. On Tuesday evening, you performed a differential backup.

4. A hard disk failure occurs on Wednesday morning.

5. To restore as much of the database as possible, you immediately back up the transaction log.

6. Next, restore the database from the full database backup taken on Sunday.

7. Then, restore the Tuesday differential backup.

8. Finally, restore the Wednesday morning transaction log.

You don't have to restore the Monday differential backup because the Tuesday backup contains everything the Monday backup contained *in addition to* the Tuesday changes. When restoring from differential backups, all files except the very last file restored need to leave the database able to restore additional transaction logs so that subsequent files can be applied.

Applying Database File Backups

You don't need to perform a restore of the most recent full database backup prior to performing a database file restoration. Database file backups are used to back up part of a database when time doesn't permit a full database backup. After you restore a single database file using a database file restore, you should restore the transaction log to bring the tables in that database file up to date with the rest of the database. Figure 15.5 shows the logical contents of a database file backup.

Applying database file backups

1. On Sunday, you backed up the full database. The database resides on two files: pubs.mdf and pubs.ndf. The transaction log is on pubs.ldf.

2. On Monday evening, you backed up pubs.ndf and pubs.ldf.

3. On Tuesday evening, you backed up pubs.mdf and pubs.ldf.

4. A hard disk failure occurs on the hard drive containing pubs.ndf on Wednesday morning.

FIGURE 15.5

A database file restoration restores just part of the database.

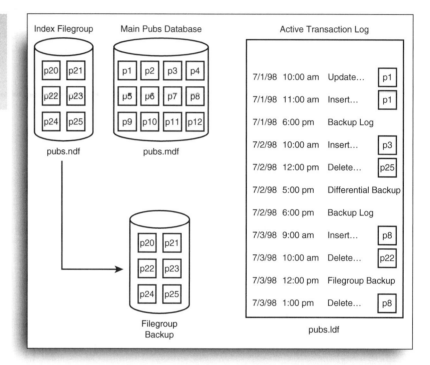

5. To restore as much of the database as possible, you immediately back up the transaction log.

6. Next, restore the backup of pubs.ndf taken on Monday. You don't need to first perform a full database restore because pubs.mdf and pubs.ldf are intact.

7. Then, restore the transaction log backup from Tuesday evening.

8. Finally, restore the transaction log backup made on Wednesday morning immediately after the failure.

If you are unable to back up the transaction log in step 5, the data stored on pubs.ndf may not be synchronized with the rest of the database. The transaction log contains all modifications made to the database after the Monday evening backup. Without the transaction log, the tables on pubs.ndf cannot be brought up to date with the tables in pubs.mdf. This may result in a lack of data integrity between the tables in the different database files.

When the transaction log is restored, it will *not* attempt to re-apply modifications to data in pubs.mdf. The process only applies changes to dbFile1 that occurred since the last backup of dbFile1. The Tuesday file backup of pubs.mdf isn't applied because that portion of the database was not affected by the failure.

Restoring to a Specific Point in Time

When restoring transaction logs, you can specify a date and time that the restoration is performed through. Point-in-time restorations are useful when data was accidentally changed or deleted and you know when the modifications occurred. When restoring the transaction logs, you can specify a time just prior to the data corruption; the transaction log restores will not recover any transactions that occurred after that time, as shown in Figure 15.6.

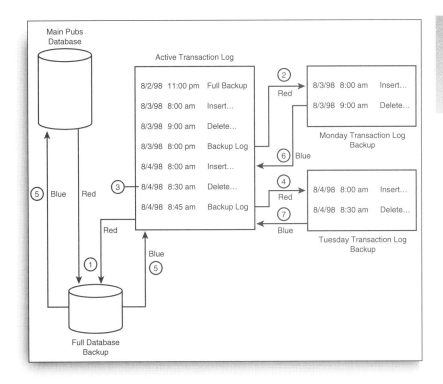

FIGURE 15.6
Restoring to a point in time helps to minimize data lost.

1. On Sunday, you backed up the full database. This would back up pubs.mdf and pubs.ldf.

2. On Monday evening, you backed up the transaction log.

3. On Tuesday at 8:30 AM, data is accidentally deleted.

4. To recover the deleted data, you immediately back up the transaction log.

5. Next, restore the database from the full database backup.

6. Then, restore from the Monday transaction log backup. This re-applies all the transactions in the log to the pubs database as well as the log.

7. Finally, restore from the Tuesday morning transaction log backup, specifying that the restore process recovers transactions through 8:25 AM. This re-applies all the transactions in the log prior to 8:25 AM to both the pubs database and the log.

Important Restoration Considerations

There are a number of miscellaneous options and facts you should be aware of when restoring a database. These include the following:

- If a hard drive fails, but SQL Server is still running, you may be able to back up all the transactions that occurred up to the moment of the failure. If the hard drive containing the transaction log is available, back up the transaction log using the With No_Truncate option to capture the contents of the log before stopping the server to fix the hard drive.

- If the hard drive containing the transaction log is lost, users cannot make modifications to the data portion of the database. To make your database operational again, stop and restart SQL Server. SQL Server will create a new transaction log for the database automatically.

- The database being restored must not be in use when the restore is attempted.

- Any transactions that are active when a transaction log is backed up are not applied during restoration. Instead, they are eliminated from the log. This ensures that SQL Server never writes partial transactions to the database.

- Transaction logs must be restored in sequence. If a full database backup is performed on Sunday, and transaction log backups are performed each day of the week, restoration requires the Sunday backup to be recovered first, followed by each daily transaction log backup in sequence. If the Monday backup is unavailable, no further transaction log backups can be applied.

- Some database options such as ANSI NULL DEFAULT and READONLY may need to be reset if the database doesn't exist when it is restored.

- If the database doesn't exist when a restore is attempted, you must select the Restore as Database option and type in the database name to create.

- When restoring a database to a different server, the server must have the same sort order and code pages installed as the server the backup was created on. This isn't necessary for servers using the binary sort order. In this case, the character sets used on the two servers may be different and the database can still be restored. However, extended characters, those with an ASCII value greater than 127, may be interpreted differently.

- To restore the database into a different file or directory than it was originally in, type in a path different from the default path supplied in the Restore Database Files As list box.

- To continue a restore that was interrupted, perhaps because the server was shut down, begin the restore again and specify the RESTART option.

- Upon startup, SQL Server marks a database *suspect* when it is unable to access the database. If you have a backup to restore from, you can drop the suspect database. SQL Server will re-create it during the restore process.

How to Restore Data

This section provides the step-by-step instructions for restoring databases. Hopefully, you will never need to use these instructions in a production environment. If you have the resources, you should definitely test your restore strategy to see that it is sufficient. If you don't have the resources to test your restore strategy, you should find the resources or have a qualified consultant review your restoration plan.

You can use Enterprise Manager (SEM) or Transact-SQL to restore a database. Both methods support every possible type of restoration. Most people will find it easier to use SEM to restore a database, but you may encounter a time when SEM is unavailable. Therefore, this chapter provides the steps for performing a typical restore from both SEM and Transact-SQL. Detailed steps are covered for every type of restore using SEM, with notes where appropriate about the Transact-SQL options.

Restoring a Database and Its Log Using Enterprise Manager

Enterprise Manager provides a dialog that you can use to restore a database. The appearance of the lower half of the dialog depends on the restoration option selected in the upper half of the diagram:

- Restore Database displays the dialog shown in Figure 15.7.
- Restore Filegroups or Files displays the dialog shown in Figure 15.8.
- Restore From Device displays the dialog shown in Figure 15.9.

You can get to these dialogs with the following steps:

Restoring data

1. In Enterprise Manager, right-click the database filename.

2. Select **All Tasks, Restore Database**.

Specifying a backup device name

If the database that you want to restore doesn't exist, you must select From Device and provide a backup device name to restore the database.

FIGURE 15.7

Use this dialog to restore a database from backup.

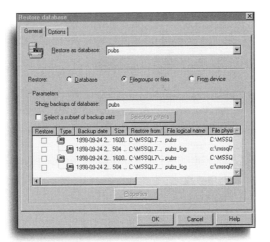

FIGURE 15.8

Use this dialog to restore a filegroup from backup..

The first option, Restore Database, displays a list of backups that you can restore from based on the history tables stored in SQL Server. By default, the most recent full database backup will be shown first, followed by the transaction log and differential backups performed after it. You can use the drop-down list to select an earlier full database backup.

The second option, Restore Filegroups or Files, also displays a list of backups that you can restore from based on the history tables. Along with a list of previous filegroup backups, you may notice that full database and transaction log backups are also listed. They are shown because a filegroup can also be restored from a full database and transaction log backup.

FIGURE 15.9
Use this dialog if restoring from a backup not recorded in SQL Server's history tables.

Caution: Restoration might not be available

Just because a backup is listed in the drop-down box doesn't mean that you will be able to restore from it. The history tables in SQL Server record where the database was backed up to when the backup was performed. If the backup files have since been overwritten or deleted, you will not be able to restore from that backup.

The third option, Restore From Device, is used when the backup you want to restore from isn't listed in the history tables. This can occur if you are restoring a database copied from another SQL Server.

How to Restore a Full Database and Differential Restores

If the database was backed up on this SQL Server, you can select Restore Database to perform the backup; otherwise you will need to select Restore From Device and select the files containing the backups manually.

When restoring from backup, the first file restored has to be a full database backup. The drop-down list, First Backup to Restore, provides a list of known full backups. In most cases, you will want to restore from the most recent full backup. The dialog will display the full backup along with subsequent transaction log and differential backups. SQL Server selects all or some of the transaction log and differential backups to be restored with the full backup automatically. The combination selected by SQL Server provides the most up-to-date image of the database in the shortest recovery time.

If you don't want to also restore the transaction log backups, you can deselect them by clicking the check box to the left of each log. If you deselect a transaction log, transaction logs that follow the deselected log on the list will also be automatically deselected. You cannot skip any transaction logs in the restoration process.

If a differential backup of the database was performed, it will also be selected along with the full database backup. Only the most recent differential backup will be selected.

If you want to restore the database backup to a specific point in time, you must select a transaction log, and then select the Point in Time Restore check box and enter the desired date and time to restore to in the dialog provided.

Select the OK button to begin the restore. If any users are in the database, the restore process will wait a short time, and then terminate unsuccessfully.

SEE ALSO
➤ *Please read "Ways to Restore Databases" on page 485, earlier in this chapter, for the reasoning behind SQL Server's selection.*

How to Restore a Filegroup or File

If you choose to restore from a filegroup backup, any transaction log backups performed after the filegroup backup will also be automatically selected. You should leave the transaction log selected so that the filegroup you are restoring can be synchronized with the other filegroups in the database.

Making a Copy of a Database Using Restore

SQL Server makes it very easy to make a copy of a database into another database. If you want to see how your database looked three days ago, but you don't want to overwrite your existing database, you can simply restore your backup of the database into a different database name. SQL Server will create the new database for you.

Making a copy of a database using Restore

1. Select the database backup you want to restore from in the lower half of the Restore dialog.

2. Then select the Options tab shown in Figure 15.10.

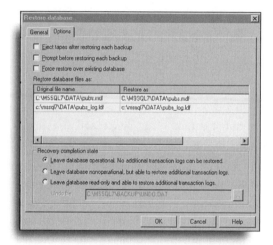

3. Select the General Tab and type in the new database name to Restore as.

4. You will also need to change the names of the physical files that the database will be restored as on the Options Tab.

5. Select the OK button and the new database will be created.

Restoring a Database and Its Log Using Transact-SQL

Use Transact-SQL to restore a database by executing the SQL from within Query Analyzer or the command prompt program ISQL. The command to restore the pubs database from a full database backup is

```
RESTORE DATABASE pubs FROM pubs_bkp WITH REPLACE
```

The REPLACE option is used to replace the contents of an *existing* pubs database. REPLACE isn't necessary if the database doesn't exist. Pubs_bkp represents a backup device, essentially a pointer to a file containing a database backup. For instructions on creating backup devices, see Chapter 14. To restore a database from a disk file without using a backup device, use

```
RESTORE DATABASE pubs FROM DISK='d:\sql70\backups\pubs.bkp'
➥WITH REPLACE
```

To place the database into different files or a different directory than the one in which the backup was created, specify the MOVE option:

```
RESTORE DATABASE pubs FROM pubs_bkp WITH MOVE 'dbFile1'
➥TO 'C:\dbs\pubs.mdf'
```

The first parameter following MOVE represents the logical database filename. Large databases may reside on multiple logical files.

Restoring a database from transaction log backups requires multiple steps. The first RESTORE command restores from a full database backup. A subsequent RESTORE LOG command is needed for each transaction log. Here is a complete example:

```
RESTORE DATABASE pubs FROM pubs_bkp WITH REPLACE, NORECOVERY
RESTORE LOG pubs FROM pubs_lg1 WITH NORECOVERY
RESTORE LOG pubs FROM pubs_lg2 WITH RECOVERY
```

Notice the NORECOVERY option is specified on the first two commands. This command informs SQL Server that this isn't the last piece of the backup. After a RESTORE is performed using WITH RECOVERY (which is the default), no additional logs can be applied.

To restore to a single point in time:

```
RESTORE LOG pubs FROM pubs_bkp
➥WITH STOPAT '1998 022717:00:00'
```

The Transact-SQL command to restore a differential backup is

```
RESTORE DATABASE pubs FROM pubs_bkpDf
```

The Transact-SQL command to restore to single database file is

```
RESTORE LOG pubs dbFile1 FROM pubs_bkp WITH NORECOVER
```

> **Load is a synonym for Restore**
>
> Previous versions of SQL Server used the **LOAD** command instead of **RESTORE**. **LOAD** is still supported as a synonym of **RESTORE** for backward compatibility but may not be supported in future versions.

How to Restore System Databases

The process for restoring system databases is similar to restoring user databases, but there are some differences. Most notable is the impact of losing the master database. When the master database is lost, you cannot start SQL Server to even attempt a database restore. This section provides instructions for recovering your system if the master database is lost. For the other system databases (model, msdb, and distribution), you can use the same recovery steps described for user databases in the preceding sections. Use the steps outlined in the following two sections to recover from the loss of the master database.

How to Restore the Master Database

Because SQL Server cannot start without the master database, you first to need create a valid master database for it to start from.

Restoring the master database

1. If possible, make copies of your msdb, model, and distribution databases. Rebuilding master will cause these databases to be rebuilt as well.

2. Run SQL Server Setup and select Rebuild Master. You are prompted for a directory and database size. Enter a size equal to or greater than your lost master database. Make sure you enter the same sort order, code page, and Unicode collation used on the previous version of master. Setup will begin building a new master database. When the rebuild process completes, a master database is created, but this master database contains no information about the user databases, backup devices, system configurations, user logins, and other information contained on your previous master. The purpose of the newly created master is to give you a way to restart SQL Server and perform a restore of the master from your backup copy.

3. Start SQL Server and log in with the sa account and no password.

4. Create a backup device pointing to the file containing the most recent backup of your original master database.

5. Restore master from the backup as you would any other database.

6. Stop and restart SQL Server.

7. If you made any changes to master since the last backup of master, you will need to re-apply them.

8. Restore your latest copies of msdb, model, and distribution databases.

In most circumstances, you will be able to start SQL Server with SQL Server Manager or SEM. However, the configuration of some SQL Servers requires you to start SQL Server in minimal configuration mode. Minimal configuration mode starts SQL Server with minimally configured resources:

- Server configurations are changed. User connections, tempdb size, open objects, and open databases are set to minimum values.

- SQL Server starts in single-user mode. Therefore, you need to make certain that no other processes are logged into the SQL Server or you will not be able to make the one connection you need to restore the master from a backup. Processes that may need to be stopped include SQL Server Agent, NT Performance Monitor, and MS DTC.

- Startup stored procedures don't run.

If you use SEM to build the backup device and issue the RESTORE command, keep your activities within SEM to a minimum. Some SEM options open additional connections to the SQL Server and these will fail in single-user mode. You may need to use ISQL from the command prompt to restore the master database.

Starting SQL Server in minimal configuration

1. Select MSSQLServer in the Service list box.

2. Type -f in the Startup Parameters box.

3. Click Start.

How to Recover the Master Database Without a Backup

If you discover that you don't have a good backup of your master database, you can still use the rebuild master operation to get SQL Server functioning again, but more work is required to gain access to all the other databases that were part of the SQL Server. You cannot really *recover* the master database if you don't

---

Use an operating system backup

It is easier to recover a lost master database if you have an operating system backup of the master database file. To create this backup, stop SQL Server and use Windows NT Explorer to copy the file to another location. To recover master using a file backup simply requires copying the backup file to the location of the original and restarting SQL Server.

have a backup, but you can attempt to recreate all the information that it contained. Your first step will be to rebuild the master as described in the preceding section. You then need to recreate user logins, database options, system configurations, backup devices, and information about other servers. Hopefully you have some of this information stored in script files or printouts. If not, you will have to reconfigure the SQL Server based on your memory of what it contained.

Recovering the master database without a backup

1. If possible, make copies of your msdb, model, and distribution databases. Rebuilding the master will cause these databases to be rebuilt as well.

2. Run SQL Server Setup and select Rebuild Master as described previously.

3. Re-create backup devices.

4. Restore your latest copies of msdb, model, and distribution databases.

5. Reattach user databases. The following is an example of the command to reattach the pubs database to the SQL Server:
```
EXEC sp_attach_db @dbname = N'pubs',
@filename1 = N'c:\mssql7\data\pubs.mdf',
@filename2 = N'c:\mssql7\data\pubs_log.ldf'
```

6. Re-associate usernames in databases with SQL Server login IDs. Use sp_addlogin to accomplish this. On servers using SQL Server Authentication, all users need to be notified of their newly assigned password.

7. Reset Database options such as Select Into/Bulk Copy to their previous values.

8. SQL Server properties need to be re-entered. This includes SQL Mail login, Security Information, Memory configuration, and other values entered in the SQL Server properties dialog.

Testing Restore Procedures

To make sure that you don't overlook any of the steps required to restore a database successfully, you should develop a plan that lists the steps to restore SQL Server to operation in the event of a disaster. After the plan is developed, you then must test it to be sure that it will actually work. Testing the plan is tedious, but it is the only way to be certain that the data you have backed up can be restored successfully. Unfortunately, many sites have a database that is so large it cannot be restored on any other SQL Servers. If this scenario applies to your SQL Server, you will have to decide if you are willing to risk overwriting your actual production database just to test the restore process. One alternative is to back up a smaller database on the same server using the same backup strategy (database file backups, differential, and so on), and then restore this smaller database and confirm that you can do so successfully to verify the strategy you will use with the larger database.

Warning: Check your backup tapes thoroughly

I have worked with multiple companies that had backup processes that ran for hours, ended successfully, and were successfully "verified" by the backup software. However, when they actually needed to restore from the backup they discovered the backup tapes were empty or unusable.

part

VI

Advanced SQL Server Administration

chapter

16

Importing, Exporting, and Distributing Data

Learn to use the DTS utility

Explore the BCP program for moving data

Use the *BULK INSERT* command

Create and install removable databases

One of the most common tasks of data management is the transfer of information from one system to another, whether this be a file for, or from, a mainframe or a file to be used within Microsoft's Excel. This allows an organization to collect data from many sources into one centrally managed, and therefore accessible, source.

With the arrival of SQL Server 7.0, you now have a number of options that allow you to choose the right tool for the task at hand:

- Bulk Copy Program (BCP), or the BULK INSERT command
- Data Transformation Services (DTS)
- Removable Databases

In this chapter, you will look at what each of these tools can do and how to use them to their full potential.

Data Transformation Services (DTS)

The Data Transformation Services (DTS) enables you to import and export data between multiple heterogeneous sources. The different sources can be based on the OLE DB architecture, ODBC, a text file, or other Microsoft SQL Servers.

This gives access to the following sources of data for the DTS to work with:

- OLE DB—MS SQL Server, MS Excel, and MS Access
- ODBC—Supported MS OLE DB providers for ODBC, such as Oracle and DB2
- Flat files—any character format you want

Using the DTS, you can transfer not only data but other database objects. These can be tables, indexes, and other physical objects, but also include users, roles, and permissions.

The DTS is in fact a lot more than a replacement for the Transfer Manager of previous versions of SQL Server. As the second part of its name indicates, you can also carry out transformations on the data that is being transferred. Transformations are series of operations that you apply to the data before it is written to the destination, which allow you to change and validate data values.

Using any language that supports OLE automation, such as Visual Basic, you can create the tasks that make up a DTS package. These tasks can be combined for execution in a coordinated sequence. After a package has been created, you can store it in one of three locations for future use and modifications:

- The `msdb` database—Central access across all SQL Server installations.
- Microsoft Repository—More overhead than storing in `msdb` but allows data lineage tracking and metadata storage. Also available across all SQL Server installations.
- COM-structured storage file—This format allows easy distribution via email or file sharing.

A stored package, because it is a self-contained unit, can be retrieved and executed using the Enterprise Manager interface or from the command line using the `dtsrun` utility.

Microsoft Repository

The Microsoft Repository is the preferred storage choice when working within a data warehousing environment because it provides the ability to track data lineage. The Microsoft Data Warehousing Framework defines database schemas and transformations that are implemented within the Repository as a set of ActiveX interfaces. Even though the Repository, by default, is installed in the `msdb` database, a single SQL Server can hold any number of Repositories.

Repository restrictions

The Enterprise Manager only supports a single Repository database per server.

Scripting

When you write transformation scripts, you can use the Active Scripting JScript and VBScript languages to make use of the following three exposed collections:

- DTSDestination
- DTSSource
- DTSGlobalVariables

511

The first two collections, DTSDestination and DTSSource, have just one property, Count, and one method, Item.

The Count property specifies the number of columns, so the number of columns in the destination is DTSDestination.Count.

The Item method takes either the column by name or position, and allows you to get and set column values. For example, to take the last_name column from the source and place it in the third destination column you would write it as:

```
DTSDestination(3) = DTSSource("last_name")
```

The DTSGlobalVariables collection allows you access to Active Data Objects (ADO).

When the DTS package is executed, the DTSSource collection is loaded with all the values from the source columns. You can carry out straight copy operations like you just saw, or more complex transformations.

Transformations

Transformations can be coded using either the OLE Automation interface implemented within DTSPKG.DLL) or directly to the data pump through the COM interface by DTSPUMP.DLL. The transformation tasks can be created on the following bases:

- Source→straight copy→Destination
- Source→Transform (VBScript/Java/COM Object)→Destination
- ActiveX Script (VBScript, JScript)
- External.exe
- SQL Server Source→object transfer→SQL Server Destination

Any transformation can occur only on columns mentioned as part of the source, and may not use others from the same table or source if they are not implicitly part of the DTSSource collection.

Using ActiveX Data Objects (ADO), your ActiveX scripts can also invoke additional objects supporting OLE Automation, including invocation of other DTS packages.

When using ADO, the DTS also provides access to the following additional properties:

- `ActualSize`
- `Attributes`
- `DefinedSize`
- `Name`
- `NumericScale`
- `OriginalValue`
- `Precision`
- `Recordset`
- `Type`
- `UnderlyingValue`
- `Value`

There is also a `DTSLookups` collection that provides you with access to lookup tables that are needed within the transformation.

In the following section, you will take a step-by-step look at how to carry out a data import with simple transformation.

Using the DTS

As an example of what the DTS can do, you will make a copy of a table and its data from one database to another.

Using DTS

1. You can create a DTS package by opening the Data Transformation Services folder, right-clicking Local Packages, and choosing New Package. This will open the DTS Package: <New Package> window.

2. Because you are taking data from one database table to another, you will be using a data source and a data destination. To specify these, you need to select and drag the first

Where to get some examples

Microsoft has provided a number of sample programs using Visual Basic 5.0 and Visual C++ 5.0 to help understand how to develop for the Data Transformation Service. These samples can be found in the `\Devtools\Samples\Dts` directory on the Microsoft SQL Server 7.0 CD-ROM.

icon in the Data area of the toolbar into the workspace. When you release the mouse button, the Connection Properties window (see Figure 16.2) appears.

FIGURE 16.1

The DTS Package: <New Package> window.

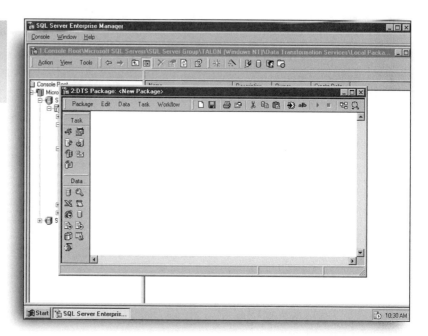

FIGURE 16.2

Connection Properties window.

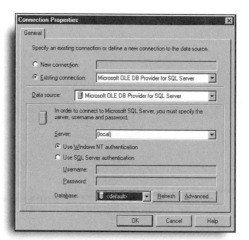

This is where you choose the current location of the data. Take a moment and have a look at the multitude of source options you have listed in the source drop-down list. You will be using Microsoft OLE DB Povider for SQL Server as your source, your local server, in fact. You can change the source type to any of the available ones, and the DTS Wizard will change the icon in the workspace appropriately. This saves you from having to delete and add a data source of the correct type. The fields below this list provide the necessary server and login information.

3. The source database you will use is pubs, so select this from the database drop-down list. If for some reason the database doesn't appear in the list, you can use the Refresh button. Name this connection Source. After you have made your choices, click OK.

4. Repeat these steps for the destination. Make the same choices you made previously except for the database, choose tempdb, and name this connection Destination.

5. The final component is to specify a Data Transform. To do this, first click in the workspace and drag the rubber band box so it encloses both the Source and Destination data sources you just created. Then, click the Data Transform icon, which is the eighth icon on the toolbar. This will draw a line between the two sources. If you double-click the line, or right-click and choose Properties, you will open the Data Transformation Properties window (see Figure 16.3).

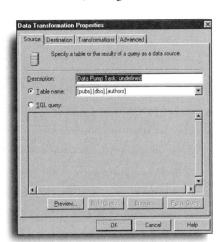

FIGURE 16.3
Data Transformation Properties window.

This window is broken out into four tabs that allow you to control the entire transfer process.

- The Source tab is where you choose the table or tables (if you choose the SQL Query option) that you are collecting the data from. By default the Authors table will already be selected along with the Source connection. This is exactly what you wanted, so let us move onto the Destination tab.

- By clicking the Destination tab, you will be shown another window, Create Destination Table (see Figure 16.4), where you can specify the structure of the receiving table.

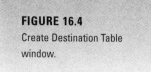

FIGURE 16.4

Create Destination Table window.

In this window, change the name of the table to my_authors and add a new column at the end of the column list with the following properties:

```
..
[contract] bit NOT NULL,
[my_id] int NOT NULL
)
```

- The Connection list should already be defaulted to the Destination connection you created earlier. If you need to change the number or properties of any column, simply click the Create New button.

6. You will now look at the transformation stage of the transfer. This is on the Transformations tab (see Figure 16.5).

FIGURE 16.5
The Transformations tab.

7. As you can see, the wizard has already created Copy mappings from the source column to a destination column. You will be carrying out a simple transformation on the au_id column to create the new my_id column in the destination my_authors table. To do this, change the New transformation selection at the bottom of this window to ActiveX Script.

Next, click the my_id column on the right and drag and release this on the au_id column on the Source table side of the window. This creates a new transformation. The ActiveX Script Transformation Properties window (see Figure 16.6) appears to allow the specification of the transformation.

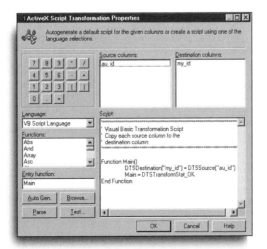

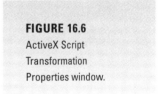

FIGURE 16.6
ActiveX Script Transformation Properties window.

8. In the script area of this window, you can code whatever transformation function that you want, using your choice of VB Script or JScript. You will carry out a simple manipulation by taking the first three characters of the au_id data and turn it into an integer. To do this, modify the code to look like this:

```
'*********************************************************
*
'   Visual Basic Transformation Script
'   Copy each source column to the
'   destination column
'*********************************************************
*

Function Main()
    DTSDestination("my_id") =
                        Int( Left( DTSSource("au_id"),
3))
    Main = DTSTransformStat_OK
End Function
```

9. After you have modified the code, click OK to return to the Transformations window. You will notice a new line has been drawn between the two columns you were working with. To edit the transformation you have defined, simply right-click the line and choose Properties. You can also delete transformation or copy operations in the same way.

10. The Advanced tab (see Figure 16.7) allows you to control the rows that get transferred as well as the error handling.

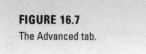

FIGURE 16.7
The Advanced tab.

11. When you have reviewed all of your settings, click OK to
finish the transformation object. You can now save this DTS
process as a package stored on the SQL Server. You do this
by right-clicking on the workspace background and choosing Save from the menu to open the Save DTS Package
window (see Figure 16.8).

FIGURE 16.8
Save DTS Package
window.

12. This is the window where you can specify the package name,
and where you want to save it. You can also assign security
to the package by specifying passwords. The owner password allows control over who can modify the behavior of
the package, and the user password allows control over
who can execute the package. Give the package a name
and click OK.

Now that you have stored the DTS package, you can execute
as and when you want, set up a schedule, and modify it any time
you want.

To make sure the package works, you can also execute it from
within this workspace. This can be done from the right mouse
button menu, or from the toolbar and will open the Executing
Package (see Figure 16.9) window, which shows each of the
steps as they are processed along with an indication of the
success or failure.

Bulk Copy Program (BCP)

Improvements to BCP

The version of BCP that comes with SQL Server 7.0 has additional enhancements that work with the Query Processor to speed up performance even more. The new addition to the data transfer toolkit is the BULK INSERT statement, which allows data loads into a table, but does so from a SQL statement rather than the command line as BCP does.

The Bulk Copy Program (BCP) is a data load and unload utility provided by Microsoft. It allows single file to single table data importation and exportation. Even with the introduction of the MS Data Transformation Services (DTS), there are a huge number of existing data load scripts that make use of BCP still in use. BCP also has the advantage over the DTS in that data loads can be made faster, and with large amounts of data. In these cases, BCP is still the mechanism of choice.

Logged and Non-logged Operations

Caution: Backup might be restricted

Remember that setting the SELECT INTO/BULK COPY option disables the ability to back up the transaction log until a full database backup has been performed. If the database had to be restored, the transaction log would not contain a record of the new data.

There are two modes that bulk-copy operations can happen in: logged and non-logged. These are also known as slow and fast BCP respectively. Usually, the ideal situation is to have them non-logged because this dramatically decreases the time to load and the consumption of other system resources such as memory, the processor, and extensive disk access. The default is for the load to run in logged mode, which causes the log to grow rapidly for large volumes of data.

To achieve a non-logged operation, the target table must not be replicated because the replication log reader needs log records to relay the changes made. The database holding the target table must also have its SELECT INTO/BULK COPY option set, and lastly, the table must not have any triggers.

Some logging still occurs

Even the so-called non-logged operation is logging some things. In the case of indexes, index page changes and allocations are logged, but mainly it's extent allocations every time the table is extended for additional storage space for the new rows.

Fast loads can still be done against tables that have indexes, although it is more advisable to drop and re-create them after the operation. Generally, you get at least a 50% drop in transfer speed if the table has an index. The more indexes, the greater the performance degradation. This is due to the logging factor, more log records are being generated and index pages are being loaded into the cache and modified. This can also cause the log to grow, possibly filling it (depending on your log file settings).

Some third-party tool vendors, notably Platinum Technologies, have fast load and unload utilities that have proved faster than Microsoft's 6.5 utilities. It will be interesting to see if they can improve any on the newest version of BCP and the BULK INSERT command.

Parallel Loading

One of the advantages of data loads using SQL Server 7.0 over previous versions is that multiple clients can work in concert to load the data from a file in parallel. To take advantage of this new feature, the following must be true:

- The bulk-copy operation will be non-logged; all requirements just specified must be met.

- There are no indexes on the target table.

The procedure is very straightforward. After you have ascertained that the target table has no indexes (which may involve dropping primary or unique constraints), and isn't being replicated, you must set the database option SELECT INTO/BULK COPY to true. The requirement to drop all indexes comes from the locking that needs to occur to load the data; the table itself can have a shared lock but the index pages are an area of contention that prevents parallel access.

Now all that is required is to set up the clients (these can be different command windows on the server/client, or on different client machines) to load the data into the table. You can make use of the -F and -L switches to specify the range of the data you want each client to load into the table if you are using the same data file; this removes the need to manually break up the file. An example of the command switches involved for a parallel load with BCP is:

```
bcp pubs..new_authors in newauthors.dat /T /Sraven /c
➡/F1 /L10000 /h"TABLOCK"
```

The TABLOCK hint provides better performance by removing contention from other users while the load takes place. If you don't use the hint, the load will take place using row level locks.

SQL Server 7.0 allows parallel loads without affecting performance by making each connection create extents in non-overlapping ranges; these are then linked into the tables page chain.

> **Parallel Loading**
>
> The parallel loading feature is only available with the ODBC- or SQLOLEDB-based APIs of version 7.0..

BCP Switches

BCP is very customizable and comes with a large number of switches. You should remember that these switches *are* case-sensitive.

521

Switch	Description
-n	Native data format
-c	Character data format
-w	Unicode data format
-N	Use Unicode for character data and native format for all others.
-C	If you are loading extended characters, this switch enables you to specify the code page of the data in the data file.
-E	Use identity values in file rather than generating new ones.
-6	Use pre-7.0 data types. This option is required when loading native 6.x BCP files.
-b	The number of rows to include in each committed batch.
-m	The maximum errors to allow before stopping the transfer.
-e	The file to write error messages to.
-f	The format file used to customize the load or unload data in a specific style.
-F	The first row to start copying from in the data file when importing.
-L	The last row to end copying with in the data file when importing.
-t	The terminating character(s) for fields.
-r	The terminating character(s) for rows.
-i	A file for redirecting input into BCP.
-o	The file for receiving redirected output from BCP.
-a	The network packet size used to send to or receive from the server.

continues...

...continued

-q	This tells BCP to use quoted identifiers when dealing with table and column names.
-k	Overrides a column's default, and enforces NULL values load as part of the BCP operation.
-h	The 7.0 hint options.
-U	The user account to login as. This account will need sufficient privileges to carry out either a read or write of the table.
-P	The password associated with the user account.
-S	The SQL Server's name
-v	The version number of BCP.
-T	Make a trusted connection to the SQL Server.

In the following sections, you will look at some of these switches, what they mean, and how and when they should be used. The remainder are obvious in their use. The syntax for all of the switches is bcp /*switch*, such as bcp /v.

Batches

By default, BCP collects all the rows being inserted into the target table and commits them as one large transaction. This reduces the amount of work that has to be done with regards the log; however, it locks down the transaction log by keeping a large part of it still active. This can make truncating or backing up the transaction log impossible or unproductive.

By using the batch (-b) switch, you can control the number of rows per batch. This controls the frequency of commits, and while increasing the activity in the log, gives you the ability to keep the transaction log trimmed down in size. You should tune

Hint for troubleshooting batches

By making the batch size just a few rows, you can more easily identify which ones are giving you problems. When used in conjunction with the -F and -L switches, it is an effective data file debugging tool.

the batch size in relation to the size of the data rows, transaction log size, and total number of rows to be loaded. One value for one load may not necessarily be the right one for a different table.

Remember that specifying a value for this switch causes batches to commit on the server. If the third batch fails, the first and second batches *are* committed, and the rows are now part of the table. However, any rows copied up to the point of failure in the third batch are rolled back.

File Datatypes

BCP can handle data in one of three forms: character (ASCII), native, or Unicode. You have the choice of what character format is used depending on the source or destination of the data file.

Character

The character format (-c) is the most commonly used of the three as it reads or writes using ASCII characters and carries out the appropriate data type conversion for the SQL Server representations. The CHAR data type is the default storage type, and makes use of tabs as the field separators, and new line as the row terminator.

Native

Native format (-n) is used when copying data between SQL Servers. This allows BCP to read and write using the same data types as used by SQL Server, leading to a performance gain. This does, however, render the data file unreadable by any other means.

Unicode

The Unicode option (-w) makes use of Unicode characters rather than ASCII. The NCHAR data type is the default storage type, and makes use of tabs as the field separators, and new line as the row terminator.

The Format File

By making use of a format file, you can customize the data file created by BCP or specify complex field layouts for data loads. There are two ways to create this file: Interactive BCP and the format switch.

Customizing a Format File Using Interactive BCP

If you don't specify any of the ·n, ·c, or ·w switches, BCP will prompt you for the following information for each column in the data set:

- File storage type
- Prefix length
- Field length
- Field terminator

BCP will offer you a default for each of these prompts, which you can accept. If you accept all the defaults, you will obtain the same format file as you would have by specifying the native format. The prompts look like this:

```
Enter the file storage type of field au_id [char]:
Enter prefix length of field au_id [0]:
Enter length of field au_id [11]:
Enter field terminator [none]:
```

By pressing Enter at the prompt, you take the default. You can type your own value at the prompt instead.

Creating a Format File by a Switch

By making use of the new 7.0 format option, a format file can be created without actually transferring any data. An example of creating a format file for the authors table in the pubs database is:

```
bcp pubs..authors format junk /Sraven /T /fauthors.fmt /c
```

①	Version of BCP			
②	Number of columns			
③	Data field position			
④	Data type			
⑤	Prefix			
⑥	Data file field length			
⑦	Field or Row Terminator			
⑧	Column position			
⑨	Column name			

The format created looks like this:

① 7.0 9	② ④		⑤	⑥	⑦	⑧	⑨
③ 1	SQLCHAR	0	11	"\t"	1	au_id
2	SQLCHAR	0	40	"\t"	2	au_lname
3	SQLCHAR	0	20	"\t"	3	au_fname
4	SQLCHAR	0	12	"\t"	4	phone
5	SQLCHAR	0	40	"\t"	5	address
6	SQLCHAR	0	20	"\t"	6	city
7	SQLCHAR	0	2	"\t"	7	state
8	SQLCHAR	0	5	"\t"	8	zip
9	SQLCHAR	0	3	"\r\n"	9	contract

You will get a different looking format file depending on your table and whether you chose character, native, or Unicode as your data type. As you can see, only the last two columns in the format file relate to the actual table, the remainder specify properties of the data file.

File Storage Type

The storage type is the description of how the data is stored in the data file. This allows data to be copied as its base type (native format), implicitly converted between types (tinyint to smallint), or copied as a string (character or Unicode format.)

If the table makes use of user-defined data types, these will appear in the format file as their base types.

If you are having problems loading certain fields into your table, you can try the following tricks:

- Copy the data in as CHAR data types, and force SQL Server to do the conversion for you.
- Duplicate the table replacing all the SQL Server data types with CHAR or VARCHAR of a length sufficient to hold the value. This enables you to carry further manipulation of the data once loaded using Transact-SQL.

Prefix Length

For reasons of compactness in native data files BCP precedes each field with a prefix length that indicates the length of the data stored. The space for storing this information is specified in characters and is the *prefix length*.

Prefix lengths are likely only to exist within data files created using BCP and it is unlikely that you will encounter a reason to change the defaults it will have chosen for you.

Field Length

When using either native or character data formats, you need to specify the maximum length of each field. When converting data types to strings, BCP will suggest lengths that are large enough to store the entire range of values for each particular data type.

You need to specify a length that is sufficiently long for the data being stored. If you see any BCP error messages regarding overflows, this indicates that the data value has been truncated in at least one of the fields. If the operation is a load, this will usually end up in BCP exiting. However, if the operation is dumping the data to a file, the data will be truncated without error messages.

The field length value is *only* used when the prefix length is 0 and you have specified no terminators. In essence, you are doing a fixed length data copy. BCP uses the exact amount of space stated by field length for each field, unused space within the field is padded out.

Using spaces

Pre-existing spaces in the data are not distinguished from the added padding.

Field Terminator

If you are not making use of fixed width fields or length prefixes, you must use a field terminator to indicate the character(s) between each field, and for the last field in the data row the character(s) add the end of each line.

BCP recognizes the following indicators for special characters:

Terminator	Escape Code
Tab	\t
Backslash	\\
Null terminator	\0
Newline	\n
Carriage return	\r

You cannot use spaces as terminators, but you can use any other printable character. You need to choose field and row terminators that make sense for your data. Obviously, you should not make use of any character you are trying to load. The \r and \n characters need to be combined to get your data into an ASCII data file with each row on its own line.

In the next few sections, you will examine how to load data into tables where there are differences in column number and layout.

Different Number of Columns in File/Table

If you have fewer fields in a data file than exist in the table, you need to dummy up an extra line in your format file.

Overriding defaults

By specifying the -t and -r switches, you can override the defaults that appear for the prompts during interactive BCP.

For our next example, let us assume that you want to load in a data file that is missing the majority of the address information for each author. By making use of the same format file you created previously in the section "The Format File," you can still load the data file, if the data file looks like this:

```
100-10-1000 Gallagher Simon 317 638-7909 Indianapolis
100-10-1001 Herbert Simon 812 462-6700 St.Paul
```

To introduce a dummy value for the missing ones, you need to make the following changes to the format file: make the prefix and data lengths 0 and the field terminator nothing (" ").

Thus the format created will look like this:

```
7.0
9
1       SQLCHAR     0       11      "\t"    1       au_id
2       SQLCHAR     0       40      "\t"    2       au_lname
3       SQLCHAR     0       20      "\t"    3       au_fname
4       SQLCHAR     0       12      "\t"    4       phone
5       SQLCHAR     0       0       " "     5       address
6       SQLCHAR     0       20      "\t"    6       city
7       SQLCHAR     0       0       " "     7       state
8       SQLCHAR     0       0       " "     8       zip
9       SQLCHAR     0       3       "\r\n"  9       contract
```

BCP can now load the data file by making use of this new format file, with the address, state, and zip columns containing NULLs for the new rows.

For data files that have more fields than the table has columns, change the format file to add additional lines of information. Consider if your new author data file contains a second address line and a country:

100-10-1000 Gallagher Simon 317 638-7809 230 S.St Ste.220
➥Indianapolis IN 46225 US 1
100-10-1001 Herbert Simon 812 462-6700 6th St. Ste.123
➥St.Paul MN 76231 USA 0

Again making use of the same format file as before, you modify it in two important areas: change the second line to reflect the actual number of values, and add new lines for each additional column in the file that isn't in the table. Notice that the column position has a value of 0, to indicate the absence of a column in the table.

Thus the format created will look like this:

```
7.0
11
1       SQLCHAR     0     11     "\t"     1     au_id
2       SQLCHAR     0     40     "\t"     2     au_lname
3       SQLCHAR     0     20     "\t"     3     au_fname
4       SQLCHAR     0     12     "\t"     4     phone
5       SQLCHAR     0     40     "\t"     5     address
6       SQLCHAR     0     40     "\t"     0     address2
7       SQLCHAR     0     20     "\t"     6     city
8       SQLCHAR     0     2      "\t"     7     state
9       SQLCHAR     0     5      "\t"     8     zip
10      SQLCHAR     0     0      "\t"     0     country
11      SQLCHAR     0     3      "\r\n"   9     contract
```

These two examples show you the possibilities that the format file offers for customizing the load and unload of data.

Renumbering Columns

Using the techniques just shown, you can also handle data files that have a different order of data to the target table. All that is required is to change the column order number to reflect the correct sequence of the columns in the table.

For example, if the new author data file came with the following layout:

```
<auid><lname><fname><phone><zip><state><city><address>
➥<contract>
```

Then the format file is modified to look like this:

```
7.0
9
1      SQLCHAR      0      11       "\t"       1      au_id
2      SQLCHAR      0      10       "\t"       2      au_lname
3      SQLCHAR      0      20       "\t"       3      au_fname
4      SQLCHAR      0      12       "\t"       4      phone
5      SQLCHAR      0      40       "\t"       8      address
6      SQLCHAR      0      20       "\t"       7      city
7      SQLCHAR      0      2        "\t"       6      state
8      SQLCHAR      0      5        "\t"       5      zip
9      SQLCHAR      0      3        "\r\n"     9      contract
```

The principal thing to remember with the format file is that all but the last two columns deal with the data file, and the last two specify the database table.

Using Views

The one big disadvantage of BCP is that it operates on a single table. Well, that's not strictly true; this is actually a limitation of the syntax. Data can actually be unloaded from a view, which allows the collection of data from multiple tables (and with distributed queries even multiple servers).

You can also bulk copy back in through the view, but as with normal Transact-SQL modifications, only into one of the underlying tables at a time.

Loading Image Data

You can also load binary large objects (BLOB) into SQL Server tables. This operation requires the use of a format file that specifies how much data is going in and into which column.

The format file would look like this:

```
7.0
1
1      SQLBINARY    0      12578         " "        1      column1
```

where column1 is the column name within the table that you are loading the image into.

You can then load a Word document using the command:

```
bcp mydb..documents in analysis.doc -T -Smyserver -fmyfmt.fmt
```

Using the format file previously defined, this will load the 12578 byte document into `column1`.

You can also make use of the BULK INSERT statement to do the same operation:

```
BULK INSERT mydb..documents FROM 'c:\analysis.doc'
WITH ( FORMATFILE = 'c:\myfmt.fmt' )
```

Supplying Hints to BCP

The new version of BCP also comes with the ability to further control the speed of data loading via the use of hints. These hints are specified using the -h switch:

```
-h "hint [, hint]"
```

This option cannot be used when bulk copying data into versions prior to SQL Server 7.0, and is because BCP can now work in conjunction with the query processor. The query processor will optimize data loads and unloads for OLE DB rowsets, which the latest version of BCP and BULK INSERT can generate.

ROWS_PER_BATCH

The ROWS_PER_BATCH hint is used to tell SQL Server the total number of rows in the data file and internally helps by SQL Server to optimize the entire load operation. This hint and the -b switch heavily influence the logging operations that occur with the data inserts. If you specify both the hint and switch, they must have the same values; otherwise, you will receive an error message.

By using the hint, you are copying the entire resultset as a single transaction, and SQL Server automatically optimizes the load operation using the batch size you specify. The value you specify does *not* have to be accurate, but you will to be aware what the practical limit is going to be based on the database's transaction log.

> **The function of this hint**
>
> Don't be confused by the name of the hint. You are specifying the total file size, not the batch size, as is the case with the -b switch.

Checking constraints shortcut

A simple way to run check constraints is to execute an UPDATE
that sets one column to its current
value. You may want to add a
WHERE clause to restrict it to the
new rows. Be aware that the
UPDATE and not the INSERT
trigger will also be fired.

CHECK_CONSTRAINTS

The CHECK_CONSTRAINTS switch controls whether check constraints are executed as part of the BCP operation. By default
check constraints are not, and this option allows you to turn this
feature back on. You should either be very sure of your data or
rerun the same logic as the check constraints you deferred after
the data has entered the table if you don't use this option.

This hint only enables constraint checking on the target table
for the BCP operation only. Any other data modifications
occurring from other users will still encounter the check constraints as normal.

ORDER

If the data that you want to bulk load is already in the same
sequence as the clustered index on the receiving table, you can
use the ORDER hint. The syntax for this hint is as follows:

```
ORDER( {column [ASC | DESC] [,...n]})
```

There must be a clustered index on the same columns, in the
same key sequence as you specify in the ORDER hint. Using a
sorted data file helps SQL Server place the data into the table.

KILOBYTES_PER_BATCH

The KILOBYTES_PER_BATCH is the size, in kilobytes, of the data
in each batch. This is an estimate and is used internally by
SQL Server to optimize the data load and logging areas of
the BCP operation.

TABLOCK

The TABLOCK hint is used to place a table level lock for the
BCP load duration; this gives you increased performance at a
loss to concurrency. This was discussed in an earlier section,
"Parallel Loading."

BULK INSERT

The BULK INSERT statement is a new introduction with version
7.0 that allows the bulk load of data into a database table. The

two main differences between this statement and BCP is that the former is load- and SQL-based, and the latter is bi-directional and command-line based.

The syntax for this command is

```
BULK INSERT [['database_name'.]['owner'].]
            {'table_name' FROM data_file}
[WITH ( [ BATCHSIZE [ = batch_size]]
      [[,] CHECK_CONSTRAINTS]
      [[,] CODEPAGE [ = ACP ¦ OEM ¦ RAW ¦ code_page]]
      [[,] DATAFILETYPE [ = {'char' ¦ 'native'¦
                             'widechar' ¦ 'widenative'}]]
      [[,] FIELDTERMINATOR [ = 'field_terminator']]
      [[,] FIRSTROW [ = first_row]]
      [[,] FORMATFILE [ = 'format_file_path']]
      [[,] KEEPIDENTITY]  [[,] KEEPNULLS]
      [[,] LASTROW [ = last_row]]
      [[,] MAXERRORS [ = max_errors]]
      [[,] ORDER ({column [ASC ¦ DESC]} [, Ön])]
      [[,] ROWS_PER BATCH [=rowsperbatch]]
      [[,] ROWTERMINATOR [ = 'row_terminator']]
      [[,] TABLOCK] )]
```

As you can see from the options for this command, the majority are the same or similar to switches you specify for the BCP program.

The CODEPAGE option is used when you need to load extended characters (values greater than 127) and enables you to specify one of the following values for char, varchar, and text data types:

- ACP—convert from the ANSI/Microsoft Windows code page (ISO 1252) to the SQL Server code page.

- OEM—convert from the system OEM code page to the SQL Server code page. This is the default.

- RAW—No conversion. This is the fastest option.

- *<value>*—Specific code page number. For example, 850 for the 4.2x default code page.

The DATAFILETYPE option allows the specification of the data character set:

- Char—Data is in ASCII format.

533

- `Native`—Data is in SQL Server native format.

- `Widechar`—Data is in Unicode format.

- `Widenative`—Data is native, except for char, varchar, and text columns, which are stored as Unicode.

The last option, `widenative`, is used when you need to transfer extended characters and want the performance offered by native data files.

To illustrate the various switches, the following example statement loads customer data from the file c:\customer.dat, which is comma separated:

```
BULK INSERT mydb..customers
FROM 'c:\customer.dat'
WITH ( FIELDTERMINATOR = ',', ROWTERMINATOR = '\n' )
```

Improving Load Performance

Other conclusions that you can draw from these values is that running without the `CHECK_CONSTRAINT` hint does speed up the data load (of course you need to be sure of our data, or perform the checks after the load), and that the choice of batch size is also an important influence on the overall speed.

So, the following should be considered as rules for BCP operations:

- You can improve load performance by two or more times by first dropping indexes from the target table.

- Determine the tradeoffs between ignoring CHECK constraints using the BCP hint, and allowing the check to take place as part of the operation. How sure of the data are you?

- Use native mode whenever possible; it is a bit faster.

- If you have a recurring load, take the time to determine the best batch size for it. Otherwise, a figure in the order of a quarter to a half is a good starting point, unless the number of rows is small (less than a few thousand).

- Examine the possibility of doing parallel data loads if you have large data files to load.

- Turn the SELECT/INTO BCP database option on prior to a load. Remember to turn it back off and back up the database afterwards!

Working with Batch Files

The BCP utility is often used in command batch files together with the isql, or the new favorite of version 7.0, osql. To illustrate the interaction between these two tools you will look at a commonly followed process for loading data into production tables (see Figure 16.9).

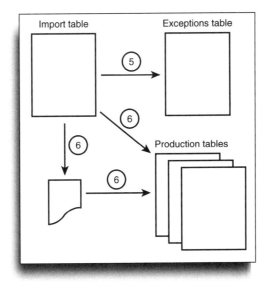

FIGURE 16.9
Loading data into production.

Loading data into production tables

1. osql -Q"create tables"—The first thing to remember is that 99% of the time you should bulk load data into a working table rather than directly into a production table. This is so that you can be sure of the data quality, distribute it among multiple production tables, and cause INSERT triggers to fire. With this in mind, step 1 is the creation of a working import table along with an exception table, which you will describe in a later step. Depending on how you do your cleanup, you might want to execute drop table statements first.

535

2. `osql -Q"sp_dboption 'select into',true"`—Optionally, set the database into SELECT INTO/BULK COPY mode. This allows a fast BCP to be carried out, but will require the database to be dumped at the end of the procedure.

3. `bcp data in`—Next, bulk load the data into the database, either using the BCP utility or with an `osql` executing a BULK INSERT command.

4. `osql -Q"create indexes"`—When you created the import table you did not specify an index creating constraints or any additional indexes in order to get the fastest possible bulk load. For the following steps, some indexes on the table will improve the speed you can carry out checks and joins. You should pick indexes appropriate for these operations.

5. `osql -Q"insert into exceptions"`—To find out which, if any, rows in the import table are bad you need to run a series of scripts that insert into the exception table key fields, or even the entire data row based on the checks, rules, and triggers you have in place on the production tables. For example, let us consider data to be bad if the state field isn't in a certain list, the SQL you might execute would be:

```
INSERT INTO exceptions
( key1, key2, reason )
SELECT author_id, title_id, 'Invalid state value.'
FROM import_table
WHERE state NOT IN ( 'IN', 'IL', 'ID' )
```

This allows us to customize an error message that is stored into the exceptions table detailing which check failed. You would follow each of these with a DELETE statement, acting on the import_table, along the same lines as the above SELECT so that you only have to work on a smaller and smaller valid data set.

6. `osql -Q"insert...select"`—The remaining data records in the import table are now ready to be moved into the production table(s). Here you have a choice depending on your requirements. You can either use INSERTs with SELECTs or use BCP again to unload the data out of the import table and then back into the production table. Using the INSERT enables you

to positively verify that the data is good as the entire range of checks that normally would occur are going to fire. You would choose this method if you have any insert triggers set up that need to be fired; remember BCP doesn't cause triggers to fire. The BCP unload and load will give you the fastest performance and you can easily go against multiple tables by careful use of format files.

7. When finished, you need to remember to turn the SELECT INTO/BULK COPY database option back off.

8. Because you just carried out a bulk unlogged data transfer, you need to backup the database. This will capture your new data, and more importantly re-enable transaction log backups.

All that is left is to clean up and record of what the operations achieved. You can use BCP to unload the exceptions table to a file that you can then email to an operator using another call to osql. Or just execute an osql to query the table and send the results to the operator. You can redirect the output of osql using the -o switch; these various log files can also be collected together for an operator to check over; place them in a certain directory, or email them.

After you have these commands set up, you can build them together into a job that is executed by the SQL Server Agent. This enables you to build in dependencies between the different tasks and enables all the other functionality provided by the agent.

Distributing Databases on Removable Media

If you need to provide a database to a number of sites, you may want to consider creating it for distribution on removable media, like CD-ROMs. This method is best used for large amounts of data that should be treated as read-only, such as product lists, historical data, or similar.

There are three distinct steps involved in creating a database on removable media: Creating the database, moving to the new media, and re-installation. You will examine each of these steps next.

Setting Up a Removable Database

Stored procedure permissions

Only the members of the sysadmin role are able to execute the sp_create_removable procedure.

Rather than using the regular CREATE DATABASE command to create a database that will be removable, you must use the special system stored procedure sp_create_removable. This stored procedure sets up the initial files for the database, one for the system tables, one for the transaction log, and at least one for the data. You will see the reason for the system tables getting their own file in a later step. The syntax for this stored procedure is

```
sp_create_removable [@databasename =] 'databasename',
        'syslogical', 'sysphysical', syssize,
        'loglogical', 'logphysical', logsize,
        'datalogical1', 'dataphysical1', datasize1
        [..., 'datalogical16', 'dataphysical16', datasize16]
```

You specify the name of the database, and then logical, physical, and the sizes of the files for the system tables, log, and data files. You can specify up to 16 data files if you need to break a large database up into a size that will fit on your distribution media of choice.

To illustrate the steps you, will create a database to hold historical_sales data. The stored procedure call would be:

```
sp_create_removable 'sales_1998',
        'sales_1998_sys',
            'c:\mssql7\data\sales_1998_sys.mdf', 2,
        'sales_1998_log',
            'c:\mssql7\data\sales_1998.ldf', 2,
        'sales_1998_data',
            'c:\mssql7\data\sales_1998_data.ndf', 640,
        'sales_1998_data2',
            'c:\mssql7\data\sales_1998_data2.ndf', 640
```

When this is executed SQL Server reports the successful creation of each of the database files and their sizes.

You are now ready to start creating your user tables, stored procedures, views, and other database objects. All objects must be created by the database owner. If you will be creating a large number of objects, you will want to make the system file larger to accommodate them.

After you have your tables created, you can use any of the techniques you have already seen in this chapter to import the data into the removable database. After the database is set up the way you want it, you will carry out the steps to move it onto the new media.

Creating a Removable Database

The first task to make the database removable is to ensure that the database is still configured in such a way that it can be made removable. This is done using the sp_certify_removable system stored procedure:

```
sp_certify_removable 'databasename' [, 'auto']
```

The second optional argument should be used if you need to transfer ownership of the database or any database objects to the system administrator. As an additional step it will drop any database users you have created and any non-default permissions. The reason for this is simple: The one user that is guaranteed to be on each and every SQL Server installation is the system administrator; therefore the ownership needs to be set this user account.

Sp_certify_removable updates the statistics on all the tables and reports any ownership problems, if you did not make use of the Auto option. It then takes the database offline and marks the data filegroups as read-only.

At the end of the procedure's execution, some verification information is provided.

After the filegroups have been set offline, you are free to copy or move them onto the removable media.

> **Adding user information**
>
> You can add roles to the database and assign permissions to these. Then, on installation the administrator of the server only needs to add users to the appropriate role(s).

Stored procedure permissions

Only the members of the `sysadmin` role are able to execute the `sp_attach_db` procedure.

Installing a Removable Database

When an administrator receives the media, in your sample CD-ROMs, they need to place the database back online for their users to access the data. The data files can remain on the CD, but you need to move the system tables and transaction log back onto read-write media, that is, the server's hard drive, along with its other database files. The reason for placing these two files back onto the server is so that you can add users to the database, assign additional roles or permissions, and allow transaction logging to take place again if required.

The data files must all be simultaneously accessible so you must either have multiple CD drives available for your two disks, or you can copy one onto the hard drive along with the system and log.

To make the database available, use the `sp_attach_db` system stored procedure:

```
sp_attach_db [@databasename =] 'databasename',
                            'filename_1' [,...16]
```

You need to provide the full path to each of the files for the database. If you continue with the example, and assume you have two CD drives G: and H:, the attachment command would be:

```
sp_attach_db 'sales_1998',
            'c:\mssql7\data\sales_1998_sys.mdf',
            'c:\mssql7\data\sales_1998.ldf',
            'g:\sales_1998_data.ndf',
            'h:\sales_1998_data2.ndf'
```

If you were keeping the same file paths you would only need to specify the primary (.mdf) file; however, in this case as in most other removable databases, the data files are going to exist on a different drive and path structure.

When you have finished with the database, or have received an update to the database, simply use the `sp_detach_db` system stored procedure, delete the files, copy the new files, and reattach the new database files.

chapter
17

Setting Up and Configuring
Data Replication

Describe what replication is and how it
can be used for your business

•

Describe and understand the different
replication topologies available from
SQL Server 7.0

•

Install, modify, and uninstall the
different types of replication topologies

•

SQL Server Replication Overview

This chapter covers how SQL Server 7.0 implements data replication. Data replication in its simplest form is copying data from its source to a destination or multiple destinations.

Data replication allows data to be replicated across the room or across the world automatically. Without data replication, multiple sites would have slow access to their data. By having multiple sites around the world with the same data, this makes the load balancing a reality, as well as making sure that the data is always reachable.

In today's client/server environment, data replication and more specifically, data warehousing, is a hot topic. Replication allows you to distribute your workload to different geographical locations and brings the data closer to your clients. With Merge replication you can guarantee that the updateable data is available around the clock.

Data replication is different from data distribution discussed in Chapter 16, "Importing, Exporting, and Distributing Data," in that data distribution is manual while replications are autonomous. After data replication is configured, no intervention is required by the DBA; data distribution, on the other hand, normally involves copying the data to a specific media device and is then distributed manually on a CD-ROM or other large storage device.

How SQL Server Replicates Data

SQL Server 7.0 replicates databases based on the publish and subscribe model, which began back in the days of SQL Server 6.0. The model is fairly simple, which is why it is so popular. It is made up of Publishers and Subscribers, articles and publications, push and pull subscriptions, and Distributors. Let's take a close look at how each of these roles work.

Publisher-Subscriber Model

If you are a Publisher, you are a server that makes its data available for replication to other servers. The publisher specifies which data is to be replicated and flags changes made to the data since the last synchronization process occurred. To make sure that data integrity is maintained, any data element that is replicated has one and only one publisher. Any number of subscribers can update this data, and this is possible because each publisher can synchronize its own data even when outside sources are modifying it.

Subscribers are servers that store the replicated data and receive updates from the publishers. In previous version of SQL Server, the publisher could typically only perform updates. SQL Server 7.0 however, allows Subscribers to make updates to the data as well. The updates a Subscriber makes are not same as the updates a Publisher makes. (For more information on this, refer to Books Online.) For the moment, just remember that it takes a specific type of replication to provide Subscriber updates; otherwise, only Publisher updates are allowed. A Subscriber can actually become a Publisher, which then allows the server to publish data to other Subscribers. For an example of this type of model, see Figure 17.1.

The Distributor is the server that contains the distribution database. This may be the same physical server as the Publisher or Subscriber, though it doesn't need to be. The Distributor may be on the same physical network or across the world. The role of the Distributor will depend on the type of SQL Server replication used. More information on the Distribution database is discussed later in this chapter.

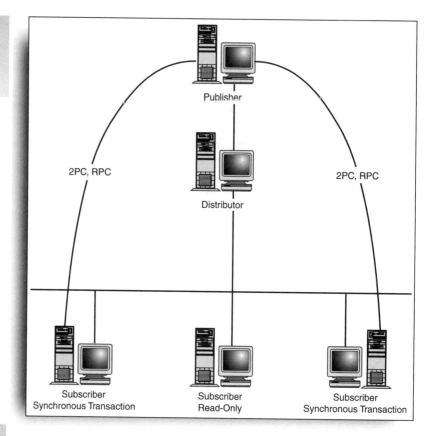

FIGURE 17.1
Publisher, Distributor, and Updateable Subscribers.

Publisher

2PC, RPC

Distributor

2PC, RPC

Subscriber
Synchronous Transaction

Subscriber
Read-Only

Subscriber
Synchronous Transaction

Publications and Articles

A Publication is simply a collection of articles, and an article is a grouping of data to be replicated. This can be an entire table, specific columns of a table (using a vertical filter), specific rows of data (using a horizontal filter), or a combination of both. A Publication often has multiple articles contained within it. Publications can then be considered a grouping of articles, and when you subscribe, you subscribe to Publications—not individual articles. Using this model makes administration much easier than managing individual articles.

Vertical Versus Horizontal Filtering

Vertical filtering is the process of altering the column list for snapshot or transactional publication (not supported for merge

Subscribing to an article

In SQL Server 6.x you could actually subscribe to an individual article. This could easily become an administrative nightmare. Realizing this, the SQL Server team remedied the situation by not supporting this functionality in the user interface. I say *the user interface* because in all actuality, subscribing to an article is still allowed, but only for backward compatibility. If you are upgrading to SQL Server 7.0 and have 6.x versions, subscribing to articles will still work with SQL Server 7.0. It is suggested, however, that you begin to migrate from these articles to publication(s).

publications). This feature enables you to show only a subset of the data on a column basis. This doesn't produce a significant performance drain on the server. It can increase performance on the Subscriber, though. This is simply because less data needs to be updated on the Subscriber. You can visualize a Vertical filter with a SQL statement.

```
USE pubs
SELECT * FROM AUTHORS
```

And

```
USE pubs
SELECT au_fname, au_lname
FROM AUTHORS
```

This isn't the way you actually set up Vertical filtering, but it should give you an idea of the difference between the two. But as you can see, the first one selects all the data, while the second only asks for the au_fname and au_lname rows of data to be returned.

Horizontal filtering is the process of replicating only a subset of the data rows. Horizontal Filter is useful when selecting data based on a certain geographical location. You could have a Northwest, Midwest, Southeast region, and so on. You could even filter on a departmental or user-level setting. The same Publisher and Subscriber effects apply to Horizontal filtering as they do to Vertical filtering. Staying with the previous analogy, let's visualize Horizontal filtering with a SQL statement.

```
USE pubs
SELECT * FROM authors
```

And

```
USE Pubs
SELECT * FROM authors
WHERE city = 'Oakland'
```

In the first example, you ask for all the authors, whereas the second asks only for authors who have an address in the city of Oakland.

Push Versus Pull Subscribing

By now you're probably familiar with push and pull technologies as they pertain to the Internet. SQL Server 7.0 push and pull subscribing is pretty much the same scenario.

Push subscriptions allow the Publisher to take control of the data flow, usually from a centralized administration perspective. The Publisher can send changes (or push out) to the Subscriber without a request. This allows changes to be reported almost instantaneously, or at least really darn quickly. If your network line is reliable, and your administrators are doing a good job of reducing bottlenecks, you should see the results in a manner of minutes. Push subscriptions are best suited for applications that need real-time data—applications that need to see (on an enterprise level) the data relatively quickly after it was entered. This does tend to create a higher processor overhead at the Publishers end. To avoid this, changes can be pushed to subscribers on a scheduled basis.

Pull subscriptions, on the other hand, don't give the Publisher any authority whatsoever (the administration is decentralized). The Subscriber has to initiate all contact (or pull) on a periodic basis. This scenario works best for Publications with a large number of Subscribers (for example, Internet Subscribers). Mobile users are a great example of pull Subscription users. When users are mobile (working on a laptop, and so on) they are often disconnected from the network (physical, Internet, or other) lines. In this case, the users need to determine when they are able to synchronize with the data.

Anonymous Subscriptions

Anonymous Subscriptions or Internet-enabled Subscriptions are special kinds of pull subscriptions, which are of course useful for Internet applications. Anonymous subscriptions aren't registered with a Publisher; however the Publisher does need to enable them. This basically means that you don't actually set one up, but you do say that it's okay for one to exist. The subscriber then makes the contact with the Publisher for data replication. The Subscriber is responsible for keeping the anonymous subscription synchronized.

Anonymous subscribers

In cases other than anonymous subscriptions, the information about each subscriber is stored at the Publisher. The Distributor maintains information about Performance. When using anonymous subscriptions, detailed information isn't being stored. If you are adding a large number of Subscribers to your Publication and don't want to maintain the information about each Subscriber, you can allow anonymous subscriptions to your publication. If anonymous publication is enabled and the server making contact isn't registered as a subscriber, the Pull subscription Wizard will create an anonymous subscription.

Initial Synchronization

After you set up a Subscription, you need to initially synchronize the publication and destination tables. In order for the data to be duplicated, the table schema needs to be duplicated as well. This doesn't mean that the databases are exact duplicates, just the tables you are subscribing to. Luckily this isn't something that needs be done manually; however, it can be, if you want. You don't have to generate scripts, have your administrators run the scripts on each database, and then fill the databases. SQL Server will automatically perform the initial synchronization for you when the subscription is created. You can, however, tell SQL Server to synchronize at a specific time, or go to the extreme and tell SQL Server not to synchronize at all.

Manual Synchronization

In some cases you may actually want to do this process manually. You might wonder why you would want to do such a thing. Let's say you have a database that is very large in size, 5 to 20GB. If you decide to let SQL Server initialize this for you across the Internet, LAN, or WAN, I have two words for you: *huge bottleneck*. To avoid this bottleneck and to possibly have the data published quicker, put the data on removable media such as a tape or detachable hard drive. Send the data across the country or wherever the subscribers may be and perform a manual initialization locally on each server.

If you have multiple sites, you might want to make multiple copies of the media device first and send them all out at the same time. This will save hours of frustration, not too mention your job. What would the boss say if you brought your network to a slow crawl for a couple of days, just because you were trying to replicate data? Better yet, what if he/she found out you could do it another way without tying up the network? Food for thought!

SQL Server Replication Architecture

When replicating data, you must ensure that the application will scale well. Setting up replication in its most simple form uses a single Publisher, a Distributor (which can be the same machine as the Publisher or Subscriber), and a single Subscriber. As your enterprise grows (you might already be at this stage) you will possibly need dozens of Publishers, Distributors, and dozens or even thousands of Subscribers. As you begin to scale your applications to these larger Enterprises, the communication plan (or topology) must be able to synchronize data and schemas at multiple locations with minimal resources. The topology is very important because it takes the following into consideration:

- How long will it take for the changes on the Publisher to be made on the Subscriber?

- Application flow—does the failure of one update on one Subscriber affect other Subscribers from being updated?

- What is the order in which the information arrives at a Subscriber, and will that affect reporting and analysis?

SQL Server topology

Currently, SQL Server only supports a topology known as Hub-and-Spoke topology. This resembles a star topology, and we will be discussing it later. Future releases will allow you to configure multi-hub and mixed hub-spoke topologies.

Replication Technologies

SQL Server provides different types of replication technologies depending on your business requirements. Each technology will provide benefits and restrictions based on the type of application you are building. These technologies cross three important dimensions for replication: transactional-based replication, site autonomy, and the ability to partition data.

Transactional Consistency Versus Site Autonomy

Transactional consistency basically means that any site involved with replication will at some point have the same data as though the transaction was performed at a single site. Site Autonomy is the effect of one site's operations on another's.

Transactional Consistency

Transactional consistency means that after the data has been replicated, the data at any site (which participated in the replication) will appear as if the transactions had actually occurred at that particular location. This means that the result of replicating the data would not in any way change the data differently than if replication was not being used at all.

Site Autonomy

Site autonomy refers to the operations of one site affecting the operations of another. You have complete site autonomy if one site can do its work independently of another site. In a transactional two phase commit (2PC), you have a low site autonomy factor. This is because if one part of the transaction fails, the other isn't allowed to be committed. *Merged replication* has high site autonomy. When using merged replication, sites can work independent of one another, allowing the work to be completed. This doesn't guarantee consistency. The 2PC has complete consistency but lacks the site autonomy.

Types of Replication

Types of replication include snapshot, transactional, and merged. Each of these includes different capabilities of the first two design requirements. The third requirement (data partitioning) is something that you design into your application.

Snapshot Replication

Snapshot replication refers to taking the data from one frozen place in time, much like taking a picture of the data—hence the name snapshot. Snapshot replication requires less of the constant drain on the processor than other types of replication. Snapshots don't need to monitor the methods in which the data is modified. Transactional replication monitors the INSERT, UPDATE, and DELETE statements, and merge replication monitors the data modifications.

Snapshot replication actually sends a complete set of data down the wire each time it updates Subscribers. This can cause a problem if the Subscribing tables are large in size. When deciding what scenario to choose, you must take this factor into account. Snapshot replication is also the simplest type of replication, and it provides latent guaranteed consistency (also known as loose guaranteed consistency) between the publisher and the Subscriber.

Snapshot replication is made possible with the help of the Snapshot Agent and the Distribution Agent.

Guaranteed consistency

Guaranteed consistency is a term you should familiarize yourself with if you have not already done so. Latent guaranteed consistency sounds like it would be great, but it's really just sufficient. It basically means that all participating sites are guaranteed to have the same data values at some point in time. It's like saying "We can't say for sure when, but soon." Keep this in mind when hearing about latent guaranteed consistency.

The short version of transfer is as follows:

The Snapshot Agent takes a Snapshot of the data and schema. It then uses BCP (see Chapter 7, "SQL Server Tools," for more information on BCP) to write the data to a file. Locks are placed to make sure that modifications aren't being done while the Snapshot Agent gathers its data. After the data is copied, the locks are released. Next, the Distribution Agent takes over moving the schema and the data to the Subscriber(s). After the data arrives at the Subscriber, locks are acquired, the schema is applied, the data is imported via BCP (if table is truncated first, if data already exits), and once complete the locks are released.

Transactional Replication

Transaction replication can replicate tables and the execution of stored procedures. When replicating a table, you can select the entire table or just part of the table using a method known as filtering. You can also select all stored procedures or just selected ones to be replicated as articles within a publication.

Transactional replication uses the transaction log for applying changes to data in an article. Instead of flagging changes to the data itself, it simply stores the transactions in the distribution database. This becomes a sort of transaction queue, and changes are sent to the Subscriber(s) and applied in the same order as they did on the originating table. These transactional updates can flow continuously or at scheduled intervals.

Changes in this replication method are made at the publisher, which avoids any data integrity problems. The Subscriber will at some point in time reflect the master table, which is the Publisher.

Transaction replication is made possible with the Snapshot Agent, the Log Reader Agent, and the Distributor Agent. If you're wondering why Snapshot Agent is also used in transactional replication, before you can update the data, the data and the schema needs to exist. This is where the Snapshot Agent comes in. This is called applying the initial synchronization, where the schema and data are copied out of the publishing database and applied to the subscribing database. Transactional replication can only occur after SQL Server knows that the Subscriber has a current copy of the schema and data. This only affects Subscribers needing initial synchronization. If the Subscriber has already received its initial synchronization, the Log Reader begins its process.

The Log Reader reads the Publication's transaction log and finds the INSERTS, UPDATES, and DELETEs, which are marked for replication. The Agent then copies only the committed transactions to the distribution database. The distribution database then forwards the changes to the Subscriber(s). After the Log Reader Agent is informed that the transactions went through, the Log Reader Agent marks where the last replication was completed. The Log on the Publisher with rows not marked for replication are purged.

Subscription initialization

When setting up a Subscription, the initial synchronization is done for you unless you specify you would like to do it manually.

Merge Replication

Here is the part you've all been waiting for. *Merge replication* is what makes updateable Publishers and Subscribers possible. Merge replication tracks the changes in each database that I will refer to as a source, and then synchronizes the Publisher and the Subscriber(s). The Publisher is still the server that actually created the publication, and the Subscriber(s) are still those subscribing to the publication. Even though the Publisher did in fact publish the data, it isn't necessarily the one who wins when a conflict arises. You, the DBA, decide who has the final say. This could be based on time, for example, who did it first or last. You could specify user level as the criteria, such as Accounting over Human Resources, and so on.

The Snapshot Agent and the Merge Agent carry out merge replication. As mentioned previously, the Snapshot Agent is used for the initial synchronization of the databases. The Merge Agent then applies the snapshot; after that, the job of the Merge Agent is to increment the data changes and resolve any conflicts according to the rules configured.

Merge Replication is possible by making some changes to the schema of the database. Actually, three important changes are made:

- A unique column for each row is identified. If a column defined with a ROWGUIDCOL property already exists, SQL Server will use that row. Otherwise, a column called rowguid is created with those characteristics. A ROWGUIDCOL property uses the UNIQUEIDENTIFIER property and the NEWID function, which generates an ID that is guaranteed unique worldwide on networked computers. This will allow the row to be unique across multiple copies of the table.

- SQL Server then installs triggers, which track the changes made to each row and optionally each column.

- SQL Server adds new system tables that are used for tracking data, efficient synchronization, conflict detection, resolution, and reporting.

The Distribution Database

For a while now I've been talking about the Distribution Database, but haven't discussed whether you really need one and, if so, how to build it. To answer the first question, yes, you need to have a distribution database. You can create a distribution database on a server that is configured to be the Distributor. This can be the same machine as the Publisher or the Subscriber; however, in most environments it is a dedicated machine configured specifically for the sole purpose of distributing data between Publishers and Subscribers.

The distribution database is used for a couple of reasons. For transactional-based replication, the distribution database tracks the transactions from other publications and Publishers. This information is queued and then forwarded when the Subscriber is ready for updates.

The Merge Agent uses the distribution database for the Merge Replication process. Merge Agents store synchronization history on the distribution database.

How to Use Wizards to Configure Replication

Configuring a system for replication is simplified by the use of wizards. The replication wizards are series of screens that lead you in a step-by-step process of the creation, modification, and even deletion of a replication system. Access to the wizards is made available through the Tools menu or through the task pads in the right window in SQL Server Enterprise Manager, as shown in Figure 17.2.

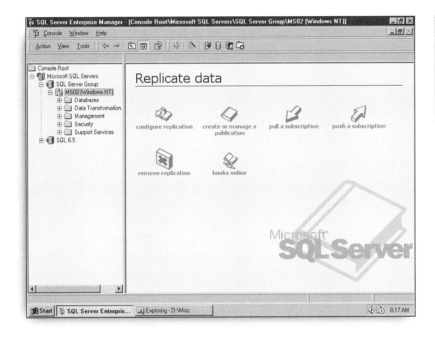

Setting Up Replication Using the SQL Enterprise Manager

SQL Server Enterprise Manager allows you to install replication using the wizards or tabular dialog box entry screens. After you install replication, you can easily view and modify the replication procedures.

Installing or Selecting the Distribution Database

As mentioned earlier, before any information can be sent out or distributed, you must configure a server to be the distributor. Again, this can be the same server as the publisher or another server elsewhere.

One of the features of SQL Server 7.0 is the ability to have multiple distribution databases on a single server. When using the wizard, the distribution database is named distribution if you accept all the defaults. If you do this manually (without the wizards), or choose the extra options during the wizard setup, you can choose a different name. You should stick with the default for this example. You can choose to change this.

To create the Distribution server, use the Configure Publishing and Distribution Wizard. This name can cause some confusion. The wizard will enable the server as both the Publisher and the Distributor or, and I stress the word *or*, you can use the wizard to create a dedicated Distributor without enabling it as a Publisher.

The wizard can be found under Tools, Replication, Configure Publication and Subscribers... or on the task pads in the SQL Server Enterprise Manager. To start the wizard, click on the Server Name in the Tree view. In the right window, you will see the Getting Started Task pads; click replicate data. The Replication options are now displayed. Locate the icon to configure replication and click on it. The wizard does a good job of walking you through the steps to create a Distribution and/or Publications. However, it doesn't tell you the reason why it's doing certain things. It assumes you already understand Replication, and in a perfect world you would before trying to tackle setting up distributors, publishers, and subscribers. However, most of you may not.

Looking at Figure 17.3, you will see that the Distribution Wizard begins by saying that you will use this wizard to specify the current server as the Distributor or select another server as the Distributor. The next two steps are optional, as you will see.

> **Permissions to create a Distributor**
>
> You must have sysadmin permissions to create a Distributor. This pertains to both the Enterprise Manager, or using system stored procedures.

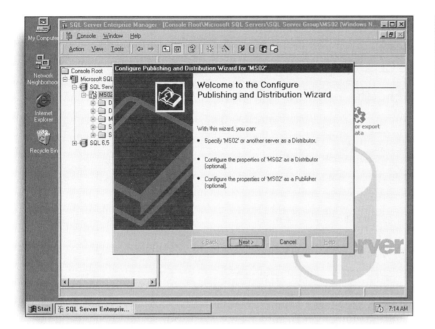

FIGURE 17.3
The Configure Publishing
and Distribution Wizard.

The next screen asks you to choose a Distributor. If you need to create one, select to use the current server. It will actually say your server name with single quotes around it. If you already have a server designated as a Distributor and you want to use that server, you need to select that option and then register the server. You cannot go any further until one of these two conditions is met.

After one of the previous conditions is met, you can continue. At this point, you can let SQL Server take all the defaults or you can customize your options. Customizations include changing the name of the distribution database (the database will be named distribution by default), the folder for the location of the distribution database, login information (default is a trusted connection by the SQLServerAgent), setting up a publication database, and enabling servers to subscribe to publications for the machine you are currently configuring.

After you have decided on what course of action to take, you will be prompted with the final wizard to finish, go back and make

Installing the distribution database

If you accept the defaults, or select the default settings on the third dialog in the wizard, only the distributor is installed on the current machine. If you do this by accident or on purpose, you can still enable publishing and/or subscribing for that machine. The only difference is you will use a different server.

changes, or cancel the whole operation. To continue to the next section, where you will set up a publisher and then the subscriber, feel free to accept the wizard's defaults.

Configuring Options for the Publishing Server

Configuring the publisher is a fairly easy process. It only gets confusing when you start thinking about all the options you have available to you. This is the point where you decide what type of replication you want to perform: Snapshot, Transaction, or Merge.

More detail on each of these types can be found earlier in this chapter. For right now just remember that a snapshot will grab a new database image or picture each time. If the database is large, that can be a lot of bandwidth you are taking up. Transactional uses the transaction logs to make database changes. Merged will actually merge the information from several databases, making them all consistent with each other. This replication process can get tricky when you come into conflicts for data modifications. You need to have policies in effect for who will win in a dispute when modifying the same data.

Creating a publication

1. To create a publication, select Tools, Replication, Create Publication Wizard. You can also use the Replication Task pads, and click the Create or Manage a Publication icon. The selected database will be the one you are publishing data from, so make sure it's the one that you actually want to publish. For the purpproses of this tutorial, select either the Pubs or the Northwind database. After you have selected your database, you will need to create the publication.

2. Again, you will have a startup or splash screen for the wizard. This screen tells you what you can expect to do with the wizard. For the Publication wizard, you can create a publication for the database you selected, filter the data, and set properties for the publication.

3. After you click Next, you will have the options that we discussed earlier available to you. These options are creating a Snapshot, Transaction, or Merge publication. Your project

design should pretty much define what you are doing. For small lookup tables that don't change much, use Snapshot replication. For larger tables, use transaction replication (this way only the changes are replicated across the wire). If users at each site want to modify their local data, and you want this data to be replicated across the enterprise, you will need to set up a merged publication.

4. For simplicity, let's select snapshot. The next screen asks you if you will be using immediate updating subscribers; this is used with two phase commit and MSDTC. This topic is beyond the scope of this book. SQL Server 7.0 Books Online can provide further guidance in this area. For now just remember that this isn't the same as merged replication. Accept the default.

5. The next screen asks you whether all subscribers will be SQL Server servers, which is selected by default. If you have MS Access, Oracle, or some other RDBMS, you may use ODBC or OLE DB for the connection. Again, take the default for simplicity at this point.

6. The next screen will show you a list of the user tables in the database selected. You can select as many or as few tables as you want to publish. The Select All button publishes all the databases for you. Publish None will clear any databases you have selected. For this example, let's just select one table, the Customers table.

   You will need to give your publication a name. When selecting a name for a publication, you should select a name that is relevant to the data within the article and publication.

7. After you click the Next button, you will be confronted with two options. You can choose to define data filters, enable subscription updates or anonymous subscribers, or accept the defaults. If you accept the defaults, you will be finished. The next wizard screen is the final one with the Finish, Go Back, and Cancel, which erases all the work you've done. Because you're here, let's explore more about filters and take a look at defining some filters and the other options available to you.

8. Click the Yes, I Will Define option as shown in Figure 17.4, and then click Next. Go ahead and click Yes and then the Next button.

9. This leads you to screens where you select only the data you want to publish. The first is vertical filters. This basically defines the select statement with graphical tools or simply, of the columns available, which ones you want to replicate to the subscriber. Check the columns that you don't want displayed. If you chose the Customers table, deselect the Address, Phone, and Fax columns, and click the Next button.

10. Next is a horizontal filter. This is a where clause of the available data that gives you only the records where the customer resides in the USA. If you like, feel free to define one here. To do this, click the button with the ellipse (...). The syntax does need to match the table you are taking information out of. If you are using the Customers table, here is an example that you can place in the box:

    country='USA'

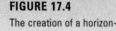

FIGURE 17.4
The creation of a horizontal filter.

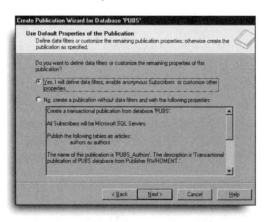

11. After you place the filter in the box and click OK, you will then see your filter in the Filter Clause text box.

12. Select the No option and click the Next button.

13. At this point, you are given the option to allow anonymous subscribers to create subscriptions, or to only allow known subscribers. This option will also help reduce overhead on the publisher.

Anonymous subscriptions

For more detail, see the section in this chapter titled "Anonymous Subscriptions."

14. The choice now is which one to create. They are relatively the same; however, you can run into more problems with authentication when asking for only known subscribers. For simplicity, select Yes, Anonymous Subscribers. The next screen indicates how often you want to create the files that will initialize the new subscriptions. For this example, create the snapshot immediately.

15. You can now click Finish to build the publications, go back and make changes, or cancel the work you've done.

After you click Finish, the publication will be created, based on what you defined with the wizard. The next section will discuss how to get the data from the publication you just created.

Configuring Options for the Subscribing Server

The subscribing server has the job of actually getting the data from a publisher. As a subscribing server, you subscribe to the publications you want replicated to your machine. This scenario represents a pull subscription. The publishers who actually push the subscriptions down to the subscribers set up push subscriptions.

Naturally, in order to subscribe to a publication, that publication must already exist. If you have not created a publication yet, follow the steps in the last section, "Configuring Options for the Publication Server." After you have a publication, you can jump back here to create a subscription.

Pull Subscription

The pull subscription does just what it sounds like it should do. It initiates contact with the publisher and pulls the information down the wire to its database. When you create a subscription, you need to have a database to hold the data. This can be a database already created or you can create one yourself. If you don't already have a database, you will need to create one; see Chapter 8, "Managing Databases."

You can start the Publication Wizard by choosing Tools, Replication, Pull Subscription, or you can access the wizard via the Getting Started Task pads by clicking on the Replicate Data icon, and then clicking the Pull a Subscription icon. Listed will be all available databases; select the database you will be using and then click Pull New Subscription.

The introduction/splash screen will be displayed, detailing what the wizard will perform for you. This wizard will assist in selecting the publisher and publications, selecting the subscribing database, setting up the synchronization schedule, and other options and properties of the subscription. Click Next.

If the server holding your publication isn't listed, it has not been registered in SQL Server Enterprise Manager. To do this, click the Register Server button. You will now need to enter the name of the server that has the publication you want to subscribe to and the authentication information. Once registered, you will be returned a list of available servers; double-click on the newly added server and the available publication will be listed. Click on it and then click Next.

In this example, the synchronization agent needs to gather some login information in order to connect to the publisher and distributor. Enter the required information and click Next.

At this point, you can change the subscription destination database or, if needed, you can create a new one or select the database you want to use as the subscribing database. Click Next. The Initialize Subscription dialog is displayed. You will have no options in this example; click Next.

Now you must determine how often you want your data refreshed. Continuously means that as the data is updated at the publisher it will be replicated immediately to the subscriber. This is good if you need your updates right away. You can also set up a schedule to have you data updated from the publisher at an interval that meets your business needs, say every 15 minutes. Your final option is to Synchronize On Demand. This option could be used for a traveling salesperson who connects to the office at random times. For this example, accept the default as shown in Figure 17.5, and click Next.

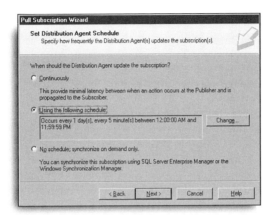

FIGURE 17.5
Distribution Agent
Scheduler.

The SQL Server Agent is required for Pull subscription. This dialog will let you know if the Agent is running, stopped, or paused. When you are sure the service is running, click Next.

The wizard now has enough information to build the subscription. You can now review your options, go back and make changes, cancel all of the work you have done so far, or finish. Click Finish.

Monitoring SQL Server Replication

Now that you have set up Replication in your environment, you need to learn more about Replication Monitoring. You can use the Replication Monitor to view publishers, publications, subscriptions, and replication agents, and to monitor the real-time heartbeat and history of each task. It can also be used to set up and monitor alerts.

chapter

18

SQL Server Optimization and Tuning Fundamentals

Learn why you need to tunel

Monitor the server and create a baseline

Learn the steps in tuning

Learn how to tune the server

Advances in Tuning for SQL Server 7.0

As anyone who has ever worked with a previous version of SQL Server knows, optimization and tuning of SQL Server can be a long and arduous task with a huge number of complicated variables to investigate. When working with advanced parameters, the user will often need to have a deep understanding of the internal workings of SQL Server itself. The worst part of tuning a SQL Server 6.5 machine is that it is a trial-and-error process accomplished over a long period of time, and it must be redone whenever a variable changes.

With the release of SQL Server 7.0, server tuning has become a much easier process. Although SQL Server 6.5 was a highly tunable environment, SQL 7.0 is a highly auto-tuned environment. SQL Server automatically monitors and changes configurations as needed with little or no interaction from the user. The few user tunable parameters are exposed when needed. The number of user tunable parameters has decreased as well. In SQL Server 6.5, there were 31 basic tunable parameters and 24 advanced parameters. In SQL Server 7.0, that number has decreased to 11 basic options and 31 advanced options.

Why Should You Tune Your Server?

Whether you are a manager, a database administrator, or a database user, there is a universal reason for you to want to tune your SQL Server: performance. When you have properly tuned the resources on the server, you will notice performance increases. Performance increases will become apparent in faster return on queries and data modifications and, overall, happier users. Users will be the first people to let you know if a server isn't performing up to their expectations. Despite the fact that Microsoft does a very good job in setting up the initial server configuration, you will need to tune the server for your specific needs.

Monitoring and Establishing a Baseline

Before you can begin tuning your server, you must first determine what areas you need to work with. To do this, you monitor the server and determine the baseline. You will then use the baseline to identify anything that is out of the normal ranges. To establish a baseline, you should routinely monitor the following:

- Server performance
- User activity
- SQL Server error log and Windows NT event log

Establishing a Baseline

To have an effective baseline, you should monitor your server over a period of time and while performing a variety of tasks. While creating a baseline, the server performance should meet your users' needs, and most importantly, their expectations. You should make sure to note peak and off-peak hours of operation, query response times, and database dumps and loads. After you have determined a baseline, you will then want to compare it to information that you gather further down the road. If you begin to see large variances in either direction, you should investigate them.

Creating a baseline involves using Performance Monitor to log server performance, as outlined later in this chapter. The type of information that you should monitor includes the following:

- Processor
- Memory
- Physical disk
- Network card

Monitoring Server Performance

As a DBA, you should create a schedule where you monitor your SQL Server frequently to determine whether it is performing the way that you and your users expect. SQL Server provides several graphical utilities and some text-based ways to monitor your server. Table 18.1 lists the various utilities and ways to monitor your server.

565

Reaching the Current Activity window

To access the Current Activity window, you first connect to the server within SQL Enterprise Manager. Next click on the Management folder, then on the Current Activity windows

TABLE 18.1 Various Utilities and Ways That You Can Monitor Your Server

Utility	Description
SQL Server Performance Monitor	This utility enables you to monitor server performance using predefined objects and counters. This utility enables you to monitor both SQL Server and Windows NT at the same time. You can also set thresholds that will generate alerts to notify operators and fire off applications when the threshold is reached. It will log information to a data file for later analysis or in a graphical fashion on the screen.
Current Activity window	This utility provides a graphical representation of the users who are logged in, blocking processes and commands that are running. You also have the ability to send messages to users and to stop processes.
SQL Server Profiler Server	This is a new and powerful tool added to SQL 7.0. This utility provides a way to monitor both server resources and database activity. This information can be fed into a table in a SQL Server database or into a log file for analysis by external applications.
sp_monitor	This system stored procedure displays statistics about how busy SQL Server has been since the last time it was started. This provides the same sort of information that is available to you when you run SQL Server Performance Monitor.
sp_spaceused	This system stored procedure will provide an estimate of how much physical space a table or database is taking up on disk. It is important to realize that this number is not always accurate.
sp_who	The sp_who system stored procedure is used to check current user and status information. This provides the same information that is available to you when viewing the Current Activity window in SQL Enterprise Manager.
sp_lock	The sp_lock system stored procedure is used to view current lock and block information. This provides the same information that is available to you when viewing lock activity in the Current Activity window in SQL Enterprise Manager.

DBCC commands

The Database Consistency Checker, or DBCC, is a set of commands that provides the ability to check performance statistics, check table and database consistency, and complete a wide number of general housekeeping functions.

Running stored procedures

Stored procedures are run from within the SQL Query Analyzer. Using this application, you can run these queries and return the results to the screen.

SEE ALSO

➤ *To learn how to use the DBCC utility for troubleshooting problems, see page 611.*

Server Monitoring Recommendations

There are three main areas that you should concentrate on when monitoring server performance:

- **Query response times**. You will use information gathered about query response times to determine the performance level of your server. Fast response times indicate that a server is performing at its peak, whereas slow response times indicate a server operating at less than peak.

- **Transactions per second**. Using information gleaned about the number of transactions per second on your server, you will be able to determine the throughput of your server. A low throughput may indicate that you need to install a faster network interface card in the computer.

- **Number of concurrent users**. When determining your baseline, you will find that there is an optimum number of users that your server can handle at one time while still performing at peak performance. If the number of concurrent users on the system approaches or exceeds the number of optimum users, you will begin to find that the server doesn't operate as well as it should.

The main tools that you should concentrate on when monitoring the SQL Server itself are the SQL Server Profiler and the SQL Server Performance Monitor.

Monitoring User Activity

Aside from monitoring server statistics to determine performance problems, you should also monitor user activity and statistics. With this information, you can pinpoint transactions that are blocking other processes as well as long running transactions that are causing the SQL Server to bog down. After you have determined what transactions and users are causing the difficulty, you can begin to reschedule the transactions for off-peak hours or retrain the user. A majority of user issues that you encounter can be resolved by retraining.

When monitoring user activity, you should concentrate on the SQL Server Profiler and the SQL Server Performance Monitor, both of which are described in detail later in the chapter. These utilities are good for collecting data for analysis over a long period of time. The Current Activity window is also a good source of information about user activity, but it is a more immediate source of information and cannot be used for data collection.

When to check the log

You should monitor and check the error logs on a daily basis. There is a great deal of useful information that can point you towards potential problems.

Monitoring the Logs

Another source of information that you can use when monitoring your SQL Server is the SQL Server error log and the Windows NT event log. SQL Server logs information to both of these locations.

The SQL Server error log contains detailed information about SQL Server only. The log contains information about the startup sequence of SQL Server, informational messages, and error messages. This information can be used to narrow down issues that are known to lie with SQL Server itself.

The Windows NT event log contains information from Windows NT, SQL Server, and any other applications that are running on the server. This information doesn't contain all the detailed information that is available in the SQL Server error log. It does, however, contain information about Windows NT that can be cross-referenced with the SQL Server error log to determine the exact nature of the problems that you are having.

Viewing the SQL Server Error Log

As part of your daily duties as a SQL Server DBA, you should set aside time to view the SQL Server error log. In the SQL

Server error log, you will be able to see if long running transactions have completed, detect any potential problems, and find any errors that have occurred. By default, SQL Server keeps six archived copies of the error log in addition to the active copy. The log is stored in the \MSSQL7\LOG directory. The error log is a text file that can be viewed with SQL Enterprise Manager or any text editor, such as Notepad.

Viewing the SQL Server error log

1. Start the SQL Enterprise Manager and connect to the server with the error log you want to view. Expand the contents of the server by clicking the plus sign next to its name.

2. Click on the plus sign next to the Management section. This will display the different management section of SQL Server.

3. Click the plus sign next to the Error Logs section. This will display the different copies of the error log that are available on the server.

4. Choose an error log to view and click its name. The contents of the error log will be displayed in the right-hand pane, as shown in Figure 18.1.

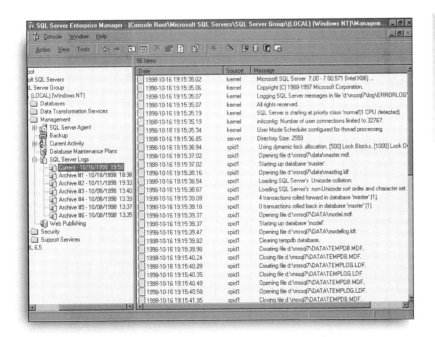

FIGURE 18.1

The SQL Server error logs contain detailed information about any errors that have occurred on the server.

5. If you are unable to read the entire text of an error message, double-click it and the SQL Server Error Log message box will open, as shown in Figure 18.2. This box contains information about the source of the error, the time and day that it occurred, and a full text of the error message.

Viewing the Windows NT Event Log

As well as spending time reviewing the SQL Server error log, you should also read the Windows NT event log to see if there are any errors that you need to act on. The log contains information about SQL Server, Windows NT, and any other applications that are installed on the server. The Windows NT event log is a special file that can only be viewed by the Windows NT Event Viewer. The other advantage you have when you are using the Windows NT event log is that you can filter the events by source.

There are three separate portions of the Windows NT event log: the System log, the Security log, and the Application log. Each portion of the log contains different information about the server.

- The System log contains information logged by Windows NT system components. Failure of drivers to load during startup would be logged here. In the case of SQL Server, one of the SQL Server services failing to start would appear in this log.

- The Security log records information about security events. A security event would include valid and invalid login attempts as well as anything to do with resource allocation and usage. The log is used to help track and identify security breaches.

- The Application log is where you will find the majority of the events logged by SQL Server. This log also records information about any other application that is installed on the SQL Server. You can match this information with the information that is contained in the SQL Server error log to help discover any problems that are occurring on the SQL Server.

Viewing the Windows NT event log

1. Log on to the server with the log you want to view. You will need to have administrative privileges on the system.

2. Click the Start button, and go to Programs, Administrative Tools, Event Viewer. The Event Viewer application, shown in Figure 18.3, will open.

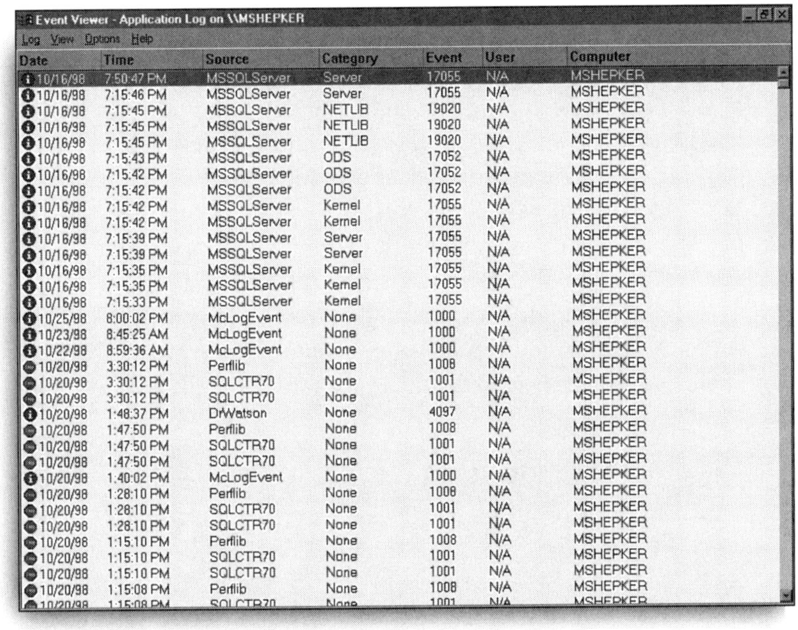

FIGURE 18.3

The Windows NT event log contains information and errors from Windows NT, SQL Server, and any other applications that are running on the server.

3. The title bar will change to show you which log you are looking at. To change the log, choose the Log menu item and then select which log you want to look at from the list that is presented.

4. To filter the event log, click the View menu and then choose Filter Events. This will open the Filter dialog box, shown in Figure 18.4.

Using the SQL Server Profiler

SQL Server 7.0 has provided a new and powerful utility that enables a DBA to collect data and monitor system performance and user activity. The types of events that SQL Server Profiler can track are login attempts, connects and disconnects, Transact-SQL INSERTs, UPDATES and DELETEs, and Remote Procedure Call batch status. After collecting information in the form of traces, you can then use the traces to analyze and fix server resource issues, monitor login attempts, and correct locking and blocking issues. A trace is simply a file where you capture server activity and events for later use. The main uses for the SQL Server Profiler are

- Monitoring performance
- Identifying problem queries and users

What to Trace

SQL Server Profiler can collect specific data about server activity. When creating a trace that will be used in monitoring performance, you should select events that are relevant to resource issues. The following trace events should be selected to assist you in tracking performance issues:

- Locks
- Stored procedures
- Transactions

Along with selecting the entire event categories, you will want to select the application name and process ID, object ID, and database ID. After collecting data from the capture, you can analyze it using one of the techniques described later in this chapter.

To start SQL Server Profiler, create a trace, and monitor it, follow these steps.

Setting up a SQL Server Profiler trace

1. Start SQL Enterprise Manager and connect to the server that you will be running a trace on. From the Tools menu, choose SQL Server Profiler. The SQL Server Profiler application, shown in Figure 18.5, will open.

2. If you want to start a predefined trace, select File, Open, and select Trace Definition.

3. To create a new trace, click the New Trace button on the toolbar, or click on the File menu and then choose New, Trace. The Trace Properties dialog box, shown in Figure 18.6, opens.

4. In the Name box, type the name that you will use to identify the trace.

5. In the Trace Type area, choose either a Private trace or a Shared trace. If the trace is going to be used by people other than the user that created it, choose Shared. The default is a Private trace.

FIGURE 18.5
The SQL Server Profiler
application enables a
DBA to collect data and
monitor system perfor-
mance and user activity.

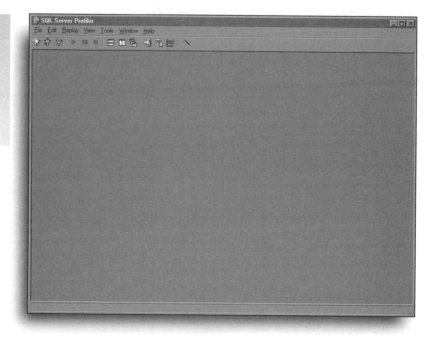

FIGURE 18.5
The SQL Server Profiler
application enables a
DBA to collect data and
monitor system perfor-
mance and user activity.

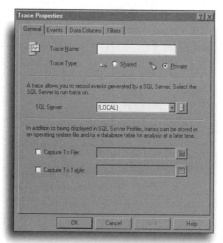

FIGURE 18.6
In the General dialog box,
you define what the trace
will capture.

6. The General tab also enables you to choose where you want
   the captured data to go. If you want to record the data for
   later analysis, choose to capture the file either to a table or
   to a file. The default option is to simply record events to
   the screen.

7. On the Events tab, shown in Figure 18.7, you can specify which SQL Server events you want to trace. In this dialog, you can choose specific options that you want to record. For the sake of this exercise, choose SQL Operators and click the Add>> button. This will track all SQL Statements such as INSERTS, UPDATES, SELECTS, and DELETES that are made against your database.

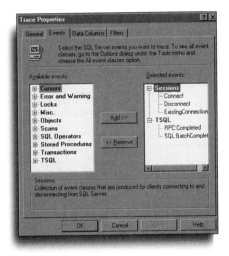

FIGURE 18.7
On the Events tab, you can choose events to monitor.

8. On the Data Columns tab, shown in Figure 18.8, you can select the data you want to capture for each traced event. This includes information about the user and any server objects that are accessed. In most cases, you will not need to change anything in this tab.

9. On the Filters tab, shown in Figure 18.9, you can choose specific criteria to include or exclude. For example, by default, any events that are generated by SQL Server Profiler are ignored. For these purposes, you will leave this with its default settings.

10. After you have set the options, click the OK button and the trace will automatically start. If you are tracing to the screen, you will begin to see information.

FIGURE 18.8

On the Data Columns tab, you can select which you can collect.

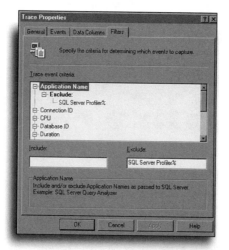

FIGURE 18.9

On the Filters tab, you can choose criteria for determining which events to capture.

Identifying Problem Queries and Users Using SQL Server Profiler

As you probably already know, users are the first people to place the blame of poor performance on you. Most users don't understand that sudden and unexpected poor performance is most often the result of either an untrained user or a badly written query. Users don't always understand that running a query that returns 100,000 rows during the busiest time of the day can cause problems.

SQL Server Profiler can be used to help outline problem queries that can either be rewritten or scheduled for off-peak hours and users who are in need of retraining. When setting up a trace that will be used in tracking this information, you should set it up with the following events:

- SQL operators
- Transact-SQL statements
- Indexes used
- Databases used
- Duration of execution

After collecting the data, you can analyze it using one of the techniques outlined later in the chapter.

Using the SQL Server Performance Monitor

SQL Server Performance Monitor is the same tool as of the Windows NT Performance Monitor and can be used to track up-to-the-minute information and statistics about SQL Server. You can use this data to provide feedback on the performance of your server and view it as a graph or store it for future use.

Monitoring Counters

Performance Monitor gathers information from SQL Server using counters. *Counters* are individual items that are monitored. For ease of use, counters are grouped together in objects. Objects are simply groups of related counters.

When SQL Server Performance Monitor starts, it monitors six default counters, which are outlined below. You can configure SQL Server Performance Monitor to track other counters aside from the default.

- **Buffer Cache Hit Ratio**. The percentage of data that was found in data cache instead of having to be read from disk.
- **Total server memory (KB)**. The amount of dynamic memory being used by the server.

- **SQL Compilations/sec**. Number of times SQL statements are being complied every second.

- **I/OPage Reads/sec**. The number of physical disk reads per second.

- **I/OPage Writes/sec**. The number of single page writes performed per second.

- **User Connections**. The number of users who are currently connected to the SQL Server at any point in time.

There are 16 different objects, outlined in Table 18.2, that can be used to track SQL Server statistics. Each object contains at least one counter.

TABLE 18.2 Each of the Following Objects Contain at Least One Counter That Can Be Used to Track SQL Server Performance

Object Name	Description
SQL Server: Access Methods	Provides information about searches and allocations of database objects.
SQL Server: Backup Device	Provides information about the status of backup devices.
SQL Server: Buffer Manager	Provides information about the usage of memory buffers by SQL Server, including the amount of free memory.
SQL Server: Cache Manager	Provides information about the procedure cache.
SQL Server: Databases	Provides information about user databases, including the size of the transaction log.
SQL Server: General Statistics	Provides server-wide statistics, such as the number of users logged into the server.
SQL Server: Latches	Provides information about latches on internal resources that are being used by SQL Server.
SQL Server: Locks	Provides information about locks that are being requested by SQL Server, including timeouts and deadlocks.
SQL Server: Memory Manager	Provides information about SQL Server memory usage.

Object Name	Description
SQL Server: Replication Agents	Provides information about any currently running replication agents.
SQL Server: Replication Dist.	Provides information on the number of transactions that are read from the distribution database and sent to the subscriber databases.
SQL Server: Replication Logreader	Provides information on the number of transactions that are read from the published databases and sent to the distribution database.
SQL Server: Replication Merge	Provides information about SQL Server Merge Replication.
SQL Server: Replication Snapshot	Provides information about SQL Server Snapshot Replication.
SQL Server: SQL Server Statistics	Provides information about SQL queries that have been sent to the server.
SQL Server: User Settable	Provides the ability to perform custom monitoring. Each counter can be a query or stored procedure that returns a value to Performance Monitor.

Analyzing Data

There are several ways to analyze data about your SQL server. SQL Performance Monitor provides a graphical presentation of information about the overall health of SQL Server. You can use the Graphical Showplan utility to display information about queries that are run. The Index Tuning Wizard takes information gathered by the SQL Server Profiler to create and modify indexes on tables.

Using Graphical Showplan

Graphical Showplan is an option within SQL Server Query Analyzer that enables you to see how SQL Server is processing your queries. This tool allows you to view the steps that SQL Server goes through. This information is displayed, as seen in Figure 18.10, showing each table accessed in the query and how they are accessed. By placing the mouse cursor over each icon displayed, you can get information about which index, if any, is used, the number of rows returned, and the estimated I/O and CPU cost. The important things to look for in this output are table scans and any portions of the query that are running for an overly long period of time.

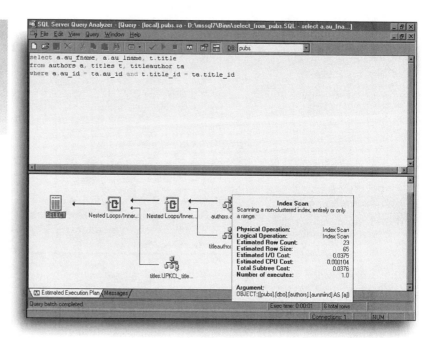

Using the Index Tuning Wizard

The Index Tuning Wizard is a tool that is new to SQL Server 7.0 that enables administrators to create and modify indexes without knowledge of the structure of the database, hardware platforms and components, or how end-user applications interact with the database. The wizard analyzes data that is collected with the SQL Server Profiler and then makes recommendations about the effectiveness of the indexes that are on the system and any new ones that may need to be created. These recommendations are in the form of a script that can be run to drop and recreate indexes on the system.

Running the Index Tuning Wizard

1. From SQL Enterprise Manager, click the Tools drop-down box and select Wizards. This will open the Select Wizard dialog box. Click the plus sign next to Management and select Index Tuning Wizard; then click on the OK button.

2. Click the Next button.

3. In the Select SQL Server and Database dialog, choose the name of the SQL Server and the name of the database that you will be analyzing and click the Next button.

4. From the Identify Your Workload dialog, choose I Have a Saved Workload File if you have already created one using SQL Profiler. If you have not, choose the I Will Create a Workload File On My Own option. This will open SQL Profiler for you to create a workload file. For these purposes, I will assume you already have a workload file.

5. From the Specify the Workload screen, select either the file or the SQL Server table that contains the trace information and click the Next button.

6. In the Select Which Tables to Tune dialog, SQL Server will automatically choose all the tables in the database for tuning. If you want to exclude any tables, you do so here.

7. When you click the Next button, the Index Tuning Wizard begins to analyze the data you collected and specify indexes based on that. When it has completed analyzing, it will open the Index Recommendations dialog box, specifying which indexed need changed or added. Examine this information and click Next.

8. The next dialog enables you to choose either to save the changes as a script file that enables you to apply the changes when you want, or allow SQL Server to make the changes for you.

What Options to Tune

As mentioned previously, there are 14 basic and 27 advanced tunable options. In this section, we will cover the different configurable options that are available to you. SQL Server 7.0

autotunes most of the options that were available to you in SQL Server 6.5. After establishing a baseline and determining which options you should change, modifications are made through SQL Enterprise Manager or the sp_configure stored procedure.

When changing configuration options, it is important to know which options are dynamic and which are static. Changes to dynamic options take effect as soon as you make them. Options such as Maximum Worker Threads and Recovery Interval are dynamic options. Changes to static options don't take effect until the SQL Server is restarted. Examples of static options are Memory and User Connections.

Affinity Mask

> **Windows NT processor options**
>
> When setting the affinity mask options, it is important to note that Windows NT uses the highest numbered processor in the system to handle all activity associated with the network interface card. For each network interface card, Windows NT will assign a processor to handle it.

Advanced Option: Yes

Dynamic Option: No

One of the features of Windows NT is the ability of process threads to move from one processor to another. Before the thread is migrated to another processor, all the information about that thread is stored in the process cache. During heavy system loads, specifying which processor a thread should run on can increase performance. This would keep the number of times that the thread cache has to be accessed to a minimum.

The affinity mask option is a bit mask that enables you to specify individual processors that SQL Server threads can run on. This option is best set on symmetric multiprocessor machines with more than four processors. With it, you can specify processors to run SQL Server tasks and exclude it from processors running Windows NT tasks. The default setting of 0 allows Windows NT to choose which tasks will execute on which processors.

Allow Updates

Advanced Option: No

Dynamic Option: Yes (Special)

The Allow Updates option specifies whether you can make direct updates to SQL Server system tables. The default setting for the Allow Updates option doesn't allow any user to update the system tables. When this option is turned on, any user who has permissions to the system tables can access the tables and update them.

It is important to turn on this option in very controlled situations. If a user were to accidentally change system tables, it is possible that SQL Server won't start or databases may become corrupt. For security purposes, when setting the allow updates option with the sp_configure stored procedure, you must also run the RECONFIGURE WITH OVERRIDE command to activate the command.

Cost Threshold for Parallelism

Advanced Option: Yes

Dynamic Option: Yes

The Cost Threshold for Parallelism option enables you to specify when SQL Server will create parallel queries. Parallel queries are queries that the query optimizer has selected to run on multiple CPUs. Long running queries are normally selected to be run as parallel queries. This option is an estimation, in seconds, for how long a particular query will take to run. If the estimated time is longer, the query is selected to be run parallel. The Cost Threshold for Parallelism option should only be set on symmetric multiprocessing machines.

Cursor Threshold

Advanced Option: Yes

Dynamic Option: Yes

The Cursor Threshold option specifies the number of rows in a cursor set at which the keysets are generated asynchronously. The default setting of −1 sets all cursor keysets to be generated synchronously. This setting is good for small cursor sets. Setting the options to 0 sets all cursor keysets to be generated asynchronously. If you set this option to any other number, SQL Server will compare the number of rows that the cursor is expected to have against the number that is in the cursor threshold option to determine how the keyset is generated. Take care not to set the cursor threshold too low, as smaller keysets are built quicker synchronously.

583

Default Language

Advanced Option: No

Dynamic Option: No

The default language option is the ID number of the language that SQL Server uses to display system messages. The default language is us_english and has an ID number of 0. As you add new languages to the server, they will be assigned new IDs.

Default Sort Order ID

Advanced Option: Yes

Dynamic Option: No (Special)

The default sort order specifies the number of the sort order that you specified during the setup of SQL Server. The default sort order is a read-only option that can only be changed using the SQL Server Setup program.

Extended Memory Size (MB)

Advanced Option: Yes

Dynamic Option: No

The Extended Memory option is a special option available only when you use SQL Server 7.0 Enterprise Edition on an Alpha platform. This setting indicates the number of megabytes of hard drive space that is to be used in addition to the amount of memory available to SQL Server.

Fill Factor (%)

Advanced Option: Yes

Dynamic Option: No

The Fill Factor option is used to specify how full SQL Server makes index pages when it creates a new index using pre-existing data. The number contained in the default Fill Factor option is the percentage full that SQL Server creates the data pages. The default value for the Fill Factor option is 0. This value means that all indexes are created with full data pages, but room is left in the upper levels of the index structure for additions to the data. When setting this option, you must take into account the amount of data that will be added to the table after the index has been created. If there will be a large amount of data added to the table, you will want to create indexes with small fill factors, as it take overhead to break up the index pages when reorganizing data.

Index Create Memory (KB)

Advanced Option: Yes

Dynamic Option: Yes

The Index Create Memory option controls the amount of memory that SQL Server uses when creating indexes. When an index is created, it must sort the data. If you frequently create large indexes, you may be able to speed up the process by increasing this number. The default for this is 1216 kilobytes.

Language in Cache

Advanced Option: No

Dynamic Option: No

The Language in Cache option enables you to specify the maximum number of languages that can be held in the language cache at any one time. The default number is 3.

Language Neutral Full-Text

Advanced Option: Yes

Dynamic Option: No

The language neutral full-text indexing option allows full-text search support to use the neutral language word breaker to process full-text indexing and queries.

Lightweight Pooling

Advanced Option: Yes

Dynamic Option: No

The Lightweight Pooling option is used to reduce the amount of system overhead associated with context switching on SMP machines. If excessive context switching is present, setting the lightweight pooling option to 1 may help improve system performance. The default for this option is 0.

Locks

Advanced Option: Yes

Dynamic Option: Yes

The Locks option is used to allocate the number of locks that are available to the server. When the Locks option is set to 0, it sets the SQL Server to autotune the number of locks based on current system needs. When the Locks option is set to 0 and the server is started, the lock manager automatically allocates two percent of the total memory available to SQL Server for use by locks. As the total pool of locks is used up, the lock manager allocates more memory for use by locks. The total amount of memory used for locks will never exceed forty percent of the total memory available to SQL Server. The recommended configuration is to allow SQL Server to autotune the amount of locks available.

Max Async IO

Advanced Option: Yes

Dynamic Option: No

The Max Async IO option is used to configure the maximum number of outstanding asynchronous I/O requests that the server can issue against a file. The default setting of 32 enables 32 reads and 32 writes to be outstanding against any file.

Servers with normal, nonspecialized disk systems won't benefit from increasing this value. High performance disk servers with intelligent disk systems may gain some performance increase by

Warning: performance

If your databases don't span multiple drives, or you aren't using an intelligent disk subsystem, don't change the Max Async IO setting, as it may decrease the performance of your server.

changing this setting. When changing this option, you should monitor system performance while slowly increasing this value. When you achieve a state where there is no further performance increase, your server is set up correctly.

Max Degree of Parallelism

Advanced Option: Yes

Dynamic Option: Yes

The Max Degree of Parallelism option specifies the number of threads that are used to execute a parallel query plan. The default value of 0 forces SQL Server to use the number of CPUs that are available for use in parallel execution. If you specify 1 as a value, SQL Server will suppress the use of parallel query execution. Any other number in this field specifies the number of threads.

Ignored in single processor environments

The Max Degree of Parallelism option is ignored on single processor servers because the server won't be able to process threads in parallel on different processors.

Max Server Memory (MB)

Advanced Option: Yes

Dynamic Option: No

The Max Server memory option enables you to configure the maximum amount of memory that SQL Server can use. When SQL Server autotunes memory, the system checks the total amount of physical memory. The system then releases or acquires memory to keep the free memory at approximately 5M to prevent Windows NT from paging. The default setting for this option is 2147483647.

Microsoft recommends that you allow SQL Server to manage the memory configuration, although you can make configuration changes as needed. Before you make changes to the SQL Server memory configuration, you must first decide the amount of memory that you will allow Windows NT to use and subtract that from the total amount of physical memory. For example, on machines with less than 64M of physical RAM, you may want to leave Windows NT at least 16M of RAM. On machine with large amounts of RAM (at least 256M), ensure that you leave 40M of RAM for Windows NT.

Max Text Repl Size

Advanced Option: No

Dynamic Option: Yes

The Max Text Repl Size option enables you to specify the size, in bytes, of text and image data that can be replicated to subscription servers.

Max Worker Threads

Advanced Option: Yes

Dynamic Option: Yes

The Max Worker Threads option enables you to set up the number of threads that are available to SQL Server processes. One thread will handle each network that SQL Server supports, one will handle all database checkpoints, and all other threads will form a pool to service user requests.

Usually you will configure SQL Server to allow one thread per user connection, but when you have hundreds of users connecting to your server, the one thread per connection rule can consume a large number of resources. When the number of user connections exceeds the number of worker threads, thread pooling occurs. Thread pooling is where SQL Server creates a pool of worker threads that will service all client connections.

Media Retention

Advanced Option: Yes

Dynamic Option: No

The Media Retention option enables you to provide a systemwide default for how long you want to retain a backup medium after you have written a database or transaction log dump to it. This option protects media from being overwritten until the number of days specified has passed. If you attempt to overwrite media before the number of days has passed, SQL Server will warn you.

Min Memory Per Query (KB)

Advanced Option: Yes

Dynamic Option: Yes

The Min Memory Per Query option is used to configure the base amount of memory that is allocated to each query for execution. The more memory that is available, the faster the query will execute and respond, especially when running queries with a large amount of sorting involved. The default for this option is 1024.

Min Server Memory (MB)

Advanced Option: Yes

Dynamic Option: No

The Min Server Memory option enables you to configure the minimum amount of memory that SQL Server can use. When SQL Server autotunes memory, the system checks the total amount of physical memory. The system then releases or acquires memory to keep the free memory at approximately 5M to prevent Windows NT from paging. The default setting for this option is 0.

Nested Triggers

Advanced Option: No

Dynamic Option: Yes

The Nested Triggers option enables you to enable cascading triggers. Cascading triggers happen when one trigger updates a table that fires off another trigger and so forth. The default setting for this option is 1, which allows triggers to be nested 16 levels deep. A setting of 0 turns off nested triggers.

Network Packet Size

Advanced Option: Yes

Dynamic Option: Yes

The network packet size option enables you to set the packet size, in bytes, for use across the entire network. The default packet size is 4096 bytes. When using multiple protocols on your network, set the network packet size option to the size of the most common protocol.

Open Objects

Advanced Option: Yes

Dynamic Option: No

The Open Objects configuration option is used to set the maximum number of objects that can be open at any time on the server. A database object is a table, view, rule, trigger, default, or stored procedure. This option is self-tuning and Microsoft recommends that you allow SQL Server to handle the configuration of it. This means that SQL Server will set the maximum number of open objects based on the current needs of the system. The default for this option is 0, which allows SQL Server to autotune it.

Priority Boost

Advanced Option: Yes

Dynamic Option: No

The Priority Boost option enables you to set the SQL Server processes to run at a higher priority than other processes on the server. The default option of 0 should only be changed if the server is dedicated to SQL Server.

> **Warning: local server performance**
>
> Changing the priority boost option, even on a server that is dedicated to SQL Server, isn't recommended. Doing so can cause problems when shutting down the server or running local administration applications, and can cause network errors.

Query Governor Cost Limit

Advanced Option: Yes

Dynamic Option: No

The Query Governor Cost Limit controls the amount of time that a query is allowed to run on the system before SQL Server will terminate its execution. If you specify a nonzero positive number for this option, SQL Server will disallow any query from running that will take more than that many seconds to run. The default for this option is 0, which allows all queries to run.

Query Wait (s)

Advanced Option: Yes

Dynamic Option: Yes

The Query Wait option specifies the number of seconds that a memory-intensive query will wait before timing out. SQL Server will queue memory-intensive queries involving sorting and hashing when there isn't enough memory to run the query. After the query is queued, SQL Server calculates a timeout value that can often be very large. SQL Server uses the value in the Query Wait option to override the calculated timeout value.

Recovery Interval (min)

Advanced Option: Yes

Dynamic Option: Yes

The Recovery Interval is the maximum number of minutes allowed for SQL Server to spend recovering databases. During the automatic recovery process, SQL Server goes through the transaction log to ensure that all completed transactions are rolled forward and all incomplete transactions are rolled back. The Recovery Interval option, along with the number of transactions that are completed per second, is used to determine the frequency of checkpoints. During a checkpoint, the SQL Server flushes all transaction logs and data pages that are written to the disk. This, in turn, limits the amount of time required for recovery by limiting the number of transactions to check. The default for this option is 5 minutes per database.

> **Truncate Log on Checkpoint overrides recovery interval**
>
> If you have the Truncate Log on Checkpoint database option turned on, a checkpoint will be performed on the database every minute, no matter what the recovery interval setting is.

Remote Access

Advanced Option: No

Dynamic Option: No

The Remote Access option is used to control logins from remote SQL Servers for the purposes of running remote stored

591

procedures. The default option of 1 allows logins from remote SQL Server.

Remote Login Timeout (s)

Advanced Option: No

Dynamic Option: Yes

The Remote Login Timeout option specifies the number of seconds that SQL Server will wait before returning from a failed login attempt. The default setting of 0 will cause the SQL Server to wait indefinitely.

Remote Proc Trans

Advanced Option: No

Dynamic Option: No

The Remote Proc Trans option protects the actions of a server-to-server procedure through a Distributed Transaction Coordinator transaction. The option, when set to 1, protects the ACID properties of the transactions.

Remote Query Timeout (s)

Advanced Option: No

Dynamic Option: Yes

The Remote Query Timeout option is used to specify the number of seconds to wait before the query times out. The default option of 0 allows SQL Server to wait indefinitely.

Resource Timeout (s)

Advanced Option: Yes

Dynamic Option: Yes

The Resource Timeout option determines the number of seconds that SQL Server will wait for a resource to become available. This option is used to set the time of asynchronous IO operations. Any operation that takes longer that the time specified will time out. In the event that you are getting many log-write or bufwait errors, you should increase this number from the default 10 seconds.

Scan For Startup Procs

Advanced Option: Yes

Dynamic Option: No

The Scan for Startup Procs is used to tell SQL Server whether to scan the system for stored procedures that are marked as startup stored procedures. This type of stored procedure is executed as soon as the system comes online. The default setting for this option is 0, which means the system isn't scanned.

Set Working Set Size

Advanced Option: Yes

Dynamic Option: No

The Set Working Set Size option is used to reserve the amount of physical memory that you have set in the memory option. When you are manually setting the amount of memory, setting this option will not allow any of its memory to be swapped out. If SQL Server is autotuning the memory option for you, don't turn this option on.

Show Advanced Options

Advanced Option: No

Dynamic Option: Yes

Show Advanced Options is used to toggle the advanced options off and on. When you set this option to 1, all options listed in this section as advanced will be displayed.

Spin Counter

Advanced Option: Yes

Dynamic Option: Yes

The Spin Counter option enables you to set the number of times that SQL Server will try to obtain a resource. Single processor machines default to 0 times and multiprocessor machines will try 10,000 times.

Time Slice (ms)

Advanced Option: Yes

Dynamic Option: No

The Time Slice option is used to determine the amount of time that a process is allowed to maintain control of the processor without voluntarily yielding control. SQL Server doesn't control the amount of time that a single process spends in the CPU. Instead, the process itself controls the amount of time that it spends in the processor. If SQL Server detects that a process has exceeded the time set in the time slice option, SQL Server terminates the process.

Unicode Comparison Style

Advanced Option: Yes

Dynamic Option: No (Special)

The Default Comparison Style option is used to determine the sorting option for all databases on the SQL Server. The default comparison style option is a read-only option and cannot be changed without reinstalling SQL Server.

Unicode Local ID

Advanced Option: Yes

Dynamic Option: No (Special)

The Unicode Local ID is used to specify the local ID used for Unicode sorting. The Unicode Comparison Style determines the sorting options when used with the local ID. The Unicode local ID is a special, read-only option that can only be changed by reinstalling SQL Server.

User Connections

Advanced Option: Yes

Dynamic Option: No

The User Connections option is used to set the number of simultaneous users who can connect to your SQL Server. This isn't necessarily the number of licenses you have, rather it is the number of clients that your server and network can handle and the number of clients that the version of SQL Server you are using allows. SQL Server 7.0 will support a maximum of 32,768 users.

> **User connections and memory**
>
> Use care when setting the number of user connections available on your server. Each user connection that you allow uses approximately 40KB of memory whether it is being used or not..

User Options

Advanced Option: No

Dynamic Option: No

The User Options option enables you to set specific defaults for the entire server. These settings enable you to set the default values for query processing options. Users can override any value set in this option using the SET command. The complete list of options is listed in Table 18.3.

TABLE 18.3 Options That You Can Specify in the User Options Option

Value	Set Command	Description
1	DISABLE_DEF_CNST_CHK	Controls whether constraints are checked immediately or deferred to later.
2	IMPLICIT_TRANSACTIONS	Controls whether a transaction is automatically started when a command is executed.
4	CURSOR_CLOSE_ON_COMMIT	Controls whether a cursor is closed once a transaction is committed.
8	ANSI_WARNINGS	Controls warnings in situations where NULLs and truncations are present.
16	ANSI_PADDING	Controls whether SQL Server pads the length of fixed length variables.

continues...

TABLE 18.3 Continued

Value	Set Command	Description
32	ANSI_NULLS	Controls NULL handling when using equality operators.
64	ARITHABORT	Controls whether a query is terminated when an overflow or divide-by-zero error occurs.
128	ARITHIGNORE	Returns a NULL when an overflow or divide-by-zero occurs.
256	QUOTED_IDENTIFIER	Controls whether SQL Server differentiates between single and double quotes when evaluating a query.
512	NOCOUNT	Turns off the message at the end of the query that informs the user of the number of rows that have been affected.
1024	ANSI_NULL_DFLT_ON	Ensures that new columns defined without explicit nullability will be defined to allow NULLs.
2048	ANSI_NULL_DFLT_OFF	Ensures that new columns defined without explicit nullability will be defined to not allow NULLs.

Setting Configuration Options

After you have monitored your server and determined where your server can be optimized, you will need to set the options. There are two ways available to you when setting configuration options. The first is through the graphical interface of SQL Enterprise Manager. The other option is by using the sp_configure stored procedure within the SQL Query Analyzer.

Setting Options with SQL Enterprise Manager

When setting options with SQL Enterprise Manager, most options listed previously are available to you, but they are listed differently. To get to the server options, right-click the server name and choose the Properties option. Table 18.4 outlines which settings are available to you on each tab.

TABLE 18.4   Setting Configuration Options

Tab	Options
General	The General tab lists information about the SQL Server and enables you to change startup parameters for the server.
Memory	The Memory tab enables you to configure SQL Server's memory options. These options include Memory and Set Working Set Size.
Processor	The Processor tab enables you to configure the processor options that include Affinity Mask, Max Worker Threads, Priority Boost, Cost Threshold for Parallelism, and the Max Degree of Parallelism options.
Security	The Security tab enables you to set the security mode that SQL Server will run under
Connections	The Connections tab enables you to set the connection options that include User Connections, User Options, Remote Login Timeout, Remote Proc Timeout, and Remote Query Timeout.
Server Settings	The Server Settings tab enables you to set the server settings that include the Default Language, Allow Updates (to System Tables), and Nested Triggers options. You can also configure SQL Mail on this tab.
Database Settings	The Database Settings tab enables you to set database settings including the Initial Database Size, Fill Factor, Media Retention, and the Recovery Interval.

Setting Options with *sp_configure*

The sp_configure stored procedure is used to configure and list options within the SQL Query Analyzer. Unlike using SQL Enterprise Manager, all possible options are available to you. The syntax of the sp_configure command is

```
sp_configure "option name", value
```

where "option name" is the text of the configuration option. The name should be contained in quotes and SQL Server will understand a unique portion of the configuration name. For example, instead of typing **show advanced options**, you could simply type **show advanced**. The *value* is an integer value that will be the new setting. After configuring many of the dynamic options, you have to tell SQL Server that it needs to begin using the new options. You do this by running the RECONFIGURE command. The syntax of the RECONFIGURE command is

```
RECONFIGURE WITH OVERRIDE
```

Configuring the show advanced options setting

Optimal timing

When setting configuration options with SQL Server, you must be careful to perform changes during off-peak hours to ensure as little downtime as possible. You should also continue to monitor the SQL Server to make sure that the changes you made had the desired effect.

1. Open the SQL Query Analyzer by clicking the Start button and choosing Programs, Microsoft SQL Server 7.0, Query Analyzer. This opens the Microsoft SQL Query Analyzer.

2. In the Query window, type **sp_configure "show advanced"**. Note that you don't have to type the full name of the configuration option. SQL Server recognizes partial option names.

3. Click the Execute Query button. This will return a message that looks like the following:

```
DBCC execution completed. If DBCC printed error
messages, contact your system administrator.
Configuration option changed. Run the RECONFIGURE
statement to install.
```

4. In the query window, type the following and execute it:

```
RECONFIGURE WITH OVERRIDE
```

This will return the following:

```
The command(s) completed successfully.
```

chapter

19

Troubleshooting SQL Server

At some point during his career, every SQL Server administrator will have to troubleshoot a broken database. This can be a very stressful time, and there will be a lot of people wanting to know why it happened and, more importantly, when it will be fixed. As a database administrator, you must be able to keep your cool and not be pressured into making any commitments that you cannot keep.

Troubleshooting is a systematic process that includes gathering data about the problem, using that data to figure out what the problem is, attempting to fix the problem, and monitoring to ensure that the problem has been fixed. You never want to jump in and attempt to solve a problem without first knowing specifically what the problem is because some fixes can cause more problems if they are improperly used.

The Troubleshooting Process

There are several distinct steps that must be followed when troubleshooting. It doesn't matter whether you are working with SQL Server or any other product; these steps are universal.

Documentation

Document Everything

It is extremely important to document every major thing that occurs on your server. This include hardware and software upgrades, database creation and deletion, and any option changes.

The first step is one that you should be following before any problems become evident. You should document anything that occurs on your server. This can include settings changes, downtime, and the installation of new software or hardware. You should document the time and date that the changes were made, as well as a detailed description of what was done. This is particularly helpful when you are troubleshooting something that has occurred due to a recent change on the server.

During the troubleshooting process, you should also document what errors you are getting and what changes you are attempting to fix those errors. This documentation will be useful in two situations. First, if the fix that you attempt doesn't work, you can use the information that you gathered to return the server to the state that it was in before the fix to try other options. Second, if you find a fix that corrects a certain problem, you have the information available to you in the event that the same problem occurs again.

Find the Facts

Finding out where the actual problem lies is the first true step in troubleshooting. Most often, the first reports of errors come from the database users. Unfortunately, this is a double-edged sword. The good side is that you will find out about errors as soon as they happen. The bad side is that users will report nearly every error that comes across their screen and sometimes exaggerate the error. For example, an error that says `Violation of PRIMARY KEY constraint 'UPKCL_auidind': Attempt to insert duplicate key in object 'authors'.` may be reported as "The server is down. Nothing works..."

When a user reports an error, you should first attempt to get the full text of the error message. This isn't always possible as many users dismiss the error as soon as they get it and then call to tell you about it. If the text of the error message isn't available to you, ask the user to repeat the action that she was taking before she found the error to see if it can be re-created. Even if the error cannot be repeated, that doesn't mean that the error never happened. Sometimes errors can be transient; they will show up and then go away for a while, only to reappear later. Ask your users to continue to look for the error and to report it to you if it reappears, making sure not to clear it from their screens before they do. If the text of the error message is still available, make sure to copy it down word for word, including any error numbers that accompany it.

Identify the Problem

After you have determined what error messages the users are getting, the next step is to determine what the actual problem is. Depending on the application that is being used, this can be a

Error Messages

When troubleshooting a SQL Server, it is important to get the full text of the message. This includes all text, error numbers, and status codes.

rather simple task, or one that could take a lot of time. The reason behind this is that some developers choose not to report the exact text of a SQL Server error message to the user. Instead, they may choose to return their own error numbers and message text to explain any errors encountered. In doing this, the application might not be telling you everything that SQL Server is.

There are two easy ways to help you determine the actual problem that your users are receiving. First is to start up the application that your users are using and attempt to re-create the error. This will often give you an idea of where the problem lies. Alternatively, you can start the SQL Query Analyzer and attempt to perform operations against the database. This will help you determine the exact nature of the error messages. The other option that you can use to determine the actual problem is to inspect the SQL Server error log. Most errors that will require inspection by the DBA are logged to the error log.

Attempt a Fix

After you have determined what the problem is, the next step that you must take is to attempt a fix. In most cases, the solutions to errors that you are getting are easily found in the SQL Server Books Online or in TechNet. In other cases, the best solution is to call your primary support provider or Microsoft's technical support, as they will usually have some sort of solution for even the most difficult of problems.

SQL Server Information Sources

There are several resources that you can use when looking for information about SQL Server and any errors that have occurred. When troubleshooting any SQL Server error, you should consult all of these to see what information you can get.

SQL Server Error Log

The error log is where SQL Server writes startup information, error messages, and informational messages that occur during everyday operation. This is a text file that can be viewed with a text editor or from within SQL Enterprise Manager. The location of the file is determined in the Registry, and the default path for the error log is `C:\MSSQL7\LOGS\ERRORLOG`. SQL Server creates a new error log every time it is restarted. The previous 6 error logs are saved with extensions numbering `.1` through `.6`.

When you are troubleshooting SQL Server, you will need to view the error log. The easiest way to do this is within SQL Enterprise Manager. The following will walk you through viewing the SQL Server error log from within SQL Enterprise Manager.

Viewing the SQL Server error log

1. Start SQL Enterprise Manager and connect to the server that you will be viewing the error log on.

2. Click the plus sign next to the name of the server to expand the view.

3. Click the plus sign next to the management folder, then click on the plus sign next to the SQL Server Logs folder. This will expand the entry to list the current error log entry, as well as the previous six.

4. You can choose which error log to view by clicking its name in the list. When you choose one, the contents of the log are displayed in the panel on the right side, as seen in Figure 19.1.

5. If the text of the error message is too long to be displayed in the window, you can double-click the message to pop up a box containing the full text of the message, as shown in Figure 19.2.

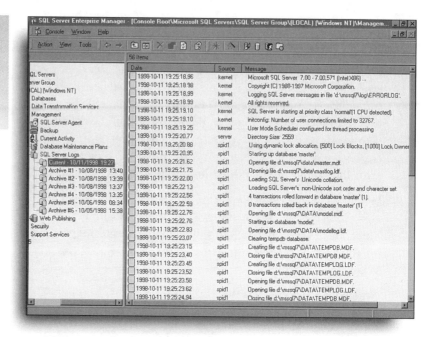

FIGURE 19.1

After choosing an error log, the contents of the log are displayed in the panel on the right side.

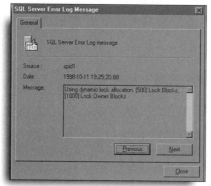

FIGURE 19.2

You can pop up a box displaying the full text of the error message by double-clicking it.

The Windows NT Event Viewer

The Windows NT Event Viewer can be used to view Application, System, and Security information.

Windows NT Application Log

Another valuable source of information about SQL Server is the Windows NT Application log. Not only does it contain information about SQL Server, but also information about Windows NT Server and any other applications that are running on the server. This can be especially useful if there is an outside event or series of events that is affecting SQL Server. The following will talk you through viewing the Windows NT Application log.

Viewing the Windows NT Application log

1. Click the Start menu, go to Programs, and then select Administrative Tools (Common) and choose Event Viewer. This will open the Windows NT Event viewer, as shown in Figure 19.3.

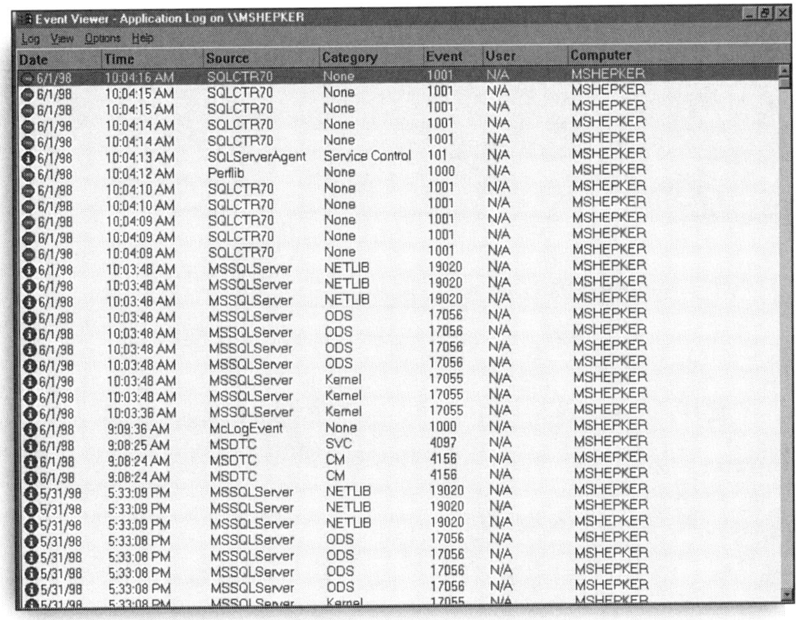

FIGURE 19.3
The Windows NT Event Viewer contains information from all applications running on the server as well as information about the server itself.

2. From the Log menu, click Application. This will change the contents of the screen to show only the information about the applications that are running on the server, and not from Windows NT itself.

3. To view more information about an event, double-click the event and it will open up the Event Detail window, as seen in Figure 19.4, that contains the event description.

When viewing the Windows NT event log, you will find that, because so much information is written there, it is difficult to discern what information comes from SQL Server and what doesn't. You can alleviate this by filtering the source of the event information to show only the SQL Server events. The following will walk you through filtering the Windows NT Application log to show only the SQL Server events.

Filtering

Filtering the Windows NT Application log can make it easier to view information that pertains only the SQL Server.

605

FIGURE 19.4

The Event Detail windows provide you with more information, including an event description.

Filtering the Windows NT Application log

1. Open the Windows NT Event Viewer and view the Application log as outlined in the previous task.

2. From the View menu, choose the Filter Events option. The Filter dialog box, shown in Figure 19.5, will appear.

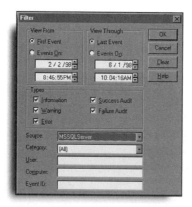

FIGURE 19.5

The Filter dialog box enables you to choose the Source of events that you view.

3. In the Source drop-down box, choose MSSQLServer. This will filter out all events except for the ones that are coming from the MSSQLServer service.

4. In the Category dialog box, you can narrow down the filter into categories such as Backup, Network Libraries, and Server events.

5. If you choose to filter by category after you have chosen the Source and Category, click OK. The Application log will be filtered, as shown in Figure 19.6, to show only the events that you have selected.

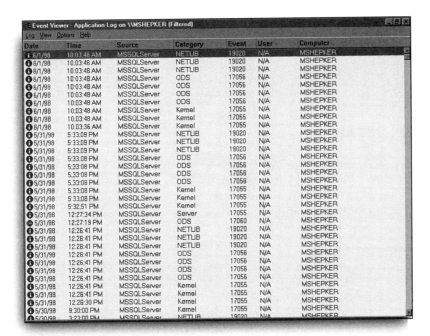

FIGURE 19.6

After filtering the Application log, it becomes much easier to discern which events come from SQL Server.

SQL Server Error Messages

When SQL Server encounters an error, it will either write a message to the error log, send a message back to the user, or both, depending on the severity level. Every SQL Server error message contains the following information:

- A unique number that identifies the message.

- A number that identifies the severity level of the error.

- A number that identifies the source of the error.

- An informational message that tells you about the error and, depending on the error, suggests some steps you can take to fix the error.

All error messages are stored in the *sysmessages* table in the *master* database. To view a complete list of all messages, run the following query listed in Listing 19.1.

```
1 use master
2 go
3 select * from sysmessages
4 go
```

Severity Levels

Every SQL Server error message contains a severity level that indicates the type of problem that SQL Server has encountered and how bad that problem can be. Error messages can be divided into two categories: nonfatal errors and fatal errors.

Nonfatal Errors

Nonfatal errors are errors that have severity levels of 0 and 10 through 18. Often, nonfatal errors are user correctable errors. These errors don't cause the connection to SQL Server to be dropped. Table 19.1 shows some examples of nonfatal errors.

TABLE 19.1 SQL Server Nonfatal Errors

Severity Level	Definition	Example
0 or 10	These messages aren't errors. These are informational messages that don't require any user correction.	Msg 2528, Level 10 State 1. DBCC execution completed. If DBCC printed error messages, see your System Administrator.
11 through 16	These errors are user correctable errors. Most often, these are due to syntax or logic errors in SQL statements.	Msg 109, Level 15, State 1. There are more columns in the INSERT statement than the values specified in the VALUES clause. The number of values in the VALUES clause must match the number of columns.

Severity Level	Definition	Example
17	Indicates that SQLServer has run out of some resource. This can be physical resources, such as disk space, or configurable resources, such as locks.	Msg 1105, Level 17, State 1. Can't allocate space for object SYSLOGS in database PUBS because the syslogs segment is full. If you ran out of space in Syslogs, dump the transaction log. Otherwise, use `ALTER DATABASE` or `sp_extendsegment` to increase the size of the segment.
18	Indicates that there is an internal error that has kept SQL Server from completing the statement, but the connection to the server isn't terminated.	Msg 1521, Level 18, State 1. Sort failed because a table in tempdb used for the processing of the query had a bad data page count. Tempdb should not have been damaged.

Fatal Errors

Fatal errors are errors with severity levels of 19 or greater. When a fatal occurs, the user's connection to SQL Server is terminated. Correcting these errors often require the database to be taken offline and the SQL Administrator to perform corrective actions. Table 19.2 shows some examples of fatal errors.

TABLE 19.2 A Listing of Fatal SQL Server Errors

Severity Level	Definition	Example
19	These errors indicate a nonconfigurable internal limit has been reached. These errors rarely happen.	Msg 422, Level 19, State 1. Too many nested expressions or logical operators to compile. Try splitting query or limiting ANDs and ORs.
20	These errors indicate that the error was in the current process. These affect only the current process, and the database was probably not damaged.	Msg 405, Level 20, State 1. Cannot route query results - query internal representation corrupted.

continues…

609

	TABLE 19.2 Continued	
Severity Level	Definition	Example
21	These errors indicate that a problem has occurred that affects all processes in the database. There was likely no corruption in the database though.	Msg 611, Level 21, State 1. Attempt made to end a transaction that is current idle or in the middle of an update.
22	These indicate that the integrity of a table is suspect. Level 22 errors are rare.	Msg 904, Level 22, State 1. Unable to find master database row in Sysdatabases. Cannot open master database.
23	These messages indicate that the integrity of an entire database is suspect. These errors are rare.	Msg 277, Level 23, State 1. A transaction that began in this stored procedure that did updates in tempdb is still active. This will cause corruption in tempdb that will exist until the server is rebooted. `All BEGIN TRANs` and `END TRANs` must have matching `COMMITs` and `ROLLBACKs`.
24	These messages indicate some sort of media failure. It may be necessary to replace hardware and reload the database.	Msg 902, Level 24, State 1. Hardware error detected reading logical page 24145, virtual page 340782 in database PUBS.
25	These messages indicate some sort of system error internal to SQL Server.	Msg 3508, Level 25, State 1. Attempt to set PUBS database to single user mode failed because the usage count is 2. Make sure that no users are currently using this database and re-run `CHECKPOINT`.

It is important to investigate all fatal errors that happen. This often involves taking the database offline and running diagnostics. Some fatal errors will occur and then, during diagnostics, will not reappear. It is better to investigate the errors when you first find them and not allow them to get any worse.

Using the Database Consistency Checker

The Database Consistency Checker, or DBCC, was originally intended to simply check the consistency of the database. Over time, Microsoft has added many useful features to DBCC that can be used when troubleshooting SQL Server problems.

DBCC is the most useful and powerful tool when trying to isolate and repair problems that you are having within your databases. Aside from the supported DBCC commands, there are many others that are undocumented and unsupported by Microsoft. If you come across any of these, it is best to use them with caution and only after contacting your primary support provider. When repairing an error, some of the commands could cause more problems to your database due to other underlying problems.

With the release of SQL Server 7.0, Microsoft has added two new DBCC commands: CHECKFILEGROUP and SHRINKFILE. The SHRINKDB command has been revamped and renamed to SHRINK-DATABASE. Following is the complete list of supported DBCC commands and the syntax:

```
DBCC {
    CHECKALLOC [(database_name [, NOINDEX])] |
    CHECKCATALOG [(database_name)] |
    CHECKTABLE (table_name [, NOINDEX | index_id]) |
    CHECKDB [(database_name [, NOINDEX])] |
    CHECKFILEGROUP [( [ {'filegroup_name' | filegroup_id} ]
    ➥ [, NOINDEX] ) ] |
    CHECKIDENT [(table_name)] |
    DBREPAIR (database_name, DROPDB [, NOINIT]) |
    DBREINDEX (['table_name' [, index_name[, fillfactor ]]])
    dllname (FREE) |
    INPUTBUFFER (spid) |
    MEMUSAGE |
    NEWALLOC [(database_name [, NOINDEX])] |
    OPENTRAN ({database_name} | {database_id})
    ➥ [WITH TABLERESULTS] |
```

Be careful with DBCCs!

Take extreme care in using and experimenting with DBCC commands. Not all DBCC commands are supported features of SQL Server and you will not receive support from Microsoft in using these commands. Microsoft may not include these commands in future releases of SQL Server.

```
        OUTPUTBUFFER (spid) ¦
        PERFMON ¦
        PINTABLE (database_id, table_id) ¦
        PROCCACHE ¦
        ROWLOCK (db_id, table_id , set) ¦
        SHOW_STATISTICS (table_name, index_name) ¦
        SHOWCONTIG (table_id, [index_id]) ¦
        SHRINKDATABASE (database_name [, target_percent]
      ➥ [, {NOTRUNCATE ¦ TRUNCATEONLY} ] ) ¦
        SHRINKFILE ( {file_name ¦ file_id } [, target_size]
      ➥ [, {NOTRUNCATE ¦ TRUNCATEONLY} ] ) ¦
        SQLPERF ({IOSTATS ¦ LRUSTATS ¦ NETSTATS ¦ RASTATS
      ➥[, CLEAR]} ¦ {THREADS} ¦ {LOGSPACE}) ¦
        TEXTALL [({database_name ¦ database_id}[,
      ➥FULL ¦ FAST])] ¦
        TEXTALLOC [({table_name ¦ table_id}[, FULL ¦ FAST])] ¦
        TRACEOFF (trace#) ¦
        TRACEON (trace#) ¦
        TRACESTATUS (trace# [, trace#...]) ¦
        UNPINTABLE (database_id, table_id) ¦
        UPDATEUSAGE ({0 ¦ database_name} [, table_name
      ➥[, index_id]]) ¦
        USEROPTIONS}
[WITH NO_INFOMSGS]
```

CHECKALLOC

The CHECKALLOC command is used to check the allocation and usage of all pages in a specified database. CHECKALLOC acquires a schema lock on database objects before running to prevent changes to the schema of the database. There is no need to run CHECKALLOC if you are currently running CHECKDB, and CHECKALLOC has been replaced by the NEWALLOC command. The syntax of the CHECKALLOC command is as follows:

```
DBCC CHECKALLOC [('database_name'[, NOINDEX])]
➥[WITH NO_INFOMSGS]
```

CHECKCATALOG

The CHECKCATALOG function checks for consistency in the system tables. The system tables don't have foreign keys, so it is up to SQL Server itself to keep track of their consistency. It is rare to find problems with the system tables, but if it happens, the results can be catastrophic. The syntax of the CHECKCATALOG command is as follows:

```
DBCC CHECKCATALOG [(database_name)][ WITH NO_INFOMSGS]
```

CHECKDB

If you only have the time to run one DBCC on your database, you should consider running CHECKDB. CHECKDB performs a comprehensive check of all tables in the database for the following:

- Makes sure that all data pages are properly linked. Data pages in SQL Server are in a double-linked list. This means that page 1 in the list points to page 2 in the list and page 2 points back to page 1.

- Makes sure that all index pages are properly linked.

- Checks to make sure that all indexes are in the correct sort order.

- Makes sure that the row offsets are reasonable. The row offset specifies where on a data page the row resides.

- Makes sure that the data on each data page is readable and in logical form.

The syntax of the CHECKDB command is

```
DBCC CHECKDB [(database_name [, NOINDEX])] [WITH NO_INFOMSGS]
```

If you leave out the database name, CHECKDB will check the database that you are currently using. The NOINDEX option allows for quick execution of the CHECKDB, but it will not do as complete a check. NOINDEX will check the clustered index and data only on user-defined tables. If a clustered index isn't present, only the data will be checked. The NOINDEX option doesn't affect the way

DBCC CHECKCATALOG

DBCC **CHECKCATALOG** command should be run frequently to check the consistency of the system tables, or system catalog.

Not enough time?

If you can only one run DBCC on your databases, you should run DBCC **CHECKDB**.

that CHECKDB handles system tables. When checking system tables, clustered indexes, nonclustered indexes, and data are checked. If you specify the WITH NO_INFOMSGS option, the command will run without returning informational messages.

The normal output of a CHECKDB run on the pubs database will look something like the following:

```
Checking pubs
Checking 1
The total number of data pages in this table is 4.
Table has 69 data rows.
Checking 2
The total number of data pages in this table is 4.
Table has 49 data rows.
Checking 3
The total number of data pages in this table is 10.
Table has 277 data rows.
      .
      .
      .
Checking 688005482
The total number of data pages in this table is 1.
The total number of TEXT/IMAGE pages in this table is 62.
Table has 8 data rows.
Checking 752005710
The total number of data pages in this table is 2.
Table has 43 data rows.
DBCC execution completed. If DBCC printed error messages,
see your System Administrator.
```

On large databases, the output of the CHECKDB can be quite long if you don't specify the WITH NO_INFOMSGS option. In this case, the easiest way to look for errors is, after the CHECKDB has completed running, go to Edit, Find, and type **Msg** in the Find box. If it comes back without finding anything, your database is clean. If not, you need to start investigating what the message is telling you.

CHECKFILEGROUP

The CHECKFILEGROUP command is new to SQL Server 7.0. This command enables you to check the structural integrity and allocation of all tables in a specified file group. CHECKFILEGROUP essentially performs all the checks that were performed by CHECKDB, NEWALLOC, and TEXTALL on every table that is contained in a file group. The output of this command is very similar to that of the CHECKDB command. The syntax of the CHECKFILEGROUP command is as follows:

```
DBBC CHECKFILEGROUP [( [ {'filegroup_name' ¦
➥filegroup_id} ] [, NOINDEX] ) ] [WITH NO_INFOMSGS]
```

CHECKIDENT

The CHECKIDENT command is used to check the current value of the identity column on a table and correct it, if needed. By specifying the NORESEED option, SQL Server will compare the current value of the identity column and what that value should be. If you specify the RESEED option, SQL Server will correct the value of the identity column. The syntax of the CHECKIDENT command is as follows:

```
DBCC CHECKIDENT ('table_name'[, { NORESEED ¦ {RESEED
➥ [, new_reseed_value] } } ] )
```

CHECKTABLE

The CHECKTABLE command performs all the same functions as the CHECKDB command does, but only to an individual specified table This is useful when you suspect problems with a single table and don't have time required to run a CHECKDB. The syntax of the CHECKTABLE command is as follows:

```
DBCC CHECKTABLE (table_name [, NOINDEX ¦ index_id])
➥ [WITH NO_INFOMSGS]
```

The table name option must be supplied for this command to work. If you want to check an index for corruption, you can supply the index ID of that index. To get the index ID, run the query in Listing 19.2. Replace dbname with the name of the database that the table resides in and replace indname with the name of the index that you want to investigate.

LISTING 19.2 This SQL Query Enables You to Obtain the Index ID for Use in the CHECKTABLE Command

```
1 use dbname
2 go
3 select indid from sysindexes where name = 'indname'
4 go
```

> **DBCC** DNREPAIR
>
> DBCC **DBREPAIR** does not repair databases. It is used only to drop corrupted databases.

DBREPAIR

The DBREPAIR command is used to drop a damaged or suspect database. This command was used in earlier versions of SQL Server and has been provided for backwards compatibility only. When running the DBREPAIR command, no one can be using the database that will be dropped. The syntax of the DBREPAIR command is as follows:

```
DBCC DBREPAIR ( database_name, DROPDB [, NOINIT] )
```

DBREINDEX

The DBREINDEX command rebuilds either one or all of the indexes in a specified table. There are two major advantages with using the DBREINDEX command instead of manually dropping and re-creating the indexes. The first is that indexes that enforce PRIMARY KEY or UNIQUE constraints can be re-created without dropping and re-creating the constraints. The second is that the indexes can be re-created without having to know anything about the structure of the table. The syntax of the DBREINDEX command is

```
DBCC DBREINDEX ([table_name [, index_name [, fillfactor
➥[, {SORTED_DATA ¦ SORTED_DATA_REORG}]]]])
➥[WITH NOINFOMSGS]
```

You must specify the table name in order for this command to work. If you only want to rebuild a single index in a table, you can specify it. To rebuild all indexes, you can 'specify' instead of a table name.

dllname (FREE)

The dllname (FREE) command is used to remove a dynamic linked library from SQL Server memory. Extended stored procedures use DLLs to provide functionality that would otherwise be unavailable. When an extended stored procedure is executed, the DLL is loaded into memory and it will remain in memory until SQL Server is shut down. The dllname (FREE) command enables you to remove a DLL from memory without shutting down SQL Server. The syntax of the command is as follows:

```
DBCC dllname (FREE)
```

INPUTBUFFER

The INPUTBUFFER command is used to display the first 255 characters of the last command that was sent to the server by a client. The command requires that you know the spid of the user who you will be investigating. You can get the user's spid by running the sp_who stored procedure. The syntax of the command is as follows:

```
DBCC dllname (FREE)
```

OPENTRAN

The OPENTRAN command is used to display information about the oldest active transaction in a specific database as well as the oldest replicated and nonreplicated transactions, if the database is published. This command is especially useful when troubleshooting problems with the transaction log filling up. When backing up the transaction log, only the inactive portion of the log is truncated. If a user's transaction is hung and the log isn't being truncated, OPENTRAN will tell you and let you kill the user's spid. The syntax of the OPENTRAN command is

```
DBCC OPENTRAN [('database_name'¦ database_id)]
➡[WITH TABLERESULTS [,NO_INFOMSGS]]
```

OUTPUTBUFFER

The OUTPUTBUFFER command enables you to view the last 255 characters that the SQL Server has sent back to the client, both in ASCII and hexadecimal format. You must pass the spid of the user that you are investigating. The spid can be obtained by running the sp_who stored procedure. The syntax of the command is as follows:

```
DBCC OUTPUTBUFFER spid
```

PERFMON

The PERFMON command returns performance information about SQL Server. PERFMON returns information on all three types of SQL Performance Monitor statistics: IOSTATS, LRUSTATS, and NETSTATS. The syntax of the command is as follows:

```
DBCC PERFMON
```

PINTABLE

The PINTABLE command marks a table as "pinned". A pinned table forces SQL Server to leave the pages associated with the table in memory. This doesn't cause SQL Server to read all pages into memory; rather, it marks them as pinned as they are read by SQL statement. SQL Server will log updates and will write the changes to disk, if needed, but doesn't flush the pages from memory. This command is useful for very small, frequently accessed tables. The syntax of the PINTABLE command is

```
DBCC PINTABLE (database_id, table_id)
```

PROCACHE

The PROCACHE command is used by SQL Performance Monitor to investigate the procedure cache. The syntax of the command is

```
DBCC PROCCACHE
```

ROWLOCK

The ROWLOCK command is used to enable insert row locking on tables in SQL Server 6.5. SQL Server 7.0 automatically uses row locking and is supported only for backwards compatibility. The syntax of the command is

```
DBCC ROWLOCK (db_id, table_id , set)
```

SHOWCONTIG

The SHOWCONTIG command scans the table that you specify for fragmentation. Fragmentation occurs when INSERTs, UPDATEs and DELETEs are made against tables. After time, the order of the pages become so disorganized that read-ahead cache can do little to keep up with the physical reads required to get the information off the disk. The syntax of the SHOWCONTIG command is

```
DBCC SHOWCONTIG (table_id, [index_id])
```

To run the SHOWCONTIG command, you will need to know the table ID of the table that you are interested in. To do this, run the query in Listing 19.3. The index ID isn't required to run this command, and it will default to index ID 0 or 1. Replace *dbname* with the name of the database that the table resides in and replace *tbl_name* with the name of the table that you want to investigate.

LISTING 19.3   This SQL Query Enables You to Get the Table ID For Use in the SHOWCONTIG Command

```
1 use dbname
2 go
3 select id from sysobjects where name = 'tbl_name'
4 go
```

The output of the SHOWCONTIG has several valuable pieces of information:

```
DBCC SHOWCONTIG scanning 'testtable' table...
[SHOW_CONTIG - SCAN ANALYSIS]
```

```
Table: 'testtable' (1625056825)  Indid: 0  dbid:1
TABLE level scan performed.
- Pages Scanned............................: 68
- Extent Switches..........................: 8
- Avg. Pages per Extent....................: 7.6
- Scan Density [Best Count:Actual Count]...: 100.00% [9:9]
- Avg. Bytes free per page.................: 51.2
- Avg. Page density (full).................: 97.46%
- Overflow Pages...........................: 67
- Avg. Bytes free per Overflow page........: 52.0
- Avg. Overflow Page density...............: 97.4%
- Disconnected Overflow Pages..............: 0
```

The first number that you need to pay attention to is the Scan Density. The optimal number for this is 100. The best count is the ideal number of extent changes if everything is contiguously linked. The actual count is the actual number of extents that the table extends across.

Use DBCC DBREINDEX to correct this problem.

SHOW_STATISTICS

One of the most important jobs of a SQL Administrator is to keep the database running quickly. Developers add indexes to their tables to help speed the performance of SELECTs made against their tables. SQL Server keeps statistics about the selectivity of those indexes and then uses those statistics to make decisions in query processing. Unfortunately, SQL Server doesn't always keep these statistics updated. After a great deal of information has been added, or the table had been truncated and reloaded, it is a good idea to run SHOW_STATISTICS to check the selectivity of the indexes in the table. The syntax of the SHOW_STATISTICS command is

```
DBCC SHOW_STATISTICS (table_name, index_name)
```

The output of the SHOW_STATISTICS command will look something like Figure 19.7. This was run on the clustered index on the authors table in the pubs database.

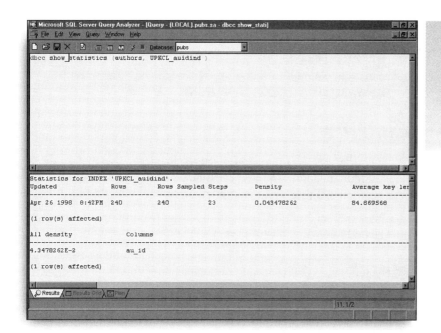

FIGURE 19.7
The results of DBCC
SHOW_CONTIG give you
valuable information
about the selectivity of
your indexes.

The most important bit of information to get out of this report is the density number. This is the number that SQL Server uses to determine the selectivity of the index. You can multiply the number of rows by the number in density to determine the selectivity. The lower the number, the more likely SQL Server will be to choose to use the index. In this case, the clustered index should have a selectivity of 1, but the statistics are off, giving us a selectivity of about 10. This will cause SQL Server to perform a table scan instead of using the index. You can use the UPDATE STATISTICS command to fix this.

SHRINKDATABASE

The SHRINKDATABASE command is used to shrink the size of all the data files in a database. If you choose to specify a target percentage, SQL Server will attempt to shrink all data files in a database to comply. SQL Server will not shrink the database files past the size that is needed to store the data. When running the SHRINKDATABASE command, you don't have to have the database in single user mode. Users can continue to work while it is being shrunk. The syntax of the command is

```
DBCC SHRINKDATABASE (database_name [, target_percent][,
➥{NOTRUNCATE ¦ TRUNCATEONLY} ]  )
```

SHRINKFILE

The SHRINKFILE command is used to shrink the size of a single data file in a database. See SHRINKDATABASE for more information. The syntax of the command is

```
DBCC SHRINKFILE ( {file_name ¦ file_id } [, target_size][,
➥ {NOTRUNCATE ¦ TRUNCATEONLY} ]  )
```

SQLPERF

The SQLPERF command is used to monitor the size of the transaction logs in all databases. This can be a good command to help you monitor your transaction logs to determine when to back them up or when to truncate them. The syntax of the SQLPERF command is

```
DBCC SQLPERF (LOGSPACE)
```

TRACEOFF

The TRACEOFF command is used to turn off trace flags that have been set using the TRACEON command. The syntax of the command is

```
DBCC TRACEOFF (trace# [,Ötrace#])
```

TRACEON

The TRACEON command is used to turn on trace flags. Trace flags are used to change or control certain characteristics of SQL Server. The syntax of the command is

```
DBCC TRACEON (trace# [,Ötrace#])
```

TRACESTATUS

The TRACESTATUS command is used to display the current status of trace flags. The syntax of the command is

```
DBCC TRACESTATUS (trace# [, ...trace#])
```

UNPINTABLE

The UNPINTABLE command is used to mark a table as unpinned. This command is used in conjunction with the PINTABLE command. This command doesn't automatically cause all pages to be flushed from memory; instead it allows SQL Server to move them from memory as needed. The syntax of the command is

```
DBCC UNPINTABLE (database_id, table_id)
```

UPDATEUSAGE

The UPDATEUSAGE command corrects inaccuracies in the sysindexes table that can result in incorrect values when viewing database information in Enterprise Manager and running the sp_spaceused stored procedure. SQL Server doesn't automatically keep track of this information, so when you view the size of you database in Enterprise Manager, it may not be accurate. The syntax of UPDATEUSAGE is

```
DBCC UPDATEUSAGE ({0 ¦ database_name} [, table_name
➥[, index_id]])
```

If you pass UPDATEUSAGE a 0 in the place of the database name, it will check the current database. The UPDATEUSAGE can take a long time to run and could result in a degradation of system performance. It should only be run if you suspect inaccuracies or during off hours.

USEROPTIONS

The USEROPTIONS command is used to show the current working set of user options that were activated using the SET command. The syntax of the command is

```
DBCC USEROPTIONS
```

Using Trace Flags

When coding SQL Server for public release, Microsoft determines a default amount of functionality and error recording that meets the needs of most of the people most of the time. There are times, though, that SQL Administrators will need more than the default. Microsoft has provided a way to add extra functionality through the use of trace flags.

Setting Trace Flags

There are three separate ways to set trace flags in SQL Server. The first is to use DBCC commands to turn the flags on and off. The second is to turn on the trace flags as a part of the startup parameters of SQL Server. Starting SQL Server from a command prompt and specifying the trace flags there is the last way to set them.

Using DBCCs to Set Trace Flags

The easiest and most frequently used way to set trace flags is to use the DBCC TRACEON command. Using the command, you can turn trace flags on and off without restarting SQL Server. The syntax for this command is

```
DBCC TRACEON (FLAG1, FLAG2, ...)
```

Be careful with trace flags!

Trace flags aren't a part of the supported feature set of SQL Server. Microsoft may not include them in future releases of the product and their technical support people may not be able to help you with their use. There are also a number of undocumented trace flags. If you come across any of these, make sure that you speak with your primary support provider before using them. Use caution when using or experimenting with trace flags.

To turn off the trace flags, you would use the following syntax:

```
DBCC TRACEOFF (FLAG1, FLAG2, ...)
```

To check to see whether you have individual trace flags turned on, the syntax is

```
DBCC TRACESTATUS (FLAG1, FLAG2, ...)
```

Setting Flags in Server Options

If you need a trace flag to be active as soon as the server is started, you can add the trace flag into the Server Properties dialog box. Click the Startup Parameters button on the General tab and add the trace flags with a –T before them. When trace flags are set in this way, they will be active as soon as the server comes online and will affect all connections to the server.

Setting Trace Flags from the Command Line

If you need a trace flag in effect as soon as SQL Server starts, you can set it at the command line by using the –T option; for example:

```
sqlservr -dc:\mssql7\data\master.mdf
➥-ec:\mssql7\log\errorlog ñld:\mssql7\
➥data\mastlog.ldf ñT3609
```

Note that the trace flag parameter is case sensitive. If you start SQL Server using a –t instead of a –T, the trace flags will still be in effect, but it will also start a number of other, internal, traces as well. Trace flags activated in this manner will affect all user connections to the server.

Informational Trace Flags

Trace flags can be divided into three separate categories: informational, behavioral and compatibility, and special trace flags. The trace flags listed in Table 19.3 are some of the more useful informational trace flags.

TABLE 19.3   SQL Server Informational Trace Flags

Flag #	Description
302	This flag details information about the use of the statistics page and what SQL Server estimated to be the physical and logical cost for using the indexes. Trace flag 302 should be used in conjunction with Trace flag 310.
310	This will print information about the join order. When used in conjunction with Trace flag 302, it will return information similar to the SET SHOWPLAN ON command.
1200	This flag will return lock information including the type of lock requested and the spid of the user who requested it.
1204	This flag will return information about the types of locks that are participating in a deadlock at the time it happens. It will also detail the spids of the users affected and the command that was running at the time.
1205	This will return detailed information about the commands that were running when a deadlock occurs. This flag is especially useful when used in conjunction with Trace flag 1204.
4030	This flag will print both a byte and ASCII representation of the receive buffer. This is useful when you need to see exactly what the client is sending to the server.
4031	This flag will print both a byte and ASCII representation of the send buffer. The send buffer is what the server sends back to the client.
4032	This flag will print only the ASCII contents of the receive buffer. This flag is commonly used in place of Trace flag 4030 when trace speed is important.

Compatibility and Behavior Changing Trace Flags

Compatibility trace flags usually emulate behaviors that were present in previous versions of SQL Server and are provided for backwards compatibility of client applications. It is important to realize that, because Microsoft doesn't support trace flags, they may change in future releases. You should use these as a temporary fix while the client applications are being retooled to take advantages the new features of SQL Server. The trace flags listed in Table 19.4 are some of the more useful compatibility and behavior changing trace flags.

TABLE 19.4   SQL Server Compatibility Trace Flags

Flag #	Description
107	This flag causes SQL Server to interpret numbers containing a decimal point as float instead of decimal.
110	This flag will disable the ANSI SELECT feature that was introduced in SQL Server 6.5. This feature disallowed the use of duplicate column names in SELECT and UPDATE statements. For example, the following SELECT statement would cause an error in SQL Server 7.0 without having Trace flag 110 set: `SELECT * FROM authors, authors`
237	Enables users who have SELECT permission on a table to create a new table that references the first table. In SQL Server 7.0, a user must have REFERENCES permission to do this.
246	In SQL Server 7.0, column names must be explicitly provided when performing SELECT INTO and CREATE VIEW queries. For example, if a column is created using an aggregate or mathematical function, SQL Server will return an error. This flag will suppress this error.
3608	This will cause SQL Server to skip the automatic recovery of all databases except the master database.
4022	This will cause SQL Server to skip the execution of all startup stored procedures. This is especially useful if you have a stored procedure that is causing SQL Server to hang on startup.

Special Trace Flags

There are three special trace flags that can be used in conjunction with any of the above trace flags. They control output of information from the traces and who is affected by them. The trace flags in Table 19.5 are the special trace flags.

TABLE 19.5 SQL Server Special Trace Flags	
Flag #	Description
–1	This flag indicates that trace flags should be set for all current client connections. This only affects the current connections to the server, not connections made after the command has been issued. This flag isn't needed when you are setting the trace from the command line or from server options, as they automatically affect all connections to the server.

3604	This flag redirects informational messages from DBCC commands and traces to the client machine. When running DBCC commands without Trace flag 3604, you will often receive no other information back except the following:
	
	`DBCC execution completed. If DBCC printed error messages,`
	`see your Systems Administrator.`

3605	This flag indicates that informational messages should be redirected to the Error Log. This will enable you to watch a sequence of events that may be causing problems instead of single errors that may not show the big picture.

Dealing with Corrupted Databases

Sometimes, after you have begun troubleshooting, you will learn that your problems don't lie with configuration issues or user training issues: You find actual corruption in the database. After you have found corruption, the next step that you must take is to decide what to do about it. When making this decision, you must take into account the amount of time that the database has been offline for you to find the problem and the amount of time that it will take to correct. Sometimes, restoring from the last known good backup is the best option. Note that even if SQL Server has marked a database as inaccessible, Microsoft has ways of getting to the data. If this is the case, you may want to contact Microsoft for assistance.

Fixing Corrupted User Tables

When dealing with corrupted user tables, it is important to remember that, although they contain all the information that your users have collected, they are the easier of the two types of tables to repair.

The first step in repairing a corrupted user table is to make a full backup of the database in the current state. This backup should be clearly marked and put in a safe place. This backup will provide a two-fold purpose. First, it will be a record of what was wrong in the database. This can be useful at a later time when you have more time to investigate exactly what was wrong with the database. Second, it can be used to restore the database after you have attempted a fix that didn't work.

The second step is to figure out exactly where in the table the corruption lies. If the corruption lies within an index on the table, oftentimes dropping and re-creating the index will fix the problem. If the corruption lies in the table itself, you will need to drop and re-create the table.

Dropping and re-creating a table isn't as easy as it sounds. Before dropping the table, you must figure out what to do with the data that is contained in the table. Depending on the age of the last backup and the activity level in the database, you may be able to restore the information from backup. Unfortunately, this isn't always an option. If the activity level in the database isn't that great, you may be able to have the users re-create the data by reentering it. Otherwise, you will need to use the Bulk Copy Program, or BCP, to get the data out.

After you have removed the data from the corrupted table, the last step is to drop and re-create the table. After that is complete and you have loaded the data back into the table, you should run DBCCs on the database to ensure that there are no more errors.

SEE ALSO
➤ *BCP is covered in more detail on page 520.*

Fixing Corrupted System Tables

Corrupted system tables, while they contain no user data, are the most difficult failure to recover from. The system tables contain all the data that make the rest of the tables in your database work. When a system table fails, the results can be catastrophic.

The first step is to make a backup of the database in its nonfunctional state. As with corrupted user tables, you will need this as a record of the state that the database was in when you started troubleshooting.

The next step that you should take is to call your primary support provider or Microsoft's technical support. There are a number of undocumented DBCC commands and trace flags that they may be able to help you implement to repair your database.

Next, restore a previous backup and run a DBCC against it. System table corruption doesn't always make itself evident as soon as it occurs. If you are running DBCCs on a daily basis, you may have caught the corruption on the day that it occurred. If not, don't be overly surprised if your previous backups were corrupted too.

As a last resort, you may need to BCP all the data out of your user tables. After all the data is out, you should drop the database and the devices that it resided on, and completely re-create the database. When the database has been re-created, you can BCP the data back in.

Maintain it

You create a plan of preventive maintenance and then implement it.

Preventive Maintenance

In Microsoft's literature regarding SQL Server 7.0, one of the advances it claims is that you no longer need to run DBCCs against your database. Although that may be what they are striving for, what they may be trying to say is that you don't have to run them as often as you did in previous versions. Not running DBCCs would be akin to telling the National Spelling Bee Champion that he doesn't need to run spell check on his latest book report. He may be good...but no one is perfect. With that aside, there are a few things that you can do to help ensure that your databases are online as much as possible.

First, one cannot stress enough the importance of making daily backups of production databases. You should always have some sort of backup scheme in place in the event that something catastrophic happens. Many SQL Administrators have lost sleep trying to repair a database that could have been back online in a short time if there had been a current backup.

Second, it is important to run DBCCs against your databases as frequently as you can. In a 7X24X365 production situation, this can be difficult to do. You should try to find at least one time during the week to run a DBCC CHECKDB. The best time to do this is late at night after you have run your backup. That way you will know if the database you have on tape is consistent.

Last, document everything that you do to your database. It may seem that it is one extra, inconsequential step that you take during day-to-day operation, but you will find your documentation to be invaluable during troubleshooting.

Other Common Problems

During the daily operation of a database, you will find that there are several problems that seem to come up more frequently than others. Sometimes, they are difficult to troubleshoot, other times they are quite simple. Two of the most common problems are a full transaction log and a blocking process.

Full Transaction Log

Every operation in SQL Server is logged in the transaction log. This functionality enables SQL Server to roll back, or cancel, transactions that have not been completed. This allows for a very stable database environment, but it can be very frustrating when the transaction log fills up. A full transaction log is usually seen as error 1105:

```
Can't allocate space for object syslogs in database dbname
because the logsegment is full. If you ran out of space in
syslogs, dump the transaction log. Otherwise use
ALTER DATABASE or sp_extendsegment to increase the size of
the segment.
```

If the transaction log is completely full, a BACKUP TRANSACTION WITH TRUNCATE_ONLY will fail because SQL Server cannot write a checkpoint record to the transaction log. If this is the case, the only option that you have is to dump the log WITH NO_LOG. The syntax for dumping the transaction log is

The transaction log is important

After you have fixed a full transaction log, it is important that you make a full backup of the database. This will ensure that the database is recoverable in the event of failure.

```
BACKUP TRANSACTION WITH NO_LOG
```

After this completes, you will need to back up the database as soon as possible because you have lost that extra measure of redundancy.

Blocking

To provide multiuser functionality, SQL Server uses locking to make sure that two user's actions don't interfere with each other. Locking stops one user from using the same resources as another. A block arises when one user has a lock on a resource that another user is attempting to access. If the first user doesn't relinquish its lock quickly, it will effectively lock up the second user. You can use the sp_who stored procedure within ISQL/w to find users who are blocking.

```
spid status    loginame hostname blk  dbname  cmd
----------------------------------------------------------------

1    sleeping sa                 0    master  MIRROR HANDLER
2    sleeping sa                 0    master  LAZY WRITER
3    sleeping sa                 0    master  CHECKPOINT SLEEP
4    sleeping sa                 0    master  RA MANAGER
10   sleeping Jack     12-102    0    pubs    AWAITING COMMAND
11   runnable Larry    07-468    10   pubs    SELECT
```

In this example, you will notice that there is a number in the blk column of spid 11. This indicates that spid 10 is blocking spid 11. Transactions should complete quickly and rarely block, but in some circumstances, you will need to use the KILL command to clear up the block. The syntax of the KILL command is as follows:

```
KILL spid
```

where you put the spid of the user connection that you are going to terminate. The spid of the user is the number that is listed in the first column before the username. This will kill the user connection, roll back their current transaction, and clear up the blocks, but you will need to investigate why the blocks are taking place and how to alleviate them in the future.

Other Sources of Information

Other than the SQL Server Books Online, there are several other sources of information available to you in helping you troubleshoot databases. Some of these resources are free and some aren't, but all of them will be useful to you at one time or another.

Online Knowledge Base

If you have access to the Internet, the most extensive source of information that is frequently updated is Microsoft's Online Support site. It is located at `http://www.microsoft.com/KB`. You can search the entire site for bug notices, fixes, and tips.

Microsoft's Newsgroups

Microsoft makes newsgroups available to the general public. These are available by pointing your newsreader at `msnews.microsoft.com`. There are hundreds of groups available that you can post to and ask questions. One thing to remember is that some people who respond to your posts may not always know the correct answer to your questions. In other words, take their advice with a grain of salt.

TechNet and MSDN

Both TechNet and the Microsoft Developers Network Library contain articles, white papers, and knowledge bases on nearly all of Microsoft's products. The MSDN library is updated and sent out on a quarterly basis, and TechNet is updated monthly. Although both of these are excellent resources, TechNet is aimed more at the administrator and you will find a great deal of useful information there.

Technical Support

When your own resources have run out, the last resource that you can call is Microsoft's technical support. The people at Microsoft technical support may not always have all the answers, but they do have one advantage that all the other resources don't: access to the people who wrote the software. They will be able to help you implement many undocumented fixes and features in SQL Server that would normally be unavailable to you.

sqldiag

There is one utility you should know about before requesting support: The sqldiag utility. It may be requested by Microsoft Product Support when diagnosing problems. The sqldiag utility [sqldiag.exe] gathers and stores diagnostic information for SQL Server into a text file - Sqldiag.txt; it can be found in the `c:\MSSQL\BINN\` directory.

If SQL Server is running, sqldiag will report on the following:

- Text of all error logs.
- Registry information.
- .dll version information.
- `xp_trace_flushqueryhistory` information, if previously used.
- Output from

    `sp_configure`

    `sp_who`

    `sp_lock`

    `sp_helpdb`

    `xp_msver`

    `sp_helpextendedproc`

    `sysprocesses`

- Input buffer SPIDs/deadlock information.

- Diagnostics Report for the server, reporting on:

    Contents of <servername>.txt file

    Operating System Report

    System Report

    Processor List

    Video Display Report

    Hard Drive Report

    Memory Report

    Services Report

    Drivers Report

    IRQ and Port Report

    DMA and Memory Report

    Environment Report

    Network Report

SEE ALSO

➤ *BCP is covered in more detail on page 520.*

Transact-SQL Quick Reference

The focus for this chapter is to describe the elements in the Transact-SQL (T-SQL) language. I will go through most of the language constructs in T-SQL. This isn't intended to be a learning book for the general SQL language. There are several such books on the market from beginner's level to advanced level; some describe the standard ANSI SQL syntax and some specialize on T-SQL. Look for the *Sams Teach Yourself* line of books on SQL and Transact-SQL and *SQL Unleashed* and *SQL Server Programming Unleashed* from Sams Publishing for more specific information on each of these.

New in SQL Server 7.0

Transact-SQL is an evolving language. As with any new release of SQL Server, version 7 includes enhancements to the Transact-SQL dialect. Here follows a brief outline of some of the major enhancements.

Unicode Support

The character set chosen at installation time cannot be changed without transfer of data and rebuild of the installation. Because storage usage for each character is one byte, the maximum number of characters that can be represented is 256. Some of these characters are special characters, so the actual number of available characters is lower. Unicode uses two bytes storage area for each character, which means that 65,536 characters can be represented. Unicode is supported through three new datatypes: *nchar*, *nvarchar*, and *ntext*. Note, however, that twice as much storage area is needed for Unicode data than for the old *char*, *varchar*, and *text* data.

ALTER TABLE, ALTER PROCEDURE, ALTER TRIGGER, ALTER VIEW

It's now possible to change the definition for an object without having to drop and re-create the object. When re-creating an object, permissions have to be re-granted or re-revoked.

ALTER TABLE was restricted in earlier versions of SQL Server. Except for adding and dropping constraints, adding a column was all that could be done. This column had to allow NULL as well.

Many scripts have been written over the years to create an intermediate table with the desired table structure, copying over data and renaming the tables. Some tools, such as Visual Database Tools, found in Visual InterDev, could perform these operations behind the scenes.

With version 7, columns can be dropped from a table, datatypes can be altered, and a column with NOT NULL can be added if a default value or identity attribute is defined for that column.

T-SQL and ANSI/ISO SQL-92

T-SQL has evolved significantly over the years, and so have the ANSI standards for the SQL language. ANSI SQL-92 is a significantly larger standard than its predecessors. There are three levels defined in ANSI SQL-92: Entry, Intermediate, and Full.

SQL Server supports the Entry Level of ANSI SQL-92. Naturally, you will find a number of special statements and features in SQL Server, not defined by the ANSI standard. Examples of such features are as follows:

- Operating system–dependent statements, such as defining physical database storage.

- Legacy syntax and commands. Even if the current version supports the ANSI way of expressing a command, backward compatibly is a major issue.

- Extensions to the ANSI standards. All vendors strive at implementing competitive features. Microsoft is no exception.

So, version 7.0 is a superset of the Entry level of the ANSI SQL-92 standard. Although this was achieved in version 6.5, Microsoft continues to add support for the ANSI standard. This includes new language constructs as well as encouraging developers to express statements as defined by the ANSI standard.

Cursor Enhancements

You are now given the same expressive power when working with SQL cursors as you have with API cursors. Microsoft has introduced an alternative syntax to declaring a cursor in T-SQL. You can explicitly define whether the cursor should be STATIC, INSENSITIVE, or DYNAMIC.

If you don't declare the cursor as read-only, you can also define the level of concurrency with our cursor definition. You can define a cursor for READ_ONLY, SCROLL_LOCKS, or OPTIMISTIC concurrency.

In version 6, all cursor's scope was global; that is, a cursor ran out of scope when the connection was terminated. You now have the ability to define local cursors, which scope is within the creating batch.

You can also return a cursor variable from a stored procedure and process the cursor from the calling batch or stored procedure. This can improve re-use because you can define a generic cursor and call it from several stored procedures or batches.

Creating Database Objects

A database consists of a number of elements or objects. Information about a particular object is found in a system table.

In Table A.1, you find the various object types and where information about the objects is stored.

TABLE A.1 Objects and System Tables in SQL Server

Object Type	System Table
Table, View, Stored Procedure, Trigger, Default, Rule	`sysobjects`
Constraints	`sysconstraints, sysreferences`
Index	`sysindexes`
Datatypes	`systypes`

To create a database object, CREATE permissions must be granted to the user. The creator of an object becomes the object owner (sometimes referred to as DBOO, or Database Object Owner). The database owner (dbo) can create an object with another username as the owner. The object will be created in the current database unless another database is specified. The following lists some examples:

```
CREATE TABLE customers
```

The `customers` table will be owned by the creator and created in the current database.

```
CREATE TABLE pubs..customer
```

The customers table will be created in the pubs database, if the login ID that executes the statement has a username in pubs.

```
CREATE TABLE steve.customer
```

This command can be executed by the dbo and creates a table, which will be owned by the username `steve`. The table will be created in the current database.

Tables

The table is the only type of information carrier in a relational database. The table has a structure containing a set of rows and a set of columns. Well, perhaps not a proper set. Columns can be addressed not only by name but also by position when performing an INSERT. Rows can contain duplicates. A debate has been going on for a rather lengthy time regarding these subjects, but I won't dive further into that debate here.

Each column (or rather, the data to be stored in the column) is based on a datatype, which limits the possible "values" that can be stored in the column and also defines behavior when adding, subtracting, and so on. The column can have further restrictions as well.

Restrictions can be defined at the table level as well; for instance, that a combination of two columns has to be unique within the table.

A table can be created using the CREATE TABLE statement. You can also use Enterprise Manager, which has been given a better and more powerful interface in version 7. Note that Enterprise Manager act as a graphical front-end which, in turn, generates the CREATE TABLE command.

This is the basic syntax for the CREATE TABLE command:

```
CREATE TABLE table_name
(column_name datatype {identity NOT NULL ¦ NULL}
[, ...])
```

The following example creates a customer table with three columns: customer ID, the customer's name, and a comment:

```
CREATE TABLE customers
(customer_id INT IDENTITY NOT NULL,
customer_name VARCHAR(100) NOT NULL,
customer_comments VARCHAR(5000) NULL)
```

SQL Server Object Names

All objects in SQL Server are named. Examples of objects are tables, views, stored procedures, and so on. Names for objects must be unique within the database, but remember that the object owner is a part of the name. So the table steve.customer isn't the same as john.customer.

> **Terminology in the relational model**
>
> The relational model uses different terminology for tables, columns, and rows. A table is called a relation; a column is called attribute, and a row is called tuple. Note, however, that the current ANSI SQL standard doesn't use this terminology, nor is it widely used.

> **Object ownership**
>
> It is recommended that the dbo owns all objects in most cases. This simplifies administration and makes it easier for programmers and end-users when referring to the object. Handling permissions on Stored Procedures and Views is also easier if the same user owns all objects.

Determining case sensitivity

To determine case-sensitivity for a SQL Server installation, execute the stored procedure `sp_help-sort`.

Whether object names are case sensitive depends on the case sensitivity chosen at installation time of the SQL Server. Case sensitivity applies to object names as well as character data stored in tables.

Object names (or Identifiers) can be up to 128 characters, including letters, symbols (_, @, or #), and numbers. The first character must be an alphabetic (a–z or A–Z) character. Variables and temporary tables have special naming schemes. Note that an object name cannot include spaces. By using Quoted Identifiers, characters that otherwise would be illegal in object names can be used. However, avoid using Quoted Identifiers if possible. You might find a great utility application that doesn't support quoted identifiers. An example of this is SQLMAINT.EXE in SQL Server 6.5.

Column Properties

A column can have several properties. Some restrict what can be stored in the column, whereas others provide functionality (a counter for instance).

NULL | NOT NULL

The NULL and NOT NULL keywords define whether a column can contain the null symbol. You cannot define NULL for a column that is to be used as the Primary Key or the Identity column. It is generally recommended to keep the columns that allow NULLs to a minimum because it is difficult to deal with missing information.

IDENTITY(seed, increment)

IDENTITY defines a counter. A new value will be generated for each row that is inserted into the table.

The identity property can only be defined for integer types of columns. This includes INT, SMALLINT, TINYINT, DECIMAL, and NUMERIC, provided that the last two have scales of 0.

ROWGUIDCOL

ROWGUIDCOL defines the column as a row global unique identifier. It can only be defined for columns of the datatype

UNIQUEIDENTIFIER. The purpose of this property is to generate values that are unique across tables and SQL Servers. To generate the unique value, the function NEWID() is used, which returns a value that is useful only for the UNIQUEIDENTIFIER datatype.

<column_constraint>

Available constraints are Primary Key, Unique, Foreign Key, Check, and Default. A constraint does exactly what the name implies—constraint the possible values that can be used within the column. The feature is used to achieve as consistent data as possible within the database.

Example

You want to create an order table with the following columns:

- Order number. A globally unique ID. This column is defined as a primary key. For each value inserted, a new value is issued through a default constraint.

- Customer number. A customer number that is a foreign key to the customer table.

- Order Date. This can be automatically inserted through a default constraint. Note that the default constraint removes the time part of the value returned from GETDATE().

Listing A.1 is the CREATE TABLE statement for an orders table.

Listing A.1   The *CREATE TABLE* Statement for the Orders Table

```
1 CREATE TABLE orders
2 (order_id UNIQUEIDENTIFIER DEFAULT NEWID() PRIMARY KEY
  ➥ NOT NULL,
3 customer_id INT REFERENCES customers(customer_id),
4 order_date DATETIME DEFAULT CONVERT(CHAR(8),
  ➥ GETDATE(), 112))
```

Notes on Identity Columns

The identity functionality isn't designed, in all situations, to produce continuous values. If a row is deleted, that value won't be reused. If an insert is rolled back, the value won't be reused.

An explicit value cannot be inserted for the identity column unless SET IDENTITY_INSERT <table_name> ON has been run. Only the table owner can explicitly insert the identity value.

To reset the value to the current highest (or lowest) value, run DBCC CHECKIDENT(<table_name>).

A Primary Key constraint (or Unique constraint) should always be defined for a column if the column is a key. The identity feature isn't designed for uniqueness per se. Duplicates can occur if IDENTITY_INSERT is used, or if SQL Server looses track of its internal counter for the identity value and starts over again at the seed value. This behavior happened quite often in versions 6.0 and 6.5, especially if SQL Server was unexpectedly shut down.

Renaming Objects

Check dependent objects

Make sure that the objects that depend on the renamed object are handled (Views, Stored Procedures, and so on). SQL Server will give you a warning that changing an object name may break script and stored procedures, which is absolutely true.

I strongly encourage you to check which objects depends on the object, edit the dependents' source code, and re-create them. The system stored procedure sp_depends will give a report of which objects depend on another object.

An object can be renamed, using the sp_rename system stored procedure. The syntax for renaming an object is

```
sp_rename {'object_name'} [, 'new_name'] [, 'object_type']
```

Where object_type can be COLUMN, DATABASE, INDEX, OBJECT, or USERDATATYPE.

Adding Columns to a Table

Sometimes a column has to be added to a table. This is generally because you find out that there are more attributes that you want to store for the entity described by the table. A column can be added with the ALTER TABLE command.

A column added to a table with earlier versions of SQL Server had to allow NULL. This was a bit annoying because you generally try to avoid NULL, if possible.

But what do you insert in the current rows for the new column? With version 7, you can define a default value, or the added column can be defined with the identity attribute.

Let's say that you want to add a column to the customer table. To increase customer service, an estimated shipping date must be given for each order. The estimated shipping date for existing orders will be set to 1900-01-01 to clearly mark the rows that were inserted before this column was added.

```
ALTER TABLE orders ADD estimated_shipping_date DATETIME
➡ NOT NULL DEFAULT '19000101'
```

The default value could later be removed or changed to something more meaningful.

Temporary Tables

A *temporary table* is a table that exists for the duration of the connection that created it. By using a hash sign (#) as the first letter in the table name, SQL Server makes the table a temporary table. A temporary table can be explicitly created with the use of the CREATE TABLE statement or implicitly with the use of SELECT INTO.

The temporary table is only available for the connection that created the table. All temporary tables are created in the tempdb database, but don't worry about name clashes. SQL Server will append a unique identifier on the table name, so even if another connection creates a temporary table with the same name, they will be named differently in the *tempdb* database.

So, why create temporary tables? If you have a complex query, it might be easier to solve it by breaking it up in steps. Or you might want to store some values so that you can do further calculations on them.

Global and Permanent Temporary Tables

A global temporary table is available for other connections. You create a global temporary table by preceding its name with two hash signs (##). This can be useful if an application uses several connections and you want the temporary table to be available for all connections. If a stored procedure creates a local temporary table, it will be removed when the procedure terminates. The procedure is considered a connection in this aspect. But a global temporary table will be available after the procedure executed.

Sizing tempdb

The default size of the tempdb database is too small for almost all production installations. It is impossible to recommend a "right" size for tempdb offhand, but a good rule of thumb is to either make it as big as your biggest table in the system, or half the size of your biggest database.

The tempdb database is also used to store the internal worktables that SQL Server creates for some operations, for instance sorting, group by, and so on.

You can also create a permanent temporary table. By explicitly creating the table in the tempdb database, it will be available after the connection that created it terminates. It will disappear when SQL Server restarts because tempdb is re-created at startup.

SELECT, INSERT, UPDATE, and DELETE

These four basic statements enable us to retrieve and modify data in our tables. SELECT retrieves data from one or more tables, INSERT inserts rows into one table, UPDATE modifies rows in one table, and DELETE removes rows from one table.

You could easily fill a book with examples and explanations for these statements. This section covers the major parts of the syntax and shows some simple examples.

The SELECT Statement

The SELECT statement has the following basic syntax:

```
SELECT column1[, column2, ...]
 FROM table1[, table2, ...]
 WHERE search_conditions
```

You want to return all author's first and last names, living in Utah, from the authors table. You also want to rename the column heading in our result.

```
SELECT au_lname AS 'First', au_fname AS 'Last'
 FROM authors
 WHERE STATE = 'UT'
```

By default, SQL Server returns all rows that meet our search conditions. By specifying SELECT DISTINCT, duplicates are removed.

The column(s) that you base your search condition on don't have to be returned in the resultset. You can filter rows in several ways with the WHERE clause. The following predicates are available for the WHERE clause:

Operators: =, <> (not equals), <, >, >=, >=.

BETWEEN expression1 AND expression2. Between is inclusive.

Dropping tables for space

It is always a good idea to drop the table when it isn't needed anymore. This will free up space in tempdb, which might become critical if your connections live for a long time.

IN(*element1*, *element2*, ...). Returns all rows with values that are equal to the elements specified in the list.

LIKE *string_expression*. Used for pattern matching. Table A.2 lists the available wildcard characters.

Table A.2 Wildcards and *LIKE*

Wildcard	Meaning
%	Any number of characters
_	Any single character
[ ]	Any character listed in the bracket

Logical OR and AND are used to connect multiple search arguments.

The ORDER BY clause sorts the resultset by the specified column or columns. Ascending sorting is default, ORDER BY column_name DESC can be used to specify descending ordering. You should always specify ORDER BY if you expect a certain order for your data. Rows in a table constitute a set, and a set isn't ordered.

Listing A.2 shows an example that exemplifies some of the clauses described.

LISTING A.2 Using *WHERE* and *ORDER BY*

```
1 SELECT au_lname, au_fname, state
2  FROM authors
3  WHERE state IN('CA', 'KS')
4    AND au_lname LIKE 'S%'
5 ORDER BY au_lname
```

The TOP keyword can be used to restrict the number of rows returned. In Listing A.3, you want to retrieve the title and price for the five most expensive books.

LISTING A.3 Using *TOP* to Restrict the Number of Rows Returned

```
1 SELECT TOP 5 price, title
2 FROM titles
3 ORDER BY price DESC
4 price                   title
5 ------------------------------------------------------------------
6 22.9500                 But Is It User Friendly?
7 21.5900                 Computer Phobic AND Non-Phobic Indi...
8 20.9500                 Onions, Leeks, and Garlic: Cooking ...
9 20.0000                 Secrets of Silicon Valley
10 19.9900                The Busy Executive's Database Guide
```

You can add WITH TIES, which might produce more than the requested rows. There are several books with the price of $19.99. In Listing A.4, add WITH TIES so all those books are returned.

LISTING A.4 Using *TOP WITH TIES*

```
1 SELECT TOP 5 WITH TIES price, title
2 FROM titles
3 ORDER BY price DESC
4 price                   title
5 ------------------------------------------------------------------
6 22.9500                 But Is It User Friendly?
7 21.5900                 Computer Phobic AND Non-Phobic Indi...
8 20.9500                 Onions, Leeks, and Garlic: Cooking ...
9 20.0000                 Secrets of Silicon Valley
10 19.9900                The Busy Executive's Database Guide
11 19.9900                Straight Talk About Computers
12 19.9900                Silicon Valley Gastronomic Treats
13 19.9900                Prolonged Data Deprivation: Four Ca...
```

Replacing ROWCOUNT

The TOP keyword is new to version 7.0. To get the same functionality, SET ROWCOUNT *n* was often used in previous versions. TOP is used by the optimizer, though, so it will often result in better performance than using ROWCOUNT.

If you don't use ORDER BY with TOP, the actual rows returned will be chosen arbitrarily, based on the execution plan chosen by the optimizer. You can also specify TOP n PERCENT to restrict the number of rows based on a percentage value instead of an absolute value.

You can store the resultset in a table instead of retrieving it with the use of SELECT column(s) INTO table_name. The table specified will be created with the same structure as the resultset. A temporary table is created in tempdb if you precede the table name with one or two hash signs. If you want to create a permanent table with SELECT...INTO, you must set the database option select into/bulkcopy to TRUE.

With the UNION keyword, a logical union between two or more resultsets is returned. This query returns the city and state of each author and publisher as a single resultset:

```
SELECT city, state FROM authors
UNION ALL
SELECT city, state FROM publishers
```

By default, SQL Server removes all duplicates. You can add the keyword ALL if you don't want duplicates to be removed.

GROUP BY and HAVING

GROUP BY and HAVING are used with aggregated functions (which are described in the functions section of this chapter). GROUP BY enables us to calculate aggregates for groups within our tables. The following example calculates the average price for each book category in the titles table:

```
SELECT type, AVG(price)
FROM titles
GROUP BY type
```

```
business       13.7300
mod_cook       11.4900
popular_comp 21.4750
psychology     13.5040
trad_cook      15.9633
UNDECIDED      NULL
```

If a WHERE clause is used, it is applied before the grouping takes place. The following query calculates the average price per book category for books published by the publisher with ID 1389:

```
SELECT type, AVG(price)
FROM titles
```

```
WHERE pub_id = 1389
GROUP BY type


business    17.3100
popular_comp 21.4750
```

HAVING enables us to restrict the number of aggregations returned. The clause is applied after the grouping is applied. You want to return the average price for book categories, but only the categories with an average that is higher than $14:

```
SELECT type, AVG(price)
FROM titles
GROUP BY type
HAVING AVG(price) > $14


popular_comp 21.4750
trad_cook    15.9633
```

CUBE, ROLLUP, and the *GROUPING* Function

CUBE, ROLLUP, and GROUPING clauses are used in conjunction with GROUP BY.

When you use CUBE, you will get extra rows in the resultset. The extra rows are super aggregates. If you add CUBE to the query that returns the average price for book categories, you will get an extra row with the average price of all books, as shown in Listing A.5.

LISTING A.5 Using *CUBE* to Calculate Super Aggregates

```
1 SELECT type, AVG(price) AS average
2 FROM titles
3 GROUP BY type
4 WITH CUBE
5
6 type          average
7 ----------------------------
8 business      13.7300
9 mod_cook      11.4900
10 popular_comp 21.4750
```

11	psychology	13.5040
12	trad_cook	15.9633
13	UNDECIDED	NULL
14	NULL	14.7662

The book type is returned as NULL for the extra row. In Listing A.6, you use the grouping function to present the extra row in a more explicit manner:

LISTING A.6 Using the *GROUPING* Function

```
1 SELECT type, AVG(price) AS average, GROUPING(type) AS
  ➥super
2 FROM titles
3 GROUP BY type
4 WITH CUBE
5
6 type           average              super
7 --------------------------------------------
8 business       13.7300              0
9 mod_cook       11.4900              0
10 popular_comp  21.4750              0
11 psychology    13.5040              0
12 trad_cook     15.9633              0
13 UNDECIDED     NULL                 0
14 NULL          14.7662              1
```

The value 1 is returned for each super aggregate presented for the grouped column specified.

CUBE is more useful if you group over several columns. In Listing A.7, you want to return the average price grouped by book type and publisher.

Listing A.7 Grouping Over Several Columns

```
1 SELECT type, pub_id, AVG(price) AS average
2 FROM titles
3 GROUP BY type, pub_id
4
5 type           pub_id average
6 --------------------------------------------
```

continues…

Listing A.7 Continued

```
 7  business      0736    2.9900
 8  psychology    0736   11.4825
 9  mod_cook      0877   11.4900
10  psychology    0877   21.5900
11  trad_oook     0877   16.0633
12  UNDECIDED     0877   NULL
13  business      1389   17.3100
14  popular_comp  1389   21.4750
```

In Listing A.8, you add WITH CUBE. This gives you the total average, the average for each book type, and the average for each publisher.

Listing A.8 Grouping Over Several Columns with *CUBE*

```
 1  SELECT type, pub_id, AVG(price) AS average
 2  FROM titles
 3  GROUP BY type, pub_id
 4  WITH CUBE
 5
 6  type          pub_id average
 7  -------------------------------------------
 8  business      0736    2.9900
 9  business      1389   17.3100
10  business      NULL   13.7300
11  mod_cook      0877   11.4900
12  mod_cook      NULL   11.4900
13  popular_comp  1389   21.4750
14  popular_comp  NULL   21.4750
15  psychology    0736   11.4825
16  psychology    0877   21.5900
17  psychology    NULL   13.5040
18  trad_cook     0877   15.9633
19  trad_cook     NULL   15.9633
20  UNDECIDED     0877   NULL
21  UNDECIDED     NULL   NULL
22  NULL          NULL   14.7662
23  NULL          0736    9.7840
24  NULL          0877   15.4100
25  NULL          1389   18.9760
```

ROLLUP is similar to CUBE, but it produces a subset of the super aggregates. It is sensitive to the position of the column in the GROUP BY clause; it goes from right to left and produces super aggregates along the way. In Listing A.9, super aggregates are calculated for publishers and for all titles, but not for book types.

Listing A.9   Using the *ROLLUP* Clause

```
1 SELECT type, pub_id, AVG(price) AS average
2 FROM titles
3 GROUP BY type, pub_id
4 WITH ROLLUP
5 type          pub_id average
6 -------------------------------------------
7 business      0736   2.9900
8 business      1389   17.3100
9 business      NULL   13.7300
10 mod_cook     0877   11.4900
11 mod_cook     NULL   11.4900
12 popular_comp 1389   21.4750
13 popular_comp NULL   21.4750
14 psychology   0736   11.4825
15 psychology   0877   21.5900
16 psychology   NULL   13.5040
17 trad_cook    0877   15.9633
18 trad_cook    NULL   15.9633
19 UNDECIDED    0877   NULL
20 UNDECIDED    NULL   NULL
21 NULL         NULL   14.7662
```

Joining Tables

You can also correlate two tables, performing a join. Generally, you "connect" the tables using a common column, which is most often a column for which a FOREIGN KEY - PRIMARY KEY relationship has been specified.

There are two ways that you can specify a join:

- Specifying the join condition in the WHERE clause. This is an older way of specifying a join, but it is still supported. Those

ANSI JOIN syntax

The ANSI-92 join syntax (or ANSI JOIN for short) was introduced in version 6.5, and is now the preferred way of expressing joins.

One advantage with the ANSI JOIN syntax is that the actual join operation performed is easier to read because it is explicitly stated in the **FROM** clause. You can also assume that Microsoft is more eager to fix problems regarding ANSI JOINs than the older T-SQL join syntax.

of you who have been using SQL for a while are probably more familiar to this method.

- Specifying the join condition in the FROM clause. This is compliant to the ANSI-92 standard.

The following example shows both ways of expressing a join. Both statements return the same resultset:

```
SELECT title, qty
 FROM titles t, sales s
 WHERE t.title_id = s.title_id


SELECT title, qty
 FROM titles t INNER JOIN sales s ON t.title_id = s.title_id
```

You also introduced a table alias in the example. You aliased the title table to the name t and sales to s. This is useful when you have to refer to a table in several places in the query; you don't have to type the whole table name each time.

The different types of joins are INNER, OUTER, and CROSS. An INNER join is based on equality between the column values. The OUTER join returns all rows from a controlling table (specified with LEFT OUTER or RIGHT OUTER) even if there is no match from the other table. Columns returned from that other table will have the NULL symbol for the returned rows. A CROSS join returns all possible combinations of rows, also called a *cartesian product*.

With the ANSI syntax, you specify the join type explicitly in the FROM clause, whereas the join type in the older join syntax is specified in the WHERE clause.

Subqueries

You can use a subquery in place of an expression. Depending on the context, restrictions exist on the subquery. The query might only be allowed to return one column and even one row.

If the subquery only returns one row and one column, it can be used in place of any expression. This example returns all books published by "Binnet & Hardley":

```
SELECT title FROM titles
```

Subquery or join?

You will often find that you can achieve the same result with a subquery or a join. A join is often more efficient that a subquery (with the exception of when you want to remove duplicates, where a subquery with EXISTS is more efficient).

```
WHERE pub_id =
(SELECT pub_id FROM publishers
 WHERE pub_name = "Binnet & Hardley")
```

An error message is returned if the subquery would have returned several rows.

A subquery must always appear in parentheses.

You can use a subquery that returns one column and several rows with the IN predicate. The following example returns all publishers of business books:

```
SELECT pub_name FROM publishers
 WHERE pub_id IN
 (SELECT pub_id FROM titles
  WHERE type = 'business')
```

A subquery that returns several rows and several columns (in fact, all columns) can be used with the EXISTS keyword. The following example returns the same resultset as the above example:

```
SELECT pub_name FROM publishers p WHERE EXISTS
   (SELECT * FROM titles t
   WHERE p.pub_id = t.pub_id
   AND type = 'business')
```

You return all columns from the subquery. And you don't have a column relationship between the queries. Your relationship is between the tables; the subquery is a *correlated subquery*. The inner query refers to the outer in the WHERE clause (WHERE p.pub_id = t.pub_id). SQL Server executes the inner query for each row in the outer query, testing for a match on pub_id.

Adding Rows with *INSERT*

You use the INSERT statement to add rows to a table. The following example adds one row to the authors table:

```
INSERT authors (au_id, au_lname, au_fname, phone, contract)
VALUES('123-65-7635', 'Johnson', 'Lisa', '408 342 7845', 1)
```

The number of values in the VALUES list must match the number in the column list. You can omit the column list, but I recommend strongly against it. That INSERT statement is dependent on the column ordering and would break if the table were re-created with another column ordering.

655

You can also omit columns from the table, but the column must allow NULL, have a default value, be of the timestamp datatype, or have the identity property defined for it.

To insert more than one row, you must use INSERT with a subquery. The following query inserts all authors from California into a table called authors_archive:

```
INSERT authors_archive
 (au_id, au_lname, au_fname, phone, city, state, zip)
SELECT au_id, au_lname, au_fname, phone, city, state, zip
FROM authors WHERE state = 'CA'
```

A useful feature is that you can EXECute any statement as the subquery, as long as it returns a resultset that is compatible with the table. Listing A.10 creates a table to hold information from DBCC SQLPERF(logspace) and inserts the resultset returned by that command into the table.

Listing A.10   Using **INSERT** with a Subquery That Isn't an Ordinary **SELECT** Statement

```
1 CREATE TABLE log_space
2 (cap_date DATETIME DEFAULT GETDATE(),
3  db sysname,
4  log_size FLOAT,
5  space_used FLOAT,
6  status BIT)
7
8 INSERT log_space(db, log_size, space_used, status)
9 EXEC ('DBCC SQLPERF(logspace)')
```

Modifying Rows with *UPDATE*

The UPDATE statement is straightforward. You specify the table to be updated, and which column(s), new value(s), and rows should be updated. The following statement changes the royalty to 15% and price to $25 for title 1032.

```
UPDATE titles
 SET royalty = 15, price = $25
 WHERE title_id = 'BU1032'
```

If you omit the WHERE clause, all rows will be updated.

Removing Rows with *DELETE*

To remove rows from a table, use the DELETE statement. To remove the title BU1032:

```
DELETE titles WHERE title_id = 'BU1032'
```

If you omit the WHERE clause, all rows will be removed.

If you really want to remove all rows, it's much more efficient to use the TRUNCATE TABLE statement, which doesn't log each deleted row to the transaction log.

SQL Server Functions

Microsoft has added more then 30 functions in version 7, and this to an already quite large number of functions. Some of the functions are shortcuts to get information that could be retrieved in other ways. For instance, there is a function to get an object ID if you know the object's name, but looking it up in the sysobjects table also does this.

```
USE pubs
SELECT OBJECT_ID('authors')
SELECT id FROM sysobjects WHERE name = 'authors'
```

Other functions are more essential, like some of the mathematical functions (okay, it could be argued that you could calculate the square root, for instance, in T-SQL, but it wouldn't be very efficient).

Most functions have the structure

```
FUNCTION_NAME(parameter1, parameter2, ...)
```

The parameters might be an expression (like a column name), a constant, or a special code (for instance, a formatting code).

A function returns a value. The datatype for the value depends on what function you are using. Let's have a look at available functions, grouped by category:

Splitting columns

Excessive use of string functions against a column might indicate that the column should be split up to several columns. For example, if you find yourself often parsing out first name and last name from a name column, perhaps you should split up the name into two columns.

String Functions

The string functions enable you to perform concatenation, parsing manipulation, and so on of strings.

Table A.3 lists the available string functions. They can be used against any string expression.

Table A.3 String Functions

Function Name	Returns	New in 7.0
ASCII(*char*)	The ASCII code for the leftmost character in *char*.	
CHAR(*int*)	A character for *int* (an ASCII code).	
CHARINDEX(*char_pattern*, *char*, [*int_start*])	Starting location of *char_patthern* within *char*; optionally, starting search at *int_start*.	
DIFFERENCE(*char1*, *char2*)	The difference between the two character expressions. Used for phonetic match.	
LEFT(*char*, *int*)	*int* characters from left of *char*.	
LEN(*char*)	Number of characters in *char*, excluding trailing blanks.	*
LOWER(*char*)	*char* in lowercase.	
LTRIM(*char*)	*char* without leading spaces.	
NCHAR(*int*)	The character for a given Unicode value.	*
PATINDEX(*char_pattern*, *char*)	Starting position of *char_pattern* in *char*, or 0 if the pattern is not found.	

Function Name	Returns	New in 7.0
REPLACE(*char1*, *char2*, *char3*)	Replaces all occurrences of *char2* with *char3* in *char1*.	*
QUOTENAME(*char*, [*char_quote*])	*char* as a valid quoted identifier. Adds the characters [and] (default, can be changed to ' or ", specified as *char_quote*) at beginning and end of char. Returns a Unicode string.	*
REPLICATE(*char*, *int*)	Repeats *char*, *int* times.	
REVERSE(*char*)	Reverses *char*.	
RIGHT(*char*, *int*)	*int* characters from right of *char*.	
RTRIM(*char*)	*char* without trailing spaces.	
SOUNDEX(*char*)	A four-character string, used for comparison of phonetic match.	
SPACE(*int*)	A string of *int* spaces.	
STR(*float*, [*length*, [*decimal*]])	*float* as a character string, with length of *length* and *decimal* numbers of decimals. Default *length* is 10 and default number of *decimal*s is 0.	
STUFF(*char1*, *start*, *length*, *char2*)	Replaces *length* of characters from *char1* with *char2*, starting at *start*.	

continues…

Table A.3 Continued

Function Name	Returns	New in 7.0
SUBSTRING(*char*, *start*, *length*)	Returns *length* number of characters from *char*, from *start* position.	
UNICODE(*char*)	Returns the Unicode code for the leftmost character in *char*.	*
UPPER(*char*)	Returns *char* in uppercase.	

The operator + can be used to concatenate strings.

The following example uses SUBSTRING and string concatenation to present each author's first letter in the first name and then the last name.

```
SELECT SUBSTRING(au_fname,1,1) + '. ' + au_lname FROM authors
```

Mathematical Functions

The mathematical functions listed in Table A.4 perform calculations based on the input values and return a numeric value. There are no new mathematical functions introduced in version 7.

TABLE A.4 Mathematical Functions

Function Name	Returns
ABS(*numeric*)	The absolute (positive) value of *numeric*.
ACOS(*float*)	The arc cosine for *float*.
ASIN(float)	The arc sine for *float*.
ATAN(*float*)	The arc tangent for *float*.
ATAN2(*float1*, *float2*)	Returns the arc tangent whose tangent is between *float1* and *float2*.
CEILING(*numeric*)	The smallest integer value, which is higher than orequal *numeric*.

Function Name	Returns
COS(*float*)	The trigonometric cosine of *float*.
COT(*float*)	The trigonometric cotangent of *float*.
DEGREES(*numeric*)	The number of degrees for a given angle, *numeric*, given in radians.
EXP(*float*)	The exponential value of *float*.
FLOOR(*numeric*)	The largest integer value, which is lower than or equal *numeric*.
LOG(*float*)	The natural logarithm of *float*.
LOG10(float)	The base-10 logarithm of *float*.
PI()	The constant pi.
POWER(*numeric1*, *numeric2*)	The value of *numeric1* to the specified power, given in *numeric2*.
RADIANS(*numeric*)	Radians of *numeric*, given in degrees.
RAND([seed])	A random value between 0 and 1. Seed can be specified as the starting value.
ROUND(*numeric*, *length*, *func*)	Rounds the specified *numeric* to specified *length*. If *func* is specified and not 0, *numeric* is truncated to *length*.
SIGN(*numeric*)	1 if *numeric* is positive, 0 if *numeric* is 0 and –1 if *numeric* is negative.
SIN(*float*)	The trigonometric sine of *float*.
SQUARE(*float*)	The square of *float*.
SQRT(*float*)	The square root of *float*.
TAN(*float*)	The trigonometric tangent of *float*.

The operators +, -, *, /, and %(modulo) are also available for numeric expressions.

Date Functions

The date functions perform operations such as formatting and subtraction. The expression given is of a datetime datatype.

Some of the functions take a *datepart* as an argument. The *datepart* specifies what part of our datetime datatype you want to operate on. Table A.5 shows the elements of datepart that you can specify.

Table A.5 Available Codes for Datepart

Datepart	Abbreviation	Possible Values
year	yy	1753–9999
quarter	qq	1–4
month	mm	1–12
day of year	dy	1–366
day	dd	1–31
week	wk	1–53
weekday	dw	1–7
hour	hh	0–23
minute	mi	0–59
second	ss	0–59
millisecond	ms	0–999

The date- and time-related functions are listed in Table A.6.

Table A.6 Date- and Time-Related Functions

Function Name	Returns	New in 7.0
DATEADD(*datepart*, *int*, *date*)	Adds *int dateparts* to date.	
DATEDIFF(*datepart*, *date1*, *date2*)	The number of *dateparts* between *date1* and *date2*.	
DATENAME(*datepart*, *date*)	A character string with the *datepart* name of *date*.	
DATEPART(*datepart*, *date*)	The *datepart* of *date*.	
GETDATE()	The current date and time.	
DAY(*date*)	The day-of-month part as an integer.	*
MONTH(*date*)	The month as an integer.	*
YEAR(*date*)	The year as an integer.	*

The operators + and – can be used directly on datetime expressions in version 7.0. The implied datepart is days. Here is an example where you use the + operator to add one day to the current date.

```
SELECT GETDATE(), GETDATE() + 1


1998-03-28 16:08:33    1998-03-29 16:08:33
```

System Functions

The system functions (shown in Table A.7) are useful for retrieving information such as column names, table names, and so on. Basically, many of them are shortcuts for querying the system tables.

Using system functions

It is better to use the system functions than directly query the system tables. If the system tables change in forthcoming releases of SQL Server (as they did with version 7.0), your applications and scripts will still work if you use the system functions. You can also use a new set of views in SQL Server 7 for retrieving system table–related information. The views are independent of the system tables and all have the object owner INFORMATION_SCHEMA.

Table A.7 System Functions

Function Name	Returns	New in 7.0
CAST(*expression* AS *datatype*)	The cast function is a synonym for the CONVERT function and converts *expression* to *datatype*.	*
COALESCE(*expr1*, [*expr2*,,,])	The first non-null expression.	
COL_LENGTH(*table*, *column*)	The length of *column* in *table*.	
COL_NAME(*table_id*, *column_id*)	The name of *column_id* in *table_id*.	

continues…

663

Table A.7 CONTINUED

Function Name	Returns	New in 7.0
COLUMNPROPERTY(*id*, *column*, *property*)	Information about a *column* in a table, given the *id*. Or returns information for a parameter, given in *column*, for a stored procedure. The *property* parameter defines the type of information to be returned.	*
CONVERT(*datatype[(length)]*, *expression*, *style*)	Converts *expression* to *datatype*. For conversion of datetime or float expression, *style* defines formatting (see below).	
CURSOR_STATUS(*local*, *cursor_name* ¦ *global*, *cursor_name* ¦ *variable*, *cursor_name*)	A code to the caller of a stored procedure that indicates whether the procedure has returned a cursor and if the resultset contains any rows.	*
DATABASEPROPERTY (*database_name*, *property*)	Information, defined in *property*, for *database_name*.	*
DATALENGTH(*expression*)	The storage area of *expression*, including trailing blanks for character information.	

Function Name	Returns	New in 7.0
DB_ID([*db_name*])	The database id of *db_name* or the current database.	
DB_NAME([*db_id*])	The database name of *db_id* or the name of the current database.	
GETANSINULL([*db_name*])	The default nullability of *db_name* for the current database.	
GETCHECKSUM(*col_name*)	A checksum value for the values in *col_name*.	*
HOST_ID()	The process id of the client applications process.	
HOST_NAME()	The client's workstation name.	
IDENT_INCR(*table*)	The identity increment for the identity column in *table*.	
IDENT_SEED(*table*)	The identity seed for the identity column in *table*.	
INDEX_COL(*table*, *index_id*, *key_id*)	The column name for the specified *table*, *index_id*, and *key_id*.	

continues...

665

Table A.7 CONTINUED

Function Name	Returns	New in 7.0
IS_MEMBER(*group* ¦ *role*]	1 if user is member of specified NT *group* or SQL Server *role*; otherwise 0.	*
IS_SRVROLEMEMBER (*role* [, *login*])	1 if users login id is member of specified server *role*; otherwise 0. An explicit *login* name can be specified.	*
ISDATE(*char*)	1 if *char* is in a valid datetime format; otherwise 0.	
FILE_ID(*filename*)	The id for *filename*.	*
FILE_NAME(*file_id*)	The filename for *file_id*.	*
FILEGROUP_ID(*filegroupname*)	The id for *filegroupname*.	*
FILEGROUP_NAME(*filegroup_id*)	The filegroup name for *filegroup_id*.	*
ISNULL(*expression, value*)	*value* if *expression* is NULL.	
ISNUMERIC(*char*)	1 if *char* can be converted to a numeric value; otherwise 0.	
NEWID()	A generated global unique identifier.	*
NULLIF(*expr1, expr2*)	Null if *expr2* equals *expr2*.	

Function Name	Returns	New in 7.0
OBJECT_ID(*object_name*)	The ID for *object_name*.	
OBJECTPROPERTY(*object_id*, *property*)	Information of *object_id*. *property* defines type of information to be returned.	*
PARSENAME(*object_name*, *object_part*) *object_part* of *object_name*.		*
PERMISSIONS(*object_id*[, *column*])	A bitmap indicating permissions on *object_id* and optionally *column*.	*
STATS_DATE(*table_id*, *index_id*)	Date when the distribution page was updated for *index_id* on *table_id*.	
SUSER_ID(*login_name*)	The loginid of specified *login_name*. Included for backward compatibility, use SUSER_SID instead.	
SUSER_NAME([*login_id*])	The login name of *login_id*. Included for backward compatibility, use SUSER_NAME instead.	
SUSER_SID([*login*])	Security identification number (SID) for *login*.	*

continues…

Table A.7 CONTINUED

Function Name	Returns	New in 7.0
SUSER_SNAME([*login_id*])	The login name of *login_id*.	*
TRIGGER_NESTLEVEL([*tr_object_id*])	Nesting level of specified or current trigger.	*
TYPEPROPERTY(*data_type*, property)	Information, defined in *property*, for *data_type*.	*
USER_ID([*user_name*])	The user id for *user_name*.	
USER_NAME([*user_id*])	The username for *user_id*.	

Niladic functions as aliases

These are basically aliases to SQL Server system functions. If you use them for default values in tables and run **sp_help** for the table, edit the table, or script the table in Enterprise Manager, you will notice that they have been translated to the corresponding system function.

The following example returns the title ID and price for all books. If the price isn't set (NULL), you return a price of 0:

```
SELECT title_id, ISNULL(price, 0) FROM titles
```

Let us expand the example a little bit. You want to display a string, 'Not Priced' for those who have NULL. You have to convert the price to a character value before replacing NULL with our text string:

```
SELECT title_id, ISNULL(CONVERT(CHAR(10),price),
➡'Not Priced') FROM titles
```

Niladic Functions

This group of functions is basically a set of system functions. The reason for grouping them separately is that they are used without parentheses after the function name. They are defined in the ANSI SQL-92 standard and shown in Table A.8.

You often find niladic functions used as defaults in CREATE TABLE and ALTER TABLE.

Table A.8 Niladic Functions

Function Name	Returns	Corresponding System Function
CURRENT_TIMESTAMP	Current date and time	GETDATE()
CURRENT_USER	The user's username	USER_NAME()
SESSION_USER	The user's username	USER_NAME()
SYSTEM_USER	The user's login name	SUSER_NAME()
USER	The user's username	USER_NAME()

In Listing A.11, you create a table with three columns, with defaults for the current datetime, the user's login name, and the username. The INSERT statement inserts default values for all columns and the SELECT statements retrieve the row inserted.

Listing A.11 Using Niladic Functions with the *INSERT* Statement

```
 1  CREATE TABLE my_defaults
 2  (the_datetime DATETIME DEFAULT CURRENT_TIMESTAMP,
 3  users_login CHAR(20) DEFAULT SYSTEM_USER,
 4  users_name CHAR(20) DEFAULT CURRENT_USER,)
 5
 6  INSERT my_defaults DEFAULT VALUES
 7
 8  SELECT * FROM my_defaults
 9
10  1998-03-29 19:09:52.377     sa                    dbo
```

Aggregate Functions

The aggregate functions differ from the other groups. Aggregate functions perform an aggregation for a column over a set of rows.

Table A.9 lists the aggregate functions available in SQL Server.

669

Table A.9   Aggregate Functions

Function Name	Returns	New in 7.0
AVG([ALL ¦ DISTINCT] *expression*)	The average of all values given in *expression*.	
COUNT([ALL ¦ DISTINCT] *expression* ¦ *)	The number of non-NULL values in *expression*. NULL are counted if * is specified.	
MAX([ALL ¦ DISTINCT] *expression*)	The maximum value in *expression*.	
VARP(*expression*)	The statistical variance for the population for all values in the given *expression*.	*
STDEVP(*expression*)	The statistical standard deviation for the population for all values in the given *expression*.	*
MIN([ALL ¦ DISTINCT] *expression*)	The minimum value in *expression*.	
SUM([ALL ¦ DISTINCT] *expression*)	The sum of all values in *expression*.	
VAR(*expression*)	The statistical variance of all values in the given *expression*.	*
STDEV(*expression*)	The statistical standard deviation of all values in the given *expression*.	*

By adding the keyword DISTINCT, only distinct values will be aggregated. The default is ALL. You should note that NULL values aren't included in the aggregates. The one exception to that is COUNT(*), which counts the number of rows returned from the relational expression.

Say that you want to count the number of rows, prices, and distinct prices in the title table:

```
SELECT COUNT(*) AS Total, COUNT(price) AS Prices,
➡ COUNT(DISTINCT price) AS "Distinct prices"
 FROM titles
```

Total	Prices	Distinct prices
18	16	11

Apparently, two books aren't priced yet or you don't know the price (NULL), and you have a total of 5 duplicate prices.

Now you want to perform some real aggregation over the prices:

```
SELECT MAX(price) AS 'Max', MIN(price) AS 'Min', AVG(price)
➡ AS 'Average' FROM titles
```

Max	Min	Average
22.9500	2.9900	14.7662

Note that even though NULL usually counts low, the minimum price is $2.99 because NULL is excluded from the aggregate.

Aggregate functions are often used in conjunction with GROUP BY. The following example retrieves the average price for each book category:

```
SELECT type, AVG(price) AS Average
 FROM titles
 GROUP BY type
```

type	Average
business	13.7300
mod_cook	11.4900
popular_comp	21.4750
psychology	13.5040
trad_cook	15.9633
UNDECIDED	NULL

Programming Constructs

The languages that interface with Database Management Systems are sometimes divided into three categories:

- DML (Data Manipulation). This includes the ability to read and manipulate the data, for instance, SELECT, INSERT, DELETE, and UPDATE.
- DDL (Data Definition Language). Creating and altering the storage structures like CREATE TABLE.
- DCL (Data Control Language). Defining permissions for data access, for instance, GRANT, REVOKE, and DENY.

T-SQL includes other statements that can be useful, for instance, to "tie together" the DML statements in a stored procedure.

The *IF* Statement

The IF statement uses the following syntax:

```
IF boolean_expression
    statement_block
ELSE
    statement_block
```

The IF statement takes one argument: boolean_expression, which is an expression that can evaluate to TRUE or FALSE. The code to be conditionally executed is a statement block. You define a statement block with the statements BEGIN and END. In Listing A.12, you have a script that checks for the existence of a table, prints a message if the table exists and, if so, drops the table.

Listing A.12 Using the *IF* Statement to Perform Conditional Processing

```
1 IF OBJECTPROPERTY(OBJECT_ID('orders'), 'istable') = 1
2 BEGIN
3   PRINT "Dropping orders Table"
4   DROP TABLE orders
5 END
6 ELSE
7   PRINT "Table orders does not exist"
```

WHILE, BREAK, and CONTINUE

The WHILE statement enables you to loop while an expression evaluates to true. The syntax for WHILE is

```
WHILE boolean_expression
statement_block
BREAK
statement_block
CONTINUE
```

BREAK exits the WHILE loop and CONTINUE stops unconditionally and evaluates the boolean_expression again.

RETURN

RETURN is used to stop execution of the batch and thus, the stored procedure and trigger. When used in a stored procedure, RETURN can take an integer as an argument. The value zero indicates successful execution. Microsoft reserves the values –1 to –99 (currently –1 to –14 are in use), so you should use values outside that range.

GOTO

GOTO (yes, there is a goto statement in T-SQL) branches to a defined label. GOTO can be useful for error handling in stored procedures, for example. In Listing A.13, you have a fragment of a stored procedure where you check for errors after each statement and exit the procedure with a return code if an error occurred.

Listing A.13 Use of *GOTO* and *RETURN*

```
1 BEGIN TRAN
2 INSERT orders(customer_number) VALUES(1)
3  IF @@ERROR <> 0 GOTO err_handle
4 RETURN 0
5 ...
6 err_handle:
7 RAISERROR ('An error occured in the stored procedure.
  ➥ The transaction has been rolled back', 12, 1)
8 ROLLBACK TRANSACTION
9 RETURN -101
```

WAITFOR

You can use WAITFOR to halt execution for a specified delay (WAITFOR DELAY) or until a specified time (WAITFOR TIME). In the following example, you want to generate a deadlock (for instance you might have defined an alert for the deadlock error and want to test it). You must be able to start execution of both batches more or less simultaneously for the deadlock to occur, so introduce a wait for 10 seconds.

Execute the two code blocks in Listing A.14 from two separate windows (connections) in the Query Analyzer.

Listing A.14 Using *WAITFOR* to Introduce a Delay of 10 Seconds

```
1 --Execute from one connection
2 BEGIN TRAN
3 UPDATE authors SET au_lname = au_lname
4 WAITFOR DELAY '00:00:10'
5 UPDATE titles SET title = title
6 ROLLBACK TRAN
7
8 --Execute from another connection
9 BEGIN TRAN
10 UPDATE titles SET title = title
11 UPDATE authors SET au_lname = au_lname
12 ROLLBACK TRAN
```

Workaround for character limitations

If the string you want to execute is longer than 8000 characters (or 4000 if you use Unicode), you can concatenate the contents of two or more variables in the EXECUTE command:

```
EXEC(@var1 + var2)
```

This is a more useful trick if you are running version 6.x because the maximum length of a CHAR or VARCHAR is 255 characters on version 6 and previous versions.

EXECute

The EXEC (or EXECute) command is used as a keyword for executing stored procedures. Introduced in version 6, you also were given the ability to execute strings and variables containing strings. This can be very useful.

You want to perform UPDATE STATISTICS for all tables in the database. The UPDATE STATISTICS command doesn't accept a variable as its parameter. So you build the command in a variable and execute the contents of the variable:

```
DECLARE @tbl_name NVARCHAR(128)
SELECT @tbl_name = 'authors'
```

```
EXEC('UPDATE STATISTICS ' + @tbl_name)
```

This is powerful in conjunction with cursors, which you will have a look at further on.

Another example is if you want to write a stored procedure that will SELECT rows from a table name passed to it as an argument.

The following syntax will produce an error message:

```
SELECT * FROM @tbl_name
```

because SQL Server doesn't accept variables for table names, column names, and so on:

```
CREATE PROC general_select @tbl_name NVARCHAR(128) AS
 EXEC('SELECT * FROM ' + @tbl_name)
GO
EXEC general_select authors
```

Batches

A *batch* is quite simply a set of commands sent to SQL Server for execution. The batch term as used here is not to be confused with traditional batch processing, where mass modifications are being performed, often at low-activity periods.

Basically, SQL Server receives a string (hopefully containing T-SQL commands) from the client application. SQL Server parses this string as a unit, searching for keywords. If a syntax error is found, none of the statements in the batch are executed, and an error message is returned to the client application.

Avoid mixing T-SQL text on the same line as the GO command. You can do it if GO is the first command on the line, but the text is easier to read if GO is on its own row. If you have any other text before GO, the string "GO" is sent to SQL Server for parsing, and is not used to separate batches. This generally leads to syntax error.

In the Query Analyzer, ISQL, and OSQL, the string GO is used to separate batches. When the tool finds the string GO, it takes all text up to the previous GO and submits it to SQL Server for execution.

675

There are restrictions for batches, such as what commands can be combined with other commands within a batch. Some examples are

- You cannot combine any command within a batch. Most CREATE commands have to be executed in a single batch. The exceptions are CREATE TABLE, CREATE INDEX, and CREATE DATABASE.

- When calling a stored procedure, you must precede the procedure name with EXECute, if it's not the first string in a batch. If SQL Server doesn't recognize the first string in a batch, it quite simply assumes that it's a call to a stored procedure.

A related concept is the script. A *script* is quite simply a text file containing one or more batches. Scripts are often used with the Query Analyzer, ISQL, and OSQL. GO doesn't have to be specified after the last command in a script file; the tools will automatically generate an end of batch signal.

Listing A.15 creates a table and then a view. Note that the CREATE commands have been separated with GO.

Listing A.15 Create a Table and a View That Only Display Recent Orders

```
1 CREATE TABLE orders
2 (order_number UNIQUEIDENTIFIER DEFAULT NEWID()
  ➥ PRIMARY KEY NOT NULL,
3 customer_number INT REFERENCES
  ➥ customers(customer_number),
4 order_date DATETIME DEFAULT CONVERT(CHAR(8),
  ➥ GETDATE(), 112))
5 GO
6 CREATE VIEW recent_orders AS
7 SELECT order_number, customer_number, order_date
8 FROM orders
9 WHERE order_date > GETDATE() - 14
```

Comments

Everyone who has to review or change code knows the importance of comments. Even if it feels obvious during writing what the code does, it certainly won't be that obvious at a later time.

When SQL Server finds a comment, it doesn't execute anything until the end of the comment. The Query Analyzers syntax coloring indicates commented text with a green color by default. SQL Server supports two types of comment markers:

```
/* Comments */
```

These comment markers are useful when commenting several lines. None of the text between the comment markers is parsed, compiled, or executed.

```
-- Comments
```

SQL Server won't execute the text following the markers until end of the line. The -- comment markers are defined in ANSI SQL-92.

Both types of comments can be nested within a /*...*/ comment block. The end of batch (GO) separator can't be specified within a /*...*/ comment block.

Here is an example of a batch with a comment block first that describes what the batch performs and with a comment block further down that can be removed for debugging purposes.

```
/* Retrieves all orders that have been submitted the last
/* day.
The SELECT COUNT is only for debugging purposes */
SELECT order_number, customer_number, order_date
 FROM orders
 WHERE order_date > GETDATE() -1
--SELECT 'Number of orders returned':, @@ROWCOUNT
```

Local Variables

Local variables enable you to store values temporarily. The variable is always declared as a certain datatype. The datatype can either be system supplied or user-defined. The variable's name always begins with the @ sign and it is declared with the DECLARE statement.

The variable is assigned a value with the SELECT statement, or (new in version 7.0) the SET statement.

Listing A.16 prints out the number of distinct book types in the titles table. First you declare a local variable, then you assign it a value, and finally you print the contents of the variable.

677

Batches and variable life span

The life span of a local variable is a batch. After the batch has processed, the variable ceases to exist.

If you want to store a value to live between batches in T-SQL, you have to create a (temporary) table to store the value in.

Listing A.16 Assigning a Value to a Local Variable and Printing the Contents of That Variable

```
1 DECLARE @user_msg VARCHAR(255)
2 SELECT @user_msg = 'There are ' + CONVERT(VARCHAR(3),
3 (SELECT COUNT(DISTINCT type) FROM titles))
  ➥ + ' book types in the titles table.'
4 PRINT @user_msg
5
6 There are 6 book types in the titles table.
```

Local variables are often used in stored procedures.

Functions That Were Called Global Variables in Earlier Releases

This set of functions was called Global Variables in earlier releases of SQL Server. The name Global was quite confusing because it implies that the scope of the variable is longer than a local variable. They were often mistaken for variables that a user can declare and that live across batches, which isn't the case. You can name a variable starting with two at signs (@@), but it will still behave just as a local variable.

These functions contain information that is maintained by SQL Server. They exist so that an application can check things like the error code for the last executed command, and so on. The functions are very useful because some of them contain information that cannot be found elsewhere, or would be hard to obtain with other means.

For *connection-specific* functions (see Table A.10), SQL Server maintains separate values for each connection.

Table A.10 Connection-Specific Functions

Variable Name	Description
@@CURSOR_ROWS	Number of rows populated in the last opened cursor.
@@DATEFIRST	Indicates the first day of week (7 is Sunday, 1 is Monday, and so on).

Variable Name	Description
@@ERROR	The error number generated by the last executed command. This is very valuable for error checking in stored procedures, batches, and triggers.
@@FETCH_STATUS	Indicates whether a fetch operation from a cursor was successful or not.
@@IDENTITY	The identity value generated by the last insert statement. The @@IDENTITY value isn't affected by other connection inserts.
@@LOCK_TIMEOUT	The locking timeout value, in milliseconds.
@@LANGID	The connections language ID in use.
@@LANGUAGE	The connections language in use, a character string.
@@NESTLEVEL	The nesting level for stored procedures and triggers.
@@PROCID	The ID of the currently executing stored procedure.
@@ROWCOUNT	The number of rows affected (modified or read) by the last command.
@@SPID	The connection ID.
@@TEXTSIZE	The maximum number of bytes returned by a SELECT statement when reading text and image data. Note that this can be further limited by the client application.
@@TRANCOUNT	The transaction nesting level.
@@ERROR	Useful for error handling in stored procedures and triggers. In the Listing A.17, you check @@ERROR after each statement and branch into an error handling routine if an error occurred.

Listing A.17 The Use of the @@***ERROR*** Function to Check for Errors

```
1 BEGIN TRAN
2 INSERT orders(customer_number) VALUES(1)
3  IF @@ERROR <> 0 GOTO err_handle
4 RETURN 0
5 ...
6 err_handle:
```

continues...

679

Listing A.17 CONTINUED

```
7 RAISERROR ('An error occured in the stored procedure.
  ➥ The transaction has been rolled back', 12, 1)
8 ROLLBACK TRANSACTION
9 RETURN ñ101
```

In Listing A.18, you need to find out the identity value generated by our last insert, so you use the @@IDENTITY function. Note
that you need to save the value returned from @@IDENTITY into a
local variable if you need it after the next INSERT statement. All
INSERT statements update @@IDENTITY, even those that insert into
a table without an identity column. You don't have to worry
about other connections inserts because @@IDENTITY is maintained
per connection.

Listing A.18 Using the *@@IDENTITY* Function to Get the Latest Generated
Identity Value

```
1 CREATE TABLE customers
2 (customer_id INT IDENTITY PRIMARY KEY NOT NULL,
3 customer_name NVARCHAR(100) NOT NULL,
4 customer_comments NVARCHAR(1000) NULL)
5
6 CREATE TABLE orders
7 (order_number UNIQUEIDENTIFIER DEFAULT NEWID() PRIMARY
  ➥ KEY NOT NULL,
8 customer_number INT REFERENCES customers(customer_id),
9 order_date DATETIME DEFAULT CONVERT(CHAR(8),
  ➥ GETDATE(), 112))
10 GO
11
12 DECLARE @cust_id INT
13 INSERT customers (customer_name, customer_comments)
14 VALUES ("Hardware Suppliers AB", "Stephanie is contact.")
15 SELECT @cust_id = @@IDENTITY
16 INSERT orders (customer_number)
17 VALUES (@cust_id)
```

The monitoring-related functions are mostly listed here in Table
A.11 for completeness. Typically, DBCC SQLPERF and SQL

Performance Monitor gives similar information in a more useful fashion.

Table A.11 Monitoring-Related Global Variables

Variable Name	Description
@@CONNECTIONS	The number of login attempts since the last restart of SQL Server.
@@CPU_BUSY	The number of time-ticks (currently 1/100 second) that the machine's CPU has been doing SQL Server work since the last restart of SQL Server.
@@IDLE	The number of time-ticks (currently 1/100 second) that the machine's SQL Server has been idle since the last restart of SQL Server.
@@IO_BUSY	The number of time-ticks (currently 1/100 second) that SQL Server has been doing I/O operations since the last restart of SQL Server.
@@PACK_RECEIVED	The number of packets received by SQL Server since the last restart of SQL Server.
@@PACK_SENT	The number of packets sent by SQL Server since the last restart of SQL Server.
@@PACKET_ERRORS	The number of times that an error occurred while sending a packet since the last restart of SQL Server.
@@TOTAL_ERRORS	The number of times that an error occurred while reading or writing since the last restart of SQL Server.
@@TOTAL_READ	The total number of physical reads since the last restart of SQL Server.
@@TOTAL_WRITE	The total number of physical writes since the last restart of SQL Server.

The *general* functions (see Table A.12) are mostly useful for administration purposes. The most useful one is @@VERSION, which returns the version number, including the service pack level.

Table A.12 General Global Variables

Variable Name	Description
@@DBTS	The current timestamp for the database.
@@MAX_CONNECTIONS	The maximum number of user connections that the installation can support. @@MAX_CONNECTIONS doesn't reflect the currently configured value of user connections.
@@MAX_PRECISION	The maximum precision value for decimal and numeric datatypes.
@@MICROSOFTVERSION	A Microsoft internal version number. This shouldn't be used for version checking and handling. Use @@VERSION instead.
@@SERVERNAME	The name of the SQL Server. This should match the machine name; if it doesn't, you might want to drop the old (wrong) name with sp_dropserver and add the new (correct) name with sp_addserver.
@@SERVICENAME	The name of the service that executes SQL Server. This should be MSSQLServer if the service name isn't changed.
@@TIMETICKS	The number of microseconds per time-tick.
@@VERSION	The SQL Server version number.

Listing A.19 shows how you can use @@VERSION to check the version number of the SQL Server.

Listing A.19 Using the *@@VERSION* Function to Determine the Version of SQL Server

```
1 SELECT @@VERSION
2
3 SELECT
4 SUBSTRING(@@VERSION, (CHARINDEX('Server    ',
   ➥ @@VERSION) + 8), 1) AS Major,
5 SUBSTRING(@@VERSION, (CHARINDEX('Server    ',
   ➥ @@VERSION) + 10), 2) As Minor,
   SUBSTRING(@@VERSION, (CHARINDEX('Server    ',
   ➥ @@VERSION) + 20), 3) AS 'Service Pack'
6
```

continues...

```
 7
 8 Microsoft SQL Server  7.00 - 7.00.390 (Intel X86)
 9 Dec 13 1997 03:16:48
10 Copyright  1988-1997 Microsoft Corporation
11
12 Major Minor Service Pack
13 7    00    390
```

RAISERROR

The RAISERROR command originates from the Db-Library programming API. A Db-Library application registers two callback functions. SQL Server executes a callback function when it sends a message or an error message to the client.

The *message handler* is called when messages are sent from SQL Server to the clients, such as messages generated from the PRINT command.

The *error handler* is called from SQL Server when an error occurs. You can generate an error message with the RAISERROR command.

An ODBC application cannot register callback functions, so a program can check for these messages and errors by the use of function calls. The same applies for OLE-DB applications, which can retrieve message and error information through the SQLOLEDB interfaces.

Managing SQL Server Errors

Most error messages are stored in the sysmessages table in the master database. An error message consists of the error number, a severity level, and a description. Table A.13 shows the details available in the sysmessages table.

Table A.13   Columns in the *sysmessages* Table

Column Name	Description
Error	The error number. Every error message has a unique error number.

•

continues...

Table A.13 CONTINUED

Column Name	Description
Severity	The severity level. Higher severity level (generally) indicates a more severe problem. SQL Server will terminate the connection and perform a rollback (if a transaction was started) for severity levels over 19.
Description	The message string with placeholders.

Some error messages are stored in the sysservermessages table in the msdb database. Some of these are informational messages. One example of these messages is the message written to NT's Event log for each backup that SQL Server performs. The messages in the sysservermessages table have severity levels of 110, 120, and 130.

When a message is written to the Eventlog or sent to a client application, it also includes state. The state is an internal value, which can describe the error further. If you report a problem to Microsoft, you might be asked for the state, for example.

Microsoft has done a rough grouping of the severity levels. This isn't as consistent as you might wish it were. This is because the messages have evolved over a long time, and from two companies (Sybase and Microsoft). So take Table A.14 with a grain of salt.

Table A.14 Descriptions of Severity Levels

Severity Level	Description
0–10	Informational messages
11	Object not found
12	Not used
13	Transactional syntax errors
14	Insufficient permissions
15	Syntax errors in SQL
16	Miscellaneous
17	Insufficient resources

Severity Level	Description
18	Internal Errors, non-fatal
19	Resource problems, fatal
20–25	Fatal errors
110	Server information
120	Server warnings
130	Server errors

You can also add your own error messages. This can be useful for centralizing error reporting from your application. Messages can also be managed with the stored procedures sp_addmessages, sp_dropmessage, and sp_altermessage. The error number has to be greater than 50000.

The *RAISERROR* and PRINT *Commands*

A message can be generated with the RAISERROR command. This is a good way to communicate that an error has occurred to a client application from triggers and stored procedures. The RAISERROR command has the following syntax:

```
RAISERROR([err_no]¦[err_string], severity, state,
➥ [argument1[, ...]] options
```

If you supply an err_string, the error number will be 50000. If you supply an error number, that error number has to be defined in the sysmessages table. Arguments are used to insert data (table names and so on) into the message string. If you want to use arguments, you have to define the error message with placeholders for the arguments.

The available options are

- LOG. The message will be sent to NT's Eventlog.
- NOWAIT. The message is sent directly to the client. This is useful for long running operations so that the application can display s status indicator, for instance.
- SETERROR. The global variable @@error will be set to 50000, even if severity is lower than 11.

Listing A.20 adds a user-defined message and calls it from T-SQL code.

685

Listing A.20   Adding an Error Message to SQL Server and Generating the Error

```
1 sp_addmessage 50001, 16, 'The row(s) from table %s could not
➥ be deleted. There are rows in table %s that
➥ refers to this row. Delete those rows first.'
2 RAISERROR (50001, 16, 1, 'Titles', 'Titleauthor')
3 Server: Msg 50001, Level 16, State 42000
4 The row(s) from table Titles could not be deleted.
   ➥ There are rows in table Titleauthor that
   ➥ refers to this row. Delete those rows first.
```

One situation where you might find the state parameter useful is if you execute a script using ISQL or OSQL. By executing the RAISERROR with a state of 127, the processing of the script file terminates. Let us say that you have a simple batch file, which executes as follows:

```
ISQL /Usa /P /iMyBatch.SQL /n
```

The script file (MyBatch.SQL) contains the code in Listing A.21.

Listing A.21   Using State 127 to Terminate a Batch Processed with ISQL or OSQL

```
1 -- Exit if users connected to database.
2 IF (SELECT COUNT(*) FROM master..sysprocesses
3     WHERE dbid = DB_ID('pubs')) > 0
4 RAISERROR ('Cannot proceed with batch, users connected
  ➥ to database.', 16, 127)
5 GO
6 -- If not, continue with whatever you want to do
7 SELECT au_fname, au_lname FROM pubs..authors
```

If the IF statement evaluates to true, the RAISERROR statement will terminate the processing of the script file. This isn't the same as if you would have issued a RETURN statement. The return statement would have terminated the batch, but the following batch(es) would have been executed.

The PRINT command returns a string to the client application's message handler. This should not be considered an error. PRINT is quite commonly used for batch processing where you want to print information to the log about the processing. The print command takes one argument, a string expression. This can be a string constant, local variable, or global variable. In version 7, string expressions can be concatenated in the print command. The following example shows that feature to display the name of the current month:

```
PRINT 'The current month is ' + DATENAME(mm, GETDATE())
➥ + '.'
The current month is April.
```

SET Options

The SET command can be used to alter the connection's behavior. Options set with the SET command stay active until the connection terminates. Most SET commands take ON or OFF as arguments, while some take a specific value. Many of the SET statements don't take effect until the next batch. In the follows tables, the default behavior is displayed in a bold typeface.

The tuning-related SET parameters (shown in Table A.15) are generally used when analyzing and optimizing queries. They can give you information as to how a query is executed by SQL Server and also, to some extent, control how a query is executed.

Table A.15 Tuning-Related *SET* Parameters

Default Options Are Noted by an Asterisk (*)

Parameter	Arguments	Description
FORCEPLAN	ON¦OFF *	Makes SQL Server process a JOIN in the same order as specified in the FROM clause.
NOEXEC	ON¦OFF *	SQL Server will optimize the query but not execute it. Used in conjunction with SHOWPLAN in earlier releases of SQL Server.
PARSEONLY	ON¦OFF *	SQL Server will parse the query but not optimize or execute it.

continues...

687

Table A.15 Continued

Parameter	Arguments	Description
SHOWPLAN_ALL	ON¦OFF *	Displays the query plan that SQL Server uses to execute the query, and doesn't execute the query. This is intended for programs that parse the output, like the Query Analyzer. For textual output, use SHOWPLAN_TEXT instead.
SHOWPLAN_TEXT	ON¦OFF *	Displays the query plan that SQL Server uses to execute the query, and doesn't execute the query.
STATISTICS_IO	ON¦OFF *	Displays information regarding I/O activity for each query.
STATISTICS_TIME	ON¦OFF *	Displays information regarding execution time for each query.

In Listing A.22, you turn on SHOWPLAN_TEXT so that the execution plan is returned to the client.

Listing A.22 Use of *SHOWPLAN_TEXT*

```
 1 SET SHOWPLAN_TEXT ON
 2 GO
 3 SELECT title, au_fname, au_lname
 4   FROM titles t
 5     JOIN titleauthor ta ON t.title_id = ta.title_id
 6     JOIN authors a ON ta.au_id = a.au_id
 7
 8 StmtText
 9 SELECT title, au_fname, au_lname
10   FROM titles t
11     JOIN titleauthor ta ON t.title_id = ta.title_id
12     JOIN authors a ON ta.au_id = a.au_id
13
14 StmtText
15 ¦--Nested Loops(Inner Join)
16         ¦--Nested Loops(Inner Join)
17         ¦     ¦--Index Scan(pubs..authors.aunmind)
18         ¦     ¦--Index Seek(pubs..titleauthor.UPKCL_taind,
   ➥ titleauthor.au_id=authors.au_id)
19         ¦--Index Seek(pubs..titles.UPKCL_titleidind,
   ➥ titles.title_id=titleauthor.title_id)
```

With the transaction handling–related SET parameters (see Table A.16) you can override SQL Server's default transaction-handling semantics. By default, one transaction (connection) cannot read or modify another transaction's modified data, but a transaction can both read and modify data that another transactions has read.

Table A.16 Transaction Handling–Related *SET* Parameters

Default options are noted by an asterisk (*)

Parameter	Arguments	Description
CURSOR_CLOSE_ON_COMMIT	ON¦OFF *	Controls whether cursors should be closed on commit.
IMPLICIT_TRANSACTIONS	ON¦OFF *	An implicit BEGIN TRANSACTION is triggered for most DML statements when turned ON.
REMOTE_PROC_TRANSACTIONS	ON¦OFF *	A distributed transaction is started when a remote procedure is executed from a local transaction when turned ON.
TRANSACTION_ISOLATION_LEVEL	READ_ COMMITTED * ¦READ_ UNCOMMITTED¦ REPEATABLE_ READ¦ SERIALIZABLE	Specifies the degree of isolation between concurrent transactions.
XACT_ABORT	ON¦OFF *	When turned on, SQL Server will roll back the current transaction if an error occurs.

In Listing A.23, you turn on IMPLICIT_TRANSACTIONS, issue two DELETE statements, print out the nesting level, and perform a ROLLBACK.

689

Listing A.23 Setting IMPLICIT_TRANSACTIONS to Get Implicit BEGIN TRANSACTION

```
1 SET IMPLICIT_TRANSACTIONS ON
2 GO
3 DELETE FROM titles WHERE title_id = 'BU1032'
4 DELETE FROM titleauthor WHERE title_id = 'BU1032'
5 SELECT 'Transaction nesting level is: ' +
  ➥ CAST(@@TRANCOUNT AS VARCHAR(5))
6 ROLLBACK TRAN
7 Server: Msg 547, Level 16, State 23000
8 DELETE statement conflicted with COLUMN REFERENCE
  ➥ constraint 'FK__sales__title_id__1CF15040'.
  ➥ The conflict occurred in database 'pubs',
  ➥ table 'titleauthor', column 'title_id'
9 Transaction nesting level is: 1
```

With the formatting-related SET parameters (see Table A.17) you can specify, for instance, the order for which day, month, and year part is specified when entering data.

Table A.17 *SET* Parameters, Which Control Formatting of Data

The default specified applies for the US English language. Default options are noted by an asterisk (*).

Parameter	Arguments	Description
DATEFIRST	<number>	Specifies which day is the last weekday. The default is 7 (Saturday).
DATEFORMAT	<mdy>	Specifies how SQL Server will interpret the date, month, and year part when inserting datetime data in numeric format.
FMTONLY	ON¦OFF *	SQL Server will only return meta-data to the client when turned ON.
IDENTITY_INSERT	<tblname> ON¦OFF *	Enables you to enter an explicit value for an identity column when turned on.

Parameter	Arguments	Description
LANGUAGE	\<language_name\>	Controls in which language error messages should be returned. The language must be available on the server. It also controls the language used when returning name of weekday and month with the DATENAME function.
NOCOUNT	ON¦OFF *	Controls whether the number of rows affected by the last command should be returned to the client application. Even if turned off, the count is still available in the @@ROWCOUNT global variable.
OFFSETS	ON¦OFF *	Controls whether the offset for certain T-SQL keywords should be returned to DB-Library applications.
PROCID	ON¦OFF *	Controls whether the ID of a stored procedure should be returned to the calling DB-Library application.
ROWCOUNT	\<number\>	Causes SQL Server to stop processing the query after a specified number of rows are processed. Note that this also applies to data modification statements. In version 7, use the TOP keyword if you want to control how many rows should be returned from a SELECT statement.
TEXTSIZE	\<number\>	Controls how many bytes a SELECT statement returns from text and ntext columns. Note that ntext uses two bytes per character.

In Listing A.24, you want to return the weekday and month that a book is published in the Swedish language. First the language is added with the call to sp_addlanguage. The call to sp_addlanguage is found in the script file instlang.sql.

691

Listing A.24 Using *sp_addlanguage* to Add a Language to SQL Server

```
1 exec sp_addlanguage 'Svenska','Swedish',
2 'januari,februari,mars,april,maj,juni,juli,augusti,
  ➥ september,oktober,november,december',
3 'jan,feb,mar,apr,maj,jun,jul,aug,sep,okt,nov,dec',
4 'måndag,tisdag,onsdag,torsdag,fredag,lördag,söndag',
5 ymd,1
6 SET LANGUAGE swedish
7 GO
8 SELECT '"' + RTRIM(title) + '" is published on a '
  ➥ + DATENAME(dw, pubdate) + ' in ' +
  ➥ DATENAME(mm, pubdate) + '.'
10 FROM titles
11 WHERE title_id = 'PC1035'
12 "But Is It User Friendly?" is published on a söndag in juni.
```

Listing A.25 sets the date format for specifying datetime data. Note the SELECT statement shows the three available options to specify datetime data. SET DATEFORMAT only applies to the Numeric format.

Listing A.25 Using *SET DATEFORMAT* to Specify Default Date Part Interpretation for Numeric Date Format

```
1 SET DATEFORMAT ymd
2 GO
3 SELECT CONVERT(smalldatetime, '1999.12.31') as 'Numeric',
4   CONVERT(smalldatetime, '19991231') as 'Unseparated',
5   CONVERT(smalldatetime, 'Dec 1999 31') as 'Alphabetic'
6
7 Numeric              Unseparated          Alphabetic
8 1999-12-31 00:00:00  1999-12-31 00:00:00
  ➥ 1999-12-15 00:00:00
```

The ANSI-related and miscellaneous SET parameters (listed in Table A. 18) control behavior for comparison to NULL, division by 0, and so on.

Table A.18 ANSI and Miscellaneous *SET* Parameters

Default options are noted by an asterisk (*).

Parameter	Arguments	Description
ARITHABORT	ON¦OFF *	Terminates a query if overflow or divide-by-zero occurs when turned on. Note that rows can be returned before the abort occurs.
ARITHIGNORE	ON¦OFF *	Returns NULL is overflow or divide-by-zero occurs if turned on. No warning message is sent to the client. Default behavior is that NULL and a warning message is returned.
NUMERIC_ROUNDABORT	ON¦OFF *	Controls level of reporting when loss of precision occurs.
ANSI_NULL_DFLT_OFF	ON¦OFF *	Set this to ON if you don't want a column to allow NULL when you create a table and don't specify NULL or NOT NULL.
ANSI_NULL_DFLT_ON	ON¦OFF *	Set this to ON if you want a column to allow NULL when you create a table and don't specify NULL or NOT NULL.
ANSI_NULLS	ON¦OFF *	Controls how comparison to NULL should be handled. By default, NULL = NULL equals true. SET ANSI_NULLS to ON changes evaluation to false.
ANSI_PADDING	ON¦OFF *	Specifies whether char, varchar, and varbinary columns should be padded with blanks and zeroes, respectively. Behavior is specified at CREATE time of the table.
ANSI_WARNINGS	ON¦OFF *	Generates a warning if an aggregate function is applied over rows that contain NULL and if INSERT or UPDATE specifies data with length that exceeds the column definitions for character, Unicode, or binary data. A division by 0 or overflow will result in rollback of the statement if this option is set.

continues...

Table A.18 CONTINUED

Parameter	Arguments	Description
ANSI_DEFAULTS	ON¦OFF *	If set to ON, the following set parameters will be activated: ANSI_NULLS, ANSI_NULL_DFLT_ON, ANSI_PADDING, ANSI_WARNINGS, CURSOR_CLOSE_ON_COMMIT, IMPLICIT_TRANSACTIONS, and QUOTED_IDENTIFIER.
DEADLOCK_PRIORITY	NORMAL *¦LOW	If LOW, this connection will be the preferred victim if a deadlock occurs. If your application handles deadlock gracefully set, this to LOW, to increase the chance that an application that doesn't handle deadlock can continue processing in the event of a deadlock situation.
DISABLE_DEF_ CNST_CHK	ON¦OFF *	Set to ON if you want SQL Server to halt execution immediately if a statement is performed that violates to a constraint. By default, SQL Server will continue processing and recheck at the end of the statement.
FIPS_FLAGGER	OFF *¦ENTRY¦ INTERMEDIATE¦FULL	Specifies whether SQL Server will generate a warning if a statement doesn't comply with the specified level of the FIPS 127-2 standard.
QUOTED_IDENTIFIER	ON¦OFF *	Will not check for keyword violation for strings surrounded with double quotes.

In Listing A.26, you explore the differences when checking for the NULL symbol depending on how ANSI_NULLS is set. The preferred way of checking for the NULL symbol is by using IS NULL and IS NOT NULL, which is consistent regardless of how ANSI_NULLS is set.

Listing A.26 Checking for *NULL*

```
1  SET ANSI_NULLS OFF
2  GO
3  SELECT title_id, price FROM titles WHERE price = NUL
4  SELECT title_id, price FROM titles WHERE price IS NULL
5
6  title_id price
7  MC3026    NULL
8  PC9999    NULL
9  title_id price
10 MC3026    NULL
11 PC9999    NULL
12
13 -- Note that both statements return two tows.
14 SET ANSI_NULLS ON
15 GO
16 SELECT title_id, price FROM titles WHERE price = NULL
17 SELECT title_id, price FROM titles WHERE price IS NULL
18
19 title_id price
20 title_id price
21 MC3026    NULL
22 PC9999    NULL
23 Note that the first statement returns zero rows.
```

You can specify many of the SET parameters in the ODBC client configuration (the ODBC DSN). This feature introduced some problems. For instance, a stored procedure could have been written so that the parameters were assigned NULL as default, and a check for a value was done inside the procedure. This check was sometimes written as IF @parameter = NULL (which evaluates to false when ANSI_NULLS is ON).

Cursors

The SQL language is a set-based language, in contrast to most programming languages. This leads to an impedance mismatch between the languages. You need some way to interface between the two languages. Most programming interfaces to SQL Server are based on function calls: you specify a query to execute through one function call, and execute the query through another function call, and so on. But what do you do with the result?

If this were a data modification statement, you probably only check for the return code and give the user some feedback. If it were a SELECT statement, you probably want to read through the rows returned and display them or perform further processing for the rows (unless you only retrieve one row, and know that in advance).

So, you build some kind of loop to go through your resultset and perform some processing for each row. If you only want to display the rows, you can simply fetch them as they arrive to the client, reading from your input buffer. But what if you need to perform further processing for each row, for instance do some calculations and update the "current row"? This can be done though a cursor.

A cursor is a placeholder in a resultset from a query. You cannot navigate in a table because a table (or rather the contents in a table) is a set, but you can navigate through the result from a query.

Let's say that you have a leads table, and you want to predict the value of sales for the forthcoming three months. You find the leads table in Listing A.27.

Listing A.27   The Leads Table

```
1 CREATE TABLE leads
2 (l_id INT IDENTITY,
3 customer INT,
4 est_sale FLOAT,
5 close_date SMALLDATETIME DEFAULT DATEADD(dd, 30,
   ➥ GETDATE()),
6 prob FLOAT DEFAULT 20,
7 sales_person CHAR(8),
8 category VARCHAR(30))
9
10 SELECT * FROM leads
11
```

```
12  l_id customer est_sales close_date prob salesperson
➥   category

13  -- -- -- -- -- -- -- -- -- -- -- -- -- -- --
14  1    1      600    Apr 15 199 30   Steve      books
15  2    1      200    Apr 25 199 55   John       paper
16  3    5      400    May  1 199 40   Kelly      books
17  4    3      900    May 12 199 25   Lisa       misc
18  5    7      200    Jun  1 199 15   John       misc
19  6    6      700    May 10 199 50   Bob        paper
20  7    5      450    Apr 10 199 10   Richard    books
21  8    13     600    May 15 199 80   John       misc
22  9    5      1200   Apr 10 199 50   Ann        books
23  10   16     200    Jun 15 199 50   Andy       books
24  11   7      800    May 20 199 40   Bob        misc
25  12   9      600    Apr 20 199 30   Lisa       paper
26  13   3      900    Apr 15 199 60   John       paper
27  14   16     300    May 25 199 25   Kelly      misc
28  15   11     700    Jun 20 199 45   Lisa       books
```

You want to do a projection based on multiplying the estimated sale to the probability of a sale occurring, and them summarize the projections:

```
SELECT SUM(est_sale * probability/100) FROM leads
```

But what if you want to try to be a bit more precise? Based on experience

- Some salespeople are too optimistic, whereas others are conservative. Lisa's probability is usually 20% low and Steve's is usually 30% high.

- In June, you always have an additional 20% discount.

- The book projections are usually low, so you want to increase it by 15%.

- Customer 2 has a tendency to ask for a bid, but seldom buys. You want to lower the probability with 50% for customer 2.

Some Approaches

You certainly could retrieve all rows to the client computer and perform all aggregations in the client application. This would make a rather poor use of SQL Server's power. You would have to write a lot of code and retrieve many records to the client computer. You could imagine what amount of network bandwidth it would take if the table has tens of millions of rows.

So, you decide to use a cursor. You loop through each row, save relevant column information in variables, and perform your calculations.

Cursor Example and Some Syntax

In Listing A.28, you find the code for performing your projection. Have a look at it, and I will explain it in detail further on.

Cursors vs. set-based operations

You might think that you should use a set-based operation instead of a cursor. I agree, so hold on. I will get to that later.

Listing A.28 Calculating Sales Projection Using a Cursor

```
1 DECLARE lead_cur CURSOR FOR
2 SELECT customer, est_sale, close_date, prob,
  ➥ sales_person,
3       category
4  FROM leads
5 FOR READ ONLY
6
7 DECLARE
8 @sum_sales FLOAT,
9 @customer INT,
10 @est_sale FLOAT,
11 @close_date SMALLDATETIME,
12 @prob FLOAT,
13 @sales_person CHAR(8),
14 @category VARCHAR(30)
15
16 SELECT @sum_sales = 0
17 OPEN lead_cur
18
19 FETCH lead_cur INTO
20 @customer, @est_sale, @close_date, @prob,
  ➥ @sales_person,
21 @category
22
23 WHILE @@FETCH_STATUS = 0
24   BEGIN
```

```
25 IF @sales_person = 'Lisa'  — Lisa usually
   ➥ projects low
26 SELECT @prob = @prob * 1.2
27 IF @sales_person = 'Steve' — Steve usually
28 ➥ projects high
29 SELECT @prob = @prob * 0.7
30 IF @customer = 2 — Customer 2 has a low buying rate
31 SELECT @prob = @prob * 0.5
32 IF DATEPART (mm, @close_date ) = 6 — Discount
   ➥June sales
33 SELECT @prob = @prob * 0.8
34 IF @category = 'Books' — Increase book projections
35 SELECT @est_sale = @est_sale * 1.15
36
37 SELECT @sum_sales = @sum_sales + @est_sale * @prob / 100
38 FETCH lead_cur INTO
39 @customer, @est_sale, @close_date, @prob,
   ➥ @sales_person,
40 @category
41 END
42
43 CLOSE lead_cur
44 SELECT @sum_sales AS "Estimated Sales"
45 DEALLOCATE lead_cur
```

Declaring Cursors

A cursor is declared for a SELECT statement. The ANSI defines the following syntax to declare a cursor:

```
DECLARE cursor_name [INSENSITIVE] [SCROLL] CURSOR
FOR select_statement
[FOR {READ ONLY ¦ UPDATE [OF column_list]}]
```

In version 7, an alternative way of declaring a cursor was introduced to give the cursor the same capabilities as the API-based cursor. I will discuss API Cursors further down.

The syntax for Transact-SQL cursors is the following:

```
DECLARE cursor_name CURSOR
[LOCAL ¦ GLOBAL]
[FORWARD_ONLY ¦ SCROLL]
[STATIC ¦ KEYSET ¦ DYNAMIC]
```

> **SQL and API level code**
>
> The cursor types actually use the same code in SQL Server, so it is quite natural that you have the ability to use the same features at the SQL level as you have at the API level.

```
[READ_ONLY ¦ SCROLL_LOCKS ¦ OPTIMISTIC]
FOR select_statement
[FOR {READ ONLY ¦ UPDATE [OF column_list]}]
```

You cannot use COMPUTE, COMPUTE BY, FOR BROWSE, and INTO in the select_statement.

Let us use our example to discuss the DECLARE statement:

```
DECLARE lead_cur CURSOR FOR
SELECT customer, est_sale, close_date, probability,
➥ sales_person, product_category
 FROM leads
FOR READ ONLY
```

Our cursor declares a SELECT statement that reads from a single table. You don't want to update any data based on cursor position, so declare the cursor as READ ONLY.

As for all queries, it is a good idea to limit the number of rows that the cursor will process through a WHERE clause. And if SQL Server can use an index to find the rows, even better.

The cursor name must follow the general rules for identifiers.

Local and Global Cursors

A new feature in version 7 is that you can specify whether the cursor should be local or global.

If you have used cursors with version 6, you have used global cursors. The cursor is implicitly deallocated at termination of the connection.

A local cursor's scope is a batch (which implies stored procedure and trigger). The cursor is implicitly deallocated when the batch terminates, unless a reference to it is passed to calling stored procedure, batch, and so on. Then it will go out of scope when the last variable referring to it goes out of scope.

In Listing A.29, you write a general stored procedure that returns the name of all tables in a database. Then you can use that procedure for performing certain maintenance routines against our tables, like UPDATE STATISTICS, rebuilding indexes, and so on. Listing A.29 shows the stored procedure definition.

```
1 CREATE PROC cur_tbl_names @tbl_cur CURSOR VARYING
  ➥ OUTPUT AS
2 SET @tbl_cur = CURSOR LOCAL FORWARD_ONLY FOR
3 SELECT TABLE_NAME FROM INFORMATION_SCHEMA.TABLES
4 WHERE TABLE_TYPE = 'BASE TABLE'
5 OPEN @tbl_cur
```

First, you can see that the parameter @tbl_cur is defined as CURSOR VARYING OUTPUT. This is needed if you want to return a "reference" to the cursor from the procedure.

The SELECT statement returns all table names in the database. It might look a bit strange for those of you who have worked with SQL Server's earlier versions. INFORMATION_SCHEMA.TABLES is one of the system table–independent views that are used for looking at catalog information. These views are defined in the ANSI standard, so I encourage you to use them when possible.

In Listing A.30, you have the code that calls the procedure.

```
1 DECLARE @tbls CURSOR
2 DECLARE @table_name sysname
3 EXEC cur_tbl_names @tbl_cur = @tbls OUTPUT
4 FETCH NEXT FROM @tbls INTO @table_name
5 WHILE @@FETCH_STATUS = 0
6  BEGIN
7   EXEC('DBCC DBREINDEX( ' + @table_name + ')')
8   FETCH NEXT FROM @tbls INTO @table_name
9  END
```

You get a reference to the cursor, execute your stored procedure and then you have a standard loop for that cursor. Now you can write several batches (or stored procedures) that uses the same cursor, and if you want to exclude any tables, you only modify the code once—in the stored procedure.

You might wonder what sysname is. It is a built-in datatype, used for identifiers.

Declaring Variables

So how do you process values from the cursor?

You could quite simply display each row to the user, as a number of one-row resultsets. But that doesn't make much sense. It would be much simpler to issue an ordinary SELECT statement and display the rows to the user as you read the rows from the input buffer.

What you really want to do is store the value for some of the columns into local variables and perform some processing based on those values.

Note that I have chosen the same variable names as those returned from the SELECT statement. This makes it easier to remember the variable names when processing the cursor, and it makes it easier to maintain the code.

```
DECLARE
 @sum_sales FLOAT,
 @customer INT,
 @est_sale FLOAT,
 @close_date SMALLDATETIME,
 @probability FLOAT,
 @sales_person CHAR(8),
 @product_category VARCHAR(30)
```

You also need to initialize the summary variable:

```
SELECT @sum_sales = 0
```

Opening Cursors

When you open a cursor, the SELECT statement is executed and the cursor becomes populated. At that point in time, the cursor will be positioned above the first row:

```
OPEN lead_cur
```

You can check how many rows the resultset contains with the global variable @@CURSOR_ROWS. If the value is –1, the cursor is being populated asynchronously.

If you close a cursor and open it again, the SELECT statement is re-executed. Bear this in mind, so you don't re-execute your SELECT statement if you don't have to.

Fetching Rows

Now it's time to start reading rows from your cursor. This is done with the FETCH command.

```
FETCH lead_cur INTO
  @customer, @est_sale, @close_date, @probability,
  @sales_person, @product_category
```

The default for FETCH is to get the next row from the cursor. You will look at scrolling capabilities further on. If you specify too many or too few variables after INTO, you will get a runtime error. The same happens if you specify a variable type for which SQL Server cannot perform an implicit datatype conversion.

The Main Loop

This is where the real processing occurs. The loop looks like this:

```
WHILE @@FETCH_STATUS = 0
 BEGIN
  IF @sales_person = 'Lisa'  — Lisa usually projects low
     SELECT @probability = @probability * 1.2
  IF @sales_person = 'Steve' — Steve usually projects high
     SELECT @probability = @probability * 0.7
  IF @customer = 2 — Customer 2 has a low buying rate
     SELECT @probability = @probability * 0.5
  IF DATEPART (mm, @close_date ) = 6 — Discount June
➥ sales by 20%
     SELECT @probability = @probability * 0.8
  IF @product_category = 'Books' — Increase book
➥projections
     SELECT @est_sale = @est_sale * 1.15

  SELECT @sum_sales = @sum_sales + @est_sale *
➥@probability / 100
  FETCH lead_cur INTO
   @customer, @est_sale, @close_date, @probability,
➥@sales_person, @product_category
 END
```

You loop while @@FETCH_STATUS = 0. A value of –1 means that you have navigated outside the cursor. A value of –2 means that the row that you are trying to fetch has been deleted—all columns will contain the NULL symbol.

Closing the Cursor

You want to close the cursor as soon as you don't need it anymore. Open cursors hold locks on the underlying tables and use valuable resources.

You can re-open the cursor, which means that the statement is executed again and the cursor is repopulated:

```
CLOSE lead_cur
SELECT @sum_sales AS "Estimated Sales"
```

Deallocating Cursors

When you are finished with the cursor definition, you deallocate it. You cannot declare a cursor with the same name until you have deallocated the previous cursor.

```
DEALLOCATE lead_cur
```

It is a good idea to deallocate a cursor when you don't need it anymore. The query plan will be released from memory at that time, and it makes the structure of your code clearer.

Updating with Cursors

How can you update a cursor when the cursor is a resultset, and not the data itself? What you do is update based on the cursor position. The modification can be either an UPDATE or a DELETE.

Declaring a Cursor *FOR UPDATE*

To be able to update based on the cursor position, the cursor must be declared FOR UPDATE:

```
[FOR {READ ONLY ¦ UPDATE [OF column_list]}]
```

If you don't specify a column_list, all columns will be updateable.

If your SELECT statement is a join, you could update several tables through the same cursor. This doesn't probably have that much meaning for ANSI cursors, but it is possible.

Listing A.31 shown an example of an updateable cursor.

Listing A.31 An Updateable Cursor

```
1 DECLARE upd_cur CURSOR FOR
2 SELECT title, au_lname, au_fname
3  FROM titles t
4  JOIN titleauthor ta ON t.title_id = ta.title_id
5  JOIN authors a ON ta.au_id = a.au_id
6  WHERE state = 'CA'
7  ORDER BY title
8 FOR UPDATE
```

Obviously, columns with computed values and aggregates cannot be updated.

Scrolling Capabilities

If you declare the cursor with the SCROLL keyword, you can navigate as you choose within the resultset. An example of the leads cursor declared with scroll capabilities would look like:

```
DECLARE lead_cur SCROLL CURSOR FOR
SELECT customer, est_sale, close_date, probability,
 sales_person, product_category FROM leads
FOR READ ONLY
```

For a scrollable cursor, you can use the FETCH statement to navigate in a more flexible way:

```
FETCH [NEXT ¦ PRIOR ¦ FIRST ¦ LAST ¦ ABSOLUTE n ¦ RELATIVE n]
```

If you omit the navigational argument, NEXT will be performed. You don't need a scrollable cursor in order to FETCH NEXT.

Scrollable cursors are most useful as API cursors, where a user, for instance can move up and down a list box and choose some entry based on a cursor value.

INSENSITIVE Cursors

A cursor declared as insensitive won't be affected by updates done through the table(s) that it is based on. SQL Server will

705

quite simply make a copy of the cursor data and store it in the tempdb database.

An insensitive cursor is useful if you want to take a snapshot of the data and don't want to be disturbed by changes to the underlying data while you process the cursor data.

An insensitive cursor isn't updateable.

Cursors and Concurrency

Cursors in a transaction

If a cursor is used inside a transaction, shared locks are held on all rows that are fetched until the end of transaction. This can lead to poor concurrency.

You must be careful when using cursors so you don't block other users' access to the data. If the code executing isn't in the scope of a transaction, SQL Server will only apply shared locks for the duration of the fetch request. SQL Server will automatically implement optimistic concurrency. If you try to update a row through the cursor, and some other user updated it, SQL Server will issue an error message to the client application.

If you use the T-SQL extension to DECLARE CURSOR, you can control the cursor concurrency behavior:

```
[READ_ONLY ¦ SCROLL_LOCKS ¦ OPTIMISTIC]
```

- If you use READ_ONLY, you cannot update through the cursor and shared locks are only held during each fetch operation.
- When using SCROLL_LOCKS, SQL Server acquires scroll locks as you read data into the cursor. Subsequent updates based on the cursor are guaranteed to succeed.
- With OPTIMISTIC, you get optimistic concurrency as described in the preceding text.

API Cursors

So far, you have looked at how you can use cursors through T-SQL. The most common use of cursors, though, is through the application programming interface, API. Each API has calls or methods for defining cursor capabilities.

In fact, you can say that all results from SQL Server are returned through a cursor. The simplest case is that the client retrieves rows one at a time scrolling forward (reading from the input buffer) through the resultset. This is called a *default resultset*.

If you need more advanced scrolling capabilities, part of the resultset needs to be cached somewhere, so you can use, say, a key when searching for the previous row. This caching can be done at the client or at the server.

Client cursors are implemented at the client side. ODBC or OLE-DB caches the necessary information. There are no cursor calls sent to SQL Server. Client cursors are useful if

- You have a slow network connection to the SQL Server.
- There are not too many rows in the resultset or you will navigate through a major part of the resultset.
- You will allow the user to interact rapidly through the cached resultset.

A Web-based application is a good example where client cursors can be valuable. For example, a SQL statement is sent to SQL Server to retrieve a number of customer names. This resultset is buffered at the client side. When the user chooses a customer, another SQL statement is executed and customer details are presented in the Web browser.

API Server Cursors are implemented through the API cursor support in SQL Server. SQL Server has a number of sp_cursor extended stored procedures used by ODBC and OLE-DB, which implement API Server Cursors.

By default, server-side cursors are used in the programming APIs, but the programmer can choose to use client cursors instead.

You can also choose how many rows are to be returned with each fetch operation sent to SQL Server (*fat* cursors). This isn't possible with Transact-SQL cursors; it wouldn't make any sense because all processing is done at the server.

> **Cursor models and performance**
>
> The cursor model chosen can have a severe impact at performance. See the section "Avoiding Cursors" for some examples.

Avoiding Cursors

I have encountered numerous situations where performance was slow due to improper use of cursors. You should always aim at letting SQL Server perform what it's good at: set-based operations. It makes little sense having advanced RDBMS and only using it for retrievals of one row at a time.

Your cursor example can be performed with one SELECT statement, as shown in Listing A.32.

Listing A.32   The Leads Cursor Example Performed with One *SELECT* Statement

```
1 SELECT "Sum of Sales" = SUM(
2 est_sale * prob / 100
3 *
4 CASE category WHEN 'Books' THEN 1.15 ELSE 1 END
5 *
6 CASE DATEPART (mm, close_date ) WHEN 6 THEN 0.8
  ➥ ELSE 1 END
7 *
8 CASE sales_person WHEN 'Lisa' THEN 1.2 WHEN
  ➥ 'Steve' THEN 0.7 ELSE 1 END
9 *
10 CASE WHEN customer = 2 THEN 0.5 ELSE 1 END)
```

The advantage with this approach is a significant performance improvement. The possible disadvantage is that you obviously need to know SQL.

As another example, imagine that you want to increase the discount for all customers who have bought for a certain amount of money.

You could retrieve all rows, check the amount bought, and if it is over that amount, update that customer's discount. This would require that you retrieve all rows, one network roundtrip for each customer, and one UPDATE statement for each row that you want to update.

Thinking set based, you could quite simply issue an UPDATE statement that raises the discount for all customers who meet the requirements (the WHERE clause). SQL Server can use an index to find the rows and all processing is done at the server. This update statement would be easier to construct than the procedural processing as well.

The performance implications are obvious. Okay, it is a simple example, but the same applies for more advanced operations.

On the companion CD, you find a Visual Basic application that demonstrates the differences. I performed some timing and the following table presents the results.

Let us have a look at some details first. My server was a Pentium, 333 MHz with 128MB of RAM. I used the Leads table with 50,000 rows. Several tests were performed:

- SQL-based cursors through RDO and ADO.
- A SELECT statement, using CASE through RDO and ADO.
- Performing all calculations at the client side, fetching all rows. Both the Default Resultset and fetching a number of rows at a time (executing an sp_cursor procedure at the server for each fetch) were used. I fetched 100 rows at a time with RDO and 1 row at a time with ADO.

The client I used was a Pentium 120 MHz with 72MB of RAM. The machines were connected through an isolated 10 Mb Ethernet. Table A.19 displays execution time in seconds both when running the Visual Basic program at the server and at the client.

Table A.19 Performance Comparison Between Different Cases of Cursors

Cursor	API	Server	Client
SQL	RDO	8.8	8.5
SQL	ADO	8.8	8.6
None	RDO	2.0	2.0
None	ADO	1.9	1.9
Default resultset	RDO	20	106
Server cursor	RDO	23	101
Default resultset	ADO	20	116
Server cursor	ADO	650	983

ADO and RDO

Note the difference between ADO and RDO when using server cursor. Without any further investigation, you can safely assume that this is due to the difference in the number of rows retrieved with each fetch. SQL Server executes an sp_cursor procedure for each fetch. I used a block size of 100 for RDO and 1 for ADO.

There is quite a difference between 2 seconds and 983 seconds of execution time!

The numbers speak for themselves.

Glossary

Alert Manager Part of the SQL Server Agent's service of monitoring and managing alerts. When an event occurs that is written to the Windows NT application event log, the event engine captures the message and passes it to the Alert Manager. The Alert Manager determines whether the alert is one that it has been configured to watch for, and if so, it will launch a job or send an email/page. Then the job might also cause a message to be written to the Windows NT event log, and the cycle starts over again.

AppleTalk An IPC supported by SQL Server. See also *Interprocess communication*.

Applications Programming Interface (API) An intermediary between the application software and SQL Server, allowing communication between the client and the database system. Supported APIs include OLE DB, ODBC, DB-Library, and Embedded SQL.

Application role Involved in user management; as their name implies, they are activated by an application.

These roles are inactive by default and do not contain any users. In addition, application roles require a password to activate them.

Authentication security mode An established mode of security (differing from a method) that uses the NT Windows Authentication method only to authenticate users. This means that whenever a user attempts to access SQL Server, Windows NT Security is used to authenticate the user. If the user cannot be authenticated by Windows NT Security, the user is denied access.

Banyan VINES An IPC supported by SQL Server. See also *Interprocess communication*.

BLOB A datatype, a binary large object.

Checkpoint A type of process that causes transactions to be either rolled back or committed to the underlying data; it creates a marker in the transaction log.

Client/server An application design technique in which all the data processing of a program does not occur on a single computer. Instead, different parts of the application run on two or more computers at the same time.

Clustered index An index that forces the rows in a table to be physically stored in sorted order, using one or more columns (indexes can include one or more columns) from the table to sort the rows by. A table may have only one clustered index.

Columns The aspect of a table where field values are stored for each record or left null. The column contains datatype information.

Constraints Used to enforce data integrity; they define specific rules regarding what can and cannot be allowed in a column. Constraints are generally added to a table by the SQL developer when the table is first created. There are five types of constraints: Primary Key, Foreign Key, Unique, Check, and Default.

Database administrator (DBA) The person responsible for the day-to-day administration of SQL Server.

Database catalog tables The 18 tables (for example, `syscolumns`) used by each database to track information on how the database is designed and used. They are automatically generated when a database is created.

Database objects SQL Server follows the object-based model so that all components are treated as objects.

These include tables, views, queries, and so on.

Database role A role that might be predefined or set and that applies specifically to a database and doesn't cross databases.

Data control statements Transact-SQL statements that are used to provide a way to protect a database from corruption.

Data definition statements Transact-SQL statements that are designed for defining a database, modifying its structure after it is created, and dropping it when you are done with it.

Data manipulation statements Transact-SQL statements that are used for entering, changing, and extracting data in a database.

Data mart A data storage facility or set of servers used to store departmental or divisional data for either OLAP or OLTP systems.

Datatype The type of data that can be entered into a column.

Data warehouse A data storage system used to store virtually all an organization's data, which might be in various formats; it typically interacts with the client via the creation of data cubes and an OLAP server.

DBA See *Database administrator*.

DB-Library A client-side programming API.

Decision support environment
Typically speaking, a data management system in which one or more managers issue complex queries that affect thousands of records, if not all the database's records, more or less simultaneously. Large queries cause many records to become *locked*, which prevents them from being changed by other users. Also known as OLAP (Online Analytical Processing).

DECNet An IPC supported by SQL Server. See also *Interprocess communication*.

Default Values that are automatically entered into columns when a user enters no values into them during data entry. When a SQL developer creates a table, the developer has the option of creating a default entry for any column in the table.

Distributed computing See *Client/server*.

Distributed Transaction Manager (MS DTC) An optional SQL Server service that acts as a transaction manager and is used when a SQL Server application has been written that modifies data on two or more SQL Servers as part of a single transaction. It guarantees that each data modification on each server will be 100% complete on all the servers, or in the event of an aborted transaction, any partial modification is rolled back on all the affected servers so that the data doesn't become corrupted.

Extent By combining eight contiguous pages (64K) together, you have an extent. An extent is the basic unit used to create tables and indexes. There are two types of extents: uniform and mixed. A uniform extent's space is dedicated to a single object, such as a single table or index. A mixed extent can be shared by up to eight different objects.

Identifier An object name. Rules for identifiers include

- Names must not exceed 128 characters. NT Server NetBIOS names must not exceed 15 characters.

- Names must not include any spaces. NT Server NetBIOS names should also not include spaces.

- Names must begin with an uppercase or lowercase letter or the symbol _. Names can also begin with @ or #, but these have special meaning and should not be used in most cases. NT Server NetBIOS names can begin with any letter, number, and most symbols.

- Characters in names after the first letter may be any letter, any number, or the symbols @, _, #, or $. NT Server NetBIOS names may include all letters, numbers, and most symbols.

Index Database objects used to speed up data access and to ensure entity integrity of a table. Indexes contain ordered pointers that point to data stored in tables, allowing SQL Server to quickly locate data. Without indexes, SQL Server would have to search every row in a table to find a particular piece of data. Indexes, like indexes in a book, enable SQL Server to quickly locate data in a table.

Interprocess communication (IPC) For the SQL Server client process to speak to the SQL Server process, an interprocess communication (IPC) must occur. This can be a local IPC or a network (remote) IPC. If it is a local IPC, both the client and SQL Server process must be running on the same computer. If it is a network IPC, the client process and the SQL Server process communicate over a network connection. SQL Server supports these IPCs: named pipes, shared memory, multiprotocol, Windows sockets, Novell SPX/IPX, DECNet, AppleTalk, and Banyan VINES.

IPC See *Interprocess communication*.

Latency The amount of time your users have to wait, from when they query SQL Server until they receive their first results from SQL Server based on the query.

Log file Every database has a log file, which is used to log all information before it is written to a primary or secondary data file. This data is used to help recover a database, should it be damaged. A single database may have a single log file or multiple log files if the original one runs out of room. The file extension for a log file is .ldf.

Logical database The part of the database that is visible to a user.

Master The Master database is used to track all SQL Server system-level information. It is also used to track all other databases and to store SQL Server configuration information.

Model The Model database is used as a template to create all new user databases. It includes all the 18 standard database catalog tables.

MSDB The Msdb database is used by the SQL Server Agent service to track job, alert, and operator information.

Multiprotocol An IPC supported by SQL Server. See also *Interprocess communication*.

Multithreaded The capability of an application to take advantage of multiple CPUs during processing, with each thread executing independently of one another. This ability is one of the reasons SQL Server scales so well.

Named pipes An IPC supported by SQL Server. See also *Interprocess communication*.

Net-Library The programming code, generally as a dynamic link library (DLL), that SQL Server implements to support each IPC mechanism. The mechanism/Net-Library is loaded by both a client and SQL Server in order to have a common way to communicate.

Network Monitor A tool used to determine current bandwidth utilization; this began shipping with NT Server 4.0 (and is also included with Microsoft's Systems Management Software).

Non-clustered index A physical data structure, separate from the table, that points to the data in a table. The pointers themselves are sorted, making it easy to quickly locate data within a table. A table may include an index for every column in a table, although this would be uncommon. Generally, only columns that benefit from sorting have indexes.

Novell SPX/IPX An IPC supported by SQL Server. See also *Interprocess communication*.

Objects See *Database objects*.

OLAP See *Online analytical processing*.

Online analytical processing (OLAP) A newer term adopted by Microsoft to describe decision support-oriented systems.

Open Data Services (ODS) A server-side programming applications programming interface (API) used for creating client/server integration with external application systems and data sources. It acts as an interface between the server Net-Libraries and server-based applications. Developers can use ODS to write applications to distribute SQL Server data to the outside computing environment. Developers can access ODS through such client-side programming APIs as DB-Library and open database connectivity (ODBC).

Page The smallest unit used in SQL Server. A page holds 8KB (8192 bytes) of data and is used to hold database objects. Seven kinds of pages are used in SQL Server, including data, index, log, text/image, global allocation map, page free space, and index allocation map.

Physical database The physical files that make up a database; composed of two or more physical operating-system files. At a minimum, one of these two files will contain the database information, and the other will contain the database's transaction log.

Primary data file Every database includes at least one primary data file. This file is designed to hold database objects, such as tables and indexes. This file is also used to point to the rest of the files that constitute the database. Primary data files have a file extension of `.mdf`.

Process All the resources allocated on a computer that are necessary to run a program. Because of this, the term *process* is often used to refer to either client software or SQL Server as it is running.

Pubs A sample database included with SQL Server.

Relational database system A type of database architecture that has been widely adapted by software vendors. A relational database is divided into multiple tables of data, each of which is further divided into rows (records) and columns (fields).

Role Enables you to group one or more users into a single unit that can be used to apply a given set of permissions. Any user who is assigned to that role takes on the permissions assigned to that role. One or more roles can be defined per database, each one enabling you to grant a different set of permissions to each role, depending on the needs of the organization. Every SQL Server database comes with several default role objects.

Script A collection of one or more batches of Transact-SQL statements designed to perform some specific action.

Secondary data file A file type used for databases if all the data for the database will not fit into a single primary data file. A database may have as many secondary data files as necessary. The file extension for a secondary data file is `.ndf`.

SQL Server Authentication The method of user login security subordinate to the operating system (such as Windows NT Authentication) and specifically for SQL Server objects. This might be used in a mixed operating-system environment.

Stored procedure Database objects that enable you to automate many tasks. They are made up of precompiled Transact-SQL statements that carry out a predetermined task or series of tasks.

Symmetrical processing (SMP) A method of processing in which the processing load is evenly distributed among each CPU for the greatest efficiency. Out of the box, NT Server supports up to 4 or 8 CPUs (depending on which version of NT Server is used) and can support up to 32 CPUs under certain circumstances. This enables support for a multithreaded application.

System database Special databases used to keep track of the SQL Server services and the databases it manages. These databases are created when SQL Server is first installed and are constantly used by SQL Server as it carries out its various tasks.

System catalog Also called the *data dictionary*. Refers to the 19 systems tables included in the Master database used to manage SQL Server.

System tables Tables used to store data that tracks information on all SQL Server and database activities. Every database, whether system or user, includes 18 identical system tables, commonly referred to as *database catalog tables*. In addition to these common system tables, the Master and Msdb databases each include special system tables that are unique to themselves.

System-stored procedure One of the many predefined stored procedures, beginning with the `sp_` prefix. One example of a system-stored procedure is `sp_help`.

Table The most important object within a database; where data is stored. Each database can store up to two billion tables. Tables are made up of *rows* (records) and *columns* (fields). Each table can have up to 1,024 columns and an unlimited number of rows (limited only by disk space and performance issues).

Tempdb The Tempdb database is used to hold all temporary tables or other objects created as SQL Server performs its work.

Three-tier client/server architecture A client/server application that divides into three components: 1) the user-interface tier, which provides user services, running on a user's desktop; 2) a server tier running on a separate server that supports business services; and 3) a data tier running on another server that supports data services.

Transaction A set of operations (Transact-SQL statements that change a database) that are to be completed at one time, as if they were a single operation.

Transaction log Used to automatically record all changes made to a database before the changes are actually written to the database. This is an important fault-tolerant feature of SQL Server that helps prevent a database from becoming corrupted.

Transaction-oriented environment A data management system in which a single record, or set of related records, is affected by each transaction. As long as each transaction is distinct, hundreds or even thousands of records can be open simultaneously by hundreds of users. Also known as *online transaction processing* (OLTP).

Transact-SQL Virtually all modern relational database systems use the SQL language to manipulate the data in a database. SQL was developed by IBM in the 1970s and has become an industry standard. Although SQL Server is fully compliant with the latest ANSI SQL-92 standard of the SQL language, it also extends the language, adding important new features. Because of this, the version of SQL included with SQL Server is referred to as *Transact-SQL*.

Transport protocols One of the communications standards by which a network operates to interact with the client/server components, such as TCP/IP.

Trigger A special type of stored procedure that executes when specific events occur to a table. For example, when data in a table is inserted, updated, or deleted, a trigger can be made to automatically fire, executing a series of Transact-SQL statements. SQL developers often use triggers to help ensure data integrity and perform other tasks.

Universal data access A Microsoft term for the technology that enables SQL Server to easily connect widely diverse data into one central location where it can be easily queried.

User database Databases that you create and fill with data. A single copy of SQL Server can maintain a single user database or hundreds of separate databases. SQL Server manages each database separately from one another and the system databases from the user databases.

View A virtual table created to provide alternative ways to view data stored in tables. Views can be created to display a subset of data from a table, or two or more tables can be linked and combined to create a view. Views themselves don't contain data; they only point to selected data and present it visually.

Windows sockets An IPC supported by SQL Server. See also *Interprocess communication*.

Windows NT Authentication An operating system–level security method that integrates Windows NT login security for restricting use of SQL Server objects.

Wizard A tool that steps you through configuring a specific aspect of SQL Server. The wizards are available from the Enterprise Manager.

Index